DATA TYPING

CHARACTER: defines a symbol as a character (string) variable

```
CHARACTER  ONELET, TENLET*10, MULTIL(10)*80
```

Chapters 3, 4, & 12

COMPLEX: defines a symbol as a complex variable, storing two real values

```
COMPLEX  X, C(3,8)
```

Chapter 13

IMPLICIT: defines a range of initial symbol letters as defining a certain type

```
IMPLICIT  REAL  (A-H, L, N)
```

Chapter 3

INTEGER: defines a symbol as an integer variable

```
INTEGER  SUM, VALUES(200)
```

Chapter 3

DOUBLE PRECISION: defines a symbol as a double-precision real variable

```
DOUBLE PRECISION  A(20), H, XY
```

Chapter 3

LOGICAL: defines a symbol as a logical variable

```
LOGICAL  ISNUM, OK
```

Chapter 5

REAL: defines a symbol as a single-precision real variable

```
REAL  LENGTH, COORDS(2,1000)
```

Chapter 3

SUBPROGRAM LINKAGE

CALL: link to subroutine

```
CALL  SORT  (BLOCK, NUMEL)
```

Chapter 8

ENTRY: allows multiple entry points into external subprogram

```
ENTRY  MYSUB  (BLOCK, NUMEL)
```

Chapter 13

RETURN: return to calling program from called program

```
RETURN
```

Chapter 8

SAVE: saves value of local variables in subprogram between accesses

```
SAVE
```

Chapter 14

(Continued inside back cover)

F O R T R A N

FOR TODAY & TOMORROW

FORTRAN

FOR TODAY & TOMORROW

MICHAEL H. PRESSMAN

Long Island University
C. W. Post Campus

WCB **Wm. C. Brown Publishers**

Dubuque, Iowa • Melbourne, Australia • Oxford, England

Book Team

Editor *Earl McPeek*
Developmental Editor *Linda M. Meehan*
Publishing Services Coordinator (Production) *Julie A. Kennedy*

Wm. C. Brown Publishers

A Division of Wm. C. Brown Communications, Inc.

Vice President and General Manager *George Bergquist*
National Sales Manager *Vincent R. Di Blasi*
Assistant Vice President, Editor-in-Chief *Edward G. Jaffe*
Marketing Manager *Elizabeth Robbins*
Advertising Manager *Amy Schmitz*

Managing Editor, Production *Colleen A. Yonda*
Manager of Visuals and Design *Faye M. Schilling*
Publishing Services Manager *Karen J. Slaght*
Permissions/Records Manager *Connie Allendorf*

Wm. C. Brown Communications, Inc.

Chairman Emeritus *Wm. C. Brown*
Chairman and Chief Executive Officer *Mark C. Falb*
President and Chief Operating Officer *G. Franklin Lewis*
Corporate Vice President, Operations *Beverly Kolz*
Corporate Vice President, President of WCB Manufacturing *Roger Meyer*

Cover design by Lachina Publishing Services
Cover image © Nicholas Foster/The Image Bank
Copyediting and production by *Lachina Publishing Services*

Copyright © 1993 by Wm. C. Brown Communications, Inc. All rights
reserved

Library of Congress Catalog Card Number: 92–72530

ISBN 0–697–04483–1

Printed in the United States of America by Wm. C. Brown Communications, Inc.,
2460 Kerper Boulevard, Dubuque, IA 52001

10 9 8 7 6 5 4 3 2 1

To my daughter Dana, who is so very special.

Brief Contents

Contents

Preface

Purpose

FORTRAN for Today & Tomorrow is designed as an introduction to this oldest of high-level computer languages, a language that, despite the predictions of its demise many years ago, continues to be used extensively. FORTRAN has gone through several revisions since its introduction in the late 1950s, the latest being Fortran 90 (note the use of lowercase to denote the new version). With this further refinement of the language, FORTRAN will undoubtedly continue to be a dynamic tool in computer programming.

In this text, the teaching of the language is approached carefully and completely, so that the reader is encouraged to write programs at the earliest possible stage. The emphasis is on simplicity of presentation, without any sacrifice in precision. The text is extremely thorough, covering the complete 1977 version of FORTRAN; the more advanced features are presented separately so that the reader who doesn't need such detailed coverage is not distracted. A separate chapter is devoted to Fortran 90.

The exercises and examples come from a variety of areas, including business, science, the arts, and the humanities, in order to appeal to students with a variety of backgrounds and interests.

FORTRAN is a language of few words, and our desire is to show how much can be done with so little. This should not lead you to think that FORTRAN is a limited or limiting language. On the contrary, the implementation of most logic often requires less work in FORTRAN than in most other languages. FORTRAN 77 is extremely flexible, as it incorporates techniques that appeared first in other languages or were suggested by academic and professional users. It is FORTRAN's lack of rigidity that allows it to expand and adjust to the needs of the professional community.

Audience

Users of this text do not have to have previous computer programming experience. The book is intended for courses in which FORTRAN is the primary teaching language, or in courses in which FORTRAN is the advanced language to be used for problem solving or graphics communication. It may also be used in a programming languages course in which students are expected to become familiar with the language independently.

As very few computer languages have facilities for higher mathematics built in, students need only a background in algebra; familiarity with trigonometry would be helpful but is not necessary. Some applications include numerical methods that border on the theory of calculus, but they do not require a knowledge of that subject. The text purposely does not assume a specific operating system or editor, so that it will have a broader appeal. These specific systems must be covered independently.

Organization

Following a two-chapter introduction to computer hardware and software, the study of FORTRAN begins in Chapter 3 with the simplest input/output (I/O) techniques available in the language: list-directed I/O. You will write your first program in this chapter, which also introduces the first of four large application problems that are developed throughout the text. The chapter includes the input and output of numeric, alphameric, and literal data, as well as the use of disk access to both input and output sequential files. The concept of data typing also appears here because it is germane to I/O and permits a treatment of the topic with immediate application.

Chapters 4 through 6 cover in great detail the general topics of assignment, logic (branching), and looping. Flowcharts demonstrate the logic used in each of the instructions, and the question of programming structure is continuously addressed. The LOGICAL type is introduced here, and its use is demonstrated throughout the rest of the text. Techniques of debugging are introduced to provide some of the necessary programming tools often passed over in other presentations. Thus, the text offers a very easy introduction to programming by first demonstrating the language's value in problem solving, before getting involved with more complex linguistic problems.

Chapter 6A introduces some of the new features of Fortran 90, in particular the new variations of the DO loop and the CASE statement. The chapter shows how programs may be written completely without statement numbers, resulting in far superior readability and structure. The new free source form is described, with the changes in comments and continuations. This introduction will ease the transition into Fortran 90, giving the student an advantage when seeking a job as a programmer. This chapter is distinctively marked with a red tab.

Chapter 7 is devoted to the study of the FORMAT statement. Special attention is given to the details of I/O buffers to illustrate just how input/output functions. In addition, all of the data types (except COMPLEX) are implemented and most of the positional options are described. The chapter is written so that it can be read following Chapter 3, for students who wish to incorporate the features described in the chapter into their programs earlier in their study of the language.

Chapter 8 contains probably the most important topic in an introduction to FORTRAN: subprograms. The ability to develop external modules and libraries is one reason for FORTRAN's long life. The topic of subprograms is treated as an extension of programming structure. Generated random data (including normalized random data) is described as a tool for program testing. Subprograms are supplied in the chapter, for cases in which none are available on the student's computer system.

Chapters 9 through 11 cover arrays and array applications, with emphasis on how their use significantly improves program structure. A description of the mapping function is included in order to provide a better understanding of array storage and the transmission of arrays to subprograms, as well as some pitfalls of incorrect array usage. Various I/O techniques are displayed as a means of reducing program effort. Exercises include simple sorting, searching, and control breaks.

Chapter 12 is devoted to alphameric manipulation. It is a thorough treatment, with many demonstrated programs and exercises involving such advanced topics as substrings and internal files.

Chapters 13 and 14 provide details about many of FORTRAN's advanced commands, which can be useful to the student as well as the professional programmer. Included are extensions of statements discussed earlier in the text and statements useful in specialized programming systems and applications. Some obsolete statements are included for the sake of completeness.

The final chapter, Chapter 15, contains several projects that should provide interesting challenges for students. These projects will enhance programming skills while acquainting students with methodologies used in a professional programming environment.

Four appendixes provide helpful reference information: the complete application problems, intrinsic functions, character code tables, and solutions to selected exercises.

Pedagogy

The text features four large application problems: (1) Bowling scores, (2) Computer Time Accounting, (3) Automated Teller Machine, and (4) Parking Violations. The solutions to these problems are developed throughout the chapters, beginning in Chapter 3 and reaching completion in Chapter 14. These problems provide continuity and reinforce the relationship of concepts, since with each new chapter students are given a new tool for solving the problem. Each chapter contains as complete a solution of the problem as possible, given the material covered to that point. Extensions to the problem may be suggested as an exercise or project.

A major strength of this text is the number and variety of exercises. There are more than 400 exercises; approximately 40 percent relate specifically to FORTRAN, and the other 60 percent involve applications in math, science, business, and general interest. The wide range of exercises will appeal to students of varying backgrounds and interests.

Chapters include the following components, in addition to the main text:

Chapter Outline: lists the topics discussed in the chapter.
Chapter Objectives: lists the main concepts that students should
    understand upon completing the chapter.
Statement of the Problem: describes the problem to be solved using the
    tools presented in the chapter.
Review Questions and Exercises, integrated with the chapter material to
    provide an immediate check of student understanding.
Chapter Review: repeats and reinforces the main concepts of the chapter.

The author believes that this text should stand on its own, enabling the student to learn independently without the need for more formal presentations. This approach gives the instructor more time to concentrate on either programming theory or specific applications.

FORTRAN 77

The version of FORTRAN used herein (with the exception of Fortran 90 in Chapter 6A) is the one specified by the American National Standards Institute (ANSI Specification X3.9–1978) and is known as FORTRAN 77. The specifications are adhered to completely, and extensions of the language (such as the DO WHILE) are not used. However, Chapter 6 describes the extensions DO UNTIL and LOOP EXIT and presents methods of simulating them.

The standards for Fortran 90 are upward-compatible, so that all programs written in FORTRAN 77 will run under Fortran 90. Thus, a user adhering solely to the new standard or using a Fortran 90 compiler will not find the text outdated.

All the programs herein were tested on an "industry-standard" microcomputer (i.e., an IBM clone), using Microsoft's Fortran Compiler, version 4.1. Testing was also done on VAX and Prime super minicomputers. It is important to understand (as the text emphasizes) that although the language is standardized, there are still places where the standards are not precise enough and "dialects" still exist.

Supplements   The following supplements are available to enhance the effectiveness of the text:

- An instructor's manual containing the philosophical approach of each chapter, how it is integrated into the text and organized, the pedagogy used, alternative methods and suggestions, and solutions to all review questions and exercises. The manual also contains an index to the review questions and exercises and an index to the demonstration programs in the text.

- An instructor's solutions disk, containing the solutions (in the form of programs) to all exercises and the data to be input for many programs. This disk is available in 3 1/2- and 5 1/4-inch IBM formats.

Acknowledgments   Special thanks to Dwight Peltzer, who has reviewed the text and exercises and has helped the author correct a number of errors. Grateful acknowledgment also to the following reviewers:

Manfred R. Ruess
Norwalk State Technical College

Thomas B. Murtagh
San Jacinto College–South Campus

Carl Penziul
Corning Community College

Bill Courter
Jackson Community College

Ervin Eltze
Fort Hays State University

Dr. Billy D. Graves
Hinds Community College

Elmer Raydean Richmond
Tarrant County Junior College/South
  Campus

Dr. Charles Beard
Blinn College

Gordon C. Kimbell
Everett Community College

Susan Harrington
Columbia Union College

Lester Hays
Pima Community College

Ijaz A. Awan
Savannah State College

Laura Cooper
College of the Mainland

Nelda Cuppy
Allen County Community College

Al Cripps
Middle Tennessee State University

Douglas W. Kirk
University of Southern Colorado

Dr. Gerald E. Gau
University of Wisconsin–Stevens
  Pointe

Dr. Janet E. Spears
Black Hawk College–East Campus

Keith B. Olson
Montana Tech

1 Computer Hardware

CHAPTER OBJECTIVE

■ To provide a short but precise description of the hardware used to write, compile, and execute FORTRAN programs.

1.1 FUNCTIONAL DEFINITION OF A COMPUTER

What is a computer? The word *computer* evokes many images and triggers many emotions. The images range from huge, menacing machines to small, intriguing toys. The emotions run a similar gamut, from nervous apprehension to pure delight. Yet, in reality, the computer is just a combination of simple tools that can be used, as can many tools, to either improve or lessen the quality of life.

Computers range in size from portable laptops (Figure 1-1), to the more familiar personal computer and workstation (Figure 1-2), to the older and more powerful office systems (Figure 1-3), mainframes (Figure 1-4), and supercomputers (Figure 1-5). Prices range from less than a thousand to hundreds of millions of dollars. Our lives are constantly affected by the millions of computers around us, and most people will use a computer of some type within their lifetime.

In this text, we are not concerned with how a computer is designed (its architecture) or how it is built (its electronics); nor do we consider its cabinetry (ergonomics) or its marketing. Our concern is with what the computer can do as a result of our programming. Therefore, we will define a computer as "a machine capable of storing and manipulating information as dictated by the instructions of a human being." The key words in this definition are *machine* and *instructions*.

Figure 1-1
A Laptop Computer

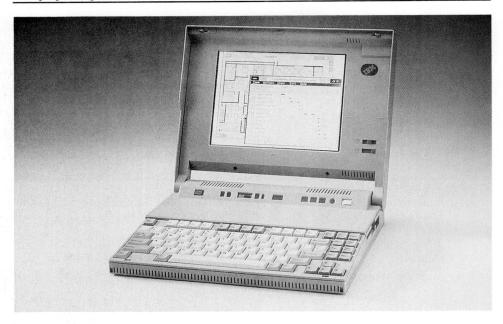

Source: Courtesy of International Business Machines Corporation

Figure 1-2
A Desktop System

Source: Courtesy of International Business Machines Corporation

Figure 1-3
A Small Office System/Network

Source: Courtesy of International Business Machines Corporation

Figure 1-4
A Typical Mainframe Computer Room

Source: Courtesy of International Business Machines Corporation

Figure 1-5
A Supercomputer Configuration

Source: Courtesy of International Business Machines Corporation

In discussing computers, we also use the terms *hardware* and *software*. Hardware is the actual computer itself; it is "hard" because it does not change until we physically modify it or replace it. Software is the set of instructions (programs) that tell the machine what to do; it is "soft" because it is easily changeable. In this chapter we will look briefly at the hardware, delaying our study of software until Chapter 2.

A programmer needs at least a rudimentary knowledge of computer hardware. Although a thorough study is beyond the scope of this text, we will define and describe the computer's basic components in this chapter. Today, most programmers are well informed about hardware; and often they are involved in its selection so that their programs will run efficiently.

As generally defined, computer hardware consists of four main parts:

1. Control unit
2. Memory
3. Arithmetic and logic unit (ALU)
4. Input and output (I/O) devices

A symbolic representation of how the parts relate to each other is shown in Figure 1-6. As you can see, information passes in only one direction between the control unit and the I/O devices: (1) from the input device(s) to the control unit and (2) from the control unit to the output device(s). Reverse flow is not possible. However, information can move in either direction between the control unit and the memory and between the control unit and the ALU. The information-handling characteristics of these components are determined by two parameters: capacity and speed.

Capacity is determined by the number of units the device can store. The standard unit is the byte, a number storable in eight binary digits (bits). These numbers range from 0 to 255 and can represent letters (both upper- and lowercase), numer-

Figure 1-6
Basic Computer Configuration

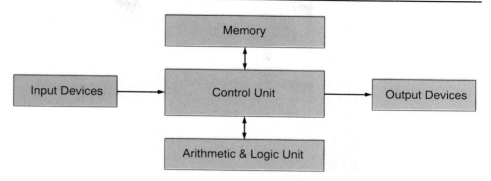

als, punctuation marks, and the control codes needed to operate the various I/O devices (clear a screen, sound an audible signal, end a line, etc.). They may also represent graphic characters displayed on monitors (computer screens), such as lines and symbols. Since many of these values represent printable and displayable characters, the term *character* is often synonymous with *byte*. Today we talk of thousands of bytes (kilobytes or Kbytes or KB), millions of bytes (megabytes or Mbytes or MB), and billions of bytes (gigabytes or Gbytes or GB).

Speed is measured in terms of how fast the information is accessed within a unit or moved to or from it. One measure of speed is how long a process takes. The following units are used:

$$\text{millisecond} = 1 \times 10^{-3} \text{ second}$$
$$\text{microsecond} = 1 \times 10^{-6} \text{ second}$$
$$\text{nanosecond} = 1 \times 10^{-9} \text{ second}$$
$$\text{picosecond} = 1 \times 10^{-12} \text{ second}$$

Another measurement of speed is the number of operations per unit time. This is related to the computer's clock speed, measured in megahertz (MHz), or millions of pulses per second. Still another measurement is millions of instructions per second (Mips).

As might be expected, all of these factors relate to cost. The general rule is that the larger (capacity, not physical size) and faster the computer is, the more it will cost. However, the cost of hardware has dropped so significantly as the technology has improved that purchasing and developing software has now become the major cost factor in data processing.

1.2 CONTROL UNIT

As an aid to understanding some of the hardware used in all computers, we can develop an analogy using a familiar subject, a commercial parking lot. The cars (information) coming in represent the input; those going out are the output. The parking spaces, set up in well-ordered rows, are similar to the computer's memory (see Figure 1-7). The movement of the cars into, out of, and within the lot (the data processing) is under the control of a traffic manager (control unit), who assigns each car to a spot, keeps track of available spots, and remembers whose car is in which spot (memory management).

Figure 1-7
Single-Level Parking Lot

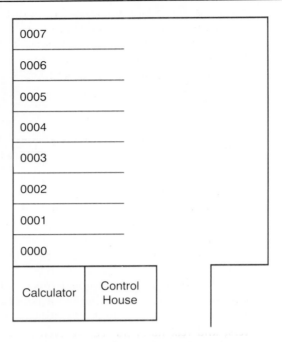

The control unit is like the traffic manager, following a set of logical procedures each time another car comes in or one is taken out. During input, an unused parking spot must be located and the incoming car directed to that spot. During output, the desired car must be found and directed to the exit.

In order to do this job, the traffic manager must be given a set of instructions about how these tasks are performed. After all, a human being, just like a machine, must be taught (programmed) how to perform a task. (The major difference is that a human being can learn from observation and may not need overt teaching; nonetheless, a learning process is taking place.) And just as we would expect higher performance from a highly paid individual, we would expect better performance from a more expensive piece of hardware.

If we think of a traffic manager who "works by the book"—that is, one who consults the operations manual each time a task is to be performed—we will have an understanding of how the control unit operates. The traffic manager who wants to park a car must go through a series of distinct steps:

1. Locate an available parking space.
2. Direct the car to that space.
3. Keep a record of the car's location.

Thus, the instruction "park a car" requires a series of lower-ordered directives.

The control unit is a conglomeration of electronic parts that is able to accept a limited number of instructions and respond by producing the necessary electrical impulses to execute the steps needed to implement those instructions. The lower-level instructions, which are either hardwired or encoded in a computer chip, are called microcode. (This code is not considered software, since it cannot be changed by the user but must be modified by the manufacturer.) Should any of the micro-code be defective, that piece of hardware might just as well be thrown out, for it costs less to produce a new chip than to try to fix the old component.

Thus, functionally, the control unit is the piece of hardware that controls the movement of information into, around, and out of the other parts of the computer. It is the control unit that obeys our program of logical instuctions and converts it to the electrical impulses that make computers work.

1.3 INTERNAL MEMORY

The computer's memory is composed of a large number of addressable locations, each capable of storing a piece of information. By "addressable" we mean that each of these locations is numbered, providing a means for the control unit to access them. Although different memory architectures exist, the standard memory address-ing unit is the byte or character.

This is little different from our parking lot analogy, wherein each parking spot is numbered and holds one car. For instance, a medium-size truck is larger than a car and may have to be allocated two parking spots. A truck and trailer might require four spaces. The same situation occurs within the computer's memory. Integer numbers require more space (two to four bytes) for storage than do charac-ters, and real numbers require even more (four to eight bytes), depending on the number of significant digits to be stored.

The cost of memory has become so affordable that capacity is not as limited as it was in the past. Whereas 30 years ago a computer with 64 kilobytes of memory was considered a large computer, 1 megabyte is now minimum in most personal computers. At one time, the difference between the various classes of computers (supercomputers, mainframes, superminis, minis, and micros) was measured in memory size; it is now measured in speed. Access times are now measured in nano-seconds (billionths of a second) for high-speed computers and microseconds (mil-lionths of a second) for slower ones. An access time of 1 microsecond means that 1 million bytes can be moved within the memory in 1 second.

To return to our analogy, the ability to move a car into and out of a parking lot quickly is also a measure of service. Just as we would expect to pay more for the convenience of quick service, we must pay more for fast memory access.

There is one major difference between computer memory and our parking lot analogy. When information is accessed from the computer's memory, it is read but not removed; that is, it is still there for later access. (The term for this is *nondestruc-tive readout*.) This is similar to playing a music recording; the recording medium, whether tape, record, or compact disc, may be accessed many times without destroy-ing the information (music). But just the opposite is true with our parking lot: once a car is moved from its parking place, it is no longer there.

On the other hand, the input processes for the parking lot, the recording medium, and the computer memory are very similar, since two things cannot occupy the same space at the same time. Thus, whatever was in the memory location is destroyed when a new piece of information is put in its spot. (This is called *destruc-tive read-in*.) In the same way, we can replace information by writing a new piece into the memory location; and the old information is then lost forever. (However, driving a car into an occupied parking space would probably destroy both the old occupant and the new one.)

1.4   ARITHMETIC AND LOGIC UNIT (ALU)

The arithmetic and logic unit (ALU) performs the manipulation done on the data, such as numeric calculations and string operations. It is like the cashier in our parking lot who computes the parking fee from given information, either manually or with a calculator (see Figure 1-7).

ALUs have many variations, much like calculators. Some are very simple and perform only basic calculations; others are more powerful and can perform complex algorithms. For example, some calculators do not have a square root key. The user who wants to find a square root must use a combination of whatever operations are available. Likewise, if no calculator is available, our parking lot cashier may have to compute the fee manually.

But just as our cashier can compute manually, ALUs that do not have the hardware capability to do all the desired operations rely on software to do the calculation with the available operations. (The early computers had very simple ALUs that could only add and complement integer numbers, yet these computers could subtract, multiply, and divide both real numbers and integers by using software to emulate the processes unavailable with that simple hardware.) Even today, the purchaser of a microcomputer can choose to add a math coprocessor chip to do real arithmetic with hardware or not to add the chip and let the software do the work, albeit much more slowly. Again, the more functions that an ALU can perform, the more expensive the computer will be—but it will also be faster.

In many small computers, the functions of the ALU are incorporated into the control unit chip. In others, the ALU chip may be mounted on the same circuit board as the control unit chip. However, despite their physical proximity, they are completely separate logically and are therefore represented by a separate box in Figure 1-6.

1.5   PERIPHERAL STORAGE

The internal memory of a computer has two major limitations, volatility and capacity. Volatility means that the computer cannot retain the information stored in its memory if the power to the computer is interrupted. Thus the internal memory is primarily used for short-term storage.

Furthermore, although the size of available memory today is far greater than in early computers, programs are also much larger today, as is the amount of data normally handled by those programs. Since the internal memory can handle only a limited number of programs and data at one time, we need some kind of more massive, permanent memory. This kind of storage is termed *peripheral* (or secondary) because it is not part of the main memory and information must be specifically input from it or output to it. (Some of those operations may occur without direct programmer instructions, but they are controlled by either the operating system software or the application program software. Because the user is not concerned with this type of peripheral memory access, it is termed "transparent" to the user, since it cannot be seen.)

The most common peripheral storage device in use today is the magnetic disk, which now comes in many sizes and capacities. Even the least expensive computer (excluding those used only for games) comes equipped with at least one drive (or can have one added to it) for the storage of programs and data. Programs on the disk are loaded to internal memory, and programs written by the user—and initially in internal memory—can be stored on the disk. Likewise, data can be transferred between the peripheral memory and the internal memory. In addition, programs can be written to read or write data selectively to and from the disk, so that a portion of the data on a disk can be manipulated by a program without the necessity of bringing all of it into internal memory. This feature allows us to work with data bases whose size is far in excess of the internal memory capacity.

Disk storage is far less expensive than internal storage. It is possible to store a megabyte of information on a disk costing about $1.00, but equivalent internal memory costs about 500 times as much. Of course, there is a trade-off, since peripheral memory requires much greater access time. To illustrate, we can extend our parking lot analogy by assuming a multilevel lot with the upper levels accessible only by a car elevator (see Figure 1-8). Although we now have additional storage capacity, the need to use the elevator definitely increases the time required to reach one of these parking spaces. Continuing the analogy, the cars on the upper level are also more secure against theft, since the elevator is a form of security.

Another method of bulk information storage is magnetic tape, which is the cheapest—but also the slowest—medium. Now that disk drives have become less expensive, magnetic tape is usually used primarily for backup and for transferring large amounts of data from one computer to another.

Figure 1-8
Multilevel Parking Lot

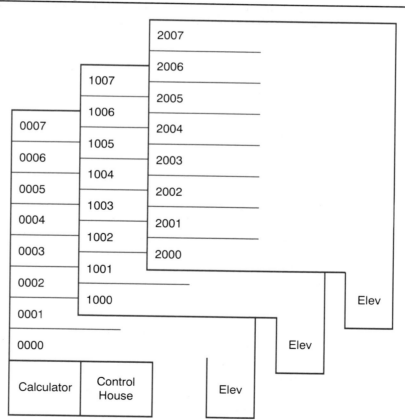

Figure 1-6 shows only a single box for memory, although we have seen that there are actually two types:

1. Primary memory, also called RAM (random-access memory)
2. Secondary memory, also called peripheral memory

To keep this explanation simple, since both types of memory serve a similar purpose despite differences in access method, we will leave the diagram as is.

The issue is further complicated by the different types of magnetic disk storage now available, including:

1. Diskettes: slow access, low storage capacity (0.3 to 1.4 MB), removable, inexpensive (available on micros)
2. Hard disks: fast access, much greater storage capacity (20 to 500 MB, fixed, moderate to very expensive (available on micros through mainframes)
3. Removable mass storage: moderate access, high storage capacity (20 to 40 MB), expensive (available on micros through mainframes)

Another type of storage is the CD-ROM (compact disc–read-only memory). Similar in appearance to the music CD, this disc is used to store large, permanent data bases such as encyclopedias, maps, dictionaries, etc. CD-ROMs have more than half a gigabyte of capacity. Manufacturers are also promising a writable CD for computer data in the near future.

Further consideration of the various types of storage media is beyond the scope of this text, but the reader should become familiar with the disk system used on his or her computer.

1.6   INPUT/OUTPUT (I/O) DEVICES

For most computer users today, the normal input device is the keyboard and the normal output device is the screen. Yet there are many other devices that can be used for moving information into and out of the computer. Among the many input devices are:

Punch card readers	Paper tape readers
Bar code readers	Badge or credit card readers
Optical scanners	Magnetic ink character readers (MICR)
Touch-tone telephones	Optical character readers (OCR)
Mice	Light pens
Joysticks	Voice recognition systems
Digitizers	Magnetic tapes
Disks	Touch-sensitive screens

Output devices include:

Printers	Plotters
Graphics screens	Voice/music generation systems
Disks	Magnetic tapes

Note that disks and magnetic tape qualify as I/O units as well as peripheral storage units. When dealing with large amounts of input data, it is often more efficient to store the data in a disk file than to enter it directly from a keyboard; in this way corrections can be made to isolated pieces of data without having to reenter all the data again from the keyboard. It is also more efficient to write output to a disk file and print it later, as a separate process, rather than having to rerun the program for each additional printout of the data. (On many large multiuser systems, the operating system stores the printer output in a disk file and then prints it when a printer becomes available, a process called spooling. The files to be printed are queued to print one file after the other.)

As a minimum, the computer must have some way of communicating with the human user with at least one input and one output device. Normally the standard input device is a keyboard and the standard output device is a screen, with an option to produce printed copy (hard copy). We will assume that type of minimum configuration in this text, plus at least one disk device for permanent storage.

1.7   CHAPTER REVIEW

Although this chapter does not purport to be a comprehensive study of computer hardware, it does introduce the hardware terms used in this text and in other references (FORTRAN manuals, computer manuals, etc.) that you may have to use. Furthermore, it has introduced some of the measuring units (speed and capacity) that can guide the user in examining or selecting hardware.

More detailed information can be found in a multitude of books on these topics. They not only describe the hardware properties in great detail, they also describe the methods used for storing and accessing the data, as well as explaining what data integrity is and how it is maintained. The inquiring reader will find that the more knowledge he or she has about the hardware, the more able he or she will be to understand the implementation of computer operating systems and languages. Furthermore, this knowledge will enable the programmer to produce software systems that run faster, minimize storage, and are more user-friendly. We can safely say that learning a computer language is only one step in using a computer to its full extent.

Exercises

In order to write a computer program, it is necessary to understand the process to be programmed. It is a basic axiom that if a human being cannot perform the process manually, then a computer cannot be programmed to do it. Therefore, a programmer often must ask, "How would I do it by hand?" Once the process is understood, then it only needs to be translated into a computer language.

The questions below will help you see how the process works. First, assume that the problems are based on the parking lot analogy from the chapter. They are to be solved manually (that is, without the help of a computer). Also assume that you are writing an operations manual for the parking lot personnel. Next, assume that each parking space is identified by a sequential number and each vehicle by its license plate.

1.7a   Assume a single-level lot with 64 parking spaces and a chalkboard to implement parking space management. What information needs to be maintained in order to locate a given car once it is in a parking space? What information is permanent and what is going to change?

1.7b What procedure must the traffic manager follow when a car leaves to indicate that the parking space it previously occupied is now available?

1.7c Assume that business has been so good that three more levels have been added to the parking lot. Each level has 64 parking spaces, with the original numbering scheme. This means that space number 1, for example, is in the same position on each level (making it easier to locate a car). Furthermore, self-parking has been eliminated and a parking attendant hired to aid the traffic manager. How must the parking space management scheme be modified to accommodate this additional storage capacity?

1.7d What instructions would you write for the traffic manager so that access time to the next available parking space is kept to a minimum?

1.7e The parking fee schedule is as follows:

$2.00 for the first hour or fraction thereof
$1.00 for the next hour or fraction thereof
$0.50 for each additional hour or fraction thereof
$8.00 maximum fee

What instructions would you write for the cashier?

1.7f Assume a car is to be parked above street level at the same time that another is to be retrieved from above street level. A single attendant can be instructed to do both sequentially. What instructions would you give?

1.7g With the increase in business, it has become necessary to hire a second parking attendant. When only one car at a time is to be retrieved, the retrieval is by first come, first served. However, when two customers arrive simultaneously, a decision must be made as to which car is to be retrieved first. The cars may be on the same level or on different levels. Assuming that the elevator to the upper three levels can handle only one car at a time, what instructions should be given to the two parking attendants to optimize retrieval time? The parking attendants will also use the elevator to get to any levels other than street level; however, after completing any transaction they must always return to the street level before beginning the next transaction.

1.7h Now that the two attendants have agreed to split their tips, it is possible to assign one to the street level and the other to the upper levels. The upper-level attendant will only drive the car into the elevator, and the elevator will move the unattended car. The street-level attendant will access parking spaces on that level and will move vehicles to and from the elevator. Furthermore, in order to speed up access, the upper-level attendant, when not in a vehicle, will use the stairs between the levels instead of the elevator. Instantaneous communication between the attendants and the control booth is done with portable radios. Write the instructions to be used to:

a. Park a car on one of the upper levels
b. Retrieve a car from one of the upper levels

2   Computer Software

CHAPTER OBJECTIVES

- To define the multiple levels of software that the FORTRAN programmer works with.
- To describe the development of the FORTRAN language.
- To discuss the various dialects of the language.
- To define the syntax of the language.
- To illustrate the way in which the programs are written, compiled, and executed.

2.1   OPERATING SYSTEMS

The purpose of software is to establish a modifiable means of communicating with the computer. The term *soft* indicates the ability to modify or reshape. There are three main types of software used on a computer:

1. Operating system: communicates with the hardware facilities and allows the user to perform the functions necessary to run the computer
2. Programming languages: allow the user to write the programs to be run on the computer
3. Application programs: used to perform the desired calculations and other processing

In this text, we will be concentrating on the programming aspect of software and on how the programs that we write are to be run. However, we must be familiar with the operating system of the computer we are working with in order to do our programming.

The operating system (OS) is the software that provides the user with a mechanism for controlling the basic operations of the computer. These operations include disk maintenance (formatting, copying to and from, backing up, etc.), file maintenance (copying, renaming, deleting, printing, sorting, cataloging, etc.), and I/O device control. Unfortunately, operating systems are not standardized and differ from manufacturer to manufacturer. Since a command on one system may not work on another, a computer user may have to become familiar with many different operating systems.

For years there have been attempts to standardize the operating systems on larger computers to eliminate the need for users to know multiple systems. The most notable effort is a system called UNIX, invented at Bell Laboratories; but so far it has met with only limited success.

On the early microcomputers, an operating system called CP/M (control program/monitor) showed promise of becoming a standard, but the failure of the developer of that operating system to keep pace with the hardware technology (with which an operating system must coordinate) prevented its success. When IBM entered the microcomputer market, its reputation caused many other manufacturers to develop compatible systems (clones). As a result, the operating system introduced by IBM, PC DOS (personal computer disk operating system), and Microsoft, the manufacturer of the generic version (MS DOS), has become a pseudostandard among almost all major manufacturers of these smaller computers—with the notable exception of Apple. However, even among these similar operating systems there are slight variations, or dialects, either in order to make use of some of the slightly different features of the hardware or to give the purchaser some additional advantages.

Nonetheless, the computer user is faced with the necessity of learning different operating systems, just as he or she must learn different layouts on the many different types of keyboards. The user must have confidence that even when the desired key (or operating system instruction) is not immediately locatable, it is probably there somewhere!

It is beyond the scope of this textbook (or any language textbook, for that matter, unless it's specifically addressed to a particular piece of hardware) to discuss the vagaries of the various operating systems. It is the responsibility of the reader to learn about the necessary procedures for entering, editing, and running programs on his or her particular machine.

2.2   LEVELS OF PROGRAMMING LANGUAGES

There are many different computer languages for writing programs, and more are being developed even today, since no language has ever been created (and may never be) that can meet all our programming needs. The purpose of a computer language is to permit a human being to give instructions to a machine, just as a spoken language allows communication of information from one person to another. And just as we have come a long way from the primitive communication of our prehistoric ancestors, computer languages have also significantly improved over the past 40 years or so.

Programming languages are of two types:

1. Machine-dependent: intimately tied to the hardware and executable only on the machine for which the language is written
2. Machine-independent: can be run on any machine that has a program which can translate that language to the host computer's hardware requirements

A machine-dependent language communicates directly with the hardware. That language may be a real "machine language" in that the instructions are written in the numeric code (either binary or a related number system) that the hardware responds to. Or it might be written in "assembly language," in which the programmer can use a more recognizable instruction that is later translated (assembled) into machine code by a very simple program (assembler).

A machine-dependent language has the advantage of being able to access every part of the hardware, utilizing all of its features. It allows the programmer to produce the most efficient code in terms of speed and minimum size. That is why most good application programs are written in assembly language. However, this type of language is cost-effective only if it is used with a large number of computers of the same type, so that the program can be installed in many locations. This explains why some programs are not available on all machines: the economic risk of writing a program for a particular machine may outweigh the economic return if not enough copies can be sold.

On the other hand, a machine-independent language is written more with the programmer in mind than with the hardware constraints (or facilities) as the prime consideration. Additionally, the machine-independent language is generally written to solve a particular type of problem or to process a particular kind of data. In general, the cost of programming far exceeds the cost of hardware and any technique that reduces the time a programmer must spend in writing, testing, and debugging programs makes the computerization of a procedure more efficient. Although the program written in the machine-independent language may run slightly slower and use a bit more memory than the same program written in assembly language, its portability to almost every machine ensures it a higher sales base and greater profitability.

Although all machine-independent languages try to place as much power as possible in the hands of the programmer, each has limitations and restrictions. Thus, there is no general-purpose language that can satisfy all needs. (However, many people, like the author, believe that FORTRAN comes closest to that goal— but this is an admittedly biased opinion.)

The machine-independent language must be translated to the machine language of the host computer (the one on which it is to be run). The program that performs the translation is called a *compiler*. This is a machine-dependent program that must be available if a particular language is to be used on the host machine. Some compilers attempt to optimize the code a program generates by reviewing the translated code and substituting more efficient ways of performing the desired process. This optimization is only partially successful and can seldom produce the kind of highly efficient code that a good assembly-language programmer can.

2.3   MACHINE LANGUAGE

The earliest computer language was machine language, which meant that each instruction had to be entered in exactly the way the machine's hardware required. It also meant that each computer had its own language, intimately tied to the hardware. A typical instruction might read:

```
210051200647
```

which might mean "add the contents of memory location 00512 into the value already in location 00647." The 21 at the beginning of the instruction would be the operation code (opcode) for addition. Most computers allowed the instruction to be entered in decimal, octal, or hexadecimal form if using a keyboard or punch cards and the system did the necessary translation to binary. However, some systems required the programmer to enter the program bit by bit using bit switches, little toggle switches whose two possible positions represented either 0 or 1. The programmer was not only responsible for keeping track of what was in the various memory locations, but had to place the instructions in a part of memory so that they did not interfere with the data the program was to manipulate.

This type of memory management is not too different from the method of accessing cell locations in a spreadsheet, although the cells are located two-dimensionally, not one-dimensionally as in a computer memory. Macros (instructions) and tables are also located within the spreadsheet but must be kept separate from the data.

One can imagine the difficulty of writing programs under such circumstances. In all fairness, it must be mentioned that memories were very small (32 kilobytes was considered a large memory) and there were usually fewer than 40 kinds of instructions available. An analogy might be made with simple calculators that accept only one instruction at a time; i.e., those that cannot interpret a formula. (These are identified by not having a set of parentheses keys.) Only functions for which there are buttons can be entered. Any complicated function, such as a square root or an exponential, is done by some numerical method that must be programmed by the user entering the appropriate keystrokes in the proper order.

Occupying the next step on the language ladder was assembly language, which is actually just an extension of machine language in that no additional instructions are available. The differences include the use of mnemonic opcodes (e.g., ADD instead of 21) and labels for addresses (X for location 00512 and Y for location 00647), so that an assembly language instruction appears as:

```
ADD   X   Y
```

The computer took care of the memory management, assigning locations to the labels. In addition, the computer segregated data and programs automatically, relieving the programmer of this major responsibility. The source code, written in the assembly language, had to be translated to machine language by an *assembler* so that the machine could execute it. The process of assembling is rather simple, since there is a one-to-one correspondence between assembly instructions and machine code.

Unfortunately, just as a machine language is machine-dependent, so is its assembly language. This meant that programs written for one computer had to be rewritten for another, preventing the sharing of code (which, in the early days, was not unethical but was considered very professional). At a time when computer hardware was becoming obsolete within a four-year cycle and new computers with improved hardware—and also different machine and assembly languages—were appearing almost daily, software conversion became the major obstacle to the expansion of computer usage. There was a distinct need for a *machine-independent* language that could be run on more than one computer and provide a basis for sharing of code and easy transportability to other computers.

2.4 COMPILERS

In order to simplify the programmer's task, and thereby to develop computer programs far more quickly, it is necessary to permit instructions that are closer to the solution of the problem without regard to the limitations of the hardware. A simple formula such as:

```
X = (a - b)/(c - d)
```

requires assembly language code that looks like this:

```
MOVE      A          X
SUB       B          X
MOVE      C          TEMP
SUB       D          TEMP
DIV       TEMP       X
```

(This is optimized code; i.e., code that uses the least number of instructions to implement the formula.)

The advantages to the programmer of writing the formula in place of the assembly code are that it is faster and the code is self-documenting, since it looks exactly like the calculation being performed. In the early days of computers, many attempts were made to develop languages that were easy to use; however, the cost of developing translators (later called *compilers*) was high and their efficiency doubtful.

The compilation process can be simplified by having the compiler translate into assembly language, and then the assembler would take over to complete the translation to machine code. The concept of using a compiler to translate a machine-independent language into machine language has one very important property. If a compiler can be written for more than one computer, then that higher-level instruction can be run on more than one computer. This means that portability is possible.

2.5 LINKERS

Another important property of an operating system is the ability to tie different pieces of code together. This would make possible the use of the same code for many different programs and eliminate the need to write the same instructions over and over. A programmer could build up a library of routines (read an input record, calculate a square root, etc.) and include these routines in the operating program by setting up linkage with that code.

These routines (later called *subprograms*) are not included in the original program; however, they are accessed by branching to them when the program is being executed. Thus they need to be assembled or compiled only once and stored in some form whereby they can be later linked to the main program prior to execution. The machine-dependent program that ties together the main program and its subprograms is called a *linker*.

The ability to link together many pieces of previously assembled or compiled code significantly speeded up the programming activity. The larger the subprogram library, the less time it would take to develop a complex program. The fact that these subprograms did not need repeated translation to machine code also significantly reduced the computer time necessary to develop, test, and debug programs. Once a subprogram was debugged, it was known to be reliable and would need no further maintenance.

The linker serves another purpose: to link the user's program with the operating system. This is critical in our present computers, where programs are run either in batch (one program after another) or in a multiprogramming environment (multiple programs sharing the computer's memory and other hardware facilities). When an executing program is completed, control returns to the operating system, which then awaits the next command, either from a human user or from a command (or batch) file, a disk file containing a list of operating system commands. In this way the computer system can process multiple programs without human intervention.

As we will see, every program must go through a translation (either assembling or compiling) and a link operation in order to run. The commands for this translation are a function of the operating system and are therefore machine-dependent. An elaboration of these commands is beyond the scope of this text. It is the reader's responsibility to learn about the necessary commands for each of the computers on which the language is to be run.

2.6   THE DEVELOPMENT OF FORTRAN

FORTRAN was developed in the mid-1950s as an experiment to determine if code could be written in an algebraically oriented fashion and translated by computer to efficient machine language. In the days of slow computers, the cost-effectiveness of automatic translation of a high-level language versus handwritten machine or assembly language had yet to be proven. The project went so well that FORTRAN (derived from *formula tran*slation) became an instant success. By the early 1960s it had become the de facto standard for scientific and engineering work, and was also being used for general-purpose and commercial programming.

One reason for FORTRAN's success was its ability to be implemented on computers with memories as small as 8 kilobytes. At a time when memory costs were extremely high, 32 kilobytes was normal and 128 kilobytes was considered gigantic. Thus FORTRAN could be implemented on almost all the computers being manufactured at the time.

The design of FORTRAN was based on two requirements: (1) the language syntax should be easily translated (compiled) into machine code and (2) the language should be programmer-friendly. Programmers of the day wrote in assembly language, which afforded almost complete programming freedom. To be useful, FORTRAN had to allow programmers to write code quickly and with a minimum of restrictions. Since the language was intended to be production-oriented and used by experienced professionals, there was little thought to what has become today's watchword: *structure.* (Good assembly language programmers must provide their own structure and should not need language constraints to force good style.)

FORTRAN was first released by IBM, and other manufacturers soon followed by copying the syntax of the uncopyrighted language. One of the advantages of this high-level language was that once compilers were written to translate FORTRAN into the computer's own machine code, FORTRAN programs written for one computer would be portable and could be moved to another computer. However, the concept of portability almost died a quick death as the various versions of FORTRAN started to diverge. Even within IBM, different versions appeared on different computers. Furthermore, manufacturers of computers competed with each other by offering enhanced versions with no standardization of the new features. Additionally, one of the faults in the language was that a different input/output command was used for each I/O device, so diverting identical output from a typewriter to a printer, for example, required a program revision.

2.7 FORTRAN DIALECTS

By the early 1960s, FORTRAN had become a plethora of dialects. Although conversion from one dialect to another was not difficult, it was sufficiently annoying that the promise of FORTRAN becoming the first truly portable language was in danger of not being fulfilled. At that time the American Standards Association (ASA) was involved in standardizing many areas of data processing, and it accepted the responsibility of drafting standards for three commonly used languages: FORTRAN, COBOL, and ALGOL.

X3.9-1966 is the ASA specification for FORTRAN IV, a version that required a medium to large computer; X3.10-1966 is the specification for a subset called Basic FORTRAN IV, which could be implemented on small computers. FORTRAN IV and its subset were sparse and efficient. All I/O was reduced to two major commands, one for input, the other for output, with the I/O device specifiable as a variable; therefore a change in the I/O unit required the change of only one value, either in the program or in the data. It had one assignment statement, two conditional branches, one unconditional branch, and one looping command, plus a halt command. The assignment command allowed the use of any valid algebraic expression and could also access built-in (intrinsic) functions. The language provided the programmer with a small number of flexible commands, and all program logic was written using these commands.

Because of sales competition in those days, the FORTRAN compiler was usually supplied without charge by the manufacturer as an inducement to purchase the hardware. As the first high-level language available, and the only one implemented on the more reasonably priced small computers, FORTRAN was used in all kinds of applications, commercial as well as technical. Its inherent precision problem when dealing with money (or any real number) was overcome by clever programming techniques. To this day, many commercial applications—including payroll, accounts payable and receivable, job costing and estimate programs—are still being written in FORTRAN.

Standardization, however, did not solve all the problems. Because of hardware or cost constraints, some manufacturers did not fulfill all the ASA requirements for the language. At the same time, some supplied additional features that were nonstandard, often leading to programming practices that destroyed the portability of the program. But more important, the ASA specifications (26 pages plus appendixes, longer than anything ASA had previously written) were unclear in many respects and did not say what should occur if a FORTRAN instruction did not conform to the standard.

One of the aims of the writers of the FORTRAN standards was to be permissive, to let the rules specify only the minimum requirements of the language. Experimental extensions were not only permitted but encouraged. All versions of the compilers had to treat standard programs similarly, but there were no such requirements for nonconforming code and extensions. The only major rule that was sacred was that the full FORTRAN IV must not exclude any of the features included in the Basic FORTRAN IV. Therefore, programs written in the subset had to always run under either compiler.

As a result of this permissive approach, there were many proposed improvements to the language. As the language spread into the academic area, many schools provided their students with versions of FORTRAN that assisted in error detection and debugging. Among the more interesting names were MAD (Michigan Algorithmic Decoder), WATFOR and WATFIV (University of Waterloo FORTRAN and its successor), IITRAN (Institute of Illinois FORTRAN), and NDFOR (Notre Dame FORTRAN). Industry needed the language to work with some of the newer I/O devices, including graphics hardware. Some of the features of the other production languages (BASIC and COBOL) were also desired.

In time, it became easier to draft a new set of specifications than to attempt elaborating on the old. Although this task began in 1970, it was not until 1977 that the new specifications were announced. By then, the ASA had become the American National Standards Institute (ANSI), and ANSI X39-1978 covered both the full implementation of the language, which has come to be called FORTRAN 77, and its subset.

By the 1970s, manufacturers had learned that there was more profit in "unbundling," selling their hardware and software separately. As a result, it is very unlikely that FORTRAN 77 will ever be given away. Since the cost of a new compiler may run into a few thousand dollars for a mini, supermini, or mainframe, the industry may not always consider the movement to the newer version to be cost-effective. In the micro field, a FORTRAN 77 compiler may cost from $250 to more than $1000.

It is expected that a new set of FORTRAN specifications will be adopted in 1992. Formerly called FORTRAN 8x (the x represents the year it was to be adopted), but now revised to Fortran 90 (note the change to lowercase), it will be an enhanced version of the language with new facilities that will permit it to remain competitive with the newer languages being used in production environments. The new version is upward-compatible and thus will accept all the features of FORTRAN 77.

Whatever the version of FORTRAN, it is imperative that the programmer read the manufacturer's manual very carefully, especially searching out the ANSI specifications that are unsupported on the computer and avoiding the nonstandard features that are so tempting to use but destroy the portability of the program.

2.8 FORTRAN SYNTAX

FORTRAN was developed during the period of punch card operations and therefore utilizes an 80-column record. The column ranges are rigidly defined, but within those ranges there is a degree of freedom. The sections of the FORTRAN instruction are described in the following paragraphs.

The character C in column 1 indicates that the rest of the record, columns 2 through 80, is a comment and is not to be treated as a FORTRAN instruction. The purpose of the comment is documentation, a very important part of program writing. Some implementations will accept a completely blank line as a comment, and others will additionally accept an asterisk (*) in column 1 in place of the C. (See Figure 2-1 for a useful rocket-firing program.)

Columns 1 through 5 are used for statement numbers, better called statement labels. These integer values are used to provide connections between related statements in the program. Although not all statements need to be labeled, those accessed by other statements must be. Each label must be unique; i.e., no two statements may have the same label. The labels themselves appear as numbers in the range 1 to 99999. They may be placed anywhere in the field (right-justified, left-justified, centered, or however the programmer desires). Blanks and leading zeros have no effect; thus, 00213 is treated the same as _ _213.

Column 6 is used to indicate that a given record is a continuation of the previous record. Although the first record of an instruction must never contain any entry in column 6, all continuation records must. In old compilers, the character in column 6 can be any nonzero digit; in newer versions, any nonblank character or nonzero digit may be used. Columns 1 through 5 must be blank. A continuation record is treated as though column 7 of that record follows right after column 72 of the previous record. However, the FORTRAN specifications place a limit of 19 continuation records for any instruction, and some implementations have an even lower limit.

Columns 7 through 72 contain the FORTRAN instructions in what is called free format. There are no rules as to what columns to use; and since blanks are removed during compilation, the programmer has complete freedom to develop a

Figure 2-1
FORTRAN Instruction Syntax

Columns:

Sample Program:

1	2	3	4	5	6	7	8	9	10	11	12	13	14	15	16	17	18	19	20	21	22	23	24	25	26	27	28	29	30	31	...
C																s	a	m	p	l	e		p	r	o	g	r	a	m		
						D	O					4	0		K	=	1	0	,	0	,	—	1								
			4	0		P	R	I	N	T				*	,		K														
						P	R	I	N	T				*	,		'	F	i	r	e	!	'								
						S	T	O	P																						
						E	N	D																							

style of instruction layout that he or she prefers. Because blanks are not relevant to the compiler, instructions can be indented and spacing within the instruction can be arbitrary. However, some implementations have restrictions on the case of the letters used and will not accept lowercase letters within instructions; to play it safe, it is best for programmers to always use uppercase letters for FORTRAN instructions.

Columns 73 through 80 are comment columns and may contain any information the programmer wishes to place there. When FORTRAN was a card-based language, it was the usual procedure to identify (number) the cards in those columns just in case a card got misplaced or the deck of cards was dropped. In disk-based systems, the columns are not used as often, but one suggestion is to place the date of a modification in those columns on the statement modified; this, again, is a very useful documentation technique. The FORTRAN 77 specifications ignore these columns, but most implementations use them as previously defined.

The actual layout of the FORTRAN instructions is a matter of style; and like most things that are a matter of style, there is no right or wrong method. Throughout this text, the author will present and discuss his style and the rationalization for it. However, the author's style continues to change (and to improve, he hopes), even after 30 years of FORTRAN programming. The intent of developing a style is of no concern to the FORTRAN compiler; the style's purpose, like the purpose of any documentation, is to make it easier for a human being to read the program. Thus, the author's rationalization of his style is that it serves as additional documentation for the reader of the program, whether that reader is the author himself, another programmer, or a student trying to understand the logic of the program.

As far as statement labels (numbers) are concerned, the author always right-justifies them so that they are easier to scan when looking for a given value. For the same reason, he tries to keep the numbers in numerical order, where possible. To help preserve that order, the author initially numbers the necessary statements in steps of 20 (20, 40, 60, etc.), thus leaving numbers available for any necessary insertions required if the program needs modification. An exception is made in the case of FORMAT statements, which are given numbers 1000 higher than the preceding statement number.

When using continuation indicators in column 6, the author uses the digits 1 through 9 consecutively as needed, and continues with the alphabet, should that be necessary (assuming that the FORTRAN being used accepts more than nine continuation lines).

Since it is always safest to use uppercase letters for FORTRAN instructions, the author uses lowercase letters for comments so that they stand out a little better. Furthermore, after the C in column 1, the author places the rest of the comment after column 20 for the same reason. Blank lines (with a C in column 1) are used quite often for better readability and to separate different modules of a program.

Within the instructions themselves, the author uses a number of indention schemes, which will be displayed and discussed later. The importance of column 6 as the separator between the statement number and the statement itself cannot be emphasized too strongly. The most common error made by FORTRAN programmers is the accidental placing of either part of the statement number or the statement itself in column 6.

2.9 A SIMPLE FORTRAN PROGRAM

According to some critics, the whole problem with FORTRAN is that it has no structure! That's somewhat true, but it's also what gives the language its flexibility and efficiency. However, there are some rules about the order of certain types of FORTRAN instructions. First of all, a FORTRAN program must end with an END statement so that the compiler recognizes that it has reached the physical end of the list of instructions. As we will see, it is possible to batch a series of FORTRAN programs one after another, and it is important that the compiler be able to separate one program from another; the END statement does just that. The shortest possible program is:

```
           column 6
  I END
```

Another statement, the STOP command, indicates the logical end of a program, which is the end of a logical path when no more program statements are to be executed. Normally, the logical end will be just before the physical end of a program, but it need not be. When it does immediately precede the END, as above, it can be left out. However, earlier versions of FORTRAN required at least one STOP statement, so it is conventional to include it even when not required:

```
           column 6
   STOP
   END
```

As described above, the FORTRAN command is placed in columns 7 through 72 in free format. Since statement numbers are not needed in this short program, columns 1 through 5 are blank. And since there are no continuation records, column 6 is also blank.

In the above short program, we have shown column 6 but will not do so in future examples. It is simple enough for the reader to realize that, except for comment records, only numbers appear in columns 1 through 5 and all instructions start in column 7.

The program above consists of only one executable instruction, STOP; when executed, this instruction causes the computer to cease execution of the FORTRAN program and return to the operating system. The END statement does not cause anything to be executed (unless the STOP statement is missing); it serves primarily as information to the compiler.

On most systems, the execution of the STOP statement will usually display a message on a screen indicating that the program has reached its conclusion; this is usually followed by the system prompt for a new operating system command. The programmer can embellish the STOP message by including a number of up to five digits or a character string enclosed in apostrophes, thus providing his or her own message or indicator. Examples of permissible embellishments are:

```
STOP  10
STOP  'END OF RUN'
STOP  'That''s all folks'
```

Note that if you wish to include an apostrophe in the message, a double apostrophe must be used; the compiler requires an even number of apostrophes in any

FORTRAN statement so that there is no confusion as to where the character string ends.

Although this program is rather useless, it does serve as a starting point for our first exercise. (In all exercises, it is the reader's responsibility to determine which processes are system-dependent.)

2.10   CHAPTER REVIEW

Once you have completed the chapter, including the exercises below, you will know all you need to know about the operating system and compiling a FORTRAN program, as well as almost all you need to know about linking. Furthermore, you will have learned about the development of FORTRAN, received a warning about dialects and nonstandard features, and learned about an enhanced version of FORTRAN (which will not make anything in this text obsolete) that should soon be available.

You are also prepared to begin writing FORTRAN programs, now that the instruction layout has been fully described. All that is left before we continue is to do the exercises below.

You should now start a personalized system logbook, documenting how the FORTRAN language is implemented on your system. First, make a note of any additions that must be made to your source program file before the FORTRAN compiler will accept it. Then record the operating instructions that you used to compile, link, and run. Finally, make an entry about what happens when each of the program versions described below is executed. Is there a message? What can someone else running your program expect to happen?

This logbook becomes a most useful reference and memory aid. Often, the rewriting of procedures in your own words is an aid to understanding and remembering. It is especially useful if you are working on more than one computer with different operating systems and/or FORTRAN compilers. Update the logbook as new information becomes available and additional experiences are accumulated.

Another suggestion is to save listings of all programs written and any I/O files used. Since many systems produce wide listings (14-7/8 inches wide), a top-mounting binder (available from most stationery stores) will be useful.

Figure 2-2 below shows the standard relationship between the files used and the operating system procedures that unite and generate them. The suffixes (the characters after the period) given correspond to those present on many systems.

Figure 2-2
Files Used When Programming in FORTRAN

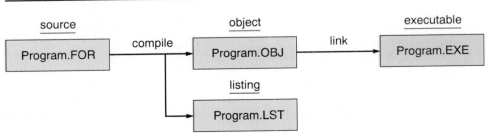

Your own system may differ, so this would become an important entry in your log-book. A brief description of the files might be as follows:

Source: the original program (in this case, in FORTRAN)

Object: the program translated into machine language (binary)

Listing: a listing of the source program with error messages (if any) and storage information

Executable: linked to the operating system (and any subprograms) and ready to run

Exercises

2.10a   *Editing* Enter the above two-statement program (STOP and END) on your computer through whatever editor is available. Use the short version of the STOP statement (without number or character string). Find out what control records are needed for your compiler. In some cases, the program must be stored in a disk file with a certain file name or file name suffix. In other cases, a control record may have to precede the program to tell the operating system that a FORTRAN program is coming and that the FORTRAN compiler is needed. The system may also require a program name within the program.

Compiling Next, find out what commands must be given to the operating system to compile the program and give you a listing of the compiled programs (not a listing of the source program you have entered into the editor but the listing produced by the compiler, which includes your source program, any error messages the compiler finds, as well as other information produced by the compiler about program storage). Compile the program and print out the compiler listing.

    If there are errors (and don't be too discouraged if there are—even STOP or END can be spelled wrong!), correct them in the editor and recompile the program. Continue this process until all errors are removed. At this point, the disk should also contain an object (sometimes called a binary) file or machine language version of your program. (Do *not* try to display or print this file; however, if your computer has a DUMP command, you can dump it to the screen, although it probably won't make much sense.) Examine the listing file to see if any of the compilation information has any meaning to you. (Some compilers will also place the assembly language code in the listing file, if you are interested in looking at it. Others will let you request the assembly language listing as an option.)

Linking Next, determine the operating system command necessary to link your program and do so. It is unlikely that you will get any linking errors for so simple a program, but then, nothing is impossible. After a successful link, another disk file is produced—an executable version of your program, linked with the operating system.

Executing Now execute (run) the program. If you are not using a terminal, you may see nothing happen. If you are on a terminal, you will probably see some kind of message that the program has executed a STOP; however, some systems will just display the operating system prompt.

    Find out how a file directory is obtained and enter the appropriate commands. Look for the various versions of the program in your directory; there should be a source file, an object or binary file, a list file, and an executable or run file.

Actually, this exercise may prove to be the most frustrating one in this book. You are responsible for learning much on your own that a text cannot teach, and the chances for error are manifold. However, once you learn the process of compiling and linking, you can use it almost without modification throughout the rest of the text.

2.10b   Revise your program and use the enhanced version of the STOP statement. First try the number and see what is displayed, entering the result in your logbook. (Sometimes the number is displayed in octal or hexadecimal, so use a number greater than 9 to test that.) Then try a character string. Some systems have restrictions on the length of the string. Experiment with strings of different lengths until you find the limit, if any; again, record the results in your logbook.

2.10c   Revise your program to use lowercase letters in the STOP and/or END statement to see if your system allows that flexibility.

2.10d   Revise your program by putting in some spelling errors. Recompile the program and examine the error messages produced. Correct the spelling errors until the program compiles and runs again.

2.10e   Remove the STOP statement and rerun the program. Note whether any message appears when the program is executed.

2.10f   Replace the STOP statement, remove the END statement, and recompile the program. Don't be surprised to see an error message! Find out how to look up error messages if your compiler simply indicates an error number and doesn't supply a description of the error.

3 Simplified Input/Output (List-Directed)

CHAPTER OBJECTIVES

- To describe FORTRAN instruction formats, including continuation.

- To define literal, character, and numeric data (integer and real).

- To define and use implicit and explicit variable typing.

- To define and use logical unit numbers.

- To keyboard input and screen output.

- To input and output list-directed mixed data.

- To use disk files for sequential input and output.

- To introduce program structure and flowcharting.

STATEMENT OF THE PROBLEM

Appendix A of this text presents complete descriptions of a number of application problems that will be used throughout the book as a kind of theme. The purpose of each of the following chapters is to develop techniques in the FORTRAN language; the applications will help to tie the material together in that the solutions to those problems will thread their way through the chapters. Thus the examples (and some of the exercises) are focused in a certain practical direction.

The beginning of each chapter will mention which of the applications will be used, but the reader might like to refer to the complete descriptions at times in order to understand the full scope of the problem. For example, in this chapter we concern ourselves with an application involving an automated teller machine (ATM) in which a bank customer is able to deposit checks and/or withdraw money. The chapter describes the input, storage, and output of both alphameric and numeric data. A very simplified method of input and output (I/O) will be developed, but the programmer will still be able to access a direct input device (keyboard) and a direct output device (screen), as well as disk files for both input and output.

Among the techniques to be developed are the prompting for input data, the storage of said data, the display of that data, and the storage of the data in a disk file. Additionally, the programs will also be able to input from a disk file. The data will consist of both character information and numeric values. The output will consist of fully annotated data, presented graphically for easy readability. When applied to our Automated Teller Machine problem, the programs will be prompting for and reading in the user's name, access code, and desired amounts.

Of course, to provide a greater depth of treatment, not all of the examples and exercises will relate to the ATM problem. Certainly it would be impossible to develop one clear problem demonstrating all of FORTRAN's capabilities; that is why several application problems are included. Part of the responsibility of the author is to show the range of applications for which this general-purpose language called FORTRAN can be used. Thus many examples and exercises will be self-contained in that they relate to no larger problem; in some cases they will be providing an academic exercise just to demonstrate or emphasize a specialized technique.

The material in this chapter provides sufficient background in input and output for the following three chapters. And by the end of this chapter, you will be writing and executing complete programs.

3.1 OUTPUT OF LITERAL DATA

The hardest part of any computer language is the input/output, and so the many variations in its handling will be presented as gently as possible, starting with very simple constructs and moving through the text to some of the more involved methods available in this most flexible of high-level languages.

It would be wonderful if we could teach a computer language without I/O, but without it we could never enter our data or see the answers we generate. Thus I/O is a most necessary evil. As FORTRAN evolved into this 1977 version, a number of simple methods (some derived from the language BASIC, others from extensions to FORTRAN written at various universities) were included in order to simplify the programmer's task.

Literal data refers to information that is fixed or unchanging. A literal statement is one that is taken to mean exactly what it says; thus literal data is a collection of characters, usually referred to as a string, which will be displayed or printed exactly as set forth in the program. Literal data is specified between apostrophes, not quotes, although quotes might be more fitting because we often say, "...and I quote" when we are repeating something literally. Nonetheless, since the quotation mark was not an available character for the early versions of FORTRAN, the apostrophe was used.

The command to send output to the principal output device, the device determined by the system as the one to which undirected output should be sent, is called PRINT. The principal output device is usually a terminal screen, but it can be a typewriter or printer; the choice is system-dependent. Furthermore, we may accept the default output formatting done automatically by the system by specifying free-format output (often called list-directed output) with an asterisk following the PRINT command. Therefore, the simplest I/O command we can issue is:

```
PRINT *
```

which will merely display or print a blank line.

If we wish to do something more interesting, like displaying a message, we could add the literal data to the command, preceded by a comma, in the following form:

```
PRINT *, 'Here is my first message'
```

As mentioned before, literal data must be enclosed in apostrophes. Although the FORTRAN character set used for instructions is limited, any available character may be placed in a literal string.

The only problem that might arise has to do with including an apostrophe within the string. The solution dictated by the FORTRAN specifications is that any two apostrophes in a row are treated as a single apostrophe. Thus we might see a statement like this:

```
PRINT *, 'Here''s to you, Tim O''Shea!'
```

which will produce the following output:

```
Here's to you, Tim O'Shea!
```

The spacing within a literal statement is maintained during output so that it is possible to place the characters into desired columns. As our first example, let us produce output as shown below in the specified columns:

```
                    1........12........23........34
        columns     12345678901234567890123456789012345678 90
                    U. S. Presidents

                    Last name      First name

                    Washington     George
                    Adams          John
                    Jefferson      Thomas
```

```
      C                    Presidential Names
      C
            PRINT *, 'U. S. Presidents'
            PRINT *
            PRINT *, '     Last name        First name'
            PRINT *
            PRINT *, '     Washington       George'
            PRINT *, '     Adams            John'
            PRINT *, '     Jefferson        Thomas'
      C
            STOP
            END
```

Exercises

3.1a   Write a program to output three lines of data:

    1. What name you like to be called by
    2. A blank line
    3. Something of interest about yourself

3.1b   Write a program to output the following message, complete with border, on the screen:

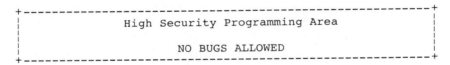

```
+ --------------------------------------------------------- +
|                                                           |
|              High Security Programming Area               |
|                                                           |
|                    NO  BUGS  ALLOWED                       |
|                                                           |
+ --------------------------------------------------------- +
```

3.1c   Write a program to generate a mailing label for yourself. Assume a maximum of five lines with 32 characters per line.

3.1d   Write a program to generate the following three-line (including the blank line) map legend:

```
        Map of Atlantis, the Lost Continent

            Scale:  1'' = 2000'
```

3.1e   Write a program to output the following tick-tack-toe playing field:

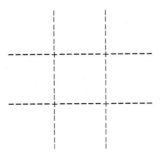

3.1f Write a program to output the following questionnaire form:

```
Name - Last:_____  First:_____

Address:_____

Town:_____  State:_____  Zip:_____

Age:_____  Gender (M/F):_____  Annual income:_____
```

Use the underscore character (usually the uppercase hyphen) for horizontal lines. Exact spacing is not critical.

3.2 CHARACTER DATA

In the previous section we looked at what is called literal data. A more precise term would be "literal constants," since the character strings do not change. The word *data* usually refers to information that can be variable and may change from application to application.

Variable information must be accessed by some method that gives the programmer the ability to access and use that information. All information is stored in the computer's memory in locations defined by the computer and accessed using a symbol of some kind—hence the "symbolic location." In FORTRAN these symbols are called "variable names"; they begin with a letter and are followed by up to five additional alphameric characters. No special characters are permissible. Thus the following are valid variable names:

```
    I          XYZ          K8NN90          AMESS
```

Here are some examples of invalid variable names:

2BAD	does not begin with a letter
TOO BAD	contains an embedded blank
MONEY$	contains a special character (not a letter or number)
A+B	contains a special character
VARIABLE	too many characters

The choice of variable name is up to the programmer. It is very wise to design variable names that describe the information as precisely as possible. The valid sample names given above do not convey too much meaning (except maybe the last one). Variable names such as the ones below have much more significance, even when they are abbreviated because of the six-character limitation:

```
    LAST          FIRST          MESSGE          PROMPT
```

Some FORTRANs allow up to 32-character variable names, but only the first 6 or 8 characters are valid. On those FORTRANs, the variable names MESSAGESIX and MESSAGESEVEN are treated the same since the beginning characters are the same. Some others allow more significant characters. However, the use of more than 6 characters automatically destroys the portability of the program and is to be discouraged.

In FORTRAN, the programmer defines the kind of information that a variable name represents or contains (thinking of the variable name as symbolizing a location). Undefined variable names have certain default characteristics, which will be described later; at present it is sufficient to know that the storage of character data requires that the variable be defined as one designed to contain a character string. FORTRAN can store only fixed-length strings (unlike BASIC, which stores variable-length strings), and the maximum length of the character string to be stored must be specified. Within that variable can be stored shorter strings, which are automatically padded with trailing blanks.

The statement used to define a character variable is:

```
CHARACTER*n  name
```

where n is the length of the string. If *n is not specified, a value of 1 is assumed. Thus a program may begin with the following definitions:

```
CHARACTER     LETTER
CHARACTER*12  LAST
CHARACTER*10  FIRST
CHARACTER*24  ADDRSS
```

Here's another way of defining different-length strings in the same line:

```
CHARACTER     LETTER*1,   LAST*12,   FIRST*10,   ADDRSS*24
```

The statements that allocate storage are among the so-called specification statements which appear at the beginning of the program. These allocation statements are more specifically called TYPE statements because they define the data type (or mode). Since each character requires 1 byte of storage, the variable LETTER, as allocated above, requires 1 byte, LAST requires 12 bytes, FIRST requires 10 bytes, and ADDRSS requires 24 bytes—for a total storage allocation of 47 bytes.

The order of specification is immaterial as long as all statements of the same type are together. Thus it is possible to change the order of the CHARACTER statements, and even intermix the two alternative methods of storage, so that we can use the following:

```
CHARACTER * 24  ADDRSS
CHARACTER       FIRST * 10,  LAST * 12,  LETTER * 1
```

The spacing shown is strictly the author's style; it is an attempt to make the program more readable to another person. The only requirement is that the statement be placed between columns 7 and 72. In fact, it could have been written like this:

```
CHARACTER*24ADDRSS
CHARACTERFIRST*10,LAST*12,LETTER
```

This form wouldn't confuse the FORTRAN compiler, but it is more difficult for the author or anyone else to read.

Review Questions

3.2a Which of the variable names below are valid? Indicate why the others are invalid.

a. CHRCTR *valid*
b. 123ABC *does not begin with a letter*
c. REAL *valid*
d. LETTER *valid*
e. FORTRAN
f. PL/1 *contains special character*
g. NUMBER *valid*
h. C*B*L *contains special character*
i. $10 *contains special*

3.2b Write the necessary statements to define the following character variables according to the length given:

STATE   2 characters
TOWN   18 characters
COMMNT 50 characters

*CHARACTER STATE *2, TOWN *18, COMMNT *50*

Show two alternative methods and calculate the total number of bytes required.

3.2c Determine the total byte storage required by the following:

```
CHARACTER*5  DECK, TURRET, MAST
CHARACTER*7  HULL, PROP
CHARACTER    PORT*12, STRBRD*14
```

3.2d Set up the character allocations necessary to specify a five-line label. Each line can contain up to 32 characters, and a separate variable is needed for each line.

3.2e Set up the character allocations necessary to specify a four-line label including name, address, and telephone number. Each line is limited to 32 characters, including spacing between the fields:

Line 1: First name, initial with period, last name

Line 2: Street address

Line 3: Town, 2-character state code, 9-digit zip code (with hyphen between first 5 and last 4 digits)

Line 4: Telephone number, including area code and punctuation

3.2f Set up the character allocations necessary to specify the following automobile descriptions:

a. Car manufacturer
b. Year of manufacture
c. Model name
d. Style (2-door, etc.)
e. Color (leave room for 2)
f. State and license plate

3.3 INPUT OF CHARACTER DATA

The simplest input statement available is of the form:

```
READ *, variable_list
```

which reads from the principal input device (usually the keyboard). The variable list is a list of variable names corresponding to the data being read in. When using this statement, the character data being input must be enclosed in apostrophes. Since blanks are valid string characters, another symbol, called a *delimiter,* must be used to indicate the extremes of that string; the apostrophe is that symbol. Let us look at a simple program and its execution.

```
C            Test of Character I/O
C
      CHARACTER*20  STRING
C
      PRINT *, 'Enter string of up to 20 characters'
      PRINT *, '''_____'''
      READ  *, STRING
      PRINT *
      PRINT *, 'Echo check of input data:', STRING, ':'
C
      STOP
      END
```

Note that the second prompt is written using a triple apostrophe at each end. At the beginning of the literal constant, the first apostrophe opens the literal statement and the next two cause a single apostrophe to be output. The reverse happens at the end; the double apostrophe causes a single one to be output and the third apostrophe closes the literal string. The apostrophes are displayed in the prompt as a reminder that they need to be used (see sample execution below). The underscore (usually the uppercase hyphen on the keyboard) in the prompt between the apostrophes shows the length of a 20-column input field, which is the limit of what can be stored in the variable STRING.

The output of this prompt in the fashion shown is a way of making the program user-friendly. It shows the user the length of the allowable input string, thus saving him or her from the annoyance of having to count characters.

The last PRINT statement shows how multiple fields of literal and variable character data can be intermixed so long as they are separated by commas. The term *echo check* refers to the output of an input record so that the user may observe how the computer is storing the information. Again, the spacing is arbitrary within the statement and is merely a reflection of the author's style.

In the execution, we use the symbolism ⟨EOL⟩ to indicate the key used for end-of-line, or carriage return. On the keyboard it is marked ENTER, RETURN, or CR, or it has a down-left arrow.

Sample Execution

Note: User responses are in bold type.

```
      Enter string of up to 20 characters
      '_____'
      'MICHAEL H. PRESSMAN'<EOL>

Echo check of input data:MICHAEL H. PRESSMAN :
```

In the sample execution above, the entered string is only 19 characters long. It is not necessary for the person entering the data to space out all 20 characters, since FORTRAN will pad the field with blanks. In this case, only 1 blank is needed. The final colon (:) is displayed just so the user can see where the literal field ends. The literal string appears between the two colons.

However, if the line entered does not contain the final apostrophe, the program will not complete the READ but will wait for additional input. Look at the next sample execution, and also notice the 5 blanks following the input of 15 characters:

Sample Execution

```
        Enter string of up to 20 characters
      '_____'
      'MICHAEL<EOL>
      PRESSMAN'<EOL>

      Echo check of input data:MICHAELPRESSMAN      :
```

Since the first entered line does not contain the closing apostrophe, the READ is not finished. Characters entered on the next and subsequent lines will be treated as part of the input line until that final apostrophe appears. In the input immediately above, no blank was entered between the two names and thus they run together. The total of 15 characters is padded with 5 trailing blanks to fill out the 20-character allocation.

If the input data exceeds the string size, the string will be truncated, as can be seen in the next sample execution. However, even if the string is too long, the final apostrophe must be there for the READ to begin processing the input data.

Sample Execution

```
        Enter string of up to 20 characters
      '_____'
      'MICHAEL PRESSMAN, P.E.'<EOL>

      Echo check of input data:MICHAEL PRESSMAN, P.:
```

Review Questions and Exercises

3.3a With the following program:

```
CHARACTER*12  INSTR
READ *, INSTR
```

indicate what will be stored for each data record shown:

    a. 'MESSAGE NUMBER ONE'
    b. 'Help me!'
    c. '10 o''clock'
    d. 'Good <EOL>
        day'

3.3b Write a program that can read and echo-check any of the above records in full.

3.3c Write a program to prompt for and read in a line of 40 characters and then display it.

3.4 INPUT/OUTPUT OF CHARACTER DATA

You are now able to write complete programs utilizing character data in a way that is somewhat useful. With what has been learned—the unformatted READ—we can read data if it is enclosed in apostrophes. Multiple data can also be read, provided the data is separated by commas or blanks.

Likewise, in output, multiple-character data can be combined with literal data, providing a graphic layout. As an example, let us look at the program below, which requests name and address and then displays the information in a slightly different format.

```
C                       Enter and display name and address
C
      CHARACTER  FIRST*10, LAST*16, ADDRS*32, TOWN*16
      CHARACTER  STATE*2, ZIP*5
C
      PRINT *, 'Enter all requested data embedded in apostrophes'
      PRINT *, '  and separated by commas or blanks.'
      PRINT *
      PRINT *, 'Enter first name (limit 10), last name (limit 16)'
      READ  *, FIRST, LAST
      PRINT *
      PRINT *, 'Enter address (limit 32)'
      READ  *, ADDRS
      PRINT *
      PRINT *, 'Enter town (limit 16), state (2), zip (5)'
      READ  *, TOWN, STATE, ZIP
      PRINT *
      PRINT *
      PRINT *, 'Name:    ', FIRST, ' ', LAST
      PRINT *, 'Address: ', ADDRS
      PRINT *, '         ', TOWN, ' ', STATE, ' ', ZIP
C
      STOP
      END
```

Sample Execution

```
      Enter all requested data embedded in apostrophes
        and separated by commas or blanks.

      Enter first name (limit 10), last name (limit 16)
      'Michael','Pressman'

      Enter address (limit 32)
      'Long Island University'

      Enter town (limit 16), state (2), zip (5)
      'Greenvale','NY','11548'


      Name:    Michael    Pressman
      Address: Long Island University
               Greenvale      NY  11548
```

The PRINT statements with no other information simply output a blank line. The input data must be enclosed in apostrophes, which slows up the manual input process significantly. Furthermore, since entering data without the required apostrophes will cause the program to fail, the data entry must be done very carefully.

Note the spacing in the output. The program purposely puts spacing between some of the variables so that any adjacent output which completely fills their character variables will still have some spacing, making it easier to read. However, where the input does not fill up a character variable, that variable is padded with blanks. Look, for example, at the output of the name. The first name is 7 characters long. The output shows 4 blanks between the names, the last of which is specified as part of the PRINT statement. The other 3 blanks are the padding placed in a 10-character variable when only 7 characters are input. FORTRAN places no spacing between the literal output fields (as BASIC does), so the programmer must supply any wanted blanks.

The next program gives an idea of how the properties of character variables can be used to produce desired output without any fancy programming.

```
C                        Entering and display of edited date
C
      CHARACTER  MONTH*3, DAY*2, YEAR*4
C
      PRINT *, 'Enter month in full or abbreviated to 3 characters'
      Read  *, MONTH
      PRINT *
      PRINT *, 'Enter day of month, full year (with apostrophes)'
      READ  *, DAY, YEAR
      PRINT *
      PRINT *, DAY, '-', MONTH, '-', YEAR
C
      STOP
      END
```

Sample Execution

```
      Enter month in full or abbreviated to 3 characters
      'July'

      Enter day of month, full year (with apostrophes)
      '16' '1991'

      16-Jul-1991
```

By using a character variable length of 3, only the first 3 characters of the month are saved and displayed. Also note that in the input a space is used to separate the day and year instead of a comma.

As will be seen later, in Chapter 7, there are other ways in which character data can be entered without the need for the apostrophes, but the trade-off is that the data will have to be entered in specific columns (formatted). Chapter 5 presents a method in which the input command checks for erroneous input and gives the programmer the opportunity to branch to an error routine. Later in this chapter (section 3.8), we will see how data is read in from disk files, greatly reducing the chances of input errors.

Review Questions and Exercises

3.4a   Write a program to prompt for and input the month, day, and year as three 2-digit numbers (entered as character data), and which displays them in this form:

```
nn/nn/nn
```

3.4b   Write a variation of the above program to output in this form:

```
Day nn of month nn, 19nn
```

3.4c   Write a program to prompt for and input the first and last names, but which displays the first initial, a period, a space, and the first 16 characters of the last name. For example, the input *Eleanor Roosevelt* would output as *E. Roosevelt*.

3.4d   Indicate what the output will be for the following program:

```
CHARACTER  IN1*4, IN2*2
READ  *, IN1, IN2
PRINT *, IN2, IN1
STOP
END
```

with this data input:

```
'NEW','YORK','YANKEES'
```

3.4e   Correct the above program so that the full name of the team appears with the message "will be the next World Champions."

3.5   NUMERIC CONSTANTS

FORTRAN was designed primarily to work with numeric data. When considering such data, we speak of two modes (types) of numbers, integers and reals. Integers are whole numbers, including positives, negatives, and zero. Reals are numbers containing both an integral and a fractional portion, although they can be integer-valued. These different kinds of numbers are stored differently, used differently, and handled differently in computations.

Integers are constrained to a defined range. Furthermore, most FORTRANs define two modes of integers: short or single integers and long or double integers. The former utilize 2 bytes of storage (16 bits); the latter, 4 bytes (32 bits). The programmer will often choose a specific type to minimize storage requirements and increase computational speed (short integers compute significantly faster than long integers). Fortunately, FORTRAN allows us to work with a mixture of long and short so that we can optimize performance with little effort. The defined ranges are:

Short (INTEGER*2) or single $\quad\quad$ $-32,768$ to $+32,767$
Long (INTEGER*4) or double $\quad$ $-2,147,483,648$ to $+2,147,483,647$

Real numbers are stored differently. So that both very small and very large numbers can be stored efficiently, the numbers are converted to normalized, exponential form in which the decimal point is moved to the left of the first significant digit and the number is multiplied by the appropriate power of 10 so that its value is maintained. For example,

$$3.14159 \quad = \quad 0.314159 \times 10^1$$
$$-0.00002543 = -0.254300 \times 10^{-4}$$
$$187650.00 \quad = \quad 0.187650 \times 10^6$$

The range of real numbers is defined in terms of the number of significant digits and range of exponents. For example, 3.14159 has 6 significant digits; -0.00002543 has only 4, since leading zeros do not count; and 187650 has 5, since trailing zeros don't count. Thus the number of significant digits is measured from the first nonzero digit to the last nonzero digit in a number.

With real numbers, there are also two modes: single-precision reals and double-precision reals. Generally, the former utilize 32 bits (4 bytes) and the latter, 64 bits (8 bytes). Although there are differences in implementation, a good general rule is that single-precision reals can store 6 significant digits precisely and double-precision reals can store 14 significant digits precisely. Any digits beyond that range are approximate. Both have an exponential range of at least 10^{-38} to 10^{+38}.

Integer constants are always written *without* a decimal point, and real constants are always written *with* a decimal point. Thus:

3 is an *integer* $\quad\quad$ 3. is a *real*

It is considered good practice to write integer-valued reals with a zero after the decimal point, such as 3.0, so that the point is not confused with a spot on the paper.

Plus signs might be used, if desired, but they are purely optional for the programmer and completely unnecessary for the computer. The only valid characters usable for writing integers are the 10 digits and the minus and plus signs; any other characters, including commas and dollar signs, are invalid and will cause an error when used either within a program or in input data.

Real numbers may be expressed in a variety of ways, but they must contain a decimal point. First, there is the standard decimal method, such as 3.14159. In addition to the characters valid for integers, the decimal point becomes an additional valid character, but only for real numbers. However, a real number may be expressed in exponential form by replacing the power of 10 (since superscripts cannot be entered on a terminal) with the following notation:

> *Esnn* where: *s* is the sign of the exponent, and
> *nn* is the exponent

Thus, 3.14159 can be expressed as 0.314159E+01.

In fact, exponential form provides complete flexibility when entering a value. If the exponent is positive, the plus sign can be omitted. If the exponent is only one digit, it can be expressed that way. Furthermore, the number does not have to be entered in normalized form but can be entered with the decimal point placed anywhere in the number—provided, of course, that the exponent is properly adjusted. Here are some allowable alternatives for the value of pi:

$$3.14159 = 0.314159E+01 = 0.00314159E3 = 314159.E-5$$

Double-precision constants are entered with *D* representing the exponential notation rather than *E*. For example:

$$3.14159265 = 0.314159265D+01 = 3.14159265D0$$

The allowable characters when defining a number in exponential form now include *D* and *E*.

In the earlier versions of FORTRAN, integer numbers were called *fixed-point numbers* because the decimal point, had there been one, is fixed at the right end. Real numbers were called *floating-point numbers* because the decimal point can be entered at any point in the number. Electronic calculators on which the decimal point may be entered in any column are called floating-point calculators. (This brief history is given because the terms *fix* and *float* show up at times in the language, as well as in some application programs; at least now the reader knows where they come from.)

Review Questions

3.5a   Below is a list of constants. Indicate whether each is a short integer (I), a long integer (J), a standard-precision real (E), a double-precision real (D), or invalid (X). If the number is given in exponential form, rewrite it in decimal form.

a. 13.887654	I	J	E	(D)	X
b. −48000	I	(J)	E	D	X
c. 0.517662E−5	I	J	(E)	D	X
d. 17	(I)	J	E	D	X
e. $123.45	I	J	E	D	(X)
f. 1890000235.50	I	J	E	(D)	X
g. 0.72E+18	I	J	(E)	D	X
h. −0.57328D7	I	J	E	(D)	X
i. 124,782	I	J	E	D	(X)
j. 3 1/7	I	J	E	D	(X)
k. 0.00	I	J	(E)	D	X

3.5b Convert each of the exponential numbers below to standard decimal form:

    a. 0.004572E+4   *4572*   **e.** 18765.32D−4   *1.876532*

    b. 1875.E−2   *18.75*   **f.** 99.5E−01   *9.95*

    c. 0.299E2   *29.9*   **g.** 0.7526D0   *0.7526*

    d. 2.4D5   **h.** 8345.7665D−01   *834.57665*

240000.0

3.5c Convert each of the decimal numbers below to normalized (decimal point to the left of the first significant digit) exponential form:

  0.12545 E+03

  a. 125.45   **d.** 18710.98   *0.1871098 D+05*

  b. −0.000000208   **e.** 2147483647.0   *0.2147483647 D+10*

    −0.208 E−06

  c. 0.10   **f.** −32768.0   *−0.32768 E+05*

    0.1 E+00

3.6 NUMERIC VARIABLES

The rules for generating variable names for numeric data are the same as for character data: up to 6 alphameric characters, beginning with a letter. As with character data, the variable must be typed; i.e., the program must be informed about the type of data the variable represents. The CHARACTER statement is called a *type* statement in that it specifies to the FORTRAN compiler the mode of data storage. These type statements are the very first statements in a program, because the compiler must "know" how the programmer wishes to store the data before the variables are used. For numeric data, there are four possible types:

```
INTEGER*2                short or single integers
INTEGER or INTEGER*4     long or double integers
REAL                     about 6 significant digits
DOUBLE PRECISION         about 14 significant digits
```

Each of the above types is then followed by a list of variables, separated by commas. For example, a program might start with the following statements:

```
INTEGER    AMOUNT, NUMBER
REAL       LENGTH, WIDTH, HEIGHT
DOUBLE PRECISION  AREA, VOLUME
```

INTEGER*2 and INTEGER*4 are not part of the ANSI FORTRAN 77 Specifications but are available on almost all modern compilers in order to maintain consistency with practices in early versions of FORTRAN. The specifications merely state that the storage unit of an integer and standard-precision real must use the same storage unit, which on most computers is 32 bits. Thus, it can be expected that INTEGER and INTEGER*4 are synonymous.

However, FORTRAN also contains a default typing for numeric data which allows the programmer to use untyped variable names. If a variable is not explicitly typed and it begins with the letters I, J, K, L, M, or N, the compiler assumes a long-integer variable (note that the range, I through N, is bounded by the first two letters of the word *integer*). Variables that begin with any other letter—A through H, O through Z—are assumed to be single-precision reals. Thus it is not unusual to see variables like ICHNGE if integer mode is wanted or XLNGTH if real mode is needed.

With the movement toward structured programming, it is considered good practice to type every variable explicitly by using one of the statements above and to make sure that each variable is covered somewhere. The default typing remains in the language so that previously written FORTRAN programs that did not use typing can still run. (This is called *upward compatibility,* which means that a new version of a language will still include all the features of the older versions.)

There is some controversy about the need for explicit typing, since it requires additional programming effort and is more likely to cause errors than default typing does. In a long program, a programmer may forget how a variable was typed; default typing eliminates that problem.

FORTRAN also provides implicit typing, in which the programmer may specify a range of beginning letters for a given type. For example, some professional programmers, deferring to the need for structure but still using the default rules, may begin a program with:

```
IMPLICIT INTEGER      (I-N)
IMPLICIT REAL         (A-H, O-Z)
```

The two statements define all variables starting with letters in the range I through N as long integers and the rest of the letters as real. These statements do exactly what the default does and add nothing to the program except a bit of documentation. What is more likely to be seen in a professional program are statements like these:

```
IMPLICIT INTEGER*2         (I-J, L-N)
IMPLICIT INTEGER*4         (K)
IMPLICIT REAL              (A-H)
IMPLICIT DOUBLE PRECISION  (O-Z)
```

These statements define ranges of variable names to be used for various purposes. Thus, any variable starting with I, J, L, M, or N is a short integer; one starting with the letter K is a long integer; one starting with H or any letter before it is a single-precision real; and a variable starting with any letter from O to Z is a double-precision real.

The IMPLICIT statements must be the very first statements in a program. They can also be followed with explicit type statements which define a particular variable in a particular mode, overruling the implicit definition. Any variable not beginning with a letter implicitly defined, and itself not explicitly defined, follows the default rule of I through N for long integers; otherwise, they default to single-precision reals. Obviously, any use of a short-integer, double-precision real or character requires a type statement, either implicit or explicit.

Within a group of IMPLICIT statements, the order is flexible. Likewise, so long as all of the type statements are together, their order is flexible.

In some implementations of FORTRAN, there may be a control record which informs the compiler that the integer default is to be the short integer. This record is usually at the beginning of the program, or the compiler may be preset to assume it. This is useful because short integers require much less storage space and compute faster, and thus they are used far more often than long integers except where the data values fall outside the short-integer range.

As an example of typing, consider the following allocations:

```
      IMPLICIT INTEGER*2          (I-J)
      IMPLICIT INTEGER*4          (K)
      IMPLICIT REAL               (A-H)
      IMPLICIT DOUBLE PRECISION   (R-Z)
C
      CHARACTER*12        LASTNM, FRSTNM
      INTEGER             CHANGE
      REAL                LENGTH
      DOUBLE PRECISION    DSTNCE
```

The variables explicitly typed (LASTNM, FRSTNM, CHANGE, LENGTH, DSTNCE) are as they are defined, despite the implicit typing. Any variable not explicitly typed obeys the implicit rules if its first letter falls within the range specified; thus XCOORD and YCOORD would be double-precision reals, HEIGHT would be a single-precision real, KOUNT would be a long integer, and INDEX would be a short integer. Variables neither implicitly nor explicitly typed would follow the default rules; thus, POS would be a single-precision real and NUM would be a long integer.

Review Questions

3.6a   For the given typing, indicate the mode of each variable below as short integer (I), long integer (J), single-precision real (E), double-precision real (D), or character (C).

```
      IMPLICIT INTEGER*2          (I-J)
      IMPLICIT INTEGER*4          (K)
      IMPLICIT REAL               (D-H)
      IMPLICIT DOUBLE PRECISION   (R-Z)
      IMPLICIT CHARACTER*8        (C)
C
      CHARACTER*12        LASTNM, FRSTNM
      INTEGER             CHANGE
      REAL                LENGTH
      DOUBLE PRECISION    DSTNCE
```

a. CODE	I	J	E	D	C
b. LAST	I	J	E	D	C
c. CHANGE	I	J	E	D	C
d. NAME	I	J	E	D	C
e. J	I	J	E	D	C
f. ZCOORD	I	J	E	D	C

g. REAL	I	J	E	D	C
h. SHORT	I	J	E	D	C
i. LONG	I	J	E	D	C
j. K	I	J	E	D	C
k. OUT	I	J	E	D	C
l. N	I	J	E	D	C

3.6b   Write the necessary type statements for the following list of variables. Use implicit typing wherever possible and avoid default typing.

Integer:	ANUM, BOUND, ERRORS
Real:	CALC, X, Y, Z
Double Precision:	MAX, MIN
Character*2:	PMAM, STORE
Character*16:	FILE, NAME

3.7   INPUT/OUTPUT OF NUMERIC DATA

The input of numeric data is not very different from that of character data, except that no apostrophes are needed. However, whereas character data allows any characters between the apostrophes, in numeric data only the valid numeric characters are permissible (0 to 9, minus and plus signs for all modes, and the decimal point and E or D with reals).

The unformatted (list-directed) output of numeric values is not within the control of the programmer. The compiler sets the amount of space allowed for each mode, and it differs from system to system. As a result, the output is not especially nice-looking because the numeric quantity may be preceded by a large number of blanks. Furthermore, a real number may be output with a very large and unnecessary number of decimal places (as in the sample below run on a microcomputer with the FORTRAN compiler written by Microsoft, version 4.1). Later in the text we will be devoting a great deal of study to the topic of formatting output (Chapter 7), and you will then understand why we delay that study for a while. For now we will concentrate on other areas of FORTRAN.

The sample program below demonstrates the I/O of numeric values, both integer and real, using this unformatted method. It should be noted that as data, real numbers can be entered without a decimal point.

Automated Teller Machine

```
      C              Data Entry for Automated Teller Machine
      C
            CHARACTER  NAME*12, PASSWD*6, YESNO*1
            INTEGER*2  WITHDR
            REAL       DPOSIT
      C
      C                prompt and input identification
            PRINT *, 'Enter ''name'''
            READ  *, NAME
            PRINT *, 'Enter ''password'''
            READ  *, PASSWD
```

```
C                          enter amount of deposit and withdrawal
      PRINT *, 'Enter amount of deposit (with decimal point)'
      READ  *, DPOSIT
      PRINT *, 'Enter amount of withdrawal (no decimal point)'
      READ  *, WITHDR
C                    verification
      PRINT *, NAME,        ' wishes to deposit  $', DPOSIT
      PRINT *, '             and to withdraw $', WITHDR
      PRINT *, 'Enter ''YES'' or ''NO'' to verify'
      READ  *, YESNO
      PRINT *, YESNO
C                       termination
      STOP
      END
```

Sample Execution

```
      Enter 'name'
      'PRESSMAN'
      Enter 'password'
      'SESAME'
      Enter amount of deposit (with decimal point)
      123.45
      Enter amount of withdrawal (no decimal point)
      400
      PRESSMAN     wishes to deposit  $      123.450000
                    and to withdraw $          400
      Enter 'YES' or 'NO' to verify
      'YES'
      Y
      Stop - Program terminated.
```

The spacing in the FORTRAN PRINT statements (in the program above) following the *verification* comment was purposely done so that the program resembled the output. The character variable NAME is 12 characters long and would output 12 characters regardless of the length of the input; there is also an additional blank before the *w* of *wishes,* for a total of 13 spaces. Thus, 16 spaces were placed at the beginning of the sixth PRINT statement so that the output lined up. Since FORTRAN instructions have no fixed columns—other than being between columns 7 and 72—8 optional blanks were placed in the statement following the comma after NAME as a documentation aid to show the program reader what output was attempted.

As with character data, multiple numeric data may also be entered on a single input line as long as the data is separated by commas and/or blanks. Likewise, as before, if the READ statement has, for example, three variables, three values must be entered. Zeros must be entered explicitly; two adjacent commas will not imply a zero. If the user enters less than the number of values requested, the program will wait until all are entered. Of course, multiple numeric data may be output by the same method as character data, but the programmer does not have control over the output spacing.

The numeric data input routine for the program above could be adjusted as follows:

```
C                          enter amount of deposit and withdrawal
      PRINT *, 'Enter deposit (real), withdrawal (integer)
      READ  *, DPOSIT, WITHDR
```

The execution would now appear as:

```
Enter 'name'
'PRESSMAN'
Enter 'password'
'SESAME'
Enter deposit (real), withdrawal (integer)
123.45, 400
PRESSMAN      wishes to deposit  $      123.450000
              and to withdraw $         400
Enter 'YES' or 'NO' to verify
'YES'
Y
Stop - Program terminated.
```

The spacing of the monetary values (after the dollar sign) is a function of the FORTRAN compiler being used and is not under programmer control.

The entering of real data allows for great flexibility. Real data may be entered as an integer (no decimal point), in decimal form, or in either exponential form (single or double precision). However, attempting to enter a double-precision value into a variable defined as single-precision will yield a truncated value, reduced to what can be stored in a single-precision location. Furthermore, as input data, the exponent may be shortened to eliminate either the E (or D) or the sign. Additionally, a one-digit exponent can be entered. Therefore the following input values are identical:

$$123.45 = 0.12345E+03 = 0.12345E3 = 0.12345+3$$

For consistency, we will assume that unformatted integer output is right-justified in 11 columns, standard-precision reals are output right-justified in 15 columns with 6 decimal places, and double-precision reals are in 24 columns with 15 decimal places.

Exercises

3.7a   Write a program to read in four real numbers entered on one input line (separated by commas and/or blanks) and then display them on one line. Define the first three variables as REAL, the last as DOUBLE PRECISION. Enter the numbers as follows:

   a. Without a decimal point
   b. With a decimal point
   c. In single-precision, exponential form (.......Esnn)
   d. In double-precision, exponential form (.......Dsnn)

Observe the spacing. Rerun the program, trying to place a double-precision number (such as 123.456789) into a single-precision location and see how it truncates the number.

3.7b   Modify the above program to output a separate line for each variable and place "borders" around each numeric field; i.e., output some character (such as a colon) on each side of the numeric field so you can measure how many columns are set aside for each mode.

3.7c Write a program that would be useful in a car rental agency. It would prompt for and accept input for:

- **a.** Car name
- **b.** Car type (compact, intermediate, full size)
- **c.** Number of days of rental

An acceptable response for item *b* would be a single letter. Display the responses after all the input is complete.

3.7d Write a program that would be useful in a computer retail store. It would prompt for and accept input for:

- **a.** Amount of memory (256K, 512K, 640K, 1M, 2M, or 4M)
- **b.** Amount of hard disk space (20M, 40M, 70M, 110M, or 200M)
- **c.** Number of diskette drives (1 or 2)
- **d.** Size of diskettes ($3^{1}/_{2}$ in. or $5^{1}/_{4}$ in.)
- **e.** Serial communications adaptor (yes or no)
- **f.** Monitor (monochrome or color)
- **g.** Printer (dot matrix, daisy wheel, ink jet, or laser)
- **h.** Amount user wishes to spend

Items *a–d* and *h* should be treated as numeric data, the last as a real number. When input is complete, present a summary.

3.8 SIMPLE DISK FILE ACCESS

As we proceed to more extensive programs, the practice of using only a keyboard for data input and a screen for data output becomes unworkable. On a computer having direct access to a printer, there is the ability to get an immediate printout (hard copy) of the computer run. But on most minicomputers and on mainframes, there is no direct access to a printer and so we must consider other methods for the programmer to set up permanent input files and printable output files. This section is not intended to present a definitive explanation of files and file structure (Chapter 13 will do that), but only to provide as much guidance as necessary for the reader to set up the minimum files needed to efficiently run and test programs.

Both the input and the output files needed are defined as sequential, formatted (or character) files in which the information is stored just as it would be entered and as it would be displayed. The records in the file are of variable length, containing just as much information as required, followed by an end-of-line (EOL) character, an internal code invisible to the user. Thus, even if we are using a 132-character printer, an output line of 70 characters requires only a 71-character record, the additional character being the end-of-line indicator.

Input files may be generated by using a text editor or a word processor, or as the output file of a program written to generate the data. Often, in a classroom situation, the instructor may generate an input file to be used by the students. Output files can be generated by a program and may be designed for screen or printer output, or both.

When inputting or outputting to or from disk, the I/O command must now include a file identifier, a number called the logical unit number (lun) which the programmer relates to a named disk file. As we will see later, more than one file may be read from or written to. The syntax of the READ statement is slightly modified, and a WRITE statement with the same syntax as the READ statement is required instead of the PRINT statement. The general forms are:

```
READ   (lun,*)  variable_list
WRITE  (lun,*)  variable_list
```

The lun may be a variable or a constant.

The process of accessing a disk file involves three procedures:

1. OPEN the file for either reading or writing.
2. Access the file as often as desired with READ or WRITE.
3. CLOSE the file before termination of the program.

The purpose of the OPEN statement is to provide the name of the file (according to the file-naming provisions of the particular computer) and assign it a logical unit number to be used in the FORTRAN I/O commands. The general form of the OPEN statement is:

```
OPEN  (lun, FILE='aaaaaaa')
```

where lun is a programmer-chosen logical unit number to be used by the READ or WRITE commands and 'aaaaaaa' is the file name.

On some systems, the above statement may need another clause, STATUS='OLD' for input or STATUS='NEW' for output. There is one problem with the use of 'NEW' and that is that the file must not already exist. Depending on the system, it may be necessary to either delete the output file or change the STATUS='NEW' to STATUS='OLD' before running the test program the second time. Some systems allow STATUS='UNKNOWN' to take care of any problem; by leaving out the STATUS clause, 'UNKNOWN' is the default assumption.

On the IBM PC and compatibles, the printer may be accessed directly with this statement:

```
OPEN  (lun, FILE='PRN')
```

wherein the desired logical unit number is substituted for lun.

Prior to the termination of the program, the files used must be closed. In FORTRAN 77, the command is:

```
CLOSE  (lun)
```

wherein lun is the logical unit number of the file.

Often, especially during the program development cycle when much testing is done, it is expedient to have simultaneous output to both screen and disk so that the results can be seen immediately and the printing of erroneous results can be eliminated. However, since the screen is usually only 80 characters, it might still be necessary to have two WRITEs. Some screens will optionally operate in 132-character format, eliminating the inconsistency. *merpodusic*

Another useful technique is to provide an echo check of the input data. The output file should contain all that is necessary to communicate the complete data to the user; it should not be necessary for the user to have to examine the input file to see what the input data was. An echo check is the writing of the input data into the output file to provide a complete picture of the computation in one place.

As an example of the use of disk files for input and output, let us use the program from section 3.7 and read the data from a disk file called INDATA. The output will go to a file called OUTDATA.

Automated Teller Machine

```
C                       Disk Data Entry for Automated Teller Machine
C
      CHARACTER   NAME*12, PASSWD*6
      INTEGER*2   WITHDR
      REAL        DPOSIT
C
C                    open files
      OPEN  (2, FILE='INDATA')
      OPEN  (3, FILE='OUTDATA')
C                    input data
      READ (2,*)  NAME, PASSWD, DPOSIT, WITHDR
C                    screen verification
      PRINT *, NAME,       ' wishes to deposit  $', DPOSIT
      PRINT *, '                   and to withdraw $', WITHDR
C                    write to output file
      WRITE  (3,*)  NAME, 'Deposit =', DPOSIT, ', Withdrawal =', WITHDR
C                    close files and terminate
      CLOSE  (2)
      CLOSE  (3)
      STOP
      END
```

For a sample execution, the input file INDATA might contain:

```
'PRESSMAN','SESAME',123.45,400
```

The screen will show:

```
      PRESSMAN      wishes to deposit  $      123.450000
                         and to withdraw $         400
      Stop - Program terminated.
```

The output file will contain:

```
PRESSMAN        Deposit =        123.450000,  Withdrawal =              400
```

Note the literal data between DPOSIT and the "Withdrawal =" annotation; the comma and two spaces yielded a purposeful separation between the amount of the deposit and the annotation.

The principal output device, for which we have used the PRINT command, can also be accessed with the WRITE instruction using the appropriate logical unit number (lun) for that device. Assuming that the lun for the screen is 6, we can rewrite the above program for output to either file or screen, with the user choosing during execution of the program; however, the screen does not need to be "opened" or "closed."

```
      C                 Disk Data Entry for Automated Teller Machine
      C
            CHARACTER  NAME*12, PASSWD*6
            INTEGER*2  WITHDR
            REAL       DPOSIT
      C
      C                    open files
            OPEN (2, FILE='INDATA')
            OPEN (3, FILE='OUTDATA')
      C                    input data
            READ (2,*)  NAME, PASSWD, DPOSIT, WITHDR
      C                    screen verification and select output device
            PRINT *, NAME,        ' wishes to deposit  $', DPOSIT
            PRINT *, '                 and to withdraw $', WITHDR
            PRINT *
            PRINT *, 'Enter 3 for file output, 6 for screen output'
            READ  *, IOUT
      C                    write to output file
            WRITE (IOUT,*)  NAME,'DEPOSIT =',DPOSIT,', Withdrawal =',WITHDR
      C                    close files and terminate
            CLOSE (2)
            CLOSE (3)
            STOP
            END
```

Exercises

3.8a   Generate a file called LABEL which will contain a mailing label for yourself. The file should consist of 5 lines with a maximum of 32 characters per line (standard 1- by 3⅓-inch label). The program should accept input from the keyboard and write it to the file. This version of the program should be very simple, with just a single prompt at the beginning to instruct on the input of the 5 lines. Structure the program into the following sections:

    a. Prompt.
    b. Input all 5 lines.
    c. Open output file and output all 5 lines.
    d. Close file and terminate program.

The strings going to the output file must be enclosed in apostrophes because this file will be used in the following exercise for input.

3.8b   Now write a second program to read the file LABEL and display the 5-line label on the screen. Perform all the input first, before any of the output. No keyboard input is needed from the user, and prompts are unnecessary.

3.8c   Modify exercise 3.7d, eliminating the prompts and reading the input values from a disk file with one line per entry. Continue to display the summary on the screen. Set up a disk file with the input values so that the program can be tested.

3.8d   Write a program to accept 14 input values from a disk file, representing the high and low temperatures for one week. The first record should contain the 7 high values; the second, the 7 low values. Write the output to a disk file in the following form:

```
Temperature Data

                    (2 blank lines)

High        Low
                    (1 blank line)
  73         58
  78         62
  75         65
  82         64
  85         68
  79         55
  75         53
```

Align the headings according to the numeric output spacing used on your computer system so that they are right-justified over the values (i.e., the last letter of the heading is over the last digit).

3.9   CONTINUATION

Since the FORTRAN instruction space is limited to 66 characters, from column 7 to column 72, there are times when a desired instruction will not fit on a single line and we must make use of the continuation facility.

The first line of any FORTRAN instruction (other than a comment line that contains a C in column 1) must have a blank in column 6. Any subsequent line which is intended to be a continuation of the preceding line must be blank in columns 1 through 5 and contain a nonblank and nonzero character in column 6. Column 7 of the continuation line is treated as though it follows column 72 of the preceding line.

As an example, we will use the prompt statement from section 3.4:

```
PRINT *, 'Enter town (limit 16), state (2), zip (5)'
```

This statement is 52 characters long and displays a prompt that is 41 characters long, far shorter than the 80 columns available on a standard display terminal. In fact, the author would have preferred that the statement include the word *limit* within all three of the parentheses, not just the first one, and would have liked to insert the word *code* after *zip*, but this would have added 17 additional characters (including the appropriate blanks), for a total statement of 69 characters and a prompt of 58 characters. Although the prompt would still fit on the screen, the necessary FORTRAN instruction could not be placed on one line.

The solution is to use more than one line with the continuation indicator:

```
 PRINT *, 'Enter town (limit 16), state (limit 2), ',
1          'zip code (limit 5)'
```

Notice how the statement was broken up into two literals with a comma between. This is a standard technique used by programmers to eliminate the problem that occurs when the statement crosses over the boundary from column 72 of the first line to column 7 of the second. That problem has to do with the unwanted blanks at the end of the first statement and the beginning of the second. For example, had the last apostrophe of line 1 been left out, there would have been 20 blanks between column 52, where the last comma is, and column 72; leaving out the apostrophe in column 16 would have left 10 blank columns from column 7 to column 17, where the *z* is; thus our prompt would have had 30 unwanted blank columns in its middle and would have totaled 86 columns.

The alternative is to run the statement right across the boundary, possibly breaking up a word, missing a blank, and making the statement harder to read and more difficult to modify, should we want to. It would appear as:

```
 PRINT *, 'Enter town (limit 16), state (limit 2), zip code (limit
15)'
```

Therefore, breaking the literal at a logical column under control of the programmer is the preferred technique.

There is another minor problem that occurs with display output. When an output line is sent to the screen, an end-of-line control character is tacked on to signal to the display device that the line has ended and the cursor should move to the next line; that is, perform a line feed and carriage return. If the line is longer than 80 characters, the display will wrap around, or move to the beginning of the next line. If we send an 80-character line to the screen, that end-of-line control character, which is automatically added on, will cause wraparound, although nothing will appear on that next line. What results is an apparent line skip. Thus, sending an 80-character string to the display should be avoided.

Exercise

3.9a   Revise exercise 3.3c to prompt for and read in a line of 72 characters and then display it. Use the continuation facility to break the underscore prompt over two lines. Try it first with one continuous literal field; then try a second time with the literal field broken into two segments, one on each line. Don't forget the comma between the two fields.

3.10   SIMPLE PROGRAM STRUCTURE

Even though we are working with very elementary programs (you may not think so now, but you will as we move on in this text!), it is proper to begin considering the subject of program structure. This chapter is concerned only with input and output, ignoring any other kind of logic (such as calculations and decision making), but even here the structure of the program has significance.

Program structure is important not to the computer but to the person who is responsible for testing, debugging, and maintaining a program. More time is spent on program maintenance than on the original writing of the program. By program maintenance we mean not only that all future bugs that show up are corrected; most programs that are in use are expanded and enhanced as time goes on. Thus it is important for the person maintaining the program to figure out what the program is doing and how it is doing it. If the program is well documented and the code well commented, that is a great help. But the code itself must be as easy as possible to read, and that requires the programmer to structure the code in some logical fashion. Let us look at an example of a program to prompt for and input a name and telephone number and then write it to a disk file.

```
C                      Write Name and Telephone Number to Disk File
C
        CHARACTER  FIRST*10, LAST*16, PHONE*26
C
C                       prompt for and read names
        PRINT *, 'Enter first name'
        PRINT *, '''_____'''
        READ  *, FIRST
        PRINT *, 'Enter last name'
        PRINT *, '''_____'''
        READ  *, LAST
C                       prompt for and read telephone number
        PRINT *, 'Enter telephone number with area code and extension'
        PRINT *, '''_____'''
        READ  *, PHONE
C                       open file, write records to it and close
        OPEN   (3, FILE='PHONLIST')
        WRITE  (3,*) '''',LAST, FIRST,''''
        WRITE  (3,*) '''',PHONE,''''
        CLOSE  (3)
C                       terminate program
        STOP
        END
```

The following screen display and keyboard input:

```
          Enter first name
          '_____'
          'William C.'
          Enter last name
          '_____'
          'Brown'
          'Enter telephone number with area code and extension
          '_____'
          '(319) 555-4920, ext 555'
```

will generate these file entries:

```
          'Brown            William C.'
          '(319) 555-4920, ext 555   '
```

The four apostrophe fields at the beginning and end of each file WRITE statement places the character records in the file enclosed in single apostrophes. The first apostrophe of each field opens the literal string, the next two put in a single apostrophe, and the last one closes the literal field. In this way another program reading this file with list-directed input will be able to accept the data. Without the apostrophes in the data file, the READ program would bomb during input.

The structure of this program is fairly obvious:

1. Prompt for and input the data.
2. Output.

The program might have been written slightly differently, with the first WRITE placed before the last prompt and READ. However, a program is considered far more structured if like processes are kept together.

In fact, one way of describing the program is to look only at the comments:

```
C                    Write Name and Telephone Number to Disk File
C
C                    prompt for and read names
C                    prompt for and read telephone number
C                    open file, write records to it and close
C                    terminate program
```

This method gives us a description in an English-like form called *pseudocode* (definition: deceptively similar to code); it has words that look like program code (READ, OPEN, WRITE, etc.), but it resembles our spoken language.

Another way of showing program logic and structure is a graphic method called a flowchart in which there are symbols for various processes, descriptions within those symbols, and lines connecting the symbols to show either logical flow or program structure. The symbols representing the operations which we have used thus far are shown in Figure 3-1.

Figure 3-1
Terminal and I/O Flowchart Symbols

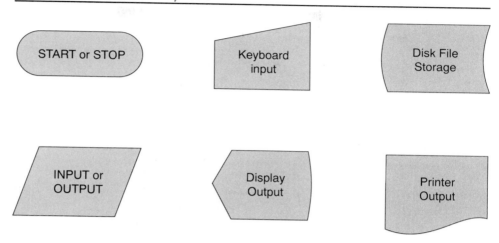

The symbols are connected with horizontal and vertical lines, with arrowheads (preferably downward or to the right) indicating the flow of the logic at the point where the line touches a symbol (or another line). Each of the symbols used thus far only allows one line to leave it (although, as we will see later on, multiple lines may enter it). Each flowchart begins with a terminal symbol marked START and ends at one marked STOP.

A flowchart may be drawn in a number of ways. First, a chart may be drawn to show every program instruction (we will call this a micro-flowchart). Also, a chart may be drawn to place the instructions into logical groups (we will call this a macro-flowchart, since each symbol represents a number of program statements); the detail is lacking, but the logic is obvious. Finally, there is the system flowchart, which illustrates only the general logic and serves as a summary of the code. Figures 3-2, 3-3, and 3-4 illustrate the three flowchart types. In the micro-flowchart, the variable names can be found wherever they appear in the program. In the macro-flowchart, the variable names may appear wherever convenient. In the system flowchart, variable names are seldom seen. Study the correlation between each of the flowcharts and the preceding program.

Exercises

3.10a Draw a micro-flowchart for the sample program in section 3.3 (Test of Character I/O).

3.10b Draw a micro-flowchart and a system flowchart for the first sample FORTRAN program in section 3.8 (Disk Data Entry for Automated Teller Machine, version 1).

3.11 CHAPTER REVIEW

This chapter has covered all the capabilities of list-directed (or unformatted) I/O. Furthermore, it also has discussed almost all of the types of data that will be used throughout the text. Additionally, it has covered simple sequential file disk access.

Figure 3-2
Micro-flowchart

Start
'Enter first name'
FIRST
'Enter last name'
LAST
'Enter telephone number with area code and extension'
PHONE
Write 'LAST, FIRST, PHONE'
Stop

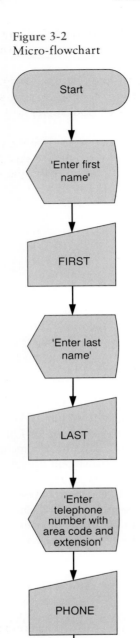

Figure 3-3
Macro-flowchart

Start
Prompt for names
FIRST, LAST
Prompt for telephone number
PHONE
Write 'LAST, FIRST, PHONE'
Stop

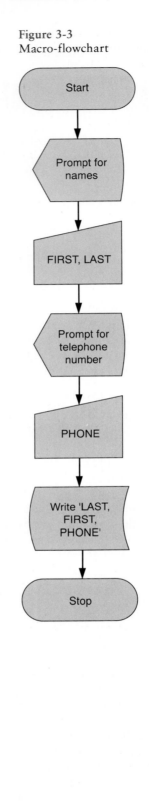

Figure 3-4
System Flowchart

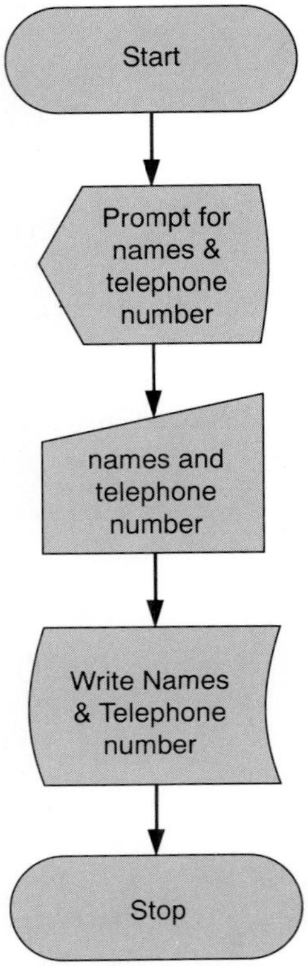

Start
Prompt for names & telephone number
names and telephone number
Write Names & Telephone number
Stop

The use of the continuation column also has been completely described. This treatment will be sufficient for the next three chapters, in which the primary concern is with getting answers to problems.

You now have enough tools to write very interesting and useful programs. Additionally, you have become acquainted with the important topic of program structure, with an introduction to pseudocode and flowcharts. Both topics will be expanded upon in later chapters.

What has not been covered is the system-dependent operating system command to send a disk file to a printer and the logical unit numbers used for the various I/O devices. It will have to be the responsibility of the reader to discover this for himself or herself.

The topics covered in this chapter include:

Topic	Section
CHARACTER	3.2, 3.4
CLOSE	3.8
Continuation	3.9
Disk files	3.8
DOUBLE PRECISION	3.6
Echo check	3.3
Exponential form	3.5
Flowchart	3.10
FILE =	3.8
IMPLICIT	3.6
INTEGER	3.6
Numeric data	3.5, 3.7
OPEN	3.8
PRINT *	3.1
Prompting	3.3, 3.7
Pseudocode	3.10
READ *	3.2
READ (n,*)	3.8
REAL	3.6
STATUS =	3.8
WRITE (n,*)	3.8

Exercises

3.11a Write a program that generates a file for a single 5-line mailing label. The prompts and field sizes are as follows:

Line 1, output columns 2–12:	First name
Line 1, output columns 14–33:	Last name
Line 2, output columns 2–33:	Title and/or company name
Line 3, output columns 2–33:	Address
Line 4, output columns 2–19:	Town
Line 4, output columns 21–22:	State code
Line 4, output columns 24–33:	Zip code (nnnnn-nnnn)
Line 5, output columns 2–33:	Special instructions

Each line should be prompted for separately, using a prompt that also displays the appropriate field length. Each record should be enclosed in apostrophes (columns 1 and 34) so that they can be read by the program in the following exercise (3.11b). Before you start, draw a macro-flowchart of the structure.

3.11b   Write a program that will read the above label file and output a 6-line (not 5 lines, as in 3.11a) test pattern consisting of a row of 32 asterisks, 3 blank lines, another row of 32 asterisks and another blank line, and a 6-line label consisting of the 5 lines in the file and a blank line. The blank line will correspond to the space between the labels on the mounting paper. (The actual size of a 1-inch label is 7/8 inch and its top is mounted 1 inch from the top of the previous label; at 6 lines per inch on the standard printer, there is room for only 5 lines on the label.) Read only complete lines, not individual fields. By alternating input and output, a single-character variable may be used for the file label.

3.11c   Write a program to set up an account file for a bank. This version of the program will only read in a single record. The file will consist of an account number (4-digit integer), an access code (6 characters), and an account balance (real number). The program should prompt for each of the fields separately but write only a one-line record on the output file (enclosed in apostrophes). Before starting, draw a micro-flowchart of the program, showing all variable names. When writing the program, first write the comments, which will serve as pseudocode, and then insert the appropriate code.

3.11d   Write a program to read the file from exercise 3.11c as a single record; use a large character variable of about 50 to make sure that the entire record is read. First display a "ruler," such as:

```
        1         12        23        34        45
12345678901234567890123456789012345678901234567890
```

Then display the record and examine each field in the output line to see how many columns your compiler sets aside for the integer and real fields.

4

Evaluation and Assignment

CHAPTER OUTLINE

CHAPTER OBJECTIVES

- To present the calculation functions of FORTRAN.

- To define the priorities of calculation.

- To demonstrate assigning values to variables by a number of methods.

- To describe the precision problems of real numbers.

- To define the available functions built into FORTRAN and their use.

STATEMENT OF THE PROBLEM

In this chapter, we continue developing the FORTRAN techniques needed to solve the problems detailed in Appendix A, as well as several other types of problems. By the end of the chapter, we will have developed enough methodology to be able to show some of the beginning calculations for the Automated Teller Machine application, begun in the previous chapter, and the Computer Time Accounting application.

Although this chapter provides all the mathematical tools needed for any future calculations, it still lacks some logical tools necessary for making decisions. Thus, our progress in solving the stated problems remains constrained. Be assured, however, that this progress will increase rapidly with each succeeding chapter.

Figure 4-1
General Structure

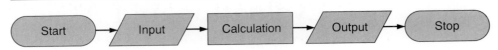

The rules presented here are but a continuation of the rules of arithmetic and algebra you learned in earlier mathematics classes. There are some implementation rules, as well as some rules required for the storage of different types of values. But remember, the programmer is able to do all that an electronic calculator can do, no matter how sophisticated that calculator is. Chapter 3 concentrated on getting information into and out of the computer. Now we are beginning to do manipulations to extract new information. In this chapter, our programs will be linear; i.e., one instruction after another, with no change in logical path. Multiple logical paths will be the feature of the next chapter.

The structure of the programs also will be expanded to include calculation functions. To accommodate this feature, we introduce a new flowchart symbol, the rectangle (called the process symbol), where we can list the calculations being performed. The symbol is also used to describe a series of steps (a *process*) in later chapters. Figure 4-1 shows the new general program structure.

4.1 ARITHMETIC OPERATORS

One of the reasons FORTRAN was developed was to simplify the programmer's job of entering algebraic formulas into a program. Its purpose was to replace the one-step-at-a-time process required in assembly language (the only other working language available at the time, 1957). FORTRAN did this task admirably by simply following the rules of arithmetic and algebra, with only a few representational exceptions. For example, since there was no division sign on the old keypunches (most modern keyboards don't have one either) the solidus, or slash (/), was used to indicate division. The ×, which in algebra represents multiplication, was replaced with the asterisk (*) so that there would be no confusion with the letter X as a real variable name. Finally, the inability to represent a superscript or exponent made it necessary to introduce a symbol for exponentiation. The absence of any suitable symbol, such as the caret (ˆ), on the old keypunches necessitated the use of other symbology; thus, the double asterisk (**) was adopted.

A few other rules had to be modified. All implied actions, such as implied multiplication when no symbol is present (like *mn*, where *m* and *n* are different variables, or like *m*(*n* − 2)), have to be explicitly stated in FORTRAN, since the computer is not as clever as the human being in separating what is obvious from what is not. And, as we will see later (Chapter 9), symbology such as *m*(*n* − 2) does not imply multiplication.

Finally, there is the question of arithmetic priorities; i.e., which process is done first. Although this matter has been settled for many centuries, many readers may not remember the rules. For example, although the expression 3 + 4 * 5 might seem ambiguous, it really isn't—the answer is 23. There is a specific hierarchy of operations in arithmetic expressions, regardless of their length, and the operations must be done in the correct order to get the correct answer. The sequence of operations is determined by their priorities, as summarized in the following table:

Process	Symbol	Priority
Exponentiation	**	1
Multiplication	*	2
Division	/	2
Addition	+	3
Subtraction	−	3

Exponentiation has the highest priority; thus, 3 * 2 ** 3 equals 24, not 216. The next priority goes to multiplication and division; and finally, we give the lowest priority to addition and subtraction; thus:

```
3 + 4 * 5 = 23        (not 35)
3 * 2 + 4 * 3 = 18    (not 54)
```

One special notation, called the unary minus, is the application of a minus sign in front of a variable. Thus, −N stands for −1 * N and has the same priority as multiplication (priority 2). Therefore:

```
-N + 2 = 2 - N    not: −(N + 2)
```

(The same rule applies to the plus sign placed before the initial variable, but that sign is so unnecessary it usually is not used.)

When priorities are equal among processes in an expression, they are evaluated from left to right. This usually has little effect on most evaluation, except when it applies to integer division. Since integer arithmetic will yield a truncated quotient when the dividend is not a multiple of the division (e.g., 8/3 = 2), the expression 8/3 * 2 will yield a different answer than 8 * 2/3 (the answers are 4 and 5, respectively). One exception to the left-to-right rule has to do with evaluating continuous exponentiations; thus, the expression 2 ** 3 ** 2 is evaluated as 2 ** (3 ** 2) = 512.

Although integer division seems to give what some might consider to be the "wrong" answer, it does prove very useful in many practical situations. For example, the program for an automated teller machine must break down a desired withdrawal into integer components: $330 does not yield 3.30 $100 bills but rather 3 $100 bills with $30 left over; the $30 then can be broken down into 1 $20 bill and 1 $10 bill. Integer arithmetic gives the programmer a perfect tool for such calculations.

As in algebra, balanced sets of parentheses may be used to control the evaluation of expressions. The terms within the innermost set of parentheses are evaluated first, and the evaluation continues by working outward. Thus: (3 + 4) * 5 = 35. Likewise:

```
  2 * (3 + (9 - 2 ** 2))
= 2 * (3 + (9 - 4))
= 2 * (3 + 5)
= 2 * 8 = 16
```

The FORTRAN compiler has no problem with unnecessary sets of parentheses, so the programmer has no need to keep notation to a minimum. It is a general rule among professionals to add as many sets of parentheses as necessary to make the program more readable to the human user. Sometimes an extra set of parentheses gives the programmer a sense of security, and that is worth the extra keystrokes.

Most programmers use the free-format spacing available in FORTRAN to make their expressions somewhat self-documenting to the reader (and themselves). For example, to emphasize the priority of the multiplication, they might enter an expression like this:

```
3  +  4 * 5
```

(Note the additional spaces before and after the plus sign.) However, this spacing does *not* influence the computer and does *not* replace the priority arrangement; it is strictly a programmer's documentation method.

A final rule states that no two operational symbols may be next to each other. Thus: N * (−M) is the proper way to express $n * -m$. Likewise, X ** (−B) is the proper way to raise a number to a negative exponent.

Since the output list of a PRINT or WRITE statement allows the inclusion of an expression, an arithmetic equation may be included. Thus, it is very easy to test priorities with the brief sequence given below.

```
PRINT *, 3 + 4 * 5
STOP
END
```

Review Questions

4.1a   For each integer expression below, evaluate the final result.

   a. 6 + 3 * 2 ** 4
   b. (6 + 3) * 2 ** 4
   c. 6 + (3 * 2) ** 4
   d. ((6 + 3) * 2) ** 4
   e. 8/3 + 6/5
   f. 3/8 + 5/6
   g. 244/5/7
   h. 100/50 * 50 − 100
   i. 103/50 * 50 − 103
   j. 9 ** (−2)

4.1b   Write a FORTRAN expression for each of the following algebraic formulas. Assume that each letter is a separate variable and that all calculations are integer.

   a. $\dfrac{n(n - 1)}{2}$

b. $\dfrac{i + j}{k + m}$

c. $i + \dfrac{j}{k + m}$

d. $j^3 - 4mn$

e. $\dfrac{i}{k^m}$

4.1c For each FORTRAN expression below, write the corresponding algebraic expression.

a. `I/J - K`
b. `I + J * K/M * N`
c. `(I + J) * K/(M * N)`
d. `J/K + M/L`
e. `M * N ** 3 + K ** J`

4.2 ASSIGNMENT

There are a number of ways to place a value into a variable location. The first, shown in the previous chapter, inputs with a READ statement. Another way is to define the location as the result of an expression; i.e., to assign it a value. As with input, the mode of storage depends on the mode of the variable into which the value is being stored. The general syntax is:

```
variable = expression
```

Unfortunately, the use of the equal sign (again, one of the few symbols available on the keypunch machines) may lead the reader to see the statement as an equation to be solved. Nothing could be further from the truth! The proper way to interpret this statement is:

```
Assign to the "variable" the value generated by the "expression"
```

To reduce confusion about the use of the equal sign, from now on we will refer to it as the *assignment* symbol.

An expression can consist of any valid combination of constants, variables, and operational symbols. The value calculated may be of any type, but the storage of the value depends on the type of the *variable* to the left of the assignment sign. Thus, type conversion can take place across the assignment sign. Any variable in the *expression* (to the right of the assignment sign) remains unchanged unless that variable is also the one being assigned the value. The variable on the left side (the storage location) is always modified to the new value, destroying the previous contents of that location. (An analogy may be made with a tape cassette recorder:

Playing the tape does not destroy the information, but recording onto the tape does destroy the previously stored sound.) Below are some examples of expressions and their interpretations.

FORTRAN Statement	Interpretation
K = 10	Place the value of 10 into K.
J = K + 1	Take the value in K, add 1 to it, place it into J. (If K = 10, J = 11.)
K = K + 1	Take the value in K, add 1 to it, place it back into K. (If K = 10, it now = 11.)
M = 12.8	Place the constant 12 into M, truncating.
M = X	Take the value in X, truncate it and store its integral value in M; X is unchanged. (If X has the value 12.8, M becomes 12.)
Z = 18	Take the integer constant 18, convert it to real (18.0), and place it into Z.
TOTAL = TOTAL + COST	Take the value in TOTAL, add to it the value in COST, and put the sum into TOTAL.

Although some of the statements above look quite simple, two of them are statements typically found in many FORTRAN programs:

1. K = K + 1 is used to keep a count. It is usually initialized to 0 at the beginning of the program and incremented by 1 each time the count is to be increased. At the end of the program, K contains the number of times the count has been incremented.
2. TOTAL = TOTAL + COST is used to generate an accumulated total. Again, this variable is usually initialized to 0.0 at the beginning of the program and added to each time COST is to be included in TOTAL. At the end of the program, TOTAL contains the accumulated sum.

If a counter or a total is not initialized to 0, it is possible that the wrong answer will be generated. The FORTRAN compiler does not place any value into a location other than those defined within the program. An attempt to get information from a location that has not been defined (called an *undefined variable*) will yield a "garbage" value, one whose value is system-dependent and may vary from execution to execution. It is the responsibility of the programmer to define every location that is to be used. Unfortunately, most FORTRAN compilers do not provide a warning message for an undefined variable.

The value calculated by the expression will be in the mode of the expression. (*Mode* is another word for *type;* they are often used interchangeably.) If all the terms are integer, the result will be integer; if all the terms are real, the result will be real. However, if the expression contains both real and integer terms (called a mixed-mode expression), the result will be real but the evaluation may be a combination of real and integer arithmetic.

Professional programmers usually avoid mixed-mode expressions because such expressions are so prone to error. The rule used by the FORTRAN compiler states that if two terms are to be operated on, the operation is done in the least restrictive mode. Thus, if an integer and a real are combined, the operation will be done in real mode. Observe the following:

$$
\begin{aligned}
X &= 8/5 + 8./5 &&\text{integer division + mixed division}\\
&= 1 + 8./5 &&\text{integer value + mixed division}\\
&= 1 + 8./5. &&\text{integer value + real division}\\
&= 1 + 1.6 &&\text{integer value + real value}\\
&= 1.0 + 1.6 &&\text{real value + real value}\\
&= 2.6 &&\text{real value}
\end{aligned}
$$

The first division is in integer mode, yielding a truncated integer quotient (1). In the second (mixed-mode) division, the value of 5 is changed to 5.0 (real) and then the division takes place, yielding a real quotient (1.6). The attempt to add an integer to a real causes a conversion from integer to real (1 to 1.0), and then the addition takes place. Had the left-hand part of the expression been 8.0/5.0 or 8.0/5 or 8/5.0, the result would have been 3.2.

Mixed-mode expressions can be avoided in two ways. One is to add additional statements; but another, more efficient way is for the programmer to control the conversions by using the special functions discussed in section 4.5. At that point we will resume this discussion; but until then, we will avoid mixed-mode expressions by using extra statements and by taking special care. For example, X = 2 * Y is a mixed-mode expression that should read X = 2.0 * Y. (The zero after the point is not necessary; it is just there to emphasize the existence of the decimal point to the human reader.) Because most professionals consider mixed-mode expressions to be poor style (as well as very prone to error), we will not use them in the text.

There is one exception to the mixed-mode rule: Integer-valued exponents on a real base may be expressed as integer. Thus, the following are not considered mixed-mode expressions:

```
A = X ** L    A = X ** 4
```

Actually, this results in faster and more precise exponentiation, since the calculation can be done by continuous multiplication whereas a real exponent leads to a calculation that uses logarithms and antilogarithms.

The reader should be careful not to write expressions such as:

```
A = X ** (1/2)
```

in an attempt to take a square root. The exponent will be computed by integer arithmetic, generating a 0, and yielding a value of 1.0 for A.

Now that we can do computation with FORTRAN, let's add that facility to some of our earlier programs. Figure 4-2 shows the flowchart for the following program.

**Automated
Teller
Machine**

```
C                           Data Entry for Automated Teller Machine
C
      INTEGER  WITHDR, N100, N20, N10, N5, N1, LEFT
C
C                     enter amount of withdrawal
      PRINT *, 'Enter amount of withdrawal (integer)'
      READ  *, WITHDR
C                     verification
      PRINT *, 'Withdrawal = $', WITHDR
C                     calculate breakdown
      N100 = WITHDR / 100
      LEFT = WITHDR  -  100 * N100
      N20  = LEFT   / 20
      LEFT = LEFT      -   20 * N20
      N10  = LEFT   / 10
      LEFT = LEFT      -   10 * N10
      N5   = LEFT   / 5
      N1   = LEFT       -    5 * N5
C                     output breakdown
      PRINT *
      PRINT *, '      $100        $20        $10        $5        $1'
      PRINT *,       N100,      N20,      N10,      N5,      N1
C                     termination
      STOP
      END
```

Figure 4-2

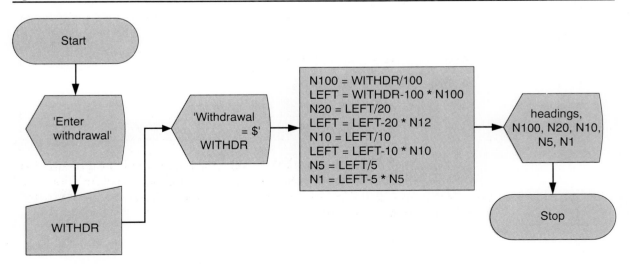

A sample run would appear as follows:

```
Enter amount of withdrawal (integer)
1034
Withdrawal = $          1034

        $100         $20         $10         $5         $1
          10           1           1          0          4
```

The type statement INTEGER was used here to change the variable WITHDR to integer. An alternative method would have been to start the program with:

```
IMPLICIT  INTEGER  (A - Z)
```

since all the variables used are integer.

Another, more mathematically oriented problem involves finding the hypotenuse of a right triangle.

```
C                        Hypotenuse of a Right Triangle
C
C                             input
      PRINT *, 'Enter two sides of right triangle'
      READ  *, SIDE1, SIDE2
C                             calculation
      HYPOT = (SIDE1 * SIDE1  +  SIDE2 * SIDE2) ** 0.5
C                             output
      PRINT *, 'Hypotenuse =', HYPOT
      STOP
      END
```

A sample run appears as follows:

```
Enter two sides of right triangle
1, 1.732
Hypotenuse =          1.99956
```

The squaring of the sides was done by multiplication instead of exponentiation purely as a matter of style; it is faster and more accurate than exponentiation, and most professionals do it that way. Here the mode of the variables was not typed and the default of standard precision reals was used.

Review Questions and Exercises

4.2a   Evaluate all the variables calculated by the following statements.

```
I = -86
J = 2 * I / 3
K = -I - J
L = -2 * (I / 5 * 5)
M = -I / 17 + 7 ** 2
N = 27 + I / 10
```

4.2b   Evaluate all the variables calculated by the following statements.

```
A = 18.7
B = 23.2
N = 7
I = A / B
J = B / A
K = -A
C = N
D = 3 + N / 2
```

4.2c   Write a program to read in the cost of a meal, calculate the tax at 4% of the cost, the tip at 15% of the cost, and the total as the sum of cost, tax, and tip. All variables should be real.

4.2d   Write a program to read in a number of units and break it down to gross, dozens, and units (1 gross = 144 units, 1 dozen = 12 units). Use integer variables only.

4.2e   Write a program to read in the diameter of a circle. Calculate and output the circumference and the area of the circle.

4.2f   Write a program to read in an integer value. Calculate and output its square, cube, square root, and cube root. Do not use any mixed-mode arithmetic.

4.2g   Write a program to read in two real values representing the sides of a rectangle. Calculate and output its perimeter, area, and diagonal length.

4.2h   Write a program to read in three real values representing the three dimensions of a rectangular prism. Compute the volume and the surface area of the prism.

4.2i   The equation for a falling body is $y = h - 16.1t^2$, where h is the initial height, in feet; and t is the time, in seconds. Write a program to read in the initial height and the number of seconds of falling, calculate the value of y, and output the results. If the value calculated is negative, it means that the body has already reached the ground.

4.2j   The equation for projectile motion is $y = vt - 16.1t^2$, where v is the vertical velocity at which the object is thrown upward and t is the time, in seconds. Write a program to read in the initial velocity and the number of seconds, calculate the value of y, and output the results. If the value calculated is negative, it means that the body has already reached the ground.

4.3 CHARACTER ASSIGNMENT

Character data may also be assigned by a process similar to that for numeric data. The available character storage as defined in the CHARACTER statement will affect the assignment. The expression may contain a character constant or a character variable, but no operations will be possible within that expression (until you learn how to manipulate substrings, in Chapter 12).

The following sample program shows some of the ways in which character assignment works.

```
C                          Assignment of CHARACTER Variables
C
        CHARACTER C2*2, C4*4, C6*6, C8*8
C
        C8 = 'ABCDEFGHIJKL'
        C4 = C8
        C6 = C4
        C2 = C4
C
        STOP
        END
```

Since the CHARACTER variable C8 has a capacity of eight characters, only the first eight letters of the string (ABCDEFGH) can be stored within it. C4 can store only the first four (ABCD). However, C6 can store six characters; when the contents of C4 are moved there, FORTRAN pads the trailing two characters with blanks. And finally, C2 can store only the first two letters (AB). Thus, using the vertical element (l) to represent blanks, the result of the above program would be:

Location	Contents
C2	AB
C4	ABCD
C6	ABCD||
C8	ABCDEFGH

Actually, the input of character data described in section 3.3 is no different from the assignment described above. The input data is read into an area of memory called the *input buffer*, and from there it is treated as a character constant. The assignment to a storage location (the input variable) follows the same rules of truncation (when the location is too small) and padding (when the location is larger).

Review Question and Exercises

4.3a Below is a small program that reads in character data and then assigns it to various locations of different size.

```
        CHARACTER S1*1, S4*4, S8*8
C
        READ *, S4
        S8 = S4
        S1 = S4
C
        STOP
        END
```

For each input string below, show what will be stored in each of the three storage locations:

    a. `'1234567890'`
    b. `'FORTRAN'`
    c. `' HI!'`   (2 blanks followed by three characters)

4.3b Write a program that will read in the first, middle, and last names of a user and output the user's initials. For example, for *Michael Howard Pressman,* the output should be *MHP.*

4.3c Adjust the above program to place a period after each initial. The input from 4.3b would yield *M.H.P.*

4.3d Write a program that will read in a telephone area code, the three-digit exchange, and the four-digit number, and display the full telephone number in this form: (nnn) nnn-nnnn.

4.4   PRECISION OF REAL NUMBERS

A part of FORTRAN that most users would like to ignore is the method by which real values are stored. However, since this same problem occurs in all mathematically oriented languages (BASIC, Pascal, Modula-2, C, PL/1, Ada, etc.), it must not be avoided.

The storage of values requires that they be converted to pure binary. This conversion is completely precise for integer and integer-valued reals but not with decimal (or fractional) values. Just as the conversion of 1/3 to decimal form yields a nonterminating number, the conversion of most decimal quantities to binary creates the same kind of situation—a nonterminating binary number. (The exceptions are those which are combinations of the powers of 1/2, such as 0.50, 0.75, 0.1875, etc.) When a nonterminating binary is generated, practicality tells us that we must terminate it somewhere; with a set number of bits for each mode of storage, a real number is restricted to 32 bits and a double-precision real to 64 bits. The unstorable bits of a nonterminating number are simply truncated and forgotten.

Thus, the storage of numbers such as 0.10 or 3.40 is not precise. Most manufacturers of FORTRAN compilers try to compensate by adding a small amount during output and hiding the problem. The error is out in the seventh significant digit for standard-precision reals and is much farther out for double-precision reals. But this imprecision will show up—much to our chagrin—when we do multiple calculations. Later, when we learn how to control our output (Chapter 7) and print out only a fixed number of decimal places, we will have some more control over the problem; but for now, using the default list-directed output formats provided by the manufacturer, we are stuck with the problem.

The problem can be very well illustrated with multiple versions of a small program that adds up one cent 1000 times. (In this example, we borrow a construct from a later chapter, the DO loop, to allow the repetition of the same operation several times. It saves writing the same statement 1000 times. The variable I is a counter that starts at 1, counts the number of repetitions, stopping after the second value, 1000, is reached.)

```
C                          Test of Precision
C
        SUM = 0.00
        DO 20  I = 1,100
    20 SUM = SUM + 0.01
        PRINT *, 'SUM =',SUM
        STOP
        END
```

The result of the above program is:

    SUM = 10.000130

The imprecision begins at the sixth significant digit. Apparently, the compiler has attempted to adjust the output of the sum upward to compensate for the truncation that takes place internally and has overcompensated.

We can modify the program to define the variable as double-precision, as shown below.

```
C                          Test of Precision
C
        DOUBLE PRECISION  SUM
        SUM = 0.00
        DO 20  I = 1,1000
    20 SUM = SUM + 0.01
        PRINT *, 'SUM =',SUM
        STOP
        END
```

The result is:

    SUM = 9.999999776482582

Although SUM is defined as a double-precision variable, the imprecision is still appearing in the eighth significant digit, a far more imprecise result than would be expected. This is because the constant, 0.01, is being treated as a single-precision number. Correcting this by adding the exponential factor D+00 to the number does not change its value but forces the FORTRAN compiler to store the constant using 64 bits, as we can see below.

```
C                          Test of Precision
C
        DOUBLE PRECISION  SUM
        SUM = 0.00
        DO 20  I = 1,1000
    20 SUM = SUM + 0.01D + 00
        PRINT *, 'SUM =',SUM
        STOP
        END
```

The result is now:

    SUM = 9.999999999999831

The imprecision now is in the fourteenth significant digit, as expected with double-precision numbers.

Obviously, the user of FORTRAN (and the other similar languages) must be cognizant of the imprecision of real numbers and be prepared to develop some special handling techniques later on. FORTRAN itself provides some, as we will see in the next section (4.5). However, never let it be said that this imprecision prevents certain types of programs from being written in FORTRAN; it just requires some special care and precautions. In the field there are hundreds of thousands of commercially oriented programs written in languages other than COBOL and RPG in which the programmers have solved the imprecision problem with some sophisticated, but not inefficient, techniques.

Exercise

4.4a   Run the above three versions of the program on your computer and compare the results.

4.5   INTRINSIC FUNCTIONS

One of the primary features of a useful programming language is the ability to write complete routines that can be included in many other programs. These separately compiled and testable routines are called subprograms because they are not executable by themselves but are accessible only from other programs. Some subprograms are supplied by the publisher of the compiler, and the programmer can write his or her own and include them in the system. Furthermore, these subprograms can be shared by many users. Chapter 8 presents a complete treatment of this most important programming feature, but this present topic is actually a form of subprogram.

Built into FORTRAN are functional computations, much like the function buttons on a calculator. These subprograms are considered part of the language and require no special linking into the program; in some references they are called library functions because they are members of the library of FORTRAN subprograms that make the language work. Although there are different extensions to the library, depending on the implementation, a basic group of routines is built into all versions of the language.

The intrinsic function names are reserved words in the sense that any attempt to use them as regular variable names may cause problems and thus should be avoided. Otherwise they are formed under the same rules as variable names, with the first letter of the name dictating mode (real or integer) of the returned value; their mode cannot be modified either implicitly or explicitly.

A function is used in the expression portion of an assignment statement and consists of the function name followed, in parentheses, by the list of arguments (shared information) sent to the function:

```
Function_name (argument_1, argument_2, etc.)
```

A function can be included in the expression just as it would be in an algebraic equation. The answer, the result calculated by the function, is returned to a memory location addressed by the function name. The number, mode, and order of the arguments are rigidly fixed, and any deviation will cause serious errors either in the running of the program or in the answer returned. Furthermore, there are limitations in the values sent to many of the functions, and it is the responsibility of the programmer to make sure that the values sent are within the proper range. An invalid argument may cause different results on different systems, yielding *system-dependent* outcomes. For example, an attempt to take the square root of a negative number may cause a "bomb out" of the program on one system; yet another system may produce some erroneous result (such as the square root of the absolute value, or maybe even zero) and continue to execute the program.

Appendix B contains a complete table of the intrinsic functions available in the ANSI standard for FORTRAN 77. Several will be introduced in this chapter in a simplified form, and some examples of their usefulness will be demonstrated. Additional functions will be utilized as the need and applications arise.

The name of the function indicates its type or mode. The answer the function returns will be in that type. This explains some names used. The types used are:

D = double-precision
I = integer
R = real

Each of the three tables in the following section gives the description and name of the function, followed by its type. The type and number of the arguments to the function are also given.

Arithmetic Manipulation

Description	Name	Mode	Arguments	
Truncation	AINT	R	R	1
	DINT	D	D	1
Nearest whole number	ANINT	R	R	1
	DNINT	D	D	1
Remaindering (modulus function)	MOD	I	I	2
second argument cannot be 0 or 0.0	AMOD	R	R	2
	DMOD	D	D	2
Positive difference	IDIM	I	I	2
$a1 - a2$ if $a1 > a2$	DIM	R	R	2
0 if $a1 < a2$	DDIM	D	D	2
Absolute value	IABS	I	I	1
	ABS	R	R	1
	DABS	D	D	1
Square root	SQRT	R	R	1
argument must be nonnegative	DSQRT	D	D	1
Transfer of sign	ISIGN	I	I	2
$ABS(a1)$ if $a2 \geq 0$	SIGN	R	R	2
$-ABS(a1)$ if $a2 < 0$	DSIGN	D	D	2
Choosing largest value	MAX0	I	I	>1
	AMAX1	R	R	>1
	DMAX1	D	D	>1
	AMAX0	R	I	>1
	MAX1	I	R	>1
Choosing smallest value	MIN0	I	I	>1
	AMIN1	R	R	>1
	DMIN1	D	D	>1
	AMIN0	R	I	>1
	MIN1	I	R	>1

Some of these functions require explanation. The absolute value functions (IABS, ABS, and DABS) are obvious, returning the positive value of their argument, as are the two square root functions (SQRT and DSQRT). A sample usage might be:

```
C = SQRT  (ABS (X - Y))
```

The square root function is more precise and faster in execution than exponentiation to the 0.5 power.

The transfer-of-sign functions combine the sign of the second argument with the absolute value of the first. They are useful in calculating rounded decimal numbers. With money, a half-cent is added to a positive value and subtracted from a negative value to round to the nearest cent. Using the SIGN function, we get the same result with:

```
RNDED = AMOUNT  +  SIGN (0.005, AMOUNT)
```

If AMOUNT is positive, +0.005 is added to AMOUNT; if it is negative, −0.005 is added to AMOUNT. In this way,

54.657 yields 54.662, which is 54.66 to two decimal places.
−54.657 yields −54.662, which is −54.66 to two decimal places.

Another application involves "saving" the sign, which might look like:

```
ISGN = ISIGN (1, K)
```

If K is positive or zero, ISGN is +1; if K is negative, ISGN becomes −1.

The truncation routines AINT and DINT convert a real number to the truncated integer-valued real and are the equivalent of converting a real to an integer and then back to real. Y = AINT (X) might be simulated with:

```
I = X
Y = I
```

The rounding routines ANINT and DNINT convert a real number rounded to the truncated integer-valued real. Thus:

```
Y = ANINT (X)
```

could be simulated with:

```
I = X + SIGN (0.5, X)
Y = I
```

or with:

```
Y = AINT (X + SIGN (0.5, X))
```

This provides an easy method for trimming money values to exactly two places. Using double-precision variables:

```
Y = DNINT (100.0 * X) / 100.0
```

The modulus function (the one called *remaindering* in the table) gives us the remainder after a division wherein the quotient is integer. Thus:

```
MOD (27, 4) = 3
```

since the quotient = 6 and the remainder = 27 − (4 * 6)

```
AMOD (8.4, 1.5) = 0.9
```

since the quotient = 5 and the remainder = 8.4 − (5 * 1.5) = 0.9. This technique reduces the change-making code shown in section 4.2 to the routine shown below.

```
C                       calculate breakdown
         N100 = WITHDR / 100
         LEFT = MOD (WITHDR, 100)
         N20  = LEFT / 20
         LEFT = MOD (LEFT, 20)
         N10  = LEFT / 10
         LEFT = MOD (LEFT, 10)
         N5   = LEFT / 5
         N1   = MOD (LEFT, 5)
```

or

```
C                       calculate breakdown
         N100 = WITHDR / 100
         N20  = MOD (WITHDR, 100) / 20
         N10  = MOD (MOD (WITHDR, 100), 20) / 10
         N5   = MOD (MOD (MOD (WITHDR, 100), 20), 10) / 5
         N1   = MOD (MOD (MOD (MOD (WITHDR, 100), 20), 10), 5)
```

The positive-difference routines (IDIM, DIM, and DDIM) yield the difference in argument 1 minus argument 2 if that difference is positive, or zero if that difference is negative. Thus:

```
IDIM (12, 5) = 7
IDIM (5, 12) = 0
```

The maximum and minimum functions are unusual in that they allow an undefined number of arguments; however, a minimum of two is assumed, since the function would have no purpose otherwise. The arguments are listed with commas between and can contain constants, such as:

```
BIG = AMAX1 (A, B, C, D, E, 87.5)
```

Thus:

```
N = MAX0 (1, 3, 8, -2, 7)  yields 8
N = MIN0 (1, 3, 8, -2, 7)  yields -2
```

Note the routines that do mode conversion automatically: AMAX0, AMIN0, MAX1, and MIN1. The first two accept integer arguments and produce a real result; the last two, just the opposite.

Mode Conversion

Description	Name	Mode	Arguments	
Conversion to integer, truncating if fractional	IFIX or INT	I	R	1
	IDINT	I	D	1
Conversion to real	FLOAT or REAL	R	I	1
	SNGL	R	D	1
Conversion to double-precision	DBLE	D	I	1
	DBLE	D	R	1
Nearest integer, rounding	NINT	I	R	1
	IDNINT	I	D	1

These functions solve the problems of mixed-mode expressions and should be used by the programmer for better control over the calculation. When mode conversions occur across an assignment sign—when a value is assigned a location—the compiler automatically inserts the appropriate function, although this will be transparent to the programmer (the programmer will not see any evidence of this unless he or she observes the compiled assembly code). However, within an expression the programmer should explicitly control the conversion, writing statements like these:

```
A = B + REAL (K)      K = I + INT (X)
```

Several intrinsic functions are used for computational purposes and are thus real-number oriented. Their purpose is to provide high-speed algorithms for common computations.

Mathematical Functions

Description	Name	Mode	Arguments	
Exponentiation ($e ** a$)	EXP	R	R	1
	DEXP	D	D	1
Natural logarithm (base e)	ALOG	R	R	1
argument must be greater than 0.0	DLOG	D	D	1
Common logarithm (base 10)	ALOG10	R	R	1
argument must be greater than 0.0	DLOG10	D	D	1
Sine	SIN	R	R	1
argument in radians	DSIN	D	D	1
Cosine	COS	R	R	1
argument in radians	DCOS	D	D	1
Tangent	TAN	R	R	1
argument in radians, $<\pm\pi/2$	DTAN	D	D	1
Arcsine	ASIN	R	R	1
answer returned in radians	DASIN	D	D	1
Arccosine	ACOS	R	R	1
answer returned in radians	DACOS	D	D	1
Arctangent	ATAN	R	R	1
answer returned in radians	DATAN	D	D	1
two arguments are a_1/a_2	ATAN2	R	R	2
	DATAN2	D	D	2
Hyperbolic sine	SINH	R	R	1
argument in radians	DSINH	D	D	1
Hyperbolic cosine	COSH	R	R	1
argument in radians	DCOSH	D	D	1
Hyperbolic tangent	TANH	R	R	1
argument in radians	DTANH	D	D	1

These functions require little explanation if the user understands the mathematics involved. Their ease of use is obvious from the following sample statements:

```
A = SIN(A) + COS(B)
T = ALOG (ATAN (X/Y))  or its equivalent: T = ALOG (ATAN2 (X, Y))
```

Since functions may also be included in the output variable list, it is possible to write code such as:

```
PRINT *, IABS(I - J), SQRT(X)
```

Review Questions and Exercises

4.5a For each expression below, determine the result calculated. Pay special attention to mode:

a. AINT (-5.6)
b. AINT (87.9)
c. ANINT (-5.6)
d. ANINT (87.9)
e. MOD (12, 5)
f. MOD (-12, 5)
g. AMOD (-12,0, 4.3)
h. IDIM (5, 2)
i. IDIM (2, 5)
j. DIM (-12.5, -18.7)
k. IABS (5)
l. ABS (-22.7)

m. SQRT (25.00)
n. SIGN (2.5, -87.2)
o. MAXO (18, -2, 23, 7, 13)
p. AMAXO (18, -2, 23, 7, 13)
q. MIN1 (18.0, -2.0, 23.0, 7.0, 13.0)
r. INT (7.8)
s. NINT (7.8)
t. REAL (7)
u. SIN (0.0)
v. COS (0.0)
w. ALOG (1.0)
x. EXP (0.0)

Note: In all the exercises below, avoid mixed-mode expressions by using the appropriate intrinsic functions for mode conversions. Also, any logic called for can be done using the FORTRAN intrinsic functions.

4.5b Write a program to input an angle in degrees, minutes, and seconds (all integer); convert that angle to decimal degrees and then to radians (3.14159 radians = 180 degrees). Using the angle in radians, calculate the sine and cosine of that angle. Display all the input values as well as all the calculated values. Also, try angles greater than 90 degrees and less than 0 degrees to see the results obtained for the quadrants other than the first one.

4.5c Write a program to determine the ratio of the natural logarithm to the base 10 logarithm. This program requires no input, since the programmer can assume the use of any real number as the argument for both functions. Display both logarithms and the ratio.

4.5d Prove the trigonometric identity that the sine squared plus the cosine squared of the same angle equals 1.0. No input is required, since the program can be run with any assumed value for the angle. However, the program might be written to accept the input of an angle in integer degrees, convert it to radians, and then apply the identity.

4.5e Write a program to enter a number in the range 0 to 1439, representing minutes from midnight. Convert the time into a real number in the form nn.mm, where nn is hours and mm is minutes. For example, 800 minutes converts to 13.20 hours. Also display the nearest hour.

4.5f Write a program to read in an integer number of items and break that number down into gross, dozens, and items (1 dozen = 12 items, 1 gross = 12 dozen = 144 items). Compute a real cost based on $10.00 per gross, $1.00 per dozen, and $0.10 per item.

4.5g Write a program to read in a real cost and compute a real tax based on a rate of 8%. The tax should be converted to a real number rounded to two decimal places.

4.5h   Write a program to read in five examination grades (integer) and to compute and display the maximum value, the minimum value, and the real average.

4.5i   Write a program to read in two integer numbers and to display a 2 if both are of the same sign and a zero if they are of opposite signs.

4.5j   Write a program to input an integer number and to display a real zero if that number is a perfect square and a nonzero real number if not.

4.5k   Write a program to input an integer number and to display a zero if that number is even and a 1 if it is odd. Make sure that your alogorithm works for both positive and negative numbers.

4.5l   Write a program to input two integer numbers and then display a zero if both are of the same parity (both even or both odd) and a 1 if of opposite parity.

4.5m   Write a program to read in an integer number of hours worked and a real rate of pay. Compute and display the amount paid as rate times all hours, plus 50% additional pay for hours above 40 (time and a half). (Hint: The DIM function is useful here.)

4.5n   Using the ALOG function, determine the number of digits in an entered integer number. Test with such numbers as 99 (two digits) and 100 (three digits).

4.5o   Test the following functions using invalid values and observe the results on your computer:

Function	Value of Argument(s)
a. ABS	10
b. MAX0	no arguments, such as M = MAX0 ( )
c. REAL	10.0
d. SQRT	< 0.00
e. MOD	10, 0

4.6   THE DATA AND PARAMETER STATEMENTS

Two other statements available in FORTRAN allow the programmer to assign values to locations. They work differently than the assignment statement in that they are not *executable* statements but do their work during the compilation process.

The DATA statement allows the programmer to define initial values for a given location or set of locations and is useful in speeding up program execution as well as reducing coding effort. The general syntax is:

```
DATA  list of variables/ list of values/
```

The list of variables (one or more) must agree in number and mode with the list of values. Multiple lists may be specified as follows:

```
DATA list_1/values_1/, list_2/values_2/, list_3/values_3/, etc.
```

with the pairs of specifications separated by commas.

The DATA statement appears after other specification statements (like the IMPLICIT and type statements) and before any executable statements in the program. The variables initialized therein may be modified either by input or by assignment at some later time in the program and, although the DATA statement can be used to define constants, the location should not be thought of as unchangeable.

To illustrate the different ways in which the data statement may be formed, assume the initialization of the following integer variables to zero:

```
      DATA  IDISTR/ 0/, NUMERR/ 0/, ISUM/ 0/
  or: DATA  IDISTR, NUMERR, ISUM/ 0, 0, 0/
  or: DATA  IDISTR, NUMERR, ISUM/ 3*0/
```

Note the use of the repetition factor when the values are all the same.

Of course, the following coding could have been used:

```
  IDISTR = 0
  NUMERR = 0
  ISUM   = 0
```

However, there is more coding involved and execution time is required whenever the program is run. When a DATA statement is used, the compiler places the value in the location at compilation time. Thus, the compilation time may be slightly longer; but since a production program is executed far more times than it is compiled, the saving in execution time becomes more significant, especially when initializing a large amount of data.

There are some strict rules regarding DATA statements:

1. The number of variables and the number of values must agree. There is a one-to-one correspondence between the list of variables and the list of values; i.e., the first value goes with the first variable, the second with the second, and so on.
2. The modes of the variables and the values must agree. This requires the programmer to be careful in differentiating between reals and integers, such as:

```
DATA  NTOTAL/ 0/,  TOTAL/ 0.0/
```

3. A variable must not appear in more than one DATA statement.

There do exist implementations in which the programmer might place the DATA statement within the executable statements instead of before them, giving the mistaken impression that the variables listed will be reset. Again we repeat that the DATA statement acts during the compilation phase and cannot be used to reset the value of any variables once the program is executing.

We also have a PARAMETER statement which, although it looks like an assignment, actually represents a string substitution, as you can see in the following program.

```
      PARAMETER  (PI = 3.14159265,  TWOPI = 2.00 * PI)
C
      READ  *, RADIUS
      AREA   = PI * RADIUS * RADIUS
      CIRCUM = TWOPI * RADIUS
      PRINT *, AREA, CIRCUM
C
      STOP
      END
```

Any place the string PI appears as an apparent variable name, it is replaced with 3.14159265; any place the string TWOPI appears, it is replaced with 2.00 * PI, which in turn becomes 2.00 * 3.14159265. Thus, to the compiler, the two statements following READ appear to be:

```
AREA   = 3.14159265 * RADIUS * RADIUS
CIRCUM = 2.00 * 3.14159265 * RADIUS
```

Therefore, since the PARAMETER statement defines a variable that remains constant at all times, it is more appropriate to use it to represent a constant rather than the DATA statement.

A PARAMETER equivalence consists of a symbolic name, an equal sign, and either a constant, the symbolic name of a constant, or a constant expression. The PARAMETER statement cannot be used in some I/O constructs, but it can be used anywhere else, including the DATA statement. It must appear after any type statement that affects it and before it is used elsewhere in the program.

Review Question and Exercises

4.6a Rewrite the following program as the computer will finally see it; i.e., with the PARAMETER variables replaced. Then determine the output for costs of $10.00 and $20.00. (This program shows a practical application of the DIM function.)

```
      PARAMETER  (TAXRAT = 8.5, TAXLIM = 1.00)
      READ  *, COST
      TAX   = DIM (COST * TAXRAT / 100.0, TAXLIM)
      PRINT *, COST, TAX
      STOP
      END
```

4.6b Rewrite the program in 4.6a using the DATA statement to set the values of TAXRAT and TAXLIM.

4.6c If the statement

```
      TAXRAT = 10.0
```

is inserted after the READ statement, why will the program in 4.6a not compile while the one in 4.6b will compile without error?

4.7   SAMPLE APPLICATIONS

To illustrate the use of some of the techniques discussed above, we will return to two of our sample applications.

First, the Automated Teller Machine routine is rewritten. It is now refined to give only $50, $20, and $10 bills. This is accomplished by rounding the withdrawal amount up to the next higher multiple of $10 when it is not already a multiple of $10. Note the routine used to convert the withdrawal amount to the next higher multiple; it is a standard algorithm in which you add an amount 1 less than the multiple desired and, using integer arithmetic, divide by the desired multiple, automatically truncating; you then multiply the result by the multiple.

Next, a fee is applied—2% of the withdrawal or $2, whichever is higher—to be deducted from the customer's account. Note the use of the NINT function, which converts the fee to the nearest whole number, rounding, and the MAX0 function to determine the final fee.

 Automated Teller Machine

```
C                        Automated Teller Machine
C
        PARAMETER  (RATE = 0.020)
        INTEGER*2  WITHDR, N50, N20, N10, LEFT
        INTEGER*2  WITH10, FEE, TOTAL
C
C                  enter amount of withdrawal
        PRINT *, 'Enter amount of withdrawal (integer)'
        READ  *, WITHDR
C                  convert to next highest ten dollars, if not multiple
        WITH10 = (WITHDR + 9) / 10 * 10
C                  verification
        PRINT *, 'Withdrawal = $', WITH10
C                  calculate breakdown
        N50  = WITH10 / 50
        LEFT = MOD (WITH10, 50)
        N20  = LEFT    /20
        LEFT = MOD (LEFT, 20)
        N10  = LEFT    / 10
C                  output breakdown
        PRINT *
        PRINT *, '     $50        $20        $10'
        PRINT *,      N50,       N20,       N10
C                  compute fee
        FEE = NINT (RATE * REAL (WITH10))
        FEE = MAX0 (FEE, 2)
        PRINT *, 'Fee   = $', FEE
        TOTAL = WITH10 + FEE
        PRINT *, 'Total = $', TOTAL
C                  termination
        STOP
        END
```

It is also possible to begin the solution of the Computer Time Accounting routine by developing the part of the program that converts the minutes from midnight (the method used for registering logging on and logging off times) to hours and minutes and then computes the charge for that time. The charge will be $2.50 per minute for the first 120 minutes and 80% of that rate for any additional time (representing a 20% discount).

**Computer
Time
Accounting**

```
C                          Computer Time Accounting
C
      PARAMETER  (RATE = 2.50, DSRATE = 0.20 * RATE)
      INTEGER*2  LOGIN, LOGOUT, MINUTE, EXCESS
      REAL       TIMIN, TIMOUT, CHARGE, DISCNT, FEE
C
C               enter logging in and logging out times in minutes
      PRINT *, 'Enter time in, time out as minutes since midnight'
      READ  *, LOGIN, LOGOUT

C               convert to hours.minutes
      TIMIN  = REAL (LOGIN  / 60) + REAL (MOD (LOGIN,  60)) / 100.0
      TIMOUT = REAL (LOGOUT / 60) + REAL (MOD (LOGOUT, 60)) / 100.0
      MINUTE = LOGOUT - LOGIN
      PRINT  *, 'On system from', TIMIN,' to', TIMOUT
      PRINT  *, MINUTE,' minutes'
C                   compute fee
      CHARGE = RATE * REAL (MINUTE)
      EXCESS = IDIM (MINUTE, 120)
      DISCNT = DSRATE * EXCESS
      FEE    = CHARGE - DISCNT
      PRINT  *, 'Charge of $', CHARGE,' minus discount of $', DISCNT
      PRINT  *, '  for final fee of $',FEE
C                   termination
      STOP
      END
```

Note the use of the IDIM function to determine the number of minutes greater than 120 and that, if the value is less than 120, a value of zero negates any discount.

4.8 CHAPTER REVIEW

This chapter has covered all the computer mathematics needed for the study of FORTRAN. This should set aside the fears of any readers who expected to see a very theoretical approach. All that is available in most computer languages is merely basic arithmetic, simple algebra, and the usual computational functions. Of course, some "higher mathematics" will appear in some of the applications in the form of numerical methods, that is, methods of arithmetic that can be used to solve complex problems in calculus, differential equations, linear algebra, and other advanced fields, but you need not fear them; as we will see, they will be explained in such a way that no theory is involved.

Furthermore, all the methods used to assign values to a location have been covered. Some of the precision problems encountered in the mathematically oriented languages have been pointed out and will be solved in later chapters.

At this point the reader is able to write programs for the solution of any formulas that can be solved by the insertion of values. The following topics are covered in this chapter:

Topic	Section
Arithmetic operators	4.1
Assignment	4.2
CHARACTER assignment	4.3
DATA	4.6
Intrinsic functions	4.5
Mixed-mode arithmetic	4.2
PARAMETER	4.6
Precision of reals	4.4

Exercises

4.8a   The FORTRAN statement Y = 70 * T − 16.1 * T ** 2 computes the height of an object thrown vertically into the air with a velocity of 70 feet per second at a time T. Write a program to read in a real value of time and output the vertical height, Y. If the value of Y is negative, redefine Y as zero, indicating that the object is on the ground, not below it. (Hint: Use the DIM function.) Test with sufficient values of time to obtain answers both in the air and on the ground.

4.8b   The FORTRAN statement AMT = PRIN * (1.0 + RATE) ** NPER computes the amount of interest plus principal in a savings account with an interest rate (RATE) (in decimal form, not percent) for a number of periods NPER. For example, 12% interest compounded quarterly for five years is 20 periods at a rate of 3%; 12% interest compounded monthly for two years is 24 periods at a rate of 1%. Write a program that will input the principal, interest rate (in percent), and number of periods, and computes and displays the total amount. Round the answer to two decimal places. (As a check of the accuracy of the program, $1000 compounded monthly for two years at 12% is $1269.73.)

4.8c   In the year 1986, one automobile user bought 700 gallons of gas for her car at an average cost of $1.20 per gallon and 4 quarts of oil at $1.50 each. She spent $720 for insurance for the year and $360 for maintenance. The car travelled 14,000 miles. Write a program to accept all of the above data; compute the total cost of running the car and the cost per mile.

4.8d   A degree-day is the number of degrees the mean temperature for a day falls below 65 degrees Fahrenheit. When the mean temperature is above 65 degrees, the degree-day equals zero. This unit of measurement is used to compute the approximate amount of heating energy required to warm a house. Write a program that will input the high and low temperatures for the day and output the mean and the degree-days.

4.8e   The equations of two straight lines can be expressed as:

$$ax + by = c \quad \text{and} \quad dx + ey = f$$

The solution for these equations (the point where they cross) is:

$$x = (ce - fb)/(ae - bd) \quad \text{and} \quad y = (af - cd)/(ae - bd)$$

This solution is valid provided the term $(ae - bd)$ is not zero, which indicates that the lines are either parallel or coincident. Write a program to input the six coefficients $(a, b, c, d, e, \text{and } f)$ and to compute and output the values of x and y. Run it with several sets of data, including one in which the denominator is zero; this will show you how your computer reacts to attempted division by zero.

4.8f   Write a program to input the hypotenuse and one angle of a right triangle and to compute and output the lengths of the sides and the area of that triangle.

4.8g   The law of sines states that the sides of a triangle are proportional to the sines of their opposite angles. Write a program to input one side and its opposite angle, and then another angle; the program should compute and output the side opposite the second angle.

4.8h   The sum of the angles of a polygon is equal to (sides − 2) times 180 degrees. Write a program to accept the number of sides in the polygon and output the sum of the angles.

4.8i   Write a conversion program to accept the number of degrees Fahrenheit and output the equivalent degrees Celsius. The equation is:

$$C = (5/9) * (F - 32)$$

4.8j   Write a program to reverse the procedure in 4.8i—to input degrees Celsius and output degrees Fahrenheit.

4.8k   The distance between two points is the square root of the sum of the difference in x-coordinates squared and the difference in y-coordinates squared. Write a program that reads in the coordinates of two points and outputs the distance between them. Also compute the slope of the line joining them as the ratio of the difference in y-coordinates divided by the difference in x-coordinates. That slope now becomes the argument to the arctangent function that will return the angle with the x-axis in radians. Output that angle in degrees. *PI* radians = 180 degrees. (Do not use a vertical line to test this program, since the slope is not definable due to division by zero.)

4.8l   The area of any triangle (right or otherwise) may be determined from the lengths of its three sides. First, the semiperimeter (s) is the sum of the three sides divided by 2. The area is then defined as:

$$\text{SQRT } (s * (s - a) * (s - b) * (s - c))$$

Write a program to determine the area of a triangle given the x- and y-coordinates of its three corners.

4.8m   Write a program to determine the difference of the slope angles between two lines, given the coordinates of the end points of each line. The answer should be given in degrees, minutes, and seconds—the first two integer, the last real.

4.8n Write a program to accept the x- and y-coordinates of a point and the azimuth (angle from north) and length of a line emanating from that point. Output the coordinates of the point at the end of that line.

4.8o Write a program to return the y-coordinate of the point on the circumference of a unit circle given an input x-coordinate between 0.0 and 1.0. Except for the extreme cases, there will be two correct y-coordinates for each x-coordinate.

5

Programming Logic

CHAPTER OUTLINE

CHAPTER OBJECTIVES

- To present the logical constructs available in programming for decision making.

- To show the application of these logical constructs in FORTRAN.

- To introduce concepts and rules for structured programming.

- To demonstrate the method of inputting multiple data until end-of-data is encountered.

- To demonstrate the methods of editing input data.

- To describe the processes of counting and accumulating totals.

- To explain the use and application of decision-making logic.

- To illustrate the use of logical variables.

STATEMENT OF THE PROBLEM

At the very end of Chapter 4, we began generating larger chunks of code that will eventually be integrated into our full applications. Still, a careful perusal of the programs suggests the limited nature of what can be done at this point. The logic is linear because each statement is executed immediately after the previous one, and after passing once through the code, the program is finished. This means that the program can execute only one set of data or (another way of looking at it) that each set of data requires a separate run of the program. This is extremely inefficient. There must be some way of using the same code again without having to exit and restart the run—and of course there is a way.

The quality of the code should not be deprecated just because it is linear. It still enables the solution of many problems in which the logic is simple. The basic logic of all programs is apparent: the input of the known data, the manipulation of that data, and the output of the newly obtained information. This chapter will develop the technique that allows for the reading of multiple records while still using the same computational logic. With this feature, the program can perform analyses on all the records as a group, such as accumulating totals from multiple input.

Nor will the programs be restricted to linear logic. A closer look at the two sample applications (section 4.7) does show some alternative logic, although that logic is transparent to (not seen by) the programmer. In the Automated Teller Machine application, the use of the function MAX0 has the computer compare the list of values and select the highest one. Likewise, the function IDIM in the Computer Time Accounting application also compares two values and either returns the positive difference or a zero. From the programmer's point of view, the logic is linear, but there are decisions and alternative logical paths taken within the function.

The main deficiency in our present knowledge of FORTRAN is the inability to execute alternative logical paths other than through the intrinsic functions. In the Automated Teller Machine application, for example, what if the user enters an invalid value for a withdrawal? In the previous chapter, the problem was solved by raising any value not a multiple of $10 to the next higher multiple; this is a possible solution, but not one that the user might like. A good program would display an error message to the user and allow the user to correct the input. But what should the program do if the user enters zero or a negative amount? Shouldn't the program also display an error message in this case—and give the user a chance to reenter the data? Also, real-life applications limit the amount of money that can be withdrawn each day; that, too, must be considered. And finally, what if the amount in the user's account is insufficient for this withdrawal? Banks don't just give money away! The need for other logic and commands to treat these extensions to our present knowledge becomes apparent as our applications become more realistic.

5.1   LOGICAL CONSTRUCTS

As every assembly (or machine) language programmer knows, all computer logic is controlled by two elemental constructs:

1. The test instruction, which compares a numeric value to zero. This instruction then sets zero and negative status indicators in the machine, with the following possible combinations:

Zero	Negative	Meaning
Off	On	Value less than zero
On	Off	Value equal to zero
Off	Off	Value greater than zero

2. The branch instruction, which directs the logical path to an instruction other than the one immediately following the present one.

The branch instruction has three versions:

2a. The unconditional branch, which directs the logic to another instruction under any conditions.

2b. The conditional branch, which first tests the status indicators for the possible conditions or combinations thereof and then branches only if the tested condition is true. The possible conditions are:

Condition	Symbol	FORTRAN Code
Less than	<	.LT.
Less than or equal to	<=	.LE.
Equal to	=	.EQ.
Not equal to	<>	.NE.
Greater than	>	.GT.
Greater than or equal to	>=	.GE.

If the tested condition is false, execution of the program continues with the next sequential instruction.

2c. An unconditional branch that also stores the address of the next sequential instruction for later use. This version is used when accessing subprograms (to be discussed in Chapter 8).

All other logical controls are but combinations of the above with the evaluation of expressions and the assignment of values. For example, two values are compared by subtracting the second from the first and testing the result.

If value 1 is less than value 2, the result is negative.
If value 1 is equal to value 2, the result is zero.
If value 1 is greater than value 2, the result is positive.

Additionally, the values above can be expressions, like the ones we have been using.

Also encountered will be logical relationships (such as $A > B$) and combinations thereof ($A > B$ *and* $C < D$). These relationships, although appearing to have values corresponding to true or false, are also numeric internally. As numerics, they can be compared and tested by the methods explained above.

The FORTRAN control statements presented in Chapters 5 and 6 will be explained by reducing them to their elemental structure so that the reader may fully understand how the compiler interprets them. Only in this way can you get a complete understanding of the code. The purpose of these available instructions is twofold:

1. To reduce the effort in programming
2. To make the logic more obvious and less error-prone

However, without complete comprehension of how an instruction works, there is the ever-present danger of programming error.

Although FORTRAN could have been designed like an assembly language with a TEST instruction and a series of conditional branches, the developers of the language placed almost all decision making into a single statement, the IF statement. This very inclusive statement combines expression evaluation, testing, and branching. This IF statement appears in a number of versions:

1. Arithmetic IF
2. Logical IF
3. IF .. THEN .. ENDIF
4. IF .. THEN .. ELSE .. ENDIF
5. IF .. THEN .. [ELSE IF] .. ELSE .. ENDIF

The first four versions are simplifications of the fifth one. The bracketed [ELSE IF] indicates that multiples of that term may be present in the statement, thus providing for an almost unlimited number of conditions.

This chapter fully develops the concepts of branching, both conditional and unconditional, as it is implemented in FORTRAN. Also described are some previously used statements in which the IF and GO TO are hiding, just as alternative logical paths are hiding within some of the intrinsic functions.

The next chapter will describe another FORTRAN construct, the DO loop, which enables the programmer to set up looping procedures very easily. The DO is a combination of evaluation, assignment, testing, and branching, as will be shown. The three statements—GO TO, IF, and DO—provide almost 100% of the logic used in FORTRAN.

5.2 PSEUDOCODE AND FLOWCHARTS

Moving into the area of alternative logical paths and loops, it is critical to have a formal method of representing the logic of the code other than the code itself. Code can become quite cryptic to someone else reading it, and even to the writer of the code after a sufficient lapse in time. Although the writer of code should use variable names that are as self-documenting as possible, other types of documentation—such as program description and information at the beginning of the program, as well as comments within the code—are required. The coding process should not begin until the logic has been completely worked out, if only to find out if the problem is solvable.

There are two generally used methods of logic documentation, one graphically oriented, the other verbally oriented. The former is a flowchart (introduced in

Chapter 3) in which there are defined symbols for various processes connnected with vectors (lines with arrowheads) to show the direction of logic flow. Although easy to read, flowcharts are quite annoying to draw, since they require much planning and effort.

The other method, pseudocode, uses a make-believe language somewhat like abbreviated English to express what the computer language should do. Instead of variable names, a description of what the variable is to represent can be used. The statements may be numbered so that branching might be described simply. Furthermore, by using techniques of indenting, the pseudocode might also take on a graphical appearance that emphasizes alternative logical paths and loops. Pseudocode has another advantage in that it can become the comments in the final coded program. However, pseudocode has the same weakness of any spoken language in that its intent may not always be clear.

Pseudocode is very free in its use. The terms used need not be available instructions and can reflect human needs more than computer language restrictions. Sometimes it sounds like instructions we wish we had in a particular language. Its purpose is clarity, but pseudocode must be precise enough to be converted into a computer language.

These two chapters (5 and 6) illustrate both methods, although later chapters will use whatever method is most illustrative of the necessary logic. The theoretical constructs will be shown with flowcharts, since such charts are more precise, but large sections of program will be shown using pseudocode.

Figure 3-1 illustrated the flowchart symbols used for input/output (I/O) and to begin and end the chart. Chapter 4 introduced the process symbol used for calculations. This chapter introduces an additional symbol for decision making (Figure 5-1). The decision symbol is the only one that allows more than one exit, i.e., more than one logical path leaving that point.

Two types of decisions are possible in FORTRAN. First, the logical, or two-branched, decision depends on whether an expression is true or false. For example, the program might test to see if an expression is greater than zero. If it is, the "true" branch will be executed. But if the expression is either equal to or less than zero, the alternate "false" branch will be executed. The question being asked is shown with a question mark (?) inside the decision symbol.

The other type of decision is the arithmetic, or three-branched, decision in which an expression is compared with zero. This comparison results in three possible branches: less than, equal to, and greater than. (The branches might be combined, such as having one branch for less than or equal to; but in such cases, it would be better to use the two-branched logical decision described above.) This same method is used to compare two values or expressions. In the program, the two

Figure 5-1
The Decision Symbol

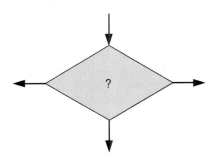

expressions are subtracted, but in the flowchart they are separated by a colon (:) in the decision symbol and the decision is based on the arithmetic relationship of the first expression to the second. There are no specifications for the pseudocode to represent this logic, except that the writer is expected to make every effort to make that code obvious. A few simple examples will illustrate the type of logic that we are trying to document, starting with a very easy one and moving to ones that are more involved but still very elementary.

Example 1: Determination of the Absolute Value of a Number

This example describes how the intrinsic function for absolute value works. A number is input; if it is negative, the sign is reversed; then it is output. The flowchart is shown in Figure 5-2.

The pseudocode reads almost like the description above:

```
1. Input the value.
2. If the value is negative, multiply the value by -1.
3. Output the value.
```

Example 2: Generating a Table of Squares from 1 to 50

```
1. Set a counter to 1.
2. Square the counter.
3.     Output the counter and the square.
4.     Add 1 to the counter.
5. If the counter is less than or equal to 50, go to step 2.
```

In steps 3 and 4, the pseudocode is indented to emphasize the loop structure. Note that this program generates its own data so that no input is required. To give the program more flexibility, the number of terms could have been requested as input rather than always processing 50 terms. The flowchart is shown in Figure 5-3.

Example 3: Determine If a Given Integer Is a Perfect Square

Here the logic is a bit more involved. It could be done by taking the square root (if the number is positive), converting it to integer, squaring that number, and determining if the new square is the same as the original input. Instead, a trial-and-error

Figure 5-2
Absolute Value of a Number

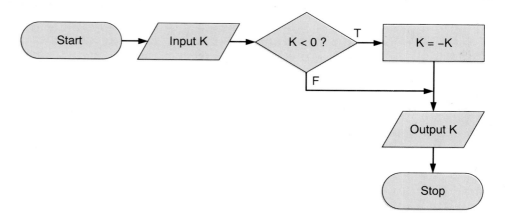

Figure 5-3
Table of Squares

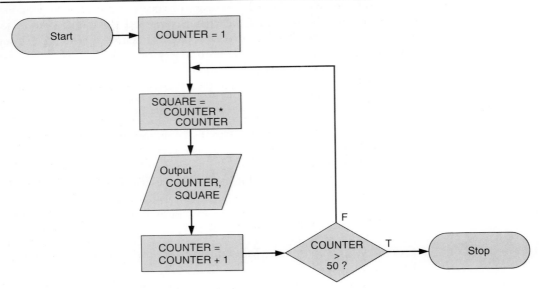

approach is demonstrated, more like the way a person who does not have a calculator might approach the problem. (This method is the only one usable for an equation that is extremely complex and does not have a simple solution.) The program generates the squares, starting at zero, until it reaches a square that is either equal to or greater than the given value. This algorithm gives the correct answer for negative numbers, which cannot be perfect squares, and for zero, which is a perfect square ($0 * 0 = 0$). This solution eliminates any mode problem.

```
1. Input the value.
2. Set a counter to 0.
3. Square the counter.
4.      If the square is less than the input value:
            add 1 to counter.
            go to step 3
5.      If the square is equal to the input value:
            output "Perfect Square."
6.      If the square is greater than the input value:
            output "Not a Perfect Square."
```

Alternatively, steps 5 and 6 might be combined:

```
5.      If the square is equal to the input value:
                output "Perfect Square."
            else output "Not a Perfect Square."
```

At step 5, only two possibilities are left to be considered, since the "less than" logic has already branched elsewhere.

Yet another alternative combines steps 4, 5, and 6:

```
4.      If the square is less than the input value:
                add 1 to counter.
                go to step 3
            else if the square is equal to the input value:
                output "Perfect Square."
            else output "Not a Perfect Square."
```

The flowchart is shown in Figure 5-4. Note the use of the colon in the decision symbol to indicate a comparison.

These examples should be enough to illustrate the general principles of both flowcharts and pseudocode. You will certainly see enough of both of them in the rest of the text. You should, however, spend some time observing the style used in drawing flowcharts:

1. All vectors are horizontal and vertical, preferably downward and to the right.
2. Arrowheads are placed where a vector leads into a symbol or joins another vector, and then only on the vector joining, not on the one continuing.
3. Crossing vectors need no special indication. If a vector does not end on a continuing vector, it is assumed that the two do not touch but cross without interaction.
4. Multiple statements may be placed in a process box (rectangle), and they will be executed from top to bottom within the box.
5. Only one decision may be made at a time within a decision box. (Later you will see how multiple conditions may be linked into a single decision.)
6. Messages or annotations are embedded within quotes or apostrophes to distinguish them from variable names.

Figure 5-4
Is a Number a Perfect Square?

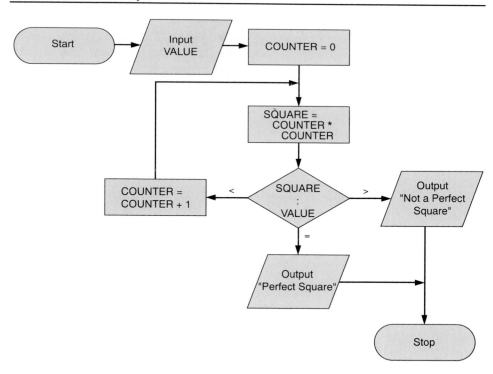

5.3   PROGRAMMING STRUCTURE

Generally there is more than one way to solve a problem, even in computer programming. Although many possible methods may result in the correct answer, other factors must be considered when selecting a preferred solution. For instance, sometimes it is more critical for programming logic and code to reflect the needs of the person reading the code than the efficiency of the computer executing the code. (This is exactly the opposite of the priorities in assembly language programming, where speed and efficiency are the most critical factors.) The pseudocode solutions given in the previous section illustrate this concern, since there are a number of ways in which correct logic would supply a solution; the method chosen, however, followed very distinct rules so that the code would be built with a certain structure.

The problem centers on the GO TO unconditional branch. Improper use of this basic construct can lead to logic and code that are difficult, sometimes almost impossible, to follow. A study of the history of programming language development shows major attempts to remove that instruction from the vocabulary of the high-level languages (i.e., languages above the assembly language level). Unfortunately, situations do arise in which GO TO is necessary, and all languages still contain some version of the unconditional branch.

The key phrase used today is *structured programming,* although there seems to be no precise definition of what this means. But we can define it functionally as the type of logic (coding, programming) that leads to understandable, error-free programming, eliminating the confusion of undisciplined multiple branching. Our goal here is to eliminate that four-letter combination (GO TO) as much as possible when introducing new constructs, using it only when there is no other recourse.

Another element of structuring is to break a program down into small sections of code or modules, each somewhat self-contained in that no entrance is made into it except at the beginning and no exit is made from it except to the beginning of another module. As an example, the pseudocode for finding perfect squares, discussed in the previous section, is repeated here using modularization. Note that the step numbers have been replaced with module numbers.

Module

1. Input and initialization

```
Input the value.
Set a counter to 0.
```

2. Process

```
Square the counter.
If square < value,
   add 1 to counter and
   go to module 2.
If square = value,
   output "Perfect Square."
If square > value,
   output "Not a Perfect Square."
```

3. Termination

```
Stop.
```

Note how "go to" branches only to the beginning of a module. One other useful branch is to the last statement in a module. Thus, in situations in which it is impossible to avoid the use of "go to," the following rules apply:

1. A "go to" may branch to the last statement in a module from within the module.

2. A "go to" may branch to the first statement in a module from within the module.
3. A "go to" may branch from any point in a module to the beginning of any other module, either before or after it, but preferably to the one immediately following it.
4. The number of upward branches to the beginning of a module should be limited to one.

Expanding the above pseudocode for input looping—the ability to return to the beginning of a program for more input until reaching the end of data—the structure becomes:

Module

1. Input

Input the value.
If end of data, go to module 4.

2. Initialization

Set a counter to 0.

3. Process

Square the counter.
If square < value,
add 1 to counter and
go to module 3.
If square = value,
output "Perfect Square."
If square > value,
output "Not a Perfect Square."

4. Termination

Stop.

In module 1, it is possible to replace "go to module 4" with "Stop," thereby eliminating the need for module 4; but it seems more psychologically satisfying to place the last logical statement in a program at the physical end of it.

One way to observe the structure of logic or a program is to draw vectors from every "go to" in the pseudocode to the target module. If they can be drawn without crossing each other, the structure is good. The more crossings, the less structured the program.

Exercises

Note: In the exercises below, draw a flowchart and write the pseudocode that illustrates the desired logic. Use the rules stated above to give your logic appropriate structure.

5.3a Input two numbers; output the message "SAME SIGN" if both numbers are of the same sign and "OPPOSITE SIGN" if they are of opposite signs. Assume that zero is positive. This exercise can be solved by two methods. One uses a multitude of branches. The other uses some of the properties of arithmetic to generate intermediate values that require less decision making; however, be sure to take into account the possibility that one or both of the values may be zero.

5.3b Input two numbers; output the message "SAME PARITY" if both numbers are even or both are odd and the message "OPPOSITE PARITY" if they are different. Zero is an even number. Arithmetic combination of the numbers reduces some of the decision making. This exercise does not depend upon division or mode manipulation but can be easily done (like the logic for finding perfect squares) by keeping in mind the definition of an even number.

5.3c   Generate a table of the powers of 2 from 0 to 15.

5.3d   Generate a Fibonacci series of 20 terms. A Fibonacci series has the form 1, 1, 2, 3, 5, 8, 13, 21, 34, etc. Each term is the sum of the previous two terms. The first two terms must be defined, and the others can then be computed.

5.3e   Input two values representing the high and low temperatures for the day. Compute the average. Determine the number of degree-days, the number of degrees the average temperature is below 65. If the average is 65 or greater, the number of degree-days is 0.

5.3f   Input the number of hours worked and the rate of pay. Compute the salary by multiplying hours times rate for the first 40 hours (straight time) and hours over 40 times rate times 1.5 (time and a half) for all hours above 40. There is another way of obtaining the same answer by varying the computation slightly; it involves paying straight time for all hours and a surcharge of 50% for the hours above 40.

5.3g   The income tax on salary is computed as follows:

If salary is less than $100, tax = 2% of salary.

If salary is greater than or equal to $100, but less than $300,
tax = $2.00 + 4% of salary in excess of $100.

If salary is greater than or equal to $300, tax = $10.00 + 5% of salary in excess of $300.

Input a value for salary and compute the tax and the net pay (the salary minus the tax).

5.3h   Social security taxes are based on a percentage of the gross salary up to a maximum taxable salary. Assume the tax rate is 8% up to a maximum of $50,000 per annum (or a maximum tax of $4000). Input the weekly salary and the accumulated salary (total salary paid so far in the year) and determine the social security tax to be withheld. Make sure that the logic covers these three cases:

   1. Full salary to be taxed (below maximum)
   2. Partial salary to be taxed (maximum exceeded during pay period)
   3. No salary to be taxed (maximum exceeded prior to pay period)

5.3i   Using the equation presented in exercise 4.8a, involving projectile motion ($Y = 70 * T - 16.1 * T ** 2$), illustrate the logic to track the projectile by calculating its height above the ground every tenth of a second until it returns to the ground. Display the values of T and Y as long as Y is nonnegative.

5.3j   Using the appropriate trigonometric functions, generate a table of x- and y-coordinates for a unit circle as the angle varies from 0 to 360 degrees by increments of 15 degrees. (Ignore the need to convert degrees to radians in the pseudocode or flowchart.)

5.4 UNCONDITIONAL BRANCHING

The statement

```
GO TO nn
```

causes an unconditional branch to the executable statement numbered nn. The branch is unconditional because it must always be executed, regardless of any other conditions. ("GO TO JAIL; go directly to jail; do not pass GO; do not collect $200.") The branched-to statement may be before or after the GO TO. There is no flowchart symbol for the GO TO; the vector describes it. In pseudocode, however, we must specify it explicitly.

As described in the previous section, the improper use of GO TO can lead to very convoluted code. In slang terms, this is called "spaghetti code" because the logical paths intertwine so extensively that following them is difficult for a human being. Although GO TO will appear in this chapter, its use will diminish significantly as new constructs are added, eliminating the need for most of them. After the next chapter, GO TO will appear only in situations where it is impossible to complete logic without it.

Although there has been a trend toward banning the GO TO statement altogether and new constructs were developed to reduce its use, there are still situations in which it is necessary. The GO TO statement still exists in the newer language Pascal and in the new versions of structured BASIC. One highly structured language, Modula-2, has eliminated GO TO altogether, but it has an EXIT statement that acts as a GO TO to the beginning of the next module. Unfortunately, some of these replacement constructs are quite restrictive and cannot handle some problems that arise without resorting to rather inefficient logic.

You will discover from the following discussions that even when the GO TO statement does not appear explicitly, it is implicitly contained within other instructions. For instance, the STOP statement is a GO TO, since it causes a branch to the operating system (OS) of the computer. (The branch is made to a fixed point in the memory where the OS is stored, and the OS takes over the running of the computer.)

5.5 INPUT LOOPS

An input loop is the logic required to repeat the processing of data for multiple records, exiting from the loop when the data is exhausted or, more precisely, when the end-of-data has been reached. With the unconditional branch, we can loop back to the beginning of our program and read another data record, continuing the process ad infinitum (although we will probably run out of data first). What is obviously needed is a way of getting out of the loop when there is no more data.

First we must define some terms and abbreviations. When a line of input (either a line of program code or a data record) is entered at the keyboard, that line is terminated by entering a carriage return (the actual key on the keyboard may be labeled RETURN or ENTER, or it may just have an arrow going down and then to the left). This places a special code into the memory or onto a disk file (usually hex code 0D = decimal 13) and is referred to as a carriage return (CR), end-of-line (EOL), or end-of-record (EOR) mark. When we exit from an editor and store a file, the system places an end-of-data (EOD) or end-of-file (EOF) mark (usually hex code 1A = decimal 26) after the last record or, to be more precise, at the beginning of the next record. On most systems, this is done at the keyboard with a control-Z (holding down the CTRL key while pressing the Z). When a FORTRAN READ inputs this record, it finds invalid data and would bomb out if FORTRAN did not supply a remedy.

By using an expanded version of the READ statement, a test for end-of-data can be included which, acting as a combination test and GO TO, causes a branch to a statement that should be outside the input loop. This expanded version (described in section 3.8) requires the use of a logical unit number (LUN), a number that represents a particular input device. Here we run into a system-dependent situation in which LUNs vary on different systems for the same device. Since many systems use the asterisk (*) as a LUN for the keyboard, we have adopted that convention for this text.

As also described in section 3.8, another asterisk is needed to indicate list-directed input. When we add the END= clause, the statement takes the form:

```
READ (*,*, END=nn) variable_list
```

The END= clause instructs the computer to branch to a specified statement numbered nn when it reaches the EOF. The flowchart for general input loop processing is shown in Figure 5-5.

The program for finding the hypotenuse of a right triangle, described in section 4.2, can be used to illustrate this technique.

```
C                       Hypotenuse of a Right Triangle
C
C                       input
   20 PRINT *, 'Enter two sides of a right triangle, (ctrl-Z to end)'
      READ (*,*, END=90) SIDE1, SIDE2
C                       calculation
      HYPOT = SQRT (SIDE1 * SIDE1 +  SIDE2 * SIDE2)
C                       output hypotenuse and blank line
      PRINT *, 'Hypotenuse =', HYPOT
      PRINT *
   GO TO 20
C                       termination
   90 STOP
      END
```

When read from a disk file, the EOF code is already there and there is no need for a displayed prompt or for input by the user.

Another useful feature is the ERR= clause, which causes the program to branch to some specified location should an error occur in the input data, such as

Figure 5-5
General Input Loop

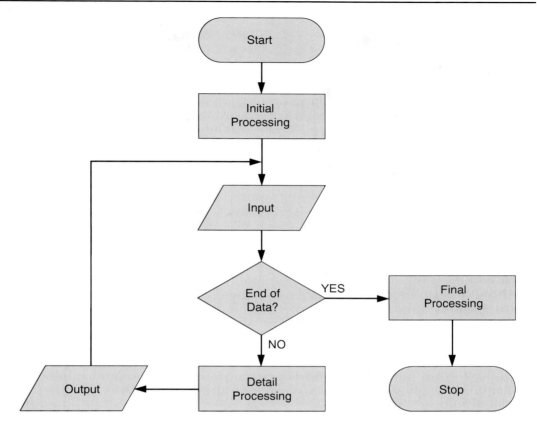

an alphabetic character or two decimal points. The order of the END= and ERR= clauses in the READ are irrelevant; the keywords END and ERR completely identify them. Thus we can code either:

```
READ   (*,*, END=90, ERR=80)   SIDE1, SIDE2
```

or

```
READ   (*,*, ERR=80, END=90)   SIDE1, SIDE2
```

Now our program might read (*with the new code italicized*):

```
C                    Hypotenuse of a Right Triangle
C
C                       input
   20 PRINT *, 'Enter two sides of right triangle, (ctrl-Z to end)'
          READ  (*,*, END=90, ERR=60)  SIDE1, SIDE2
C                       calculation
          HYPOT = SQRT (SIDE1 * SIDE1  +  SIDE2 * SIDE2)
C                       output hypotenuse and blank line
          PRINT *, 'Hypotenuse =', HYPOT
          PRINT *
             GO TO 80
```

```
C                      input error
   60      PRINT *, 'Error in input data  -  try again!'
C                      return for more data
   80 GO TO 20
C                      termination
   90 STOP
      END
```

These techniques apply to all programs that accept multiple input. The ERR= clause should be used in all READs, whether or not they test for the EOF condition.

In the above program, the GO TO 80 could be eliminated by placing the error-handling module after statement number 80. This would result in an input error causing a termination of the program after displaying the error message. Although this would eliminate a GO TO, the program would become far less efficient, requiring restarting each time an error occurred. This would be especially wasteful if continuous output was desired or if totals (see next section) were being accumulated. This is one of the cases in which a GO TO cannot be eliminated or replaced with another construct.

Exercises

Note: One of the prime uses of small programs like the last sample shown for Hypotenuse of a Right Triangle, complete with the END= and ERR= clauses, is to test small pieces of code for correctness. By entering multiple data, many different conditions may be tested efficiently. The intent of each of the exercises below is to give the reader practice in this kind of activity which is performed by professional programmers as part of program development. Each program should include multiple input with END= and ERR= clauses.

5.5a   Write a simple program to input an integer variable and then output it. Utilize the program to test first for end-of-data. If CTRL-Z does not work, try CTRL-C, CTRL-P, and CTRL-Y; if none of those work, try the BREAK key, if it exists. If none of them work, ask for some support from the person who runs your system. (If your system does not support keyboard entry of end-of-data, see section 5.7 for a method that uses a "sentinel value.") Once end-of-file is working (and even if it does not), try various error conditions, such as alphabetic characters, decimal points, punctuation characters, etc.

5.5b   Modify the program from exercise 5.5a to input and output a real variable. Try different error conditions, such as two decimal points, alphabetic characters, punctuation characters, etc.

5.5c   One of the more difficult intrinsic functions to understand is the IDIM function. Write a test program to accept multiple data records of two integers entered from the keyboard to be used as arguments to IDIM. Output the input values as well as the returned value. Test with positive, negative, and zero values.

5.5d   Another difficult function is the ISIGN and SIGN. Replace the IDIM function in exercise 5.5c with the ISIGN and test it thoroughly until you understand exactly how it works.

5.5e The AINT, ANINT, and NINT functions are very useful, but they are also somewhat confusing. Write a test program inputting a real variable to be used as the argument for all three functions. The program should output the input value and the three returned values, one from each function. Test with all manner of data, including negative values, until you are sure that you understand how it works.

5.5f The equation $xy = 2$ represents a hyperbola, part of which falls within the first (upper right) quadrant of the x, y coordinate system. Write a progam to determine the distance of any point on the curve from the origin $(0, 0)$, given a positive value for x. Then, by trial and error, enter different values for x until a point on the curve is found which is a distance of about 2.5 from the origin, with an allowable tolerance of 0.001.

5.6 COUNTING AND ACCUMULATING

We can now cover a very important technique: counting records and accumulating totals. Although the operations are called by different names, the processing is similar, except that the first adds a 1 and the second adds some variable value. Each of these processes requires three additional steps, one in each of the processing modules shown in Figure 5-5:

Module	Counting	Accumulating
Initial processing	Set counter to 0.	Set total to 0.
Detail processing	Add 1 to counter.	Add value to total.
Final processing	Output counter.	Output total.

Initializing the total or counter is done either with an assignment or in a DATA statement. This usually results in code such as the following:

```
      TOTAL = 0.00          or          DATA  TOTAL/ 0.00/
        :
 nn    :
      READ  (*,*, END=mm)  xxx
        :
       TOTAL = TOTAL + AMOUNT
        :
      GO TO nn
 mm PRINT *,  TOTAL
```

Counters are used for a multitude of purposes, such as counting input records, counting lines and pages of output, and tabulating different types of data.

> If a counter or total is not initialized to zero, no error message is provided by the FORTRAN compiler and the results are system-dependent. It is possible that the location assigned by the compiler for the counter or total contains a nonzero value left over from an earlier program; obviously, the final result will be wrong. It is the responsibility of the programmer to control his or her memory locations and initialize them properly, just as the user of a calculator would clear the display before adding up a new set of numbers.

Below, the Automated Teller Machine program is expanded to include multiple input records, terminate on end-of-data, contain an ERR= branch, and accumulate the total withdrawals. The new statements are italicized.

**Automated
Teller
Machine**

```
C                       Multiple Data Entry for Automated Teller Machine
C
        PARAMETER  (RATE = 0.020)
        INTEGER    WITHDR, N50, N20, N10, LEFT
        INTEGER    WITH10, FEE, TOTAL
C                         initialize total withdrawals, number transactions
        DATA       TOTWTH, NTRNS/ 0.00, 0/
C
C                       enter amount of withdrawal
   20 PRINT *
        PRINT *, 'Enter amount of withdrawal (integer)'
        READ  (*,*, END=90, ERR=60)  WITHDR
C                       convert to next highest ten dollars, if not multiple
        WITH10 = (WITHDR + 9) / 10 * 10
C                       verification
        PRINT *, 'Withdrawal = $', WITH10
C                       calculate breakdown
        N50  = WITH10 / 50
        LEFT = MOD (WITH10, 50)
        N20  = LEFT    / 20
        LEFT = MOD (LEFT, 20)
        N10  = LEFT    / 10
C                       output breakdown
        PRINT *
        PRINT *, '         $50        $20        $10'
        PRINT *,            N50,       N20,       N10
C                       compute fee
        FEE = NINT (RATE * REAL (WITH10))
        FEE = MAX0 (FEE, 2)
        PRINT *, 'Fee   = $', FEE
        TOTAL = WITH10 + FEE
        PRINT *, 'TOTAL = $', TOTAL
C                       accumulate into total and increment counter
        TOTWTH = TOTWTH + WITH10
        NTRANS = NTRANS + 1
           GO TO 80
```

```
C                           error processing
   60     PRINT *
          PRINT *, 'INPUT ERROR  -  reenter'
C                           return for more input
   80 GO TO 20
C
C                           output total, count, average and terminate
   90 PRINT*
      PRINT *, 'Total withdrawn      = $', TOTWTH
      PRINT *, 'Number of transactions =',  NTRANS
      PRINT *, 'Average withdrawal    = $', TOTWTH / REAL (NTRANS)
      STOP
      END
```

Note that there is only one backward branch, the one at the statement numbered 80. Both the counter and the accumulator (NTRANS and TOTWTH) were initialized using a DATA statement.

Exercises

5.6a   Write a program to accept multiple grades from the keyboard. The program should count and add up the grades. At end-of-data, display the number of grades and the average.

5.6b   Write a program to accept multiple input from a disk file of the number of hours worked and the pay rate, both real numbers. Compute salary as hours times rate. Accumulate total hours and total salary, outputting the values before terminating.

5.6c   Write a program to accept multiple input from a disk file of two integer values per record representing the high and low temperatures for a number of days. Compute a rounded average for each day using real arithmetic, but without using mixed-mode arithmetic. Output the record number (the counter), the input values, and the computed average with appropriate annotation for each day. Accumulate and output the number of days on the file and the average mean temperature over the period.

5.6d   Write a program to balance your checkbook. Enter the opening balance first. Enter deposits as positive numbers, checks and bank expenses as negative numbers. Output the total after each transaction; no final output is needed after the end-of-data is entered.

5.6e   Write a program to compute the total time of a musical record or compact disc by adding up the times of the individual tracks. Enter the times as real numbers representing minutes and seconds (*mm.ss*). Convert the time to seconds in the program and add up the seconds. Then output the sum as a real number, again representing minutes and seconds.

5.6f   Write a program to compute your car's gas mileage and the cost of fuel per mile. Enter starting and ending odometer readings to get miles traveled. Then loop through the input of the amount of gas purchased and the cost of the purchase, accumulating total gas and total cost. At the end, determine miles per gallon and cost per mile.

5.7   CONDITIONAL BRANCHING

The purpose of the conditional branch is to separate a program into multiple logical paths based on conditions that become known only during the running of a program. For example, the input of the Automated Teller Machine application may be examined to see if it is valid. The pseudocode would look like:

```
1.   Input desired withdrawal.
2.   If desired withdrawal is less than or equal to zero, then:
         display "DESIRED WITHDRAWAL LESS THAN OR EQUAL TO ZERO";
         go to step 5.
3.   If desired withdrawal is greater than the limit, then:
         display "DESIRED WITHDRAWAL GREATER THAN LIMIT";
         go to step 5.
4.   Process withdrawal:
         compute breakdown of bills:
         compute fee;
         add withdrawal and fee to get total;
         display breakdown, fee, and total.
5.   Terminate.
```

Note that the form of the pseudocode appears different as it is broken down into modules, each representing a different logical path and each mutually exclusive. In flowchart form, it would appear as in Figure 5-6. Logical decisions, rather than

Figure 5-6
Automated Teller Machine Application

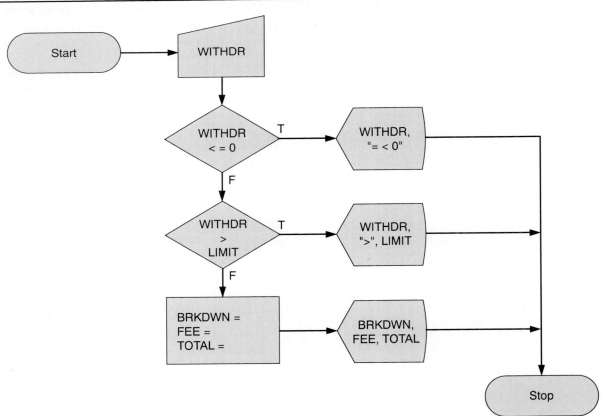

arithmetic decisions, are used in the chart so that the branches are based on True and False. The computations are not detailed in the processing box at lower left; the main purpose of a flowchart is to display logic, not obvious calculations.

The conditional branch is called an IF statement and has a number of forms. The basic syntax is:

```
IF (expression) procedure to be executed
```

The Arithmetic IF

The early FORTRANs contained only a conditional branch based on the arithmetic evaluation (test) of an expression. The procedure consisted of three branches (three GO TOs) to other statements, depending on whether the expression was:

1. Less than zero
2. Equal to zero
3. Greater than zero

in that order. This statement is called the three-branch IF; and its syntax is:

```
IF (expression) statement_1, statement_2, statement_3
```

Actually, the three branches do not have to be unique; two branches could have the same statement number. (The three branches could even be the same, thereby creating an unconditional GO TO; the compiler doesn't check for such idiocy.) Furthermore, there is no restriction on the expression, so that one could even test to see if a constant is less than, equal to, or greater than zero.

Because the arithmetic IF is difficult to follow and tends to destroy program structure, it has fallen out of favor. The statement still exists in the FORTRAN specifications for purposes of upward compatibility with older versions of the language. The reader should be familiar with its existence because there are hundreds of thousands of programs written using this statement.

Below is a simple code segment illustrating the use of the arithmetic IF. The indentation is a matter of the author's style and has no effect on the execution of the program; it is merely an attempt to make the program more readable.

```
      IF (I - J)  10, 20, 30
10      PRINT *, 'I is less than J'
            GO TO 40
20      PRINT *, 'I is equal to J'
            GO TO 40
30      PRINT *, 'I is greater than J'
40  . . . . .
```

This code compares the values of I and J by subtracting the second from the first; the difference is an indication of their relationship. This was how comparisons were done in the early versions of FORTRAN. If I is less than J, the subtraction yields a result less than zero; if I is equal to J, the difference is equal to zero; if I is greater than J, the result is greater than zero. Note the use of the unconditional branch to rejoin the logical paths of the three alternatives. One advantage of this method is that no possible condition can be ignored.

The absolute value logic in section 5.2 can be coded as follows:

```
      IF (A)  10, 20, 20
10      A = -A
20  . . . . .
```

Two branches have the same statement number. The expression is compared to zero (there is no need to code A − 0.00), and if the value is equal to or greater than zero, the sign reversal statement is skipped.

The Perfect Square problem can be solved with the following:

```
      PRINT *, 'Enter an integer number'
      READ  *,  I
      ICOUNT = 0
  20 ISQ    = ICOUNT * ICOUNT
         IF (ISQ) - I)  40, 60, 80
  40     ICOUNT = ICOUNT + 1
      GO TO 20
  60     PRINT *, I, ' is a perfect square'
      GO TO 90
  80     PRINT *, I, ' is not a perfect square'
  90 STOP
      END
```

From the few examples above, you can see how much branching is required, how difficult it is to follow, and why it should be avoided. One of the keys to bad code is the density of statement numbers. In subsequent sections, the same problems will be solved with more obvious (structured) programs.

The Logical IF (Single Statement)

With the logical (or two-branched) IF, the value of the expression is tested for truth or falsity, not numeric value. When true, a single statement (which cannot be another IF statement) is executed; when false, that statement is ignored and execution continues with the next sequential statement. The flowchart is given in Figure 5-7; the work to be done is the single statement following the expression.

To implement this statement, some new operators (called *relational operators*) are available to the programmer:

.LT.	less than
.LE.	less than or equal to
.EQ.	equal to
.NE.	not equal to
.GE.	greater than or equal to
.GT.	greater than

Figure 5-7
Logical IF and Block IF

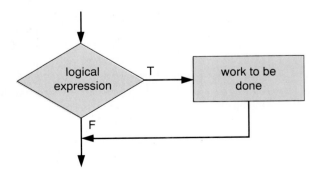

The previous sample code becomes:

```
IF  (I .LT. J)  PRINT *, 'I is less than J'
IF  (I .EQ. J)  PRINT *, 'I is equal to J'
IF  (I .GT. J)  PRINT *, 'I is greater than J'
IF  (A .LT. 0.00)  A = -A
```

The Perfect Square example, which has three logical branches, will be solved by other constructs to be presented later.

In addition to the relational operators, there are also *logical operators*, which allow us to combine conditions. They are:

```
.NOT. negates the expression segment following it
.AND. combines the expression segments in a logical conjunction
      true only when both expressions are true
.OR.  combines the expression segments in a logical disjunction
      true when either expression, or both, is true
```

A few examples are in order here:

```
IF  (A .GT. -0.005  .AND.  A .LT. 0.005)  A = 0.00
```

is a statement used to reduce any monetary amount between plus and minus a half-cent to zero. The expression is true only if A satisfies both conditions.

```
IF  (A .LT. 0.00  .OR.  B .LT. 0.00)  C = 0.00
```

is a statement that sets C to zero if either A or B is (or both are) negative.

There is a hierarchy of priority in the evaluation of an expression containing different kinds of operations:

```
• arithmetic
• relational   (.LT., .LE., etc.)
• logical in the order:    .NOT.
                           .AND.
                           .OR.
```

Spacing within the statement is a matter of style and in no way affects the evaluation process. Thus, in this expression:

```
IF  (I + 2 .GT. J - 7 .OR. M .LT. 2 .AND. N .EQ. 0)
```

the arithmetics (I + 2 and J − 7) are done first, then the .AND., and finally the .OR. Assuming:

$$I = 6, \quad J = 9, \quad M = 0, \quad N = 8$$

the expression is evaluated in this order:

```
IF  (6 + 2 .GT. 9 - 7 .OR. 0 .LT. 2 .AND. 8 .EQ. 0)
IF     (8   .GT.   2   .OR. 0 .LT. 2 .AND. 8 .EQ. 0)
IF         (.TRUE.     .OR.   .TRUE. .AND.  .FALSE.)
IF         (.TRUE.     .OR.          .FALSE.)
IF                     (.TRUE.)
```

The terms .TRUE. and .FALSE. are logical constants that will be defined fully in section 5.9; they are not variable names.

Just as with arithmetic expressions, however, the programmer can use extra sets of parentheses to ensure evaluation in the desired way. If the above expression is modified to:

```
IF  ((I + 2 .GT. J - 7 .OR. M .LT. 2) .AND. N .EQ. 0)
```

the evaluation then becomes:

```
IF    ((8   .GT.   2   .OR. 0 .LT. 2) .AND. 8 .EQ. 0)
IF        ((.TRUE.     .OR.  .TRUE. ) .AND.  .FALSE.)
IF                   (.TRUE.          .AND.  .FALSE.)
IF                                   (.FALSE.)
```

It is rather critical that the programmer fully understand the implications of the logical operators. For example:

```
IF  (A .LT. -0.005  .AND.  A .GT. 0.005)  A = 0.00
```

will always be false, since no values can be both less than −0.005 and greater than +0.005 simultaneously. On the other hand:

```
IF  (A .GT. -0.005  .OR.  A .LT. 0.005)  A = 0.00
```

will always be true because every number is either greater than −0.005 and less than +0.005, or both.

There is an alternative method of processing the end-of-data condition which depends not upon an EOD code (such as CTRL-Z) but on the value of the data. This method is *not* recommended, since it is very error-prone and might be confusing; but under some circumstances it might be necessary. This method requires a data value, called a *sentinel value,* to indicate end-of-data that cannot be confused with any valid data. For example, a negative grade or a temperature of 9999 are values outside the normal range. Below is a version of the hypotenuse program using two sides of 0.00 as sentinel values.

```
C                      Hypotenuse of a Right Triangle
C
C                  input
   20 PRINT *, 'Enter two sides of right triangle, (0,0 to end)'
        READ  (*,*, ERR=40)  SIDE1, SIDE2
C                  check for end-of-data
        IF  (SIDE1 .EQ. 0.00  .AND.  SIDE2 .EQ. 0.00)  GO TO 90
C                  eliminate invalid data
        IF  (SIDE1 .LE. 0.00  .OR.  SIDE2 .LE. 0.00)  GO TO 60
C                  calculation
        HYPOT = SQRT (SIDE1 * SIDE1  +  SIDE2 * SIDE2)
C                  output hypotenuse and blank line
        PRINT *, 'Hypotenuse =', HYPOT
        PRINT *
            GO TO 80
C                  data error
   60   PRINT *, 'Invalid data:', SIDE1, SIDE2
            GO TO 80
```

```
C                        input error
   40      PRINT *, 'Error in input data  -  try again!'
C                        branch back for more data
   80 GO TO 20
C                        termination
   90 STOP
      END
```

The logical IF also permits decisions on alphameric data. For example, the program shown below prompts for approval of the amount to be withdrawn and allows the user to enter a single-letter response, either a Y or an N for yes or no. Actually, the code considers only the positive response, assuming any non-Y to be negative. It also handles both uppercase and lowercase letters. Any variable compared must be defined as a character variable, and any constant used or value input must be placed between apostrophes; additionally, both compared quantities must be of the same length (same number of characters), otherwise they cannot be equal. The code might be written like this:

```
CHARACTER  RESPNS
      :
      :
IF  (RESPNS .NE. 'Y'  .AND.  RESPNS .NE. 'y')  STOP
```

Block IF (IF..THEN.. ENDIF)

The block IF gives the programmer a mechanism for performing a number of steps when the tested expression is true. The flowchart is the same as that given for the single-statement IF (Figure 5-7), except that the work to be done can include more than one statement. The required syntax includes the command THEN between the tested expression and the statements to be performed and an ENDIF after the statements to be performed. Rewriting the Perfect Square program, we get:

```
      PRINT *, 'Enter an integer number'
      READ  *,  I
      ICOUNT = 0
   20 ISQ   = ICOUNT * ICOUNT
      IF (ISQ .LT. I)  THEN
         ICOUNT = ICOUNT + 1
         GO TO 20
      ENDIF
      IF (ISQ .EQ. I)  PRINT *, I, ' is a perfect square'
      IF (ISQ .GT. I)  PRINT *, I, ' is not a perfect square'
      STOP
      END
```

This program shows both the use of the block IF and the single-statement IF. The choice depends on the logic, and choosing the easiest form of the statement is good programming style. You will have further opportunities to choose, since this problem will be solved by two more methods later in the text.

The Automated Teller Machine program is now enhanced to include the logic presented in the pseudocode at the beginning of this chapter and includes an IF structure embedded within another IF structure.

Automated Teller Machine

```
C                        Automated Teller Machine
C
      PARAMETER  (RATE = 0.020, LIMIT = 400.00)
      INTEGER    WITHDR, N50, N20, N10, LEFT
      INTEGER    WITH10, FEE, TOTAL, TOTWTH
      CHARACTER  RESPNS
C                        initialize total withdrawal
      DATA   TOTWTH/ 0/
C
C                        enter amount of withdrawal
   20 PRINT *, 'Enter amount of withdrawal (integer)'
      READ (*,*, ERR= 40, END=90)  WITHDR
C                        check for positive value
      IF  (WITHDR .LE. 0)  THEN
          PRINT *, 'DESIRED WITHDRAWAL LESS THAN OR EQUAL TO ZERO'
      ENDIF
C                        check for value within limit
      IF  (WITHDR .GT. LIMIT)  THEN
          PRINT *, 'DESIRED WITHDRAWAL GREATER THAN LIMIT'
      ENDIF
C                        check for correct input
      IF  (WITHDR .GT. 0 and  .AND.  WITHDR .LE. LIMIT)  THEN
C                          convert to next highest $10, if not multiple
          WITH10 = (WITHDR + 9) / 10  *  10
C                        verification
          PRINT *,'Withdrawal = $',WITH10,' Do you approve (Y/N)?'
          READ  *, RESPNS
          IF  (RESPNS .EQ.  'Y'  .OR.  RESPNS .EQ. 'y')  THEN
C                        calculate breakdown
              N50  = WITH10 / 50
              LEFT = MOD (WITH10, 50)
              N20  = LEFT    / 20
              LEFT = MOD (LEFT, 20)
              N10  = LEFT    / 10
C                        output breakdown
              PRINT *
              PRINT *, '         $50        $20        $10'
              PRINT *,        N50,        N20,        N10
C                        compute fee
              FEE = NINT (Rate * REAL (WITH10))
              FEE = MAX0 (FEE, 2)
              PRINT *, 'Fee   = $', FEE
              TOTAL = WITH10 + FEE
              PRINT *, 'Total = $', TOTAL
C                        add to total
              TOTWTH = TOTWTH + WITH10
          ENDIF
      ENDIF
      GO TO 60
C
C                        error in input
   40     PRINT *, 'Invalid character in input  -  Re-enter'
C                        loop back for more input
   60 GO TO 20
C
```

```
C                        termination
   90 PRINT *, 'Total withdrawn = $', TOTWTH
      STOP
      END
```

Another construct, alternative conditional branching, will be used to solve this same problem in the next section.

Exercises

Note: The exercises below are derived from those in section 5.2 of this chapter using flowcharts and pseudocode. Having that material completed will help with the coding of these programs. Error checking of the input should be included in each exercise.

5.7a Write a program to input multiple sets of two integer numbers; output the message "SAME SIGN" if both numbers in the pair are of the same sign and "OPPOSITE SIGN" if they are of opposite signs. Assume that zero is positive. Output should include the input values. The entire logic, including output of the answer, should be reduced to two long, single-statement IF statements.

5.7b Write a program to input multiple sets of two integer numbers; output the message "SAME PARITY" if both numbers in the pair are even or both are odd and the message "OPPOSITE PARITY" if both are not either even or odd. Zero is an even number. Output should include the input values. The MOD function is very useful here.

5.7c Write a program to generate a table of the powers of 2 from 0 to 15. Work entirely in integer. Output should consist of appropriate headings and two columns of numbers, the power and the result.

5.7d Write a program to generate a Fibonacci series of 20 terms. A Fibonacci series is in the form 1, 1, 2, 3, 5, 8, 13, 21, 34, etc., wherein each term is the sum of the previous two terms. The first two terms must be defined, and the others can then be computed. Output should consist of appropriate headings and two columns of numbers, the term number and the term value. Output should include the first two terms.

5.7e Write a program to input multiple records containing two integer values, each representing the high and low temperatures for the day. Compute a rounded average without using real or mixed-mode arithmetic. Determine the number of degree-days, the number of degrees the average is below 65; if the average is 65 or greater, the number of degree-days is 0. Output both the input values and the computed values with appropriate annotation. Accumulate the degree-days and the total average. At the end, display the total degree-days and the average temperature for the period.

5.7f Write a program to input the number of hours worked and the rate, both real numbers. Compute the salary as hours times rate for the first 40 hours and hours more than 40 times rate times 1.5 for hours above 40. Output the hours, the rate, and the salary. The program should handle multiple input records. Also check that hours are positive.

5.7g   The income tax on salary is computed as follows:

>   If salary is less than $100, tax = 2% of salary.
>
>   If salary is greater than or equal to $100, but less than $300,
>   tax = $2.00 + 4% of salary in excess of $100.
>
>   If salary is greater than or equal to $300, tax = $10.00 + 5% of salary
>   in excess of $300.

Write a program to input multiple values for salary and to compute the tax and the net (the salary less the tax), outputting all three values. Accumulate the total salary and tax. At the end, compute the total net from the other two totals and display all three.

5.7h   Social security taxes are based on a percentage of the gross salary up to a maximum taxable salary. Assume the tax rate is 8% up to a maximum of $50,000 per annum (or a maximum tax of $4000). Write a program to input records containing the weekly salary and the accumulated salary (total salary paid so far in the year) and determine the social security tax to be withheld. Make sure that the logic covers these three cases:

1. Full salary to be taxed (below maximum)
2. Partial salary to be taxed (maximum exceeded during pay period)
3. No salary to be taxed (maximum exceeded prior to pay period)

Output the input values and the tax to be withheld, plus any intermediate values determined as part of the computation, if desired for debugging purposes. Accumulate the total weekly salary and tax to be withheld. At the end, compute the average tax rate by dividing the total tax by the total salary (it should be no greater than 8%).

5.7i   Using the equation presented in exercises 4.8a and 5.3i for projectile motion ($Y = 70 * T - 16.1 * T ** 2$), write a program to track the projectile by calculating its height above the ground every tenth of a second until it returns to the ground. Display the values of T and Y as long as Y is nonnegative.

5.7j   Write a program to implement the logic of exercise 5.3j using the appropriate trigonometric functions to generate a table of x- and y-coordinates for a unit circle as the angle varies from 0 to 360 degrees by increments of 15 degrees. Remember that the angles must be converted to radians before being used as arguments to the functions (2 pi radians (2 * 3.14159) = 360 degrees).

5.8   ALTERNATIVE CONDITIONAL BRANCHING

The IF statements above provided for only one working logical path to be executed when the expression was true. If the expression was false, no statements were to be executed. However, a variation of the IF statement provides two (or more) working logical paths.

**IF .. THEN ..
ELSE .. ENDIF**

The IF .. THEN .. ELSE .. ENDIF construction allows the programmer two logical paths, one for true and one for false. The pseudocode looks like this:

```
If expression is true
     then
          perform statements for 'true' condition
     else
          perform statements for 'false' condition
```

The flowchart is shown in Figure 5-8.

The Hypotenuse of a Right Triangle program is an example of how this construct is used.

```
C                           Hypotenuse of a Right Triangle
C
C                           input
   20 PRINT *, 'Enter two sides of right triangle, (ctrl-Z to end)'
          READ (*,*, END=90, ERR=40) SIDE1, SIDE2
C                           check for valid data
          IF (SIDE1 .GT. 0.00 .AND. SIDE2 .GT. 0.00)  THEN
C                           calculation
               HYPOT = SQRT (SIDE1 * SIDE1 + SIDE2 * SIDE2)
C                           output hypotenuse and blank line
               PRINT *, 'Hypotenuse =', HYPOT
C                           invalid data message
          ELSE
               PRINT *, 'Invalid data:', SIDE1, SIDE2
          ENDIF
          PRINT *
          GO TO 60
C                           input error
   40     PRINT *, 'Error in input data  -  try again!'
C                           branch back for more data
   60 GO TO 20
C                           termination
   90 STOP
      END
```

Figure 5-8
IF .. THEN .. ELSE .. ENDIF

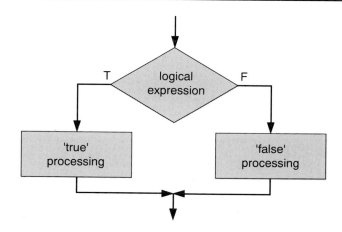

In the above program, no calculation is done unless both sides are greater than zero. The distinction between an input error and invalid data must be understood. An input error occurs when there is a mode conflict, as when numerics are expected and an alphabetic character is entered, or a real number is entered (with a decimal point) when an integer variable is expected. The machine is unable to convert the input string into a number of the appropriate mode. Invalid data occurs when the input line consists of valid characters but the data values do not make sense, such as zero or negative values for the sides of a triangle. The program can do a computation with invalid data, but the answer will not be correct. On the other hand, any attempt to divide by zero will cause a program to bomb out.

IF .. THEN ..
[ELSE IF] ..
ENDIF

This construct, with repeating ELSE IFs (as indicated by the brackets), allows for multiple logical paths, each independent of the other or, to put it another way, each mutually exclusive. Only one ENDIF is required to complete the construct, no matter how many ELSE IFs are used. The pseudocode (assuming three conditions) is:

```
If expression_1 is true,  then
     perform statements for expression_1 true
   else if expression_2 is true,  then
         perform statements for expression_1 false
                             and expression_2 true
     else if expression_3 is true,  then
         perform statements for expression_1,
                           expression_2 false
               and expression_3 true
     else
           perform statements for expressions 1, 2 and 3 false
```

The flowchart is given in Figure 5-9. The expressions within the process symbol (rectangle) represent the logical conditions that brought the execution to that location.

In FORTRAN, the construct appears as:

```
IF   (condition 1)  THEN
          block 1
     ELSE IF (condition 2)  THEN
          block 2
     ELSE IF (condition 3)  THEN
          block 3
     ELSE
          block 4
ENDIF
```

In tabular form, the logic is:

Conditions			Executed
1	2	3	
T			Block 1
F	T		Block 2
F	F	T	Block 3
F	F	F	Block 4

If the last ELSE with block 4 were not present, nothing would have been executed if all conditions were false. Good programming practice would at least place an error message there.

Figure 5-9
IF .. THEN .. [ELSEIF] .. ENDIF

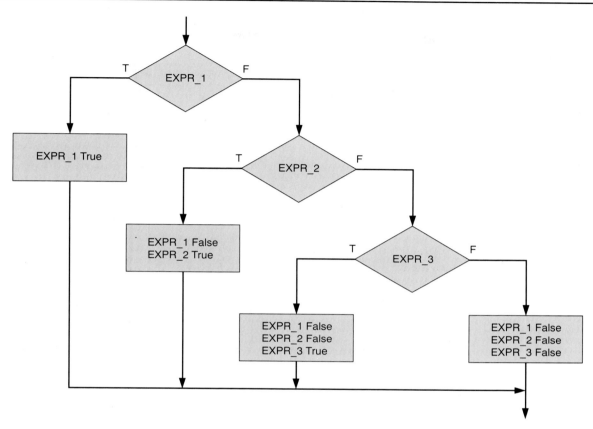

The blocks can have any statement in them except an END. Branches can be made to the ENDIF, but only from within one of the blocks; branches can also be made within a block, but not from one block to another block. Block IFs can also be nested completely within another block IF, but only if the constructs do not overlap.

The following is an illustrative and easy example, which assigns a letter grade to a numeric value.

```
C                    Test of IF .. THEN .. ELSE IF .. ENDIF
C
   20 PRINT *, 'Enter numeric grade'
      READ   (*,*, END=90)  IGRADE
      PRINT *, IGRADE
      IF        (IGRADE .GE. 90)  THEN
               PRINT*,'A'
        ELSE IF (IGRADE .GE. 80)  THEN
               PRINT*,'B'
        ELSE IF (IGRADE .GE. 70)  THEN
               PRINT*,'C'
        ELSE IF (IGRADE .GE. 65)  THEN
               PRINT*,'D'
        ELSE
               PRINT*,'F'
```

```
              ENDIF
          GO TO 20
 C
      90 STOP
         END
```

Now here's another solution to the Perfect Square problem:

```
         PRINT *, 'Enter an integer number'
         READ  *,  I
         ICOUNT = 0
      20 ISQ    = ICOUNT * ICOUNT
         IF  (ISQ .LT. I)  THEN
             ICOUNT = ICOUNT + 1
             GO TO 20
          ELSE IF (ISQ .EQ. I) PRINT *, I,' is a perfect square'
          ELSE                 PRINT *, I,' is not a perfect square'
         ENDIF
         STOP
         END
```

In the application problem Computer Time Accounting, the cost of computer usage is based on how long the user is on the system. The problem was solved by one method in section 4.7 using intrinsic functions; here we do it with our new IF instruction. Again the charge is $2.50 per minute for the first 120 minutes and 80% of that rate for any additional time:

```
     IF  (MINUTE .LE. 120)  THEN
         FEE = 2.50 * REAL (MINUTE)
      ELSE
         FEE = 2.50 * 120.00  +  0.80 * 2.50 * REAL (MINUTE - 120)
     ENDIF
```

Exercises

5.8a   Expand exercise 5.7e by adding to the output a message based on the average temperature, as follows:

Temperature Range	Message
< 11	Frigid
11–31	Freezing
32–55	Cool
56–70	Moderate
71–85	Warm
> 85	Hot

5.8b   Expand exercise 5.7f to three pay brackets:

1. Up to 40 hours (straight time)
2. 40 to 60 hours (time and a half)
3. More than 60 hours (double time)

Compute the salary using the IF .. THEN .. ELSE .. ENDIF construct. Test with appropriate data.

5.8c   Rework exercise 5.7g to use the IF .. THEN .. [ELSE IF] .. ENDIF construct. Only two decisions will be necessary, each doing a .LT. comparison.

5.8d   Rework exercise 5.7h to use the IF .. THEN .. [ELSE IF] .. ENDIF construct.

5.9   LOGICAL VARIABLES

A variable defined as a LOGICAL can only store values corresponding to True and False. These variables are used to hold the results of logical expressions and can lead to faster execution when certain conditions are used more than once to trigger the logical branches. Furthermore, logical variables, if properly chosen, often make a program easier to read.

There are two logical constants, .TRUE. and .FALSE., which are assignable to a logical variable or usable in a DATA statement. In addition, the results of logical expressions can be assigned to them.

Logical variables are first typed using a statement in the very beginning of the program (similar to the INTEGER and REAL statements), called LOGICAL. The IMPLICIT LOGICAL statement is also available for typing a group of variables. A program may begin with:

```
LOGICAL  NEW, FIRST
DATA     NEW, FIRST/ 2 * .FALSE./
```

When a logical variable has a value assigned to it, that value can be one of the logical constants (.TRUE. or .FALSE.) or the kind of logical expression that we have been placing in logical IF statements. For example:

```
LOGICAL  YES
YES = J .GT. 0 .AND.  J .LE. 10
```

would place .TRUE. into YES if J is in the range 1 to 10 and into .FALSE. into YES if J is less than 1 or greater than 10.

Logical variables are used in decisions and may be combined with logical operators (.AND., .OR. and .NOT.). This statement:

```
IF  (YES)  GO TO 20
```

will cause a branch to the statement numbered 20 if YES is true; otherwise the program continues with the next sequential statement. Likewise, there can be a construct like:

```
IF  (NEW .AND. .NOT. FIRST)  THEN
   :
   :
ENDIF
```

which will execute the block if NEW is true *and* FIRST is false.

Logical values may also be input and output. For those purposes only the letters T and F are necessary; during input, any additional characters are ignored.

Below is a sample program illustrating the use of these logical variables. The program is strictly for demonstration and thus contains some code that would not normally be used, but it does show some of the many ways in which logicals may be used.

```
C                       Logical Variables
C
        LOGICAL ZERO, POSTVE, NEGTVE, EVEN, ODD, INTGER, REALN
C
   20 PRINT *
      PRINT *, 'Enter a number (integer or real)'
      READ (*,*, END=90)X
C               determine if integer or real
         I = X
         IF  (REAL(I) .EQ. X)  THEN
              INTGER = .TRUE.
         ELSE
              INTGER = .FALSE.
         ENDIF
         REALN = .NOT. INTGER
         PRINT *, X,' is an integer:',INTGER,' or a real:', REALN
C               determine if equivalent to zero
         ZERO = X .GT. -0.005  .AND.  X .LT. 0.005
         IF        (ZERO)  PRINT *, X,' is close to zero'
         IF  (.NOT. ZERO)  PRINT *, X,' is non-zero'
         POSTVE = X .GT. 0.00
         NEGTVE = X .LT. 0.00
         PRINT *, X,' is positive:',POSTVE,' or negative:', NEGTVE
C               check for integer even or odd
         EVEN = INTGER  .AND.  MOD(I,2) .EQ. 0
         ODD  = INTGER  .AND.  .NOT. EVEN
         IF  (INTGER)  PRINT *,I,' is even:',EVEN,' or odd:', ODD
      GO TO 20
C
   90 STOP
      END
```

A detailed explanation is in order. The program reads in a real number (X) and determines if it is integer-valued by comparing it with the truncated integer to which it was assigned (I). The results of this comparison will place either a .TRUE. or a .FALSE. into the logical variable INTGER. The statement following ENDIF places the reverse condition into REALN by using the .NOT. operator to reverse the truth or falsity of the variable INTGER. The output was so arranged that both conditions are shown, but one will have a T following it and the other will have an F. (A sample run is shown below.)

Zero is then defined as any value within 0.005 of actual 0.00; two output messages are selected from, based on the results of that condition. Next, the positivity or negativity of the input is determined, each based on mutually exclusive conditions. If X is exactly 0.00, then neither POSTVE nor NEGTV is .TRUE. Again, both conditions are output, but both may be false this time. Finally, the parity of the number, if integer, is obtained; if INTGER is .FALSE., both EVEN and ODD will be .FALSE. because of the .AND. relationship. Only if the number is integer will there be output showing the results of this test.

A sample run looks like this (using the Microsoft Fortran Compiler, version 4.1):

```
Enter a number (integer or real)
0
    0.000000E+00 is an integer:T or a real:F
    0.000000E+00 is close to zero
    0.000000E+00 is positive:F or negative:F
           0 is even:T or odd:F

Enter a number (integer or real)
-0.007
   -7.000000E-04 is an integer:F or a real:T
   -7.000000E-04 is close to zero
   -7.000000E-04 is positive:F or negative:T

Enter a number (integer or real)
28
    28.000000 is an integer:T or a real:F
    28.000000 is non-zero
    28.000000 is positive:T or negative:F
           28 is even:T or odd:F

^Z

Stop - Program terminated.
```

Logical variables use only one bit in the storage word. A 1 represents true and a 0 represents false. In most computer systems, the last bit is used so that a true condition can be represented by any positive or negative odd number and false by an even number or zero. For simplicity, assume .TRUE. = 1 and .FALSE. = 0. When the logical IF is testing, it (just like the arithmetic IF) is testing the relationship of the expression with zero and branching according to .TRUE. > 0, .FALSE. = 0.

In the logical IF, the evaluation of a relation (.LT., .GE., etc.) is done arithmetically by subtracting and storing the logical result (.TRUE. or .FALSE.) in a temporary location.

Logical operations do not use an arithmetic process but a bit manipulation process. The tables below give the beginning and ending conditions of the three logical operations. The left column represents the truth or falsity of one condition; the top row, the same for the other condition. The .NOT. logical has only one condition. Within the box are the results of the logical combination. For example, if condition 1 is true (row 1) and condition 2 is false (column 0), the .AND. relationship yields .FALSE. but the .OR. relationship yields .TRUE. (intersection of row 1 and column 0).

.AND.	0	1
0	0	0
1	0	1

.OR.	0	1
0	0	1
1	1	1

.NOT.	
0	1
1	0

Thus, all decisions eventually reduce to arithmetic.

Exercises

5.9a   Write a program to input two integer numbers for temperature and humidity. If the temperature is outside the range −20 to +110, or the humidity is outside the range 0 to 100, output error messages for each number out of range and for the combination of either or both being outside of range. Use one logical variable for each quantity.

5.9b   Write a program to input hours worked. If the hours worked are greater than 40, turn on (make .TRUE.) the logical variable HALFTM. If the hours worked are also greater than 60, turn on the logical variable DBLETM. Use the variables to trigger these output messages:

    `STRAIGHT TIME` if the time worked is less than or equal to 40 hours
    `DOUBLE TIME`   if the time worked is greater than 60 hours
    `OVERTIME`   if the time worked is between 40 and 60 hours

5.9c   Combine exercises 5.7a and 5.7b into a single program to input multiple integer pairs and provide the appropriate messages about sign and parity. Use logical variables to control the output. There should be only one output line for each data record, so there must be four separate output messages available, each combining the two conditions. The output line should also include the input values.

5.10   CHAPTER REVIEW

In this chapter, we have covered almost all the decision-making instructions available to the FORTRAN programmer. The two not covered here are minor (and unstructured) variations of GO TO and will be discussed in Chapter 13.

At this point, you have all the rudimentary tools necessary for writing useful programs to get answers to almost any kind of problem. From here on, the text will be adding language features that provide for easier programming, better data handling, and better input/output formatting. Effectively, we have given you a hammer, a saw, and a screwdriver; the electric drills and other fancy appliances are yet to come. But you can do a lot of construction with these basic tools.

Most important, we have introduced the concepts of structure and the rules of structure will be rigidly enforced throughout the text. Except for implementing the ERR= clause, the GO TO statement should disappear from our programs after the next chapter. The requirement that computer programs must be readable by human beings cannot be overemphasized. The majority of programming work is the revision and enhancement of existing programs. Thus, if the logic in the program is not clear, any improvement to it is impossible without a complete rewrite.

The following topics are covered in this chapter:

Topic	Section
End-of-data (EOD)	5.5
End-of-file (EOF)	5.5
END= clause	5.5
ERR= clause	5.5

Topic	Section
Flowcharts	5.2
GO TO	5.4
IF (arithmetic)	5.7
IF (block)	5.7
IF (logical)	5.7
IF .. THEN .. ENDIF	5.7
IF .. THEN .. ELSE .. ENDIF	5.8
IF .. THEN .. ELSEIF .. ENDIF	5.8
LOGICAL	5.9
Logical operators	5.7
Pseudocode	5.2
Relational operators	5.7
Sentinel value	5.7
Structure	5.3
Total processing	5.6

Exercises

5.10a   Write a program to input a file of examination grades (integer, range of 0 to 100). The program should count the number of grades and calculate a real average. Then, using the following distribution, count and output the number of As, Bs, Cs, Ds, and Fs.

0–64	F
65–69	D
70–79	C
80–89	B
90–100	A

5.10b   Write a program to track the repayment of a loan. The input includes the principle, the annual interest rate, and the monthly payment. The monthly payment must exceed the monthly interest so that the loan will eventually be paid off. A reasonable assumption is that the annual interest will be between 8% and 25% (with the monthly interest being one-twelfth of that amount) and that the payment should be between 2% and 5% of the principle.

The interest is simple interest on the existing monthly balance. The balance for the next month is the existing balance, plus the interest, minus the payment. For example, a loan of $10,000 at an interest of 18% per annum and a payment of $300 per month would yield a table like this:

Month	Balance	Interest	Payment
1	10000.00	150.00	300.00
2	9850.00	147.75	300.00
3	9697.75	145.47	300.00
4	9643.22	(etc.)	(etc.)
5	(etc.)		

Your program should compute interest to the nearest cent (use the intrinsic function ANINT). Special care must be taken on the last month's payment, which will be less than $300 (otherwise the payer will be owed money) yet enough to cover the interest generated; thus, the calculation for the last month is different from the others. The output cannot be as nice as the above example, because you do not have all the available I/O tools yet, but do the best you can.

5.10c   The equation $y = v * t - 16.1 * t * t$ represents the vertical height of a body thrown upward with a velocity of v feet per second after t seconds. Write a program to input an initial velocity and produce a table of y versus t for as many integer seconds as the body is in the air or just touching the ground. Do not output any record for time after the body has hit the ground (i.e., when y is negative).

5.10d   The general solution of a second-order equation of the following form:

$$y = a * x ** 2 + b * x + c$$

has two solutions. If the discriminant ($b ** 2 - 4 * a * c$) is nonnegative, the solutions are:

$$x1 = (-b + \text{sqrt} (b*b - 4*a*c))/(2*a)$$
$$x2 = (-b - \text{sqrt} (b*b - 4*a*c))/(2*a)$$

If the discriminant is zero, both solutions have the same value. If the discriminant is negative, the solution becomes two complex conjugate numbers having a real portion and an imaginary portion in these forms:

real + imaginary   and   real − imaginary
Real value $= -b/(2*a)$
Imaginary value $= \text{sqrt} (-(b*b - 4*a*c))/(2*a)$ i,
where i is the square root of -1.

If the coefficient a is zero, the equation reduces to a straight line whose solution is easy to derive. Should both a and b be zero, with c nonzero, we have an impossible case.
    Write a program to input values of a, b, and c and output the solutions with appropriate annotation to fully describe them. Test all possible cases.

5.10e   Write a program to input the end points of a line as x- and y-coordinates. The end points may have positive or negative coordinates but must be at some nonzero distance apart. Then input an increment to be used to mark off coordinates on that line, starting at the first point. The increment should be less than the length of the line; your program should test that it is true and that it is also greater than zero. Calculate the x- and y-coordinates of the marked-off points.
    As a test case, the line from coordinates $(2, 4)$ to coordinates $(14, 13)$ with an increment of 2 will have marks at $(3.6, 5.2)$, $(5.2, 6.4)$, $(6.8, 7.6)$, $(8.4, 8.8)$, $(10.0, 10.0)$, $(11.6, 11.2)$, and $(13.2, 12.4)$. No mark should fall on an end point or outside the range of the line. Test your program with the above data, then with data that includes combinations of positive and negative coordinates (the line may even go down and to the left).

This program can be written without using the trigonometric functions by using the concept of proportions. However, if you do it that way, make sure that your program works for both horizontal and vertical lines.

5.10f When a line is drawn either to a display screen or to a graphic plotter, that line must be "clipped" to fit within the "window" which limits the graphic to the size of the screen or desired drawing. Write a program to enter the coordinates of the window and the endpoints of the line. The window coordinates may be specified with the x- and y-coordinates of the frame, the former giving the horizontal limits, the latter the vertical limits. The end points should be given as x- and y-coordinates of each end.

To keep the program simple, assume lines that extend beyond the window and that do go through the window. Thus two intersections with the window borders should be calculated. The program must work with both positive and negative coordinates and with lines that slope in any direction, including horizontally and vertically.

5.10g Now it's time for some fun! You are going to amaze your friends with a program that will guess which number they pick in a very small number of trials. For example, the program can pick any number from 1 to 30,000 in 16 guesses. The method to be used is called a binary search, which keeps cutting the guessing range in half.

For example, take the smaller range 1 to 30 and assume the number to be guessed is 20. The logic assumes the range to go from 1 to one higher than the top of the range (i.e., 31), so that the truncation done by the integer division does not prevent guessing the top of the range. The first guess is $(31 + 1)/2 = 16$. The program must now determine if the guess is too high, too low, or correct. If the guess is incorrect, the range is adjusted. If the guess is too high, it becomes the new upper value. If the guess is too low, as in our example, it becomes the new lower value. The next guess is $(31 + 16)/2 = 23$. That guess is too high. The next guess is $(23 + 16)/2 = 19$. Since this last guess is too low, the next guess is $(23 + 19)/2 = 21$. The next guess is $(21 + 19)/2 = 20$, the correct answer. A graphic representation of this process is shown on the next page.

You can also predict how many guesses are needed at most. Taking the top of the range, find the next higher power of 2—in this case, 32. (If the top of the range is a power of 2, use it.) 32 is 2 to the fifth power; adding one to the power gives us the maximum number of guesses required. It may be even less, as in the example above.

This exercise is to be developed in a number of steps so that each part may be tested thoroughly before proceeding to the next.

Part a Write a program to input the top of the range and the number to be guessed. Test the input value to see that it is greater than zero and less than or equal to the top of the desired range. Write the code necessary to implement the binary search, letting the program adjust the range when its guess is not equal to the value input. Count the number of guesses, including the final one, and verify that it does not exceed the expected number.

Part b Write a routine to determine the maximum number of guesses from the number input as the top of the range. It can be done by a looping procedure similar to that used to determine perfect squares or by a more sophisticated version using base 2 logarithms. (Base 2 logarithms = 1.4427 * natural logarithms.) Test this against known values, such as:

Range	9–16	17–32	33–64	...	16,385–32,767
Maximum guesses	5	6	7	...	16

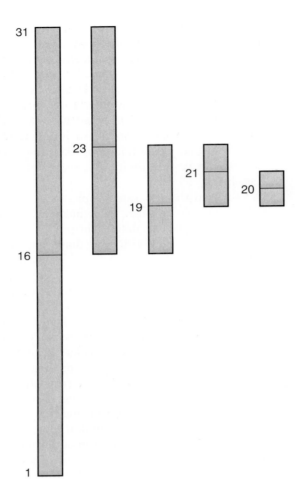

Part c   Convert the program interactive, in which a user must specify whether the machine's guess is too high (H), too low (L), or correct (C). Remove your input and set the top of the range with a data statement. Display a message introducing your program, asking the user if he or she believes that the computer can do it. Save the yes or no response for a later output message.

Next, display a message describing the interaction required, especially the need to place apostrophes around the responses.

Prepare yourself for someone trying to outsmart your program. For example, the user may enter a response other than the allowable H, L, or C or their lowercase equivalents. In that case, display an error message and let the user reenter a response. To make it interesting, count the number of errors and use that counter to trigger a series of different error messages, making them nastier as they go. (However, use good taste; you would not want to display "GO TO HELL" because it contains the forbidden four-letter word, "GOTO"!) If you have three error messages, you can use the MOD function to choose them in sequence, letting the sequence start over again after the third message is displayed.

Also be prepared for a liar! Your user may try to fool the computer by giving it incorrect high and low messages. You know the maximum number of guesses required, so once that number is exceeded, terminate your program with a stinging remark about the unprofessionalism of the user—or maybe a curse such as "May your programs breed a million bugs!"

At the end of the program, display two possible messages, dependent on the initial yes/no response. Either praise the user for his or her ultimate faith in the power of computers or condemn the user for being so cynical.

6

Looping Structures

CHAPTER OUTLINE

CHAPTER OBJECTIVES

- To show the methods of constructing loops using the DO statement.

- To describe the internal workings of the DO instruction.

- To analyze structured looping methods and their simulation.

- To explore practical applications.

- To define structured programming more precisely.

- To introduce the concept of top-down design.

- To describe various debugging methodologies.

STATEMENT OF THE PROBLEM

As new applications are introduced in any programming text, it becomes obvious that very few programs are linear in nature. Most programs repeat their logic a number of times before terminating their run. These loops may be used for a variety of reasons, including:

1. An input loop to handle multiple data
2. A logic loop to solve certain algorithms
3. An output loop to produce multiple pages in a long report

You can create loops with the FORTRAN tools you have already learned. However, a specialized tool just to control loops has a number of distinct advantages, such as:

1. Reducing the number of statements that must be written
2. Reducing the programming effort
3. Making the program easier to read (for the human)
4. Helping to structure the program
5. Aiding in counting

Item 4 is probably the most important. The use of a specialized instruction just to control loops establishes a module of instructions within the program that leads to better and less error-prone coding. By specifically setting up this structure, both the programmer and the compiler can spot attempts to branch into the middle of a loop from outside its range, a technique which is usually not intended by the programmer. (Some compilers will display a nondestructive warning if such an attempt is made.)

One characteristic of FORTRAN is its paucity of instructions; and indeed, the instruction introduced in this chapter can be simulated by other means. However, it is so helpful (even indispensable in some I/O situations) that it was put into the very first version of the language. It has remained the only available looping structure specified in FORTRAN; all others are optional add-ins and do not appear in the ANSI specifications (ANSI X3.9-1978).

6.1 SIMPLE LOOPS

The previous chapter presented the pseudocode and flowchart for the logic that generates a table of squares from 1 to 50 but gave no solution. Now we will introduce a new looping construct that can be used to find a solution. First, however, examine the program below, which uses only the tools available until now.

```
C                      Table of Squares from 1 to 50
C
        ICOUNT = 1                              initialization
   20 ISQURE = ICOUNT * ICOUNT
        PRINT *, ICOUNT, ISQURE
        ICOUNT = ICOUNT + 1                     incrementation
      IF (ICOUNT .LE. 50)  GO TO 20             termination
```

```
C
      STOP
      END
```

Three processes are required in any looping code:

1. Initialization: setting the counter to an initial value
2. Incrementation: applying a constant to the counter
3. Termination: ending the loop when a final value has been exceeded

There is one FORTRAN statement that does all three of these processes; it is the DO statement, a term derived from the abbreviation for *ditto*. Using the DO statement, the above program takes the form shown below.

```
C                   Table of Squares from 1 to 50
C
      DO 20  ICOUNT = 1,50,1
           ISQURE = ICOUNT * ICOUNT
   20 PRINT *, ICOUNT, ISQURE
      STOP
      END
```

The DO statement consists of:

1. A statement number that designates the end of the loop. All statements, up to and including the designated one, are executed. Those statements are said to be within the range of the loop.
2. An index (or counter) used to control the loop. It may also be used as part of an expression at any time, but its value must not be reassigned within the loop.
3. A beginning value for the index.
4. A terminating value for the index. When the index is within the range of the beginning and terminating values, execution continues with the statement following the DO statement. When the index is outside the range, execution continues with the statement following the last statement in the loop (the one with the statement number on it).
5. An increment applied to the index when the work within the loop is completed. The increment may be positive or negative, but it can never be zero.

If the increment is not stated, it is assumed to be 1; thus, the above DO statement might have been written as:

```
DO 20  ICOUNT = 1,50
```

The three values which control the index are called the *DO loop parameters* and may be all integer or all real. The index must be of the same mode. They may also be positive, negative, or zero (except the increment, which cannot be zero). Thus, it is possible to write the following program to generate a tax table:

```
C                       Tax Table for 8% Taxes
C
      PARAMETER  (RATE = 0.08)
C
      DO 100  AMOUNT = 0.01, 1.00, 0.01
          TAX = ANINT (RATE * AMOUNT * 100.00) / 100.00
  100 PRINT *, ANINT (AMOUNT * 100.00) / 100.00, TAX
C
      STOP
      END
```

The function ANINT adjusts reals to the nearest whole number; and in the construction shown above (introduced in section 4.5), it rounds the argument to the nearest cent. The function was used directly in the PRINT statement so that the value of the index AMOUNT will not be modified.

The same table might have been generated in reverse order with:

```
DO 100  AMOUNT = 1.00, 0.01, -0.01
```

Certain rules apply to these simple loops. They must be fully understood so that the contained logic of DO loops will not lead to errors and problems. First of all, the value of the index must *never* be modified within the loop itself. FORTRAN sets up a loop control methodology before the loop starts executing to control the number of times the loop will be executed. Symbolizing the three parameters as m1, m2, and m3, the number of times the loop is executed is:

```
MAX (INT ((m2 - m1 + m3) / m3), 0)
```

This means that the integer results of the calculation involving the parameters is compared with zero and the greater of those two values is the number of times the work within the loop is repeated. This prevents such ridiculous situations as going from 1 to 10 with an increment of −5. For example:

DO controls	Number of Executions
DO 20 I = 1, 10, 3	MAX (12/3, 0) = MAX (4, 0) = 4
DO 20 I = 1, 20, −5	MAX (14/(−5), 0) = MAX (−2, 0) = 0
DO 20 X = −0.8, 1.5, 0.2	MAX (2.5/0.2, 0) = MAX (12, 0) = 11

FORTRAN maintains its own internal counter to keep track of the number of repetitions the loop has performed, decrementing that counter until its value reaches zero. The pseudocode is as follows:

```
1.   counter = MAX (INT ((m2 - m1 + m3) / m3), 0)
2.   set index to m1
3.   if counter = 0, go to step 8
4.       do work of loop
5.       add m3 to index
6.       decrement counter by 1
7.   go to step 3
8.   continue to next instruction
```

The flowchart is shown in Figure 6-1. The rounded process and decision symbols are used to indicate the work that the DO statement does automatically once the program has defined the parameters. The squared process symbol is the work done in the loop by the programmed statements.

The work of the loop may include any kind of logic, including branching within the loop or to a point outside the loop. However, *no branching may be made into the range of the DO loop except by going through the DO statement;* otherwise, the loop controls are not properly set. The terminal statement of the DO loop (the one with the statement number on it designated by the DO statement) *cannot* be one of these:

GO TO	STOP	Arithmetic IF	ELSE
DO	END	Block IF	ELSE IF

A single statement IF is allowed. Where logic is required that places one of the forbidden constructions at the logical end of the loop, a dummy statement, CONTINUE, that does nothing except allow a statement number to be attached to it, is used.

Figure 6-1
DO-loop logic

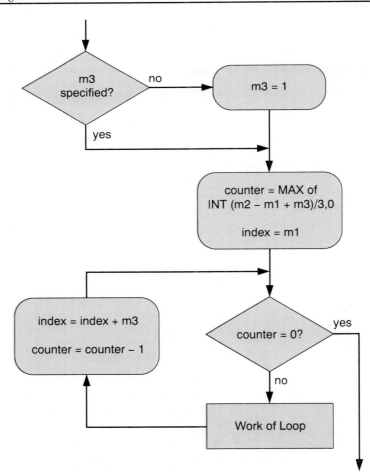

Some programmers always end a DO loop with a CONTINUE because it emphasizes the structure. Indenting of the statements within the loop also makes the coding easier to read. Note, too, that the need for a GO TO back to the beginning of the loop is eliminated by the DO statement.

To illustrate the use of the allowable single statement IF, the tax table program above might have been modified to display only the values in which the tax is nonzero:

```
C                        Tax Table for 8% Taxes
C
        PARAMETER  (RATE = 0.08)
C
        DO 100   AMOUNT = 0.01, 1.00, 0.01
            TAX = ANINT  (RATE * AMOUNT * 100.00) / 100.00
   100  IF (TAX .GE. 0.01) PRINT *, ANINT (AMOUNT * 100.00) / 100.00, TAX
C
        STOP
        END
```

DO loops may also be included within an IF, ELSE or ELSE IF block only if that loop is contained entirely within the block. Inversely, if an IF block appears within a DO loop, the END IF must also be within the range of that loop.

Review Questions and Exercises

6.1a   For each of the following DO statements, determine the number of times the work of the loop will be executed.

    a. DO 20   I = 4,16
    b. DO 20   I = 4,16,-2
    c. DO 20   I = 3,23,7
    d. DO 20   I = 3,24,7
    e. DO 20   X = 0.85,5.65,0.5

6.1b   For the loops given below, determine the final values of *L*.

    a.   L = 1
            DO 20   I = 2,6
      20 L = L * I

    c.   L = 0
            DO 20   I = 2,6
      20 L = L + 2 * (I - 1)

    b.   L = 10
            DO 20   I = 20,3,-7
      20 L = L + I / 5

    d.   L = -8000
            DO 20   I = -16,-8,4
      20 L = L / I

6.1c   Using a DO loop, write a program to generate a table of the powers of 2 from 0 to 15. Work entirely in integer. Output should consist of appropriate headings and two columns of numbers: the power and the result.

6.1d   Using a DO loop, write a program to generate a Fibonacci series of 20 terms. A Fibonnacci series is in the form 1, 1, 2, 3, 5, 8, 13, 21, 34, etc., wherein each term is the sum of the previous two terms. The first two terms must be defined and the others can then be computed. Output should consist of appropriate headings and two columns of numbers: the term number and the term value. Output should include the first two terms.

6.1e   Using a DO loop, generate a table of squares, cubes, square roots, and cube roots for the integers in the range of 1 to 50. The output should include appropriate headings and five columns of numbers.

6.1f   Using a DO loop, generate a temperature conversion table from Fahrenheit to Celsius using the formula C = (F − 32)/9 * 5. Loop from Fahrenheit = −40 to +120. The output of the Celsius temperature should be rounded to the nearest integer.

6.1g   Reverse the formula in exercise 6.1f to convert from Celsius to Fahrenheit with a Celsius range from −40 to +50. Place messages alongside the following Celsius temperatures:

    0 Freezing
   20 Room temperature
   37 Body temperature

6.1h   Write a table of conversions from feet to inches, yards, centimeters, and meters. (1 foot = 12 inches = 1/3 yard = 30.48 centimeters = 0.3048 meters.) Use a range of 1 to 20 feet. Use integer variables where possible and real variables otherwise. Avoid mixed-mode expressions.

6.1i   Write a program to vary hours from 5 to 70 by 5. Using a rate of $8.00 per hour, calculate and display the salary paid using straight time up to 40 hours, time and a half up to 60 hours, and double time above 60 hours.

6.1j   A music store sells compact discs for $11.50 each, but it offers a discount for bulk purchases. From the tenth to the nineteenth CD, the discount is 10%; after the twentieth CD, the discount is 18%. Write a program to output the costs for 2 to 30 CDs.

6.2   INPUT LOOPS AND COUNTING

One of the major uses of a DO loop is to facilitate multiple input. In the previous chapter, there is a program to calculate the hypotenuse of a right triangle. Now we can place that program into a DO loop:

```
C                       Hypotenuse of a Right Triangle
C
C                       loop through input
         DO 80  I = 1,20000
              PRINT *, 'Enter two sides of right triangle, (ctrl-Z to end)'
              READ   (*,*, END=90, ERR=60)  SIDE1, SIDE2
              IF  (SIDE1 .GT. 0.00  .AND.  SIDE2 .GT. 0.00)  THEN
C                       calculation
                   HYPOT = SQRT (SIDE1 * SIDE1  +  SIDE2 * SIDE2)
```

```
C                           output hypotenuse and blank line
                    PRINT *, 'Hypotenuse =', HYPOT
                ELSE
                    PRINT *, 'Invalid data:', SIDE1, SIDE2
                ENDIF
                PRINT *
                    GO TO 80
C                           invalid characters in input
      60      PRINT *, 'Invalid character in input data'
C                           return for more data
      80 CONTINUE
C                           termination
      90 STOP
         END
```

Looping from 1 to 20,000 is almost as good as an infinite loop; if the programmer wants more, real parameters might be used with a very small increment. This version eliminates the GO TO back to the prompt, but it cannot eliminate the GO TO around the error message. There are alternatives that could eliminate the GO TO:

1. Eliminate ERR= clause and statement 60 (and the GO TO before it). The elimination of error checking can lead to disastrous results.
2. Reset to ERR=90 and remove statement 60 (and the GO TO before it). One error and the program exits without an error message, a very inefficient method.
3. Move statement 60 to a point between statements 80 and 90, providing the error message before terminating. If the loop becomes exhausted (by 20,000 sets of input data), the error message will appear at the termination of the program.
4. Reset to ERR=80 and remove statement 60 (and the GO TO before it). This method displays no result and leaves the user uninformed about why no output appeared.

This is one situation wherein the GO TO does provide an efficient method. Its use follows one of the rules given in Chapter 5; namely, that an unconditional branch can be made to the end of a loop. However, for those who wish to fully purge the GO TO, here is a possibility:

```
C                       Hypotenuse of a Right Triangle
C
         LOGICAL  VALID, GOOD
C
C                       loop through input
         DO 80  I = 1,20000
             VALID = .FALSE.
             GOOD  = .FALSE.
             PRINT *, 'Enter two sides of right triangle, (ctrl-Z to end)'
             READ (*,*, END=90, ERR=60) SIDE1, SIDE2
             VALID = .TRUE.
             GOOD  = SIDE1 .GT. 0.00  .AND.  SIDE2 .GT. 0.00
C                           calculation
      60      IF (VALID .AND. GOOD) THEN
                 HYPOT = SQRT (SIDE1 * SIDE1 +  SIDE2 * SIDE2)
```

```
C                         output hypotenuse
                  PRINT *, 'Hypotenuse =', HYPOT
            ENDIF
C                         data error
            IF (VALID .AND. .NOT. GOOD)
      1           PRINT *, 'Invalid data: ', SIDE1, SIDE2
C                      invalid characters in input
            IF (.NOT. VALID)
      1           PRINT *, 'Invalid character in input data'
C                      output blank line and return for more data
      80 PRINT *
C                      termination
      90 STOP
            END
```

The number of working statements (excluding STOP, END, and comments) increased from 13 to 15, and two more variables were added. Note the assignment of a condition to the logical variable. It does, however, make the program free of the GO TO statement (except those inherent in the END= and ERR= clauses)—although it did not reduce the number of labels. I also believe the program is harder to follow.

Many professionals agree that occasional use of a GO TO in highly structured situations with strict, restrictive rules should be allowed in cases where the FORTRAN code is simplified significantly. The exercise of adding too much additional code just to avoid a GO TO is inefficient, both in coding and in execution. There will be a number of other situations (to be discussed in the next section) wherein the GO TO cannot possibly be eliminated, so that judgment about the occasional use of that despised statement should be reserved until that time.

Another feature of using a DO loop to define the input loop is that the index of the loop can be used as a counter when the initial value is 1 and the increment is 1. (Other parameters can also give a count if a computation is added.) This index variable is a regular variable whose value (although it should not be reassigned within the loop) is available both inside the loop and after the program has exited from the loop. (That same variable may be used for other purposes once the loop is exited.) For example, the display in the preceding program could have been enhanced to:

```
      PRINT *, 'Hypotenuse =', HYPOT,' for input set', I
```

Yet another method would be to display the total number of input sets (including sets in error) at the end of the program using the value of the index when the exit is made from the loop. However, the logic must be examined carefully so that the reader understands that the value of the DO loop index upon exiting the loop is 1 more than the number of data sets handled. For example, assume four sets of data followed by end-of-data. The index equals 1 for the first set of data, 2 for the second, 3 for the third, 4 for the fourth, and 5 for the end-of-data entry. Thus, on exiting the loop, the value of the index must be decremented by 1 to provide the correct answer. The final statements of the above program may be revised to:

```
      80 CONTINUE
C                      termination
      90 PRINT *, I-1,' sets of data processed'
         STOP
         END
```

The logic is also correct in those cases in which the loop is exhausted; i.e., all values of the index have been executed. As Figure 6-1 shows, the index is incremented before the counter is tested so that it will be equal to the final value plus 1. Subtracting 1 gives the correct answer.

Exercises

6.2a Write a program to input and edit hours worked and rate of pay from a data file, using a DO loop to handle the multiple input and the index of that loop to count the records. Edit the records according to these parameters:

Hours: 1 to 80
Rate of pay: $3.75 to $60.00 per hour

Keep a count of the number of errors in the hours, rate, and invalid characters in the record. Display each record with its record number, the data (if not in error due to invalid characters), and one of the following messages if the data is in error:

```
'Invalid character in input record'
'Invalid number of hours'
'Invalid rate of pay'
'Invalid hours and pay'
```

At the end of the input, display the number of records read and the total errors in each category.

Design test data for all of the above conditions, as well as a few sets of correct data.

6.2b Using correct payroll data, as edited by the program in exercise 6.2a, write a program to read in the same records, using the index of the DO loop as the counter for the number of records. Compute the salary as follows:

Up to 40 hours: straight time
40 to 60 hours: time and a half
More than 60 hours: double time

At the end of the input, display the total hours worked, the total salary earned, the average hours worked, the average salary, and the average rate of pay per total hours worked.

6.2c Revise exercise 5.7e (temperature input and analysis) to use a DO loop.

6.2d Revise exercise 5.6f (gas mileage and travel analysis) to use a DO loop. Add to the analysis the average number of miles and the average cost of gas per fillup.

6.3 OTHER LOOPING STRUCTURES

The FORTRAN DO statement only gives the programmer the ability to specify the termination of the loop when all the values of the index have been executed (when the loop is exhausted). It is an excellent structure when the number of repetitions is known or can be calculated, but often it is necessary to get out of the loop before that occurs. If it is an input loop, the END= clause of the READ statement can generate the branch to some statement outside the loop. However, in a calculation loop, if exit from the loop is wanted—based on a calculation or comparison of a variable other than the index—then it is necessary to have a conditional branch out of the loop.

Structured programming uses three types of loop structures that permit branching to the statement immediately following the end of the loop:

1. WHILE loop for repetitions to continue while a specified condition is true, with testing at the beginning of the loop. If the tested condition is false upon entering the loop, the work of the loop is not done. If the tested condition becomes false while still in the loop, the work of that repetition is completed before exiting.
2. UNTIL loop for repetitions to continue until a specified condition becomes true. The work of the loop is always done at least once because testing is at the end. If the tested condition becomes true while still in the loop, the work of that repetition is completed before exiting.
3. LOOP with EXIT for repetitions to continue until a specified condition becomes true at a specified point in the loop. When it becomes true, exit is made from the loop immediately.

Flowcharts for WHILE and UNTIL are shown in Figure 6-2. Not all of these constructs are implemented in all languages, and *none of them exist in the FORTRAN 77 specifications.*

Figure 6-2
DO WHILE and DO UNTIL

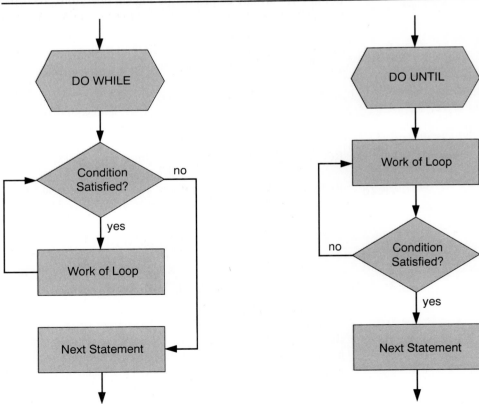

Although some implementations do contain either a WHILE .. DO or a DO WHILE instruction, such an instruction is not in the FORTRAN 77 specifications and thus we cannot, in all good conscience, endorse its use. To do so would make our programs not standard and destroy their portability. In the specifications for Fortran 90, the DO WHILE construct has been included.

FORTRAN has no real need for such statements because it can simulate them with a conditional branch placed anywhere within the code. Actually, all of the structured constructs above are the same except for the placement of the decision. They differ from the FORTRAN conditional branch in that the structured constructs can branch only to the statement following the end of the loop; the FORTRAN conditional branch can branch to any statement in the program.

It is this very freedom that causes FORTRAN to be unstructured, and that is why this text has placed very restrictive rules on the use of the GO TO. By following these rules, we can simulate the constructs above, thereby maintaining the structure so essential for good programming.

None of the above structures exist, but they can be simulated. And although the example below shows only one condition, like the IF statement, there can be multiple conditions connected by logical operators. To demonstrate this, below are hypothetical programs using the statements as though they did exist.

```
C                       Demonstration of DO WHILE
C
      I   = 0
      ISQ = 0
      DO 20  WHILE  (ISQ .LT. 100)
          I   = I + 1
          ISQ = I * I
   20 PRINT *, I, ISQ
C
      STOP 'all done'
      END
```

```
C                       Demonstration of DO UNTIL
C
      I = 0
      DO 20  UNTIL  (ISQ .GE. 100)
          I   = I + 1
          ISQ = I * I
   20 PRINT *, I, ISQ
C
      STOP 'all done'
      END
```

The output file will look like this:

```
                    1        1
                    2        4
                    3        9
                    4       16
                    5       25
                    6       36
                    7       49
                    8       64
                    9       81
                   10      100
            all done
```

Both programs above should leave us with some questions. If the purpose of the programs is to print the squares up to and including 100, why do we specify that the WHILE condition be less than 100? And why does the UNTIL test for equal to 100 when we want to display 100? The answer is that the complete work of the repetition is done even when the tested condition changes during that work. Thus, if the WHILE control had read "less than or equal to 100," the next square (121) would have been displayed; likewise, the UNTIL has to read "equal to or greater than 100" to terminate the loop after displaying the 100 because "greater than 100" alone would not have terminated it.

It is possible to fix the above problem, but the cure may be worse than the illness. One way is to place the same conditional before the output statement so that the test occurs twice. Another method rearranges the statements as shown below; the calculation must appear twice (not serious here, but it would be if it consisted of many statements) and the output of a previous case appears in the same module as the calculation for the next case. Although only the DO WHILE is shown, the DO UNTIL could be rearranged the same way.

```
      C                       Demonstration of DO WHILE, cured
      C
            I   = 0
            ISQ = I * I
            DO 20  WHILE  (ISQ .LT. 100)
                PRINT *, I, ISQ
                I = I + 1
         20 ISQ = I * I
      C
            STOP 'all done'
            END
```

The LOOP .. EXIT construct below requires no adjustment, since it will stop executing the loop as soon as the condition changes.

```
      C                       Demonstration of LOOP .. EXIT
      C
            I = 0
            LOOP 20
                I   = I + 1
```

```
              ISQ = I * I
              IF  (ISQ .GT. 100)   EXIT
       20 PRINT *, I, ISQ
C
          STOP 'all done'
          END
```

We can simulate the DO WHILE using valid FORTRAN 77 instructions in two ways. The first uses the block IF with the desired condition, staying within the loop if true; a single GO TO is used to get back to the beginning of the loop. The second uses the regular IF with a GO TO to get out of the loop if the opposite (or undesired) condition is true; it also uses a GO TO to get back to the beginning of the loop. These versions of the DO WHILE are simulated below.

```
C                      Demonstration of Block IF .. GO TO to simulate DO WHILE
C
       I   = 0
       ISQ = 0
    20 IF  (ISQ .LT. 100)   THEN
           I   = I + 1
           ISQ = I * I
           PRINT *, I, ISQ
           GO TO 20
       ENDIF
C
       STOP 'all done'
       END
C                      Demonstration of IF .. GO TO to simulate DO WHILE
C
       I   = 0
       ISQ = 0
    20 IF  (ISQ .GE. 100)   GO TO 40
           I   = I + 1
           ISQ = I * I
           PRINT *, I, ISQ
       GO TO 20
C
    40 STOP 'all done'
       END
```

The DO UNTIL can be simulated in standard FORTRAN in the following manner.

```
C                       Demonstration of IF .. GO TO to simulate DO UNTIL
C
       I = 0
    10 I = I + 1
           ISQ = I * I
           PRINT *, I, ISQ
       IF  (ISQ .LT. 100)   GO TO 10
C
       STOP 'all done'
       END
```

The LOOP .. EXIT structure is the easiest to simulate and allows us to use the DO loop to aid in counting. However, the upper range of the DO loop must be high enough to ensure that the tested value is reached. Without using the DO loop, the program reduces to a combination of IFs and GO TOs, as in Chapter 5.

```
C               Demonstration of IF .. GO TO to simulate LOOP .. EXIT
C
      DO 20  I = 1,20000
          ISQ = I * I
          IF  (ISQ .GT. 100)  GO TO 40
 20 PRINT *, I, ISQ
C
 40 STOP 'all done'
      END
```

Exercises

6.3a   For each of the programs below, determine what the final output line will display.

a.
```
      I   = 0
      ISQ = 0
      ICB = 0
      DO 20  WHILE (ISQ .LT. 40  .AND.  ICB .LT. 200)
          I   = I + 1
          ISQ = I * I
          ICB = I * I * I
 20 PRINT *, I, ISQ, ICB
      STOP
      END
```

b.
```
      I = 0
      DO 20 UNTIL (ISQ .GT. 40  .OR.  ICB .GT. 200)
          I   = I + 1
          ISQ = I * I
          ICB = I * I * I
 20 PRINT *, I, ISQ, ICB
      STOP
      END
```

c.
```
      I = 0
      LOOP 20
          I   = I + 1
          ISQ = I * I
          ICB = I * I * I
          IF (ISQ .GT. 40  .OR.  ICB .GT. 200)  EXIT
 20 PRINT *, I, ISQ, ICB
      STOP
      END
```

Note: All of the exercises below are phrased in terms of DO WHILE or DO UNTIL. If your compiler has one or both of these statements implemented, try them; but write a standardized version of the program using no more than the regular DO statement.

6.3b Write a program to generate a table of the powers of 2 while that power is less than or equal to 20,000.

6.3c Write a program to generate a Fibonacci series (see exercise 6.1d) until the term exceeds 200.

6.3d Write a program to input a variable for the number of terms to be generated in a Fibonacci series (see exercise 6.1d). Generate terms while the value of the term is less than 200. Test this program with input of 10 and 15 terms.

6.3e Write a program to generate a Celsius to Fahrenheit conversion table (see exercise 6.1g) while the Fahrenheit temperature is below 100 degrees.

6.3f The formulas for calculating the vertical and horizontal motion of a particular projectile are:

```
Y = 70 * T - 16.1 * T ** 2    and    X = 80 * T
```

Write programs to use these equations and vary time from 0.00 by 0.10 second with the following conditions:

    a. While the projectile is above the ground
    b. Until the projectile exceeds an elevation of 50
    c. Until the projectile begins to descend (previous value of Y exceeds current value of Y)
    d. Until either the projectile begins to descend or the horizontal distance exceeds 120
    e. While the projectile is ascending and the horizontal distance is less than 100

6.3g Generate points along the circumference of a unit circle every radial degree while the angle with the *x*-axis (measured counterclockwise) is between 30 and 40 degrees, inclusive.

6.4 COMPLEX LOOPS

DO loops are among the most powerful tools in the FORTRAN programmer's toolbox. They can be used in a variety of ways, as we will see now and in the forthcoming chapters. Loops may be nested within other loops, provided that each loop is nested completely within the other; that is, if their ranges do *not* cross. For example, the code:

```
DO 40  I = 1,20

    DO 20  J = 5,100,5

20 CONTINUE

40 CONTINUE
```

is perfectly valid in that the range of the inner loop is completely contained in the outer loop. It is also critical that the indexes are different variables. As an aid to the reader, it is the writer's style to indent the statements within the loop so that the ranges are more obvious (to the human, not the machine). Thus, the above code would appear as:

```
      DO 40  I = 1,20
               |
               |
           DO 20  J = 5,100,5
                    |
                    |
   20          CONTINUE
               |
               |
   40 CONTINUE
```

The first example below is an application solved with a doubly nested loop that generates a table of total amount in a savings account for interest ranging from 6% to 18% by increments of 2% and for every five years from 5 to 25.

```
      C                     Table of Interest for $1000.00
      C
            DO 40  I = 6,18,2
               DO 20  N = 5,25,5
                  AMT = 1000.00 * (1.0 + REAL(I)/100.00) ** N
         20     PRINT *, 'At',I,'% for',N,' years, total amount = $',AMT
         40 CONTINUE
      C
            STOP
            END
```

Sample output would appear as follows:

```
   At        6% for        5 years, total amount = $        1338.226000
   At        6% for       10 years, total amount = $        1790.848000
                                   :
                                   :
   At       18% for       20 years, total amount = $       27393.040000
   At       18% for       25 years, total amount = $       62668.630000
```

There is a slightly shorter version of the above, based on the fact that the final statement in the outer loop follows immediately after the final statement in the inner loop and that the final statement in the outer loop does nothing (CONTINUE). It appears as follows:

```
      C                     Table of Interest for $1000.00
      C
            DO 20  I = 6,18,2
               DO 20  N = 5,25,5
                  AMT = 1000.00 * (1.0 + REAL(I)/100.00) ** N
         20 PRINT *, 'At',I,'% for',N,' years, total amount = $',AMT
```

```
C
        STOP
        END
```

The FORTRAN compiler treats the terminal statement as a part of the inner loop and infers a CONTINUE for the outer loop. Where more than two loops end on the same statement, only the innermost one executes that statement.

Another version of this program, giving a slightly different output, would be:

```
C                       Table of Interest for $1000.00
C
        DO 40  I = 6,18,2
            PRINT *, 'Interest =',I,'%'
            DO 20  N = 5,25,5
                AMT = 1000.00 * (1.0 + REAL(I)/100.00) ** N
   20       PRINT *, '  After',N,' years, total amount = $',AMT
   40 PRINT *
C
        STOP
        END
```

Here the amounts are grouped by interest rate, with the interest rate displayed first, followed by the five amounts for that rate and a blank line to separate the different rates.

The index of an outer loop might be used as one of the controlling parameters of an inner loop. To generate a multiplication table for the numbers from 2 to 12 without duplicating any calculation, we will use the index of the outer loop as the first parameter in the inner loop. After all, 2 * 5 is the same as 5 * 2. Thus, a possible solution would be:

```
C                       Multiplication Table
C
        DO 40  I = 2,12
            DO 40  J = I,12
                K = I * J
   40 PRINT *, I,' *',J,' =',K
C
        STOP
        END
```

Here the output will start with 2 * 2 and run through 2 * 12; then, as *I* becomes 3, the output will continue with 3 * 3 through 3 * 12, and so forth, finishing up with 11 * 11, 11 * 12, and 12 * 12. Thus no calculation appears more than once.

There appears to be no specified limit as to the number of loops that may be nested within other loops. However, few programs will ever need more than five nested loops, well below any limit that might exist in any implementation of FORTRAN.

Branching within nested loops must be done with care. The general rule is that no branch may take place into a loop from outside the loop; all entrance to the loop must be at the DO statement. Branching to statements within the loop or outside the loop is perfectly permissible. Here is where a GO TO statement becomes most dangerous and restrictions must be applied!

If a module approach is taken to nested loops, then the diagram below illustrates that a nested loop is contained completely within the outer loop or module. The outer loop (1) can be entered only at the DO 1 statement. The inner loop (2) can be entered only at the DO 2 statement and, since loop 2 is within loop 1, 2 can be entered only from within loop 1.

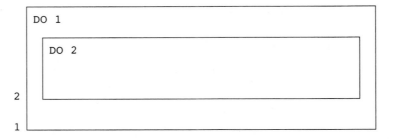

Our restricted GO TO rules allow a branch out of either loop to the beginning of another module. Branches from within these loops could be made to its own DO statement or to the DO statement of an outer loop, but that could lead to possible infinite looping if not properly coded with additional escapes.

Allowed branching from within loop 1 would be:

1. Branching to the end of loop 1
2. Branching to the beginning of a module outside loop 1

Allowed branching from within loop 2 would be:

1. Branching to the end of loop 2
2. Branching to the end of loop 1 (Loop 2 is part of module 1.)
3. Branching to the beginning of a module outside loop 1

A DO loop may be encapsulated within an IF .. THEN .. ENDIF, giving the programmer excellent control over the execution of a nested loop.

To illustrate some simple branching within nested loops, our multiplication table will be restricted to products no larger than 100. The program is modified as follows:

```
      C                     Multiplication Table Up to Products of 100
      C
            DO 40  I = 2,12
               DO 20  J = I,12
                  K = I * J
                  IF (K .GT. 100)  GO TO 40
      20     PRINT *, I,' *',J,' =',K
      40 CONTINUE
```

```
      C
              STOP
              END
```

The reader might suggest that the GO TO could be eliminated by using a conditional on the PRINT statement to restrict the output instead. This is a perfectly valid suggestion that will work, but it will be most inefficient since it generates many unused calculations. The topic of program efficiency (using this example) is discussed in the next section.

Although the discussion above illustrates only a few of the simplest examples, this text will be using these tools so often that more complex applications will become apparent.

Review Questions and Exercises

6.4a   For each of the loops below, determine what values will be output:

a.
```
      DO 20  K = 1,5,2
           DO 20  J = K,7,3
   20 PRINT *, K, J
```

b.
```
      DO 20  K = 1,5,2
           DO 20  J = 1,8,K
   20 PRINT *, K, J
```

6.4b   Write a program to generate a division table for values from 1 to 20, but do not compute any quotients of zero. No conditional branches are needed to solve this program.

6.4c   A factorial is defined as the product of itself and all of the positive integers less than itself down to 1. n factorial (written $n!$) $= n * (n - 1) * (n - 2) * (n - 3) *.....*$ $3 * 2 * 1$. Thus, $4! = 4 * 3 * 2 * 1 = 24$. $1! = 1$ and $0! = 1$ by definition. A factorial is very easily calculated by using a DO loop and multiplying upward from 1 to the value. $(4 * 3 * 2 * 1 = 1 * 2 * 3 * 4)$. Write a program to generate a table of factorials from $0!$ to $10!$, using long integers. The outer loop will go from 0 to 10, and the inner loop will compute the factorial for that number. Output should consist of headings and two columns of numbers. (Although this exercise can be done with only one loop if the method is known, use the two-loop algorithm.)

6.4d   Write a program to generate a table of fees earned by a consultant who charges by the hour. The consultant charges different rates, ranging from $40.00 to $60.00 per hour, depending on a number of factors. The program should have an outer loop with rates from $40 to $60 by $5 increments and an inner loop with hours from 10 to 60 by 10-hour increments. Skip a line between rates.

6.4e   Generate a table of x- and y-coordinates of points along the circumference of a circle from 0 to 90 degrees by increments of 15 degrees. The outer loop should vary the radius of the circle from 0.5 to 2.5 by 0.5. Do not output any points outside the rectangular window beginning at the origin and extending to $x = 1.5$ and $y = 2$.

6.4f   Using the equation for projectile motion ($y = Vt - 16.1t^2$, where V is the initial upward velocity and t is the time in seconds), write a program to vary V from 10 to 100 by increments of 10 and, as the inner loop, to vary time from 0.00 by increments of 0.10 while the projectile is still above or on the ground (y is nonnegative).

6.4g   Generate a gas mileage table with the outer loop being the number of gallons from 5 to 20 and the inner loop being the miles traveled, from 60 to 600 by increments of 20.

6.5   STRUCTURED PROGRAMMING

FORTRAN, like the older languages COBOL and BASIC, and like C, is not by definition a structured language. In other words, instructions in these languages can create very convoluted code. The GO TO statement is the chief perpetrator; that is why its use is so strongly discouraged, if not banned outright. Attempts to do away with it entirely are impossible. Even the more modern structured language Pascal still has the instruction in its vocabulary. Only Modula-2, Pascal's successor, does not have a GO TO, but it does include all four (DO, WHILE, UNTIL, EXIT) of the loop structures discussed in this chapter, albeit under slightly different names.

This means that the programmer using FORTRAN must impose a structure on his or her writing of code. No compiler will enforce it. (Some teachers may do so, however.) It is a matter of following certain rules and guidelines and using some good sense. The basic question to be asked is, "Will a human being be able to read, understand, and modify the code with ease?"

The concept to be emphasized here is modularization. A *module* is a block of code that can be entered only at its beginning. For example, every assignment statement could be a separate module because it can be executed only as a complete statement; one cannot jump into the middle of it. (If jumping into the middle sounds ridiculous, remember that in assembly language, anything is possible.) An assignment statement can be reached only from the statement before it or by a branch to it if it is numbered. A series of unnumbered assignment statements (or a numbered assignment followed by a series of unnumbered assignments) becomes an elemental module, since the logic starts at the first and progresses to the last of the series. That is why the processing flowchart symbol can contain more than one assignment statement.

The IF .. THEN .. ELSEIF .. ELSE .. ENDIF structure may be many statements long, but execution must begin with the IF; it is also not possible to jump into the middle of it. Every IF statement (with the exception of the arithmetic IF) is a subset of the IF .. THEN .. ELSEIF .. ELSE .. ENDIF, and thus every IF instruction is an elemental module. The exception, the arithmetic IF, can easily be replaced by logical IFs. For that reason, the arithmetic IF should not be used—and will not reappear in the remainder of this text.

Because a block IF may contain a module of assignment statements, it is obvious that modules may be contained within other modules, just as we described for nested DO loops. This introduces a new concept called "top-down programming," which states that the programming activity begins with a main module, the program as an entirety, and continues to break down into smaller and smaller modules until the elemental modules are reached. Every time we are able to put a box around our code indicating only one entrance to that box from outside the box, we have found a module. And when we write code, you and I, we must think in terms of writing modules.

The Hypotenuse example at the beginning of section 6.2 provides the following *top-down* design:

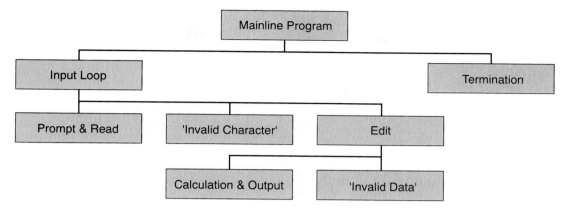

Whenever a line from a module leads to lower modules, it means that those modules are contained within the upper module. Modules on the same line are separated modules which may or may not be executed as the computer executes the module containing them, depending upon the logic in the upper module. The important rule is that a module may be entered only at its first statement.

The statement that can destroy this modular structure if not properly used is the GO TO and the constructs that use it inherently: the END= clause and the ERR= clause of the READ statement. The rules specified in Chapter 5 for the use of the GO TO are repeated here again to emphasize their importance:

1. A GO TO may branch to the last statement in a module from within the module.
2. A GO TO may branch to the first statement in a module from within the module.
3. A GO TO may branch from any point in a module to the beginning of any other module, either before the present one or after it, but preferably to the one immediately following it.
4. The number of upward branches to the beginning of a module should be limited to one.

Wherever practical, the use of the GO TO will be replaced by other methods—as we illustrated by controlling an input loop with a DO statement, even if the value of the index is irrelevant.

One important consideration must be added to these structuring guidelines: There *are* times when the avoidance of the GO TO will lead to very inefficient or unclear code; e.g., the last section the following program:

```
C                        Multiplication Table Up to Products of 100
C
      DO 40  I = 2,12
          DO 20  J = I,12
              K = I * J
              IF (K .GT. 100) GO TO 40
20        PRINT *, I,' *',J,' =',K
40 CONTINUE
```

```
C
      STOP
      END
```

uses a GO TO to exit the inner loop rather than a conditional on the PRINT statement:

```
C                    Multiplication Table Up to Products of 100
C
      DO 40  I = 2,12
         DO 20  J = I,12
            K = I * J
  20     IF  (K .LE. 100)  PRINT *, I,' *',J,' =',K
  40 CONTINUE
C
      STOP
      END
```

The justification is twofold. First, using the GO TO and exiting the inner loop before it is exhausted saves a significant number of multiplications, thus improving the execution speed. Although execution speed is not too important in these small programs, it is critical in many situations. FORTRAN is used primarily for large scientific, engineering, statistical, and financial programs, applications that are generally *compute-bound*, meaning that the bulk of execution time is spent doing calculations. It is critical that the professional programmer think in terms of efficient algorithmic execution.

Second, the GO TO construct tells the human reader of the program that once the first value in the loop exceeds 100 (i.e., once it reaches .GT. 100), no other value will be less than or equal to 100 until the next time the loop is initialized. The conditional on the PRINT, on the other hand, may leave the reader suspicious about the possibility that maybe another value will come around that will again be less than or equal to 100. The GO TO clearly indicates the impossibility of that situation.

6.6   DEBUGGING TECHNIQUES

Every good programmer knows that his or her program is flawed! That conclusion comes from the humility gained with experience. The human brain is not perfect and, no matter how careful the programmer, there usually is lurking somewhere in the middle of our code some little bug just waiting for an inconvenient moment to appear. This paranoid attitude is not uncommon among experienced programmers, and in fact leads to the care which they (should, at least) take in developing, testing, and documenting code.

With this attitude in mind, professionals often build into their code some debugging statements; i.e., statements that provide intermediate output when desired. Let us now take a look at our Perfect Square program enhanced for debugging.

```
C                       Is a Given Number a Perfect Square?
C
      LOGICAL     IDBG
      CHARACTER*1 YN
C
C'                      debugging output?
      PRINT  *, 'Debugging output (Y/N)?'
      READ   *, YN
      IF  (YN .EQ. 'Y'  .OR.  YN .EQ. 'y')  THEN
         IDBG = .TRUE.
        ELSE
         IDBG = .FALSE.
      ENDIF
C                       input loop
      DO 80  N = 1,20000
         PRINT  *
         PRINT  *, 'Enter an integer number'
         READ  (*,*, END=90)  I
C                       calculation
         DO 40  ICOUNT = 0,20000
            ISQ = ICOUNT * ICOUNT
            IF  (IDBG)  PRINT *, ICOUNT, ISQ, I
            IF  (ISQ .GT. I)  THEN
               PRINT *, I,' is not a perfect square'
               GO TO 80
            ENDIF
            IF  (ISQ .EQ. I)  THEN
               PRINT *, I,' is a perfect square'
               GO TO 80
            ENDIF
  40     CONTINUE
  80  CONTINUE
C                       terminations
      STOP  'Input out of range'
  90  STOP
      END
```

The program allows for the entry of either an uppercase or lowercase letter. Actually, more than one letter can be entered, but since the variable is defined as CHARACTER*1, only the first will be stored. Any non-'Y' entry will suppress the debugging output.

The extra STOP after statement 80 is placed there just in case the input is so large that the calculation loop is exhausted before the square is reached. The input value would have to be over 400,000,000 for this to occur, but the careful programmer can take no chances.

Debugging output usually is just a simple listing of the values, without any fancy annotation, since it is designed strictly for the programmer, not for the general user.

Most important is an echo check of the input data (the variable I in this program) so that the programmer knows exactly what value the computer is working with and can be assured that it has not changed. A sample run would appear as:

```
Debugging output (Y/N)?
'Y'
Enter an integer number
20
                0               0               20
                1               1               20
                2               4               20
                3               9               20
                4              16               20
                5              25               20
               20 is not a perfect square
Enter an integer number
16
                0               0               16
                1               1               16
                2               4               16
                3               9               16
                4              16               16
               16 is a perfect square
Enter an integer number
^Z
Stop - Program terminated.
```

A slightly modified version of the program allows the programmer to hide the debugging option by using the input of an unusual value that would not be confused with a possible valid input value. In this case, a negative value (which can never be a perfect square and thus becomes a most unlikely piece of data) is used to trigger the optional output.

```
C                       Is a Given Number a Perfect Square?
C
      LOGICAL     IDBG
      CHARACTER*1 YN
C
C                         input loop
      DO 80  N = 1,20000
          PRINT *
          PRINT *, 'Enter an integer number'
          READ (*,*, END=90) I
C                   check for debugging output
          IF (I .LT. 0) THEN
              IDBG = .TRUE.
            ELSE
              IDBG = .FALSE.
          ENDIF
          I = IABS (I)
C                   calculation
          DO 40  ICOUNT = 0,20000
              ISQ = ICOUNT * ICOUNT
              IF (IDBG) PRINT *, ICOUNT, ISQ, I
```

```
              IF  (ISQ .GT. I)  THEN
                  PRINT *, I,' is not a perfect square'
                  GO TO 80
              ENDIF
              IF  (ISQ .EQ. I)  THEN
                  PRINT *, I,' is a perfect square'
                  GO TO 80
              ENDIF
     40       CONTINUE
     80 CONTINUE
C                          terminations
         STOP  'Input out of range'
     90 STOP
         END
```

Even after a programmer thinks that a program has been completely debugged, the debugging statements are left in or are "commented out," the latter meaning that C's are put into column 1 so that the statement is treated as a comment and not included in the executable code; in this way the C's can be removed, and the debugging statements again become part of the executable code if necessary.

There is another most important tool now implemented on most FORTRAN compilers: the symbolic debugger. This tool allows the user to debug programs by stepping through them one instruction at a time; the user can examine the values in each of the variables, trace the branches, and watch the variables change. We highly recommend that you become familiar with this tool (the greatest programming aid ever invented), which is found in almost all languages, not just FORTRAN.

6.7 CHAPTER REVIEW

Chapters 5 and 6 have covered almost all the logical structures available to the FORTRAN programmer. The few others we have not covered are of very minor importance and will be covered in Chapter 13. These constructs will carry us through the rest of this text, and our main concern from now on will be their application in some of the new situations that will arise.

In addition to having all the rudimentary tools needed to handle any kind of logic operating on simple data, you now have some sophisticated constructs to ease the programming effort. Also, you have been given some guidance on program design and structure, as well as an insight as to how professional programmers debug their code. The programs written from now on should show a clarity of logic and a simplicity of code.

The topics covered in this chapter include:

Topic	Section
Counting records	6.2
Debugging	6.6
DO loop	6.1, 6.4
DO UNTIL	6.3
DO WHILE	6.3
Input loops	6.2

Topic	Section
LOOP .. EXIT	6.3
Modules	6.4, 6.5
Nested loops	6.4
Structure	6.5
Symbolic debugger	6.6
Top-down design	6.5

Exercises

6.7a   Newton's method for finding a square root is to approximate the value based on a previous approximation. If the number whose root is sought is symbolized as a, and the old and new approximations as x and x' respectively, the equation becomes:

$$x' = (x + a/x)/2$$

In order for the method to work, it is necessary to assume a first approximation; it is good enough to use the value itself as this first approximation. The method requires continuous approximations, each time using the newly derived value as the old one. Convergence is assumed when the relative precision (i.e., the difference between the new and old values divided by the new value) is less than some specified tolerance. For standard-precision reals using six significant digits, a value of 0.000001 serves as a good relative-precision tolerance. The number of approximations attempted should be controlled so that a nonconvergent value (such as zero) does not cause an infinite loop; 50 terms is usually sufficient, since most numbers will converge in less than 15 terms.

     Write a program to implement Newton's method for finding square roots. Input should consist of real numbers, edited to eliminate negative and zero values (the last does have a valid square root of zero). Output should be displayed for each approximation so that the process may be watched; it should consist of the trial number, the new approximation, and the relative precision. Test with sufficient data to ensure that the program works for all numbers, including numbers between 0 and 1.

6.7b   A number of functions are evaluated using the concept of an infinite series. For example, the exponential function can be derived as follows:

$$e^x = 1 + x + x^2/2! + x^3/3! + x^4/4! + \ldots + x^n/n!$$

Of course, generating an infinite number of terms can take a very long time. Therefore a test is made for convergence using the relative precision of the new term divided by the new sum; when that value falls below 0.000001, it is considered good enough for single-precision reals. Generally, convergence is reached in about a dozen terms, but to play it safe, the logic is usually encapsulated in a loop with a reasonable limit (about 50). All values of x (negative, positive, and zero) will work, except that special precautions must be taken for $x = -1$.

     Write a program to accept a value of x and output each term, the sum, and the relative precision until convergence (or nonconvergence) is reached.

6.7c   (a) Numerical integration consists of dividing the area under the curve to be integrated into small vertical trapezoids, computing the areas of the trapezoids, and adding them together to get a sum. An interesting application is to derive the value of π as the area of a circle with a radius of 1. This is done by using the quarter-circle in the first quadrant and multiplying the result by 4. The more strips used, the more accurate the result. The heights of the sides of the trapezoids are obtained by rearranging the equation of a unit circle:

$$x^2 + y^2 = 1$$

to solve for y when the value of x is known. The basic method is to start with one strip (in this case, it reduces to an isosceles right triangle) and then keep doubling the number of strips until the relative precision between each successive approximation reaches some reasonable tolerance, such as 0.0001.

Write a program to use the trapezoidal method to find the value of π from the area of the unit quarter-circle, displaying each new approximation and the accompanying relative precision. It might also be valuable for debugging purposes to list the trapezoids used and their areas.

(**b**) The above method might be modified to use the rectangular method, which assumes rectangular strips whose height is equal to the y-value at their midpoint. Repeat the above program using this method.

(**c**) Yet a third method uses the circumscribed/inscribed method wherein two rectangles are assumed for each strip, one using the greater height (in this case, the left-hand edge) and the other using the lesser height (the right-hand edge). In this way we generate two areas, one larger than that of the quarter-circle (circumscribed) and one smaller than the quarter-circle (inscribed). When these two areas approach each other within some prescribed tolerance (say, 0.0001), the area can be assumed to be the average of the two areas. Repeat the above program using this method.

6.7d   The pharaoh has commissioned us to build a solid pyramid. The construction will consist of stone cubes, one yard on each side. The pyramid will have a square base, and the sloping sides will be at 45 degrees to the horizontal. The basic construction will consist of a square of square cubes laid upon a lower square that is two lengths larger, as can be seen in the vertical cross section below. Course 1 is $2 \times 2 = 4$ cubes, course 2 is $4 \times 4 = 16$ cubes, etc.

After the basic cubes (marked B) are put in place (using special Pyramid Power cement for structural integrity), smooth slopes are formed using side and corner pieces, as seen in the horizontal detail below. The side blocks (marked S) are cubes halved into two triangular prisms; thus, one cube supplies two side blocks. The corner blocks are each cut from one side block by trimming off a tetrahedron shape, leaving a block with a square base, two perpendicular triangular sides to match up with the side blocks, and two triangular sloping sides for the face of the pyramid. Since only one corner block can be cut from one side block, one cube supplies two corner blocks. The apex of the pyramid is formed from four corner blocks; a minimum pyramid consists only of these four corners.

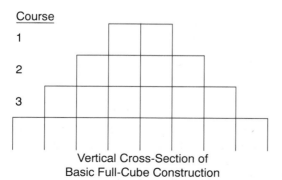

Vertical Cross-Section of
Basic Full-Cube Construction

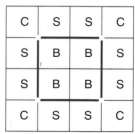

Horizontal Detail
of Course 1

(a) Generate a table of courses (from 0 to 20) versus blocks needed for that course. (0 courses means no basic blocks, only the four corner block apex.) Break down the structure into basic blocks, side blocks, and corner blocks. Accumulate the total number of basic, side, and corner blocks needed so that the output will consist of the blocks needed for that course and the ones above it (the completed pyramid). Also calculate the total number of cube blocks from which all the structural blocks will be cut. Output the accumulated values. (A second-order equation can be derived for the total number of cubes needed per course, and a third-order equation derived for the accumulation; see if you can derive it!)

(b) Each cube costs $30, delivered to the site. If a delivery is more than 300 blocks, a 2% discount is applied to the total order; if more than 1500 blocks, a 5% discount is applied to the total order. It costs $5 to cut a cube into two side blocks and $3 to cut a side block into a corner block. Expand your program to include the cost of materials and the cost of cutting the stone. Your output can consist of course number, accumulated total cubes, cost of materials, cost of cutting, and total cost.

(c) The cost of placing each basic block depends on the number of sides to which the cement must be placed and the level to which the block must be raised. The first block is cemented only to its base. The rest of that row and the side perpendicular to it need cement on the bottom and one side. The rest of the blocks on that level need cement on the bottom and two sides. The cost of raising the block is:

$$\$2 \times (\text{number of levels above the ground} + 1)^2$$

The level on the ground is considered 0 levels above ground, so the cost is $2 per block. On the second level, the cost is $8 per block, and so forth. The cost of applying the cement is $0.50 per face. Expand your program to include the cost of placement of the basic blocks.

(d) The cost of placing each side block also depends on the number of sides to which cement must be applied. The first side block needs cement on the bottom and the square back; the rest of the blocks on that side need cement on the bottom and two sides (one triangular, one square). There are four sets of side blocks for each level. Each of the corner blocks has a square bottom and two triangular faces. The cost of applying the cement is $0.50 per square face and $0.35 per triangular face. The cost of raising the side and corner blocks is the same as in part c, above. Expand your program to include the cost of placement of all the blocks.

(e) Your consulting fee is 1% of the total cost of the job, with an upper limit of $10,000. Compute your fee, based on the costs calculated above, and determine the minimum number of levels that will pay your full fee.

6A Control Structures in Fortran 90

CHAPTER OUTLINE

CHAPTER OBJECTIVES

- To introduce the reader to some of the extended constructs in Fortran 90.
- To demonstrate the techniques available for easier coding.
- To show how Fortran 90 programs may be structured more precisely.
- To warn the reader about the pitfalls of a new version of a language.

COMMENTS ON FORTRAN 90

After more than a decade of discussion, the adoption of Fortran 90 (formerly called FORTRAN 8x) is imminent. However, as with the adoption of any new version of the language, it will be many years before it gains full acceptance and is fully implemented. Fortunately, the new version is a superset of FORTRAN 77 and will thus accept all previously written code.

A number of commercially available compilers contain some of the Fortran 90 features. Software publishers do this in an attempt to provide a more up-to-date product. Therefore, some of the structures illustrated in this chapter have been tested with present Fortran compilers (notably, Microsoft and DEC VAX). However, those compilers do not contain all of the new features and cannot be called truly Fortran 90–compatible. Thus, some of the programs in this chapter have not been tested (leaving the author somewhat unhappy); however, they have been carefully written, closely following the proposed new specifications.

The reader is warned that the placement of any of the new commands found in Fortran 90 destroys its portability to machines without that compiler. But, more important, the use of FORTRAN 77 extensions that seem to be "look-aheads" to Fortran 90 may be more destructive of portability, even in the future, because they may deviate from the final language standards! A comparison of the compiler manual with the information provided in this chapter will point up those differences. Keep in mind that once the publisher does release Fortran 90, those extensions which are not compatible will have to be removed.

(Just to further warn the reader, the author is referencing the proposed specifications as printed in May 1991. It is extremely unlikely that any changes will be made at this late date, but one cannot be too careful.)

Although there are some new methods for handling arrays and data structures, the major enhancements for the relatively inexperienced programmer are the introduction of additional controls within the DO loop. Most obvious is the introduction of the DO WHILE, which has existed in other languages for some years. However, the GO TO has *not* been eliminated because, as we showed earlier, some problems are difficult to solve without it.

As a compromise, two additional loop controls, the CYCLE and EXIT statements, have been introduced which provide conditional branches to the end of the loop and to the statement immediately following the loop, respectively. Although these statements are implied GO TOs, they do not require a statement number since their action is so restricted.

6A.1   NEW INSTRUCTION FORMATTING

The Fortran 90 programmer will be able to enter in-line comments on the same line as the Fortran instruction. The Fortran 90 compiler treats an exclamation mark (!) that is neither in column 6 nor within a literal field (between apostrophes) as the beginning of a comment. All characters to its right are treated as comments, not as part of the Fortran instruction. For example, the following program has comments on the same line as the DO statements.

```
C                        Table of Interest for $1000.00
C
        DO 40  I = 6,18,2      ! loop by even years from 6 to 18
           DO 20 N = 5,25,5        ! loop by percentage interest rates
              AMT = 1000.00 * (1.0 + REAL(I)/100.00) ** N
  20       PRINT *, 'At',I,'% for',N,' years, total amount = $', AMT
  40 CONTINUE
C
        STOP   'end-of-run'
        END
```

Another feature is the ability to place multiple statements on the same line separated by semicolons, as in the following partial FORTRAN program:

```
        :
     N100 = WITHDR / 100 ; LEFT = MOD (WITHDR, 100)
     N20  = LEFT   / 20 ; LEFT = MOD (LEFT,    20)
```

```
N10   = LEFT   /  10 ; LEFT = MOD (LEFT,    10)
       :
       :
STOP ; END
```

Fortran 90 also provides for the use of "free source form," wherein the instruction is no longer restricted in column location. A comment begins with an exclamation mark in any column, including column 1. The Fortran statement begins in any desired column. If the statement begins with a numeral, the compiler knows that the numeral is the beginning of a statement number and that the first letter begins the statement proper. If the statement starts with a letter, then there is no statement number.

The purpose of this freedom is to allow easier input of code from the keyboard. A comment line no longer can be indicated with a C in column 1, and continuation can no longer use column 6. The ! becomes the comment indicator, and continuation is indicated on the line to be continued with an ampersand (&) as the last nonblank in the line. In addition, the input line can be as long as 132 columns. For example, a long PRINT statement might appear as:

```
PRINT *, 'Radius of', RADIUS,' generates a circle with area =', &
         AREA,' and circumference =', CIRCUM
```

With all the new features, we could expect to see programs that look like this:

```
!       Table of Interest for $1000.00
DO 40  I = 6,18,2 ; DO 20 N = 5,25,5 ; AMT = 1000.00 * (1.0 + REAL(I)/100.00) ** N
20 PRINT *, 'At',I,'% for',N,' years, total amount = $', AMT ; 40 CONTINUE ; STOP 'end-of-run' ; END
```

It should be fairly obvious that the abuse of this new freedom can make the programs much harder to read. The use of separate lines for most statements is highly recommended, and the indentation suggested in previous programs should be maintained for readability.

As we continue to develop the new constructs in Fortran 90, the reader will see that statement numbers can be eliminated completely and that the concept of starting the statement proper in column 1 is very useful. However, statement separators should be used with caution.

6A.2   A MEASURE OF STRUCTURE

Although it can be very difficult to define structured programming, there are some very obvious measurements that can be applied to a program. The command that should be avoided whenever possible is the GO TO; it can produce some very convoluted code that is difficult to follow and, more important, difficult to debug.

One way to eliminate the GO TO is to eliminate its target, namely, a labeled statement. If statement numbers can be eliminated, then the possibility of improper branching is also eliminated. This was done to the BASIC language in the newer "structured" versions now available. However, there must be control structures available that allow the programmer to solve the necessary logical problems. The trade-off is that statement numbers can be significantly reduced, if not eliminated entirely, by using some of the new constructs in Fortran 90.

By the end of this chapter, every statement number will have been removed from our programs by using the new facilities of Fortran 90, in addition to one from FORTRAN 77 that requires additional conditional statements but eliminates statement numbers.

6A.3   THE END DO AND THE DO CONSTRUCT NAME

Since the ranges of DO loops cannot overlap, but nested loops must fit entirely within one another, the statement number is not really necessary as long as there is no branching to the terminating statement. Fortran 90 uses the END DO or ENDDO to indicate the end of a DO loop.

For example, the Table of Interest program becomes:

```
!                    Table of Interest for $1000.00
DO   I = 6,18,2
    DO   N = 5,25,5
        AMT = 1000.00 * (1.0 + REAL(I)/100.00) ** N
        PRINT *, 'At',I,'% for',N,' years, total amount = $', AMT
    END DO
END DO
STOP   'end-of-run'
END
```

Although the indenting makes the program obvious, it is not necessary in order for the program to work properly. Free source form has been used to simplify coding the program.

It is allowable to combine numbered and unnumbered loops, such as:

```
!                    Table of Interest for $1000.00
DO   I = 6,18,2
    DO 20   N = 5,25,5
        AMT = 1000.00 * (1.0 + REAL(I)/100.00) ** N
        PRINT *, 'At',I,'% for',N,' years, total amount = $', AMT
 20 END DO
END DO
STOP   'end-of-run'
END
```

As an aid in documentation, Fortran 90 allows the programmer to "name" the DO loop uniquely. The name appears twice, once before the DO (separated by a colon) and again after the END DO:

```
!                    Table of Interest for $1000.00
RATE: DO   I = 6,18,2
        YEARS: DO   N = 5,25,5
```

```
              AMT = 1000.00 * (1.0 + REAL(I)/100.00) ** N
              PRINT *, 'At',I,'% for',N,' years, total amount = $', AMT
        END DO YEARS
    END DO RATE
    STOP  'end-of-run'
    END
```

Named DO loops and unnamed DO loops can be mixed, but if any loop is named, that name must appear twice.

6A.4   THE CYCLE STATEMENT

The CYCLE statement is an unconditional branch to the terminating statement of the loop. Usually that statement is the END DO, but if a numbered terminal statement is used, execution continues *after* that statement with the transparent part of the DO loop logic that modifies the loop index. Thus, the CYCLE statement serves to skip over all executable statements from just below its position to the end of the loop.

The CYCLE statement is usually coupled with a decision-making IF statement so that its execution becomes conditional. For example, in the Table of Interest program above, the output might be restricted to amounts of at least $1500 by amending it as follows:

```
    !                   Table of Interest for $1000.00
    DO  I = 6,18,2
        DO  N = 5,25,5
            AMT = 1000.00 * (1.0 + REAL(I)/100.00) ** N
                IF (AMT .LT. 1500.00) CYCLE
            PRINT *, 'At',I,'% for',N,' years, total amount = $', AMT
        END DO
    END DO
    STOP  'end-of-run'
    END
```

Where there are nested loops, the CYCLE applies to the loop in which it appears; in this case the inner loop.

Although the CYCLE statement in this simple example seems to be unnecessary because it could be replaced with an IF on the PRINT statement, the advantage of CYCLE is that it can appear more than once within the loop to eliminate different parts of the execution cycle. Although this might also be done with IF statements, the numerous IF blocks required might make the program more difficult to read.

Actually, the CYCLE is a hidden GO TO; this was one of the compromises made in Fortran 90 to satisfy both users who saw the need for the GO TO and those who wished to eliminate it entirely. The net gain is that the CYCLE can be used in an unnumbered DO loop.

If the programmer wishes to skip over interest rates of 10 and 14 percent also, the program could be modified to:

```
    !                     Table of Interest for $1000.00
    DO   I = 6,18,2
        IF  (I .EQ. 10  .OR.  I .EQ. 14)  CYCLE
        DO   N = 5,25,5
            AMT = 1000.00 * (1.0 + REAL(I)/100.00) ** N
                IF  (AMT .LT. 1500.00)  CYCLE
            PRINT *, 'At',I,'% for',N,' years, total amount = $', AMT
        END DO
    END DO
    STOP   'end-of-run'
    END
```

The CYCLE in the outer loop branches to the last END DO.

6A.5   THE EXIT STATEMENT

The EXIT statement is an unconditional branch to the statement following the end of the loop. Although it is a disguised GO TO, its target is severely restricted and does not require a statement number. This compromise almost completely eliminates the need for the GO TO within DO loops.

For example, if we wished to restrict our table of interest to amounts between $1500 and $2000 in the most efficient fashion, the program might be amended to:

```
    !                     Table of Interest for $1000.00
    DO   I = 6,18,2
        DO   N = 5,25,5
            AMT = 1000.00 * (1.0 + REAL(I)/100.00) ** N
                IF  (AMT .GT. 2000.00)  EXIT
                IF  (AMT .LT. 1500.00)  CYCLE
            PRINT *, 'At',I,'% for',N,' years, total amount = $', AMT
        END DO
    END DO
    STOP   'end-of-run'
    END
```

This modification forces the logic to get out of the inner loop and proceed to the next rate of interest in the outer loop as soon as the first amount greater than $2000 for that interest rate occurs. The problem could also have been solved with a CYCLE statement, but the solution would not have been as efficient because more repetitions of the inner loop with its calculation would take place.

Just as with the CYCLE statement, the EXIT statement might appear multiple times in a loop. As we will see later, in section 6A.9, it can be used to terminate input loops as well.

6A.6   THE DO FOREVER

With the inclusion of the EXIT statement for termination of loop execution, it is not always necessary to establish a counter. In some of our earlier examples, there were loops from 1 to 20,000 just for the purpose of having a looping structure; the loop control index was never used. The choice of 20,000 was arbitrary, just a large number used to represent infinity.

Fortran 90 allows a DO statement in which no index is used, which effectively is an infinite loop. However, it is expected that the loop contains an EXIT statement based on some certain condition; otherwise an infinite loop would occur, which takes an awfully long time to execute!

Below is our same Table of Interest using this new construct:

```
!                     Table of Interest for $1000.00
DO  I = 6,18,2
    N = 0
    DO
        N = N + 5
        AMT = 1000.00 * (1.0 + REAL(I)/100.00) ** N
            IF (AMT .GT. 2000.00)  EXIT
            IF (AMT .LT. 1500.00)  CYCLE
        PRINT *, 'At',I,'% for',N,' years, total amount = $', AMT
    END DO
END DO
STOP   'end-of-run'
END
```

Obviously, special care must be used to avoid an infinite loop.

6A.7   THE DO WHILE

The DO WHILE construct has existed in many other languages, and even in some extensions of FORTRAN 77, for some time. Its arrival in Fortran 90 was the cause of much discussion, since it can be confusing in its application. Also (as we saw in section 6.3 and will reiterate here and again in section 6A.9), additional statements must be written to make it work, and at times the logic used within the loop is quite different from what might be normally written.

As an example, here is the Table of Interest program above, using the DO WHILE to restrict the output to amounts between $1500 and $2000:

```
!                     Table of Interest for $1000.00 with DO WHILE
DO  I = 6,18,2
    N = 5
    AMT = 1000.00 * (1.0 + REAL(I)/100.00) ** N
    DO  WHILE (AMT .LE. 2000.00)
        IF (AMT .GE. 1500.00)  &
            PRINT *, 'At',I,'% for',N,' years, total amount = $', AMT
```

```
          N = N + 5
          AMT = 1000.00 * (1.0 + REAL(I)/100.00) ** N
      END DO
    END DO
    STOP  'end-of-run'
    END
```

Because the condition in the WHILE is tested at the beginning of the loop, it is necessary to calculate the initial value *before* beginning the loop. Thus the calculation of AMT appears twice: once before and once within the loop. It is also impossible to include the test for amounts less than $1500 in the WHILE condition, because to do so would terminate the inner loop in any case where the interest rate at 5 years is below that lower limit; the other years for that interest rate would not be calculated and tested. It was also necessary to use an IF statement instead of a CYCLE statement because it is critical that the incrementation of N be executed each time; the CYCLE statement skips it, resulting in an infinite loop.

The initial calculation (or any condition that the WHILE tests) prior to the loop is called a primal statement. (We will see it again when setting up input loops in section 6A.9.) The logic within the loop is also reversed from the "first calculate, then output" order. It was for this reason that there was much discussion about adopting the DO .. WHILE construct in the new Fortran. To those Fortran programmers who were not using it for decades, it seemed unnecessary and confusing. In all fairness, it must be said that there are times when this construct provides more structured and more easily readable code. The inclusion of the EXIT and CYCLE statements along with the DO WHILE represents a compromise between the opposing positions.

6A.8 THE CASE STATEMENT

The CASE statement, which exists in a number of other languages, is one of the new constructs introduced into Fortran 90 which provides the programmer with an alternative and more elegant way of doing multiple conditional branching. A single value is selected and compared against various ranges; should the variable fall within one of the ranges, a series of instructions can be executed. Although the CASE does nothing more than the IF .. THEN .. [ELSEIF] .. ENDIF, it does it in a way that is far easier to code and to read.

The CASE instruction is encapsulated between a SELECT CASE (expression) and an END SELECT. The expression may be logical, integer, or character.

Each range is specified, with the command CASE followed in parentheses by a definition of the range, as:

1.	Single value	`CASE (10)`	or `CASE ('K')`
2.	List of values	`CASE (8,10,11)`	or `CASE ('Y','y')`
3.	Range of values	`CASE (5:15)`	or `CASE ('A':'N')`
4.	Upper bound	`CASE (:20)`	or `CASE (:'R')`
5.	Lower bound	`CASE (-5:)`	or `CASE ('a':)`

In the second numeric example, the range is either of the three values 8, 10, or 11. In the third alphameric example, the range includes any character between capital A and capital N, inclusive. In the fourth numeric example, any value less than or equal to 20 is within the range. In the fifth alphameric example, any lowercase letter is within the range.

The instruction also includes a CASE DEFAULT option to cover situations where the selected expression is not within the specified ranges. For example, section 5.8 presented a program to accept a numeric grade and display the corresponding letter grade. With the new construct, it can be written as:

```
!                 Assigning Grades
DO
    PRINT *, 'Enter numeric grade'
    READ   (*,*, END=90)  IGRADE
    SELECT CASE  (IGRADE)
          CASE  (90:)
                PRINT *, 'A'
          CASE  (80:89)
                PRINT *, 'B'
          CASE  (70:79)
                PRINT *, 'C'
          CASE  (65:69)
                PRINT *, 'D'
          CASE  (0:64)
                PRINT *, 'F'
          CASE  DEFAULT
                PRINT *, 'Invalid Grade'
    END SELECT
END DO
!
90 STOP 'end-of-run'
END
```

Only one block within the CASE construct will be executed. If the programmer specifies overlapping ranges, only the first one will be executed for a given value. Many statements may exist for a particular range, not just the single statements shown above. Those statements may include loops, I/O, additional branching, etc.

As further examples of the use of the CASE, the above program is modified and expanded as follows:

```
!                 Assigning Grades and Evaluations
CHARACTER  GRADE
DO
    PRINT *
    PRINT *, 'Enter numeric grade'
    READ   (*,*, END=90)  IGRADE
    SELECT CASE  (IGRADE)
          CASE  (90:)
                GRADE = 'A'
          CASE  (80:89)
                GRADE = 'B'
          CASE  (70:79)
                GRADE = 'C'
```

```
                    CASE   (65:69)
                          GRADE = 'D'
                    CASE   (0:64)
                          GRADE = 'F'
                    CASE   DEFAULT
                          GRADE = 'G'
                          PRINT *, 'Invalid Grade'
             END SELECT
             PRINT *, GRADE
             IF  (GRADE .EQ. 'G')  CYCLE
             SELECT CASE  (IGRADE .GE. 65)
                    CASE  (.TRUE.)
                          PRINT *, 'Pass'
                    CASE  (.FALSE.)
                          PRINT *, 'Fail'
             END SELECT
             SELECT CASE  (GRADE)
                    CASE  (:'B')
                          PRINT *, 'Doing OK'
                    CASE  ('C','D')
                          PRINT *, 'Need to work harder'
                    CASE  ('F')
                          PRINT *, 'See you again next semester'
             END SELECT
         END DO
         90 STOP 'end-of-run'
         END
```

6A.9   THE IOSTAT OPTION

In the previous program, the only remaining statement number is that used to end the input loop. An option that already exists in FORTRAN 77 eliminates the implied GO TOs of the ERR= and END= clauses and still checks for error conditions and end-of-file. Using this option with the new constructs from Fortran 90 allows the programmer to remove all statement numbers.

The IOSTAT= clause with an integer variable places a return code from the I/O routine into that variable, indicating the success or failure of the I/O process. Instead of using the END= and ERR= clauses in a READ statement, the programmer can code:

```
    READ  (*,*, IOSTAT = INCHK)  IGRADE
```

where INCHK is a programmer-selected integer variable name. If there is an input error, INCHK is assigned a positive run-time error number; that number is system-dependent but will always be positive. If the end-of-file is detected, INCHK is assigned a value of -1. And if the input is successful, INCHK is assigned a 0. Thus, the value deposited therein can be used for programmer-controlled branching and numbered statements are no longer required.

Below is our shorter grade assignment program, modified to completely avoid the use of statement numbers and implied GO TOs:

```
!                   Assigning Grades
CHARACTER GRADE
DO
     PRINT *
     PRINT *, 'Enter numeric grade'
     READ   (*,*, IOSTAT=INCHK)  IGRADE
     IF  (INCHK .LT. 0)  EXIT
     IF  (INCHK .EQ. 0)  THEN
          SELECT CASE  (IGRADE)
                  CASE  (90:)
                          PRINT *, 'A'
                  CASE  (80:89)
                          PRINT *, 'B'
                  CASE  (70:79)
                          PRINT *, 'C'
                  CASE  (65:69)
                          PRINT *, 'D'
                  CASE   (0:64)
                          PRINT *, 'F'
                  CASE  DEFAULT
                          PRINT *,  'Invalid Grade'
        ELSE
            PRINT *, 'Invalid character in data'
        ENDIF
END DO
STOP 'end-of-run'
END
```

A slightly different version of the program can use the DO WHILE construct, although this version must include the "primal READ," since the end-of-file condition is tested prior to entering the loop. Also, a second READ occurs at the end of the loop before going back to the beginning, where the end-of-file condition is tested.

```
!               Assigning Grades
!                   primal READ
PRINT *, 'Enter numeric grade'
READ   (*,*, IOSTAT=INCHK)  IGRADE
!                    loop while not end-of-file
DO WHILE  (INCHK .GE. 0)
      IF  (INCHK .EQ. 0)  THEN
          SELECT CASE  (IGRADE)
                  CASE  (90:)
                          PRINT *, 'A'
                  CASE  (80:89)
                          PRINT *, 'B'
                  CASE  (70:79)
                          PRINT *, 'C'
```

```
                        CASE  (65:69)
                              PRINT *, 'D'
                        CASE  (0:64)
                              PRINT *, 'F'
                        CASE  DEFAULT
                              PRINT *,  'Invalid Grade'
                  END SELECT
              ELSE
                  PRINT *, 'Invalid character in data'
              ENDIF
              PRINT *
              PRINT *, 'Enter numeric grade'
              READ   (*,*, IOSTAT=INCHK)  IGRADE
        END DO
        STOP 'end-of-run'
        END
```

6A.10   CHAPTER REVIEW

Although Fortran 90 does not give the programmer any new abilities, it does provide tools that are easier to use for programming. These new tools have the advantage of being shorter to code, more self-documenting, easier to debug, and far more structured. They ensure that Fortran will still be a viable language right into the next millennium and that the prediction of its death some years ago, to paraphrase Mark Twain, was "an exaggeration."

Exercises

Special exercises are not needed for this chapter. Instead, you can refer to the following list of exercises from Chapter 6. If you have a Fortran 90 compiler available, you can convert the previously written programs to the newer format using the new statements. Even if you only have available a FORTRAN 77 compiler with some of the extensions that were incorporated into Fortran 90, it might be good practice to try writing a few programs with those features included, just for the experience. However, the author again warns about the necessity of portability: You should never forget that for many years it may be necessary to write in FORTRAN 77, until the time that Fortran 90 is fully implemented in industry.

Where possible:

1. Use free form for your source code.
2. Include comments on some of the source code lines.
3. Eliminate statement numbers on DO loops.
4. Eliminate DO loop ranges when an index is not needed.
5. Use CYCLE to eliminate branching within the loop.
6. Use EXIT to eliminate branching out of the loop.
7. Use DO WHILE to control input through end-of-data.
8. Use CASE to code multiple branching.

Suggested Exercises

Exercise	Topic
6.1c	Using an unnumbered DO and the END DO
6.1d	Using an unnumbered DO and the END DO
6.1g	Using CASE to control the output
6.1i	Using CASE to control the calculations
6.2b	Using DO WHILE to control the input loop with the IOSTAT clause
6.2c	Using DO WHILE to limit the loop
6.3f	Using the EXIT statement
6.4f	Using the EXIT statement
6.7a	Using the IOSTAT clause with the DO WHILE to test for end-of-data and the DO WHILE to test precision
6.7c	Using the EXIT statement

7

The FORMAT Statement

CHAPTER OUTLINE

CHAPTER OBJECTIVES

- To present a full description of the FORTRAN FORMAT statement, with all its features.

- To show techniques for the efficient use of the FORMAT statement.

- To develop a sophisticated approach to input and output.

STATEMENT OF THE PROBLEM

The major restriction encountered up to this point is the dependence upon the default output formats when displaying or printing information. It is difficult for the programmer to control this kind of output and to produce columns that align. Furthermore, money values could not be controlled so that only two decimal places were output. An additional problem was that alphameric input had to be surrounded with apostrophes. But now we move on to a higher plateau that will give us complete control of our input and output. We will not lose the ease with which we can I/O data, just enhance that feature with precise control when we want it.

Peculiarly, this topic of formatting has often been considered the most difficult in FORTRAN—and it can be, if it is not properly presented. Because earlier versions of the language did not have the list-directed methodology available, formal formatting had to be learned early so that I/O would be possible; otherwise, doing a computation and not being able to display the results is rather unproductive. All too often, the topic was presented by throwing in all the details at one time, before the student had compiled and run the first program, and it was confusing.

Our presentation here also will be throwing in many details, but we will do so slowly and carefully, with tight definition and precise explanation. Furthermore, since you have been doing some programming for a while, you are accustomed to I/O; much of what will be done now is simply enhancement and expansion of previous practices. In addition, we use examples introduced earlier in the text, giving you the opportunity to concentrate on I/O and without being distracted by the rest of the program.

Each topic is developed with a minimum of other programming techniques so that you can concentrate on formatting and absorb the material easily. Each technique is demonstrated and the section exercises are designed so that you can practice these constructs without too much other programming. However, the "technical" details in the first two sections are necessary for the precise understanding that a good programmer needs, and we strongly urge that you spend the time necessary to understand the concept of I/O buffers.

7.1   THE INPUT BUFFER

When a READ command is issued, the system awaits a response from an input device. The characters read in (and all information, both numeric and nonnumeric, is in character form during I/O) are transmitted from the input device when an end-of-record character is sent; this EOR character can be triggered by the RETURN or ENTER key on a keyboard or by an end-of-line character in a disk file. The information transmitted is placed into an input buffer, an array of memory locations, just as it is received from the input device, one character per location. The information is then parsed—separated into its different fields and converted to the appropriate mode (integer, real, character, logical, etc.)—and sent to its assigned memory location.

With list-directed (or free-formatted) input, the parsing depends on separating characters (delimiters) between each of the fields, which in FORTRAN can be one or more blanks or single commas; extra blanks surrounding the commas are permitted and have no effect on the value. Alphameric information must be further

defined, otherwise it would always be necessary to put in the full number of characters to fill the variable—something the programmer knows but the user may not be
aware of. Thus, apostrophes are required for alphameric input so that a subsequent
field which would fit within the character variable is not absorbed incorrectly.

All of the data expected by the READ (i.e., all of the variables in the input list)
must be read, or else the system will wait for the rest of the data. This problem can
be avoided by using a slash (/) to indicate the end of the input for the record. Repeat
values may be entered with two adjacent commas, with or without blanks between
them; the value of the variable remains the same as it was before the READ. As an
example, let us look at the following statements:

```
DATA  I, J, K/  11, 12, 13/
READ  *, I, J, K
```

If the input values (assume they are from a keyboard) are

```
7  5  <enter>
```

the program will wait until another value is entered for K before moving to the
next statement.

For the same READ, if the entered record is

```
7,,5   <enter>
```

the 7 is assigned to I, J remains what it was before, namely 12, and the 5 is assigned
to K.

On the other hand, if the entered record is

```
7  5  /  <enter>
```

the input is complete. The 7 is assigned to I, the 5 to J, and the value in K remains
the same as before, namely 13.

Although list-directed input is often very convenient, it is prone to invalid character errors due to improper spacing, incorrect delimiters, or missing apostrophes.
Furthermore, a user who does not enter all the expected information can sit and
wait for a computer response that will never come.

With formatted input, the use of the input buffer remains the same but the
FORMAT statement will direct the parsing function to defined columns for each
field. As a result, alphameric input does *not* require apostrophes, and blank numeric
fields are interpreted as zero. Furthermore, the approach clears the input buffer
before any data is transmitted to it, and the system accepts that data as the full
record, assuming that all fields for which no input appears are blank. As will be
shown, the parsing may be done in any order, not necessarily from left to right, and
columns may be reread if so desired.

7.2   THE OUTPUT BUFFER

The output buffer works in the reverse manner from the input buffer in that
the computer puts characters into it prior to its transmission to the output device.
Numeric data is converted from pure binary to characters. The output buffer can
be filled in any order, not necessarily from left to right. The buffer is automatically

cleared (with blanks) before any output information is transmitted to it and is then filled with the desired output. Any undefined column is left blank.

However, there is one major difference between the input and output buffers because of the nature of the output device most often used, the printer. In the early days of computers, when most output was printed on rolled paper, vertical spacing was controlled by inserting blank lines. However, modern printers allow more sophisticated paper movement (called "carriage control," since it is the printer's paper carriage that is being controlled), and our output buffer must provide for that. The technique used in FORTRAN is to send a carriage control character out to the printer at the beginning of the output line. Since this character occupies the first position in the buffer and is not printed, the author finds it convenient to call it column 0 and think of the first print position as column 1. Pictorially, it might look like this:

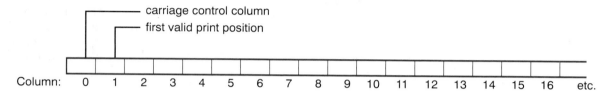

The character placed in column 0 by the FORMAT statement controls the vertical movement of the paper prior to printing. Four characters are specified in the standards (although some manufacturers provide a few more):

Character	Movement
Blank	Move to next line before printing.
Zero	Skip a line before printing (line is left blank).
One	Move to top-of-form (new page).
Plus	Suppress movement (print on same line), allowing overprinting.

Any other character is usually treated as a blank.

Any output to the printer, including files written to disk for later printing, must contain a carriage control at the beginning of each output line. If column 0 contains output, that character will not be printed, but it could cause some unwanted movement of the paper.

Some manufacturers, to provide consistency of output generation, require carriage control in output sent to the screen. The "blank" control provides the same movement to the next line, and "zero" causes skipping a line. The "plus" causes overwriting of the screen line, erasing the previously displayed characters. The "one" results in the skipping of multiple lines, either 6, 12, or 24. A skip of 24 lines will clear the screen, and you should test for this (see exercise 7.4b). The text assumes this consistency and will use carriage control in all future screen output.

Most output buffers have 145 columns to accommodate a 144-column printer, which, although rare, still does exist. The majority of printers utilize 132 print positions, at 0.1 inch each, for an output line of 13.2 inches. (136-character printers are also not unusual these days.) Characters in the buffer may be overwritten by later-placed characters prior to transmitting that line to the output device.

7.3 INPUT/OUTPUT COMMANDS

Until now, you have been using the simplest possible I/O instructions so that you could write useful programs without getting into the more formalized I/O procedures possible with FORTRAN. When writing to the screen, for example, we used (in section 3.7) the following statement:

```
PRINT *, NAME, ' wishes to deposit  $', DPOSIT
```

This statement contains two types of information, variable (the values in NAME and DPOSIT) and literal (the character string between the apostrophes). Automatically, the PRINT command refers to the screen and the asterisk (*) indicates unformatted output or, to be more precise, the system default format.

It is also possible to write to an output device other than the screen by opening a file, giving it a number (LUN, or logical unit number) of our choice. In section 3.8, we saw this sequence:

```
OPEN  (3, FILE='OUTDATA')
   |
   |
   |
WRITE  (3,*)  NAME, 'Deposit =', DPOSIT, ', Withdrawal =',WITHDR
   |
   |
   |
CLOSE  (3)
```

The WRITE statement is a more generalized output statement that allows the programmer to specify a device and a format; again, the asterisk (*) indicates default formatting. The logical unit number could be a variable, so that we could write:

```
WRITE  (IOUT,*)  NAME, 'Deposit =', DPOSIT, ', Withdrawal =',WITHDR
```

with IOUT assigned a value corresponding to the desired device or file prior to executing this statement.

When the system default formatting is used, we have little control over spacing or number of decimal places output. Nor can we move to a new page easily, unless we want the bother of coding a running line count and then printing blank lines to reach the end of the page. In the more formalized approach being introduced here, the programmer will gain full control of both vertical paper movement and horizontal location of information. (This was the only kind of I/O available in the early versions of FORTRAN; free format [list-directed] I/O was available only in some versions of FORTRAN IV [or FORTRAN '66].)

The general form of I/O consists of two statements:

1. An I/O command indicating what is to be input and output
2. A FORMAT statement indicating where the information is to be found or placed in the I/O buffer

The I/O command has four parts:

1. The I/O mode: input or output; i.e., READ or WRITE
2. The logical unit number
3. The FORMAT statement number reference
4. The variable list (optional)

The above WRITE statement would become:

```
WRITE  (3,1000)  NAME, DPOSIT
```

wherein 1000 is a user-chosen FORMAT statement number reference. The variable list consists of the two shown variables. The literal information and the specifications for how to space the variable values are placed in the FORMAT statement. The corresponding FORMAT statement might look like this:

```
1000 FORMAT  (' ', A12, 'Deposit =', F10.2, ', Withdrawal =', F10.2)
```

The details relating to the terms A12 and F10.2 will be discussed in later sections.

Input statements and their formats would be similar, except that a variable list is almost always included with the READ statement and the FORMAT contains no literal fields or carriage control.

For the sake of consistency throughout the rest of this text, we will use the logical unit number of 5 for the keyboard (input) and 6 for the screen (output). You should be aware, however, that each system has its own default; there is no consistency from manufacturer to manufacturer. Of course, we could use the asterisk (*) for our logical unit identifier, which automatically refers to the keyboard for input and to the screen for output; but it is good practice to use a number—or better yet, a variable—for the LUN so that it is easy to change. Many programmers will initially write programs to input from the keyboard and output to the screen during the testing and debugging phases, and then change the LUNs so that the input and output comes from and goes to disk files. As an example of good practice, and to ease portability of the program from computer to computer, this text will use the following:

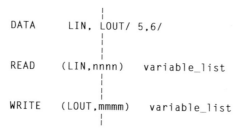

```
DATA      LIN, LOUT/ 5,6/


READ      (LIN,nnnn)   variable_list


WRITE     (LOUT,mmmm)  variable_list
```

Furthermore, it is assumed that our output screen expects a carriage control character placed in column 0 of the output buffer so that it is consistent with the practice used for printer files. (See exercise 7.4b to check out your system.) Only output disk files used to store data will not have carriage control.

7.4 LITERAL AND POSITIONAL SPECIFICATIONS

Literal fields are those that contain a constant character string which is to be output literally; i.e., just as spelled out. There are two ways to define them:

1. Literal specification: placing the string between apostrophes
2. Hollerith specification: specifying the number of characters to be output and the characters themselves

Hollerith specification is named after Herman Hollerith, who first conceived, in the 1890s, the idea of storing numeric information (in his case, it was census data) on punch cards so that it could be read mechanically.

Below are examples of the two ways to specify the seven-character string representing the name of this language:

```
'FORTRAN'  or  7HFORTRAN
```

The latter method requires careful counting of characters, since an incorrect value of the counter would yield a syntax error in the FORMAT statement. In the sample used in the previous section, the statements would become:

```
1000 FORMAT (' ', A12, 'Deposit =', F10.2, ',  Withdrawal =', F10.2)
```

or

```
1000 FORMAT (1H , A12, 9HDeposit =, F10.2, 15H,  Withdrawal =, F10.2)
```

The Hollerith version is hard to read, especially the second 15-character field, which contains a comma. However, there are complications when using a literal field that contains apostrophes; here, a double apostrophe is required for every apostrophe to be output and thus a FORMAT will always contain an even number of apostrophes. For example, to output the string 1″ = 10′ (1 inch = 10 feet), the choices are:

```
9H1'' = 10'  or  '1'''' = 10'''
```

Keep in mind that Hollerith and literal specifications may be mixed in the same FORMAT statement, so the programmer is free to choose the most convenient arrangement.

Note the first specification in the FORMAT statement above, the one following the opening parenthesis. Shown below are two ways of placing a blank in column 0 of the output buffer. Both specify one blank character to be placed in the beginning of the buffer, resulting in vertical movement of the paper to the next line before printing. The following formats are all equivalent:

```
FORMAT (1H , 7HFORTRAN)       FORMAT (' ', 'FORTRAN')
FORMAT (1H , 'FORTRAN')       FORMAT (' ', 7HFORTRAN)
FORMAT (8H FORTRAN)           FORMAT (' FORTRAN')
```

The statements shown on the last line combine carriage control and literal field, a method that could easily lead to error (the author avoids it like the plague, having made so many errors of that type in the past). The author's style is always to use a specification of one character so that the carriage control character is obvious.

Also available are two FORMAT specifications that allow the placement of information on the I/O line:

1. Skip specification, nX, where n is the number of columns to be skipped, or left blank
2. Tab specification, Tn, where n is the column at which the placement of data is to begin

Since the output buffer is cleared to blanks prior to the execution of an output statement, any column left undefined remains blank. So another way of specifying a carriage control of blank would be:

```
FORMAT  (1X, 'FORTRAN')
```

which skips over column 0, leaving it blank.

Likewise, if tab specification is used and column 0 is ignored, it will also be left blank. However, tab specification does not follow our "column 0" construct; it refers to the carriage control column as column 1. Thus, to specify print position 11, it is necessary to use T12.

Tab specification allows the placement of data into the output buffer in any order, not necessarily from left to right. For example:

```
      WRITE   (LOUT,1000)
1000 FORMAT  (T22,'Column A', T7,'Column B')
```

places the string *Column B* in print positions 6 to 13 and the string *Column A* in print positions 21 to 28. The following specification,

```
      WRITE   (LOUT,1000)
1000 FORMAT  (T22,'Column A', T7,'Column B', T1,'0')
```

performs similarly after skipping a line due to the 0 placed in the carriage control column with the tab format T1.

We can summarize the various carriage control characters and the method whereby they are placed into column 0 as follows:

Movement	Character	Method
Next line	Blank	(' ', or (1H , or (1X,
Skip a line	Zero	('0', or (1H0,
Top-of-form	One	('1', or (1H1,
Same line	Plus	('+', or (1H+,

There are some other rules regarding FORMAT statements that make them easier to use. First of all, they are not executable; i.e., nothing is done when they are encountered in a program. Rather, they are auxiliary statements to the READ and WRITE I/O commands and serve to amplify them. The READ and WRITE statements are executable statements and will cause something to happen. What all this means is that the location of the FORMAT statements in a program has no effect (provided they are placed before the END statement); nor does their order have any effect on the execution of the program. (Actually, the FORTRAN compiler moves the FORMAT statements to an area where data is stored, so that in the machine code they are not in the same place as in the source code.) Also, a single FORMAT statement may be accessed by more than one READ or WRITE statement. For instance, the following code:

```
      WRITE    (LOUT,1000)
1000  FORMAT   (' ', '==================')
      WRITE    (LOUT,1002)
1002  FORMAT   (' ', 'Here is a message!')
      WRITE    (LOUT,1000)
```

will produce the output in columns 1 to 18:

```
==================
Here is a message!
==================
```

but, then, so will this one:

```
      WRITE    (LOUT,1000)
      WRITE    (LOUT,1002)
      WRITE    (LOUT,1000)
1000  FORMAT   (' ', '==================')
1002  FORMAT   (' ', 'Here is a message!')
```

as will this form:

```
1002  FORMAT   (' ', 'Here is a message!')
1000  FORMAT   (' ', '==================')
      WRITE    (LOUT,1000)
      WRITE    (LOUT,1002)
      WRITE    (LOUT,1000)
```

Another feature of the FORMAT statement is the repetition factor, which allows the repetition of single fields and groups of fields. For example, the 18 equal signs could have been specified as:

```
1000  FORMAT   (' ', 18('='))
```

Groups of fields may also be repeated:

```
      WRITE    (LOUT,2000)
2000  FORMAT   ('1','Column 1    Column 2    Column 3')
      WRITE    (LOUT,2002)
2002  FORMAT   (' ', 3('--------', 4X))
```

to produce the following output in columns 1 to 32 on lines 1 and 2 of a new page:

```
Column 1    Column 2    Column 3
--------    --------    --------
```

The variety of ways in which the FORMAT statement can be used is endless. Throughout the text, we will demonstrate embellishments that make I/O programming easier than it seems to be at first. In the beginning, the FORMAT seems to add complications to our programming, but the careful reader will soon see just how powerful this statement is; it is the opinion of many professional programmers that the FORTRAN FORMAT statement provides the optimal flexibility when compared with other computer language facilities.

Review Questions and Exercises

7.4a   For the following statements, describe the lines and columns in which the literal fields will appear.

```
        WRITE   (LOUT,1000)
   1000 FORMAT  ('1', 20X, 'TITLE')
        WRITE   (LOUT,1002)
   1002 FORMAT  ('0', T12, 2(3X, 'Headings'))
        WRITE   (LOUT,1004)
   1004 FORMAT  (T32,'Detail', T2,'Identification', T1,'0')
```

7.4b   Include the following code in a program to write to the screen, using the appropriate logical unit number.

```
        WRITE   (LOUT, 1000)
   1000 FORMAT  ('Will we see the first letter?')
        WRITE   (LOUT, 1002)
   1002 FORMAT  ('1', 'Do we skip lines or get a "1"?')
```

If your terminal requires carriage control, the *W* in *Will* will not appear and some lines (how many depends on your compiler and terminal) will be skipped before the second message. If carriage control is not expected, the whole first message will be seen and the second message will start with the digit 1.

7.4c   Repeat exercise 3.1a using two WRITE and FORMAT statements. Use the carriage controls to space your output.

7.4d   Repeat exercise 3.1b using FORMAT statements; although only four are necessary, there must be five WRITE statements.

7.4e   Repeat exercise 3.1c using FORMAT statements.

7.4f   Repeat exercise 3.1d using FORMAT statements. Again, only two pairs of WRITE and FORMAT statements are needed.

7.4g   Repeat exercise 3.1e. Only two FORMAT statements are needed. DO loops can reduce the number of WRITE statements to five and a doubly nested loop to three. Adding an IF statement can reduce the number of WRITE statements to two.

7.4h   Repeat exercise 3.1f using FORMAT statements. If your compiler will accept the underline character, use it. Otherwise, use periods to represent the underline.

7.4i   Write a program to clear the screen. This involves some experimentation, since there are a number of possible ways. See what effect the new page carriage control character has on your screen, and also try the line skip. The worst case will involve writing 24 blank lines. Whatever method you use, the screen will not be completely clear, since the operating system prompt will be displayed on the line after your last one. Hint: An output format with only carriage control serves to define a blank line. You can even try using FORMAT ().

7.4j   Write a program to time a DO loop. The program should consist of an outer loop from 1 to 10 and two nested inner loops from 1 to some very large values (start with 10,000 and 100) with CONTINUEs in them. Display a message in the outer loop to indicate when the program is there and, with a watch, time the duration between messages. Modify the upper value of the inner loop to get a time of about 1 second. A good approximation of the loop time would be from the first message to the STOP message, divided by 10. (On multiprogramming systems in which many users are sharing the system, the times will vary.)

7.5   CHARACTER (ALPHAMERIC) SPECIFICATION

Alphameric specification allows specification of the number of characters that will be printed from character strings. The general form is: **Aw,** where w is the field width, or number of columns allocated for the output.

For example, the following program:

```
        CHARACTER*8  NAME
        DATA  LOUT/ 6/
        NAME = 'Pressman'
        WRITE   (LOUT,1000)   NAME, NAME, NAME
1000 FORMAT  (' ',A8, 4X, A12, 4X, A4)
        STOP
        END
```

will output:

```
                                    1111111111222222222333
columns:    12345678901234567890123456789012
            Pressman     Pressman          Pres
```

The first field specification (A8) is the same size as the string and uses columns 1 to 8. Columns 9 to 12 are skipped (4X). Next, 12 columns are allocated (13 to 24), but since the string needs only 8, the remaining 4 (columns 21 to 24) are left blank. Alphameric format left-justifies the characters; i.e., it places the available characters in the leftmost positions and leaves the remaining rightmost positions blank. Columns 25 to 28 are skipped (4X). Finally, the first four characters are placed in the allocated four columns, 29 to 32, truncating the last four, which did not fit within the allocation. (The memory storage is not modified, only the way the string is output.)

Input is greatly simplified because the computer knows that it is looking for alphameric data and knows in what columns that data can be found. Therefore it is not necessary to place apostrophes around the input data. For example, the following program:

```
        CHARACTER  FIRST * 10, LAST * 12
C
        DATA  LIN, LOUT/ 5,6/
C
        WRITE    (LOUT,1000)
  1000 FORMAT   (' ','Enter first and last names')
        WRITE    (LOUT,1002)
  1002 FORMAT   (' ',10('-'), 1X, 12('-'))
        READ     (LIN,1004)  FIRST, LAST
  1004 FORMAT   (A10, 1X, A12)
        WRITE    (LOUT,1006)  FIRST, LAST
  1006 FORMAT   (' ',A1,'. ',A12)
C
        STOP
        END
```

inputs the strings in columns 1–10 and 12–23, respectively. A sample execution would appear on the screen as:

```
    Enter first and last names
    ---------- ------------
    Michael     Pressman
    M. Pressman
```

with the first name truncated to its initial letter. The program does not search for the first character of the first name; it uses whatever is entered in column 1 as the initial. Thus, entering the names right-justified would result in:

```
    Enter first and last names
    ---------- ------------
       Michael      Pressman
      .         Pressman
```

Obviously, the placement of the input data in the record becomes critical. When reading from a disk file, there is less of a problem, but for keyboard input, the prompt shown above indicating the appropriate columns for the fields is extremely useful. (There is always a trade-off; either apostrophes or careful placement is required for alphameric input.)

Alphameric input has one quite marvelous feature: There are no invalid characters. Thus an ERR= clause would be a waste. However, an entered end-of-file character would cause a bomb-out in the above code, since the END= clause was not included; in this program, such a provision would serve no useful purpose, as it would in other applications.

Input exceeding the size of the storage location, such as entering 10 characters into an 8-character variable, will result in the loss of the last 2 characters. Input less than the size of the variable will cause the rightmost undefined columns in the variable to be filled with blanks, since the system assumes that all undefined columns are blank.

Tab specification allows the FORMAT to access the input buffer in a number of ways, including in an order that is not from left to right. For example, the following input pairs might be used to get the same result:

```
      READ    (LIN,1004) FIRST, LAST
 1004 FORMAT  (A10, T12,A12)
```

or

```
      READ    (LIN,1004) LAST, FIRST
 1004 FORMAT  (T12,A12, T1,A10)
```

And, of course, the output FORMAT may combine different types of information. For example, combining literal and alphameric:

```
      WRITE   (LOUT,1006) FIRST, LAST
 1006 FORMAT  (' ',6HName: , A1, '. ', A12)
```

Another interesting application involves using variable names for the carriage control character so that a single FORMAT statement may be used for similar output but with different line movement:

```
      CHARACTER  CARCON, NEWPAG, NEWLIN, SKPLIN, SAMLIN
      DATA               NEWPAG, NEWLIN, SKPLIN, SAMLIN/
     1                   '1',    ' ',    '0',    '+'/
                          ┊
                          ┊
                          ┊
      IF (LINE .GT. 54) THEN
            CARCON = NEWPAG
            LINE   = 0
         ELSE
            CARCON = NEWLIN
      ENDIF
      WRITE   (LOUT,1000) CARCON, FIRST, LAST
 1000 FORMAT  (A1, 'Name: ', A1, '. ', A12)
      LINE = LINE + 1
```

Here a line counter triggers a new page after 54 lines have been printed. The carriage control characters '1' and '0' could also have been specified as integer, with an I1 instead of A1 specification (since all numerics are converted to alpha when sent to the printer), but that would eliminate the ability to use the ' ' and '+' control characters.

Exercises

7.5a Write a label-making program according to the following specifications. The input file consists of multiple records, each with three fields:

Columns	Information
1–25	Name
26–50	Street address
51–75	Town, state, and zip code

The program should read the file and, for each record, produce a label in the following format:

Line	Columns	Information
1		(blank)
2	4–28	Name
3	4–28	Street address
4	4–28	Town, state, and zip code
5		(blank)
6		(blank

7.5b Write a program to prompt for and input the information needed to reproduce a filled-out questionnaire, as shown in exercise 3.1f. Write the filled-out questionnaire to a disk file. (Note: No carriage control should be written to a disk file.)

7.5c The file name in an OPEN statement can be an alphameric variable, such as:

```
CHARACTER*12  FLNAME
          |
          |
OPEN  (3, FILE=FLNAME)
```

Write a program to request a file name (use 12 characters) and open it. Then have the program set up an input loop that will prompt for 75-character input lines, allowing you to type information into the lines, and will write them to the file as each line is completed (as indicated by the end-of-line key). An end-of-file key completes the input of the file. Test by entering at least three lines of information; then display the file on the screen.

7.5d In the same manner as in the above exercise, write a program to request a file name (use 12 characters), open and list the file on the screen, counting the number of lines in the file and displaying that number at the end. The output should consist of a header with the file name, a blank line, the listing of the file, another blank line, and the record count (using unformatted output). Test by using any text file available, including the source file for this program.

7.5e   Rewrite the sample program at the beginning of section 3.4 using FORMAT statements and appropriate field size prompts. Produce output identical to that presently provided.

7.5f   Write a program to accept the input of the date as a two-character month number, a two-character day number, and a four-character year. Output as 3 two-character fields separated by slashes. For example, input of 07 16 1934 becomes 07/16/34.

7.6   INTEGER (NUMERIC) SPECIFICATION

> Numeric I/O can be performed using one of two assumptions, either that all blank columns are treated as blanks or that all blank columns are treated as zeros. The default is that blank columns are treated as blanks, except that an all-blank numeric field is input as the value 0. We will use this default condition, symbolized as BN, in our treatment of numeric data; we will discuss the alternative method, symbolized as BZ, in Chapter 13.

All examples in this section will assume the following variable specifications:

```
DATA  I,   J,    K, L,    M, N
1        12, -320, 18471, 5, -10000, 0/
```

Integer specification is of the form **Iw,** where w is (as in all specifications) the field width, the number of columns set aside for the value. For example, starting with output (which is easier), this code:

```
      WRITE  (LOUT,1000) I, J, K, L, M, N
1000 FORMAT  (' ',I4, 2I6, I4, 2I6)
```

will output as follows:

```
                          1111111111222222222333
columns:  1234567890123456789012345678901012
            12  -320 18471    5-10000        0
```

with the values right-justified in the six fields—columns 1–4, 5–10, 11–16, 17–20, 21–26, and 27–32, respectively—with leading blanks. (Note the use of the repetition factor 2I6.) Obviously, better spacing is needed in the code above to isolate the term −10000 from the 5 preceding it. The FORMAT might also have been written as:

```
1000 FORMAT (' ', 2 (I4, 2I6))
```

by repeating a group of specifications.

If a value cannot fit in the allocated field width, the field is filled with asterisks. The code

```
      WRITE  (LOUT,1000) K, J, I
1000 FORMAT (' ',I4, 2I6)
```

will output as follows:

```
                          1111111
columns:      1234567890123456
              ****  -320    12
```

During input, the columns in the input buffer specified by the format are scanned and the entered digits extracted, ignoring blank columns; however, any field completely blank is translated as a zero. Look at the following program segment:

```
      READ   (LIN, 1000) I, J
1000 FORMAT (I4, 2X, I4)
```

Here, columns 1–4 and 7–10 are specified (columns 5 and 6 are skipped and thereby ignored), with the following result:

	Input	*Storage*	
	1		
columns:	1234567890	I	J
	1 20	1	20
	1234567890	1234	7890
	123	0	23
	1 2 3 4	12	34
		0	0
	817 -817	817	-817
	817 -817	817	817

It is obviously easier to enter unformatted numeric input when the data is entered at the keyboard because spacing is not critical, as it is with formatted input. Since FORTRAN accepts both the comma and the space as a delimiter, generally either READ statement can be used for the same data. In the seven examples above, however (almost all are unusual cases), only the first and next to last will result in similar values with both an unformatted READ and a formatted READ.

Inputting numeric data might result in an input error if an invalid character is entered. In integer mode, only the 10 digits (0–9), minus sign, plus sign (which is unnecessary), and the blank are valid characters. The ERR= clause would protect against a bomb-out in case of invalid characters. The test program below is useful for checking out the use of the error branch:

```
C                           Test of Integer Input
C
        DO 40  NUMREC = 1,20000
          WRITE   (6,1000)
 1000     FORMAT  ('0','Enter two integers'/ ' ',',____  ____')
          READ    (5,1002, ERR=20, END=90)  I, J
 1002     FORMAT  (I4, 2X, I4)
          PRINT   *, I,J
            GO TO 40
C                           error routine
   20     WRITE   (6,1020)
 1020     FORMAT  ('0','INVALID CHARACTER IN INPUT  -  RE-ENTER!')
   40 CONTINUE
C
   90 STOP
      END
```

Review Questions and Exercises

7.6a   For the following code:

```
      READ    (LIN, 1000)  I, J, K
 1000 FORMAT  (I2, 1X, I4, T11,I3)
```

show what will be stored in the locations I, J, and K for the given input records:

```
                            111111
         columns:  123456789012345
     a.          12789     99999
     b.          987654321
     c.
     d.          123456789012345
```

7.6b   If the format shown in the FORTRAN program above is revised as follows:

```
 1000 FORMAT  (I5, 2X, 2I4)
```

show what will be stored in the locations
for the input records given in exercise 7.6a.

7.6c   If the format above is revised to:

```
 1000 FORMAT  (3I4)
```

show what will be stored in the locations
for the input records given in exercise 7.6a.

7.6d If the format above is revised to:

```
1000 FORMAT (I4, 3X, 2 (2X,I2))
```

show what will be stored in the locations
for the input records given in exercise 7.6a.

7.6e If the format above is revised to:

```
1000 FORMAT (I2, T11,I1, T1,I4)
```

show what will be stored in the locations
for the input records given in exercise 7.6a.

7.6f Rewrite each of the five FORMATS above, using the T specification before each I specification.

7.6g For the following code:

```
DATA   L,   M,   N/
1      -12, 12345, 9876/
WRITE  (LOUT, 1000) L, M, N
```

what will be the printer output according to the following FORMATs?

```
1000 FORMAT (' ', I3, 2I8)
1000 FORMAT (' ', 3I4)
1000 FORMAT (' ', 2(I5,','), I4)
1000 FORMAT (T12,I3, 1X,I6, T2,I6)
1000 FORMAT (1X, I2, I5, I4)
1000 FORMAT (1X, 3(2X, I4))
1000 FORMAT (' ', 'GO TO = ',3I2)
```

7.6h Using the DATA and WRITE statements from exercise 7.6g, write the printer FORMAT statements (using the repetition factor wherever possible) to be used to produce the following output:

```
output              111111111122222
columns:  12345678901234567890123 4
                 -12    12345      9876
          -12  12345   9876
            -12 12345    9876
          -12987612345
           -12 12345    9876
          -12,12345,9876
          -12-12345-9876
          X = ** -12345 **
```

7.6i Write a program to generate the first 20 powers of 2. Start with a heading on the first line of a new page with the character N in column 5 and "2 ** N" in columns 10–15. Skip a line after the heading. Then output the 20 sets of values, right-justified under the headings, skipping a line after each output record.

7.7   REAL (NUMERIC) SPECIFICATIONS

Real values may be input and output in three basic forms: decimal, exponential, and general (the default format used in list-directed output).

Decimal (or "floating-point," in the old nomenclature) uses the specification **Fw.d** where w is again the field width and d is the number of decimal places. For output, there will always be a column used for the decimal point, possibly one for a leading zero if the value is less than 1.00 (this is optional and compiler-dependent), and one for the leading minus sign if the number is negative. Thus, it is a general rule for w to be at least "d+3" in value to avoid overflowing the field and outputting a string of asterisks.

The analysis of what will be output is very straightforward. For example, a specification of F10.2 means that 10 columns will be allocated for the value and 2 of them are to the right of the decimal point. Allocating a column for that decimal point leaves 7 columns in front of the point for the integral portion of the number and a possible minus sign. The values are output right-justified in the specified field and rounded. Below are some examples of different numbers with the same format and the same number with different formats.

```
                                          output            11111111112
                                          columns:  12345678901234567890
      Format         Value                              -123.46
   ('  ', F10.2)    -123.456                                 0.00
   ('  ', F10.2)     0.002                             1234567.89
   ('  ', F10.2)     1234567.89                        **********
   ('  ', F10.2)    -1234567.89                           -87.00
   ('  ', F10.2)    -87.0                                  -87.
   ('  ', F10.0)    -87.0                         -87.0000000000
   ('  ', F20.10)   -87.0                                  -87.0
   ('  ',15X,F5.1)  -87.0
```

Note how the decimal points in the values output with the F10.2 specification are all aligned in the same column. Also note the rounding in the first example. (The value stored in memory is not modified.) Even with zero decimal columns specified, the decimal point is still output. Additional requested decimal positions beyond the defined numeric value are padded with trailing zeros.

The third example above is actually out of the range of significant digits for standard precision reals, which usually amounts to about seven digits. Since some compilers will output "garbage" digits beyond that range, the programmer must be very careful. It is possible to see the next-to-last example output as -87.0000063572 with some compilers.

To handle numbers of greater significance than seven digits, there is double-precision specification, **Dw.d**, which is used for that mode of variable; it follows the same rules as the **Fw.d** specification. The variable must be defined as double-precision, not just the FORMAT specification.

Exponential I/O uses the specification **Ew.d**; again, w is the field width and d the number of decimal places, which in the case of exponential output corresponds to the number of significant digits. Exponential output is in normalized, exponential form in which the decimal point is placed to the left of the first significant digit and the value of the exponent is so adjusted that the numeric value is maintained. For example, 3.14159 would appear as 0.314159E+01.

Unless specified otherwise, the output will always show an exponent consisting of the letter E followed by a sign and a two-digit exponent. (Often, the place for the sign is left blank if the sign is positive.) This is preceded by the normalized form of the number, consisting of a possible minus sign, an optional leading zero, a decimal point, and d significant digits. Thus, the general rule is that w should exceed "$d+7$." A number of examples are shown below:

```
                                   output              11111111112
       Format        Value         columns:   12345678901234567890
     (' ', E10.2)    -123.456                     -0.12E 03
     (' ', E14.4)    -123.456                     -0.1235E 03
     (' ', E20.6)    -123.456                         -0.123456E 03
     (' ', E12.8)    -123.456                  ************
     (' ', E12.5)    -123.456                  -0.12346E 03
     (' ', E12.5)    1.0                        0.10000E 01
     (' ', E12.5)    0.10                       0.10000E 00
     (' ', E12.5)    0.01                       0.10000E-01
     (' ', E12.5)    0.002                      0.20000E-02
     (' ', E12.5)    3.14159                    0.31416E 01
     (' ', E12.5)    1000000000.00              0.10000E 10
```

The main advantage of exponential format is that significant digits will always appear. This is not true for real format when the number is either very small, yielding a zero (see the second real example above, 0.002 with F10.2) or very large, yielding a row of asterisks.

General format, **Gw.d,** is very useful when the range of the output value is not known. Here the system selects an output format, either real or exponential, that is convenient for the size of the value. General format is the default for unformatted I/O.

Input of real values is very flexible, allowing the user to enter them in decimal or a variety of exponential forms. The input specification used, either F, D, E, or G, is not important, since the system will examine the syntax of the entered data and determine whether it is in real or exponential form and translate it accordingly. In addition to the 10 digits, the decimal point, and the plus and minus signs, the letters E and D (for double-precision numbers entered in exponential form) are also valid characters.

The presence of a decimal point in the input field is critical. If that point is entered, the number is accepted as is, regardless of its location in the field and regardless of the number of decimal places called for in the "d" part of the specification. However, if a point is not entered, then the number of decimal places in the "d" part of the specification tells the computer just how many digits are to be assumed to the right of the point. For example, the following input format:

```
FORMAT  (F10.2)
```

will scan columns 1–10 of the input buffer and extract the value therein. If that value contains a decimal point, the value is translated as read. If there is no decimal point, the last two nonblank columns are assumed to be to the right of the point; in other words, an implied decimal point exists before those last two columns.

Exponential data entry can utilize a few shortcuts, since the exponent need not always be in the usual four-character form. The sign need not be entered if the exponent is positive, nor are leading zeros needed. It is also possible to enter the number without the E by using the sign as the indication that the entry is in exponential form. If the number is entered in exponential format without a decimal point, the decimal point is assumed in the columns to the left of the E or the sign. Below are some examples using the F10.2 specification, although the specifications D10.2, E10.2 or G10.2 would yield the same results.

Format	input columns:	1 1234567890	Value
(F10.2)		1234.56	1234.56
(F10.2)		123456	1234.56
(F10.2)		123456	1234.56
(F10.2)		1234.E2	123400.00
(F10.2)		1234.+2	123400.00
(F10.2)		1234+2	1234.00
(F10.2)		1234.E-2	12.34
(F10.2)		1234.00-2	12.34
(F10.2)		1234E0	12.34
(F10.2)		1 2 3 4	12.34

Note the convenience of entering the data left-justified with decimal point to eliminate the need to count columns for right justification.

As a practical example, we present the Hypotenuse program using formatting. The I/O uses data files, and the output has the printer carriage control. The output of each line includes the input sides and the hypotenuse, plus any error messages:

```
C                           Hypotenuse of a Right Triangle
C
C                        open files
      OPEN  (3, FILE='SIDES.IN')
      OPEN  (4, FILE='HYPOT.OUT')
C                        output headings
      WRITE  (4,1000)
 1000 FORMAT ('1,'    Side 1    Side 2   Hypotenuse   Messages')
      WRITE  (4,1001)
 1001 FORMAT (' ')
C                        loop through input
      DO 80  I = 1,20000
         READ   (3,1002, END=90, ERR=60)  SIDE1, SIDE2
 1002    FORMAT (2F8.0)
         IF (SIDE1 .GT. 0.00  .AND.  SIDE2 .GT. 0.00)  THEN
C                        calculation
            HYPOT = SQRT (SIDE1 * SIDE1  +  SIDE2 * SIDE2)
C                        output hypotenuse
            WRITE  (4,1004)  SIDE1, SIDE2, HYPOT
 1004       FORMAT (' ', 2F10.2, F12.2)
         ELSE
            WRITE  (4,1006)  SIDE1, SIDE2
 1006       FORMAT (' ', 2F10.2, 14X, 'Invalid Data')
         ENDIF
         GO TO 80
C                        invalid characters in input
   60    WRITE (4, 1060)
 1060    FORMAT (' ', T36, 'Invalid character in input data')
C                        return for more data
   80 CONTINUE
```

```
C                              termination
  90 CLOSE (3)
     CLOSE (4)
     STOP
     END
```

FORMAT 1001 is used to skip a line (i.e., print a blank line). The input is in columns 1–8 and 9–16; it has been entered left-justified with decimal points:

```
        3.0      4.0
        5.0     12.0
        1.0      1.0
        1.0      2..0
        1.0      1.732
                18.0
        8.0     15.0
```

The output has been lined up under headings and includes the input so that it becomes a complete record of the computer run. The "invalid character" situation, caused by two decimal points, shows no input data because there is no way to convert it to numeric if it is erroneous:

Side 1	Side 2	Hypotenuse	Messages
3.00	4.00	5.00	
5.00	12.00	13.00	
1.00	1.00	1.41	
			Invalid character in input data
1.00	1.73	2.00	
0.00	18.00		Invalid Data
8.00	15.00	17.00	

The blank field, interpreted as a zero value of side 1, does show up with data and the error message.

Review Questions

7.7a For the following code:

```
     READ    (LIN, 1000) X, Y
1000 FORMAT  (E10.2, 1X, F10.4)
```

show what will be stored in the locations X and Y for the given input records.

```
                              111111111122
          columns:   123456789012345678901
      a.            12.34      1234
      b.          8742.56-2
      c.          15200E+5   32.50-7
      d.           20.2      87654321
      e.           1.00      100
      f.                 100 100.-2
```

7.7b　For this code:

```
    DATA     W,       X,           Y,        Z/
    1      -12.50,  123.45,  8790.5E+02,  -0.0003/
    WRITE   (LOUT, 1000)  W, X, Y, Z
```

what will be the output according to the following FORMATs?

```
1000 FORMAT  ('  ', 4F9.3)
1000 FORMAT  ('  ', 4F9.2)
1000 FORMAT  ('  ', 4E9.1)
1000 FORMAT  ('  ', 4E9.0)
1000 FORMAT  ('  ', 4F9.0)
1000 FORMAT  ('  ', 4F6.2)
```

7.7c　Revise exercise 6.1f (Fahrenheit to Celsius conversion) to output the resulting Celsius temperature to one decimal place. Fahrenheit can be left as integer. Output the data right-justified against columns 6 and 18 and place the appropriate headings over the columns. Skip one line after the headings. Modify the loop increment to 5, producing 33 lines of output.

7.7d　Revise exercise 6.1h (conversion table from inches) to output appropriate headings; then output the values in the following forms:

Feet	Integer
Inches	Integer
Yards	4 decimal places
Centimeters	1 decimal place
Meters	3 decimal places

7.7e　Revise exercise 6.1j (CD discounts) to output the money values to two decimal places.

7.8　LOGICAL SPECIFICATION

Logical variables contain only the conditions .TRUE. and .FALSE. Seldom are they input or output, although they are output in a program shown in section 5.9. Output consists only of the letters T or F, requiring only one column. However, logical specification, **Lw,** allows for more than one column and the output letter will be right-justified in the "w" columns, preceded by w-1 blanks.

For input, the number of columns specified by "w" is scanned and the value of the logical variable may be entered as a T or an F. It may be preceded by optional blanks and an optional period. (This latter option allows the value to be entered as .TRUE. or .FALSE.) Any letters beyond the T or F are ignored.

The following program indicates how logical I/O is done:

```
      LOGICAL  LOG
C
      DATA  LIN, LOUT/ 5, 6/
C
      DO 80  I = 1,20000
         WRITE   (LOUT,1000)
1000     FORMAT  ('0', 'Enter a logical value')
         READ    (LIN,1002, ERR=40, END=90)  LOG
1002     FORMAT  (L8)
         WRITE   (LOUT,1004)  LOG
1004     FORMAT  (' ',L1)
         IF      (LOG)  PRINT *, 'True'
         IF  (.NOT. LOG)  PRINT *, 'False'
            GO TO 80
C
   40    WRITE   (LOUT,1040)
1040     FORMAT  (' ', 'INVALID LOGICAL CHARACTER')
   80 CONTINUE
C
   90 STOP
      END
```

The following input will yield either true or false values or will be invalid:

.TRUE.	.FALSE.	invalid
T	F	G
t	f	?
.TRUE.	.FALSE.	neither
.TRUTH.	FIRE	.LIE.

7.9   MULTILINE OUTPUT

The closing parenthesis of a FORMAT statement indicates end-of-I/O-record (EOR). The next I/O command will proceed to the next record and start at the first column of that record. Also, the slash (/) indicates end-of-I/O-record and allows the generation of multiple I/O records within the same FORMAT.

We must distinguish very carefully between the next record and the next line. With an output FORMAT, the next record may not be the next line, because carriage control may cause the next record to skip a line, be on the next page, or even be on the same line. For example:

```
      WRITE    (LOUT, 1000)
1000 FORMAT   ('1',10X,'Title'/ '0','Heading 1',5X,'Heading 2')
```

replaces:

```
      WRITE    (LOUT, 1000)
1000 FORMAT   ('1',10X,'Title')
      WRITE    (LOUT, 1001)
1001 FORMAT   ('0','Heading 1',5X,'Heading 2')
```

Note that the slash must be followed by the carriage control for the next output record. The title appears on line 1 and the headers on line 3, with line 2 skipped because of the zero placed in carriage control.

Using the continuation indicator, many programmers like to enter multiline FORMAT statements in such a way that the multiline nature of the instruction is emphasized:

```
      WRITE    (LOUT, 1000)
1000 FORMAT   ('1',10X,'Title'/
     1             '0','Heading 1',5X,'Heading 2')
```

With some long FORMATS coming up, continuation will be necessary. We recommend that you use it as a documentation aid.

There are a number of different ways of obtaining the same output. The above FORMAT might have been coded:

```
      WRITE    (LOUT, 1000)
1000 FORMAT   ('1',10X,'Title'//
     1             ' ','Heading 1',5X,'Heading 2')
```

The first of the two slashes at the end of the first FORMAT line indicates the end of line 1. The second slash indicates the end of line 2. The blank carriage control moves the output to line 3 prior to printing the headers. The answer to the question about what is on line 2 is obvious: nothing. Since the output buffer is filled with blanks before the FORMAT is processed, the entry of nothing into it leaves a blank in column 0, thus moving to the next output line and leaving it blank.

This introduces another useful construct, multiple slashes for skipping multiple lines. The rule is that n slashes followed by a blank carriage control symbol leaves $n - 1$ blank lines; n slashes followed by a 0 carriage control symbol yields n blank lines.

One inconsistent usage is the skipping of a line at the end of the FORMAT. In the following construction:

```
      WRITE    (LOUT, 1000)
1000 FORMAT   ('1',10X,'Title'/
     1             '0','Heading 1',5X,'Heading 2'/)
```

one might expect that a blank line (line 4) is left after the headings are output and the next record would be on line 5, assuming we use the "next line" carriage control symbol (blank). The FORTRAN specifications are not specific on this, and there are two interpretations of the construct; namely, no skipped line (since the adjacent slash and closing parenthesis both indicated EOR) and one skipped line. One way the programmer can play it safe is to place a carriage control symbol on the new line and thus assure that the desired blank line is supplied:

```
      WRITE   (LOUT, 1000)
 1000 FORMAT  ('1',10X,'Title'/
    1          '0','Heading 1',5X,'Heading 2'/ ' ')
```

Another, but somewhat illogical, alternative to the three-line title and heading output is:

```
      WRITE   (LOUT, 1000)
 1000 FORMAT  ('1',10X,'Title'///
    1          '+','Heading 1',5X,'Heading 2')
```

in which the three slashes represent the ends of lines 1, 2, and 3 and the '+' carriage control means "stay on line 3."

This brings us to yet another rather useful construct, multiple printing on the same line. The '+' carriage control allows this, but it is useful only in a printing operation; on a screen, the overlaid information replaces what was there before. For example:

```
      WRITE   (LOUT, 1000)
 1000 FORMAT  ('1',10X,'Title'/ '+',10X,'____')
```

will underline the title on printers that have an underline character. The construct can also be used to generate bold type by printing the same line more than once:

```
      WRITE   (LOUT, 1000)
 1000 FORMAT  ('1',10X,'Title')
      DO 20   I = 1,2
   20 WRITE   (LOUT, 1020)
 1020 FORMAT  ('+',10X,'Title')
```

or simply:

```
      WRITE   (LOUT, 1000)
 1000 FORMAT  ('1',10X,'Title'/ '+',10X,'Title'/ '+',10X,'Title')
```

Of course, variable and literal specifications may be interspersed in these FORMATs, just as in previous cases, such as:

```
      WRITE   (LOUT, 1000)  NPAGE
 1000 FORMAT  ('1',10X,'Title', T48,'Page',I3/
    1          '0','Headings')
```

Review Questions and Exercises

7.9a   For the following code, indicate the page and line number where each of the capital letters will appear:

```
      WRITE   (LOUT,1000)
 1000 FORMAT  ('1'/ '0','A'//// '0','B'/ '1','C'/// '+','D'/ ' ')
      WRITE   (LOUT,1001)
 1001 FORMAT  ('0','E'/ '0','F'/ '1','G')
```

7.9b   Produce the following output using one WRITE and one FORMAT statement:

```
                    1111111111222222222233333333334444
columns:   12345678901234567890123456789012
           Hypotenuse of a Right Triangle          new page
                                                   skipped line

           Side 1     Side 2   Hypotenuse   Messages
                                                   2 skipped
                                                   lines
```

7.9c   Repeat exercise 7.4c (which repeats exercise 3.1a,), using a single WRITE and FORMAT statement.

7.9d   Repeat exercise 7.4e (which repeats exercise 3.1c), using a single WRITE and FORMAT statement.

7.9e   Repeat exercise 7.4g, generating a tick-tack-toe diagram, but this time specify two character variables to define the two different output records and use them with a single WRITE and multiline FORMAT pair to output the diagram.

7.10   INPUT/OUTPUT LIST AND FORMAT INTERACTION

The I/O list and its associated FORMAT statement work together to locate the desired variables in the specified columns. Usually there is one FORMAT specification for each variable in the I/O list; but this need not be so. In fact, the interaction between the two associated statements can be manipulated very efficiently by the programmer to save coding effort.

If the I/O list is exhausted before the available FORMAT specifications are, I/O ends with the first unsatisfiable specification. For example:

```
     DATA    X, Y/ 183.56, -48.17/
     WRITE   (LOUT,1000)  X, Y
1000 FORMAT  (' ','x =',F10.2, 4X, 'y =',F10.2)
```

produces the output:

```
     x =    183.56    y =      -48.17
```

Revising the output command to:

```
     WRITE   (LOUT,1000)  X
```

produces the output:

```
     x =    183.56    y =
```

since the second F10.2 is the unsatisfiable specification.

The cure for this is to place a colon (:) in the FORMAT statement where you wish output to end if the I/O list is exhausted, such as:

```
1000 FORMAT  (' ','x =',F10.2, :, 4X, 'y =',F10.2)
```

which produces the output:

```
     x =    183.56
```

Another useful technique is to "steal" the carriage control from another FORMAT. For example:

```
      WRITE    (LOUT,1000)  X, Y
1000 FORMAT   (' ', 2F10.2)
      WRITE    (LOUT,1000)
```

The second WRITE has no I/O list, but it will still access FORMAT 1000 up to the unsatisfiable F10.2, executing only the carriage control. As a result, a blank line is output (a line is skipped).

Input works similarly. These statements:

```
1000 FORMAT   (3I8)
      READ     (LIN, 1000)  I, J, K
      READ     (LIN, 1000)  L
      READ     (LIN, 1000)  M, N
```

will read:

Record	Columns:	1–8	9–16	17–24
1		I	J	K
2		L		
3		M	N	

Another very useful construct is called "reversion." It comes into play when the end of the FORMAT has been reached but there are still values to be input or output. As stated above, the closing parenthesis indicates the end-of-I/O-record. The system then goes to the *rightmost opening parenthesis* and continues to I/O as though that were the beginning of the FORMAT. If that parenthesis is preceded by a repetition factor, that factor is included.

This combination:

```
      WRITE    (LOUT,1000)  I, J, K
1000 FORMAT   ('1', I5)
```

results in the values of I, J, and K being printed in columns 1–5 of line 1 on three separate pages. Each time the end of the FORMAT is reached and there are more variables to be output, control reverts back to the opening parenthesis and the '1' carriage control character.

Using the same WRITE:

```
1000 FORMAT   ('1', I5/ ' ', I5)
```

will result in I output in columns 1–5 on line 1 of page 1, J in the same columns on line 2 of page 1, and K in the same columns on line 1 of page 2.

An additional set of parentheses provides additional control. For example, with the same WRITE statement:

```
1000 FORMAT   ('1', I5/ (' ', I5))
```

will now place K in columns 1–5 of line 3 of page 1. Reversion takes us back to the rightmost opening parentheses, not to the first opening parenthesis.

To show the use of the repetition factor, the following statements:

```
      WRITE    (LOUT,1000)  I, J, K, L, M, N
1000 FORMAT   ('1', I5/ 2(' ',I5))
```

will result in the following layout:

Page	Line	Columns:	1–5	7–11
1	1		I	
	2		J	K
	3		L	M
	4		N	

since the FORMAT statement is interpreted as:

```
1000 FORMAT ('1', I5/ (' ',I5, ' ',I5))
```

Reversion will prove to be indispensable in later chapters on arrays.

Review Questions and Exercises

7.10a In the examples below, indicate the page number, line number, and column locations for each of the variables. Assume that all output will start on page 1, line 1, unless the carriage control yields otherwise.

```
        WRITE   (LOUT,1000)  I, J, K, L, M
a. 1000 FORMAT ('1', 3I5)
b. 1000 FORMAT ('1', 3I5/ ' ', I5)
c. 1000 FORMAT ('1', 3I5/ (' ', I5))
d. 1000 FORMAT ('1', I5/ ' ', 2I5/ '0', I5)
e. 1000 FORMAT ('1', 30X, I5/ '+', 4I5)
f. 1000 FORMAT ('1'/// ('0', 3I5))
```

7.10b Real data is arranged in a disk file in three columns, four records:

```
                             111111111
         columns:  123456789012345678
                    27.45 82.37 53.21
                   117.42 -3.76 -0.12
                    37.11 40.50 77.91
                   105.64100.00 -9.99
```

Indicate the value for each element read according to the FORMATs given below:

```
        READ    (LIN,1000)  R1, R2, R3, R4
a. 1000 FORMAT (F6.2)
b. 1000 FORMAT (2F6.2)
c. 1000 FORMAT (3F6.2)
d. 1000 FORMAT (4F6.2)
e. 1000 FORMAT (2F6.2 // 2F6.2)
f. 1000 FORMAT (/ 2F6.2)
g. 1000 FORMAT (2F6.2 / (12X, F6.2))
h. 1000 FORMAT (F6.2/ 6X, F6.2/ (F6.2))
i. 1000 FORMAT (F6.2/ 12X, F6.2)
```

7.11 CHAPTER REVIEW

Although in this chapter we have presented many of the rules relative to the FORMAT statement, we have only scratched the surface of the possible I/O variations. Additional facilities are covered in Chapter 13. However, the material in this chapter is very extensive and covers about 95% of the needs of most professional programmers. You are encouraged to experiment with the FORMAT statement; almost any logical construct will work. (Even after almost three decades of programming in FORTRAN, the author is still discovering new FORMAT applications—in some cases from his students.)

The topics covered in this chapter include:

Topic	Section
Alphameric specification (**Aw**)	7.4, 7.5
Blank input fields	7.1
Carriage control	7.2, 7.4
Colon editing	7.10
DATA	7.3
End-of-record (/)	7.1
ERR= clause	7.6
FORMAT	7.3
Hollerith specification (nH)	7.4
Implied decimal point	7.7
Integer specification (**Iw**)	7.6
I/O buffer	7.1, 7.2
Literal specification	7.4
Logical specification (**Lw**)	7.8
Logical unit number (LUN)	7.3
Multiline output	7.9
Positional specifications (nX, Tn)	7.4
READ	7.3
Real specifications (**Fw.d, Dw.d, Ew.d, Gw.d**)	7.7
Reversion	7.10
Tab specification (Tn)	7.4
WRITE	7.3

Exercises

7.11a Revise exercise 6.1e (table of squares, cubes, square and cube roots) to calculate values from 1 to 100 and print out on two pages, with values 1–50 on the first page and values 51–100 on the second page. Each page should have appropriate headings followed by a blank line. Also skip a line after each tenth value; the MOD function is very useful here. Output the value and its powers as integers and the roots as reals to four decimal places. Use a single DO loop.

7.11b Revise exercise 7.11a to calculate values from 1 to 200 and to use two nested DO loops. The outer loop controls the pages (from 1 to 4), and the inner loop controls the values printed on those pages. The initial and final parameters for the inner loop should be calculated from the index of the outer loop. Also print out a page number.

7.11c   Revise exercise 6.2b (computation of salaries from filed data) to print out hours to two decimal places, rates to three decimal places, and the salaries earned to two decimal places. Modify the input file as follows:

```
                              1
   columns:   1234567890
              3550 18625
              4225 14584
              6300 11555
```

where columns 1–4 contain the hours and columns 6–10 the rates. The input FORMAT is to place the implied decimal points between columns 2 and 3 and between columns 7 and 8. The first input record reads, for example, 35.50 hours at a rate of 18.625.

   After the input records are processed, skip a line before printing the totals. Annotate that line so that the totals are identified.

7.11d   Combine the three parts of exercise 6.7c into a single program that will output the computed value of pi for each of the three methods on the same line. Output the number of strips as integer and the three values of pi to five decimal places. Continue generating approximations until the relative precision has reached 0.0001 in two of the methods. Use an appropriate title and headings.

8

Subprograms

CHAPTER OUTLINE

Statement of the Problem

8.1 Subprogram Concepts
Topics Introduced:
Programming System
LINK Command

8.2 Subprogram Linkage
Topic Introduced:
Arguments

8.3 The Arithmetic Statement Function

8.4 The Function Subprogram

8.5 Subroutines

8.6 Generating Random Data
Topic Introduced:
Normally Distributed Values

8.7 Programming Systems

8.8 Chapter Review

CHAPTER OBJECTIVES

- To present the most powerful tool available in FORTRAN for developing structured, modular code and top-down design.

- To present the method whereby code usable in many programming systems may be packaged for multiple use.

- To show the techniques used in the professional environment for sharing tested and debugged code.

- To show the methods used by professional programmers for writing efficient code.

- To demonstrate a method for generating random test data.

STATEMENT OF THE PROBLEM

As programs become larger and more complex, it is often difficult to follow the logic unless it is structured in such a way that it is broken down into small modules of code, each somewhat self-contained. In addition, many processes, such as maximum, minimum, and sorting, are so often used in programming that it would be most efficient to incorporate them into a program without having to enter the source code each time.

You have already seen how FORTRAN allows the use of the intrinsic functions simply by coding their names. These functions, although providing relatively simple calculations, contain a number of logical steps and not only save us from having to write them ourselves, but also provide the convenience of not having to include their code with our own source code. FORTRAN also enables us to write our own functions and subroutines, storing them externally, so that their source code is not embedded within our source program but is accessible with a single statement that specifies their name.

External subprograms are useful not only because they can be used with many separate programs, they can also be shared with other programmers, thereby reducing the overall programming effort in a professional environment. Even in an academic environment, certain basic routines needed by an entire class can be made available and shared, saving the students from each having to "reinvent the wheel."

This most powerful property of FORTRAN is what has allowed it to survive in a world filled with a plethora of competing languages. We now see versions of BASIC emerging that can be modularized with external subprograms. There are also versions of Pascal that allow the same, although the design of that language does not include that ability.

An even more interesting trend exists that calls for a standardization of subprogram structure among many languages so that a subprogram written in one language can be called by another language. Soon we will see I/O routines written in COBOL, with computational subprograms written in FORTRAN, string-handling routines in BASIC, complex data structure routines in C, and bit manipulation routines written in assembly language, all linked together into one programming system. This is not a new concept, since all languages can call assembly language routines now. The future intent is that all languages will be compatible and that the accessed routines need not be written only in assembly language or in the language of the initial (mainline) program.

The use of external subprograms in the programming environment also allows for the "programming team" concept in which the work is shared. Since subprograms are self-contained and isolated from the programs that will eventually access them, they can be compiled and tested, guaranteeing that they will be bug-free when they are used. When they are as general-purpose as possible, their use within many programming systems increases the efficiency of the programmers and the reliability of the code.

Chapter 6 introduced the concept of modularization and top-down design. In this chapter, the concept is emphasized and expanded, since the subprogram is self-contained and thus becomes the ultimate module. The subprograms written by the programmer can be standardized, stored, and shared, just like the intrinsic functions. In many applications, the mainline program often becomes little more than a series of calls to subprograms, each written for one of the prime functions of the program. Since subprograms can call other subprograms, the top-down structure is further enhanced. The ideal would be to keep each part of the modulated program down to about 60 lines of code so that each of these parts occupies no more than one page.

8.1   SUBPROGRAM CONCEPTS

A subprogram is an independently written piece of code, packaged so that it can be compiled separately and stored apart from the programs that will utilize it. The user need not know anything about the logic of the subprogram, the variables used, or the statement numbers used; all the user must know is the name of the subprogram and the structure of its argument list; i.e., the number, order, and mode of the variables used to transmit information back and forth between the calling program and the subprogram.

We have already been using subprograms in our study of FORTRAN. The intrinsic functions introduced in Chapter 4 are subprograms supplied by the publisher of the FORTRAN compiler and are considered a part of the language. Now we begin writing our own subprograms to be included with our main program. This combination of the main program (called the mainline) and the subprograms is called a programming system.

Placing a piece of code into subprogram form has many advantages. First of all, it allows a large program to be broken into modules, thus aiding in the structuring of the program. Each module can be independently tested without concern about the integration of that module, which may take place at some later time.

Furthermore, the subprogram may be accessed many times within the same programming system, yet its code occupies memory only once. For example, a program may use the square root function (SQRT) many times, but the same code is used over and over. The access to the subprogram does not cause the code to be inserted into the program each time that subprogram is accessed. Rather, a branch is made to the one copy of the code sitting in memory, with a return to the statement following the one accessing the subprogram after the subprogram code has been executed. An additional access branches to the same code, but the return will be to the statement following the second access. In small computer systems, this space savings is of significant importance.

In addition, once the subprogram is written it may be accessed by many different programs. Thus, a properly generalized subprogram is valuable not only to the writer of the subprogram but to the other programmers who might need it. Most systems provide a means by which subprograms may be stored in a common library accessible to all system users in a very simple fashion.

And, finally, to emphasize the advantages of subprograms, a subprogram can call another subprogram. Thus we talk of calling and called programs without the need to differentiate between a mainline program and its subprograms. The only limitation is that a circular reference cannot be used; i.e., subprogram A cannot call subprogram B, which calls subprogram A.

Nor, except in some very advanced, nonstandard versions of FORTRAN, can recursion exist wherein a subprogram can call itself. (Recursion is a favorite topic of many theoretical computer scientists, but a study of the linkage procedures used in most computers will show that recursion uses an exorbitant amount of memory and is significantly slower compared with other ways of solving a problem. Only in a very few instances is the use of recursion efficient in both memory usage and execution time.)

The term *programming system* represents the mainline program plus its called subprograms. Every system must have a mainline, which is the anchor of the system. Subprograms cannot be executed separately but must be accessed from a mainline. During the linking operation, the machine-language versions of the mainline and the called subprograms (and *their* called subprograms) are tied together, as are the intrinsic functions and the subprograms contained in the FORTRAN subprogram library, as well as the necessary parts of the operating system.

Thus far you have probably used the linking operation without any knowledge of exactly what was happening. Now we are concerned with what is going on because the inclusion of a user-written subprogram requires an extra step during the linking operation—specifying the user-written subprograms. This step is computer-dependent, but the user can expect to find operating system instructions of the following type:

```
LINK   MAINLN+SUB1+SUB2+SUB3
```

or

```
LINK   MAINLN,SUB1,SUB2,SUB3
```

Every user-written subprogram used in the programming system must be listed in the link command. It is your responsibility to determine what the link instruction for FORTRAN is on your own computer system.

8.2   SUBPROGRAM LINKAGE

Subprogram linkage is concerned with three elements:

1. How transfer is made to the subprogram
2. How information is transmitted back and forth between calling and called programs
3. How return is made to the proper location in the calling program

Illustrating with some partial code that calls one of the intrinsic library programs a number of times, the SQRT function requires one real argument. That argument must be a real constant, a real variable, or a real expression. The function returns a real value, which can be assigned to either a real or an integer location (the latter truncating). In this sequence of code:

```
X = SQRT (C)
N = SQRT (A + B)
Y = SQRT (2.5 * D  -  E)
Z = X - SQRT (Y - 2.00)
```

the subprogram SQRT is accessed four times, yet, as previously mentioned, the actual code for SQRT resides in memory only once. Linking to a subprogram requires a simple GO TO, or more generally put, a branch statement. However, the linkage mechanism also requires that there be a way of saving a "return address" so that the logic continues at the appropriate point (called a "branch back" or "return") after the subprogram is executed. Furthermore, each time the subprogram is accessed, a different value of the argument is transmitted to it; a mechanism must thus exist so that only the appropriate value is used for the calculation. The beauty of this is that the linkage mechanisms set up by FORTRAN are transparent to the programmer and of no concern, *provided that the code is correctly written.*

When a programming system is linked together, the memory of the computer is first loaded with the portion of the operating system needed to execute a program, then with the mainline, then with the user-written subprograms called by the mainline, then with the system subprograms called by the mainline and the subprograms.

Since the user-written subprograms themselves might call other system or user-written subprograms, the linking operation continues until all accessed subprograms are tied together. Should the machine code for a called subprogram not be available (possibly because the user forgot to compile it or to list it in the linking command), the linkage operation will fail, hopefully with an informative error message. The executable program system appears as one big program within the memory, with all of its parts linked together by GO TOs, as shown in Figure 8-1. In this hypothetical diagram, the memory increases from bottom to top, although each program module reads downward.

Figure 8-1
Memory map of a programming system

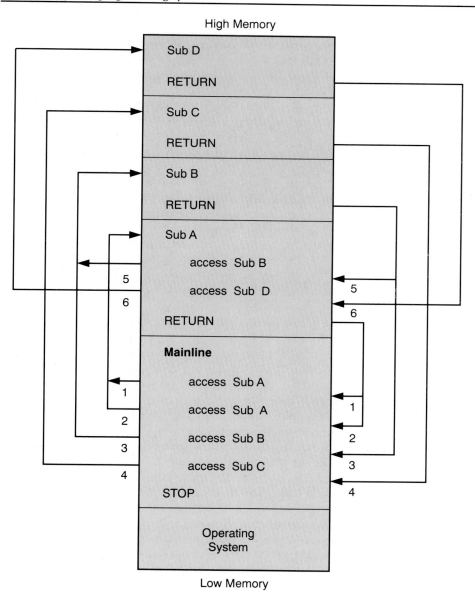

As the diagram shows, the mainline is where all branching begins. The main-line can link to any of the subprograms, and it does link to all except Sub D (paths 1, 2, 3, and 4 on the left side). In fact, it links twice to Sub A (paths 1 and 2). How-ever, as mentioned above, the code for Sub A appears only once in the memory; the two branches go to the same code but return to different locations in the calling program, the mainline (return paths 1 and 2 on the right side). Sub A links to Sub B and Sub D (paths 5 and 6 on the left, with returns on the right), showing how sub-programs can access other subprograms. However, note that the mainline can also access Sub B (path 3). The only limit, as mentioned in the previous section, is that a subprogram cannot reference itself directly (recursively) or indirectly (through another subprogram).

Since it is the intention to have subprograms return to the calling program, the last logical executable statement in a subprogram is a RETURN; the subprogram, like all programs, will have an END statement, which is the last physical statement in the program. (A subprogram can have a STOP also, but it must have at least one RETURN in order to compile.)

There are two main types of subprograms:

1. Functions: used (primarily) to calculate a single value
2. Subroutines: used in all other situations

The functions break down further into three subtypes:

1a. Intrinsic functions: supplied by the manufacturer and automatically linked into the calling program. They usually are high-speed, very efficient algorithms written in assembly language. (These were cov-ered in Chapter 4.)
1b. Arithmetic statement functions: consist of a single assignment state-ment placed directly into the calling program
1c. Function subprograms: independently compiled code with no restric-tion in logic except that only one value is to be returned

The accessing of a function, regardless of subtype, is the same; it is only the physi-cal location of the code that is different.

The function usually has at least one argument. The returned value is stored in a location whose label is the name of the function itself. Thus, if the SQRT function is accessed, the calling program sets aside a location labeled SQRT to store the re-turned value. The arguments, numbering zero or more (virtually without limit), are the identification of the values sent to the function. These arguments may be con-stants, variables, or expressions. The function is accessed in an assignment state-ment and looks just like a function used in algebra. However, since the name of the function (unless otherwise typed) defines the mode of the returned value, it was necessary to name the logarithmic intrinsic function ALOG (instead of LOG) so that it would return a real value.

The subroutine lists all of the information going back and forth as arguments. The name of the subroutine is only for identification, and thus there is no need for the compiler to set aside a storage location for its name, as is necessary with func-tions. The number of arguments for a subroutine can be as little as none or as many as desired. Furthermore, the arguments may represent the information going to the subroutine, the variables being modified in the subroutine, or the variables being generated in the subroutine. These arguments may be specified in any order and also may be constants, variables, or expressions for information sent to the subroutine—but only variables for information being modified or generated in the subroutine. The subroutine is accessed with a CALL statement.

There are some very critical rules governing the placement of arguments. The programmer who writes the subprogram dictates the name of the subprogram and the arguments used; after all, it is the writer's subprogram, and if we want to use it we must abide by his or her terms. First, the number of arguments must agree in both calling and called programs. Second, the order of the arguments must agree; i.e., the first argument in the calling program must correspond to the first argument in the called program, the second argument in the calling program must agree with the second argument in the called program, and likewise for the rest of the arguments. As will be seen, communication between routines is done by their order in the list, not by the names of the arguments. Third, the mode of the corresponding arguments must agree; if the calling program transmits a real value and the called program treats it as integer, the value returned will be wrong because of the different methods of storage.

Try, for example, writing a program with this statement:

```
X = SQRT (9)
```

and print the value of X. The SQRT function expects a real value, like 9.0, whereas 9 is an integer value; either the program will bomb out at that point or the returned value will not be what is expected.

Character variables must be so typed in both calling and called subprograms and must be of the same length.

The mechanism used in FORTRAN for transmitting information to a subprogram consists of transmitting the address of the information, not the value. Then the subprogram can utilize that address to reach into the memory and retrieve the value. The same rule is used for information to be returned from the subprogram: The address where the result is to be placed is sent to the subprogram, which uses it to locate the repository of the modified or generated information. This is why only a variable can be in the argument list for any argument that is to be modified. If the argument for information sent to a subprogram is an expression, that expression is first evaluated and the result placed in a temporary location; it is the address of that temporary location that is sent to the subprogram. A mode change is not possible during subroutine linkage, since the only means of communication is an address and there is no way to differentiate the address of an integer from that of a real.

The result of this method is that when a variable appears in the argument list, a location is set aside for it in the calling program but not in the called subprogram. The transmitted address is moved into the appropriate location in the subprogram, but that is transparent to the FORTRAN programmer.

There is one critical concern to the user of the subprogram, and that is how the routine handles an error condition. For example, there is no rational solution to the square root of a negative number. When we start writing our own routines a little later in this chapter, we will discuss various error-handling techniques, but here we are using someone else's routine and we have no control over it. In most cases, manufacturers will document the range of the argument(s) to the intrinsic functions, in this case nonnegative; but seldom will they describe what happens if an argument is out of range. On the old IBM 1130, for example, the square root was taken of the argument's absolute value, so that the square root of -4 was 2. On other systems, a zero is returned; and others display an error message and abort the program. This is, unfortunately, just one of those "system-dependent" situations, and we can give no advice other than to be careful.

8.3   THE ARITHMETIC STATEMENT FUNCTION

The arithmetic statement function (sometimes more simply called a statement function) is a user-written function that consists of a single assignment statement. Yet despite its limited length, it is a very useful construct in many situations; it will also serve as a useful example of just how a subprogram works.

The required elements of this abbreviated subprogram are described below.

1. Name of the function: Since the name of the function also serves as the storage identification for the value derived, the mode (integer, real, character, or logical) of the function must agree with the mode of the value to be returned. Thus, the name of a function follows the same rules as that of a variable.

2. Argument list: These are the variable names for the information to be sent to the function and with which the function will perform the calculation. However, the arguments listed only serve as temporary identifiers, since different information may be sent to the function each time; thus they are called dummy arguments. No storage locations are set aside for them, and they are useful only to the programmer in describing just what the function does. The dummy argument names used in statement functions are defined only within the scope of the function and may be used elsewhere in the program for other purposes without conflict. They, of course, must reflect the mode of the information being stored.

3. Work of the function: This is the FORTRAN expression describing what the function does. It can contain only the dummy variables specified in the argument list, variables appearing in the program containing the function, constants, and intrinsic function names. As might be expected, it must follow all the rules of FORTRAN expressions.

This is the general form:

```
Function_name (argument_list) = expression
```

The arithmetic statement function, like the function in BASIC or the procedure in Pascal, is placed immediately before (exclusive of comments) the first executable statement. An arithmetic statement function is classified as nonexecutable, since its execution is based not on its location in the program but on the location of the statement that accesses it (like the FORMAT statement). Thus far, the nonexecutable statements covered are the type statements that define mode, the FORMAT statement, and now the arithmetic statement function. All the other statements covered (assignment, branch, decision, etc.) are classified as executable because they are executed according to their location in the program.

A program may contain more than one statement function. However, if one arithmetic statement function accesses another, the accessed function must appear before the one that accesses it.

As an example, assume that there is a program which must calculate the square root of the sum of the squares a number of times and, to avoid the boredom of constantly repeating the same kind of expression, a statement function will be used.

```
          :
C         statement function for square root of the sum of squares
ROOT (XXX, YYY)  =  SQRT (XXX * XXX  +   YYY * YYY)
          :
          :
HYPOT = ROOT (DX, DY)
          :
          :
SIDE3 = ROOT (X2-X1, Y2-Y1)
          :
          :
DIST = XLNGTH + ROOT (2.86, HEIGHT)
          :
```

In the above program segment, the statement function is specified once but accessed three times, each time with different arguments. XXX and YYY are the dummy arguments in the function itself. To access the function, the accessing statement must specify the name of the function and an argument list corresponding in length, order, and mode to that of the function. The value of the first argument in the accessing statement is represented in the function by the first dummy argument, the second with the second, and so forth with any other arguments. Thus, in the above program, the first time the function is accessed the value of DX is "substituted" wherever XXX appears in the function and the value of DY wherever YYY appears. The second time the function is accessed, the dummy arguments are "replaced" by the values of X2 − X1 and Y2 − Y1, respectively, and the third time by 2.86 and HEIGHT.

The actual mechanism transmits the address of the variable. Thus in the first access, the addresses of DX and DY are transmitted to the statement function. In the second access, the values of X2 − X1 and Y2 − Y1 are placed in temporary locations and the addresses of those temporary locations are transmitted to the statement function. In the third acccess, the addresses of the locations in the memory where the constant 2.86 is stored and where HEIGHT is stored is transmitted to the statement function. An examination of the generated assembly language code would show how this is done on your particular computer.

Note how the function's expression may contain an intrinsic function; it may even contain a previously defined arithmetic statement function. (The squaring of the arguments was done by multiplication rather than exponentiation because the former is both faster and more accurate.)

Because the arithmetic statement function is limited to a single calculation, there is no error-handling capability. Arithmetic statement functions and their dummy arguments may be typed explicitly or implicitly.

In order to test subprograms, we often write a driver program whose only purpose is to access the subprogram so that it can be tested in an environment isolated from any other factors. The driver program will usually contain a prompt for the input, the input statement, a statement accessing the subprogram, and an output statement to display the results. The driver program will usually be written to loop back for additional input in order to test many combinations of data. Below is a sample driver to test the arithmetic statement function ROOT:

```
C              Driver to test ASF for Square Root of Sum of Squares
       ROOT (XXX, YYY) = SQRT (XXX * XXX  +  YYY * YYY)
C
       DO 20  I = 1,20000
           WRITE   (*,1000)
 1000      FORMAT  (//' ','Enter two real numbers')
           READ    (*,*, ERR=20, END=90)  A, B
           C = ROOT (A, B)
           WRITE   (*,1002)  C
 1002      FORMAT  (F12.4)
    20 CONTINUE
C
    90 STOP
       END
```

Exercises

8.3a   Write an arithmetic statement function to return the cube of a real number. The calculation should be done by multiplication so that the speed is faster and the precision increased. Embed the function into a testing (driver) program that will accept multiple input and display the results of the calculation. Negative input is valid and should be used as test data, as well as the more obvious positive values.

8.3b   In Chapter 4, section 4.5 presented a single statement to convert a double-precision real to a value rounded to exactly two decimal places. Code this as an arithmetic statement function and test it with a driver program. This single function may prove to be the most valuable one a programmer has in his or her library.

8.3c   Write an arithmetic statement function to calculate a rounded integer quotient; use no real arithmetic. Embed it into a driver program that will accept multiple sets of data. This testing program should test to ensure that the divisor is nonzero before sending it to the function. The function can first be written for positive values only; and once that is complete, expanded to cover mixed signs.

8.3d   Write two arithmetic statement functions to receive the radius of a circle and (1) return its circumference and (2) return its area. Embed it into a driver program used to test it.

8.3e Write an arithmetic statement function to generate the tangent of an angle as a function of the sine and cosine. There should be a preceding arithmetic statement function to convert from integer degrees to radians. (Pi (3.14159265) radians = 180 degrees.) The driver program should accept the angle in degrees, use the first function to convert it to radians and then the second to determine the tangent. Once that is working, modify it so that the second function accesses the first directly instead of having the driver access both.

8.3f Write a series of arithmetic statement functions to be used to generate the cotangent, the secant, and the cosecant, all as functions of the sine and cosine. Again, a driver program should surround them for purposes of testing.

8.3g Write two arithmetic statement functions, one to convert an angle in degrees and decimals of a degree to radians (D2R) and the other to convert radians to degrees and decimals of a degree (R2D). Both are to receive a real argument and return a real result. Incorporate both into a driver program for testing.

8.3h The sum of the digits from 1 to some integer N can be calculated from N (N + 1)/2. Write an arithmetic statement function to perform the calculation and use a driver program with a DO loop from N = 1 to N = 50.

8.3i Write an arithmetic statement function to calculate the area of a right triangle from its two sides. Embed it in a driver and test. Have the driver edit for valid (positive) data.

8.3j Refer to exercise 4.8l for the method of determining the area of any kind of triangle (including a right triangle) and write two arithmetic statement functions to implement it. One should determine the semiperimeter and the second the area. Embed in a driver program that tests for valid data (positive values, all less than the semiperimeter).

8.4 THE FUNCTION SUBPROGRAM

The function subprogram is a true, external subprogram which is compiled separately from the calling program. However, like the arithmetic statement function, it can return only one value. But it is not limited to only one assignment statement and can contain any kind of logic, including branching, looping, and I/O. The function subprogram is used primarily for computation, not for I/O, but there is no inherent restriction.

Actually, the function subprogram can return more than one answer by modifying one of its arguments. However, this is not the intent of the function and such argument modification should be done only with a subroutine (next section) to avoid confusion.

A function subprogram is an independent piece of code. Thus, the algorithm must be packaged with:

1. A header identifying the program as a function, specifying its name and its (dummy) argument list.
2. The necessary terminating statements: the last logical statement, RETURN; and the last physical statement, END. A subprogram may have a STOP in it, ending the run of the program, but it must contain at least one RETURN in order to compile correctly.

Presented below is an example of a simple function utilizing two dummy arguments.

```
C                    Function SALSTX:
C                    Applies sales tax to purchases greater than $1.00
C
      FUNCTION  SALSTX (AMT, RATE)
C
      IF  (AMT .LE. 1.00)  THEN
             SALSTX = 0.00
         ELSE
             SALSTX = ANINT (AMT * RATE * 100.00)  /  100.00
      ENDIF
C
      RETURN
      END
```

Accessing this function with a 5% sales tax gives:

```
TAX = SALSTX (TOTAL, 0.05)
```

and

```
BILL = TOTAL + SALSTX (TOTAL, 0.05) + TIP
```

This function is suitable for handling up to six digits of precision, but that may prove insufficient for many situations where the amount may go above $10,000. Thus it could be rewritten for a double-precision environment using DNINT:

```
C                    Function SALSTX:
C                    Applies sales tax to purchases greater than $1.00
C
      DOUBLE PRECISION FUNCTION  SALSTX (AMT, RATE)
      DOUBLE PRECISION AMT, RATE
C
      IF  (AMT .LE. 1.00)  THEN
             SALSTX = 0.00
         ELSE
             SALSTX = DNINT (AMT * RATE * 100.00)  /  100.00
      ENDIF
C
      RETURN
      END
```

The calling program must specify the function SALSTX as double-precision. The IMPLICIT DOUBLE PRECISION (O–Z) will *not* type a called function. Furthermore, any constants sent to the subprogram must also be double-precision. Thus, the calling program takes on a few modifications:

```
IMPLICIT DOUBLE PRECISION  (A-H, O-Z)
DOUBLE PRECISION  SALSTX
       |
TAX = SALSTX (TOTAL, 0.05D+00)
BILL = TOTAL + SALSTX (TOTAL, 0.05D+00) + TIP
```

Note the method by which the constant for 5% is defined as double-precision.

Although some disk-oriented systems allow the programmer to place subprograms in the same source file as the mainline, thus compiling them simultaneously and linking in easily, this is efficient when that routine is useful only with that application. It is a more general practice to store subprograms in their own source files and compile them separately. However, an additional step is now required to link them with the mainline: It is necessary during the linking operation to specify any user-written, external subprograms, otherwise the linker will be unable to find the routine.

Another alternative is the use of subprogram libraries. In this method, the machine language version of the subprogram is stored along with other subprograms in a named library. During the linking operation, the name or names of the desired libraries are given and the linker extracts from those libraries just those routines called by the system. Most production environments utilize this method in order to simplify the work of the programmers. However, since the development of these libraries is system-dependent, it will be your responsibility to research the methodology for your system.

As an example of how this might be useful, note the need to produce a monetary value rounded to the nearest cent. This code is so relevant to most commercial applications that it will appear quite often. Thus, a general-purpose routine could be generated and stored as an external function (preferably in a library) so that it may be linked into any program that needs it without having to look at the code again. Even though the algorithm requires only one statement, it is still useful to package it as a function subprogram so that its ability to be stored externally may be utilized.

```
C            Function RND2:  rounds a monetary value to two places
C
      FUNCTION  RND2  (AMOUNT)
      RND2 = ANINT (AMOUNT * 100.00)  /  100.00
      RETURN
      END
```

Of course, a double-precision version, probably called DRND2, should also be made available. It will be assumed that both versions are available and that they can be used later in this text when needed without further comment. In the above FUNCTION SALSTX, the assignment:

```
SALSTX = DNINT (AMT * RATE * 100.00)  /  100.00
```

becomes

```
SALSTX = DRND2 (AMT * RATE)
```

greatly simplifying the programmer's effort once the rounding routines are available.

It is advisable to provide some method of error handling within a subprogram whenever possible. For example, a function to generate a factorial ($n!$ = the product of the integers from 1 to that number = $1 * 2 * 3 * ... * n - 2 * n - 1 * n$) requires that the argument be a positive integer or zero; 0! is defined as 1. Thus a negative value does not make sense. One method of indicating an error is to output an error message to the screen, but it might not be noticed; even so, the function must return some answer. One could always branch to a STOP with an error message, but that prevents the caller from programming his or her own error-handling method. One method, which the author prefers, is to return an impossible value (such as a negative 1) which should seriously impair later calculations if the caller does not check for it. (Of course, any time a subprogram is accessed with a restricted range of values for any of the arguments, the calling program should verify the validity of those argument values before the access.) The routine might look like this:

```
        DOUBLE PRECISION FUNCTION  FACTL (N)
C
        IF  (N .GE. 0)  THEN
            FACTL = 1.00
            IF  (N .GT. 1)  THEN
                DO 20  I = 2,N
  20            FACTL = FACTL * DBLE (I)
            ENDIF
          ELSE
            FACTL = -1.00
        ENDIF
C
        RETURN
        END
```

Exercises

All of these exercises require a driver program for testing.

8.4a   Write an integer function subprogram to accept three arguments: the hour, the minute, and a character (either A or P) representing time in the range 12:00 to 11:59 A.M. and 12:00 to 11:59 P.M. and return the minutes from midnight.

8.4b   Write a function subprogram (DMS2R) to accept as arguments integer values for degrees and minutes and a real value for seconds, and to return the angle in radians.

8.4c   Write a function subprogram (SALARY) to accept as arguments real values for hours worked and hourly rate paid. Compute the salary as hours times rate for hours less than or equal to 40, plus hours times rate times 1.5 for hours more than 40 and less than 60, plus hours times rate times 2.0 for hours greater than 60. Return a 0 if either hours or rate (or both) is negative.

8.4d   Write a function subprogram to accept two integer numbers and return a 1 if both are positive, a −1 if both are negative, and a 0 if they are of different signs. Assume that 0 is positive. (With a little cleverness, this can be reduced to one statement, making it eligible for an arithmetic statement function.)

8.4e Write a function subprogram to accept two integer numbers and return a 0 if both are even, a 1 if both are odd, and a −1 if they are of different parity.

8.4f Write a function subprogram ISRITE to receive three sides of a triangle and test if it is a right triangle. Use the Pythagorean theorem and a relative tolerance (difference of computed hypotenuse and suspected third side divided by computed hypotenuse) of 0.00001. The function should return a 0, 1, 2, or 3, indicating whether it is not a right triangle (0) or which of the sides is the hypotenuse.

8.4g Revise the function in exercise 8.4f to a logical one, LSRITE, which returns either .TRUE. or .FALSE.

8.4h Write a function to return the Nth term of a Fibonacci series given the value N. If N is less than 1, return a 0.

8.4i Using the equation of projectile motion ($y = Vt - 16.1t^{**}2$), write a function, TIMPAC, to determine the time to the hundredth of a second nearest to the time of impact, using the initial velocity V as input to the function.

8.5 SUBROUTINES

The subroutine is quite different from the function in a number of ways. First, it can return more (or less) than one result. In order to do so, all information, both going to the subroutine and coming from it, is placed in the argument list. The name of the subroutine is for identification only; even though the name must follow the rules of FORTRAN variable names, the mode of the subroutine name has no significance. It is also considered proper for a subroutine to change the value of the arguments, if that is the intention of the routine.

Second, since the subroutine may return multiple answers, it cannot be placed in an assignment statement, as the function can. The subroutine is accessed with a CALL statement which specifies the subroutine name and the argument list. But, similar to the function, the arguments in both calling and called programs must agree in number, mode, and order.

In no way are input arguments (values sent to the subroutines) differentiated from output arguments (values returned from the subroutine) or updated arguments (values modified by the subroutine). The order in which they are placed in the argument list by the writer of the subroutine is purely a matter of style (or whim). Thus the caller of the subroutine must carefully understand what each argument stands for and what the subroutine will do with it or to it.

The packaging of the subroutine consists of:

1. A header identifying the program as a subroutine, specifying its name and the argument list
2. The necessary terminating statements, which must include at least one RETURN and an END

As an example, let us look at a subroutine that receives a unit cost, the number of units, the rate of profit, and the tax rate and returns the price, the tax, and a variable delivery charge (nothing if the price is $100.00 or more, 2% of price if the price is less than $100.00). Since the subroutine can return many results, an error indicator is added to the argument list and set to 0 if no input values are in error and to 1 if any of them are 0 or negative. If there are any errors, then the output values are set to 0 as an additional indication that something is wrong.

```
C                          Subroutine FIGURE:   prices items and computes tax
C
      SUBROUTINE  FIGURE  (UCOST, NUNITS, PRFRAT, TAXRAT, PRICE,
     1                        TAX, DLIVRY, INDERR)
C
C                Glossary
C                --------
C           UCOST:    unit cost                         input
C           NUNITS:   number of units                   input
C           PRFRAT:   profit rate (in decimal)          input
C           TAXRAT:   tax rate (in decimal)             input
C           PRICE:    price                             output
C           TAX:      computed tax                      output
C           DLIVRY:   delivery charge                   output
C                     if price < $100.00, delivery free
C                     if price >= $100.00, = 2% of price
C           INDERR:   error indicator                   output
C                     0 if no error, 1 if error
C
      IF  (UCOST .GT. 0.00  .AND.  NUNITS .GT. 0  .AND.
     1    PRFRAT .GT. 0.00  .AND.  TAXRAT .GT. 0.00)      THEN
           PRICE = RND2 (PRFRAT *  RND2 (UCOST * FLOAT(NUNITS)))
           TAX   = RND2 (TAXRAT * PRICE)
           IF  (PRICE .GE. 100.00)  THEN
                 DLIVRY = 0.00
              ELSE
                 DLIVRY = RND2 (0.02 * PRICE)
           ENDIF
           INDERR = 0
        ELSE
           PRICE  = 0.00
           TAX    = 0.00
           DLIVRY = 0.00
           INDERR = 1
      ENDIF
C
      RETURN
      END
```

Although the results could have been obtained by three functions, the subroutine is more efficient in this situation. The subroutine is accessed by a statement looking something like this:

```
CALL FIGURE (UC, NUMBER, 1.25, 0.075, SELLPR, TAX, DCHRGE, INDERR)
```

Note how the argument lists agree in number and mode and how the order of the arguments must correspond. Only the input values may be constants or expressions, otherwise our results will be incorrect.

Another good example of how handy a subroutine can be is the Automated Teller Machine problem in which a breakdown of the dollar amount is needed:

```
C           Subroutine BRKDWN:  breakdown dollars to $50, $20 & $10
C
      SUBROUTINE  BRKDWN (IDOLLR, N50, N20, N10)
C
      N50 = IDOLLR / 50
      N20 = MOD (IDOLLR, 50) / 20
      N10 = MOD (MOD (IDOLLR, 50)), 20) / 10
C
      RETURN
      END
```

Note the rather sophisticated usage of the MOD function in the calculation of N10; a less sophisticated method would be:

```
      N10 = (IDOLLR  -  50 * N50  -  20 * N20) / 10
```

The linking of subroutines with the mainline program is done in the same way as with functions. And, of course, subroutines can also be stored in libraries.

Exercises

All the subroutines below require a driver program to test.

8.5a Write an error-message subroutine, called ERRMSG, which displays different error messages based on a single input argument. Use the table below as a starting point and add to it any messages you think will be valuable.

Input	Message
1	Value out of range
2	Invalid input
3	Excess data
4	Insufficient data
<1 or >4	Undefined error

As an added touch, if the input value is negative, skip a line in the output both before and after the message. Thus, a 2 will display (or print) the message "Invalid input", but a −2 will surround the message with blank lines.

8.5b Write a subroutine, R2DMS, which receives an angle in radians and returns the angle in degrees, minutes, and seconds; the first two as integer, the last as real. The driver program should display the reals to at least two decimal places.

8.5c Write a subroutine, TIMBRK, which receives a real value for time in the form HR.MN and returns the hours and minutes as integers.

8.5d Write a subroutine, TIMDIF, which receives two times in hours, minutes, and an A.M./P.M. indicator (see exercise 8.4a) and returns the difference between the times in hours and minutes as integer. If the second time is less than or equal to the first time, assume that the second time occurs on the next day.

8.5e   Write a subroutine, EGGBRK, which receives an integer number of eggs and returns a breakdown in gross, dozen, and units. (1 gross = 144 units, 1 dozen = 12 units)

8.5f   Write a subroutine, EXAMIN, which receives two integers and returns two logical values, SAMSGN and SAMPAR, indicating whether they are of the same sign and of the same parity. Assume 0 is positive and even.

8.5g   Write a subroutine, MILAGE, which receives the beginning mileage, the current mileage, the amount of gas put in the car, and the price per gallon. The subroutine should return the miles per gallon and the cost per mile.

8.5h   Write a subroutine, ANGLES, which receives the three sides of any kind of triangle and returns the three angles in degrees and decimals of a degree. This routine requires the law of cosines and the intrinsic function ACOS.

8.5i   Write a subroutine, SWAP (X,Y), to exchange the values in the two given reals.

8.5j   Write two subroutines, BIGGER (X,Y) and SMALER (X,Y), to place the given values in the desired order; i.e., BIGGER puts the larger value first (in X), SMALER puts the smaller value in X. (The code in subroutine SWAP in exercise 8.5i would be handy to use.)

8.5k   Revise subroutine SWAP (X,Y,IND) to use an indicator to transmit the desired order of the values. If IND = −1, the smaller one would be first; if IND = 1, the larger would be first; if IND = 0, they would be swapped regardless of values.

8.6   GENERATING RANDOM DATA

The generation of test data can be a very boring task, particularly when a large amount of it is needed. In addition, there is the psychological problem that when a programmer selects data to test a program, he or she will pick data similar to that for which the program was written. However, the correct testing of a program involves all kinds of data, valid and invalid, but especially those values which the programmer may have inadvertently ignored.

In a professional environment, the designer of test data should not be the program's author but another person whose desire is to make the program fail by presenting all varieties of possible data. Unfortunately, we cannot always afford to hire another person just to test our programs; and besides, we should do much of the testing ourselves.

One way of generating unbiased data is to use a random number generator. Of course, on a computer there is no such thing as randomness, but the algorithms used will give us a sufficient range for testing purposes. Unfortunately, a random number generator is not part of the FORTRAN language (unlike BASIC, where it is an intrinsic function). However, many manufacturers supply one as a utility program. A good random number generator makes use of the hardware facilities and thus is system-oriented. Wherever possible, the programmer should use the one supplied with his or her compiler.

A random number generator produces a series of real values between 0.0 and just less than 1.0. Each value depends on the previous value, so the series is always the same. However, since so many numbers can be generated before the series repeats (usually more than 30,000), it is possible to start at different points in the series by using a seed. The seed starts the series with a certain value and then continues from there. By supplying the same seed each time, the user will get the same series of values, a very useful property during the testing phase. By changing the seed, the user can get multiple series of values, which is very useful for random testing. The best seeds are large, positive, odd integers.

In some cases, the seed is generated by using the system time so that it changes from second to second. However, this requires a nonstandard, system-supplied routine for accessing the clock. The general procedure for the user of the function is to send it a seed and then to derive the values (like RANDOMIZE and RND in BASIC).

Following is a random number generator derived by the author from the one supplied with the Microsoft FORTRAN compiler.

```
C                       Function RND:  random number generator
C
        FUNCTION  RND (ISEED)
C
C         if ISEED = 0, return random number
C         if ISEED > 0, seed with that number
C         if ISEED < 0, seed with absolute value of that number
C
        PARAMETER  (IA=7141, IC=54773, IM=259200)
C
C                     if desired, seed generator
        IF  (ISEED .NE. 0)  SEED = IABS (ISEED)
C                     get random number
        SEED  =  MOD (INT (SEED) * IA + IC, IM)
        RND   =  SEED / REAL (IM)
C                     return
        RETURN
        END
```

If the generator is not seeded, the results are system-dependent and indeterminate.

Since the generated number is between 0.0 and just less than 1.0, it can be multiplied by an appropriate constant, adjusted for the desired range, and converted to integer. For example, if it is desired to generate random temperatures between -20 and $+100$ degrees, the range of temperatures is 121 and the base is -20. Thus, a random temperature could be obtained as:

```
    ITEMPR = INT (121.0 * RND(0))  -  20
```

Below is a sample program that generates 31 random temperatures from a user-supplied seed:

```
C                   generate a month's worth of random temperatures
C
      DUMMY = RND (12345)
      DO 20  I = 1,31
          ITEMPR = INT (121.0 * RND(0)) - 20
   20 PRINT *, I, ITEMPR
      STOP
      END
```

Note that the first access to the function RND does produce a valid random number; but rather than have a value generated outside the loop, the author prefers to treat the first value as an unused dummy number. The program could be modified to allow the user to input the seed as a variable to get different series. A more useful exercise (see exercise 8.6a below) would be to allow the user to enter the limits of the temperature to be generated as variables.

Another useful extension of the random number generator is the generation of normally distributed values; i.e., numbers which are not spread out evenly but follow a normal curve, like heights, weights, examination grades, etc. If we take a series of averages of 12 consecutive random numbers, the numbers are normally distributed. A program to do this is easy enough to write, and can even be enhanced so that the user might enter the mean of the data and the standard deviation (the spread of the curve). As a guideline, almost all of the values generated (99.7%) fall within 3 standard deviations of the mean. So if we wish to generate normally distributed examination grades, a mean of 76 and a standard deviation of 8 will usually place all grades within the range of 76 plus or minus 3 * 8, or 52 to 100. Very few grades will appear at the extremes, although that must be checked; the bulk (68.3%) fall within 1 standard deviation, and 95.4% fall within 2 standard deviations.

The easiest algorithm to use states that a normally distributed random number is equal to the standard deviation times the average of 12 random numbers plus the mean. Since random numbers naturally average about 0.50, the average can be calculated as the sum minus 6.0. A typical equation would be:

```
XNRMAL = STDEV * (SUM - 6.0)  +  XMEAN
```

SUM can be generated in a DO loop. (See exercise 8.6b.)

Exercises

8.6a   Write a general-purpose function, INTRAN, which receives the lower and upper limits (integer) of the random number to be generated. This function should access the random number generator and adjust the random number so that it falls within the appropriate range before returning the value to the driver program. Generate 14 values of Fahrenheit temperature within the range of 50 and 90 degrees. The driver program should seed the random number generator before looping through your new function. Thus the random number generator is accessed both from the driver and from your function. The driver should also display the average, minimum, and maximum temperatures.

8.6b   Write a general-purpose function, RANRML (XMEAN, STDEV), to generate normally distributed numbers according to the algorithm discussed above. Access that function with an average temperature of 70 degrees and a standard deviation of 12 degrees. Convert the temperatures to the nearest integer value. The driver should again display the average, minimum, and maximum temperatures for comparison with the results of the above exercise.

8.6c   Write a program to generate 20 normally distributed bowling scores, with a mean of 170.5 and a standard deviation of 40.5. Change any scores greater than 300 to 300 and any scores less than 0 to 0. (Although it is extremely unlikely that such out-of-range scores would appear, the possibility still exists.)

8.6d Write a program to generate 100 records of random test data to be written to a disk file in the specified format:

Columns	Data	Range
1– 2	Month	1–12
4– 5	Day of month	1–30
7–10	Year	1988–1992
11–12	Hour	1–12
14–15	Minute	0–59
17	A or P	1–2
21–30	Amount	1.00–1000.00

8.6e Write a program to generate 1000 random coordinates in the x and y ranges from −1.00 to +1.00. Count the number that fall in each of the four quadrants, generating a new number if a coordinate of 0.00 appears. Compute the deviation of the total numbers in each quadrant; i.e., the percentage of the difference in what *does* fall into each quadrant and the number that *should* fall in each quadrant (1000/4) divided by the number that should fall, converted to percentage. Output the quadrant number, the number of points that fell into the quadrant, and the deviation.

8.6f The probability of rolling a particular value (from 1 to 6) on a single die of a pair of dice is one out of 6 (0.1667). The probability of rolling a particular pair (such as 1 and 1) is 1 out of 6 squared (0.0278). The probability of rolling any value (2 to 12) with a pair of dice is the sum of the probability of rolling the various combinations which can make up that value. For example, a 4 is possible with 1 and 3, 2 and 2, and 3 and 1. Thus, the probability of rolling a 4 is 3 times 1 out of 6 squared (0.0833). The following table provides a list of the various probabilities:

Value(s)	Probability
2, 12	0.0278
3, 11	0.0556
4, 10	0.0833
5, 9	0.1111
6, 8	0.1389
7	0.1667

Write a program which accepts as input one of the possible numbers resulting from a single roll of a pair of dice (2 to 12) and the number of rolls. Test the program with some of the numbers and with various number of rolls to see how close your random number distributor comes to the correct probability. Your computed probability should approach the theoretical as the number of rolls increases.

8.7 PROGRAMMING SYSTEMS

With our background in subprograms, we can start to make some serious inroads into the application programs that are the leitmotif of this text. In this chapter, the modification of the Automated Teller Machine program will be used to illustrate the technique of modulating a program into a programming system consisting of a mainline and a series of subprograms.

In Chapter 4, section 4.7, we presented a rather interesting way of calculating the fee for this application, using intrinsic functions instead of the more usual IF.. THEN.. ELSE logic:

```
C                    compute fee
      FEE = NINT (RATE * REAL (WITHRN))
      FEE = MAXO (FEE, 2)
```

The fee was rounded to the nearest dollar and the fee structure was very simple. Writing it as a function with the logic now available seems to be more work, but it provides us with an easily modified subprogram that might also be useful in other programming systems. Furthermore, now that formatted output is available, the fee will be computed as a real number. No rounding is necessary, because 2% of the $10 increment is $0.20. It could be coded as:

```
      FUNCTION  CALCFE  (IAMT)
C
C        Abstract:  calculates a fee to be applied to the account
C
C        Input:    IAMT        amount of money dispensed (integer)
C
C        Output:  CALCFE       real fee charged according to:
C                              if IAMT <  $100, fee = $2.00
C                              if IAMT >= $100, fee = 2% of IAMT
C
      IF  (IAMT .LT. 100)  THEN
            CALCFE = 2.00
         ELSE
            CALCFE = REAL (IAMT) * 0.02
      ENDIF
C
      RETURN
      END
```

Although the coding looks more elaborate than that presented earlier, the actual number of steps executed is about the same because the intrinsic functions do contain decision-making logic. The accessing statement in the calling program becomes:

```
C                    compute fee
      FEE = CALCFE (WITHRN)
```

The mainline is also revised so that it agrees more closely with the specifications in Appendix A, which limit the breakdown to $50, $20, and $10. The programming system utilizes a subroutine specific to that breakdown:

```
      SUBROUTINE  BRKDWN  (IAMT, N50, N20, N10)
C
C        Abstract:  reduces a dollar amount (multiple of $10) to
C                   appropriate number of $50, $20 and $10 bills.
C
C        Input:    IAMT        amount, a multiple of $10
C
C        Output:   N50         number of $50 bills dispensed
C                  N20           "    "  $20   "       "
C                  N10           "    "  $10   "       "
```

```
C
      N50 = IAMT / 50
      N20 = MOD (IAMT, 50) / 20
      N10 = MOD (MOD (IAMT, 50), 20) / 10
C
      RETURN
      END
```

The accessing statement becomes:

```
C                         calculate breakdown
      CALL BRKDWN (WITHRN, N50, N20, N10)
```

A further enhancement to the program is the generation of an output file to keep track of the transactions and from which a report can be written.

 **Automated Teller Machine**

```
C                         Automated Teller Machine
C
      PARAMETER (RATE = 0.020,  LIMIT = 400.00)
      INTEGER   WITHDR, WITHRN, TOTWTH
      REAL      FEE,    TOTAL
      CHARACTER RESPNS
C                  initialize total withdrawal, I/O units
      DATA  TOTWTH/ 0/,  LIN,LOUT/ 5,6/
C
C                         open output file
      OPEN (4, FILE='TRANS.DAT')
C                         loop through input
      DO 60  I = 1,20000
C                         enter amount of withdrawal
            WRITE    (LOUT,1000)
1000        FORMAT   ('0', 'Enter amount of withdrawal (integer)')
            READ     (LIN,*, ERR= 40, END=90)  WITHDR
C                         check for positive value
        IF (WITHDR .LE. 0.00)   WRITE   (LOUT,1002)
1002         FORMAT  (' ','DESIRED WITHDRAWAL INSUFFICIENT')
C                         check for value within limit
        IF (WITHDR .GT. LIMIT)   WRITE   (LOUT,1004)
1004         FORMAT  (' ', 'DESIRED WITHDRAWAL GREATER THAN LIMIT')
C                  valid input: convert to $10 denomination
        IF (WITHDR .GT. 0.00 .AND.  WITHDR .LE. LIMIT)  THEN
            WITHRN = (WITHDR + 9) / 10 * 10
C                         verification
            WRITE    (LOUT,1006)  WITHRN
1006        FORMAT   (' ','Withdrawal = $',I3,
     1                            ', Do you approve (Y/N)?')
            READ     (LIN, 1008, END=60)  RESPNS
1008        FORMAT   (A1)
            IF  (RESPNS .EQ. 'Y' .OR.  RESPNS .EQ. 'y')  THEN
C                         calculate breakdown
                CALL BRKDWN (WITHRN, N50, N20, N10)
C                         compute fee
            FEE   = CALCFE (WITHRN)
            TOTAL = WITHRN + FEE
```

```
C                               display output
                WRITE    (LOUT,1014)  N50, N20, N10, FEE, TOTAL
    1014        FORMAT (' ','       $50     $20     $10      Fee  Total'/
        1                ' ',        3I7,                    2F7.2)
C                               add to total
                TOTWTH = TOTWTH + WITHRN
C                        write to file
                WRITE    (4,1016)  WITHRN, N50, N20, N10, FEE
    1016        FORMAT              (4I5,                    F7.2)
              ENDIF
          ENDIF
          GO TO 60
C                        error in input
      40    WRITE    (LOUT,1040)
    1040    FORMAT (' ', 'Invalid character in input  -  Re-enter')
C                        loop back for more input
      60 CONTINUE
        STOP  'excessive transactions'
C                        termination
      90 WRITE    (LOUT,1090)  TOTWTH
    1090 FORMAT  ('0', 'Total withdrawn = $', I8)
        CLOSE   (4)
        STOP  'end of run'
        END
```

The output disk file TRANS.DAT looks like this:

```
                           111111111122222222
          columns   12345678901234567890123456
                        100     2     0    0   2.00
                        310     6     0    1   6.20
                        400     8     0    0   8.00
                        160     3     0    1   3.20
                         80     1     1    1   2.00
                        240     4     2    0   4.80
```

A program to read this file and produce a report of the transactions may be coded as:

```
C                       Transaction Report
C
        REAL      AMOUNT, FEE,         TOTAMT, TOTFEE
        INTEGER*2 N50,    N20,  N10,  TOT50,  TOT20,  TOT10
C
        DATA      TOTAMT, TOTFEE, TOT50, TOT20, TOT10/
      1           2 * 0.00,      3 * 0/
C
C                       open input and output files; write title, headings
        OPEN    (3, FILE='TRANS.DAT')
        OPEN    (4, FILE='TRANS.OUT')
        WRITE   (4, 1000)
    1000 FORMAT  ('1', '        TRANSACTION       REGISTER'/
      1          '0', ' Amount    $50  $20  $10      Fee'/ 1X)
C                       loop through data and process
        DO 40  I = 1,20000
            READ    (3,1002, END=60) AMOUNT, N50, N20, N10, FEE
    1002    FORMAT              (F5.0,   3I5,              F7.2)
```

```
C                                       add to totals
                TOTAMT = TOTAMT + AMOUNT
                TOT50  = TOT50  + N50
                TOT20  = TOT20  + N20
                TOT10  = TOT10  + N10
                TOTFEE = TOTFEE + FEE
C                                       output detail record
     40 WRITE    (4, 1040)  AMOUNT, N50, N20, N10, FEE
   1040 FORMAT         (' ', F8.2,    2X, 3I5,        F8.2)
C                               calculate grand total and output totals
     60 GRTOT = TOTAMT + TOTFEE
        WRITE    (4,1060)  TOTAMT, TOT50, TOT20, TOT10, TOTFEE, GRTOT
   1060 FORMAT         ('0', F8.2,    2X, 3I5,            F8.2, 4X, 'Totals'/
      1                 '0',' Total amount and fees =',        F9.2)
C                               termination
        CLOSE (3)
        CLOSE (4)
        STOP
        END
```

Printer file TRANS.OUT will produce the following output:

```
       TRANSACTION       REGISTER

   Amount      $50  $20  $10      Fee

    100.00       2    0    0     2.00
    310.00       6    0    1     6.20
    400.00       8    0    0     8.00
    160.00       3    0    1     3.20
     80.00       1    1    1     2.00
    240.00       4    2    0     4.80

   1290.00      24    3    3    26.20    Totals

  Total amount and fees =   1316.20
```

The solution provided above meets all the program specifications in Appendix A and might be considered a complete solution. And so it is. But there are ways to further simplify and generalize the programs involved; they will be demonstrated in future chapters.

8.8 CHAPTER REVIEW

This chapter has presented one of the most powerful of the tools available in the FORTRAN repertoire, the subprogram which can be external to the programming system and yet linkable into it as needed. It allows the development of a library of commonly used routines, which are now accessible not only to the individual programmer who wrote them but also to others who wish to use them. Thus, subprograms are considered the most labor-saving device in programming.

Another advantage of breaking a mainline into subprograms is that it simplifies the program maintenance task. A change in the fee structure in the system shown in the previous section, for example, only requires a modification of that subprogram, a compilation of it only, and a new link into the mainline. No modifications to the mainline and the other subprograms are necessary, nor are compilations of them required. However, the programmer must remember that whenever a module is modified, that module *must* be recompiled and the system linked with the mainline. If that subprogram services a number of mainlines, each of them must be linked again.

This ability to link to external subprograms is responsible for the long life of FORTRAN. The use of the language has been extended by the tremendous number of libraries available for it to be linked to. Among those to be found are libraries of scientific, statistical, financial, plotting, and graphical display subprograms, as well as subprograms to communicate with many diverse I/O devices. These libraries can be purchased, although many of the algorithms are in the public domain and may be copied legally from the publications in which they appear.

You are now prepared to write general-purpose subprograms and to start developing a library of them. These subprograms should be accompanied by a testing driver. Furthermore, the subprogram should contain complete documentation of its name, arguments, calculations done, and limitations. The documentation should be so written that it can be abstracted from the program, since the user of a subprogram is not interested in how it works, only what must be given to it and what is returned. A subprogram is sometimes referred to as a "black box," since information goes in one side and new information comes out the other. No one cares what happens inside, as long as it happens correctly!

You are also prepared to write complete programming systems. At this point it would be wise to start thinking in terms of programming teams so that the work may be shared. The team would analyze the system, dividing it up into programming modules. Each module would be defined in terms of input and output. Then the individuals would work on their particular module, test it with drivers, and package it for eventual linkage into the system. If each module has been thoroughly debugged, there is no reason why the system won't work as a unit.

The topics covered in this chapter include:

Topic	Section
Argument list	8.3
Arithmetic statement function	8.2, 8.3
CALL	8.2, 8.5
Error handling	8.4, 8.5
Function subprogram	8.2, 8.4
Intrinsic function	8.2
Linking	8.1, 8.2
Programming systems	8.7
Random data	8.6
RETURN	8.2, 8.4, 8.5
Subroutine	8.2, 8.5

Exercises

The exercises that follow are relatively large compared with those presented earlier, and there is more precise definition of file structure and argument lists. The programming systems from this chapter will be enhanced and revised in later chapters. Also, you may wish to use a team approach to work through these exercises, since sharing the programming effort will more closely approximate a real-world problem-solving environment than working alone.

Where practical, each subprogram should be fully tested with its own driver before being incorporated into the programming system.

8.8a *Baseball Statistics*
Input file structure:

Columns 1–10: player's name		alpha
Columns 13–15: number of at-bats	(AB)	integer *
Columns 18–20: number of singles	(1B)	integer
Columns 23–25: number of doubles	(2B)	integer
Columns 28–30: number of triples	(3B)	integer
Columns 33–35: number of home runs	(HR)	integer
Columns 38–40: number of bases on balls	(BB)	integer *
Columns 43–45: number of strikeouts	(SO)	integer
Columns 48–50: number of runs batted in	(RBI)	integer *

*number of at-bats does not include bases on balls, only hits and outs.

Sample input file records:

```
SMITH      300  70  18  4  10  23  42  65
RONZAC     275  47  10  7  16  27  52  54
MORELLI    312  86  17  2   9  14  35  43
REILLY     243  45   8  2  21  30  42  72
```

The mainline program will:

1. Initialize the totals to zero with a DATA statement. This includes totals for all eight numeric items in the input file.
2. Open the output file and print titles and headings for all of the input data and for the values calculated in step 5, below.
3. Set up an input loop to read the file and process the data (steps 4 and 5).
4. Call a subroutine to add the input data to the totals.
5. Call a subroutine to calculate a number of averages and output them with the input data.
6. Skip a line and call the subroutine to calculate and output the team total results.

The required subprograms are:

Subroutine ADDUP: Adds the eight record values to the eight totals. The argument list *does* contain 16 entries.

Function TOTBAS: Computes the total bases as a result of hits = 1B + 2 * 2B + 3 * 3B + 4 * 4B.

Subroutine BBSTAT: Performs each of the following:

1. Computes the batting average (BATAV) as the sum of the four hit categories (1B, 2B, 3B, HR) divided by the at-bats (AB).
2. Computes the slugging average (SLGAV) as the weighted sum of the four hit categories (1B + 2 * 2B + 3 * 3B + 4 * HR) divided by

the at-bats (AB). The function TOTBAS should be called from here, not from the mainline.

3. Computes the on-base average (ONBAV) as the sum of the four hit categories plus the bases on balls (BB) divided by the sum of the at-bats (AB) and bases on balls (BB).

4. Computes the strikeout average (STRAV) as the number of strikeouts (SO) divided by the sum of the at-bats (AB) and bases on balls (BB).

5. Computes the average (RBIAV) number of runs batted in (RBI) per time at bat (AB) and bases on balls (BB).

6. Outputs an echo check of the input data and the computed values. Skip a line between players and two lines before the team totals.

Most sport averages are actually percentages. Thus, 3 hits in 10 times at bat represents a 30% chance of a hit. The calculation is 3/10 = 0.300; it is traditional to ignore the decimal point and call it a "300 average." In the program above, multiply by 1000 and round to the nearest integer value, but leave the answer as real. During output, specify no decimal places (Fn.0); the decimal point will appear, but there will be no digits to its right.

8.8b   *Accounts Receivable*

An accounts receivable (AR) file contains the following fields:

        Columns   1– 4: invoice number
        Columns   7–10: date of transaction: digits 1–2: month
                                             digits 3–4: year
        Columns 11–20: amount of sale

A sample input file might include:

```
1001    1089    2514.87
1002    1089     876.54
1003    1089    8765.00
1004    1189    5500.00
1005    1189      25.65
1006    0190    4500.75
1007    0190     540.50
1008    0190    1200.00
1009    0290     875.00
10010   0290    3560.98
```

Write a function, MONTH, to determine from the date the number of months since some datum month (say, December 1987) so that aging of the accounts can be done. The function should receive the single four-digit integer number in the form shown above and return the number of months.

Write a function, MONAGE, which accepts an input value of current month and year (in the same format as the date in the input file) and the date of the invoice and determines how many months apart the two dates are. The current month must be the same as or later than the last invoice date being processed. MONAGE should call MONTH as part of its computation. The returned value is used to provide an aging into four categories; it should be in the range 0 to 3:

        0–30 days (0 month)
       30–60 days (1 month)
       60–90 days (2 months)
         >90 days (more than 2 months)

Write subroutine ADDCHG to receive the amount and the aging category and return the discount and the surcharge, as follows:

Aging Category	Discount	Surcharge
0–30 days	2% of amount	0.00
30–60 days	0.00	0.00
60–90 days	0.00	5% of amount
>90 days	0.00	$100 + 8% of amount

The mainline should:

1. Request the current date to be entered from the keyboard. That date must be the same as or later than the last date in the input file.
2. Set totals for amount owed and four aging categories to zero.
3. Output a title and headings for the input data, the aging category, the discount, the surcharge, and those values applied to the amount ("Amount Owed").
4. Set up an input loop to read and process the data (steps 5–8).
5. Call function MONAGE to get the aging category of the entry.
6. Call subroutine ADDCHG to determine the discount or surcharge.
7. Apply the discount (subtracting) or the surcharge (adding) to the amount to compute the amount owed.
8. Add the appropriate values to the totals.
9. At the end of the input, output the totals, annotating the total line clearly.

8.8c *Coordinate Geometry*

This exercise will develop a partial-coordinate geometry system that will allow the user to enter a beginning north and south pair of coordinates, then a series of distances and compass bearings. The output will show running coordinates and total distance after each course, as well as the distance and bearing back to the original position. A program like this is useful in navigating and in surveying property lines. It requires a supporting system of five general-purpose subprograms and one specific subprogram.

Function ARCTAN: The arctangent routines (ATAN and ATAN2) supplied by FORTRAN are somewhat limited in that they do not work well with angles approaching plus or minus 90 degrees (where the tangent becomes infinite) and, although it returns either a positive or negative value for the angle, further code is needed to see which quadrant the angle is in. Write a function, ARCTAN, with the same arguments as ATAN2, which returns an azimuth, the angle measured clockwise from the north (or y) axis, in radians. The function can be made more precise and less error-prone by examining the values of the input arguments, divided appropriately so that the tangent is 1 or less, and adjusting the angle returned to produce the correct azimuth.

Subroutine AZBE: Accepts the value of an azimuth in radians and converts the angle to a bearing in degrees, minutes, and truncated seconds (3.14159265 radians = 180 degrees). A bearing is the acute angle measured from the *N-S* axis, with directions given by referring to the compass directions. The table below indicates some of the conversions:

Azimuth		Bearing
0.00	(due north)	N 00 00 00 E
0.5236 = 30 degrees		N 30 00 00 E
1.5708 = 90 degrees	(due east)	N 90 00 00 E
2.0954 = 120 degrees		S 60 00 00 E
3.1416 = 180 degrees	(due south)	S 00 00 00 E
3.9270 = 225 degrees		S 45 00 00 W
4.7124 = 270 degrees	(due west)	N 90 00 00 W
6.1087 = 350 degrees		N 10 00 00 W

The routine will have to return three integer numbers and two alphabetic characters.

Function BEAZ: Accepts the bearing, expressed as an alphabetic character (N or S), integer degrees, minutes, and seconds; and a second alphabetic character (E or W), and converts the angle to an azimuth in radians. The routine must edit the input arguments for proper characters and ranges, returning a distinctly wrong value (like a negative azimuth) to warn the calling program that a data error has occurred.

Subroutine LOCAPT: Accepts the coordinates of a point and the distance and azimuth to a new point and returns the coordinates of the new point.

Subroutine INVRSE: Accepts the coordinates of two points and returns the distance and azimuth from the first to the second.

Subroutine EDIT: Edits the input data for proper range and displays appropriate error messages. Also returns an error indicator so that the calling program is warned that the data is incorrect. Among the input items to be checked are:

a. Distance for greater than zero.
b. Bearings for proper alphabetic direction codes
c. Bearings for degrees, seconds, and minutes in the proper range: 0–90, 0–59, and 0–59, respectively.

MAINLINE:

1. Inputs a starting set of north and east coordinates.
2. Initializes total distance to zero.
3. Prints and displays headings as required for full output of data both to screen and disk file.
4. Sets up input loop to process data (steps 5 and 6).
5. Input data includes distance traveled and bearing for each course.
6. Calculate and output coordinates of new point and total distance traveled at end of each course, as well as distance and bearing to return to original position.
7. At end of data, terminate with count of number of courses traveled and average distance per course.

8.8d *Pyramid Construction*
Exercise 6.7d involves the various calculations required for building a pyramid. Convert to a programming system containing:

1. A mainline
2. SUBROUTINE COSTS to return the costs of materials and cutting
3. FUNCTION GLUCST to return the cementing costs
4. FUNCTION PLCTOT to return the cost of placing the materials
5. SUBROUTINE FEE to display when minimum fee is reached

8.8e *Delivery Service*
A delivery company bases its charges on the weight of the item to be shipped and the distance to be shipped, based on the zip codes of the locations shipped from and to. The first digit of the zip code is used to give approximate location in the United States. (Zip codes start at 0*nnnn* in the New England states and increase to 3*nnnn* for the southeastern states. They continue to increase going westward, looping first north and then south across the country, with the West Coast having codes of 9*nnnn*. The zip code has now become a nine-digit number, the additional four digits added at the end to locate the destination more precisely. Digits after the first one are used to locate into smaller geographic areas.)

Write a general-purpose function, IEXTDG, to extract a single digit from a long integer. The arguments to the function are the value itself and the digit to be extracted, numbered leftward from 1 to 9, starting at the right. Test thoroughly with a driver.

Write a general-purpose integer function, HNDRWT (hundredweight), to round an integer weight up to the next 100 pounds. For example, weights of 1 to 100 are rounded to 100 pounds; weights of 101 to 200, to 200 pounds; etc.

Write a function, DELCHG, to determine the delivery charge which combines a distance fee and a pickup fee, plus a large-weight discount. The distance fee is based on the difference in the first digits of the shipping and destination zip code locations:

Difference	Fee per Actual Pound
0	$2.00
1	$3.00
2–4	$4.00
5–9	$4.50

Weight	Discount
>100 pounds	2% applied to distance fee, rounded
>200 pounds	5% applied to distance fee, rounded

The weight used is actual, not rounded to hundredweight.

The pickup fee is based upon the weight:

Weight	Fee
up to 10 pounds	$ 2.50 based on actual weight
up to 30 pounds	$ 4.00 based on actual weight
>30 pounds	$10.00 per hundredweight, based on rounded value.

The mainline program should set up an input loop to read the data from the keyboard. The input consists of two five-digit zip codes and the weight of the package. The output should include the computed full delivery charge.

9

One-Dimensional Arrays

CHAPTER OUTLINE

CHAPTER OBJECTIVES

- To present an additional method of data handling that provides for: (1) more structured programming, (2) handling of large blocks of data of varied amounts, and (3) easier coding.

- To demonstrate the technique for manipulating arrays in subprograms.

- To present a number of professionally oriented techniques for data processing.

STATEMENT OF THE PROBLEM

With what we already know, we can write a program that would input students' examination scores and analyze them for average, maximum, and minimum. Such a program would be considered a very minor programming effort, since it is easily written, yet it can provide a significant analysis of the data with very little code. In addition, the program could handle an unlimited amount of data and could also distribute the scores (i.e., count the number in the ranges 90–100, 80–89, 70–79, 65–69, and below 65, and then tabulate the frequency).

However, there is much this program cannot do. What if the passing score was not fixed at 65 but at 15 points below the average grade? Or what if the scores were graded on a curve, with the top 10% getting an *A*, the next 35% a *B*, the next lower 35% a *C*, the next lower 10% a *D*, and the lowest 10% an *F*? Without getting too involved in the pros and cons of using a variable grading scheme, we can say that there are almost as many schemes as there are professors to implement them. But any variable scheme requires a method whereby the data may be reexamined *after* certain parameters, such as the average, have been determined.

The examples above use a scheme wherein each piece of data is input, manipulated, and output before the next piece of data is input; and that next data value erases the preceding value. But if each new piece of data destroys its predecessor, how can we look at that data again?

One approach that might seem valid at first glance would be to use a separate variable for each piece of data, but this would work only if the program was written for a known amount of data. Then, if we should want to run more data or less data, we would have to modify the program—a very inefficient approach to a general-purpose program! There is another alternative: rereading the data, either by entering it again manually (a ridiculous method) or *rewinding* our disk file (moving the file pointer back to the beginning of the file) and repeating the input code. This option has some merit in certain circumstances, but it is very slow.

Fortunately for the programmer, there is another construct available in FORTRAN which is not only much more sophisticated, it is also faster and, more importantly, leads to far superior code—superior in that it is more rigidly structured and easier to write, debug, and understand. This method involves the handling of blocks of data that are all resident in memory simultaneously and opens up new horizons of programming applications. Since it is found in almost every programming language, its importance cannot be overstressed. In this chapter and the next two, we devote a great deal of time and effort to developing the construct in complete detail.

This technique enables the programmer to handle an extremely large amount of data without inputting and outputting all the individual values every time information is needed. Imagine a situation in which we analyze temperature data for a year by inputting up to 366 numbers, representing the mean temperature for each day. A program to accept 365 or 366 manually input values would probably never run correctly because of the very great chance that at least one entered value would be incorrect, thus negating the whole effort. The usual method is to prepare the data in advance by placing it in a disk file and writing a program to read from the file. Each line of data in the input file is called a *record*.

Likewise, our results should also be sent to a disk file or a printer so that they may be viewed other than as a fleeting image on the screen. This final output should contain not only the answers but also a listing of the input so that the user can see the complete problem—input and output—at one time without having to look at two different files. The listing of the input data is called an *echo check*, since it "echoes" what comes into the machine. Not only does this echo check provide the human user with a listing of the input, it also tells the user what values the machine is working with, enabling him or her to easily correct input errors. Furthermore, the output should not only be self-contained, it also should be properly annotated so that the reader is not confused by a myriad of numbers. In this way, the user can understand what each value represents. The input file, on the other hand, is usually just a collection of numbers without annotation, arranged in a convenient format for input.

This chapter will cover the basic methods of block I/O and will also look at many variations so that the reader can see the tools that provide flexible and artistic output. Keep in mind that the purpose of developing a report is to convey information; and for good communication, the information must be provided in a clear and concise fashion to prevent confusion on the part of the reader. The purpose of mentioning "artistic" output here is to emphasize the importance of good forms design as an aid in communication. Often, the professional programmer spends more time on the design of the output than on the calculations; after all, the calculations are a matter of fact, but the artwork is a matter of individual style. Unfortunately, the style of the programmer and that of the user may differ widely, and it is not unusual for the output form to go through many revisions. Little does the nonprogrammer realize how much programming effort goes into this seemingly simple task!

9.1   CONCEPT OF THE ARRAY

An *array* is a block (or matrix) of data addressable by a single variable name. To differentiate among the members of the array, called the array elements, a numeric subscript is used to indicate the location of each element. Just as we might refer to the first house on a block or the third seat in a row, we talk about the first element, the second element, etc. An array stores the data "permanently" (i.e., as long as the program is running) so that the program has access to all of it from any place in the code.

Any type of variable—integer, real, character, or logical—can be defined as an array. Thus, blocks of any kind of information may be accessed easily. The usual rules regarding variable naming and mode defaults hold with array variable names. Arrays can be one-dimensional (a row or column or *vector* of values), two-dimensional (a table or *matrix* of values), three-dimensional (multiple tables of values), or four-dimensional (volumes of multiple tables of values). The ANSI specifications allow up to seven dimensions, although it would be difficult to find a physical analogy to picture anything beyond three. (Some compilers allow even more than seven dimensions.) We will limit the treatment in this chapter to one dimension and delay the discussion of multidimensioned arrays until Chapter 10.

Although the element locator is called a subscript, the lack of a subscripting mechanism on keyboard devices and most printers has caused the inventors of computer languages to adopt another symbol. The earlier languages, such as FORTRAN, COBOL, RPG, and BASIC, use parentheses to surround the subscript, which is written on the same line. Some of the later languages, such as Pascal, C, and Modula-2, use square brackets for the same purpose. Here, of course, the FORTRAN convention, a pair of parentheses, is used.

Subscripts are integer values defined as constants, variables, or integer expressions. The following are examples of acceptable array elements:

```
BLOCK(7)        NN(I)        X(81-5*K+L)
```

Because of the "permanent" storage of arrays, it is possible to restructure a program in an entirely different way. Rather than the approach mentioned above, in which we take care of one piece of data at a time, a program can be written to input *all* of the data first, then manipulate *all* of the data in the next section of the program, and finally to output *all* of the data at one time. Thus the program has three distinct modules, each separate from the other in terms of branches and loops but sharing common data. This segmentation of logic results in highly structured code.

There is, however, one drawback: The size of the array is bound by the size of the available memory, and thus the amount of data may be limited. In these days of large memories, even on microcomputers, only extremely large data samples will cause a problem. For the moment, then, we will ignore this restriction, assuming that the kinds of problems being solved here are well within our memory capacity.

The input module consists of reading in the data until the end-of-data is reached:

Input Module

```
            array is labeled M
            number of pieces of data is labeled ND
            counter is labeled counter
1. counter = 1
2. read data into M(counter)
3.     if End-of-Data, go to step 6
4.     counter = counter + 1
5. go to step 2
6. number of pieces of data, ND = counter - 1
```

The indentation of steps 3 and 4 emphasizes the loop and provides easier readability.

Although step 6 has already been discussed (in section 6.2), some review would be useful here. It might seem strange to have a counter that is counting ahead and must be decremented to obtain the number of actual pieces of data, but this is no different from the way the human brain works. If we look at a list of numbers, our eyes may scan the numbers very quickly without realizing just how much work our brain does in absorbing the information. If we were to imagine that we are reading the numbers from a distance through a telescope, so that we can see only one number at a time, then it would not be until we try to read the number following the last one that we realize there are no more values. For example, when viewing a list of four numbers, we do not know until we attempt to read the fifth one that there are no more numbers, and thus that the number of actual values is one less than the number of attempted reads. This process is very similar to what happens in real life.

The next process would be to determine the average of the numbers. Since the values are always available, there was no need to keep a running accumulation during the input module; but each process can be kept separate and distinct. The pseudocode is as follows:

Determine Average

```
7.    sum = 0
8.    counter = 1
9.    add M(counter) into sum
10.       counter = counter + 1
11. if counter < or = ND, go to step  9
12. average = sum / ND
```

Moving on to find the highest score:

Highest Score

```
13. high = M(1)
14. if ND = 1, go to step 19
15. counter = 2
16. if  M(counter) > high, then high = M(counter)
17.       counter = counter + 1
18. if counter is < or = ND, go to step 16
19. continue
```

Step 19 was provided just to complete this module, but it actually could be the beginning of the next process. Therefore, we will begin the numbering with 19.

Output Module: listing the input and the results

```
19. counter = 1
20. output M(counter)
21.      counter = counter + 1
22. if counter is < or = ND, go to step 20
23. output average, high
```

Note how distinct the modules are. Instead of one big loop, there are now three small loops, sharing the same data but detached logically. As you will see in a few more pages, the implementation of this program in FORTRAN in extremely short and simple.

Exercises

Note: The following exercises may be completed with either pseudocode or a flowchart (or both).

9.1a   Show the logic that would be used to generate a table of squares from 1 to 50 with two arrays, NUMBER and SQUARE. Include a second module to output the table with two values on each line, the NUMBER and its associated square. The arrays are self-generating; no input module is required.

9.1b   Show the logic required to read in two arrays, A and B, from a file in which there are exactly 20 records, one for each pair of corresponding values. In a separate module, add the corresponding values to generate a new array, C, with the same number of records. Then write the three arrays to a file.

9.1c   Show the logic required to read in a single array of unknown length (with an end-of-data indicator at the end of the file) and reverse the order of the elements in the array. (This logic differs slightly according to whether there is an even or an odd number of elements.) Then show the logic to output the array.

9.1d   Show the logic required to read in a single array of unknown length. Then replace all the negative values in the array with their absolute values.

9.1e   Show the logic required to read in all the temperatures for a month and to count the number of days the temperatures are below freezing and the number of days the temperatures are above a comfortable point, say, 80° Fahrenheit (30° Celsius). The program should be flexible enough to handle months of 28–31 days automatically, by reading in the data. In each case, list the number of days and the actual temperatures as well. Use separate modules for input, counting, and output.

9.1f   Show the logic required to read in an unknown amount of x, y coordinate pairs and determine the extremes of the coordinates (the minimum and maximum values of x and y). From those extremes, determine the midpoint of the graphic output that would display all the points. There should be seven modules: one for input, one for each of the four extremes, one to find the graphic midpoint, and an output module.

9.1g   Using $y = 70 * t - 16.1 * t ** 2$, generate values for $t = 0.00$ to the time when the projectile has reached the ground. Use a counter from 1 to 4001, each count representing 0.01 second, from 0.00 to 40.00. Store the values of t and y in arrays.

9.2 THE DIMENSION STATEMENT

The DIMENSION statement is a nonexecutable (or specification) statement which declares that: (1) a variable name represents an array, and (2) the array is so many elements in size. This statement appears before any of the executable statements but after the type statements. For example, the statement

```
DIMENSION  I(4), J(2), K(3)
```

sets aside four locations for I, two for J, and three for K—a total of nine locations. Furthermore, any appearance of the syntax I(2) or K(N), for instance, is now defined as an array element and will not be treated as a function.

A variable with the same name as an intrinsic function placed in the DIMENSION statement overrides its use as a function name. It certainly would be confusing to use an intrinsic function name for any other purpose, but it can happen accidentally; however, such a practice is to be discouraged. On the other hand, a variable coded with subscript notation, but not specified by dimensioning it, appears to the linker to be a missing function subprogram.

The DIMENSION statement merely sets aside room for the data and does not initialize any of the data values; that must be done with a DATA statement, with input of the values, or by assignment. The memory layout generated by the above example looks like this:

I(1)	I(2)	I(3)	I(4)	J(1)	J(2)	K(1)	K(2)	K(3)

With the array elements laid out in contiguous locations, the program need only locate the first element of the array; the other memory addresses can be computed with a simple arithmetic equation called the *mapping function*.

The dimensioning information may also be included in the type statement, avoiding the need for two statements. Thus, an alternative to:

```
REAL       LENGTH
DIMENSION  LENGTH(10)
```

is:

```
REAL  LENGTH(10)
```

There is always the problem of how big the dimension of an array should be. If the exact amount of data is known or limited, such as the mean temperature for each day of the year with an upper limit of 366 days, there is no problem. But if we are talking about a body of data whose size varies from application to application, the programmer must make some estimate of a reasonable size. Although our computers today have fairly large memories, it is still possible to overload them. Thus, the programmer's estimate must be a balance of what is truly necessary and safe for future expansion against what is not excessive. (The author has always doubled, where possible, the dimension specified to him by the program user as the "maximum amount of data that will ever come in." And many times throughout the years, even that was not sufficient.)

Under any circumstances, if the program is not to yield erroneous results, it is the responsibility of the programmer to ensure that arrays do not extend beyond their bounds. The FORTRAN language is not required to do any bounds checking (i.e., it does not check to see if a subscript is within the range defined in the DIMENSION statement), and it will place an assigned value into a location outside the array and destroy the information in some other location.

The location of an array member in memory is determined by a mapping function that calculates the member's address from the address of the beginning (first element) of the array. In the case of one-dimensional arrays, the mapping function reduces to the difference in subscripts plus the address of the first element. Thus, theoretically, I(6) is five locations above I(1). In the above memory layout, I is dimensioned as 4; and as the diagram shows, the fifth location above I(1) is J(2). Whereas the statement I(6) = 0 may result in a compiler error or warning, since some compilers check constant subscripts against the dimensions, I(N) = 0 is not checked. If N has been assigned the value 6, then the machine will execute I(6) = 0, assigning zero to the location J(2).

By the same token, J(N) = 0 with N = −1 would assign a zero to I(3) because the relative location of a theoretical J(−1) = (−1) − (1) = −2 locations from J(1). Obviously, carelessly calculated subscripts seem to cause many mysterious results; but in programming there are no "mysteries," only undiscovered errors. Subscripting is the first place the professional programmer looks when a "mystery" appears!

Some compilers have a bounds-checking option which includes machine code into the compiled program to check a subscript's value before executing the instruction; the error will appear during execution of the checking program. However, this option adds a great deal of code to the program, slowing it down significantly. Some professional programmers will use the option during program testing but remove it once the program has gone into the production environment.

The DIMENSION statements above (for I, J, K, and LENGTH) assume that the valid subscripts to access them will range from 1 to the value given in the parentheses. Thus, the statement:

```
INTEGER  TEMPR(366)
```

assumes that the valid subscripts for this array will range from 1 to 366. However, it is sometimes more convenient to specify a different range. For example, if we wanted to tabulate the distribution of temperatures by counting the number of times a particular temperature appeared, we could define the range with:

```
INTEGER  TMPDIS(-20:110)
```

allowing us a range of subscripts from -20 to 110, with the advantage of correlating the temperature reading with the subscript. This assumes that any temperatures outside that range will either be ignored or grouped with those at the extremes.

Another example might be the tabulation of height among a segment of the population. Assuming a range from 3.5 feet to 7.5 feet (42 to 90 inches) for adults, we would use:

```
INTEGER  HEIGHT(42:90)
```

One must be careful in measuring the size of these arrays. In the array HEIGHT, there is room for 49 values (not 48); in the array TMPDIS, there is room for 131 values (not 130). Just as the range (1:10) has 10 values $[(10 - 1) + 1]$, 1 must be added to the difference of the limits to obtain the number of elements in the array.

Once the variable is defined as an array in the DIMENSION or type statements, its use merely requires the addition of a subscript. Take a look at this partial program that implements the pseudocode from the previous section for average and high scores:

```
C                       Grade Analysis
C
C           Glossary: M:         array of up to 100 grades     integer
C                     ND:        number of grades              integer
C                     SUM:       sum of grades                 integer
C                     COUNTR:    temporary counter             integer
C                     AVRAGE:    average                       real
C                     HIGH:      high score                    integer
C
C
      INTEGER  M(100), ND, SUM, COUNTR, HIGH
C
C                       input module
                        |
                        |
                        |
C                       add up array
      SUM = 0
      DO 40  COUNTR = 1,ND
   40 SUM = SUM + M(COUNTR)
C                       calculate average
      AVRAGE = REAL (SUM) / REAL (COUNTR)
C                       highest score
      HIGH = M(1)
      IF  (ND .GT. 1)  THEN
          DO 60  COUNTR = 2,ND
              IF  (M(COUNTR) .GT. HIGH)  HIGH = M(COUNTR)
   60     CONTINUE
      ENDIF
C                       output module
                        |
                        |
C                       termination
      STOP
      END
```

Review Question

9.2a   In each of the arrays below, determine the number of elements:

a. `DIMENSION  I(19)`
b. `DIMENSION  J(1:19)`
c. `DIMENSION  K(11:100)`
d. `DIMENSION  L(-10:10)`
e. `INTEGER    DICE(2:12)`
f. `INTEGER    BSCORE(0:300)`
g. `LOGICAL    VALID(100)`
h. `REAL       X(-100:100)`

9.3   INPUT/OUTPUT OF ARRAYS

There are three basic methods for the I/O of arrays, and each has advantages and disadvantages. To illustrate, we will begin with input and assume a file of up to 366 integer mean temperature values. The program provides the flexibility to accept an input file with less than 366 values for non–leap years, or with only 28 to 31 values for analysis of a month, or with only 7 values for analysis of a week. Thus, the program allows for as many as 366 values but as few as 1.

At the same time, some simple calculations are shown as an indication of how easy it is to manipulate arrays. The program begins with the DIMENSION statement, the opening of the input file, and the integer FORMAT to be used with the files.

```
C                        Analysis of Temperature Data
C
C               read in up to 366 mean temperatures (integer)
C               compute average
C
      DIMENSION  MEANTM(367)
C
C                        open input file
      OPEN     (2, FILE='TEMPIN')
 1000 FORMAT   (7I4)
```

The overly dimensioned array allows the program to attempt reading a 367th temperature to ensure that the file does not contain too much data; i.e., more than 366 records.

Method 1: DO Loop

```
      DO 20  I = 1,367
   20 READ    (2,1000, END=40)  MEANTM(I)
         CLOSE  (2)
         STOP 'EXCESSIVE INPUT  -   ABORT!'
   40 NUMTMP = I - 1
      CLOSE  (2)
C                        compute average
      ISUM = 0
      DO 60  I = 1,NUMTMP
   60 ISUM = ISUM + MEANTM(I)
      AVRAGE = REAL (ISUM) / REAL (NUMTMP)
```

```
C                       open and output to file TMPOUT
      OPEN    (3, FILE='TMPOUT')
      WRITE   (3,1000)  NUMTMP
      DO 80   I = 1,NUMTMP
   80 WRITE   (3,1000)  MEANTM(I)
      WRITE   (3,1080)  AVRAGE
 1080 FORMAT  (F7.2, ' Average')
      CLOSE   (3)
C                       termination
      STOP
      END
```

With this method, each trip around the loop causes a new read. Each new read starts at a new record, and 367 READs are attempted. However, with only 365 days, 366 READs are issued, the last encountering the end-of-file. The output of data (the echo check) by this method results in 365 output lines, one piece of data per line.

The format of (7I4) is a format to be used throughout this exposition of array I/O. In this case, since each read and write has just a single array element in the variable list, only the first four-column format field of the I/O record is accessed; for this example, a simple format of (I4) would have sufficed.

If the amount of readable data in the file exceeds the size of the array, the program aborts. In this way, no erroneous results are computed. The input file is closed and the run terminates with an error message.

> Note how the file is closed immediately after it is read. This makes the file available to another user working on a multiuser system.

For smaller input files, less data would be read in. For example, assuming the input file TEMPIN consists of:

```
                        1111111111222222222
columns:   12345678901234567890123456 78
           68   62   74   79   82   87   90
           82   87   78   85   85   86   82
           71   63   65   62   68   70
```

The computer would read the first four columns of each of the three records before reading the end-of-file, with the result that the input temperatures would be 68, 82, and 71, with NUMTMP = 3.

Since the output file is considered to be a data file, not a printer file, no carriage control was entered. The number of pieces of data, now known, is placed at the beginning of the file. The output file for this example would be:

```
       3
      68
      82
      71
      73.67   Average
```

A program that reads the file can begin as follows, not needing the END= clause:

```
      DIMENSION  MEANTM(367)
C
C                    open input and output files
      OPEN    (3, FILE='TMPOUT')
 1000 FORMAT  (7I4)
C                    input array
      READ    (3, 1000)  NUMTMP
      DO 20  I = 1,NUMTMP
   20 READ    (3, 1000)  MEANTM(I)
                  |
                  |
                  |
```

Method 2: Implied DO Loop

The implied DO loop looks like a DO statement without the DO and the end-of-loop statement number; it generates the variable list for an I/O command. The variables may be single or subscripted; in the latter case, the DO index may be the same as the subscript. The general syntax includes the index and the two or three DO loop parameters (the third is optional, assumed to be 1 if not specified) enclosed in a set of parentheses:

```
      READ  (n,m [,END=])  (list of variables,  index = m1, m2, m3)
```

Implementing it into the code:

```
      READ    (2,1000, END=40)  (MEANTM(I), I=1,367)
         CLOSE  (2)
         STOP 'EXCESSIVE INPUT  -  ABORT!'
   40 CLOSE    (2)
      NUMTMP = I - 1
C                    compute average
      ISUM = 0
      DO 60  I = 1,NUMTMP
   60 ISUM = ISUM + MEANTM(I)
      AVRAGE = REAL (ISUM) / REAL (NUMTMP)
C                    open and output to file TMPOUT
      OPEN    (3, FILE='TMPOUT')
      WRITE   (3,1000)  (MEANTM(I), I=1,NUMTMP)
      WRITE   (3,1080)  AVRAGE
 1080 FORMAT  (F7.2, ' Average')
      CLOSE   (3)
C                    termination
      STOP
      END
```

The implied DO loop (MEANTM(I), I=1,367) is identical to the following code:

```
      READ  (2,1000, END=40)  MEANTM(1), MEANTM(2), MEANTM(3),
     1    MEANTM(4), MEANTM(5), MEANTM(6), .....................
     .    ....                                    ........
     Z    MEANTM(364), MEANTM(365), MEANTM(366), MEANTM(367)
```

but obviously much shorter, with the implied DO loop generating a variable list of 367 elements.

Since there is only a single READ command, it is possible to input multiple values per record. With the input file TEMPIN shown above, the computer would find 20 values, with the end-of-file detected at the 21st value. The program would write the data to file 3, TMPOUT, in the same format with the addition of the counter in the initial record and the average in the last:

```
20
68   62   74   79   82   87   90
82   87   78   85   85   86   82
71   63   65   62   68   70
76.30   Average
```

There is no problem with mixing methods in the same program. If, in the DO loop method demonstrated first, the array output was changed to:

```
WRITE  (3,1000)  (MEANTM(I), I=1,NUMTMP)
```

the output file would show (in addition to the counter and the average) the three input temperatures in the same record:

```
         3
68   82   71
73.67   Average
```

Unfortunately, the above method, which provides the greatest flexibility in data entry and/or preparation and also provides for the shortest possible code, does not work with all compilers. With Microsoft FORTRAN, for example, the END= clause does not become effective upon reaching the end-of-file, but rather an attempt is made to read in as many values as are defined by the upper implied DO loop parameter. The value of the implied DO loop index is set to the upper loop parameter, and the undefined pieces of data are usually set to zero. Thus the above code would yield the 21 valid values plus 346 zeros. In order to make this method work, it is necessary to write a sentinel value in the file and add some code, thus losing the conciseness of the method.

Throughout the text, the implied DO loop with the END= clause will be used as first described, since most compilers react in that way. We are in a situation in which there is no clear definition within the FORTRAN specifications, but the traditional practice in the industry has been for the instruction to respond immediately to the end-of-file. It is unfortunate when a major compiler manufacturer moves in an untraditional way!

Another application of the implied DO-loop with nonsubscripted variables can also prove to be quite handy:

```
     WRITE  (6,1000)  (I, I=60,100,10)
1000 FORMAT  (' ', 5I6/ ' ', 4(4X,'--'), '   ---')
```

This would output the values 60, 70, 80, 90, and 100, right-justified in columns 1–6, 7–12, 13–18, 19–24, and 25–30, with dashes below:

```
60   70   80   90   100
--   --   --   --   ---
```

This method also allows the output of single and array variables responding to the same subscript, such as:

```
        WRITE   (6,1000)  (I, MEANTM(I), I=1,7)
   1000 FORMAT  (' ', I3, I5)
```

The output would appear as:

```
   1    68
   2    62
   3    74
   4    79
   5    82
   6    87
   7    90
```

Had the statement been mistakenly written as follows:

```
        WRITE   (6,1000)  (I, I=1,7), (MEANTM(I), I=1,7)
   1000 FORMAT  (' ', I3, I5)
```

the output would be all the values of I followed by all of MEANTM:

```
   1     2
   3     4
   5     6
   7    68
  62    74
  79    82
  87    90
```

Method 3: Entire Array

The following statement:

```
   DIMENSION  MEANTM(366)
   READ    (3,1000)  MEANTM
```

would be useful if we had exactly 366 pieces of data. By stating the array name only, the compiler refers to the DIMENSION statement and generates the code for an implied DO loop whose range corresponds to the declared subscript range. Effectively, we are saving ourselves the effort of coding:

```
   READ  (3,1000)  (MEANTM(I), I=1,366)
```

Although limited to only certain applications, this method is often useful (primarily in output) and will appear later in some of our examples.

Review Questions and Exercises

9.3a   For the following program segment:

```
        DIMENSION  J(5), K(5)
        DO 20  I = 1,5
            J(I) = I
     20 K(I) = I+5
   1000 FORMAT  (' ', 5I4)
```

show the output generated by the following statements:

a. WRITE   (6,1000)   J
b. WRITE   (6,1000)   J(4), J(3), K

```
c. WRITE  (6,1000)  (J(I), I=1,5), (K(I), I=1,5)
d. WRITE  (6,1000)  (J(I), K(I), I=1,5)
e. WRITE  (6,1000)  (K(I), I=1,3), (J(I), I=3,5)
f. WRITE  (6,1000)  (K(I), J(I), I=1,5,2)
g. WRITE  (6,1000)  (J(I), I=1,5,3), (J(L), L=2,5,3)
```

9.3b   Using the program segment given in exercise 9.3a, show the output generated by the following I/O pairs:

```
a.      WRITE  (6,1002)  K(5), (J(I), I=1,3,2), K(4)
   1002 FORMAT  (' ', 3I4)
b.      WRITE  (6,1004)  K, J
   1004 FORMAT  (' ', 3I4/ ' ', 2I4)
c.      WRITE  (6,1006)  K, J
   1006 FORMAT  (' ', 3I4/ (' ', 2I4))
```

9.3c   For the following program segment:

```
      DIMENSION  J(5), K(5)
      DO 20  I = 1,5
         J(I) = 0
   20 K(I) = 0
 2000 FORMAT  (3I4)
```

and this input file:

```
                       11111111112
   columns:  12345678901234567890
                 1    2    3    4    5
                 6    7    8    9   10
                11   12   13   14   15
                16   17   18   19   20
                21   22   23   24   25
```

indicate which of the elements of arrays J and K are modified to nonzero values:

```
a. READ  (5,2000)  J, K
b. READ  (5,2000)  (J(I), K(I), I=1,3)
c. READ  (5,2000)  (K(I), I=1,5,2), (J(I), I=2,5,2)
d. READ  (5,2000)  K(4), J(2), K(1), J(4), J(2)
```

9.3d   Write a program to generate an array of the even numbers from 2 to 100 and write those numbers to a file using Method 3. No input is required.

9.3e   Modify exercise 6.1e (table of squares, cubes, square roots, and cube roots) to first generate the values, storing them into four arrays of 50 each. Then use a separate output module (a second DO loop) to display the table.

9.3f   Modify the sample Tax Table program from section 6.1 (use the first version) to generate the values into two arrays of 100 and then, with a separate DO loop, output the table.

9.3g Generate a 6-by-6 multiplication table, using an array to store the six answers to be placed on each line. The output should look something like this:

	1	2	3	4	5	6
1	1	2	3	4	5	6
2	2	4	6	8	10	12
3	3	6	9	12	15	18
4	4	8	12	16	20	24
5	5	10	15	20	25	30
6	6	12	18	24	30	36

9.3h Read in a 10-element array from a file with 5 values per record. Multiply the elements of the array by 5, and output to the screen one value per line and its associated subscript.

9.3i Read in two 20-element arrays from a file (see exercise 9.1b). Each record consists of a pair of corresponding values from each array. Generate a third array by adding together the corresponding values of each array. Output the subscript and the three arrays to the screen, one record (four values) per line.

9.3j Read in a 20-element array from a file containing negative, positive, and zero numbers. Using three additional loops, count the number of numbers in each group and output the results.

9.3k Read the same array described above and convert each number to its absolute value.

9.4   THE DATA STATEMENT REVISITED

In section 4.6, the DATA statement was presented as an easy way to initialize values in single variables. When used with arrays, the DATA statement becomes even more useful because it saves many lines of executable code by replacing necessary DO loops and, further, because there is no execution time taken when placing the initial values in the appropriate memory locations. (That time is taken during compilation.) The use of the repetition factor is especially useful. The following code:

```
      CHARACTER*12  MESSGE(6)
      DIMENSION     TOTALS(8), RATES(8), KOUNTR(4)
C
      DATA  TOTALS/ 8 * 0.00/,  KOUNTR/ 4 * 0/
```

initializes the values in TOTALS and KOUNTR to zero, using the appropriate mode. The arrays MESSGE and RATES are still undefined. Then:

```
      DATA  (RATES(I), I=3,7)/ 12.34, 18.77, 9.45, 22.76, 15.00/
```

initializes part of the array RATE, leaving the first two and the last values undefined. The values in the undefined locations are compiler-dependent and should be defined within the program either by input or by assignment. The following:

```
      DATA MESSGE/ 4*'            ', 'INPUT ERROR ', 'OVERFLOW    '/
```

initializes the first four elements of MESSGE to blank and the last two with distinct messages.

The three DATA statements would require at least 13 executable statements (3 DO loops and 10 assignment statements) to implement. The same rule of mode agreement that exists for regular variables still exists. Additionally, the agreement of number of variables and number of corresponding values is also critical.

The DATA statement is very useful where a fixed table is to be accessed. This kind of process is defined as *table lookup*. Below is a program used to compute taxes based on a graduated rate; it is similar to that used by the federal government and by many state governments.

```
C                         Tax Program Based on the Following Table:
C
C        Income                          Tax
C        ------                          ---
C            up   to  $8,000                      2% of income
C        $8,000  to  $12,000         $160   +   4% in excess of  $8,000
C        $12,000 to  $20,000         $320   +   5% in excess of $12,000
C        $20,000 to  $40,000         $720   +   8% in excess of $20,000
C        greater than $40,000        $2320  +  10% in excess of $40,000
C
         DIMENSION  RANGE(5),  BASE(5),  RATE(5)
C
         DATA  RANGE/  0.00, 8000.00, 12000.00, 20000.00, 40000.00/
         DATA  BASE/   0.00,  160.00,   320.00,   720.00,  2320.00/
         DATA  RATE/   0.02,    0.04,     0.05,     0.08,     0.10/
C
C                    loop through input
         DO 80  N = 1,20000
C                         prompt and input
             WRITE   (6,1000)
 1000        FORMAT  (' ', 'Enter income      ctrl-Z to terminate')
             READ    (5,*, END=90)  XINCM
C                    find proper range
             DO 40  I = 1,4
                 IF  (XINCM .LE. RANGE(I+1))         GO TO 60
   40        CONTINUE
             I = 5
C                    compute tax
   60        TAX = BASE(I)  +  RATE(I) * (XINCM - RANGE(I))
C                    output
             WRITE   (6,1060)  XINCM, TAX
 1060        FORMAT  (' ', 'For income of', F10.2,', tax = ', F8.2)
   80    CONTINUE
C                    termination
   90 STOP
      END
```

The GO TO statement in the program simulates the LOOP .. EXIT construct which is not available in FORTRAN. The coding above is the most efficient possible, using the least amount of code and executing the least number of statements. However, it is possible to remove the GO TO by adding a logical variable FOUND and revising the DO 40 loop as follows:

```
      LOGICAL  FOUND
              |
              |
              |
```

```
C                          find proper range
              FOUND = .FALSE.
              DO 40  I = 1,5
                 IF  (.NOT. FOUND  .AND.
     1              (I .EQ. 5  .OR.  XINCM .GE. RANGE(I+1)))  THEN
                    TAX = BASE(I)  +  RATE(I) * (XINCM - RANGE(I))
                    FOUND = .TRUE.
                 ENDIF
     40       CONTINUE
```

Exercises

9.4a   Write the code necessary to define an array, X, of 20 elements. Then, using a DATA statement, define the first 5 elements as −1, the middle 10 elements as 0, and the final 5 as +1. Include this in a complete program which also contains an output module so that the code may be verified by displaying the results.

9.4b   Write a program that contains a routine for converting numeric grades to letter grades. Use a DATA statement to define the ranges and the letter grade; the latter should be CHARACTER*2 mode. Then, using the table lookup method, convert singly entered numeric grades to letters according to the following table:

>100	IV	(for *invalid*)
90-100	A	
87- 89	B+	
80- 86	B	
77- 79	C+	
70- 76	C	
65- 69	D	
0- 64	F	
<0	IV	

9.4c   A program includes the following statements to define an inventory of lights for cars:

```
CHARACTER*8  DESCRP(4)
DIMENSION    INVNUM(4), UNITPR(4)
C
DATA  DESCRP/ 'Headlite', 'Taillite', 'Int.Lite', 'StopLite'/
DATA  INVNUM/ 1005,      2211,       4756,       9800/
DATA  UNITPR/ 10.95,     3.98,       2.49,       5.75/
```

Write a program that reads in the inventory number and number of parts desired and outputs the input values, the description, and the computed cost as number of parts desired times unit price.

9.4d   Extend the above program (9.4c) to allow a customer to purchase a number of different items; also have the program provide a total of the purchase. Test the program to ensure that it will handle more than one customer and provide the correct total after that first customer. The program might be extended even further to provide a grand total of all the sales during the run.

9.4e   The social security (FICA, or Federal Insurance Contributions Act) tax rate and maximum change almost every year, requiring annual modifications to the computation. The methodology is explained in exercise 5.7h, where a sample tax rate and maximum are given. Write a general-purpose FUNCTION FICATX (SALARY, ACCUM) to return the tax to be deducted according to a rate of 8% and a maximum salary accumulation of $50,000. Test with a driver. Then modify the function by changing the rate and accumulation to 8.25% and $54,000; retest. No arrays are used here.

9.5 APPLICATIONS USING ARRAYS

This section on applications starts with an extension of the temperature program from section 3 of this chapter.

In this version a file of records is read, one for each day. Each record will contain two values, the low temperature and the high temperature for the day. These are integer values, right justified in columns 1–4 and 5–8. The program will compute the mean temperature and what is called the degree-days, that is the number of degrees the mean is below 65 degrees. It will compute the average mean temperature for the period and the total degree-days, the latter being an approximate measure of how much heating is needed. And, just in case the data file is empty, the program will include an error stop for that condition.

```
C                          Analysis of Temperature Data
C
C                  read in up to 366 high and low temperatures (integer)
C                  compute daily mean and degree-days,
C                      period average mean, maximum, minimum and
C                      total degree-days
C
      INTEGER  HIGH(367), LOW(367), MEAN(366), DEGDAY(366)
      INTEGER  TOTTMP,    TOTDDY,   AVGTMP
C
      DATA     TOTTMP, TOTDDY/ 2*0/, DEGDAY/ 366*0/
C
C                      open input file
      OPEN   (2, FILE='TEMPIN')
C                      input routine
      DO 20  I = 1,367
   20 READ    (2,1020, END=40)  HIGH(I), LOW(I)
 1020 FORMAT  (2I4)
      CLOSE   (2)
      STOP  'EXCESSIVE INPUT!'
   40 CLOSE  (2)
      NUMTMP = I - 1
      IF  (NUMTMP .EQ. 0)  STOP  'NO DATA!'
C                      calculations
      DO 100  I = 1,NUMTMP
      MEAN(I) = (HIGH(I) + LOW(I)) / 2
      IF  (MEAN(I) .LT. 65)  DEGDAY(I) = 65 - MEAN(I)
      TOTTMP = TOTTMP + MEAN(I)
  100 TOTDDY = TOTDDY + DEGDAY(I)
      AVGTMP = NINT (REAL (TOTTMP) / REAL (NUMTMP))
C                      write output file
      OPEN   (3, FILE='TMPOUT')
      WRITE   (3,1100)  (HIGH(I),LOW(I),MEAN(I),DEGDAY(I), I=1,NUMTMP)
 1100 FORMAT  ('1','High Low  Mean  Degree-Day'/
     1         (' ', 2I4, I6, I12))
      WRITE   (3,1102)  AVGTMP, TOTDDY
 1102 FORMAT  ('0','Average temperature =', I5/
     1         ' ','Total degree days   =', I5)
      CLOSE   (3)
C                      termination
      STOP
      END
```

The INTEGER type statement was used not only to define the mode of the variables but to dimension the arrays as well. Whereas the input arrays, HIGH and LOW, had to allow for 367 possible values, the calculated arrays, MEAN and DEGDAY, could be limited to 366 values since that is the limit of NUMTMP. The DATA statement initialized the totals and the degree-day array. In the latter case, it simplified the conditional test within the DO 100 loop, which assigns the number of degree-days by not having to include an ELSE condition.

The input was done with a regular DO loop, which works with all compilers. An alternative for most traditional compilers is:

```
READ  (2,1020, END=40)  (HIGH(I), LOW(I), I=1,367)
```

The average temperature was computed in real mode and rounded to integer with the function NINT.

Sample Input File (seven-day period)

```
columns   12345678
              78  58
              75  60
              68  52
              66  49
              69  54
              74  63
              76  60
```

Sample Output File

```
                        11111111112222222
        columns   12345678901234567890123456

          High Low  Mean  Degree-Day
           78   58    68            0
           75   60    67            0
           68   52    60            5
           66   49    57            8
           69   54    61            4
           74   63    68            0
           76   60    68            0

          Average temperature =    64
          Total degree-days    =    17
```

A simple grading program was discussed in the introduction to this chapter; now it is presented in one of its many possible forms. In a later chapter, part of it will be enhanced as new facilities are introduced. In this example, the program inputs and outputs the student names as alphameric data.

```
      C                     Grade Analysis and Distribution
      C
      C          Abstract:Program inputs up to 60 examination grades.Grades
      C                   are edited for proper range (0 to 100).Average is cal-
      C                   culated and a grade distribution determined as follows:
```

```
C                               90 to 100:    A    DISTR(1)
C                               80 to  89:    B      :
C                               70 to  79:    C      :
C                               65 to  69:    D      :
C                                    < 65:    F    DISTR(5)
C
       CHARACTER*16   NAME(61)
       INTEGER        GRADE(61), DISTR(5), SUM, IGRBK(4)
C               initialize counters, error counter, sum, grade breaks
       DATA           DISTR, NUMERR, SUM,   IGBRK/
      1               7 * 0,                90, 80, 70, 65/
C                               open input file
       OPEN   (2, FILE='GRADES')
C                               input module
       DO 20  I = 1,61
   20 READ    (2,1020, END=40)  NAME(I), GRADE(I)
 1020 FORMAT  (A16, I4)
          CLOSE  (2)
          STOP  'EXCESSIVE INPUT!'
   40 NUMREC = I - 1
          CLOSE  (2)
          IF  (NUMREC .EQ. 0)  STOP  'NO DATA!'
C                       open output file, echo check and edit
       OPEN   (3, FILE='REPORT')
       WRITE  (3,1040)
 1040 FORMAT  ('1',' GRADE DISTRUBUTION'/
      1         '0','Name',11X,'Grade'/)
       DO 60  I = 1,NUMREC
          IF  (GRADE(I) .GE. 0 .AND.  GRADE(I) .LE. 100)  THEN
                WRITE  (3,1042)  NAME(I), GRADE(I)
 1042           FORMAT  (' ',A16, I4)
             ELSE
                WRITE  (3,1044)  NAME(I), GRADE(I),
 1044           FORMAT  (' ',A16, I4, '  INVALID GRADE')
                NUMERR = NUMERR + 1
          ENDIF
   60 CONTINUE
C                       abort if errors
       IF  (NUMERR .GT. 0)  THEN
          WRITE  (3,1060)  NUMERR
 1060     FORMAT  ('0','Program aborted with', I3,' errors')
          CLOSE  (3)
          STOP
       ENDIF
C                       compute average
       DO 120  I = 1,NUMREC
  120 SUM  = SUM + GRADE(I)
       AVRG = REAL (SUM) / REAL (NUMREC)
C                       distribution  (one of many ways)
       DO 160  I = 1,NUMREC
          DO 140  J = 1,4
             IF  (GRADE(I) .GE. IGRBRK(J))  GO TO 160
  140     CONTINUE
          J = 5
  160 DISTR(J) = DISTR(J) + 1
C                       output average and distribution
       WRITE  (3,1160)  NUMREC, AVRG, DISTR
 1160 FORMAT  ('0', 'Average of', I3,' grades =', F5.1/
      1         '0', 'Distribution: A  B  C  D  E  F'/
      2         ' ', 12X, 5I3)
       CLOSE  (3)
```

```
C                       termination
      STOP
      END
```

Note how this program is modularized. The first module is the input; it is followed by the echo check, edit, average, distribution, and output modules. What makes them separate modules is that each is isolated from the others with no branching from one to another; only the data is shared. This program could have been written by a programming team, with each member writing only one module by being given the names of the variables common to all modules and a range of statement numbers to work within.

Another interesting point is that once the input and edit modules are complete, the order of the average and distribution modules is not critical; one does not depend on the other. Also note the use of I/O method 3 (entire array) in the last WRITE statement.

The single GO TO simulates the LOOP .. EXIT and branches to the end of a module. It produces the most efficient code in this circumstance.

Sample Input File

```
                       11111111112
columns   12345678901234567890
          Smith               78
          Jones               83
          Brown               85
          Green               72
          Pressman           100
          Sunshine            98
          Klein               54
          Frank               68
          Newton              89
          Moore               77
```

Sample Output File

```
      GRADE DISTRIBUTION

   Name            Grade

   Smith              78
   Jones              83
   Brown              85
   Green              72
   Pressman          100
   Sunshine           98
   Klein              54
   Frank              68
   Newton             89
   Moore              77

   Average of 10 grades = 80.4

   Distribution: A B C D F
                 2 3 3 1 1
```

Exercises

9.5a Write a program to read from a file consisting of 10 records, each containing 8 values in the range from 0 to 300. Use an array of 8 to read in each record. For each record, compute the mean, maximum, and minimum values and store them in three arrays of 10, with the subscript representing the record number. After the file has been read, find the mean of the means and also the group maximum and minimum. Perform the group calculations in a separate module after all the data has been read and the arrays defined. It will be necessary to generate your own data; however, see exercise 8.6c for a method of generating normally distributed random data.

9.5b An input file has the following file structure:

> Record 1, fields 1–3: examination weights in percent (adds up to 100%)
> Records 2–*n*, field 1: student name (up to 12 characters)
>   fields 2–4: examination grades

Write a program to read the three examination weights into an array; the weights are three decimal values (percentages) that add up to 1.00 (such as 0.30, 0.45 and 0.25). Then read in up to 30 student names, each with three grades, into four arrays, one for name and three for grades. Generate a new array with each student's average computed as the sum of the three examination grades, with each grade multiplied by its weight. Also generate the average of each of the three examinations and the class weighted average, placing them in a real array of four elements. Output a record for each student and for the four averages.

9.5c Add to the above program the calculation of the three standard deviations for each of the examinations. The standard deviation is defined as the sum of the squares of the differences between each grade and the average grade, dividing that by the number of grades and then taking the square root:

$$\text{standard deviation} = \text{SQRT}\left[\frac{\text{sum (each grade} - \text{average grade)} ** 2}{\text{number of grades}}\right]$$

These should be placed into a real array of three elements. (The standard deviation is a measure of the spread of the grades; usually, 95% of the grades fit within 2 standard deviations of the mean; i.e., for a mean of 75 and a standard deviation of 10, 95% of the grades are in the range 55 to 95.)

9.5d Write a program to tabulate votes, using an integer array with an element for each candidate. Assume up to 12 candidates. The initial input should consist of the number of candidates, a value which should be used for editing the incoming data and for controlling the amount of elements that are output. Read from a disk file partial results with the candidates' number and votes, accumulating the votes as new data is entered. Display the total votes after each data record is read, including the percentage of the total vote (real) for each candidate.

9.5e Write a program to read in a file of records consisting of names (CHARACTER*12) and balances in an account (real), into two arrays. Determine the total and average balances. Output the arrays and the two calculated values. At the end, output the number of records read.

9.5f   Revise the program in exercise 9.5e to reverse the order of the records in the arrays. Only the original arrays should be used, although some temporary locations may be necessary. Make sure that both the names *and* balances are reversed. (This exercise is not designed to be satisfied by revising the output routine but by actually modifying the arrays.)

9.6   ARRAY HANDLING IN SUBPROGRAMS

In the previous section, the grading program calculated the real average of an integer array. The calculation of averages, minimums, and maximums appears very often in many applications; it certainly would be efficient to generate subprograms for such functions so that coding may be reduced.

There is no problem in transmitting an array to a subprogram. The array name must be placed in the argument lists of both calling and called programs, and the array must be dimensioned. Using the grading program as an example of implementing the function AVGINT (real average of an integer array), it could be coded as follows:

Partial FORTRAN Mainline

```
       INTEGER      GRADE(61)



       AVRG = AVGINT (GRADE, NUMREC)

       WRITE   (3,1160)  NUMREC, AVRG
  1160 FORMAT  ('0', 'Average of', I3,' grades =', F5.1)

       STOP
       END
```

```
       FUNCTION  AVGINT (IA, NR)
C
C          Abstract:  calculates real average of
C                        integer array IA with NR elements
C
       DIMENSION  IA(61)
C
C                  initialize sum
       ISUM = 0
C                  loop through elements
       DO 20  N = 1,NR
   20  ISUM = ISUM + IA(N)
C                  calculate average
       AVGINT = REAL (ISUM) / REAL (NR)
C                  return
       RETURN
       END
```

The initial zeroing of ISUM is assigned each time the subprogram is entered. If a DATA statement were used in the subprogram, the value of ISUM upon entering the subprogram a second time during program execution (if this were to happen) would not be zero but would be its value at the end of the previous access.

To fully understand how the argument transmission works, look at the following possible memory layout:

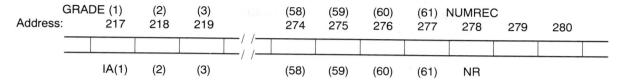

When the mainline is placed into memory, the dimensioned array GRADE is assigned 61 locations, according to the DIMENSION statement. For simplicity of this explanation, the next available location is assumed to be assigned to NUMREC.

As explained in section 8.2, when a subprogram is called, the addresses of the arguments in the list are transmitted to it. Thus the array IA (known to be an array because of the DIMENSION statement in the subprogram) accesses the locations starting at the first element of GRADE, which is 217 in this example. The single variable NR accesses the same location as the second argument in the calling statement (NUMREC), notably, location 278. The value found in location 278 becomes the upper limit of the DO loop in the subprogram, and, using the mapping function (which calculates the difference in location of one-dimensional arrays as the difference in subscripts), the locations starting with 217 are accessed for the calculation. If NUMREC = NR = 4, the memory locations 217, 218, 219, and 220 are accessed by the subprogram.

No memory is assigned in the subprogram for any variables in the argument list. In the subprogram above, only ISUM requires a memory assignment. The function name, AVGINT, would be assigned a memory location in the calling program, where the returned answer is stored.

> ISUM is called a "local" variable, since it only appears in this independent module; any reference to a variable ISUM in any other module would be treated as a different variable and have a separate memory location.

It would seem at first that this subprogram can only be used for an array of exactly 61 elements, but that is far from the truth. If the subprogram were dimensioned as:

```
DIMENSION  IA(1)
```

there would be no difference in execution. Since only the address of the beginnings of the arrays GRADE and IA are shared, the length has already been defined by the calling program. The subprogram will use the mapping function to access the other elements, regardless of the size of the DIMENSION.

The next question, then, might be: If the size of the array is specified in the calling program, why is a DIMENSION statement needed in the called program at all? Well, without it the array IA would be treated as a function name! Thus, there must be a DIMENSION statement in the called program. The final question is what should that dimension value be. The answer is straightforward: *It does not matter!* Any value will suffice.

Most professionals use the dimension value of 1 as a way of showing that the dimensioned array is not local to the subprogram. FORTRAN 77 also allows:

```
DIMENSION  IA(*)
```

This symbol is referred to as a *dummy array declarator* or an *assumed size array declarator*.

The concepts described above open up a tremendous area for writing general-purpose subprograms. (See the exercises at the end of this section for some possibilities.) As another example, below is a general-purpose integer breakdown subprogram which will be used in future programming systems (in particular, in an enhanced version of the Automated Teller Program, in the next section of this chapter).

```
C               Subroutine BRKDWN:  Break Down Integer to Denominations
C
      SUBROUTINE  BRKDWN  (AMOUNT, NUMDEN, VALDEN, NUMUNT)
C
      INTEGER  AMOUNT, NUMDEN, VALDEN(*), NUMUNT(*), LEFT
C
C           Glossary: AMOUNT:  amount to be broken down
C                     NUMDEN:  number of denominations
C                     VALDEN:  value of those denominations
C                     NUMUNT:  number of units in the denominations
C                     LEFT:    working variable
C
C                  place amount into local working variable
      LEFT = AMOUNT
C                  loop through number of denominations
      DO 20  I = 1,NUMDEN
          NUMUNT(I) = LEFT / VALDEN(I)
   20 LEFT = MOD (LEFT, VALDEN(I))
C                        return
      RETURN
      END
```

A reminder is in order here. The variable names in the argument list do not always agree with those used in the calling program, but they must agree in number and mode. Furthermore, the arrays must be dimensioned in both programs.

Another rule to follow in writing a subprogram is *never* to change a transmitted value unless the purpose of the subprogram is to change that value. To be more precise: In this case, the value in AMOUNT is transferred to a working variable so that the value in AMOUNT is not modified by the subprogram. This way the value stored in AMOUNT in the calling program (i.e., the first argument in the list) is not changed during execution of the subprogram.

This subprogram would be useful in a number of applications. Assuming one that is involved with gross (144 units), dozen (12 units), and units, the calling program could look like this:

```
          INTEGER   NUMBRK, VALBRK(3), NUMGRP(3), NMUNIT

          DATA      VALBRK/ 144, 12, 1/

     C                        calculate breakdown
          CALL BRKDWN   (NMUNIT, 3, VALBRK, NUMGRP)
```

In the next section, the ATM program will be modified as follows:

```
          INTEGER   NUMBRK, VALBRK(3), NUMBIL(3), WITHRN

          DATA   NUMBRK, VALBRK/ 3, 50, 20, 10/

     C                        calculate breakdown
          CALL BRKDWN   (WITHRN, NUMBRK, VALBRK, NUMBIL)
```

A single element of an array may be placed in the argument list if the called subprogram expects a single variable. For example, if the argument list requires three single variables, the accessing statement might appear as:

```
CALL SUBA (X(3), Y(5*I-2), N)
```

Exercises

9.6a   Write four functions:

```
IMAX (IARRAY, NUMEL)
IMIN (IARRAY, NUMEL)
RMAX (ARRAY,  NUMEL)
RMIN (ARRAY,  NUMEL)
```

and a test driver. Test the functions by reading two arrays of the same length, one real and one integer, from a disk file. Use the END= clause to determine the number of elements (NUMEL). Display the arrays, the minimums, and the maximums.

9.6b   Write a subroutine:

```
STATS (ARRAY, NUMEL, SUM, AVERAG, FMAX, FMIN)
```

which receives a real array and the number of elements and returns the sum of the elements, the average value, the maximum value, and the minimum value. The subroutine should call the functions written in exercise 9.6a. Write a driver to accept input from a disk file and display the array and the answers.

9.6c Rewrite the tax program in section 9.4 as a function subprogram. Also write a driver for testing purposes.

9.6d Rewrite exercise 9.4b to place the grade determination routine into a function subprogram that returns a character variable. Also write a driver to test the function. The numeric arrays should be defined in the driver.

9.6e Write SUBROUTINE AVGSTD to receive an array of real values and the number of valid elements and to return the average and the standard deviation. (See exercise 9.5c for a definition of standard deviation.)

9.6f Write a SUBROUTINE INITIA to initialize all the values of an integer array to a constant. The arguments to the subroutine are the name of the array, the number of elements in the array, and the initial value to be placed in the array. A simple driver with only an output routine would be sufficient.

9.6g Write a matrix arithmetic subroutine (MTRXAR) which combines the elements of two one-dimensional integer arrays into a third one-dimensional array according to the desired process. For example, if addition is requested, the subprogram will add the first elements of each of the two input arrays and place the result in the first element of the output array. The process continues for all the elements. The arguments to the subroutine should be:

   a. Name of the first input array
   b. Name of the second input array
   c. Name of the output array
   d. Number of elements in the three arrays
   e. Desired process, using the appropriate symbols: +, −, *, or /. This must be a character variable and must be checked in the subprogram. If the character is invalid, zero the entire output array.

The driver should read the arrays from a test file and the desired operation from a keyboard. The output should be a three-column listing of the arrays, showing the input and calculated values.

9.6h Write SUBROUTINE BIT32 which takes a positive 32-bit (long) integer and generates a 32-element array, each element storing one bit. The bits are numbered from 1 to 32, with 1 being the high-order bit and 32 the low-order bit.

9.6i Write FUNCTION INT32 which receives an array of 32 bits (0 and 1) and generates the integer value which they represent.

9.6j Section 5.9 has logical tables for .AND. and .OR. based on bits. It is possible to treat numeric variables logically, but only by performing a bit-by-bit operation. Thus it is necessary to convert each of the values to be operated on to bits (see exercise 9.6h), perform the bit-by-bit operations, and then convert the bits back to an integer (see exercise 9.6i). Write two integer functions, IAND and IOR, to accept two integers and return a third. The AND and OR operations can be done by clever integer arithmetic and require no decision making. Write a driver to test with input from the keyboard, sending the same values to both functions.

9.7 PROGRAMMING SYSTEMS

In this section, we will make an interesting modification to our Automated Teller Machine application program to illustrate the flexibility of writing programs using arrays and subprograms. The new SUBROUTINE BRKDWN from the previous section and FUNCTION CALCFE from section 8.7 are now included in our system.

In order to get the breakdown in $50, $20, and $10 bills, the program now specifies in a DATA statement not only the number of denominations to be used for the breakdown but also the denominations themselves. Additionally, the arrays have a capacity of 6—although the program now uses only 3 elements—to facilitate future modification.

If we also wanted to include $5 bills and $100 bills, the coding would be:

```
DATA  NUMBRK, VALBRK/ 5,  100, 50, 20, 10, 5, 0/
```

To pay with $10 bills only, the coding would be:

```
DATA  NUMBRK, VALBRK/ 1,  10, 0, 0, 0, 0, 0/
```

Thus it is easy to modify the program, should we decide to change the denominations to be issued.

There are three more variables in the modified program below—NUMBRK, VALBRK, and NUMBIL—the last two defined as arrays with capacities of six. NUMBRK will be used to store the number of denominations and VALBRK the denominations to be used in descending order. NUMBIL is the actual breakdown in number of bills. Additionally, the former variable WITH10 has been modified to WITHRN (withdrawal, rounded), since it will not be the next higher multiple of 10 but rather the next higher multiple of whatever is the lowest denomination to be used, again adding more flexibility.

In the program below, the first DATA statement indicates three denominations are to be used, with the values 50, 20, and 10. Although it is not necessary to define the unused three elements of the array, it is considered good documentation to provide some dummy values to show how much of the array is still available and to make possible future modification of the data statement simpler.

Automated Teller Machine

```
C                     Automated Teller Machine
C
      PARAMETER  (RATE = 0.020, LIMIT = 400.00)
```

```
C
      CHARACTER  RESPNS
      INTEGER    WITHDR, WITHRN,    TOTWTH
      INTEGER    NUMBRK, VALBRK(6), NUMBIL(6)
      REAL       FEE,    TOTAL
C                        initialize breakdown & total withdrawal
      DATA  NUMBRK, VALBRK/ 3,  50, 20, 10, 0, 0, 0/
      DATA  TOTWTH/ 0/
C
C                        enter amount of withdrawal
      DO 80  NTRANS = 1,20000
         WRITE   (*,1000)
 1000    FORMAT  ('0', 'Enter amount of withdrawal (integer)')
         READ    (*,*, ERR= 40, END=90) WITHDR
C                    check for positive value
       IF  (WITHDR .LE. 0)
     1    PRINT *, 'DESIRED WITHDRAWAL LESS THAN OR EQUAL TO ZERO'
C                    check for value within limit
       IF  (WITHDR .GT. LIMIT)
     1    PRINT *, 'DESIRED WITHDRAWAL GREATER THAN LIMIT'
C                        convert to next highest lower denomination
       IF  (WITHDR .GT. 0  .AND.  WITHDR .LE. LIMIT)  THEN
          WITHRN = (WITHDR + (VALBRK(NUMBRK) - 1)) /
     1                       VALBRK(NUMBRK) * VALBRK(NUMBRK)
C                    verification
          WRITE   (*,1020)  WITHRN
 1020     FORMAT  (' ','Withdrawal = $', I4,'  Do you approve (Y/N)?')
          READ    (*,1022)  RESPNS
 1022     FORMAT  (A1)
          IF  (RESPNS .EQ. 'Y'  .OR.  RESPNS .EQ. 'y')  THEN
C                        calculate breakdown
             CALL BRKDWN (WITHRN, NUMBRK, VALBRK, NUMBIL)
C                        output breakdown
             WRITE   (*,1024)  (VALBRK(I), I=1,NUMBRK)
 1024        FORMAT  ('0', 6('  $',I3,:))
             WRITE   (*,1026)  (NUMBIL(I), I=1,NUMBRK)
 1026        FORMAT  (' ', 6I6)
C                        compute fee
             FEE  = CALCFE (WITHRN)
             TOTAL = REAL (WITHRN) + FEE
             WRITE   (*,1028)  FEE, TOTAL
 1028        FORMAT  (' ', 'Fee   =', F7.2/
     1                ' ', 'Total =', F7.2)
C                        add to total
             TOTWTH = TOTWTH + WITHRN
          ENDIF
       ENDIF
       GO TO 80
C                        error in input
   40  PRINT *, 'Invalid character in input  -  Re-enter'
C                        loop back for more input
   80 CONTINUE
C
C                        termination
   90 WRITE  (*,1090)  TOTWTH
 1090 FORMAT  ('0', 'Total withdrawn = $', I5)
      STOP
      END
```

Sample Execution   *(Data entered is underlined.)*

```
Enter amount of withdrawal (integer)
-395
DESIRED WITHDRAWAL LESS THAN OR EQUAL TO ZERO

Enter amount of withdrawal (integer)
$395
Invalid character in input   -   Re-enter

Enter amount of withdrawal (integer)
395
Withdrawal = $ 400   Do you approve (Y/N)?
N

Enter amount of withdrawal (integer)
390
Withdrawal = $ 390   Do you approve (Y/N)?
Y

   $ 50   $ 20   $ 10
      7      2      0
Fee   =    7.80
Total = 397.80

Enter amount of withdrawal (integer)
85
Withdrawal = $  90   Do you approve (Y/N)?
Y

   $ 50   $ 20   $ 10
      1      2      0
Fee   =    2.00
Total =   92.00

Enter amount of withdrawal (integer)
500
DESIRED WITHDRAWAL GREATER THAN LIMIT

Enter amount of withdrawal (integer)
250
Withdrawal = $ 250   Do you approve (Y/N)?
Y

   $ 50   $ 20   $ 10
      5      0      0
Fee   =    5.00
Total = 255.00

Enter amount of withdrawal (integer)
^Z

Total withdrawn = $   730
```

The Computer Time Accounting program can also be modularized and converted to arrays. Two subprograms are included. The first is a subroutine to convert from minutes since midnight to hours and minutes from that same datum. The second is a function to compute the cost of the computer time. The algorithm was developed in section 5.8, and now it is packaged as a general-purpose subprogram.

```
      SUBROUTINE  M2HM (MIN, NEWHRS, NEWMIN)
C
C                  Abstract:   reduces minutes to hours and minutes
C
C                  Input:      MIN:    minutes since midnight
C
C                  Ouput:      NEWHRS: hours since midnight
C                              NEWMIN: remainder of minutes
C
      NEWHRS = MIN / 60
      NEWMIN = MOD (MIN, 60)
C
      RETURN
      END



      FUNCTION  CMPCST (MIN, RATE)
C
C        Abstract:   computes the cost of computer time from
C                        the minutes used
C
C        Input:      MIN:    minutes of computer usage
C                    RATE:   basic rate per minute
C
C        Output:     CMPCST: based on
C                              RATE * MIN for first 120 minutes and
C                                80% of RATE * MIN for balance
C
      IF  (MIN .LE. 120)  THEN
              CMPCST = RATE * REAL (MIN)
          ELSE
              CMPCST = 120.0 * RATE  +  0.80 * REAL (MIN - 120) * RATE
      ENDIF
C
      RETURN
      END
```

We do not yet have the tools for generating the final mainline, since that requires a two-dimensional array (which will be covered in Chapter 10), but we can write an abbreviated mainline which will test our program. Let's even go a step further and enter the log-on and log-off times in military hours and minutes and produce an output using either 'am' or 'pm' notation, along with minutes used and cost.

Computer Time Accounting

```
      C                 Computer Time Accounting
      C
            CHARACTER*2  AMPM(2)
            CHARACTER*7  MESSAG(2)
            DIMENSION    XONOFF(2), MONOFF(2), LONOFF(4)
      C
            DATA  MESSAG/ 'Log On', 'Log Off'/
```

```
C
C              Glossary: XONOFF:  input times in military time
C                        MONOFF:  input times converted to minutes
C                        LONOFF:  output times in hours and minutes
C                        AMPM:    'am' or 'pm' annotation
C
       DO 80  NTRANS = 1,20000
              WRITE   (*,1000)
  1000         FORMAT  ('0','Enter log on,log off times in military units'/
     1                 ' ','     ctrl-Z to terminate')
              READ    (*,*, END=90, ERR=60)  XONOFF
C                     get minutes since midnight, then hours and minutes
              DO 20  I = 1,2
                 ITEMP    = 100.0 * XONOFF(I) +  0.5
                 MONOFF(I) = 60 * (ITEMP / 100) +  MOD (ITEMP, 100)
                 CALL M2HM  (MONOFF(I), LONOFF(2*I-1), LONOFF(2*I))
C                     convert to am/pm notation
                 IF  (LONOFF (2*I-1) .LE. 12)  THEN
                    AMPM(I) = 'am'
                  ELSE
                    AMPM(I) = 'pm'
                    LONOFF(2*I-1) = LONOFF(2*I-1) - 12
                 ENDIF
    20        CONTINUE
C                     get minutes used & cost
              MINUSE = MONOFF(2) - MONOFF(1)
              IF  (MINUSE .GT. 0)  THEN
                 COST    = CMPCST (MINUSE, 2.50)
C                     output
                 WRITE  (*,1040)
     1           (MESSAG(I), LONOFF(2*I-1),LONOFF(2*I), AMPM(I), I=1,2)
  1040           FORMAT  (' ',A7, I4,':',I2, 1X,A2)
                 WRITE   (*,1042)  MINUSE, COST
  1042           FORMAT  ('0',I4,' minutes used for a cost of $',F7.2/)
                 GO TO 80
              ENDIF
C                     error in input
    60        PRINT  *, 'Input error  -  re-enter'
C
    80 CONTINUE
C
C                     termination
    90 STOP
       END
```

Our mainline program has a number of features worthy of comment. We have used arrays as much as possible not only because we want to utilize our new knowledge but also because they are more efficient. The use of loops in our program reduces certain sections of code by almost 50%.

The method of using the array name to read in the entire array was employed in our input routine. A loop to treat each of the values first converts from military time (input as a real number) to integer, then to minutes since midnight, and then to integer hours and minutes. An array of four elements (LONOFF) was used for our output array. Although two arrays of two elements each might have been used, using this longer array did show some new techniques in terms of calculating subscripts. Since the subroutine M2HM expects single variables, we do so by specifying single array elements.

The program also uses a two-character variable array for '*am*' and '*pm*,' again reducing programming effort. The error routine takes care of both invalid input characters (nonnumeric data) as well as invalid input values wherein the log-on time is after the log-off time. Below is a sample test run:

```
Enter log on, log off times in military units
    ctrl-Z to terminate
9.10,10.45
Log  On   9:10 am
Log Off  10:45 am

   95 minutes used for a cost of $ 237.50


Enter log on, log off times in military units
    ctrl-Z to terminate
13.15,4.45
Input error  -  re-enter

Enter log on, log off times in military units
    ctrl-Z to terminate
13.15,16.45
Log  On   1:15 pm
Log Off   4:45 pm

  210 minutes used for a cost of $ 480.00


Enter log on, log off times in military units
    ctrl-Z to terminate
^Z
```

9.8   CHAPTER REVIEW

This chapter has shown methods whereby large amounts of data can be handled with a minimum of coding. Furthermore, the chapter has demonstrated how arrays may be transferred to and from subprograms. Combining arrays with subprograms and formatted I/O, the reader is now equipped to write some very sophisticated programs. The programming systems detailed below are but a taste of what can be done. In fact, many elementary FORTRAN courses end with the information presented in this chapter.

Great emphasis was placed on the I/O of arrays, since a thorough knowledge of the workings of the READ, WRITE, and FORMAT statements greatly simplifies the coding effort. Much programming time is spent on forms design and artistic output; thus, anything that simplifies the programmer's work is important.

Despite all the material presented to this point, we have not finished with the concept of arrays. In the next chapter, we will return for an expansion of that concept into multiple dimensions; and in Chapter 11, we will show some additional critical techniques using arrays. However, even one-dimensional arrays open up new areas of applications which are almost limitless.

The reader now has about 90% of the tools available in the language and can solve about 80% of the problems which might arise, although some sophistication is still lacking.

The topics covered in this chapter include:

Topic	Section
Array concepts	9.1
Bounds checking	9.2
DATA	9.4
DIMENSION	9.2
END= clause	9.3
Implied DO loop	9.3
Input/output	9.3
Mapping function	9.2, 9.6
Memory assignment	9.2
Modularization	9.1, 9.5, 9.6
Program module	9.1
Subprograms	9.6
Subscript	9.1, 9.2
Table lookup	9.4
Type statements	9.2

Exercises

9.8a *Baseball Statistics* This exercise is a revision of exercise 8.8a. This version will manipulate the same data, but in arrays, and will produce a disk file with the results as well as a formal report. The arrays to be used are:

```
INTEGER          IN(11)
```

1 = number of at-bats
2 = number of singles
3 = number of doubles
4 = number of triples
5 = number of home runs
6 = number of bases on balls
7 = number of strike outs
8 = number of runs batted in
9 = number of hits
10 = number of total bases
11 = number of times on base

items 1– 8 are input from the disk file
items 9–11 are calculated in the program

```
INTEGER          ITOTAL(11)      team totals for the above
CHARACTER*10     NAMES(60)       10-character player names
REAL             BATAV(61)       batting averages
REAL             SLGAV(61)       slugging averages
REAL             ONBAV(61)       on-base averages
REAL             STRAV(61)       strike-out averages
REAL             RBIAV(61)       runs batted-in, averages
```

items 1–60 in the real arrays are for the players
item   61 in the real arrays are for the team

The mainline will consist of three modules—the first to input, total, calculate, store, print, and file the individual players' statistics. The second will calculate and file the team results. The third will determine team leaders.

The input module should open the input file and loop through the records until the end-of-file is reached. In that loop, subroutine BBCALC, which receives the array IN, should be written to fill out the rest of the array, items 9 through 11. Another subroutine, BBSTAT, should be written to receive the array IN, the record number being operated on, and the real arrays; that subroutine should place the computed values directly into the appropriate record in the real arrays. The computed value should be multiplied by 1000 and rounded to the nearest integer so that it becomes an integer-valued real. All output of these values should show no decimal places (format specification = Fn.0), although the decimal point cannot be avoided. The totals should be accumulated in the mainline. A record should be written to a disk file containing all of the input and calculated information for each player.

The second module takes effect after end-of-file. The subroutine BBSTAT can now be called with the totals array and record number 61 as arguments, as well as the real arrays, to compute the team averages. The output disk file entry should include a blank field in place of the player name, to distinguish that record as the team statistics.

The third module will list the players with the highest averages in a printed report. Write a general-purpose function LMAXR which receives a real array and the number of elements in that array and returns the record number of the element with the largest value. Send each of the real arrays to the function, one at a time. Print a report with title and headings for player, classification of average (batting, slugging, etc.), and average itself. List the five leading averages and the player's name associated with it.

A fourth, independent module will be a separate mainline designed to read the disk file and produce a printed report of the individual and team statistics. The file record can be read using a single variable for the player name, an integer array of 11, and a real array of 5 for the other values. The total can be isolated by a simple comparison on the order of:

```
IF  (NAME .EQ. '           ')  .............
```

with 10 blanks between the apostrophes. This report should include titles and headings, a listing of all the individual data, and a line with the team data, properly annotated so that it is obvious.

9.8b *Accounts Receivable* This exercise is a revision of exercise 8.8b. The input data is expanded and will be entered into arrays for a more structured program. The input arrays to be used are:

```
INTEGER   INVCE(101)     invoice number
INTEGER   DATE(101)      date: digits 1–2:    month
                               digits 3–4:    year
INTEGER   TYPE(101)      type of transaction:   1 = bill
                                                2 = payment
REAL      AMOUNT(101)    amount of bill or payment
```

The input file consists of bills sent and payments made. The invoice number ties them together; the dates are used to age the bills; i.e., to indicate how much overdue they are. A sample input file might include:

```
                              1111111111222
        columns:    12345678901234567890012
                    1001    1089 1    2514.87
                    1002    1089 1     876.54
                    1003    1089 1    8765.00
                    1004    1189 1    5500.00
                    1002    1189 2     876.54
                    1005    1189 1      25.65
                    1001    1189 2    2000.00
                    1006    0190 1    4500.75
                    1007    0190 1     540.50
                    1001    0190 2     400.00
                    1003    0190 2    8770.00
                    1004    0190 2    5500.00
                    1008    0190 1    1200.00
                    1007    0190 2     500.00
                    1008    0290 1     875.00
                    1009    0290 1    3560.98
                    1006    0290 2    4500.75
```

Module 1 of the mainline should open the input file, read the data in, close the file, and display the number of records on the screen. Module 2 should open an output file, print the title and headings, and perform an echo check of the input data. Module 3 should generate the total billed and the total payments received, and place those totals, properly annotated, after the echo check.

Module 4 will apply the payments to the bill. The file contains only one bill for each invoice number, but it may contain multiple payments against that invoice. The program should look at each bill and apply the payments to it, modifying the value in the bill AMOUNT by subtracting the payment and placing a zero in the payment AMOUNT. Because the payments always appear in the file after the bill, the logic is very direct; a doubly nested loop will do it. (Placing a zero in the payment AMOUNT is a safety measure; it allows the program to search for unapplied payments, or payments for which there is no invoice.) Overpaid bills will become negative.

Module 5 will generate a report on a new page listing first the invoices not fully paid. The fully paid invoices will have a value of 0.00, but the program should use a tolerance (such as <0.005) to compensate for any imprecision or else round the number to the nearest cent. Invoices with an outstanding balance will have a positive amount. Next, list the overpaid invoices, using a separate loop so that the output is separate. Use appropriate annotation to describe the alternative conditions.

Module 6 will perform an aging of the unpaid balances. The last date in the input file can be used as the current date. The function MONAGE from exercise 8.8b should be used to determine the number of months from the invoice date to the current date. The function also needs function MONTH from exercise 8.8b. The array DATE should be modified to hold the aging as a value from 1 to 4, one higher than the value returned from MONAGE. A new array, AGE(4), should be dimensioned and initialized to zero. Then the billing amounts should again be scanned for balances due (ignore overpayments) and added into the proper aging category. The aging schedule should then be added to the output file with these headings:

```
0-30 days    30-60 days    60-90 days    >90 days
```

Below the amounts due in each of the four aging categories, place the percentage of total billed with each category.

9.8c *Coordinate Geometry* The coordinate geometry program in exercise 8.8c will now be modified to store the information and to separate the program into three modules. Module 1 will input, edit, and store the data read from the input file. Module 2 will do the computations, and module 3 will print the report. The five supporting subprograms will still be needed.

The arrays to be used are:

CN(101) north coordinates
CE(101) east coordinates
DS(101) distance traveled for each course
AZ(101) azimuth of each course

Record 1 is the starting coordinates and the distance and azimuth for the first course; record 2 is the coordinates of the point reached after the first course and the distance and azimuth of the second course. The last record will contain the final coordinates and the distance and azimuth back to the starting point.

Module 1 will loop through the input file, placing the first record into CN(1) and CE(1). It will continue with the distance and bearing records, editing each one (counting the errors on the way and displaying an error message and the record number and contents if an error is detected), converting bearings to azimuths and storing the distances and azimuths into the appropriate locations in the array. At the end of the input, if any errors have been detected, the program should terminate with an appropriate message displayed.

Module 2 will compute the coordinates of the rest of the points and the distance and azimuth from the last point to the starting point.

Module 3 will print a report of the traverse, properly annotating the starting and ending points and the course numbers. Directions are to be converted back to bearings. The output is easiest to read if the lines alternate, the first giving the coordinates, the second the distance and bearing to the next coordinate, the third the next coordinate, etc. Also, the distance and bearing to the starting point should be given and annotated.

9.8d *Inventory Close-Out* A company sells and ships four close-out items on a daily basis until no more are left. The file structure, with each record having four fields (each 10 columns), one for each item, is set up as follows:

Record 1   Unit prices (real)
Record 2   Inventory (integer)
Records 3–n Transactions (integer)

A sample file might be:

```
1.234      1.862      0.798      2.230
 187       17631      17631       433
  80        9000      11000        18
  12           0       2500       150
  53        9000       3500       200
   0         100        600        75
```

Write a mainline that reads the first two records into the arrays:

```
INTEGER  INVENT(4)
REAL     UNITPR(4)
```

and then proceeds to process each of the transaction records with an input buffer ITRANS(4). However, it should first save the value of the starting inventory in another array for later use.

Write a subroutine which receives the above arrays and returns an array ISHIP(4) of the items deliverable—those for which there is inventory left. The inventory should also be updated in the subroutine.

Write a function to accept the arrays ISHIP and UNITPR and return the cost of the items deliverable. That cost should be accumulated in the mainline as a total of goods sold; use TOTAL(1) in an array of TOTAL(3).

Write a function to determine handling costs according to the following rules:

$1.00 per item handled
$0.02 per number of total items up to a maximum of $100
Minimum handling charge: $10.00

For example, in the last record (if the entire order is still available in inventory), there are three items handled ($3.00) plus 775 total items at $0.02 ($15.50), for a total handling charge of $18.50. Thus, the handling charge could range from $10.00 to $104.00. This cost should be accumulated into TOTAL(2).

Write a function to determine the shipping charge based on the following schedule:

Total Cost of Goods Sold	Shipping Charge
Less than $1000	$10.00
1000–$5000	1% of cost of goods sold
Greater than $5000	$50.00

Accumulate this total as TOTAL(3).

For each transaction, output the number of item ordered, the number of items deliverable, and the three costs with a total for the transaction. At the end of the transaction day, determine the value of goods left in inventory. The difference between that value and the starting inventory value should equal the total of goods sold to within a couple of pennies. Output those values and the three accumulated totals with a grand total.

9.8e   *Coordinate Analysis*   Generate a file of 20 x, y, and z coordinates consisting of a record for each point, each record having three fields. Read these into three arrays in a mainline program. Output the three arrays in the same order they are read in.

Using the functions RMAX and RMIN developed in exercise 9.6a, find and output the maximums and minumums of each of the three arrays.

Write a subroutine to receive the x- and y-coordinate arrays and the number of coordinates and return the average x- and y-coordinates.

Set up a new integer array, IQUAD and, thinking of the coordinate plane as being divided up into four quadrants by the midcoordinates computed in the previous module, determine the number of points in each quadrant, making sure that you make some assumption about points which fall right on either or both of the midcoordinate axes. Also set up another integer array, LQUAD(20), and place the quadrant number found into this array so that there is a record of which quadrant a given coordinate falls into. Do this in a subroutine. Output the distribution.

Determine the maximum and minimum z-coordinates for the points in each quadrant. Output the results.

9.8f   *Payroll*   File TASKS contains a table of tasks with hourly rates for performing those tasks, as well as a description of those tasks. A sample file for surveyors would look like:

```
                        11111111112222222222333
columns:    12345678901234567890123456789012
            1      18.86     Rod person
            2      20.77     Instrument person
            3      22.41     Chief of party
            4      28.75     Supervisor
```

File NAMES contains employee numbers and names and looks like this:

```
                     11111111112
columns:    12345678901234567890
            1    Lee Joker
            2    V. P. Daniels
           18    Mindy Brown
           23    Harold Harolds
           32    Evander Childs
           56    Dana Pressman
          117    Karen Vogel
          118    Thomas Thomas
```

An associated payroll input file WORKED contains records of employee activities. Each record consists of an employee number, the task worked on and the number of hours worked, and might look like this:

```
                       111111
columns:    123456789012345
            18    2    40.00
            23    1    27.25
            32    1    12.75
           117    3    42.50
```

Write a program to read all three files into appropriate arrays. Then process the data from file WORKED, looking up each employee's name and task, and computing the employees' pay as the rate for the task times the hours worked. (Ignore any consideration of overtime.) Next display a record for each working employee, showing the employee number, name, task description, rate, hours, and pay. Then display two exception lists, one listing any task that was not worked on and the other listing employees who did no work during the period.

10

Multidimensional Arrays

CHAPTER OUTLINE

CHAPTER OBJECTIVES

- To present the theory of multidimensional arrays.

- To relate to data found in the real world.

- To show the method of storing arrays using the mapping function, how it works and how its use simplifies code.

- To introduce the concepts of data structure.

- To demonstrate professional techniques of data manipulation.

STATEMENT OF THE PROBLEM

The concept of multidimensional arrays is always considered difficult to grasp, and yet so much manual data handling done is with more than a single column or row of numbers. Almost every accounting worksheet has multiple rows and columns, if not pages as well. Likewise, scientific data is usually in matrix form; something as simple as plane or spatial coordinates are arranged in tables.

The ability to work in more than one dimension is critical to the programmer if he or she is to work with "real-world" data. All that the various computer languages do is to extend the concept of labeling locations to two, three, or higher-order spaces.

Once you learn the techniques of working with multidimensional arrays, you will be pleasantly surprised at the tremendous amount of data handling possible with a minimum of code. Algorithms developed for one-dimensional arrays can be expanded easily to handle more than one dimension and, in some cases, can be used with only minor modifications.

10.1   MULTIDIMENSIONAL CONCEPTS

In the previous chapter, one-dimensional arrays were described as blocks of data defined under a single variable name and accessible with a subscript or "element locator." This construct opened up a whole new methodology for handling data, allowing the modification of program structure into small modules that are easier to code and debug, as well as making the programs far more understandable. Most critical was the ability we derived to do more data processing with less code. We will now expand our technique to include arrays of more than one dimension, thereby further expanding our ability to process data with short and precise code.

Whereas a one-dimensional array can be thought of as a column (or a row) of values, a two-dimensional array is more like a matrix of values arranged in rows and columns. A three-dimensional array can be visualized as layers of two-dimensional arrays or, as often described, a matrix of values arranged in rows, columns, and pages. Nor need we stop there and limit ourselves to the three visual dimensions; a fourth dimensional array is a collection of three-dimensional arrays arranged in volumes or files. There is theoretically nothing that stops the compiler writer, as we will shortly see, from implementing as many dimensions as desired. FORTRAN 77 allows up to seven dimensions in its full implementation, and some versions have no limit whatsoever.

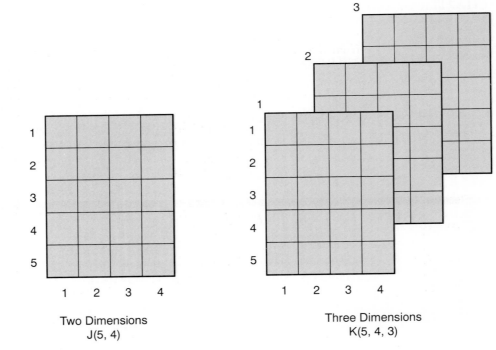

One Dimension
I(5)

Two Dimensions
J(5, 4)

Three Dimensions
K(5, 4, 3)

The rules pertaining to multidimensional arrays are very similar to those for single dimensioned arrays. There must still be a DIMENSION statement declaring the number and size of the arrays; the total number of elements that can be stored in the array is the product of the dimensions. For example, these arrays:

```
DIMENSION  I(5), J(5,4), K(5,4,3)
```

have 5, 20 (from 5 × 4), and 60 (from 5 × 4 × 3) elements, respectively. Any use of the DATA statement to initialize these arrays must reflect the array size:

```
DATA K/ 60 * 0/
```

Likewise, an I/O statement which uses just the array name will I/O the full number of elements.

One is tempted to ask which dimension of a two-dimensional array stands for the row and which for the column; likewise, one might ask which dimension of a three-dimensional array represents the page. The diagrams above show that I is a one-dimensional array of 5 rows, J is a two-dimensional array of 5 rows and 4 columns, and K is a three-dimensional array with 5 rows, 4 columns, and 3 pages. The dimensions shown seem to indicate that the order is row, column, and page; but in reality, there is no such thing as a multidimensional array! Such arrays are figments of the programmer's imagination, albeit very useful figments. The computer's memory is a big one-dimensional array, and all data, single values, and arrays are stored accordingly.

Therefore, the question about which subscript stands for which dimension will go unanswered. The author resists answering the question for two reasons: (1) any such definition is artificial, since the programmer has absolute control over how the information is input or output, and (2) there is a better way to think of the dimensions in light of our upcoming applications. It is very important for the sophisticated programmer to understand how the information is stored in memory and the techniques for controlling the I/O of that information.

This brings us to that better way of defining what our dimensions stand for from the viewpoint of data structures. Assume a situation in which temperature data is being analyzed. The data base is to hold the high, low, and mean temperatures for each day in some period. That period can be a week (7 days), a month (28, 29, 30, or 31 days), a year (365 or 366 days), or some part of a year. Each day will have three data elements; this is defined as a record. However, the number of records can vary depending upon the period selected. A better assumption is that the order of the dimensions is, first, the number of items in a record and, second, the number of records. The justification for this assumption is given in the next section.

We can diagram a 3 * 5 array in two ways:

Record:	1	2	3	4	5
Item 1					
Item 2					
Item 3					

or

Item:	1	2	3
Record 1			
Record 2			
Record 3			
Record 4			
Record 5			

Obviously, we can look at the item/record orientation either as row/column or column/row. However, the order of placement in the DIMENSION statement *does* have significance in how the matrix is arranged in memory, and the understanding of this concept brings us to a higher level of sophistication.

Review Question

10.1a   How many locations must be set aside for each of the dimensioned arrays?

        DIMENSION I(3,5), J(2,8,6), K(5,6,9), L(5,2)

10.2   THE MAPPING FUNCTION

As stated above, there is no such thing as a multidimensional array. What we conceive of as a multidimensional array is rearranged by the *mapping function*, a formula that maps multidimensional arrays into one dimension. This function was discussed in the previous chapter in relation to one-dimensional arrays, where it appears in its simplest form: the difference between the subscripts. Now it must be generalized to higher-order dimensions.

For example, look at the simple two-dimensional array:

        DIMENSION IJ(3,4)

The mapping function states that the order of storage of this array is as follows:

        IJ(1,1), IJ(2,1), IJ(3,1), IJ(1,2), IJ(2,2), IJ(3,2), IJ(1,3), IJ(2,3),
        IJ(3,3), IJ(1,4), IJ(2,4), IJ(3,4)

To remember the order of storage, note that the first subscript changes most often and the second subscript changes only when the range of the first subscript is exhausted; the first subscript is then reset to 1.

The order of storage of a three-dimensional array is defined in the same way. For example:

        DIMENSION NN(2,3,2)

is stored in the following order:

        NN(1,1,1), NN(2,1,1), NN(1,2,1), NN(2,2,1), NN(1,3,1), NN(2,3,1),
        NN(1,1,2), NN(2,1,2), NN(1,2,2), NN(2,2,2), NN(1,3,2), NN(2,3,2)

again, with the earliest subscript changing most often; and the last, least often.

The mapping function for element IJ(m,n) in the dimensioned array IJ(M,N) defines the displacement from the beginning of the array as:

        M * (n - 1) + m - 1

Using our array IJ(3,4), let's see how this works:

IJ (m,n):	1,1	2,1	3,1	1,2	2,2	3,2	1,3	2,3	3,3	1,4	2,4	3,4
Address:	1	2	3	4	5	6	7	8	9	10	11	12

Element IJ(2,3) [m=2, n=3] in array IJ (3,4) [M=3, N=4] has a displacement of 3 * (3 − 1) + 2 − 1 = 7. Adding this displacement to the address of the beginning of the array, 1, we get address 8—and lo and behold, that is where IJ(2,3) is stored! Try a few to convince yourself of the consistency of this scheme.

Furthermore, notice that the value of N does not even appear in the formula, indicating that the value of the last dimension is not critical. This is identical to the situation described in section 9.6, which states that the size of the one-dimensional array does not have to be known in an accessed subprogram; the actual last subscript value is merely added to the displacement.

In the discussion of the temperature data base, the number of items is three for all records, but the number of records could vary based on the number of days in the data. Since the value of N, the second dimension in a two-dimensional array, does not come into the mapping function, to make maximum use of that function and provide us with the facility of some very sophisticated coding later on, it behooves us to set the first dimensional value as the constant. Even where the number of records varies, the formula of the mapping function does not. This justifies the assumption that the order of the dimensions should be, first, the number of items in a record and, second, the number of records.

Look back at the diagram above which shows the layout of the two-dimensional array IJ(3,4) in memory. If the mapping formula is defined without −1 at the end, we find that the result of the formula agrees with the address below the diagram, which represents an equivalent one-dimensional array. For example, an array L(12) starting at the same location as array IJ would map exactly the same. Later, in section 10.5, this principle will be used to design general-purpose subprograms that can access arrays that are either one- or two-dimensional.

The mapping function for the element IJ(k,m,n) in the three-dimensional array IJ(K,M,N) has a displacement from the first element of:

```
K * M * (n - 1) + K * (m - 1) + k - 1
```

Note again how the last dimension, N, does not appear in the mapping function. Ignoring the −1 at the end, we get the location in the equivalent one-dimensional array.

Not much effort is required to extend the function into the higher dimensions; thus, many compilers will allow an unlimited number of subscripts. Most compilers use a general multidimensional mapping function up to the number of allowed dimensions. Note that if the three-dimensional function above is applied to IJ(1,M,N), wherein K and k equal 1, the function reduces to its two-dimensional equivalent. And if the array is further reduced to IJ(1,1,N), with K, k, M, and m all equal to 1, the function reduces to its one-dimensional equivalent, namely n.

Occasionally you might see (in other publications) a reference to "column major order" for storage of two-dimensional arrays. If one assumes that a two-dimensional array is always subscripted in the order (*row, column*), then the data is stored "by the column"; i.e., the order of storage is down the column, with one column after another. Acceptance of that definition for data storage might lead the programmer to believe that the data must be input and output in that geometric form. This places a mental restriction on the programmer and prevents the use of some very sophisticated methodology, which will be discussed in subsequent sections and in the next chapter.

Manipulation of multidimensional array elements is usually just an extension of the principles learned with one-dimensional arrays. The mapping function is transparent to the programmer, and reference to it is not necessary in simple situations. In most cases, writing for higher-level dimensions is just a matter of adding additional nested loops. For example, to calculate the sum of all the elements of a two-dimensional array, the code might look like this:

```
      DIMENSION  N(3,10)
            |
            |
            |
      ISUM = 0
      DO 20  I = 1,10
          DO 20  J = 1,3
   20 ISUM = ISUM + N(J,I)
```

Exactly the same results would have been obtained with the following:

```
      ISUM = 0
      DO 20  I = 1,3
          DO 20  J = 1,10
   20 ISUM = ISUM + N(I,J)
```

Note that the programmer has complete freedom in assigning variable names to subscripts. And for those who do not like to end two loops on the same statement:

```
      ISUM = 0
      DO 20  I = 1,3
          DO 10  J = 1,10
   10     ISUM = ISUM + N(I,J)
   20 CONTINUE
```

Review Question and Exercise

10.2a   For the given arrays:

```
DIMENSION  M(3,4,6), N(5,3)
```

determine the displacements of the following elements from the first element.

a. N(1,1)
b. N(4,2)
c. N(5,3)
d. M(1,3,2)
e. M(2,3,5)
f. M(1,1,6)
g. M(2,4,6)
h. M(3,4,6)

10.2b   Write the code necessary to set all the elements of the array N(4,5,10) to zero. Show two methods, one using DO loops and assignments, the other using the DATA statement. To check out the program, use a WRITE statement for the entire array and a FORMAT of (' ',20I3).

10.2c   Write the code necessary to place the values 1 to 40 into the array M(5,4,2) in the same order as stored by the mapping function (first subscript changes most often). Output as in exercise 10.2b; the values should come out in order. Use this technique in setting values into the arrays needed in subsequent exercises.

10.2d Write the code to transfer all the elements from the array M(3,8) to the array N(3,8) and to the array L(8,3), reversing rows and columns in the last case. Use two separate modules for each transfer. Output all three entire arrays, each with its own WRITE statement, and note carefully the order of the output. Draw diagrams in (*row, column*) form and verify that the output is what you would expect from the theory given in the text.

10.2e Write the code to transfer the elements of array M(4) to array N(4,2) wherein both items in the record have the same value. For example,

If:	M	then:		N	
	2		2		2
	5		5		5
	1		1		1
	7		7		7

Use a DATA statement to place the values into M.

10.2f Write the code to set up a matrix M(10,10), wherein the elements represent the products of a 10×10 multiplication table. Output the whole array using FORMAT (' ', 10I6).

10.2g Write the code to set up a matrix M(10,10), wherein the elements represent the differences of the second subscript subtracted from the first subscript. Output the whole array using FORMAT (' ', 10I6).

10.3 INPUT/OUTPUT TECHNIQUES

As emphasized earlier in the chapter, the programmer has full control over which dimension represents the row and which dimension represents the column (or the page). To input or output multidimensional arrays, any of the tools described in Chapter 9 can be used: the DO loop, the implied DO loop, the entire array method, or any combination of those methods. The implied DO loop can have as many indices as there are dimensions; the programmer must include the appropriate number of paired parentheses to keep the syntax correct. When the entire array is used, the I/O order agrees with that of the method of storage, namely, the earlier subscripts change most often (as dictated by the mapping function). Thus, for:

```
DIMENSION  IA (3,2)
   :
WRITE   (1,*)  IA
```

the order of output is:

```
IA(1,1), IA(2,1), IA(3,1), IA(1,2), IA(2,2), IA(3,2)
```

Assume a situation involving an array of (8,3) or (3,8). As a practical example, it might represent a fixed-size seminar class of eight students in which each student gets three grades. The array is to contain these grades. Since this matrix may be thought of as eight records with three items each, or three records with eight items each, the order of the subscripts is arbitrary. For the sake of our exposition, assume:

```
DIMENSION  IGRADE(3,8)
```

We can output this block of data in the geometric form of eight rows and three columns in a number of ways:

```
      DO 20  I = 1,8
   20 WRITE    (6,1020)  IGRADE(1,I), IGRADE(2,I), IGRADE(3,I)
 1020 FORMAT  (' ', 3I6)
```

Since there are eight executions of the WRITE statement, each starting at the beginning of the FORMAT, the number of fields may be larger than three; for example, 5I6 will give the same output, although there is no useful purpose in using any variation of the given format.

The use of the single implied DO loop simplifies the WRITE statement to:

```
      DO 20  I = 1,8
   20 WRITE    (6,1020)  (IGRADE(J,I), J = 1,3)
```

The use of the double implied DO loop reduces the output command to a single line:

```
      WRITE    (6,1020)  ((IGRADE(J,I), J = 1,3), I = 1,8)
```

However, using this method (and the next one below) requires that the format be exactly (3I6), since there is only one WRITE command and the property of format reversion is needed to place three values on a line. And, since the order of the output is the same as the order of storage (first subscript changing most often), the entire array method might be used:

```
      WRITE    (6,1020)   IGRADE
```

Now, to output the data as three lines with eight columns using:

```
 1040 FORMAT  (' ', 8I6)
```

the following methods might be used:

```
      DO 20  I = 1,3
   20 WRITE    (6,1040)   IGRADE(I,1), IGRADE(I,2), IGRADE(I,3),
    1                     IGRADE(I,4), IGRADE(I,5), IGRADE(I,6),
    2                     IGRADE(I,7), IGRADE(I,8)
```

or

```
      DO 20  I = 1,3
   20 WRITE    (6,1040)  (IGRADE(I,J), J=1,8)
```

or

```
      WRITE    (6,1040)  ((IGRADE(I,J), J=1,8), I=1,3)
```

Looking at the input, assume that the grades have been entered into a file chronologically; i.e., three rows of eight grades, each grade right-justified in a field of four columns. The input routine, using the same DIMENSION (3,8) from above, becomes:

```
      DO 10  I = 1,3
   10 READ     (5,1010)  (IGRADE(J,I), J=1,8)
```

or

```
READ      (5,1010)   ((IGRADE(J,I), J=1,8), I=1,3)
```

with

```
1010 FORMAT  (8I4)
```

This illustrates the complete control that the programmer has over the order of storage and the shape of the I/O. Thus, the programmer should choose the order of the subscripts in a way that is convenient or efficient and not based on such arbitrary definitions as (*row, column*).

Using the temperature data as another example, assume that the highs and lows for each day represent an input record and that a record is filed on one line, with the high temperature in columns 1–5 and the low temperature in columns 6–10, right-justified; the temperatures are entered without a decimal point, although they will be read in as real numbers. There are as many lines in the file as there are input records, and since each record represents a day, each line in the file is a day.

```
      C                        Input and Echo-Check Temperature Data
      C
            DIMENSION  TEMP3(3,367)
      C
      C                        open input file and read data
            OPEN    (UNIT=7, FILE='TEMPIN')
            READ    (7,1000, END=20)  ((TEMP3(J,I), J=1,2), I=1,367)
       1000 FORMAT  (2F5.0)
                  STOP 'excessive data'
         20 NUMDAY = I - 1
            CLOSE (7)
      C                        compute mean temperatures
            DO 40  I = 1,NUMDAY
         40 TEMP3(3,I) = (TEMP3(1,I) + TEMP3(2,I)) / 2.00
      C                        open output file and write array
            OPEN    (UNIT=8, FILE='TEMPOUT')
            WRITE   (8,1040)  ((TEMP3(J,I), J=1,3), I=1,NUMDAY)
       1040 FORMAT  ('1','Temperature Data'//
          1              '0','  High    Low    Mean'//
          2              (' ', 3F7.1))
            CLOSE (8)
      C                        termination
            STOP
            END
```

Note the conciseness of the I/O. The output includes title, headings, and data, all neatly lined up.

The next application shows how a very short program can utilize the tools of FORTRAN to develop a rather large report from an almost unlimited amount of input. It involves the tabulation of sales and returns for a large chain of stores. It utilizes a three-dimensional array, AMT(12,31,2), to store two values for each day of the year. The reader can think in terms of 12 pages (months), each with up to 31 lines (days) and 2 columns (sales, returns). Each of the storage locations is initially cleared to zero, and as the data is read, it is added into the proper storage location. (The large DO loop was used with a limit of 30,000 to avoid the use of a

GO TO; the GO TO would have allowed an unlimited amount of data.) The array allows for up to 31 days per month, but the output routine restricts the number of days printed out to the actual number of days in each month, stored in the array MDAY; for simplicity, February is assumed to have 29 days.

```
C                       Program to Demonstrate Multidimensional Arrays
C
C          Abstract: a program to tabulate sales and returns for a chain
C                    of retail stores by printing a chronological
C                    listing of activities on a daily basis with monthly
C                    and annual totals.
C
C          Input:    columns  1 - 2:  month  (integer, range 1 - 12)
C                       "     4 - 5:  day    (integer, range 1 - 31)
C                       "    11 - 20:  amount of sales    (real)
C                       "    21 - 30:  amount of returns  (real)
C                    Input has been previously edited for proper ranges.
C                    Data is unsorted.
C                    There may be multiple records for each day.
C
C          Output:   12 pages, one for each month.
C                    Up to 31 lines, one for each day.
C                    Monthly totals on each page.
C                    Annual totals on final page.
C
C
          IMPLICIT DOUBLE PRECISION  (A-H, O-Z)
          DIMENSION  AMT(12,31,2), TOTM(12,2), TOTA(2), XIN(2), MDAY(12)
C
          DATA       AMT, TOTM, TOTA/ 770 * 0.00/
          DATA       MDAY/ 31,29,31, 30,31,30, 31,31,30, 31,30,31/
C
C                         input loop
          OPEN  (UNIT=4, FILE='SRIN')
          DO 40  N = 1,30000
              READ  (4,1020, END=100)  MO,     IDAY,  XIN
 1020         FORMAT               (I2, 1X, I2, 5X, 2F10.2)
              DO 20  I = 1,2
   20         AMT(MO,IDAY,I) = AMT(MO,IDAY,I) + XIN(I)
   40 CONTINUE
          CLOSE  (4)
          STOP  'excessive data'
  100 CLOSE  (4)
C
C                         compute totals
          DO 140  I = 1,2
              DO 140  J = 1,12
                  DO 120  K = 1,31
  120             TOTM(J,I) = TOTM(J,I) + AMT(J,K,I)
  140 TOTA(I) = TOTA(I) + TOTM(J,I)
C
C                         output
          OPEN  (UNIT=3, FILE='SROUT')
C                         loop through months, new page for each
          DO 200  I = 1,12
              WRITE  (3,1140)  I
 1140         FORMAT  ('1','SALES & RETURNS for Month', I3//
     1                 '0','Day', 7X,'Sales', 5X,'Returns'/' ')
              NDAYS = MDAY(I)
```

```
C                         loop through days
          DO 160  J = 1,NDAYS
  160     WRITE    (3,1160) J, (AMT(I,J,K), K=1,2)
 1160     FORMAT  (' ',     I3,  2F12.2)
C                         monthly totals
  200 WRITE    (3,1200) (TOTM(I,J), J=1,2)
 1200 FORMAT  ('0', 3X,  2F12.2, 4X, 'Totals')
C                         annual totals
      WRITE    (3,1202)  TOTA
 1202 FORMAT  (//'0', 3X, 2F12.2, 4X, 'Grand Totals')
C                         termination
      CLOSE (3)
      STOP   'end-of-run'
      END
```

Note the various methods of I/O used, including implied DO loops and whole arrays. In fact, the coding:

```
          DO 160  J = 1,NDAYS
  160     WRITE    (3,1160) J, (AMT(I,J,K), K=1,2)
```

could have been shortened by using a single WRITE statement with a double implied DO loop in place of the two-statement DO 160 loop:

```
      WRITE    (3,1160)  (J, (AMT(I,J,K), K=1,2), J=1,NDAYS)
```

The module for computing the monthly and annual totals is very efficient and is similar to the way a sophisticated calculator user with one available memory location would work. The outer loop first sets up the calculation for sales, then later sets up for returns. The sales for month 1 are added up and that sum is added to the annual sales; then month 2 sales are added up, with the sum again being added to the annual sales; and so forth until month 12. Then the outer loop is set to calculate returns and the process is repeated. Having two of the three loops terminate on the same statement (140) may be confusing to the reader but not to the machine; the same results would be obtained with the following code, which might be more understandable:

```
C                    compute totals
      DO 140  I = 1,2
         DO 130  J = 1,12
            DO 120  K = 1,31
  120          TOTM(J,I) = TOTM(J,I) + AMT(J,K,I)
  130       TOTA(I) = TOTA(I) + TOTM(J,I)
  140 CONTINUE
C
```

Another interesting application is the generation of the following table:

Value	Square	Value	Square
1	1	51	2601
2	4	52	2704
:	:	:	:
:	:	:	:
50	2500	100	10000

The program is remarkably short. However, note the clever use of the triple implied DO loop!

```
C                         Table of Squares
C
        DIMENSION  ISQ(2,100)
C
C                      generate values
        DO 20  I = 1,100
            ISQ(1,I) = I
     20     ISQ(2,I) = I * I
C                      output routine
        WRITE   (3,1020)  (((ISQ(J,I), J=1,2), I=N,100,50), N=1,50)
  1020  FORMAT  ('1',2('Value', 5X,'Square', 9X)//(' ',I5,I11, I14,I11))
C                      termination
        STOP
        END
```

Review Questions and Exercise

10.3a   Indicate the order of output for the following WRITE statements:

    a. WRITE (1,1000) ((A(J,I), J=1,10,2), I=1,3)
    b. WRITE (1,1000) ((A(J,I), I=1,3,2), J=1,10,4)
    c. WRITE (1,1000) ((A(I,K), I=1,3), K=5,8)
    d. WRITE (1,1000) (((A(K,J,I), K=1,4), J=1,3,2), I=1,5,3)
    e. WRITE (1,1000) (((A(K,J,I), I=1,5,3), J=1,3,2), K=1,4)
    f. WRITE (1,1000) (((A(K,J,I), K=1,4,4), I=1,2), J=3,5)

10.3b   An array J(3,5) stores a matrix of 3 rows and 5 columns. Give the WRITE and FORMAT statements necessary to display the array in that geometric form.

10.3c   For that same array, J(3,5), assume 5 rows and 3 columns. Give the WRITE and FORMAT statements necessary to display the array in that geometric form.

10.3d   For the array J(4,7,52), assume 4 columns, 7 rows, and 52 pages. Give the WRITE and FORMAT statements necessary to display the array in that geometric form.

10.3e   For the same array J(4,7,52), assume 4 pages, 7 columns, and 52 lines. Give the WRITE and FORMAT statements necessary to display the array in that geometric form.

10.3f   For the grading program presented in section 10.3, give the READ statement necessary to read in the data if it is stored as one piece of data per line (as it might be entered from a keyboard) in the following order:

    a. 3 groups of 8 grades
    b. 8 groups of 3 grades

10.3g   Write a program to input a tax rate in percent and produce a table in the following format, using a two-dimensional array. Skip a line after every multiple of 5 cents:

Tax Table for 7.50%

Amount	Tax	Amount	Tax	Amount	Tax	Amount	Tax
0.01	0.00	0.26	0.02	0.51	0.04	0.76	0.06
0.02	0.00	0.27	0.02	0.52	0.04	0.77	0.06
:	:	:	:	:	:	:	:
0.05	0.00	0.30	0.02	0.55	0.04	0.80	0.06
0.06	0.00	0.31	0.02	0.56	0.04	0.81	0.06
:	:	:	:	:	:	:	:
:	:	:	:	:	:	:	:
0.25	0.02	0.50	0.04	0.75	0.06	1.00	0.08

10.4 COMPUTATIONAL TECHNIQUES

Multidimensional arrays allow the programmer to manipulate a large amount of data with very few instructions. Our first application program involves 3200 bowling scores collected by 40 bowlers, each playing 80 games. (In case the reader is unaware of this very frustrating sport, it is a game in which the possible scores range from 0 to 300.) In the program below, we will input those scores into an array of 80 by 40 (80 items, 40 records), determine the individual bowlers' averages, find the highest average, the lowest score, the 300 games, and the distribution of the scores into the following ranges:

0– 50	171–210
51– 90	211–250
91–130	251–290
131–170	291–300

In order for the program to be described fully, it will be interspersed with text explaining its many features.

 Bowling Scores

```
C                      Analysis of Bowling Scores
C
      DIMENSION  IBOWL(80,40), IDSTR(8), NDSTR(8), BAVG(40)
C
      DATA  NDSTR/ 50, 90, 130, 170, 210, 250, 290, 300/
      DATA  IDSTR, MIN, BMAX/ 8*0, 301, -1.0/
C
C                      glossary
C                      --------
C      BAVG:    bowler averages
C      BMAX:    maximum bowler average
C      IBOWL:   bowler scores by (game,bowler)
C      IDSTR:   counter of scores in each range
C      MIN:     minimum score
C      NDSTR:   high end of each range, used to compute IDSTR
C
```

The minimum score (MIN) is initialized to a value (301) greater than any possible score; in this way the minimum-value algorithm is simplified. The maximum bowler average (BMAX) is initialized to a value (−1.0) less than any possible average for the same reason.

```
C                     read in file
      OPEN    (2, FILE='BOWLING.RAW')
      READ    (2,1000) IBOWL
 1000 FORMAT  (I3)
      CLOSE   (2)
```

The input file contains 3200 records, with one score in each record stored in columns 1 to 3. It is assumed that the first 80 records are the scores for the first bowler; the next 80, the scores for the second bowler; and so forth. Thus, the entire array method of input can be used. Even with a different input data layout, the READ will work with an appropriate FORMAT as long as that input data is arranged in the same order. The file is opened, the data read, and the file closed.

The test file used for this program was generated using a random-number generator with the mean value theorem to produce a normally distributed collection of scores. The mean used was 170.5, and the standard deviation was 40.5. Although this produced a good distribution, it was necessary to ensure that no score was less than 0 or greater than 300 by checking the generated values and adjusting them if necessary. Also, the data was modified so that some 300 games appeared therein in order that the program logic could be checked.

```
C                     get bowler averages
      DO 40  I = 1,40
         ISUM = 0
         DO 20  J = 1,80
   20    ISUM = ISUM + IBOWL(J,I)
   40 BAVG(I) = REAL (ISUM) / 80.0
      WRITE   (*,1040) BAVG
 1040 FORMAT  (' ','Bowler averages:'/ (' ',8F8.1))
```

The computation of the bowler averages is standard. It is embedded within an outer loop which controls the bowler number. Dividing SUM by 80.0 rather than 80 was done to avoid mixed-mode arithmetic. The output method of specifying the entire array was used here and results in 10 lines of output, each line with 8 scores on it. (See the end of this section for sample output.)

```
C                     find highest bowler average
      DO 60  I = 1,40
         IF (BAVG(I) .GT. BMAX)  THEN
            BMAX = BAVG(I)
            IMAX = I
         ENDIF
   60 CONTINUE
      WRITE   (*,1060)  IMAX, BMAX
 1060 FORMAT  (' ','Bowler',I3,' has highest average of', F6.1)
```

The method of determining the highest bowler average uses the standard maximum-value algorithm, which assumes that the value has been initialized as a small value out of the normal range of the data. However, this routine does not consider the unlikely case of two bowlers tied for the maximum value. To cover that possibility, it would be necessary to rescan the array BAVG after BMAX is determined.

```
C                      find lowest score
      DO 100  I = 1,40
         DO 80  J = 1,80
            IF  (IBOWL(J,I) .LT. MIN)  MIN = IBOWL(J,I)
 80      CONTINUE
100 CONTINUE
      DO 110  I = 1,40
         DO 110  J = 1,80
            IF  (IBOWL(J,I) .EQ. MIN)  WRITE  (*,1100)  I, MIN, J
1100        FORMAT  (' ','Bowler',I3,
     1                ' has a low score of',I4,' in game',I3)
110 CONTINUE
```

Again, the standard algorithm for minimum value is used, with the assumption that MIN is initialized to a high value outside the range of the data. However, because of the more likely case of a tie, the output is included in a rescan of the data. Thus, the minimum value is determined first, then all scores are compared for equality. Here a single terminating CONTINUE has been used, although two would be easier to read.

```
C                      list 300 bowlers
      DO 140  I = 1,40
         DO 120  J = 1,80
            IF  (IBOWL(J,I) .EQ. 300)
     1         WRITE  (*,1102)  I, J
1102           FORMAT  (' ','Bowler',I3,
     1                ' has a score of 300 in game',I3)
120      CONTINUE
140 CONTINUE
```

Nothing too spectacular here! Some programmers might want to combine the code above with the computation for lowest score in the section preceding (DO 100 loop), since the loop structure is the same. Although it would lead to fewer statements, it would destroy the structure of the code by combining two functions which are better left in separate modules.

```
C                      distribution
      DO 180  I = 1,40
         DO 180  J = 1,80
            DO 160  K = 1,8
               IF  (IBOWL(J,I) .LE. NDSTR(K))  THEN
                  IDSTR(K) = IDSTR(K) + 1
                  GO TO 180
               ENDIF
160         CONTINUE
180 CONTINUE
      WRITE  (*,1180)  NDSTR, IDSTR
1180 FORMAT  ('0','Distribution:',5X, 8I5/ 19X, 8I5)
```

Here is some very short and efficient code for determining the distribution. The GO TO was used to simulate the LOOP .. EXIT construct; any other solution would be longer and less efficient in execution.

Each score is compared with the upper end of a range, and should it be less than or equal to it, its location is determined immediately because the ranges are arranged in increasing order. Once added to the counters, the program can continue with the next value (note the GO TO to the end of the middle loop) and not concern itself with the other ranges. Any score greater than 300 would be ignored.

One excellent way of auditing the results would be to compute the sum of the distribution to ensure that all 3200 scores have been assigned to one of the ranges. Even though we think we are treating edited data that is correct, sometimes a bad value sneaks in; thus, the code below should be added before terminating:

```
C                       verify that all scores have been assigned
      ISUM = 0
      DO 200  I = 1,8
  200 ISUM = ISUM + IDSTR(I)
      IF (ISUM .NE. 3200)  WRITE  (*,1200)  ISUM
 1200     FORMAT (//' ','ERROR IN DATA:  only',I5,' scores')
C                       termination
      STOP
      END
```

Running the above program produces output like the following:

```
Bowler averages:
    174.4    169.6    178.6    170.0    170.8    174.8    165.3    167.9
    170.9    171.4    169.1    169.9    166.8    171.5    163.8    172.3
    168.4    162.1    167.6    167.6    168.4    174.4    171.9    175.1
    173.0    166.9    169.6    171.5    162.3    167.1    163.9    171.9
    165.4    166.2    170.2    165.2    174.5    169.9    171.9    163.6
Bowler  3 has highest average of 178.6
Bowler 25 has a low score of  27 in game 75
Bowler  5 has a score of 300 in game 72

Distribution:       50   90  130  170  210  250  290  300
                     1   70  468 1103 1057  429   70    2
```

Exercises

10.4a   Consult the weather data from a newspaper which lists the temperatures for a number of cities. Set up a data file containing these temperatures, entering the high temperature and the low temperature in the same record. Edit the data to prevent any temperatures outside the range of $-20°$ to $+119°$ Fahrenheit, or $-30°$ to $+49°$ Celsius. Write a program to input this data into an integer array ITEMPR(5,100). If the temperatures are in Fahrenheit, enter them into items 1 and 2; if in Celsius, enter them into items 3 and 4. Then, using one of the following conversion equations:

```
Fahrenheit = Celsius  *  9 / 5  +  32
Celsius    = (Fahrenheit - 32)  *  5 / 9
```

convert to the other temperature (the one not input), filling in the appropriate item. Round the converted temperature to the nearest integer.

Next, compute item 5 as the mean of the high and low temperatures in degrees Celsius. Finally, set up a distribution array of 8 items for each 10-degree (Celsius) range and distribute the mean temperatures. (Hint: The subscript for the distribution array may be computed by adding 40 to the mean and dividing by 10.)

10.4b Set up a data file, GRADES.DAT, which contains multiple records, each with four fields:

Field	Columns	
1	1– 4	student identification number
2	6– 8	first examination grade
3	10–12	second examination grade
4	14–16	third examination grade

and the following sample data:

1007	90	85	77
1886	100	62	85
2134	62	60	69
3387	85	42	72
4176	100	88	70
4199	87	80	75
5020	61	65	78
8888	41	43	65

Write a program with a two-dimensional integer array, 7 by 101, which can handle up to 100 records. The first four items are those in the input file GRADES.DAT. The other items are:

```
5:  Integer average, rounded, of the three exams
6:  Integer average, rounded, of the second and third exams
7:  The maximum of items 4, 5, and 6, which will be used to compute
        the student's grade
```

The rounding can be done completely with integer calculations by adding the appropriate integer constant before dividing.

There is also to be a one-dimensional integer array of six fields containing the averages of items 2 through 7. Divide the program into the following modules:

a. Input file, terminating if more than 100 records.
b. Compute items 5 through 7 for each valid record.
c. Compute the six averages.
d. Generate a report in the following format:

Number	1	2	3	A13	A23	Final	
							new page
							blank line
nnnn	nn	nn	nn	nn	nn	nn	
nnnn	nn	nn	nn	nn	nn	nn	
:	:	:	:	:	:	:	
:	:	:	:	:	:	:	
nnnn	nn	nn	nn	nn	nn	nn	
							blank line
Averages:	nn	nn	nn	nn	nn	nn	

10.4c   Revise exercise 9.8c using a two-dimensional array CDZ(4,101) where the first subscript is:

  a. North coordinate
  b. East coordinate
  c. Distance to next coordinate
  d. Azimuth to next coordinate

10.4d   Generate the x- and y-coordinates of a spiral of Archimedes defined in polar notation (radius, angle) wherein the radius is equal to the angle in radians measured clockwise from the y-axis. The program should request the number of points to be calculated in one revolution from 0 to 360 degrees. Divide the revolution into equal angles; e.g., 9 points yield $360/(9 - 1) = 45$ degrees between radials. Define an array DRXY(4,361), with the first subscript defined as:

  a. Angle of radial in degrees
  b. Angle of radial in radians
  c. x-coordinate
  d. y-coordinate

Output should be arranged in four columns and as many rows as necessary, looking, for 9 points, something like this:

Degrees	Radians	x	y
0.00	0.00	0.00	0.00
45.00	0.79	0.56	0.56
90.00	1.57	1.57	0.00
135.00	2.36	1.67	−1.67
180.00	3.14	0.00	−3.14
225.00	3.93	−2.78	−2.78
270.00	4.71	−4.71	0.00
315.00	5.50	−3.89	3.89
360.00	6.28	0.00	6.28

10.4e   Write a program to prompt for the size of an integer matrix (number of rows and columns) and a real constant. Read that matrix from a disk file in which the elements are arranged in the geometric shape of the matrix. Generate and output a new real matrix in which each element has been multiplied by the constant.

10.4f   Write a program to read in two similar-size matrices and add them into a third similar-size matrix. The program should prompt for the sizes (number of rows and columns) of the matrices from the keyboard and then read them from a disk file, laid out in the geometric shape of the matrices. The output should consist of the two input matrices and the third computed one, properly annotated and in the same geometric form. (The double nested DO loop for I/O will not prove possible in this exercise because of the flexible nature of the size of the arrays.)

10.4g   Write a program to read in two matrices in which the number of columns in the first is equal to the number of rows in the second, prompting for the size of the matrices from the keyboard. The matrices should be laid out in the input file exactly as they would appear. Generate the product matrix. (The equation for the product matrix can be found in any mathematics book that discusses matrices.)

10.5   USE WITHIN SUBPROGRAMS

As discussed in the previous chapter, the use of subprograms with arrays allows the generation of a great deal of general-purpose code that is useful in many different applications. The array name goes into the argument list, and the subprogram must contain a DIMENSION statement reflecting that the variable in the argument list is an array. There are a number of concepts that must be explored first, however, if usefulness of our code is to be optimized.

Assume that we wish to modularize the bowling program presented in the previous section by performing the calculations for the bowler averages and maximum bowler average in a subroutine. The following code will be replaced:

```
C                        get bowler averages
         DO 40  I = 1,40
             ISUM = 0.0
             DO 20  J = 1,80
     20      ISUM = ISUM + IBOWL(J,I)
     40 BAVG(I) = REAL (ISUM) / 80.00
         WRITE  (*,1040)  BAVG
   1040 FORMAT (' ','Bowler averages:'/ (' ',8F8.1))
C                        find highest bowler average
         DO 60  I = 1,40
             IF (BAVG(I) .GT. BMAX)  THEN
                 BMAX = BAVG(I)
                 IMAX = I
             ENDIF
     60 CONTINUE
         WRITE  (*,1060)  IMAX, BMAX
   1060 FORMAT (' ','Bowler',I3,' has highest average of', F6.1)
```

with:

```
C                        get bowler averages and highest average
         CALL CALCBW  (IBOWL, BAVG, BMAX, IMAX)
         WRITE  (*,1040)  BAVG
   1040 FORMAT (' ','Bowler averages:'/ (' ',8F8.1))
         WRITE  (*,1060)  IMAX, BMAX
   1060 FORMAT (' ','Bowler',I3,' has highest average of', F6.1)
```

by adding to the system the following subroutine:

```
C              Subroutine CALCBW:  Bowler Calculations
C
         SUBROUTINE  CALCBW  (IBOWL, BAVG, BMAX, IMAX)
```

```
C
        DIMENSION  IBOWL(80,40), BAVG(40)
C
C                        get bowler averages
        DO 40  I = 1,40
            ISUM = 0
            DO 20  J = 1,80
    20      ISUM = ISUM + IBOWL(J,I)
    40 BAVG(I) = REAL (ISUM) / 80.00
C                        find highest bowler average
        BMAX = -1.00
        DO 60  I = 1,40
            IF  (BAVG(I) .GT. BMAX)  THEN
                BMAX = BAVG(I)
                IMAX = I
            ENDIF
    60 CONTINUE
C                        termination
        RETURN
        END
```

This would be a perfect solution if all the programs we wrote were for bowling leagues that have exactly 40 players, each bowling exactly 80 games! FORTRAN, however, has a number of alternative ways of coding which allow the writing of very flexible subprograms. The first of these alternatives is the use of variable dimensions. The subprogram then becomes:

```
C                Subroutine CALCBW:  Bowler Calculations
C
        SUBROUTINE  CALCBW  (IBOWL, NB, NG, BAVG, BMAX, IMAX)
C
C              NB = number of bowlers        NG = number of games
C
        DIMENSION  IBOWL(NG,NB), BAVG(NB)
C
C                        get bowler averages
        DO 40  I = 1,NB
            ISUM = 0
            DO 20  J = 1,NG
    20      ISUM = ISUM + IBOWL(J,I)
    40 BAVG(I) = REAL (ISUM) / REAL (NG)
C                        find highest bowler average
        BMAX = -1.00
        DO 60  I = 1,NB
            IF  (BAVG(I) .GT. BMAX)  THEN
                BMAX = BAVG(I)
                IMAX = I
            ENDIF
    60 CONTINUE
C                        termination
        RETURN
        END
```

The calling statement must be modified by adding the two additional arguments. (A PARAMETER statement to define the number of bowlers and games per bowler would make the program even more general.)

```
      DIMENSION  IBOWL(80,40)
                     |
                     |
                     |
C                         get bowler averages and find highest average
      CALL CALCBW  (IBOWL, 40, 80, BAVG, BMAX, IMAX)
      WRITE   (*,1040) BAVG
 1040 FORMAT  (' ','Bowler averages:'/ (' ',8F8.1))
      WRITE   (*,1060) IMAX, BMAX
 1060 FORMAT  (' ','Bowler',I3,' has highest average of', F6.1)
```

In section 9.6, we described why the value in the DIMENSION statement of an array in the argument list of a subprogram is not relevant; it can be given a dummy value such as a 1 or an asterisk. With multidimensional arrays, as the discussion of the mapping function in section 10.2 shows, the last dimension is not relevant but all the previous dimensions are. When dimensions are passed to a subprogram, as in the above code, it is critical that we pass the actual value of all but the last dimension. Thus, the last subscript can be undefined in the dimension statement of the subprogram, as in the slightly modified subprogram below:

```
C                     Subroutine CALCBW:   Bowler Calculations
C
      SUBROUTINE CALCBW  (IBOWL, NB, NG, BAVG, BMAX, IMAX)
C
C             NB = number of bowlers        NG = number of games
C
      DIMENSION  IBOWL(NG,*), BAVG(*)
C
C                     get bowler averages
      DO 40  I = 1,NB
         ISUM = 0
         DO 20  J = 1,NG
   20    ISUM = ISUM + IBOWL(J,I)
   40 BAVG(I) = REAL (ISUM) / REAL (NG)
C                         find highest bowler average
      BMAX = -1.00
      DO 60  I = 1,NB
         IF (BAVG(I) .GT. BMAX)  THEN
             BMAX = BAVG(I)
             IMAX = I
         ENDIF
   60 CONTINUE
C                     termination
      RETURN
      END
```

There is little gain when leaving that last dimension undefined, since the values for the number of bowlers and number of games must still be transmitted to the subprogram for calculational reasons.

However, a knowledge of the mapping function leads us to an alternative that is quite interesting. Section 9.6 presented a function for calculating the real average of a one-dimensional integer array. Repeating that function, but generalizing it, gives:

```
        FUNCTION  AVGINT (IA, NR)
C
C         Abstract:  calculates real average of
C                         integer array IA with NR elements
C
        DIMENSION  IA(*)
C
C                   initialize sum
        ISUM = 0
C                   loop through elements
        DO 20  N = 1,NR
     20 ISUM = ISUM + IA(N)
C                   calculate average
        AVGINT = REAL (ISUM) / REAL (NR)
C                   return
        RETURN
        END
```

Now, because the data is stored in (item, record) order, the 80 bowling scores for any given player occupy contiguous locations and thus each bowler's scores appear to the computer to be a series of 40 one-dimensional arrays:

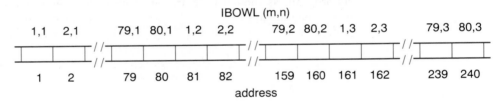

IBOWL (m,n)

And since FORTRAN transmits the address of an argument when accessing a subprogram, all we need to do is send the function AVGINT 40 one-dimensional arrays by specifying an argument IBOWL(1,n), where n is the bowler number.

Also, we add the following subprogram to return the location of the maximum value in a real array:

```
C               Function LMAXR:  returns the location of a maximum value
C                                    in a real array
C
        FUNCTION  LMAXR  (ARRAY, NUMEL)
C
        DIMENSION  ARRAY(*)
C
C           Glossary: ARRAY:  array of real elements
C                     NUMEL:  number of valid elements in array
C
C               set first element as maximum
        LMAXR = 1
```

```
C                        loop through remaining elements, if any
      IF  (NUMEL .GT. 1)  THEN
          DO 20  I = 2,NUMEL
              IF  (ARRAY(I) .GT. ARRAY(LMAXR))  LMAXR = I
   20     CONTINUE
      ENDIF
C                        return
      RETURN
      END
```

Our mainline becomes:

```
C                    get bowler averages and highest average
      DO 40  I = 1,40
   40 BAVG(I) = AVGINT (IBOWL(1,I), 80)
      IMAX    = LMAXR   (BAVG, 40)
      BMAX    = BAVG    (IMAX)
      WRITE   (*,1040)  BAVG
 1040 FORMAT  (' ','Bowler averages:'/ (' ',8F8.1))
      WRITE   (*,1060)  IMAX, BMAX
 1060 FORMAT  (' ','Bowler',I3,' has highest average of', F6.1)
```

Although the mainline code is longer by a few statements, we are using general-purpose subprograms rather than specific ones appropriate only in limited applications—and that means more efficient programming, because these subprograms can be used in other applications.

Note the flexibility we have here: Two-dimensional arrays may be treated in a subprogram as though they are one-dimensional, and vice versa. Single array elements may always be transmitted as single variables, not needing a DIMENSION statement in the subprogram. There are three constructs that we need to know:

1. FORTRAN transmits variable (including array) addresses.
2. The order in which array elements are stored
3. The mapping function

This concept can be extended even further! What if we wanted to find the average score for all the bowlers in one given game? The use of AVGINT was predicated on the 80 games for each bowler being located in contiguous locations. Now each of the 40 games to be averaged are separated by a block of unwanted games. Referring to the memory layout above, if game 2 is to be averaged, it appears in memory locations 2, 82, 162, etc. A subprogram could be written using the mapping function to calculate the location within the routine and then be usable for one- or two-dimensional arrays:

```
      FUNCTION  AVINT2 (IA, NREC, NITEMS, ITEM)
C
C       Abstract:  calculates real average of one-dimensional or
C                  item of two-dimensional integer array
C
C       Glossary:  IA:     integer array
C                  NREC:   number of records
C                  NITEMS: number of items
C                  ITEM:   desired item
C
```

```
C              Array in calling program corresponding to IA must be
C                      dimensioned either (record) or (item,record)
C              For one-dimensional array, calling program must define
C                      NITEMS = 1, ITEM = 1
C
      DIMENSION  IA(1)
C
C                      initialize sum
      ISUM = 0
C                      loop through elements
      DO 20  N = 1,NR
          MAP = NITEMS * (N - 1) + ITEM
   20 ISUM = ISUM + IA(MAP)
C                      calculate average
      AVINT2 = REAL (ISUM) / REAL (NR)
C                      return
      RETURN
      END
```

When the array transmitted is one-dimensional and NITEMS = ITEM = 1, the assignment of MAP reduces to MAP = N. The use of this technique will be developed more fully in the next chapter.

Exercises

10.5a   Write a subprogram to input any size integer matrix (assuming a limit of 20×20 and a format of 20I4). Write a subprogram to output any size matrix. Then write a mainline and design data files to test the two subprograms. The input data file should contain the size of the matrix (number of rows, number of columns) as the first line of data and then the matrix itself.

10.5b   Write a subprogram to invert a square, two-dimensional matix; i.e., the values reverse around the diagonal from upper left to lower right or, another way of describing it, the first column becomes the first row; the second column, the second row, etc. For example:

$$
\begin{vmatrix} 23 & 18 & 72 & 56 \\ 7 & 67 & 43 & 12 \\ 89 & 95 & 77 & 72 \\ 3 & 9 & 35 & 28 \end{vmatrix}
\quad \text{becomes:} \quad
\begin{vmatrix} 23 & 7 & 89 & 3 \\ 18 & 67 & 95 & 9 \\ 72 & 43 & 77 & 35 \\ 56 & 12 & 72 & 28 \end{vmatrix}
$$

Since the array is square, the subscripts are the same. The mainline program should call the subprograms written in exercise 10.5a and read a data file containing the dimension of the matrix and the appropriate number of values to fill in the matrix. Test with a number of matrices of different sizes; the program should work with only the one array and not need any temporary ones. (Refer to exercise 8.5i for subroutine SWAP.)

10.5c   Write a subprogram to do matrix addition; i.e., to accept two matrices and generate a third in which each element is the sum of the corresponding elements of the two original arrays. For example:

$$
\begin{vmatrix} 12 & -3 \\ 8 & 5 \\ -2 & 7 \end{vmatrix}
+
\begin{vmatrix} 6 & 2 \\ 14 & 11 \\ -4 & -1 \end{vmatrix}
=
\begin{vmatrix} 18 & 1 \\ 22 & 16 \\ -6 & 6 \end{vmatrix}
$$

Since the matrices need not be square, the input must consist of the two dimensions and the matrices themselves. The driver program should call the input subprogram twice, once for each matrix, and the output subprogram three times.

10.5d   Write a mainline which calls the subprograms from exercises 10.5a and 10.5c and adds up three matrices of similar size.

10.5e   Write a subroutine which accepts a matrix of any size and returns two one-dimensional arrays, the first the sums of the elements in each of the rows, the second the sums of the elements in each of the columns. The driver should use the input routine from above to read the matrix and its own routine to output the matrix with column numbers on top, row numbers on the left, row sums on the right, and column sums on the bottom.

10.5f   Modify exercise 10.4b by breaking it up into a number of modules. The first should be an input subroutine that opens the file, reads in the data, closes the file, and returns the data and the number of records.

The second should be a function which receives the two-dimensional array, the number of records, and the item number to be averaged, returning an integer average. Finally, there should be an output subroutine which receives the array and the number of records and produces the report.

Adjust the mainline to accommodate the three subprograms and test. The calculation of items 5, 6, and 7 should be done in the mainline.

10.6   PROGRAMMING SYSTEMS

Another version of the code for application program 3 (Automated Teller Machine), parts 3 and 4, can now be presented utilizing some of the new techniques involving two-dimensional arrays. The program will also use function CALCFE (from section 8.7) with parts of the two-dimensional array, but since the subprogram receives a single variable argument, not an array, the single array element is placed in the calling argument list and no new concepts are used. However, the linkage with subroutine BRKDWN (see section 9.6) will have to be explained.

Comparing this version with those given in earlier sections, you should notice three major differences:

1. The use of arrays (one- and two-dimensional) for easier data access
2. A more structured program, with separate modules for input, calculations, and output, where possible
3. The use of formatting for more flexible I/O

**Automated
Teller
Machine**

```
C                       Automated Teller Machine
C
       PARAMETER  (RATE = 0.020, LIMIT = 400.00)
```

```
C
      LOGICAL    ERROR
      INTEGER    IN(8,20000), TOTWTH, VALBRK(6)
C
C                IN(1,n):    account number
C                IN(2,n):    amount to be withdrawn
C                IN(3-8,n):  denominations of breakdown
C
      REAL       FEE(20000), TOTAL
C                    initialize total withdrawal and number of records
      DATA  TOTWTH/ 0/,  NREC / 0/
C                breakdown denominations
      DATA  NUMBRK, VALBRK/ 3,  50, 20, 10, 0, 0, 0/
C
      MULTPL = VALBRK (NUMBRK)
C                    enter account number and amount of withdrawal
      DO 60  N = 1,20000
          WRITE    (*,1020)  MULTPL
 1020     FORMAT   ('0','Enter account number',
     1             ' amount of withdrawal (multiple of $',I3,')')
          READ     (*,*, ERR=40, END=90)  (IN(J,NREC+1), J=1,2)
          ERROR = .FALSE.
C                        check for positive value
          IF  (IN(2,NREC+1) .LE. 0.00)  THEN
              PRINT *, 'DESIRED WITHDRAWAL LESS THAN OR EQUAL TO ZERO'
              ERROR = .TRUE.
          ENDIF
C                        check for value within limit
          IF  (IN(2,NREC+1) .GT. LIMIT)  THEN
              PRINT *, 'DESIRED WITHDRAWAL GREATER THAN LIMIT'
              ERROR = .TRUE.
          ENDIF
C                        check for proper multiple
          IF  (MOD (IN(2,NREC+1), MULTPL)  .NE.  0)  THEN
              PRINT *, 'NOT MULTIPLE OF $',MULTPL,'  - RE-ENTER'
              ERROR = .TRUE.
          ENDIF
C                        calculate breakdown
          IF  (.NOT. ERROR)  THEN
              NREC = NREC + 1
              CALL BRKDWN (IN(2,NREC), NUMBRK, VALBRK, IN(3,NREC))
C                        compute fee and total
              FEE(NREC) = CALCFE (IN(2,NREC))
              TOTAL     = REAL   (IN(2,NREC)) + FEE(NREC)
C                        output transaction
              NN = NUMBRK + 2
              WRITE    (*,1060)  (VALBRK(J),  J=1,NUMBRK)
 1060         FORMAT   ('0', 6('   $',I3,:))
              WRITE    (*,1062)  (IN(J,NREC), J=3,NN)
 1062         FORMAT   (' ', 6I6)
              WRITE    (*,1064)  FEE(NREC), TOTAL
 1064         FORMAT   (' ','Fee = $',F4.2,',    Total = $',F6.2)
C                     add to total
              TOTWTH = TOTWTH + IN(2,NREC)
          ENDIF
          GO TO 60
C              error in input
   40 PRINT *, 'Invalid character in input  -  Re-enter'
```

```
C                      loop back for more input
   60 CONTINUE
C
C                      end of input, open output file and write to it
   90 OPEN      (4, FILE='TRANS.DAT')
      WRITE     (4,1090) VALBRK
 1090 FORMAT    (10X, 6I4)
      WRITE     (4,1022) ((IN(J,I), J=1,8), FEE(I), I=1,NREC)
 1022 FORMAT    (2I5, 6I4, F6.2)
      CLOSE     (4)
C                      termination
      PRINT *, 'Total withdrawn = $', TOTWTH
      STOP
      END
```

Sample Display

```
    Enter account number, amount of withdrawal (multiple of $ 10)
    10783,100

     $ 50   $ 20   $ 10
        2      0      0
    Fee = $2.00,     Total = $102.00

    Enter account number, amount of withdrawal (multiple of $ 10)
    30556,-20
    DESIRED WITHDRAWAL LESS THAN OR EQUAL TO ZERO

    Enter account number, amount of withdrawal (multiple of $ 10)
    30556,319
    NOT MULTIPLE OF $          10   -   RE-ENTER

    Enter account number, amount of withdrawal (multiple of $ 10)
    30556,310

     $ 50   $ 20   $ 10
        6      0      1
    Fee = $6.20,     Total = $316.20

    Enter account number, amount of withdrawal (multiple of $ 10)
    26578,600
    DESIRED WITHDRAWAL GREATER THAN LIMIT

    Enter account number, amount of withdrawal (multiple of $ 10)
    26578,400

     $ 50   $ 20   $ 10
        8      0      0
    Fee = $8.00,     Total = $408.00

    Enter account number, amount of withdrawal (multiple of $ 10)
    10007,160

     $ 50   $ 20   $ 10
        3      0      1
    Fee = $3.20,     Total = $163.20
```

```
Enter account number, amount of withdrawal (multiple of $ 10)
5564,80

   $ 50  $ 20  $ 10
      1     1     1
Fee = $2.00,     Total = $ 82.00

Enter account number, amount of withdrawal (multiple of $ 10)
18230,240

   $ 50  $ 20  $ 10
      4     2     0
Fee = $4.80,     Total = $244.80

Enter account number, amount of withdrawal (multiple of $ 10)
^z

Total withdrawn = $          1290
```

The use of the counter NREC requires some explanation. The data must be edited for correct range and multiple, but until that is done, the data should not be added to the array as valid. NREC is maintained as the counter of accepted data; and when NREC is used in the input statements, the program is looking at the next possible record (NREC + 1). When the editing is complete and the record is found valid, then the record counter is updated (NREC = NREC + 1) and processing continues.

The LOGICAL variable ERROR was used to simplify some of the logic and make it easier to read. It is a useful alternative as coding becomes more complex.

The subprograms BRKDWN (the later, more flexible version) and CALCFE are the same as those given in sections 9.6 and 8.7, respectively, and are not repeated here. However, the linkage with BRKDWN is not simple. The fourth argument in the list is the new denominations. In the calling list it is entered as IN(3,NREC), and it is called NUMBIL(6) in the subroutine. The addresses of IN(3,NREC) through IN(8,NREC) correspond to NUMBIL(1) through NUMBIL(6); the argument lists can be used to line up arrays, not necessarily starting at the beginnings of the arrays. This can be a very useful property at times.

IN:	(1,n)	(2,n)	(3,n)	(4,n)	(5,n)	(6,n)	(7,n)	(8,n)
NUMBIL:			(1)	(2)	(3)	(4)	(5)	(6)

The allowable withdrawal multiple depends upon the lowest denomination used. Also note the considerable effort spent to output only the denominations used. This produces a more sophisticated output with no extraneous information. Because the denominations may change in later versions of the program, the ones used are sent to the transaction file, TRANS.DAT. This way, whenever that file is read, the program can work with the denominations used when it was generated.

Sample File TRANS.DAT

```
               50  20  10   0   0   0
   10783  100   2   0   0   0   0   0  2.00
   30556  310   6   0   1   0   0   0  6.20
   26578  400   8   0   0   0   0   0  8.00
   10007  160   3   0   1   0   0   0  3.20
    5564   80   1   1   1   0   0   0  2.00
   18230  240   4   2   0   0   0   0  4.80
```

In the transaction report program displayed below, we are once more using arrays to their fullest power. Again, considerable effort was made to print only the denominations used. Note how they are input with the first READ and the number of them is determined in the DO 100 loop, working backward.

```
C                       Transaction Report
C
      DIMENSION  IN(8,20000), FEE(20000), ITOTAL(6), IDNOM(6)
      DATA       ITOTAL, TOTALA, TOTALF/ 6 * 0,  2 * 0.00/
C
C                     input routine
      OPEN    (4, FILE='TRANS.DAT')
      READ    (4,1000)  IDNOM
 1000 FORMAT  (10X, 6I4)
      DO 20   I = 1,20000
   20 READ    (4,1020, END=40)  (IN(J,I), J=1,8), FEE(I)
 1020 FORMAT  (2I5, 6I4, F6.2)
      STOP  'Excessive data'
   40 NREC = I - 1
      CLOSE   (4)
C                     calculate totals
      DO 80   I = 1,NREC
         DO 60   J = 1,6
   60    ITOTAL(J) = ITOTAL(J) + IN(J+2,I)
         TOTALA    = TOTALA + REAL (IN(2,I))
   80 TOTALF       = TOTALF + FEE(I)
C               determine number of denominations
      DO 100  ND = 6,1,-1
         IF  (IDNOM(ND) .NE. 0)  GO TO 120
  100 CONTINUE
      STOP  'Error in denominations'
C                     output routine
  120 OPEN    (5, FILE='TRANS.OUT')
      WRITE   (5,1120) (IDNOM(I), I=1,ND)
 1120 FORMAT  ('1',10X,'Transaction  Register'//
     1         '0', 3X,'Account     Amount     Fee', 3(2X,'$'I3,:))
      NN = ND + 2
      WRITE   (5,1122)
 1122 FORMAT  (' ')
      DO 140  I = 1,NREC
  140 WRITE   (5,1140)  (IN(J,I), J=1,2),    FEE(I), (IN(J,I), J=3,NN)
 1140 FORMAT  (' ',    I10,' $',I3,'.00', F8.2,    6I6)
      WRITE   (5,1142)              TOTALA, TOTALF, (ITOTAL(J), J=1,ND)
```

```
1142 FORMAT  ('0','Totals:   $', F9.2,   F8.2,        6I6)
     CLOSE  (5)
C                         termination
     STOP
     END
```

Sample Output

```
          Transaction   Register

   Account     Amount     Fee  $ 50  $ 20  $ 10

     10783   $100.00     2.00    2    0    0
     30556   $310.00     6.20    6    0    1
     26578   $400.00     8.00    8    0    0
     10007   $160.00     3.20    3    0    1
      5564   $ 80.00     2.00    1    1    1
     18230   $240.00     4.80    4    2    0

  Totals:   $  1290.00  26.20   24    3    3
```

10.7   CHAPTER REVIEW

This chapter may seem somewhat overwhelming, since it presents material that is theoretical (the mapping function) and then tries to condense almost 30 years of programming experience into relatively few pages. And more is to follow in the next chapter!

At this point, you should be able to handle almost any problem involving numeric data and fixed alphameric data—which means you are equipped to face about 95% of the problems a professional programmer encounters.

We have emphasized the use of multidimensional arrays because—despite their apparent difficulty to the novice—in the long run, they enable us to write easier and more efficient code. Any reader serious about a career in programming may well consider this chapter one of the most important in the text.

The topics covered in this chapter include:

Topic	*Section*
Data storage	10.1, 10.2, 10.5
DIMENSION	10.1
Input/output	10.3
Mapping function	10.2, 10.5
Minimum/maximum value	10.4
Subprograms	10.5, 10.6

Exercises

10.7a *Egg Distribution* Presented below is a sample data file with the following structure:

Record 1:	Columns 2–10:	month, right-justified
	" 12–15:	year
	" 21–25:	unit cost per gross eggs
	" 26–30:	unit cost per dozen eggs
Records 2 – n:	Columns 5– 6:	customer number
	" 11–12:	day of month
	" 15–18:	number of eggs purchased

The records are sorted by customer and then by day of month. All purchases are in multiples of a dozen eggs.

Sample Input Data File

```
September 1993    16.50  1.80
        1     2    252
        1    13    384
        1    18     96
        1    26    216
        2     1     96
        2     3    216
        2     4    240
        2     5    240
        2     8    216
        2    10    144
        2    11    156
        2    13    288
        2    14    240
        2    15    384
        2    22    108
        2    29    228
        5     3    300
        5    12    216
        5    13    348
        8    14    348
        8    15    168
        8    22    144
        8    23    252
        8    24    216
        8    29    264
        9     1    132
        9     2    192
        9    13    384
        9    16    204
        9    29    132
```

Module 1: Use a two-dimensional array IEGGS(5,1000) to read the data into items 1, 2, and 5.

Module 2: Generate items 3 and 4 as the equivalent gross and dozen. (Subroutine BRKDWN will do it, even if the first argument is IEGGS(5,n) and the last is IEGGS(3,n); since all purchases are even dozens, only two denominations are needed.)

Module 3: The cost of each purchase is based on the number of gross and dozens purchased. For the above data, a purchase of 300 eggs (2 gross + 1 dozen) would cost 2 * $16.50 + 1 * $1.80 = $34.80. An arithmetic statement function to compute the cost would be efficient. Generate a real array to store the costs.

Module 4: The total purchase for each customer can be placed into a real array with a location for up to 10 purchasers. Generate such an array for the above data. Also generate total selling cost.

Module 5: The amount of total gross and total dozen to be sold is based on the total number of eggs purchased, before breakdown into individual orders. Calculate the total number of eggs sold, then break it down into gross and dozen. For consistency with the IEGGS, use an array NEGGS(3) in this order: total gross, total dozen, total units.

Module 6: Compute the wholesale price of the eggs purchased as 60% of the cost based upon total gross and total dozen. Calculate the profit as the difference between total selling cost and wholesale price, as well as the percentage based on profit divided by wholesale price.

Module 7: Output a detail report in the following general form:

```
EGG  REPORT  FOR  aaaaaaaaa, nnnn


Customer    Date    Gross  Dozen      Cost

    1         2       1      9       32.70
    1        13       2      8       47.40
    1        18       0      8       14.40
    1        26       1      6       27.30
    2         1       0      8       14.40
    2         3       1      6       27.30
    |         |       |      |          .
```

[etc.—with final totals for gross, dozen, and cost; wholesale price, profit, and percentage profit. On a new page, print out the customer total purchases, listing only those customers with a nonzero amount.]

10.7b *Coordinate Analysis* Using function AVINT2 from section 10.5 as an example, develop functions RMAX2 and RMIN2 with argument lists (ARRAY, NREC, NITEMS, NITEM). Use AVINT2 to find average coordinates.

Then revise exercise 9.8e to use a two-dimensional array XYZ(3,20) to store the data. Use the new routines to determine minimum and maximum *x*-, *y*-, and *z*-coordinates. Revise QUADRN accordingly.

Store the distances between the points by using an array DIFFRN (20,20), where the subscripts stand for the "from" and "to" point numbers. This may result in zero distances (where the subscripts are identical) and duplicated results, but this does simplify the logic of the program. Function RMAX2 can then be used to find the largest distance by using an argument list (DIFFRN, 400, 1, 1) thereby fooling the function to believe that it is dealing with a one-dimensional array.

Complete the program as described in exercise 9.8e.

10.7c   *Temperature Data Analysis*   Using the subprogram for generating normalized random data, generate an array of (2, 365) integer high and low daily temperatures. Assume that the mean high temperatures (in degrees Fahrenheit) for 12 months (January–December) are 42, 43, 51, 63, 72, 81, 87, 85, 78, 68, 57, and 46; and that the low is 20°F lower. Also assume a standard deviation of 10. Write the data to a disk file with the following format:

> Columns: 1– 3: month
> "   5– 6: day of month (assume 28 days in February)
> "   7– 9: high for day
> "   10–12: low for day

Module 1: Read from the above data file into an array ITEMPR (6, 365) using the following subscripts:

    1 = month
    2 = day
    3 = high temperature
    4 = low temperature

Module 2: Generate a rounded mean temperature for each day and place it into subscript 5. Also generate a mean temperature for the year.

Module 3: Generate the degree-days (subscript 6) for each day (0 if the temperature is equal to or greater than 65°F; otherwise, use the difference between 65°F and the mean temperature). Also calculate total degree-days.

Module 4: Generate an INDEX(3,12) of the beginning and ending record numbers for the month based upon the input and the number of days in each month. Using that index and two arrays MMEAN(12) and MDEGD(12), generate the average mean temperature and total degree-days for each month.

Module 5: Write a report placing three months on a page, with a total of four pages. The columns should include the day number (1–31); the high, low, and mean temperatures; and the number of degree-days for each of the three months. Identify the months either by number or by name. Use as many FORMATs as necessary to avoid printing data where none should appear for a particular month. At the bottom of each page, print the mean for the month and the number of degree-days.

Module 6: Write a report which lists all the dates with a mean temperature below freezing. On the same report, list all the dates with degree-days in excess of 45. Output a count for each group.

10.7d *Simultaneous Equations* The intersection of two straight lines can be calculated arithmetically by using determinants. A determinant is a square matrix of values whose evaluation appears as:

$$\begin{vmatrix} a & b \\ c & d \end{vmatrix} = ad - bc$$

If two straight lines are defined in the form:

$$ax + by = e$$
$$cx + dy = f$$

their solution is:

$$x = \frac{\begin{vmatrix} e & b \\ f & d \end{vmatrix}}{\begin{vmatrix} a & b \\ c & d \end{vmatrix}} \quad \text{and} \quad y = \frac{\begin{vmatrix} a & e \\ c & f \end{vmatrix}}{\begin{vmatrix} a & b \\ c & d \end{vmatrix}}$$

provided that the denominator is not zero, which would mean that the lines are either parallel or coincident.

The two straight lines can be input as a matrix of two rows, three columns. Note that the columns in the determinants agree with the columns in the original equations. Write function DETERM, which receives as arguments the original 2-by-3 matrix and the two column numbers, to be used in evaluating the determinant and returns that evaluation. The driver program should accept input from the keyboard for the six coefficients of the input lines and output the answers for x and y. Simultaneously, the program should write a report listing the input and output of the program in easily readable form.

The driver must check the denominator before dividing by it for a value close to zero (use a tolerance of 0.0001). If such is the case, there is either no solution (if the lines are parallel) or an infinite number of solutions (if they are coincident). If the e and f coefficients are in the same ratio as the a and c (or b and d) coefficients, the lines are coincident. The output should so state.

10.7e *Baseball Statistics* Revise exercise 9.8a, using array IN(11,61) to first read in all the data, before doing any calculations. The array ITOTAL is replaced by the 61st record of IN. Then put all the calculations of the averages into a single array BBAVG (5,61). The only remaining one-dimensional array is NAMES.

The function LMAXR will have to be revised to LMAXR2 in the same concept as AVINT2 in section 10.5. Also revise the report-writing module to use two-dimensional arrays, one for all the integer data and one for all the real. Again, only the NAMES array will be one-dimensional.

10.7f *Accounts Receivable* Revise exercise 9.8b to use a two-dimensional array for the integer data of (3,101). All other conditions remain the same.

11

Additional Programming Techniques

CHAPTER OUTLINE

CHAPTER OBJECTIVES

- To present the theory and concepts required in manipulating large data arrays.

- To relate to data found in the real world.

- To utilize the mapping function to design and implement general-purpose subprograms for future use.

- To extend the concepts of data structure.

- To demonstrate professional techniques of data manipulation.

STATEMENT OF THE PROBLEM

From what you have seen in the previous chapters, it might seem that the prime purpose of data processing is to generate new information from detailed data. Finding sums, averages, minimum values, etc., emphasizes this type of application. But there is another major use of data processing—the ordering of data so that detailed information is more easily abstracted.

There is no way to summarize the information in a telephone directory, but to present its data in no particular order would make that publication very difficult to use. Imagine trying to find a telephone number in the book if the names were not alphabetized! Not only is the book alphabetized, but it is indexed by first and last names on the page as an aid in finding a particular name. In addition, there are two less common versions of the telephone book, one alphabetized by address (as an aid to businesses) and a second sorted by telephone number (for use by the telephone company). These files, especially the latter directory, may not necessarily be printed and may exist only as a computer data file.

Most books and other publications have two types of aids used for finding information therein. Usually there is a table of contents in the front of the publication; it lists the various parts in the order they appear in the book. An index, which lists the information sorted alphabetically, is usually found in the back of the book. In exercise 10.7c, for example, you were asked to develop an index to chronological temperature data so that the monthly data was more easily extracted.

Many times, the order in which the information is stored in the input data file is not the way in which it is most useful. In exercise 10.7a, the data on egg distribution was already sorted by customer number, but it was most likely originally entered chronologically and then sorted. In this chapter, you will learn how to reorder data in any way desired.

Another way of extracting information is to group it with obvious breaks (a skipped line or a new page) to make it easier to read. The output from exercise 10.7a would have benefitted from such grouping, and that methodology will be presented in this chapter. Additionally, the output can be modified to print the subtotals right after the detailed output for each egg customer, rather than at the end as in the exercise.

Finally, another critical technique in data processing is finding detailed data from a large data base. Determining a balance in a bank account, a telephone number when only the name is known, the location of the nearest point to a known point, etc., are all practical examples of searching a data base for a particular record. In the bowling program, the lowest score and the 300 games were found by searching sequentially through the data base. But that method is relatively slow, and such lack of speed is not tolerable in many applications.

The reader should be aware that the data bases considered in this text are miniscule by practical standards. A telephone book of moderate size has about 1000 pages, with about 400 entries per page and about 40 characters per reference, a total of 16 megabytes. This textbook requires about 1.5 megabytes of word processing files. A moderate highway design requires the storage of about 5000 points, each point consisting of 8-byte x-coordinates, y-coordinates, z-coordinates, and descriptions, for a total of 160 kilobytes, or 0.16 megabyte. By way of contrast, the data base of 3200 bowling scores (assuming 2-byte integers) requires only 6.4 kilobytes, or 0.0064 megabyte.

This chapter is concerned with the ordering, reordering, grouping, and searching out of individual data records. Even though programs may summarize that data, such as the calculation of payroll from total hours worked, the source data is a legal document that must be maintained for a required period. Additionally, that same data, grouped by employee for payroll purposes, must be grouped by job for billing purposes and by task for cost-accounting purposes. Thus, summarization does not replace the need for maintaining and accessing source data.

11.1 TERMS AND CONCEPTS

To facilitate the development of the concepts in this chapter, it behooves us to define very precisely the constructs that we will be working with. In prior chapters, you have used files of data; those files are made up of records, and each record is made up of items. The basic record is usually called a detail record, and a file is made up of a number of detail records. All of them will have the same structure; i.e., the same number of items, each formatted or separated into distinct fields.

A data file usually contains only detail records. However, sometimes it will have a header record or records; these records may contain the date the file was generated, the number of records in the file or, as in the ATM file TRANS.DAT from section 10.6, the denominations used in the cash breakdown. Additionally, the file may have a trailer record or records containing such information as totals, or maybe a sentinel value to indicate end-of-file. If a trailer record contains only totals, it is called a totals record.

Occasionally, a data file may contain intermediate records, such as subtotals; i.e., totals from the detail records following the previous subtotal, as with the degree-days in exercise 10.7c, module 4. Total and subtotal records must have some kind of identification distinguishing them from a detail record; in exercise 9.8a, the totals record was identified by leaving the baseball player's name field blank. By using the same number of items and the same format for all kinds of records, the input routine is very straightforward; only an additional decision statement to identify the type of record is needed to direct the logic of the program.

The items within a record are usually of two types, keys and variables. For example, a file of account numbers and balances, which a bank might have, would use the account number as a means of identifying the record; the account number is the key to the record, the means whereby identification is made and access is obtained. On the other hand, the balance will change as new transactions are entered.

There might also be a file of transactions containing deposits and withdrawals, along with the month and day of each transaction. If you are searching for the activity within a given account, the account number is the key; if searching for activity within a certain month, the month is the key; if searching for activity within a certain day, the month and the day become a combined key; and if looking for the activity on a certain day for a certain account, the month, day, and account number are the keys. Thus the key in a record is not a function of the record but of the application and may vary from application to application.

It is critical that we distinguish between distinct keys and multiple occurrences of a key. It is possible for more than one activity to take place within a given account on the same day. If multiple keys are possible, then the program must search for all occurrences of that key. If the key is distinct, such as in the account and balance file or the temperature for a given day, then the search is over once the first key is found. The algorithms used by the programs to be written must reflect the kind of data to be found in a file.

It is important to know the order in which the data is filed. Fortunately, once the data is read into arrays, it can be reordered or sorted. The sorting operation refers to *keys* and, for want of a better word, *carry-alongs*. For example, the baseball data in exercise 8.8a is in no particular order. The data consists of the player names, the given data, and the derived data (the various averages). If you wanted to output the results in alphabetic order, the name is the key and the other data is "carried-along" as the records are moved around. By carrying-along, the correspondence between the player and his or her statistics is maintained. If you then want to have a second output by descending batting average, that average becomes the key and the other items are carried-along.

Occasionally the key will be made up of multiple items, such as in a chronological sort wherein the key items are year, month, and day, in that order. An alphabetic sort really involves multiple keys, with each letter being a key; the sort works on the first letter of the string, and where the first letters are the same, moves to the second letter; where the first two letters are the same, the third letter becomes critical, and so forth. If the keys of two records are the same, the programmer must decide if there is any significance with which record appears first or whether they should appear in the same order as they originally appeared (record number order); if the latter is chosen, the record number (or subscript) now becomes part of the key, although it is not part of the data record.

Once the key is determined, the method of sorting must be decided upon. There are many, many algorithms for doing sorts, some of which appear in later sections. This text will not be the definitive reference on sorting; there are volumes written on it, primarily because the sorting procedure is very time-consuming. But by the end of this chapter, you will have an excellent general-purpose subroutine which has gone through more than 25 years of testing in many applications without failure.

Sorting comes in many forms. A table of contents is a list of topics sorted by page number. An index is a list of topics sorted alphabetically. To be more specific, an index is a *key/record sort* in which the key, the topic, carries along the page or record number. A glossary, which provides a definition for the topic, is a full sort wherein the full definition is carried along.

The method used to search data for information often depends upon how the data is sorted. If it is not sorted, every record must be read until the desired record is found. If the data is sorted, as in a telephone book, one can start the search at the beginning; but once a record is reached beyond the one being looked for (like looking for *Green* after having reached *Gross*), the searcher knows that the desired record is not there. On the average, that cuts the search time in half.

A more sophisticated technique was introduced in exercise 5.10g, a binary search. Try opening a telephone book in the middle. Once you determine that the name you want is either before or after that page, half of the book is eliminated. Then go to the half that is still good and repeat the procedure. Each time you look at a new page, half of what is left is eliminated. Using this procedure, you can find a given entry in a 1000-page telephone book by viewing only 10 pages!

Once data is sorted, it can be grouped on different levels. Assume a file of sales sorted by salesperson, month, and day. It might be useful to get subtotals for all of the salesperson's activity, for his or her activity during the month and for each day. (Sales commission calculations need this information.) The program must "break" its logic to provide subtotals when the day changes, when the month changes, and when the salesperson changes. These are called *level breaks*. This example has three levels. The highest level, level 1, is the salesperson; the level 2 break occurs within that salesperson's records when the month changes; the level 3 break occurs within that month when the day changes. Finally, there is the grand or final total, summarizing all the sales for all the salespersons, which is output at the end of the report. Thus we speak of *subtotal records* and of *grand* or *final total* records.

This chapter will explore each of these topics in sufficient detail to provide firm knowledge of how data is manipulated on the professional level.

11.2   ONE-DIMENSIONAL SORTING

One of the most frequently used procedures in data processing is the sorting of data so that its access and presentation are more orderly. Sorting is not a complicated process, but it is time-consuming; in fact, it probably consumes more computer time than most other processes combined. The programmer can find volumes written on different sorting algorithms, as well as the results of many benchmark tests. This chapter will describe a simple sort which is applicable to almost all situations, although it is not the fastest one available.

For purposes of illustration, take a raw (unsorted) list of examination grades and sort them in descending order, from the highest grade to the lowest.

Unsorted	Sorted
82	98
98	85
79	82
85	79

The human eye can sort these few values very easily, almost without thinking. However, to program the sorting process for a computer requires that some general algorithm be developed that will work for all numbers. Probably the most obvious method would be to think in terms of two lists and follow the instructions below:

1. Find the largest value in the first list and transfer it to the first location of the second list.
2. Ignoring the first transferred value, find the largest value among those that are left and transfer it into the second position.
3. Continue the process, ignoring transferred values, until all values have been transferred from the first list to the second.

Watch the process and see what happens:

Original		Pass 1		Pass 2		Pass 3		Pass 4	
82	—	82	98	82	98	—	98	—	98
98	—	—	—	—	85	—	85	—	85
79	—	79	—	79	—	79	82	—	82
85	—	85	—	—	—	—	—	—	79

The implementation of this sort on the computer requires that some value be placed in the vacated positions so that those positions are ignored in later passes. The easiest way is to place a very small value into the location that never competes for the maximum. In this case, using the sort for examination grades, −1 should be sufficiently low; however, to make the sort more general, a value of −9999 will be assumed.

```
C                       Descending Sort Using Two Arrays
C
      DIMENSION  IOLD(10), JNEW(10)
      DATA       IOLD/ 82, 98, 79, 85, 6*0/,  NELEM/ 4/
C
C                  loop through positions to be filled
      DO 100  I = 1,NELEM
          LMAX = 1
          DO 80  J = 2,NELEM
              IF  (IOLD(J) .GT. IOLD(LMAX))  LMAX = J
   80     CONTINUE
          JNEW(I) = IOLD(LMAX)
  100 IOLD(LMAX) = -9999
```

```
C                    output sorted array
      PRINT  *, (JNEW(I), I=1,NELEM)
C                       termination
      STOP
      END
```

The variable name LMAX, which might stand for "location of maximum," was chosen instead of MAX to avoid confusion with the intrinsic function of that name.

Although this sort looks very simple (and it is), it is also very time-consuming. To sort four items, 4×3 comparisons are needed, or 12 altogether. For this sort, the general rule is $N * (N - 1)$ comparisons for N items. Furthermore, twice as much memory is required as the size of the array; unless it is necessary to save the original array in memory, a good sorting routine works within the original array, replacing it with a sorted array.

The program above illustrates a number of points about the testing of algorithms. The use of DATA statements saves time and effort during testing and ensures that the data is the same in all tests; the need for an input routine disappears and there is no need for input from either the keyboard or a file. The DIMENSION of the array can exceed the amount of data tested by using a variable for the actual amount of data; in this way, when it is time to package the algorithm as a subprogram or to place it in a mainline with I/O routines, it is ready to go. However, the array should be padded with garbage data (in our case, zeros) in the unused positions as an aid in finding errors in the algorithm. A useful alternative for more complete testing is to fill the array with good test data and prompt the tester to enter the number of elements to be used for the particular test run.

To convert the above sort to an ascending one, only one statement need be changed; the comparison becomes:

```
      IF  (IOLD(J) .LT. IOLD(LMAX))  LMAX = J
```

Of course, although a poorly chosen variable name does not destroy the algorithm, for esthetic reasons, all references to LMAX should be changed to LMIN.

Simple One-Array Sort

The technique of working in one array requires an interchange of values. Once the maximum value is found on the first pass, it is interchanged with the value occupying the first position so that at the end of that first pass, the first position has the maximum value. On the second pass, the first position is now ignored and the second-highest value is obtained by comparing the values from the second position on, eventually interchanging it with the original contents of the second position so that the next-highest location becomes filled. And so it continues until the next-to-last position is filled with the second-lowest value; automatically, the last position has the lowest value as a result of all of the interchanges.

This type of sort is usually referred to as a *selection sort* because the location to be filled is selected in order. Looking at the array as it is sorted, we see:

Original	Pass 1	Pass 2	Pass 3
82	98	98	98
98	82	85	85
79	79	79	82
85	85	82	79

```
C                        Descending Sort Using One Array
C
      DIMENSION   IARRY(10)
      DATA        IARRY/ 82, 98, 79, 85, 6*0/,  NELEM/ 4/
C
C                    loop through positions to be filled
      N = NELEM - 1
      DO 100  I = 1,N
         LMAX = I
C                    compare with following positions
         NN   = I + 1
         DO 80  J = NN,NELEM
            IF  (IARRY(J) .GT. IARRY(LMAX))  LMAX = J
   80    CONTINUE
C                    interchange, if necessary
         IF  (I .NE. LMAX)  THEN
             ITEMP       = IARRY(I)
             IARRY(I)    = IARRY(LMAX)
             IARRY(LMAX) = ITEMP
         ENDIF
  100 CONTINUE
C
      PRINT *, (IARRY(I), I=1,NELEM)
      STOP
      END
```

The above sort is far more efficient in terms of work done in that many less comparisons are needed, since the list becomes reduced in length by one element each time a new pass is started. Again, the sort becomes ascending with the change of LMAX to LMIN and the comparison changes to:

```
      IF  (IARRY(J) .LT. IARRY(LMIN))  LMIN = J
```

Another concept important to us is the carry-along array, values which correspond to those being sorted but which the sort is not keyed on. For example, section 9.5 has a grading application in which the input is examination grades and student names. When sorting the grades in descending order, the student names are carried along during the interchange so that their matchup with the grade is not lost. Likewise, when sorting the list alphabetically by student name, the grade is carried along during the interchange. Thus there are two parts: the *key*, the array or arrays on which the sort is based; and the *carry-alongs,* the corresponding arrays that just go along for the ride.

Below is the grading application with the two sorts, the first descending by grade (with names carried along) and the second ascending alphabetically (with grades carried along). However, there are some minor complications in the sorting of characters involving the codes used to store them. To ensure that an alphameric sort works, the following four intrinsic functions are used when testing the order of character variables:

```
LGE (character_1, character_2) lexically greater than or equal to
LGT (character_1, character_2) lexically greater than
LLE (character_1, character_2) lexically less than or equal to
LLT (character_1, character_2) lexically less than
```

The conditionals .EQ. and .NE. are used with character data for testing equality and nonequality testing; the lexicals are needed only to test order. As an example of their use, consider the following program segment:

```
      CHARACTER*16  NAME1, NAME2
      DATA  NAME1, NAME2/ 'Washington      ', 'Jefferson       '/
C
      IF  (LLT (NAME1, NAME2))  PRINT *, NAME1, NAME2
      IF  (LGE (NAME1, NAME2))  PRINT *, NAME2, NAME1
```

which prints the names in alphabetical order. Note that one of the conditions should contain the "equal" test, otherwise two equal names will never be output.

```
C              Grade Analysis & Distribution
C
C        Abstract:  Program inputs up to 60 examination grades.  Grades
C              are edited for proper range (0 to 100).  Average is cal-
C              culated and a grade distribution determined as follows:
C                   90 to 100:  A      DISTR(1)
C                   80 to 89:   B        :
C                   70 to 79:   C        :
C                   65 to 69:   D        :
C                   < 65:       F      DISTR(5)
C
      CHARACTER*12  NAME(61),  TNAME
      INTEGER       GRADE(61), DISTR(5), IGRBRK(4), SUM
C             initialize error counter, sum,
C                 distribution counters and grade range breaks
      DATA  NERROR, SUM, DISTR/ 7 * 0/,  IGRBRK/ 90, 80, 70, 65/
C
C                 open input and output files
      OPEN  (2, FILE='GRADES')
      OPEN  (3, FILE='REPORT')
C                 input module
      DO 20  I = 1,61
   20 READ     (2,1020, END=40)  NAME(I), GRADE(I)
 1020 FORMAT  (A12, I3)
          STOP  'Excessive input - ABORT'
   40 NUMREC = I - 1
      CLOSE   (2)
C                 echo check and edit
      WRITE   (3,1040)  (NAME(I), GRADE(I), I=1,NUMREC)
 1040 FORMAT  (////'GRADE DISTRIBUTION'/
     1              'Name           Grade'//
     2              (A12,           I6))
      DO 100  I = 1,NUMREC
          IF  (GRADE(I) .LT. 0  .OR.  GRADE(I) .GT. 100)  THEN
              WRITE   (3,1042)  GRADE(I), NAME(I)
 1042         FORMAT  (/'Grade of', I5,' invalid for ', A12)
              NERROR = NERROR + 1
          ENDIF
```

```
      100 CONTINUE
          IF  (NERROR .GT. 0)  STOP  'Invalid grades - ABORT'
C
C
C                              sort by descending grades, carrying along names
          N = NUMREC - 1
          DO 80  I = 1,N
              LMAX = I
C                              compare with following positions
              NN   = I + 1
              DO 60  J = NN,NUMREC
                  IF  (GRADE(J) .GT. GRADE(LMAX))  LMAX = J
       60     CONTINUE
C                              interchange, if necessary
              IF  (I .NE. LMAX)  THEN
                  ITEMP       = GRADE(I)
                  GRADE(I)    = GRADE(LMAX)
                  GRADE(LMAX) = ITEMP
                  TNAME       = NAME(I)
                  NAME(I)     = NAME(LMAX)
                  NAME(LMAX)  = TNAME
              ENDIF
       80 CONTINUE
C                              output by descending grade
          WRITE   (3,1040) (NAME(I), GRADE(I), I=1,NUMREC)
C
C
C                              sort alphabetically, carrying along grades
          DO 140  I = 1,N
              LMIN = I
C                              compare with following positions
              NN   = I + 1
              DO 120  J = NN,NUMREC
                  IF  (LLT(NAME(J), NAME(LMIN)))  LMIN = J
      120     CONTINUE
C                              interchange, if necessary
              IF  (I .NE. LMIN)  THEN
                  TNAME       = NAME(I)
                  NAME(I)     = NAME(LMIN)
                  NAME(LMIN)  = TNAME
                  ITEMP       = GRADE(I)
                  GRADE(I)    = GRADE(LMIN)
                  GRADE(LMIN) = ITEMP
              ENDIF
      140 CONTINUE
C                      alphabetic output
          WRITE   (3,1040) (NAME(I), GRADE(I), I=1,NUMREC)
C
C                      compute average
          DO 220  I = 1,NUMREC
      220 SUM  = SUM + GRADE(I)
          AVRG = REAL (SUM) / REAL (NUMREC)
C                      distribution  (one of many methods)
          DO 260  I = 1,NUMREC
              DO 240  J = 1,4
                  IF  (GRADE(I) .GE. IGRBRK(J))  GO TO 260
      240     CONTINUE
              J = 5
      260 DISTR(J) = DISTR(J) + 1
C                      output average and distribution
          WRITE   (3,1260)  NUMREC, AVRG, DISTR
     1260 FORMAT  (////'Average of',I3,' grades =', F10.2//
     1                'Distribution = A  B  C  D  F'/
     2                14X,              5I3)
          CLOSE   (3)
```

```
C                   termination
      STOP
      END
```

Sample Output File

```
      GRADE DISTRIBUTION
      Name           Grade

      Smith             78
      Jones             83
      Brown             85
      Green             72
      Pressman         100
      Sunshine          98
      Klein             54
      Frank             68
      Newton            89
      Moore             77


      GRADE DISTRIBUTION
      Name           Grade

      Pressman         100
      Sunshine          98
      Newton            89
      Brown             85
      Jones             83
      Smith             78
      Moore             77
      Green             72
      Frank             68
      Klein             54


      GRADE DISTRIBUTION
      Name           Grade

      Brown             85
      Frank             68
      Green             72
      Jones             83
      Klein             54
      Moore             77
      Newton            89
      Pressman         100
      Smith             78
      Sunshine          98


      Average of 10 grades =      80.40

      Distribution =  A  B  C  D  F
                      2  3  3  1  1
```

Exercises

11.2a Write an ascending real sort subroutine RSORT with the array name and number of elements in the array as arguments. Test with a driver that defines six real values and outputs the array both before and after the sort.

11.2b Revise the above subroutine to become a descending sort called RDSORT. Test with the same driver using the same values but stored in a second array. Output both arrays simultaneously arranged in six rows, three columns (subscript, ascending value, descending value).

11.2c Write a program to read in a file of x- and y-coordinates arranged with a pair in each record into two one-dimensional arrays, X and Y. Write a real sort subroutine RSORTC with a real carry-along. Sort by x-coordinate, carrying along the y-coordinate, and output both x- and y-coordinates; then sort by y-coordinates, carrying along the x-coordinates, and output them. (Unless otherwise specified, the term *sort* refers to an ascending sort.)

11.2d Revise exercise 11.2c to generate a new array, Z, containing both the x- and y-coordinates. This is called a *merge*. One of the easiest ways to code it is to put both arrays (X and Y) into a new single array (Z), one array stacked after the other, and then sort the new array. The size of the new array must be at least as long as the two source arrays together. Sort this new array in descending order using RDSORT.

11.2e Write a subroutine ASORT to sort a CHARACTER*16 array. Test with an array of at least six strings.

11.2f Generate a telephone list file with the followng fields:

1. Name 30 characters
2. Telephone number 12 characters

Write a driver to read the records into two arrays. Sort in a subroutine ASORTC which sorts on the name and carries the telephone number along. Output in alphabetical order.

11.2g Generate 51 terms of the equation $Y = x ** 2 - 30 * x + 50$ for $x = 0$ to $x = 50$, storing both x- and y-coordinates in arrays. Write a descending-sort subroutine RDSRTC and call it with the y-coordinate as key and the x as carry-along. Output both coordinates in a table in that order. Once sorted, the maximum and minimum values of y are at the ends of the array; indicate that. Count the number of positive y values and the number of negative y values; assume the number of values left are equal to zero.

11.2h Write a program to input a file of integer numbers and determine the median value. The median is the middle value in the sorted list; where there are an even number of values, the average of the middle two is used. To determine the median, it is necessary to sort the array (either ascending or descending will do it). Output the mean (or average) as well. Test with both an even number and an odd number of elements.

11.3 TWO-DIMENSIONAL SORTING

The previous section described some of the methods of sorting and showed a sort which, if not the fastest one around, is easy to understand. This section will present a sort using the same basic algorithm but with the flexibility of accessing either one- or two-dimensional arrays and of being able to handle both an integer and a real carry-along array, also of either one or two dimensions. This sort will be set up as a subroutine so that it can be "packaged" and ready to go whenever needed.

Sorts can be in ascending or descending order (only the decision statement in the beginning is different) and can be keyed on either integer or real arrays (only the variable name is different). The sort below is a descending, real sort with integer and real carry-alongs. It works with either one- or two-dimensional keys and/or carry-alongs; for a one-dimensional array, the number of items is specified as 1. If a particular carry-along array is not needed, the number of items is specified as 0.

```
C           RDSORT:   1-d or 2-d Descending real sort with carry-alongs
C
      SUBROUTINE  RDSORT   (XKEY,NREC,NITEM, ICARY,INDI, RCARY,INDR)
C
      DIMENSION   XKEY(NITEM,*), ICARY(INDI,*), RCARY(INDR,*)
C
C               Glossary
C               --------
C     XKEY:     the real array upon which the sort acts
C     NREC:     the number of records (last dimension) in the
C                    arrays
C     NITEM:    the number of items (first dimension) in the
C                    key array
C     ICARY:    the integer carry-along array
C     INDI:     the number of items in the integer carry-along
C                    0 if no carry-along, >0 if a carry-along
C     RCARY:    the real carry-along array
C     INDR:     the number of items in the real carry-along
C                    0 if no carry-along, >0 if a carry-along
C     All arrays may be one or two-dimensional
C     Where an array is one-dimensional, number of items = 1
C
C               if only one record, no sort necessary
      IF  (NREC .LE. 1)  RETURN
C               major loop from first record to next-to-last
      DO 200  I = 1,NREC-1
        LMAX = I
C               minor loop from next record to last
        DO 80  L = I+1,NREC
C               comparison
          DO 40  JK = 1,NITEM
            IF  (XKEY(JK,L) .LT. XKEY(JK,LMAX))    GO TO 80
            IF  (XKEY(JK,L) .GT. XKEY(JK,LMAX))    THEN
              LMAX = L
              GO TO 80
            ENDIF
40        CONTINUE
80      CONTINUE
        IF  (LMAX .NE. I)  THEN
C               interchange key
120       DO 140  JK = 1,NITEM
            TEMP      = XKEY(JK,I)
```

```
                              XKEY(JK,I)    = XKEY(JK,LMAX)
            140               XKEY(JK,LMAX) = TEMP
        C
                                    interchange integer carry-along, if necessary
                    IF  (INDI .GT. 0)  THEN
                       DO 160  JK = 1,INDI
                              ITEMP        = ICARY(JK,I)
                              ICARY(JK,I)  = ICARY(JK,LMAX)
            160               ICARY(JK,LMAX)   = ITEMP
                    ENDIF
        C
                                    interchange real carry-along, if necessary
                    IF  (INDR .GT. 0)  THEN
                       DO 180  JK = 1,INDR
                              TEMP         = RCARY(JK,I)
                              RCARY(JK,I)  = RCARY(JK,LMAX)
            180               RCARY(JK,LMAX)   = TEMP
                    ENDIF
                 ENDIF
        C                           end of loops
          200 CONTINUE
              RETURN
              END
```

The two GO TOs in the above algorithm simulate the LOOP .. EXIT construct and are required to make the code efficient.

The use of this subroutine is demonstrated by adding the following code to the bowling program:

```
      C                     sort averages and bowler number
              DO 80  I = 1,40
           80 NUMBWL(I) = I
              CALL RDSORT  (BAVG,40,1, NUMBWL,1, RDUMMY,0)
              WRITE    (*,1080)  (BAVG(I), NUMBWL(I), I=1,40)
         1080 FORMAT   ('0','Descending bowler averages:'/ 8(F7.1,I3))
```

The array NUMBWL stores the bowler numbers which, before sorting, are in order from 1 to 40, but after sorting will not be. NUMBWL is carried along as the bowler averages are rearranged in descending order. The variable RDUMMY is not an array but simply a dummy array name placed in the argument list to satisfy the requirements of the list; the dummy array will never be accessed, since the number of items indicated for it is 0. The output generated for our test data appears as:

```
Descending bowler averages:
 178.6   3   175.1 24   174.8   6   174.5 37   174.4 22   174.4   1   173.0 25   172.3 16
 171.9 39   171.9 32   171.9 23   171.5 28   171.5 14   171.4 10   170.9   9   170.8   5
 170.2 35   170.0   4   169.9 12   169.9 38   169.6 27   169.6   2   169.1 11   168.4 17
 168.4 21   167.9   8   167.6 20   167.6 19   167.1 30   166.9 26   166.8 13   166.2 34
 165.4 33   165.3   7   165.2 36   163.9 31   163.8 15   163.6 40   162.3 29   162.1 18
```

Because of the order of output used, the scores read across the page, not down the column. Associated with each score is the bowler number. Variations of this type of sort include an ascending real sort:

```
SUBROUTINE  RSORT  (XKEY,NREC,NITEM, ICARY,INDR, RCARY,INDR)
```

The only variation from RDSORT is in the comparison of the key records and the substitution of LMIN for the variable LMAX. The comparison section of the code would then become:

```
C                            comparison
           DO 40  JK = 1,NITEM
                 IF  (XKEY(JK,L) .GT. XKEY(JK,LMIN))   GO TO 80
                 IF  (XKEY(JK,L) .LT. XKEY(JK,LMIN))   THEN
                    LMIN = L
                    GO TO 80
                 ENDIF
        40      CONTINUE
```

Of course, two integer sorts could also be developed:

```
SUBROUTINE  ISORT  (KEY,NREC,NITEM, ICARY,INDR, RCARY,INDR)

SUBROUTINE  IDSORT (KEY,NREC,NITEM, ICARY,INDR, RCARY,INDR)
```

These sorts would be parallel to RSORT and RDSORT; but the real variable XKEY would be replaced by an integer variable KEY in all occurrences and the key interchange would now use an integer ITEMP in place of the real TEMP.

Section 10.6 presented a transaction register for the Automated Teller Machine application. If we modify the code ever so slightly by inserting this statement:

```
C                       sort in ascending account order
         CALL ISORT  (IN,NREC,5, IDUMMY,0, FEE,1)
```

somewhere between the end of the input routine and the beginning of the output routine, the output becomes:

```
                   Transaction Register


       Account       Amount     Fee   $ 50   $ 20   $ 10

          5564     $ 80.00     2.00      1      1      1
         10007     $160.00     3.20      3      0      1
         10783     $100.00     2.00      2      0      0
         18230     $240.00     4.80      4      2      0
         26578     $400.00     8.00      8      0      0
         30556     $310.00     6.20      6      0      1

    Totals:     $   1290.00   26.20     24      3      3
```

The variable IDUMMY is not an array, but simply a dummy array name placed in the argument list to satisfy the requirements of the list; the dummy array will never be accessed, since the number of items indicated for it is 0.

To sort by increasing amount withdrawn, there are three possible approaches. In this particular case, since the fee charged increases with the amount withdrawn (for all withdrawals greater than $100), there is also a fourth, a very easy (although imperfect) solution, which is to sort on the fee with the following statements:

```
C                       sort in ascending fee order
      CALL RSORT  (FEE,NREC,1, IN,5, RDUMMY,0)
```

However, a simple solution cannot always be found in many applications, so we move on to three general solutions.

Alternative 1—Rearranged Key: In this solution, we rearrange the key array (IN in our example) so that it is in the order of the desired sort. This alternative has the disadvantage of having to place the key back into its original order prior to the output routine or to having to modify the order of output. To illustrate, the code below reverses the positions of the account number and the amount so that the prime sort will be on the amount and the secondary sort on the account number; in any situation where the amounts are the same, the smaller (or smallest) account number will be listed first.

```
C                       rearrange key by amount, then account
      DO 100  I = 1,NREC
            ITEMP   = IN(1,I)
            IN(1,I) = IN(2,I)
  100 IN(2,I)     = ITEMP
C                       sort in ascending amount order
      CALL ISORT  (IN,NREC,5, IDUMMY,0, FEE,1)
C                       place key back in original order
      DO 120  I = 1,NREC
            ITEMP   = IN(1,I)
            IN(1,I) = IN(2,I)
  120 IN(2,I)     = ITEMP
```

The alternative to the last four statements, which place the array back the way it was, is to modify the output as follows:

```
      WRITE   (5,1040)  IN(2,I), IN(1,I), FEE(I), (IN(J,I), J=3,NN)
```

Alternative 2—Key Sort: This solution utilizes an array other than the working one just to store the key. Although it is somewhat wasteful of memory, it executes faster and is easier to code. Assuming an array KEY(2,10000), the following code applies:

```
C                       set up key by amount, account
      DO 100  I = 1,NREC
            KEY(1,I) = IN(2,I)
  100 KEY(2,I)     = IN(1,I)
C                       sort in ascending amount order
      CALL ISORT  (KEY,NREC,2, IN,5, FEE,1)
```

Here the key is sorted and the original data (array IN) is carried along. The output routine is identical to the original routine.

Alternative 3—Key/Record Sort: In this solution, the key is sorted and the record number is carried along. The original data is unchanged, but the output routine must be modified to send the data out in the right order. This method is significantly faster when dealing with carry-along arrays in which there are many items. It is extremely more efficient where the records are not in memory but in a disk file, thereby not requiring the rearranging of the disk records, which is a very time-consuming process. The only carry-along is a one-dimensional record number array. The output routine now is more involved and cannot be done with an implied DO loop; it must use a regular DO loop. In addition to KEY(2,10000), we also need IREC(1000).

```
      C                      set up key by amount, then account; set up record #
          120 DO 110  I = 1,NREC
                    KEY(1,I) = IN(2,I)
                    KEY(2,I) = IN(1,I)
          110 IREC(I)      = I
      C                      sort in ascending amount order
              CALL ISORT  (KEY,NREC,2, IREC,1, RDUMMY,0)
      C                      output routine
              OPEN    (5, FILE='TRANS.OUT')
              WRITE   (5,1120) (IDNOM(I), I=1,ND)
         1120 FORMAT  ('1',10X,'Transaction Register'//
             1           '0', 3X,'Account    Amount       Fee', 3(2X,'$',I3,:))
              NN = ND + 2
              WRITE   (5,1122)
         1122 FORMAT  (' ')
              DO 140  I = 1,NREC
                 K = IREC(I)
          140 WRITE   (5,1140) (IN(J,K), J=1,2),    FEE(K), (IN(J,K), J=3,NN)
         1140 FORMAT  (' ',    I10,'   $',I3,'.00', F8.2,    6I6)
              WRITE   (5,1142)               TOTALA, TOTALF, (ITOTAL(J), J=1,ND)
         1142 FORMAT  ('0','Totals:    $', F9.2,    F8.2,    6I6)
              CLOSE   (5)
      C                      termination
              STOP
              END
```

Exercises

Note: Additional sort routines are required in the model of RDSORT. Needed are ISORT, an ascending-integer sort; IDSORT, a descending-integer sort; IASORT, an ascending-integer sort with a CHARACTER*12 one-dimensional carry-along in place of the real carry-along; and ASORT, an alphabetic sort with a CHARACTER*12 one-dimensional key.

11.3a   Modify exercise 10.4a to sort the data by increasing mean temperature. Use ISORT with a two-dimensional key consisting of the mean and record number. Use the sorted record number to control the order of the output.

11.3b   Modify exercise 10.4b to sort the grades in decreasing order by final grade, using IDSORT prior to output. Use a two-dimensional key consisting of the mean and record number, using the latter to control the order of the output.

11.3c   Modify exercise 11.3b to do a full sort on the grade array, thus providing a sort by student number. Add last names to each of the student records in the input file of exercise 10.4b, using columns 19 through 30. Use IASORT and output student names as well.

11.3d   Enhance exercise 11.3c by producing a second output in alphabetic order using ASORT.

11.4 SEARCHING

Searching is the process of scanning an array for a particular record or group of records according to a specified key. For example, in the Automated Teller Machine application, we might want to see if a particular account was accessed, or we might want to list all transactions greater than $200. Each of these examples requires the program to examine all the records in an array and compare them with some criteria. As a first demonstration, the following is a program to display all transactions greater than $200.

Automated Teller Machine

```
C                        Search Transaction File for Amounts > $200
C
        DIMENSION   IN(2,10000)
        DATA        NFOUND/ 0/
C
C                        open file, dummy read to skip denomination header
        OPEN    (4, FILE='TRANS.DAT')
        READ    (4,1020)
C                        input data
        DO 20  I = 1,10000
    20 READ    (4,1020, END=40)  (IN(J,I), J=1,2)
  1020 FORMAT  (2I5)
        STOP  'Excessive data'
    40 NREC = I - 1
        CLOSE   (4)
C                        output title and headings
        WRITE   (*,1000)
  1000 FORMAT  ('0','Transactions greater then $200'/
       1        '0', 3X,'Account      Amount'/)
C                        search through array
        DO 60  I = 1,NREC
           IF  (IN(2,I) .GT. 200)  THEN
              WRITE   (*,1040)  IN(1,I), IN(2,I)
  1040        FORMAT  (' ',    I10,   5X,'$',I4)
              NFOUND = NFOUND + 1
           ENDIF
    60 CONTINUE
C                        final message
        IF  (NFOUND .GT. 0)  THEN
           WRITE   (*,1060)  NFOUND
  1060     FORMAT  ('0',I4,' record(s) found')
        ELSE
           WRITE   (*,1062)
  1062     FORMAT  ('0','No records found')
        ENDIF
C                        termination
        STOP
        END
```

Another type of useful search program is one in which there is interaction between the user and the computer. In the program below, the user enters the desired account number and, if corresponding records are found, they are displayed.

```
C                       Search Transaction File by Account
C
      DIMENSION  IN(8,10000), FEE(10000), IDNOM(6)
      DATA       NFOUND/ 0/
C
C                       input routine
      OPEN    (4, FILE='TRANS.DAT')
      READ    (4,1000)  IDNOM
 1000 FORMAT  (10X, 6I4)
      DO 20  I = 1,10000
   20 READ    (4,1020, END=40)  (IN(J,I), J=1,8), FEE(I)
 1020 FORMAT  (2I5, 6I4, F6.2)
      STOP  'Excessive data'
   40 NREC = I - 1
      CLOSE   (4)
C                       determine number of denominations
      DO 60  I = 6,1,-1
         IF  (IDNOM(I) .NE. 0)  GO TO 80
   60 CONTINUE
      STOP  'No denominations in file'
   80 NUMDNM = I
      ND     = NUMDNM + 2
      WRITE   (*,1060)  NREC, NUMDNM
 1060 FORMAT  ('0',I4,' transactions on file with',I2,' denominations')
C
C                       loop through input
      DO 200  I = 1,20000
         WRITE   (*,1080)
 1080    FORMAT  (/'0','Enter account number  (ctrl-Z to end):')
         READ    (*,*, ERR=180, END=900)  IACCNT
         NFOUND = 0
C                          search array; write headings on first find
         DO 100  J = 1,NREC
            IF  (IACCNT .EQ. IN(1,J))  THEN
                NFOUND = NFOUND + 1
                IF  (NFOUND .EQ. 1)
     1              WRITE   (*,1082)  (IDNOM(K), K=1,NUMDNM)
 1082           FORMAT  ('0','Account   Amount     Fee', 6I5)
                WRITE   (*,1084)  (IN(K,J), K=1,2), FEE(J),
     1                            (IN(K,J), K=3,ND
 1084           FORMAT  (' ',I7, '   $',I4, F7.2, 6I5)
            ENDIF
  100    CONTINUE
C                       final message
         IF (NFOUND .GT. 0)  THEN
             WRITE   (*,1100)  NFOUND
 1100        FORMAT  (' ',I2,' record(s) found')
           ELSE
             WRITE   (*,1102)
 1102        FORMAT  (' ','No records found')
         ENDIF
         GO TO 200
```

```
C                               input error message
  180       WRITE   (*,1180)
  1180      FORMAT  ('0','ERROR IN INPUT  -  RE-ENTER')
C
  200 CONTINUE
C                         termination
  900 STOP
      END
```

Sample Output

```
        7 transactions on file with 3 denominations


    Enter account number  (ctrl-Z to end):
    10783

    Account   Amount    Fee    50    20    10
      10783   $ 100    2.00     2     0     0
     1 record(s) found



    Enter account number  (ctrl-Z to end):
    18230

    Account   Amount    Fee    50    20    10
      18230   $ 240    4.80     4     2     0
     1 record(s) found



    Enter account number  (ctrl-Z to end):
    account

    ERROR IN INPUT  -  RE-ENTER



    Enter account number (ctrl-Z to end):
    30556
    Account   Amount    Fee    50    20    10
      30556   $ 310    6.20     6     0     1
      30556   $  90    2.00     1     2     0
     2 record(s) found



    Enter account number  (ctrl-Z to end):
    22222
    No records found



    Enter account number  (ctrl-Z to end):
    ^ Z

    Stop - Program terminated.
```

In both of the above cases, multiple records may be found and thus the entire array must be examined. However, in many applications, each record key is unique, such as a file which contains the bank balances for each of the depositors; here, there would be only one entry per account. Assume a file in which there are two items per record: (1) account number and (2) bank balance. A partial sample file might appear as follows:

```
 553   36299.86
 554   76826.81
1072   95051.02
1214   65186.10
  |       |
  |       |
  |       |
9561   93451.52
9712   32093.29
```

To determine the balance in any account, only one record can correspond; thus, the search ends with the first record found.

```
      C                     Search Balance File by Account
      C
            DIMENSION  NACCT(1000), BALANC(1000)
      C
      C                     input routine
            OPEN    (4, FILE='BALANCE.DAT')
            DO 20  I = 1,1000
        20  READ    (4,1020, END=40)  NACCT(I), BALANC(I)
      1020  FORMAT  (I4, F10.2)
              STOP  'Excessive data'
        40  NREC = I - 1
            CLOSE   (4)
      C                     loop through prompts for account number
            DO 100  NTRANS = 1,20000
              WRITE   (*,1040)
      1040      FORMAT  (/'0','Enter account number  (ctrl-Z to end):')
              READ    (*,*, ERR=80, END=900)  IACCNT
      C                     search through array
              DO 60  I = 1,NREC
                IF  (IACCNT .EQ. NACCT(I))  THEN
                    WRITE   (*,1042)  BALANC(I)
      1042          FORMAT  (' ','Account has a balance of $',F10.2)
                    GO TO 100
                ENDIF
        60    CONTINUE
              WRITE   (*,1060)
      1060      FORMAT  (' ','No record found')
              GO TO 100
      C                     input error routine
        80    PRINT  *,'ERROR IN INPUT  -  RE-ENTER'
      C
       100  CONTINUE
      C                     termination
       900  STOP
            END
```

Again, the first GO TO simulates the LOOP .. EXIT construct to produce efficient code.

If the key (the item being matched) is sorted, as in the case of a data file in which the records are sorted by ascending account number, once the program is looking at an account number which exceeds the search value, it is obvious that the record is not there. Thus, the execution of the program can be speeded up by adding an extra statement just after the DO 60:

```
C                          search through array
          DO 60  I = 1,NREC
              IF  (IACCNT .LT. NACCT(I))  GO TO 70
              IF  (IACCNT .EQ. NACCT(I))  THEN
                  WRITE  (*,1040)  BALANC(I)
 1040             FORMAT  (' ','Account has a balance of $',F10.2)
                  GO TO 100
              ENDIF
   60         CONTINUE
   70     WRITE  (*,1060)
 1060     FORMAT  (' ','No record found')
          GO TO 100
```

All of the searches shown above are called sequential searches because the data is scanned sequentially from top to bottom.

It would be terribly remiss of us not to present at this point one of the most fascinating algorithms used in searching, the binary search. (The concept was discussed and applied in exercise 5.10g.) In this search, the methodology is not to start at the beginning of the file but rather at the middle. Should the search value be less than the key found, we know that the key being sought cannot be in the last half of the file; this is like opening the telephone book in the middle when we are looking for a name beginning with G and finding ourselves on an M page. Likewise, if the search value exceeds the halfway key, the key being sought cannot be in the first half. Thus the file is cut in half.

The program then proceeds to examine the middle record in the portion of the file that is left. With each step, the file is cut in half. A file of 100 records is reduced to 50 in the first pass, 25 in the second pass, 13 in the third pass, 7 in the fourth pass, 4 in the fifth pass, 2 in the sixth pass, and 1 in the seventh pass; thus, if a matching record exists in a file of 100 records, only seven comparisons will find it. In fact, the maximum number of passes needed can be computed with the following equation:

```
Maximum number of passes  =  the truncated integer of
    ((the base 2 logarithm of the number of records)  +  1)
```

The base 2 logarithm is the natural logarithm times 1.4427, and the natural logarithm is available in all FORTRANs as the function ALOG. Just as an idea of how powerful this algorithm is, a file of 32,000 records would need only 15 passes to find the key.

Below is the modified program using a binary search. Although the coding is a little longer, the savings in execution time is tremendous. For demonstration purposes, we have added the number of passes used to the output.

```
C                      Binary Search of Balance File by Account
C
      DIMENSION  NACCT(1000), BALANC(1000)
C
C                        input routine
      OPEN    (4, FILE='BALANCE.DAT')
      DO 20  I = 1,1000
   20 READ    (4,1020, END=40)  NACCT(I), BALANC(I)
 1020 FORMAT  (I4, F10.2)
         STOP  'Excessive data'
   40 NREC = I - 1
      CLOSE   (4)
C                       determine maximum number of passes needed
      NPASS = ALOG (REAL (NREC)) * 1.4427  +  1.00
      WRITE   (*,1040)  NREC, NPASS
 1040 FORMAT  ('0','With',I6,' records, passes required =',I3)
C                         loop through prompts for account number
      DO 100  NTRANS = 1,20000
         WRITE  (*,1042)
 1042    FORMAT (/'0','Enter account number')
         READ   (*,*, ERR=80, END=900)  IACCNT
C                        search through array
         LBOT = 1
         LTOP = NREC + 1
         DO 60  I = 1,NPASS
            LMID = (LBOT + LTOP) / 2
         IF  (IACCNT .LT. NACCT(LMID))  THEN
            LTOP = LMID
          ELSE IF  (IACCNT .GT. NACCT(LMID))  THEN
            LBOT = LMID
          ELSE
            WRITE  (*,1052)  BALANC(LMID), I
 1052       FORMAT  (' ','Account has a balance of $',F10.2/
     1                ' ',I2,' passes used')
            GO TO 100
         ENDIF
   60    CONTINUE
         WRITE  (*,1060)
 1060    FORMAT  (' ','No record found')
         GO TO 100
C                         input error routine
   80    PRINT  *,'ERROR IN INPUT  -  RE-ENTER'
C
  100 CONTINUE
C                       termination
  900 STOP
      END
```

Again, the GO TOs simulate the LOOP .. EXIT construct; and they cannot be eliminated without adding a number of additional statements and slowing the execution of the code significantly.

Little needs to be said of this program, except to comment on the following statement:

    LTOP = NREC + 1

One is added to the number of records because when the top and bottom record numbers are integer-averaged to compute LMID, the truncation would prevent the algorithm from ever reaching the last record in the file if the program did not add the one.

Exercises

11.4a Generate a binary search function which responds to the accessing statement:

    LREC = IBSRCH (KEY, NREC, NVALUE)

in which KEY is a one-dimensional array being searched, NREC is the number of records being searched through, and NVALUE is the search value. Return a value of zero if the record is not found. Also write a driver program to test the function and do so with test data similar to that in BALANCE.DAT. The input would consist of the search value, and the driver would display the associated value or a "not found" message.

11.4b Expand the above function to handle a two-dimensional key and a multiple-item search array. The accessing statement should now read:

    LREC = IB2SRC (KEY,NREC,NITEM, NVALUE)

NITEM is the first subscript of the array KEY, and NREC is the second. NVALUE is a one-dimensional array of NITEM items. The mapping function will be useful here. Again, write a driver to test the function. As sample data, generate a file with a three-item key consisting of year, month, and day. For example, the following temperature data, giving the date and mean temperature for the day, would be sufficient:

    88 12 30 32
    88 12 31 22
    89 01 01 45
    89 01 02 47
    89 01 03 38
    89 01 04 40

The input would consist of the year, month, and day placed into the array NVALUE(3). The function should return the record number and the driver would display the temperature for that day (or a "not found" message).

11.4c Write a function to do a binary search on a three-letter alphameric key. Generate a data file containing the three-letter abbreviation of the month (capitalized) and the number of days in the month (ignoring leap years). Write a driver to read the file and sort it alphabetically; the 3-character sort is short enough to be placed directly in the driver. Then have the driver accept the desired month from the keyboard, access the function, and display the number of days in the month.

11.5   CONTROL BREAKS

A control break represents a point in the logic where the normal flow of instructions is interrupted so that some additional logic may be inserted. Usually this refers to the output of subtotals (or minor totals) when some group of data is complete, but it could include something as simple as a skipped line or a new page for improved output readability.

Thus far the treatment of the output of a final or grand total has been rather casual, since the logic is quite straightforward. The usual steps are:

1. Initialize the sum to zero.
2. During detail processing, add the amount to the sum.
3. Upon completion of the detail processing, output the sum.

However, the output of intermediate values based upon some change in a specific control item is a bit more involved. First of all, the data must be sorted so that all records of the same control item are together. Secondly, as each detail record is processed, it is necessary to see if a control break is required. Let's look at some sample data. Assume a data file containing a variable amount of records, each one consisting of three items:

```
1: numeric day of the week
        2: salesperson number
                3: amount sold

        1       18      3245.77
        1       21       996.32
        1       34      5400.00
        2       18      3116.50
        2       21       782.44
        .        .         .
        .        .         .
        5       21      6643.89
        5       34       125.75
```

Note that the data is sorted by day and then, within each day, by salesperson number. In this program, a subtotal of sales for each day is wanted as well as a final total of sales for the week. The output should look like this:

```
Day Salesperson      Amount

1               18     3245.77
1               21      996.32
1               34     5400.00
Daily Subtotal:        9642.09

2               18     3116.50
2               21      782.44
Daily Subtotal:        3898.94
```

```
          3              21        4450.98
          3              34        1007.89
       Daily Subtotal:             5458.87

          4              18         887.00
          4              21        5073.45
          4              34        2207.80
       Daily Subtotal:             8168.25

          5              18         225.98
          5              21        6643.89
          5              34         125.75
       Daily Subtotal:             6995.62

       Final Total:               27168.15
```

The logic requires looping through the detail records, printing each out, as usual. The subtotal logic requires the subtotal to be initialized as zero and the detail amount to be added in each time a detail record is processed. Then, when appropriate, that subtotal is output and reset to zero for the next group (in this case, the next day). The question now becomes, How do we determine when it is appropriate?

There are two methods. One is the look-back method in which, just before processing the next detail record, the previous record is compared with it to see if a control break has taken place. If so, the subtotal is output, set back to zero, and processing of the detail record continues. Special treatment must be given to the first detail record, since there is no previous record to compare it with. Assuming the array is IN(2,100), the coding might look as follows:

```
C                     Control Break:  Look-Back Method
C
        DIMENSION  IN(2,100), SALES(100)
C
        DATA       TOTAL, SUBTOT/ 2*0.00/
C
C                      open and read input file
        OPEN   (2, FILE='SALESIN')
        DO 20  I = 1,100
   20 READ    (2,1000, END=40) (IN(J,I), J=1,2), SALES(I)
 1000 FORMAT               (I1, I6,          F10.2)
          STOP  'excessive data'
   40 NREC = I - 1
        CLOSE  (2)
C                    loop though records  (detail processing)
        DO 100  I = 1,NREC
          IF (I .EQ. 1)  WRITE   (*,1040)
 1040               FORMAT ('0','Day  Salesperson    Amount'/)
          IF (I .GT. 1 .AND.  IN(1,I) .GT. IN(1,I-1))  THEN
            WRITE   (*,1042)  SUBTOT
 1042       FORMAT  (' ','Daily Subtotal:', F10.2/)
            TOTAL  = TOTAL + SUBTOT
            SUBTOT = 0.00
          ENDIF
          SUBTOT = SUBTOT + SALES(I)
  100 WRITE    (*,1100) (IN(J,I), J=1,2), SALES(I)
 1100 FORMAT   (' ',I1, I15, F10.2)
```

```
C                             final subtotal and total
        WRITE   (*,1042)  SUBTOT
        WRITE   (*,1102)  TOTAL
 1102 FORMAT   (' ','Final Total:', F14.2)
C                             termination
        STOP
        END
```

Note the two segments of conditional code within the detail loop. One is the check for headings. Of course, this could have been done prior to the beginning of the loop and would not have required an IF statement. However, the construction shown is useful if we are using a line counter to control moving to a new page and printing new headings. Secondly, and more importantly for this discussion, is the conditional logic for subtotal. Here the program is looking back, but only if at some record other than the first one, to see if a subtotal is necessary. After the detail loop is complete, it is necessary to output the last subtotal as well as the final subtotal.

The second possible method is the look-ahead method, in which the detail record is processed and then the program compares it with the next record to be processed. Should a control break occur, the subtotal is output prior to completing the loop. In this case, special care must be taken when the last record is processed because there is no valid record to compare it with. The code below does that by using a compound conditional, but later we will show an alternative method which has additional usefulness.

```
C                 Control Breaks:   Look-Ahead Method
C
        DIMENSION  IN(2,100), SALES(100)
C
        DATA       TOTAL, SUBTOT/ 2*0.00/
C
C                          open and read input file
        OPEN    (2, FILE='SALESIN')
        DO 20   I = 1,100
   20 READ    (2,1000, END=40)  (IN(J,I), J=1,2), SALES(I)
 1000 FORMAT                          (I1, I6,  F10.2)
          STOP  'excessive data'
   40 NREC = I - 1
        CLOSE   (2)
C                       loop through records
        DO 100   I = 1,NREC
          IF  (I .EQ. 1)  WRITE    (*,1040)
 1040             FORMAT  ('0','Day  Salesperson    Amount'/)
          SUBTOT = SUBTOT + SALES(I)
          WRITE   (*,1042)  (IN(J,I), J=1,2), SALES(I)
 1042     FORMAT  (' ',I1, I15, F10.2)
          IF  (I .EQ. NREC .OR.  IN(1,I) .LT. IN(1,I+1))  THEN
            WRITE   (*,1044)  SUBTOT
 1044       FORMAT  (' ','Daily Sub-Total:', F10.2/)
            TOTAL  = TOTAL + SUBTOT
            SUBTOT = 0.00
          ENDIF
  100 CONTINUE
C                       final total
        WRITE   (*,1102)  TOTAL
 1102 FORMAT   ('0','Final Total:', F14.2)
```

```
C                       termination
      STOP
      END
```

Note that in this code it was not necessary to output the final subtotal, since that is done within the detail processing loop. However, the carriage control on the final total format was modified to generate a line skip.

A slight variation within this method is to generate an "end-of-file" record just after the last valid record. This record contains a control break item larger than the one in the last valid record. Although an additional statement is needed (and the DIMENSION expanded to compensate for the additional record), the conditional logic is simplified. Furthermore, this method simplifies coding where there are multiple control breaks (i.e., where there is more than one level of control breaks) and in certain other processes, such as the merging of two or more files.

Two changes are required. One establishes the end-of-file record:

```
40 NREC         = I - 1
   IN(1,NREC+1) = 9999
```

or

```
40 IN(1,I) = 9999
   NREC    = I - 1
```

The second modifies the conditional as follows:

```
      IF  (IN(1,I) .LT. IN(1,I+1))  THEN
          WRITE  (*,1044)  SUBTOT
1044      FORMAT (' ','Daily Sub-Total:', F10.2/)
          TOTAL  = TOTAL + SUBTOT
          SUBTOT = 0.00
      ENDIF
```

Now we are ready to show our final solution to Application Problem 2: Computer Time Accounting. There are two outputs. One is chronological, in the same order as the input file, with only a final total. Then second is in user order, to be output with user subtotals and the same final total. The two subprograms M2HM and CMPCST, presented in Chapter 9, are accessed, as well as the sort ISORT, described in section 11.3. The look-ahead method is used with the end-of-file record. Notice how the + carriage control character is used to print the subtotal on the same line as the last detail record.

**Computer
Time
Accounting**

```
C                 Computer Time Accounting
C
      CHARACTER*9  MONTH
C
      DIMENSION    MT(9,2000), COST(2000)
      DATA         ITOTTM, TOTCST, SUBTOT/ 0, 2*0.00/
C
C                  open file and input data
      OPEN    (2, FILE='TIMEIN')
      READ    (2,1000)  MONTH, IYEAR
```

```
      1000 FORMAT   (A9, 1X, I4)
           DO 20   I = 1,2000
        20 READ     (2,1020, END=40)   (MT(J,I), J=1,4)
      1020 FORMAT   (I2, 1X, I2, 2(1X, I4))
               STOP 'excessive data'
        40 CLOSE   (2)
           NREC = I - 1
   C
   C                        compute minutes used and total
           DO 60   I = 1,NREC
               MT(5,I) = MT(4,I) - MT(3,I)
               IF  (MT(5,I) .LE. 0)  MT(5,I) = MT(5,I) + 1440
        60 ITOTTM = ITOTTM + MT(5,I)
   C
   C                        convert log on and time used to hours and minutes
           DO 80   I = 1,NREC
               CALL M2HM (MT(3,I),MT(6,I), MT(7,I))
        80 CALL M2HM (MT(5,I), MT(8,I), MT(9,I))
   C
   C                        get cost and total cost
           DO 100   I = 1,NREC
               COST(I) = CMPCST (MT(5,I), 2.50)
       100 TOTCST  = TOTCST + COST(I)
   C
   C                        chronological report
           OPEN  (3, FILE='TIMEOUT')
   C                                new page, title & headings
           WRITE   (3,1100)  MONTH, IYEAR
      1100 FORMAT   ('1', 'COMPUTER TIME USAGE FOR ',A9,', ',I4//
          1          '0', 'User   Day      Time    Usage        Cost'/ 1X)
   C                                loop through detail records
           DO 120   I = 1,NREC
               TIME  = REAL (MT(6,I))  +  REAL (MT(7,I)) / 100.00
               USAGE = REAL (MT(8,I))  +  REAL (MT(9,I)) / 100.00
       120 WRITE   (3,1120)  MT(1,I), MT(2,I), TIME, USAGE, COST(I)
      1120 FORMAT   (' ', I4, I5, 2F11.2, F11.2)
   C                                convert total minutes to real time and output
           CALL M2HM (ITOTTM, ITOTHR, ITOTMN)
           TOTTIM = REAL (ITOTHR)  +  REAL (ITOTMN) / 100.00
           WRITE   (3,1122)  TOTTIM, TOTCST
      1122 FORMAT   ('0', 'Totals', F21.2, F11.2)
   C
   C
   C                        user report
   C                                sort by user, date and logon time
           CALL ISORT (MT,NREC,9, IDUMMY,0, COST,1)
   C                                set end-of-file
           MT(1,NREC+1) = 9999
   C                                new page, title and headings
           WRITE   (3,1100)  MONTH, IYEAR
   C                                loop through detail records
           DO 140   I = 1,NREC
               TIME  = REAL (MT(6,I))  +  REAL (MT(7,I)) / 100.00
               USAGE = REAL (MT(8,I))  +  REAL (MT(9,I)) / 100.00
               WRITE   (3,1120)  MT(1,I), MT(2,I), TIME, USAGE, COST(I)
               SUBTOT = SUBTOT + COST(I)
   C                                check for control break
               IF  (MT(1,I) .LT. MT(1,I+1))  THEN
                   WRITE  (3,1124)  SUBTOT
```

```
 1124           FORMAT ('+', F50.2/ 1X)
                SUBTOT = 0.00
           ENDIF
  140 CONTINUE
C                                        final totals
      WRITE   (3,1122) TOTTIM, TOTCST
C
C                        termination
      CLOSE   (3)
      STOP
      END
```

Sample output for this program looks like:

```
COMPUTER TIME USAGE FOR September 1992


   User   Day     Time     Usage       Cost

      9     3    11.46     23.09     2838.00
      5     4     8.13     11.48     1476.00
      7     6     7.53     22.00     2700.00
      2     6    17.06     19.30     2400.00
      5     8     1.36      6.52      884.00
      8     8     5.17     13.03     1626.00
     10    11     9.54       .18       45.00
     11    11    22.57     23.29     2878.00
     10    12    21.22     21.47     2674.00
      6    15     3.18      8.19     1058.00
     10    15     4.39     15.04     1868.00
      2    16     1.20      7.23      946.00
      4    16    21.04     12.54     1608.00
      2    17     8.34      2.56      412.00
      6    18    16.07       .45      112.50
      4    19     2.30      1.40      250.00
     10    19    13.20      3.56      532.00
      7    19    16.41      3.46      512.00
      8    21     5.33      5.36      732.00
      8    21    10.54     21.07     2594.00
      2    21    20.51     20.40     2540.00
      8    22    22.25      7.53     1006.00
      3    23    13.02     21.11     2602.00
      2    24    12.19      1.13      182.50
      7    25     2.59     21.14     2608.00
      7    26     2.45     20.48     2556.00
      5    28    18.45     12.11     1522.00
      8    29     8.46     20.18     2496.00
      2    30    16.54     19.52     2444.00
      7    31     6.58      8.49     1118.00

   Totals               379.31    47220.00
```

```
        COMPUTER TIME USAGE FOR September 1992


     User   Day      Time      Usage        Cost

       2      6      17.06     111.30      2400.00
       2     16       1.20       7.23       946.00
       2     17       8.34       2.56       412.00
       2     21      20.51      20.40      2540.00
       2     24      12.19       1.13       182.50
       2     30      16.54      19.52      2444.00      8924.50

       3     23      13.02      21.11      2602.00      2602.00

       4     16      21.04      12.54      1608.00
       4     19       2.30       1.40       250.00      1858.00

       5      4       8.13      11.48      1476.00
       5      8       1.36       6.52       884.00
       5     28      18.45      12.11      1522.00      3882.00

       6     15       3.18       8.19      1058.00
       6     18      16.07        .45       112.50      1170.50

       7      6       7.53      22.00      2700.00
       7     19      16.41       3.46       512.00
       7     25       2.59      21.14      2608.00
       7     26       2.45      20.48      2556.00
       7     31       6.58       8.49      1118.00      9494.00

       8      8       5.17      13.03      1626.00
       8     21       5.33       5.36       732.00
       8     21      10.54      21.07      2594.00
       8     22      22.25       7.53      1006.00
       8     29       8.46      20.18      2496.00      8454.00

       9      3      11.46      23.09      2838.00      2838.00

      10     11       9.54        .18        45.00
      10     12      21.22      21.47      2674.00
      10     15       4.39      15.04      1868.00
      10     19      13.20       3.56       532.00     51111.00

      11     11      22.57      23.29      2878.00      2878.00

     Totals                   3711.31     47220.00
```

Exercises

11.5a   The following data file of 50 records consists of three items, sorted in the following order: (1) Day of week, (2) salesperson number, and (3) sale of car. Write a program that reads in the data and outputs a report with daily subtotals and a final total for sales.

```
1   1    10331.60
1   1    10447.53
1   1    12245.79
1   1    12975.27
1   2     8296.99
1   2    14093.02
1   2    15895.26
1   3    11210.01
2   1     8050.01
2   1     9303.88
2   1     9658.27
2   1    11293.98
2   1    11338.98
2   1    12050.92
2   1    12071.82
2   2     8521.17
2   2    10424.94
2   2    11660.38
2   2    12085.42
2   2    12103.58
2   2    13281.63
2   2   138811.98
2   2    15027.45
2   2   158911.72
2   3    11675.15
3   1    13672.15
3   2     8580.21
3   2    11311.58
3   2    14866.37
3   3    10598.52
4   1     9628.46
4   1     9684.80
4   1    15981.56
4   2   102011.47
4   2    14778.77
4   3    80511.31
4   3     9377.50
4   3    10033.90
4   3    11512.47
4   3    12441.25
4   3    12600.60
5   1     9201.80
5   1    10604.38
5   1    11920.02
5   1    12813.63
5   2     8781.74
5   2    10857.79
5   2    10935.02
5   2    15710.75
5   3     9114.14
```

11.5b Expand the above program to give an additional level of subtotals—the total sales for each employee for each day. Use double-precision reals.

11.5c Enhance the above program to resort the data by salesperson and day of the week. Output an additional report with two subtotals, one by salesperson for each day and a second by salesperson, as well as a final total. This will need a version of an ascending integer sort with a double-precision real carry.

11.5d   Using a random-number generator, generate an array of 100 real values in the range 0.00 to 9.99. Sort the values in descending order (using subroutine RDSORT from exercise 11.2b) and then output in groups so that there is a skipped line between the points that are in different integer ranges (e.g., the points in the range 9.00 or greater are separated from those in the range 8.00 or greater, which in turn are separated from those in the range 7.00 or greater, and so forth). For each range, output the number of points and the average points before beginning the output of the next range. An integer array with the truncated values in it would be useful in establishing the control break.

11.6   CHAPTER REVIEW

This chapter is a culmination of the methods of numeric data handling. Combining the use of multidimensional arrays, subprograms, and multiple-line I/O with advanced techniques of data manipulation, the programs written herein indicate an almost professional quality which combines concise code and full utilization of the tools of the language.

There is little more that a professional programmer is asked to do with numeric data handling, whether working with scientific or commercially based programming systems. Although many of the applications seem to be more business-oriented, the same techniques are used in scientific data processing, but the theoretical aspects of the problems to be solved in that latter field would make this text far too complex for a beginning programming reader. It should also be recognized that about 75% of the programming done is oriented to business and finance, and that much of it is done in FORTRAN because of the availability, efficiency, and calculational speed of this high-level language.

There is much you can still learn about sorting and searching; and there are many algorithms available, especially for sorting. Sorts such as the "bubble" sort and the "shell" sort are algorithms in the public domain which you can use freely to speed up the execution of your programs. (The author uses a variation of the "shell" sort, which runs about five times faster than the sort presented in the chapter.) In all of these sorts, the comparisons and interchanging are the same; only the order of the elements being compared differs.

There is still one topic that remains to be discussed—merging (the collating of two or more sorted files)—but it is covered in the exercises below.

The topics covered in this chapter include:

Topic	Section
Binary search	11.1, 11.4
Carry-along	11.1
Control breaks	11.5
End-of-file record	11.5
Header records	11.1
Interchange sort	11.2

Topic	Section
Key	11.1
Key sort	11.5
Key/record sort	11.5
Level breaks	11.1
Lexical functions	11.2
Look-ahead method	11.5
Look-back method	11.5
Mapping function	11.1
Merging	11.6
Minimum/maximum value	11.3
Searching	11.5
Sequential search	11.6
Sorting	11.1, 11.5
Subprograms	11.2, 11.4
Subtotals	11.5
Totals	11.5
Trailer records	11.1

Exercises

11.6a This is a continuation of exercise 10.7a, the egg distribution problem from Chapter 10. Add to module 4 (the subtotal gathering) the calculation of subtotals for units sold per customer. Then expand module 7, the output module, to produce subtotals for gross, dozen, and cost. The easiest way is to generate the subtotals by units and then use subroutine BRKDWN to get the subtotals for gross and dozen; note that there will never be more than 11 dozen in the output. The cost, however, is not recomputed; it is the actual subtotal of the cost for that customer. Below is a sample output:

```
EGG   REPORT   FOR   aaaaaaaaa, nnnn


Customer   Date    Gross  Dozen      Cost

        1      2       1      9      32.70
        1     13       2      8      47.40
        1     18              8      14.40
        1     26       1      6      27.30
        1  Subtotal    6      7     121.80

        2      1              8      14.40
        2      3       1      6      27.30
        ┊      ┊       ┊      ┊        .

  etc.  with final totals for gross, dozen, and cost
```

Then generate a chronological report which lists only the day of the month and the cost of eggs sold on that day. The cost is the actual cost of the individual purchases, not the computed cost based on the total gross and dozen. Thus it will be necessary to utilize the array of costs generated in the first part of the program. The data should be resorted by day of month and only print the subtotals for each day. If there are no purchases on that day, there should be no output. The final totals will be the same (they'd better be!) as in the first part of the report, so there is no need to recompute them.

```
  CHRONOLOGICAL   EGG   REPORT   FOR   aaaaaaaaa, nnnn


  Date        Gross  Dozen         Cost

     1          0     11          19.80
     2          6     11         129.00
     3          3      9          65.70
     |          |      |            .
     |          |      |            .
    29          4      4          nn.nn

  Totals       nnn     nn        nnnn.nn
```

11.6b Convert the array DIFFRN(20,20) from exercise 10.7b to a one-dimensional array containing only the nonzero values and no repeat values (i.e., the distances between points 1 and 2 and between points 2 and 1 should be represented by only one value in the new array); there should be 190 values. Also generate an array of (2,190) with the point numbers, the lower-numbered point first. Sort this information in descending order with the distance as the key and the point numbers carried along. Output the values with the following columns:

1. Point number 1
2. x-coordinate of point 1
3. y-coordinate of point 1
4. z-coordinate of point 1
5. Point number 2
6. x-coordinate of point 2
7. y-coordinate of point 2
8. z-coordinate of point 2
9. Distance from point 1 to point 2

Output onto four pages, with 50 points on the first three pages and 40 on the last. Skip a line between groups of 10 points. Output should have a title and headings on each page, with a page number.

11.6c Revise the output for exercise 11.3a so that a line is skipped every time the temperature rises into a new bracket of 10 degrees. That is, a line skip should occur between -11 and -10, -1 and 0, 9 and 10, 19 and 20, etc.

11.6d In exercise 11.2d, two arrays were merged into a third array by stacking them one after the other in the new array and sorting. Sorting is a very slow process, expanding exponentially as longer arrays are processed. It is much more efficient to merge two sorted arrays by comparing the elements in each and moving the smaller one (for an ascending set of data) into the new array. Pointers are useful, one for each array; two point to the elements being compared, and the third points to the position in the new array where the next element goes. Then the pointer is increased to the next position in the array where the next element came from, and in the target array:

1:	Array 1	Array 2	Target
	32 <	45 <	<
	47	52	
	56	62	
	59		

2:	Array 1	Array 2	Target
	32	45 <	32
	47 <	52	<
	56	62	
	59		

3:	Array 1	Array 2	Target
	32	45	32
	47 <	52 <	45
	56	62	<
	59		

4:	Array 1	Array 2	Target
	32	45	32
	47	52 <	45
	56 <	62	47
	59		<

5:	Array 1	Array 2	Target
	32	45	32
	47	52	45
	56 <	62 <	47
	59		52
			<

6:	Array 1	Array 2	Target
	32	45	32
	47	52	45
	56	62 <	47
	59 <		52
			56
			<

7:	Array 1	Array 2	Target
	32	45	32
	47	52	45
	56	62 <	47
	59		52
	<		56
			59
			<

8:	Array 1	Array 2	Target
	32	45	32
	47	52	45
	56	62	47
	59	<	52
	<		56
			59
			62
			<

The only difficulty is ending the merge. Either the pointers must be compared with the number of records in each of the arrays, or end-of-data values may be placed at the end of the input arrays and, when the compared values are equal to that sentinel value, the merge is over. The coding using the sentinel values is easy.

Write a program to merge two arrays. The above data can be used for testing.

11.6e   Using a random-number generator, generate two sets of 20 pairs of x- and y-coordinates in the range 0.00 to 10.00. Sort each set independently, using the x-coordinate as the key and the y-coordinate as the carry-along. Then merge the two sets by x-coordinates into a new two-dimensional array with the y-coordinates carried along.

12

Alphameric Manipulation

CHAPTER OBJECTIVES

■ To present the methods by which alphameric information is stored.

■ To describe the concept of strings and substrings.

■ To detail the methods by which strings are manipulated and used in FORTRAN programs and subprograms.

■ To explain the use of internal files that allow data to be reformatted.

STATEMENT OF THE PROBLEM

Almost from the very beginning of our discussion of the FORTRAN language, we have discussed character variables. In Chapter 3, section 3.2, they were used for the input and output of alphameric data. In Chapter 4, section 4.3 showed how character variables can be used in assignment statements for the movement of data from one variable to another. Chapter 5, section 5.7, showed how their values can be used to make decisions. In Chapter 7, section 7.5 demonstrated the use of the alphameric (**Aw**) format specification that gives the programmer greater control over the input and output of such variables. Chapter 9, section 9.4, showed arrays of character variables and how they can be initialized in a DATA statement, just like other variables. Chapter 11, section 11.2, introduced the lexical intrinsic functions LGE, LGT, LLE, and LLT, which are used to determine the collating sequence (sorting order) of two character variables.

In the examples given in previous chapters, the contents of the character variables—called *strings*—remained constant in that the programmer could not change the contents of the strings or add two strings or remove characters from them. A program could replace strings with new strings or trim strings by moving them into variables with a smaller capacity, but it could not manipulate the characters within the strings or examine the strings for their partial contents.

This chapter introduces the tools that allow programs to get into the strings and work with the *substrings*. For many programmers, this is the most interesting and challenging programming because of the myriad applications and complexity of the logic. It is quite different from the normal "number crunching" kind of application and often requires a different mind-set. If nothing else, it makes us aware of how powerful the human mind is, because some of the easiest functions that our mind seems to do so automatically become rather complex when we have to design a computer algorithm to do the same thing!

It should be noted in passing that the material presented in this chapter contains one of the most significant additions to FORTRAN, as the language was updated from the 1966 standards to the 1977 standards. Prior to the new upgrade, programmers had to work with string arrays wherein each element would be used to store one character and all work was done by treating each individual character numerically, similar to the way integer arrays are manipulated. Although a character could be coded as 'A' (with apostrophes), for example, instead of its stored numeric code, there were no shortcuts unless the programmer designed his/her own subprograms (or the manufacturer supplied them) to perform the desired functions. Therefore, if you are reading some old programs, you might find the coding quite different from that done in this chapter.

12.1 ALPHAMERIC CODES

All information is stored in the computer memory (and on the peripheral storage devices) as numbers. Thus there must be a numeric code for each character, and computer programs must be explicit in defining those numbers as characters when they are to be so treated. In order to implement this scheme, there must be a set of codes to represent each keyboard character. In addition, there is the need to store information pertaining to keyboard and computer operations not seen on the screen, such as carriage return (what happens when we press the RETURN or ENTER key), TAB, ESC, and the various combinations we get when we combine the ALT or CTRL keys with other keyboard characters. And finally there are codes necessary to store file and communication controls, such as end-of-file, start-of-transmission, end-of-transmission, the audible signal (beep or bell), and so on.

In almost all cases, these codes are transparent to the user or programmer; that is, the values in no way affect the implementation of a program. However, in many cases a specific knowledge of the coding scheme is useful to the programmer and an understanding of the codes leads to a better understanding of why and how a particular implementation works. If nothing else, it is critical that you be aware that there are *different* codes used on different systems and that sometimes conversion problems do occur.

Part of the reason that different codes exist is that some of them were developed before computers existed and were later applied to computer technology. The inventors of these codes could not foresee what would be happening in the future. As early as 1829, Louis Braille had invented a code for the blind which used raised dots on paper, with a 6-bit code representing the letters of the alphabet.

The first still-known (but now little used) code invented for mechanical data transmission (in 1838) was that of Samuel F. B. Morse. It uses a series of short impulses (dots) and long impulses (two quick dots or dashes) to represent a letter. This code was used on the early telegraph systems, with human operators entering the signal manually and other human operators interpreting the signal aurally. The codes varied in length, using a slight pause in transmission to indicate the end of a letter. For purposes of optimization, Morse used short combinations for more frequently used letters (*e, t, a*, etc.). Codes could be as short as one impulse or as long as four.

The first machine-readable code was invented about 1880 by J. M. E. Baudot and consisted of a fixed 5-bit code to be used in telegraph communications. With 5 bits, only 32 possible combinations exist; but Baudot used the typewriter shift scheme to almost double the set. His code thus included both upper and lower cases of all 26 letters, the 10 digits, a few punctuation and arithmetic symbols, as well as space, carriage return (return to beginning of line with no line feed), and line feed (move to next line without returning typing element). There is a code to shift to upper case and another to shift to lower case, which worked like the "caps lock" key on a keyboard, toggling back and forth from one mode to another. Hardware was developed which could also punch and read a 5-channel continuous paper tape so that information could be prepared in advance and saved in this machine-readable medium.

There exists a natural way of coding the decimal numbers in binary form, called Binary Coded Decimal (BCD), in which 4 bits can be used to represent any single decimal digit:

Decimal	BCD	Decimal	BCD
0	0000	5	0101
1	0001	6	0110
2	0010	7	0111
3	0011	8	1000
4	0100	9	1001

The bits (binary digits) represent the powers of 2—which are, reading from right to left, 1, 2, 4, and 8. For any mechanical scheme, this would seem like a logical starting place, although Baudot did not use it. All future coding schemes, however, did start from this point.

In the 1890s, when Dr. Herman Hollerith was developing his methodology for the mechanical storage and processing of census data, he used holes punched in a stiff paper card for storing that information (still called a Hollerith card). The card had 12 rows and 80 columns. The bottom 10 rows represented the decimal digits 0 to 9. The upper two rows, called the 12 row (top) and the 11 row (second), are used—occasionally with row 0—to extend the available codes; these three rows are called the zone rows. (Row 0 can serve as both a numeric punch and a zone punch.) The numeric information in rows 0 to 9 is compressed into BCD; the zone information (only one zone punch was allowed in a column) is maintained in its own 2-bits. This scheme, usually referred to as *keypunch code,* provides a 6-bit code capable of storing up to 64 different characters. Of these, only 48 were used by Hollerith; they included 12 punctuation and arithmetic symbols in addition to the 36 alphanumeric characters. This coding scheme was sufficient to handle all of the data processing needs up to the early computer period (late 1950s). One of the major shortcomings of this scheme was that, due to the lack of special characters, a single code could represent two different characters and required the compiler to interpret according to application. A typical punch card is shown in Figure 12-1.

As needs increased for additional computer character representation, two competing codes emerged. IBM developed Extended Binary Coded Decimal Interchange Code (EBCDIC), an 8-bit code which is an extension of the 6-bit keypunch code. The last 4 bits are still BCD. The third and fourth store the zone codes: a 12-row punch is stored as 00, the 11 row as 01, and the 0 row as 10; the code for no zone punch (which indicates that the stored value is a digit) is 11. The first 2 bits are assigned as needed. This code of 256 possible characters includes all of the upper- and lowercase letters, all of the necessary punctuation and arithmetic symbols (including those found only on specialized language keyboards), as well as all of the necessary communication and file-handling codes, plus room for the definition of many new ones. (There are about 100 unused codes.)

Unfortunately, EBCDIC has a number of internal problems because of its derivation from keypunch code. The *collating sequence*, the numeric order of the codes and the way it will sort if the sort is based on a numeric key, places the lowercase letters before the uppercase letters and the numbers after the letters. Also, the letters and numerals will sort before the special characters, including the blank; which means, for example, that the name "Pressmann" would sort before "Pressman " (the string ends with a blank). Furthermore, the numeric differences between adjoining letters is usually 1; but where the zones change, the difference is 7 between the letters *I* and *J* and 8 between the letters *R* and *S*. Thus, there is not a natural progression that programmers could use in sophisticated applications.

However, a more logical code was adopted by the American National Standards Institute (ANSI) in 1967 and is called the American Standard Code for Information Interchange (ASCII or, more officially, USASCII). This is a 7-bit code with a more orderly organization than the earlier codes had. Special transmission and other codes are in the first 32 positions (values 0 to 31, decimal; or 00 to 1F, hexadecimal), followed by most of the special characters, then the numerals, some more special characters, the uppercase letters, some more special characters, the lowercase letters, and some final special characters. With 7 bits, there are 128 possible combinations. With the movement to an 8-bit standard (byte), the additional bit is

Figure 12-1
An Example of a Punch Card

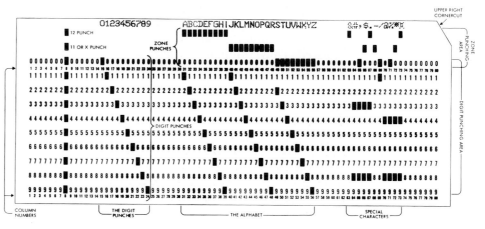

Source: Courtesy of International Business Machines Corporation

available for different uses but has not become standardized; thus computer users might find many different implementations of the additional 128 characters, including cursor control, color control, special spacing, graphics, etc.

To eliminate the conflicts between the codes, the FORTRAN language includes the lexical functions (LGE, LGT, LLE, and LLT) so that a compiler manufacturer can provide a proper collating sequence for the programmer. Some former users of EBCDIC have converted to ASCII, and most peripheral equipment, such as printers, disks, and tapes, accept only ASCII. Although ANSI could not force a particular sequence, their specifications for FORTRAN 77 (ANSI X3.9-1978) state (Appendix B: Section Notes, page B-2): "If possible, a processor should use the American National Standard Code for Information Interchange, ANSI X3.4-1977 (ASCII), sequence for the complete FORTRAN character set."

The reader will find complete EBCDIC and ASCII tables in Appendix C of this text.

12.2   STRINGS AND SUBSTRINGS*

In addition to the ability to access a complete string, FORTRAN gives us the ability to access part of that string, referred to as a substring, and to manipulate just the characters desired. The notation consists of a pair of numbers representing the beginning and ending position of the substring separated by a colon (:) and enclosed in a set of parentheses. If one of the limits is missing, the extreme of the limit is assumed; i.e., if the beginning value is missing, position one is assumed, and if the ending value is missing, the last position is assumed. For example, assuming:

```
CHARACTER   STRNG*8
DATA        STRNG/ 'ABCDEFGH'/
```

then

STRNG(1:8)	refers to 'ABCDEFGH'	(same as STRNG)
STRNG(3:6)	refers to 'CDEF'	
STRNG(:6)	refers to 'ABCDEF'	
STRNG(3:)	refers to 'CDEFGH'	
STRNG(2:2)	refers to 'B'	

The substring may appear on either side of the assignment. If it is on the right, only those characters indicated are accessed. If on the left, only those positions are replaced. Thus, assuming we start with the original contents of STRNG each time:

STRNG(5:8) = STRNG(1:4)	yields	'ABCDABCD'
STRNG(1:3) = 'WXYZ'	yields	'WXYDEFGH',
		ignoring the extra character
STRNG(2:3) = '. '	yields	'A. DEFGH'
STRNG(2:3) = '.'	yields	'A. DEFGH'

Note the blank padding at the end if the replacement string is shorter.

STRNG(1:8) = ' '	yields	' ',	as does
STRNG = ' '			

*Please review Chapter 4, section 4.3, prior to beginning this section.

Any reference to a character position outside the string, such as STRNG(9:10), is invalid. In all cases, strings are treated in a left-justified mode; i.e., the leftmost positions and characters are the ones used if the receiving string is shorter, and padding is done on the right if the receiving string is longer.

FORTRAN provides the ability to add strings together (*concatenation*) by placing a double slash between the strings to be added. The receiving string will store only as many characters as it has room for, truncating the rightmost ones. For example:

```
      CHARACTER   STRNGA*4,        STRNGB*8,            STRNGC*12
      DATA        STRNGA/'ABCD'/, STRNGB/'12345678'/
C
      STRNGC = STRNGA // STRNGB                 yields     'ABCD12345678'
      STRNGC = STRNGB // STRNGA                 yields     '12345678ABCD'
      STRNGC = STRNGB // STRNGB                 yields     '123456781234'
      STRNGC = STRNGA(2:4) // STRNGB(1:1) // STRNGB(7:8)
                                                yields     'BCD178      '
      STRNGC = 'Grade = ' // STRNGA(4:4)        yields     'Grade = D   '
      STRNGC = STRNGB(1:3) // ' GO'             yields     '123 GO      '
```

Character variables can also be arrayed. The dimensioning is done in the same way as regular variables. When dimensioning is in the CHARACTER statement, the dimension is placed before the string length. Here are a number of different ways of dimensioning the same two strings:

```
      CHARACTER*4   STRNGA
      CHARACTER*8   STRNGB
      DIMENSION     STRNGA(20), STRNGB(15)
```

or

```
      CHARACTER     STRNGA*4,    STRGNB*8
      DIMENSION     STRNGA(20),  STRNGB(15)
```

or

```
      CHARACTER     STRNGA(20)*4, STRNGB(15)*8
```

Below is a sample program utilizing some of the described concepts. It accepts an entered name and time and responds with a salutation based on the time of day.

```
      C                     Program Salutation
      C
      C           Abstract:  displays a salutation based on time of day
      C                      and user's name.
      C
      C
            CHARACTER   NAME*18, MESSGE*47, HOWDY*12, SALUT(3)*9
            INTEGER*2   LENSAL(3), LNAME
      C
            DATA   LENSAL/ 7,9,7/
            DATA   SALUT/ 'morning  ',
           1             'afternoon',
           2             'evening  '/
            DATA   HOWDY/ 'how are you?'/
      C
```

```
C                        enter name, get length
      WRITE    (*,1000)
 1000 FORMAT  ('0','Please enter your name (up to 18 characters)'/
     1          ' ', 18('-'))
      READ     (*,1002)  NAME
 1002 FORMAT  (A18)
C                  get length of name entered
      DO 20  LNAME = 18,1,-1
          IF  (NAME(LNAME:LNAME) .NE. ' ')  GO TO 40
   20 CONTINUE
      LNAME = 0
C                      enter time as real number, determine part of day
   40 WRITE    (*,1040)
 1040 FORMAT  ('0','Enter military time (00.00 to 23.99)')
      READ     (*,*)  TIME
      ITIME = TIME
      ITIME = ITIME / 6
      IF  (ITIME .EQ. 0)  ITIME = 1
C                      concatenate output string
      LSAL   = LENSAL (ITIME)
      MESSGE = 'Good '//SALUT(ITIME)(1:LSAL)//' '//NAME(1:LNAME)//
     1          ', '//HOWDY
C                      output message
      WRITE    (*,1080)  MESSGE
 1080 FORMAT  ('0', A47)
C                      termination
      STOP
      END
```

The size of the final output variable, MESSGE*47, was determined by the greatest possible length of the string: an 18-character name, a 9-character time of day, the 12-character constant string HOWDY, and the fixed literals. The DO loop to determine the length of the name is very useful for eliminating unnecessary spacing in the final message; a little later in the chapter we will package the algorithm into a subprogram for general use. Note how the loop steps backward through the string, examining each character, looking for the last nonblank. The lengths of the three salutation messages (LENSAL) are stored in a data statement so that, again, unnecessary blanks are not placed in the output. The two variables LSAL and LNAME are then used in the concatenation to control the number of characters extracted from the strings SALUT and NAME.

A sample run would look like:

```
Please enter your name (up to 18 characters)
---------------------------------------------
Mike

Enter military time (00.00 to 23.99)
9.30

Good morning Mike, how are you?
```

Review Questions and Exercises

12.2a Determine the final contents of STRNGF, assuming that it begins in each case as a blank string.

```
      CHARACTER  STRNGA(4)*6, STRNGF*18
      DATA       STRNGA/ 'Status', 'Good  ','Bad   ','Indiff'/,
     1           STRNGF/ '
```

    a. STRNGF = STRNGA(1) // ' is ' // 'STRNGA(2)

    b. STRNGF = STRNGA(1) // ': ', // STRNGA(2) // ' & ' // STRNGA(3)

    c. STRNGF = 'Enter '// STRNGA(2)(1:1) // ', '// STRNGA(3)(1:1) //
        1   ' or '// STRNGA(4)(1:1)

    d. STRNGF(3:12) = STRNGA(3)(1:4) // STRNGA(1)

    e. STRNGF(3:18) = STRNGA(4) // 'erent ' // STRNGA(1)

12.2b Write a program with terminal I/O which reads in a four-digit number and converts it to words. For example:

Input	Output
0	Zero Zero Zero Zero
16	Zero Zero One Six
123	Zero One Two Three
1704	One Seven Zero Four

12.2c Modify exercise 12.2b so that it suppresses all leading zeros in the first three positions. For example:

Input	Output
0	Zero
16	One Six
123	One Two Three
1704	One Seven Zero Four

12.2d Write a program that reads in an eight-character date sequence and outputs it in words, as shown below. It might be advantageous to read in some of the values numerically, others alphamerically.

Input	Output
10/12/92	October 12, 1992
07/16/93	July 16, 1993

12.3 ALPHAMERIC FUNCTIONS

A number of alphameric functions are supplied as part of the FORTRAN compiler. The lexical functions LGE, LGT, LLE, and LLT (Chapter 11, section 11.2) ensure that the collating sequence of sorts and merges is as close to standards as the compiler manufacturer permits.

There is a function, ICHAR(character), which returns the numeric code used to store an alphameric character. Although the programmer may not care what those values are, there are certain applications wherein computations must be done on the characters, and this can only be done when the program has access to that numeric code. The program below is a simple application which allows the user to display the code.

```
C                        Program to display alphameric code value
C
      CHARACTER  IC
C
      DO 40  I = 1,2000
          WRITE   (*,1020)
 1020     FORMAT  ('0','Enter desired character:')
          READ    (*,1022, END=90)  IC
 1022     FORMAT  (A1)
          WRITE   (*,1024)  IC, ICHAR(IC)
 1024     FORMAT  (' ','Internal code for character ',A1,' =',I6)
   40 CONTINUE
C
   90 STOP
      END
```

You might want to compile the program and execute it to see which code (ASCII or EBCDIC) is being used on your machine. Another application of this program is to see what codes are used for some of the nongraphic keys on the keyboard. Some compilers have additional codes used for the function keys (the F keys) found on most keyboards today; a programmer knowing these values can use them in the program and utilize those keys for input. They are handy because they not only transmit a value, they add a carriage return to it so that only one stroke is required when entering a single number. In addition to the function keys, there is also the code generated by the keys used in combination with the control (ctrl) key. For example, if a programmer knows that ctrl-G generates an audible signal, knowing the value of that code (usually 7), allows the programmer to have the FORTRAN program issue a beep. The coding would be something like this:

```
      DATA  IBEEP/  7/
      WRITE   (*,1000)  IBEEP
 1000 FORMAT  (' ',A1)
```

Since many compilers have filters which block certain key usage, don't be surprised to find a blank code transmitted for many of the keys.

Another available function is CHAR(integer), which converts a numeric code to the character it represents. Some FORTRAN compilers would not accept the above coding for the audible signal, but they would expect to see:

```
      WRITE   (*,1000)  CHAR (IBEEP)
```

This forces us to very carefully distinguish between numerals and their characters. For example, the number 7 in numeric format specification (**In**) outputs as the numeral 7; but in alphameric format specification (**An**), it outputs as a control character—in this case, the one that triggers the audible tone in a terminal. On the other hand, the character 7 has an internal code of either 55 in ASCII or 247 in

EBCDIC, outputting the character 7 in alphameric format or the equivalent number code in numeric format. Later on, we will be working with manipulation in which we will be converting numbers from numeric to alphameric and vice versa; thus, we must distinguish between the two.

As a general rule, if a variable is defined as numeric, it will be converted to a character with the function CHAR. Likewise, if a variable is defined as character, ICHAR will be used to get its numeric equivalent.

The program below is the opposite of the one above, accepting a number and returning a graphics character. Although both the ASCII table and the EBCDIC table have undefined areas and values specifically defined as control characters, many applications utilize those codes for a secondary purpose as additional display characters, including letters in foreign alphabets, common symbols (smiling face, arrows, etc.), and line drawing elements. The user of the program can experiment with the full set of 256 possible values, with this proviso: Since some of the values are used by the system for specific purposes, such as breaking out of a program or locking the keyboard, you might get a few surprises!

```
C                       Program to display alphameric equivalent
C
      DO 40  I = 1,20000
          WRITE  (*,1020)
 1020     FORMAT ('0','Enter desired value:')
          READ   (*,*, END=90)  IC
          WRITE  (*,1024)  CHAR(IC), IC
 1024     FORMAT (' ','Internal code for character ',A1,' =',I6)
   40 CONTINUE
C
   90 STOP
      END
```

Following is a useful program which shows how case conversions (upper to lower and vice versa) can be made with a program that runs with either EBCDIC or ASCII code.

```
C                       Program to convert from upper to lower case
C
      CHARACTER  ICH, U2L, ICR
C                       arithmetic function to perform conversion
      U2L(ICR) = CHAR (ICHAR(ICR) + (ICHAR('a') - ICHAR('A')))
C
C
      DO 80  I = 1,20000
          WRITE  (*,1020)
 1020     FORMAT ('0','Enter desired upper case letter:')
          READ   (*,1022, END=90)  ICH
 1022     FORMAT (A1)
              IF (ICH .LT. 'A'  .OR.  ICH .GT. 'Z') GO TO 60
          ICH = U2L (ICH)
          WRITE  (*,1024)  ICH, ICHAR(ICH)
 1024     FORMAT (' ','Internal code for character ',A1,' =',I6)
          GO TO 80
```

```
C                          error routine
   60      WRITE    (*,1060)
 1060      FORMAT   (' ','Invalid character  -  re-enter')
C
   80 CONTINUE
C                          termination
   90 STOP
      END
```

In both codes, the difference between the uppercase and the lowercase versions of a letter is a constant. The arithmetic statement function computes that difference as a function of their code values. (In ASCII that difference is 32, in EBCDIC it is −64; but our program is transparent to the difference in code.) It then adds that value to the numeric equivalent of the letter entered, converts it back to a character, and displays it. The program also edits the data to ensure that it is in the range A through Z; the lexical functions are not necessary here, since we are checking a single character for range and in all collating sequences the letters are grouped together and not intermixed with the numbers.

Another useful conversion is that of a number (NUMBER) to its character value (IC). This can be done in either code with:

```
IC = CHAR (ICHAR('0') + NUMBER)
```

The reverse conversion (character to numeric value) is done with:

```
NUMBER = ICHAR(IC) - ICHAR('0')
```

As an example of the use of these functions, we present a program to convert positive hexadecimal numbers to their decimal equivalent. Hexadecimal numbers (usually called *hex*) are those generated in base 16, wherein the counting numbers are:

```
0  1  2  3  4  5  6  7  8  9  A  B  C  D  E  F
```

with the letters A through F having values of 11 through 15, respectively. Thus the hex number 41CA =

```
         4  *  16 ** 3  =  16384
         1  *  16 ** 2  =    256
        12  *  16 ** 1  =    192
    +   10  *  16 ** 0  =     10
                           16842
```

The program requests input to the range 0000 to 7FFF, because that is the range of positive 16-bit integer variables.

```
C                          Hexadecimal to Decimal Conversion
C
      CHARACTER HEX*4, IC*1
C
C                          convert digit character to number
      NUMBER (IC) = ICHAR(IC) - ICHAR('0')
C                          convert letter character to number
      LETTER (IC) = ICHAR(IC) - ICHAR('A') + 10
```

```
C
C                      loop through input
        DO 100  NTIMES = 1,20000
           WRITE   (*,1020)
1020       FORMAT  ('0','Enter 4-character hex number in range ',
     1                            '0000 to 7FFF')
           READ    (*,1022, END=900) HEX
1022       FORMAT  (A4)
C                      edit for valid characters, if ok, calculate value
           IVALUE = 0
           DO 40 I = 1,4
              IF  ((HEX(I:I) .LT. 'A'  .OR.  HEX(I:I) .GT. 'F')  .AND.
     1             (HEX(I:I) .LT. '0'  .OR.  HEX(I:I) .GT. '9'))  THEN
                 WRITE  (*,1024)
1024             FORMAT  (' ','INVALID CHARACTER  -  re-enter!')
                 GO TO 100
              ENDIF
C                         generate digit
              IF (HEX(I:I) .GE. '0'  .AND.
     1            HEX(I:I) .LE. '9')            N = NUMBER (HEX(I:I))
              IF (HEX(I:I) .GE. 'A'  .AND.
     1            HEX(I:I) .LE. 'F')            N = LETTER (HEX(I:I))
C                         accumulate value
40            IVALUE = IVALUE  +  N * 16 ** (4 - I)
C                      output value
           WRITE  (*,1060)  HEX, IVALUE
1060       FORMAT  (' ','Hex value of ',A4,' =', I6,' decimal')
100     CONTINUE
C                      termination
900     STOP
        END
```

The program would have worked equally well with an array of four single characters, which would have been defined as:

```
CHARACTER  HEX(4)*1, IC*1
```

The references to the array would become HEX(I) rather than HEX(I:I).

There is a function LEN(string) which returns the length of a string. Its value will not become apparent until the next section of this chapter, because all it seems to do is tell us something we already know. For example, in the code:

```
CHARACTER  ST*8, STR*12
     |
     |
     |
L = LEN (ST)              it returns an 8
     |
L = LEN (STR)             it returns a 12
     |
L = LEN ('status')        it returns a 6
```

However, this function will serve us to much better advantage in subprograms where the length of the string is not known.

The final function to be discussed is the INDEX(string1, string2), which locates a substring within a string. For example, the code:

```
L1 = INDEX ('character', 'ract')
```

places a 4 into L1 since the substring *'ract'* starts at the fourth position in the string *'character'*. However, in the code:

```
L2 = INDEX ('character', 'race')
```

a 0 is placed in L2 since the substring *'race'* does not exist in the string *'character'*. Only the first occurrence of the substring is located.

This function will prove quite useful in applications later in the chapter.

Review Questions and Exercises

12.3a For the following code, determine the value placed in *L*.

```
CHARACTER    M*9, N*3, EEEE
DATA         M/ 'ABCDEFGHI'/,  N/ 'SEX'/,  EEEE/ 'E'/

a. L = INDEX (M, EEEE)
b. L = INDEX (N, EEEE)
c. L = INDEX (M, N)
d. L = INDEX (M, 'X')
e. L = INDEX (N, 'x')
f. L = INDEX (M, 'DEAF')
g. L = INDEX (N, 'EXTRA')
h. L = INDEX (M // N, 'S')
i. L = INDEX (M // N, EEEE//'F')
```

12.3b A data file contains a mailing list. Each record consists of 90 characters, with the critical characters being:

Town: Characters 61–80
Zip code: Characters 86–90

Due to the building of a new post office, those residences in the town of Dix Hills with a zip code of 11746 will now have a zip code of 11747. Write a program to read an input file and write a new file with the necessary zip code change.

12.3c Just as the character code of a number is related to the character code of 0, the character code of a letter is related to *A*. (In EBCDIC there are two special characters, the closing brace and the backslash, and 13 unused positions within the letter grouping; but the program has a way around this.) Thus it is possible to give each letter a numeric equivalent, such as $A = 1, B = 2$, etc. In this way a letter can be equated to a subscript.

This technique should be used in a program to read in a string of characters, ignore nonletters, convert each letter to upper case if necessary (reversing the procedure shown in the text for conversion to lower case), determine a subscript for each character in the string, and add into an array of counters, one for each letter. The output should consist of a listing of the letters that have counters greater than 0 and the value in those counters. (This last condition will eliminate those special characters embedded in the range of letters in EBCDIC.)

If working in ASCII, exactly 26 locations are needed; EBCDIC will need 41. Before testing the full program, test your algorithm that determines the subscript with the letters *A* and *Z* to make sure that they fall within the range you have dimensioned.

12.3d Write a program which reads in a string of text and determines how many times the substring *the* appears. Convert all characters to lower case before beginning. Use test data like the following sentence: "Therefore, there are those people who believe that these United States have the power to bring peace to the world!"

12.4 STRING HANDLING IN SUBPROGRAMS

Character variables are handled the same way numeric variables are in subprograms, except it is not necessary to define the number of characters. This provides us with the facility of writing many general-purpose subprograms to aid in the manipulation of strings.

In the subprogram, the length of the character variable is defined as (*) and the LEN function is used to find the length. This is very similar to the method in which transmitted one-dimensional arrays do not need a value for their dimension in the subprogram. The transmitted address is used as the beginning of the string (or of the array), and the mapping function calculates the location of the desired character (or array element).

Section 12.2 showed code for determining the location of the last nonblank character in a string. This made it possible to concatenate a number of strings without unnecessary blanks in the middle. The general-purpose function below does exactly this.

```
      FUNCTION  LNSTR (STRING)
C
C        Abstract:  determines the last non-blank character in a
C                   character variable of any length
C
      CHARACTER*(*)  STRING
C
C                  get size of character variable
      LENGTH = LEN (STRING)
C                  pass through string backwards looking for non-blank
      DO 40  LNSTR = LENGTH,1,-1
         IF  (STRING(LNSTR:LNSTR) .NE. ' ')  RETURN
   40 CONTINUE
      LNSTR = 0
C                        termination
      RETURN
      END
```

Note how the transmitted character variable length is left undefined and the function LEN provides the program with the needed value for the DO loop.

Just as a partial array may be sent to the subprogram, a substring can also be sent. For example,

```
      CHARACTER  STR*8
      STR = 'ABCDEF  '
      L  =  LNSTR (STR)          returns a 6
      L  =  LNSTR (STR(3:7))     returns a 4
```

In a previous application (Program Salutation in section 12.2), the code:

```
C                         get length of name entered
      DO 20  LNAME = 18,1,-1
          IF  (NAME(LNAME:LNAME) .NE. ' ')  GO TO 40
   20     CONTINUE
          LNAME = 0
```

could now be replaced with:

```
LNAME = LNSTR (NAME)
```

The following is a subroutine used to convert the alphabetic characters of a string from upper to lower case.

```
      SUBROUTINE  U2L (STRING)
C
C                 Abstract:  converts upper case letters to lower case
C
      CHARACTER*(*)  STRING
C
C                 get size of character variable
      LENGTH = LEN (STRING)
C                 pass through string
      DO 40  I = 1,LENGTH
          IF  (STRING(I:I) .GE. 'A'  .AND.  STRING(I:I) .LE. 'Z')
   1          STRING(I:I) = CHAR (ICHAR (STRING(I:I))
   2                             + (ICHAR('a') - ICHAR('A')))
   40 CONTINUE
C                 return
      RETURN
      END
```

Sample calling statements might look like this:

```
CALL U2L (STR)
CALL U2L (STR(2:20))
CALL U2L (STR(2:))
```

The last two leave the first character capitalized.

In many applications, there is a need to convert digits to their character equivalent. As a simple case, assume a routine to return a number as characters so that it might be output with the digits in every other column, leaving a blank between individual digits. This is sometimes required when printing on preprinted forms. The problem to be solved requires a general-purpose subprogram that returns the right character code regardless of whether the system stores the characters in ASCII or EBCDIC. The function below does just that. Note how the mode of the function is typed so that it will return a character and not a numeric value, as would be the case if default typing controlled.

```
      CHARACTER*1  FUNCTION  MYCHAR(N)
C
C       Abstract:  returns the character code for the digit received.
C                  works with all internal storage codes
```

```
      C
            CHARACTER*10   DGTCOD
            DATA           DGTCOD/ '0123456789'/
      C
            MYCHAR = DGTCOD(N+1:N+1)
            RETURN
            END
```

To test the function, here is a program which reads a positive integer of up to four digits and outputs them with blanks between the digits. A more elaborate program illustrating the use of this function is given in section 12.6.

```
      C                       Test of Function MYCHAR
      C
            CHARACTER  MYCHAR, OUTSTR*8
      C
      C                       prompt for input and edit it
            DO 60  NTIMES = 1,20000
               WRITE   (*,1020)
       1020    FORMAT  ('0','Enter a positive integer value < 10000')
               READ    (*,*, END=90) NUMBER
               IF  (NUMBER .GT. 0 .AND.  NUMBER .LE. 9999)  THEN
      C                          blank out output string
                  OUTSTR = ' '
      C                          loop to generate digits
                  DO 40  I = 1,3
                     IDIGIT = NUMBER / 10 ** (4-I)
                     NUMBER = NUMBER - IDIGIT * 10 ** (4-I)
        40           OUTSTR(2*I:2*I) = MYCHAR(IDIGIT)
                  OUTSTR(8:8)      = MYCHAR(NUMBER)
      C                       output
                  WRITE   (*,1040)    OUTSTR
       1040       FORMAT  (' ',A8)
               ENDIF
        60   CONTINUE
      C                       termination
        90   STOP
            END
```

Note that it is necessary to type the name of the function being called if it differs from the default for integers and reals; since there is no default for CHARACTER, every function of that mode must be specifically typed.

Exercises

12.4a Write and test a subroutine to convert all lowercase letters to upper case.

12.4b Write a function to return the number of blanks in a string.

12.4c Write a function which receives as input a string of characters and a single character, returning the number of times that character appears in the string. The accessing statement might look like:

```
      NAPEAR = NTIMES (LONGST, 'A')
```

when searching for the character *A*.

12.4d   Improve on exercise 12.4c so that when it receives a letter it searches for both the uppercase and lowercase versions, regardless of the case transmitted to the function.

12.4e   Using the function from exercise 12.4d, write a program which reads in a file and does an analysis of the frequency in which letters appear in that file. Sort the output in order of descending use.

12.4f   Expand the function MYCHAR to one called HEXCHR, which returns the appropriate hexadecimal character (0 to F) for an argument from 0 to 15. Then use it in a program which inputs an integer number from 0 to 32767 and outputs the hex value.

12.4g   Write a function INTERR which receives a string of characters and returns the number of characters in the string that are invalid for integer input. The valid characters are the 10 digits, plus, minus, and blank. Test with a driver.

12.4h   Write a function REALER which receives a string of characters and returns the number of characters in the string that are invalid for real decimal input. In addition to the valid characters for integer, the decimal point is also valid. Expand the driver from exercise 12.4g to test both functions simultaneously.

12.4i   Write a function EXPERR which receives a string of characters and returns the number of characters in the string that are invalid for exponential input. In addition to the valid characters for real, the characters E and D are also valid. Expand the driver from exercise 12.4h to test all three functions simultaneously.

12.5   INTERNAL FILES

It is simple enough to move partial strings from one character variable to another using the substring concept, but there are times when it would be very useful to convert from one storage mode to another. It might be necessary, for example, to modify a numeric value so that it can be output in a nonstandard form, such as with a blank column between each character, or to read a character string and convert it, or part of it, to a number. FORTRAN 77 provides a mechanism called an internal file which provides the ability to write to a memory file in one format and then read from it in another format. This *memory file* is a character variable residing in memory, but it works just like a disk file in its ability to handle input and output.

In earlier versions of FORTRAN, there existed instructions called DECODE and ENCODE which performed similar functions. They are not part of FORTRAN 77, but some manufacturers still support them for the sake of upward compatibility, so that programs written in the earlier version will still work in FORTRAN 77.

An *internal file* is a character variable of some convenient length, and that variable is used as a logical unit reference in a READ or WRITE statement. For example, assume that we wish to convert an integer variable to a string of characters so that we can output it with blanks between the digits. (This problem was shown in the previous section, but this alternative solution is of greater flexibility and more efficient of code.) A program to test the technique looks like this:

```
      CHARACTER  INTFLE*4, IOUT(4)
C                     prompt for and read input
      DO 40  NTIMES = 1,20000
         WRITE   (*,1020)
1020     FORMAT  ('0','Enter a four-digit integer')
         READ    (*,*, ERR=20, END=90)  IN
C                convert storage mode
         WRITE   (INTFLE,1022)  IN
1022     FORMAT  (I4)
         READ    (INTFLE,1024)  IOUT
1024     FORMAT  (4A1)
C                output
         WRITE   (*,1026)  IOUT
1026     FORMAT  (' ',4(A1,1X))
      CONTINUE
C
  90 STOP
      END
```

The READ and WRITE statements to the internal file look similar to the standard READs and WRITEs used previously, except that the logical unit reference is a character variable rather than a number (or numeric variable). The ERR= clause may be useful when reading into a numeric format. ANSI specifications allow only formatted I/O. The FORMAT statements do not need any carriage control character. The character variable must be large enough to handle the largest format used. In the above case, a length of four characters is enough.

Another very useful technique involves extracting a numeric value from a string. Below is a subprogram which does just that, ignoring any invalid characters, although it will fail with a double sign or multiple decimal points. The function returns a double-precision real from a string or substring sent to it. The number of columns to be treated is also sent. Blanks, commas, dollar signs, and other nonnumeric characters within the string are ignored.

```
C               Function GETVAL:  returns real number from string
C
      DOUBLE PRECISION  FUNCTION  GETVAL  (STRING)
C
      CHARACTER  STRING*(*), WORKFL*16, ICHAR*1
C
C     glossary: GETVAL:  returned value;  returns 0.00 if overflow
C               STRING:  input string or substring; all nonnumeric
C                        characters are ignored
C               NCOL:    number of columns (characters) in string
C               WORKFL:  internal file, maximum 16 characters
C               ICHAR:   character being worked on
```

```
C                   NCHAR:    number of valid characters in new string
C                                       limit = 16
C
C                       set initial values
      NCOL   = LNSTR (STRING)
      WORKFL = ' '
      GETVAL = 0.00
      NCHAR  = 0
C                       loop through characters
      DO 100  I = 1,NCOL
          ICHAR = STRING (I:I)
C                          check for numeric character, point or sign
          IF  ((ICHAR .GE. '0'  .AND.  ICHAR .LE. '9')  .OR.
     1          ICHAR .EQ. '+'  .OR.   ICHAR .EQ. '-'  .OR.
     2                                 ICHAR .EQ. '.')            THEN
C                          return 0.00 if overflow
              IF  (NCHAR .EQ. 16)  RETURN
C                          add to internal file
              NCHAR = NCHAR + 1
              WORKFL(NCHAR:NCHAR) = ICHAR
          ENDIF
  100 CONTINUE
C                       convert to double precision real
      READ    (WORKFL, 1100, ERR=900)  GETVAL
 1100 FORMAT  (D16.0)
C                       return
  900 RETURN
      END
```

The program first determines the location of the last nonblank character and sets that up as the number of columns used in the input string. It then passes through the string and develops a work string (which serves as the internal file) consisting of signs, digits, and decimal points. That string (the internal file) is then read with a numeric format. Any string that would fail under the numeric format (such as multiple decimal points) will do so here, returning a value of 0.00.

To show how the subprogram works, assume a program with the following:

```
      CHARACTER   INSTRG*30
      DOUBLE PRECISION GETVAL
C
C                                  111111111122222222223
C          columns:    123456789012345678901234567890
      DATA     INSTRG/ '$123,456.78 +-90.257 123ABC780'/
C
      A = GETVAL (INSTRG (1:10))    returns 123456.700
      B = GETVAL (INSTRG (3:9))     returns  23456.000
      C = GETVAL (INSTRG (13:20))   returns         0.000 (two signs)
      D = GETVAL (INSTRG (14:20))   returns       -90.257
      E = GETVAL (INSTRG (22:30))   returns 123780.000
      F = GETVAL (INSTRG (27:29))   returns      78.000
      G = GETVAL (INSTRG (8:11))    returns       6.780
```

The author has found this program useful for reading filed data in which the money values are in edited format (with commas and dollar signs) and when he needs to extract that value and place it into a numeric field.

A simpler variation of the program in which invalid characters yield an error and return a zero is shown below.

```
C                         Function GETVAL:  returns real number from string
C
        DOUBLE PRECISION  FUNCTION  GETVAL  (STRING)
C
        CHARACTER  STRING*(*)
C
C        glossary: GETVAL:  returned value;  returns 0.00 if overflow
C                                            or invalid character
C                   STRING:  input string or substring; all nonnumeric
C                                            characters are ignored
C
C                         set initial value
        GETVAL = 0.00
C                         convert to double precision real
        READ     (STRING, 1100, ERR=900)  GETVAL
 1100 FORMAT   (D16.0)
C                              return
   900 RETURN
        END
```

There is one restriction in this routine: A comma in the input is treated as a data terminator, not an erroneous character. Thus, input of 123,456 would yield a value of 123.00.

Exercises

12.5a   Modify function GETVAL to stop accumulating characters when it finds either a second sign, a second decimal point, or a nonnumeric character once it has started accumulating the numeric characters. Write a driver to test your new function and test it thoroughly.

12.5b   Write a program to accept a date format in any of the following four forms:

```
nn/nn/nn    n/nn/nn
nn/n/nn     n/n/nn
```

Use a subroutine IPARSE (INSTR, IVALUS, LIMIT, NUMACT) where the arguments are the input string, the returned values, the size of the IVALUS array, and the number of actual numbers found in the string. Do not overflow IVALUS if NUMACT is greater than LIMIT! Output the returned integers.

12.5c   Write a program to accept a time format in any of the following four forms:

```
nn:nn:nn.nn    n:nn:nn.nn
nn:n:nn.nn     n:n:nn.nn
```

where the decimal point separates seconds from hundredths of a second. Use a subroutine RPARSE on the same order as IPARSE above, except that all real numbers are returned. The hours and minutes can later be changed to integer. Output the returned values.

12.5d   Write a function to accept quantity information in any of the six formats below and return the number of units:

7 gross, 11 dozen, 5 units	11 dozen
15 gross, 8 units	8 units
11 dozen, 2 units	7 gross

12.6   APPLICATIONS

The possible applications using these string-handling techniques are so numerous that it is difficult to know where to start. In the early days of computing, when FORTRAN was the only available language, there was very little string-handling capability. We were very happy just to get out an answer to a problem. Furthermore, since the I/O devices were very slow, it was not efficient to tie up the computer to print voluminous documents.

As computers and I/O devices sped up and programming became more sophisticated, the demands on computer languages grew significantly. FORTRAN became standardized in 1966, and it was expanded to include many new commands in 1977. Since it has been able to grow during that period to meet the new demands, it has remained a viable language and is still a great favorite among professionals. It is very efficient in that it does a lot of computing with very few instructions, yet still remains fairly easy to read. The addition of the character variable and the string-handling facilities in FORTRAN 77 ensured that the language would be around for a long time.

Let us begin by presenting a subroutine which the author wrote some 20 years ago. (It was originally written in FORTRAN 66 but has now been updated.) This routine generates an "edited" monetary value (although it can be used for nonmonetary applications as well). The term *edited* is used in the sense that it is used in the commercial languages COBOL and RPG, wherein the numeric string is modified before output to include commas and an optional floating dollar sign, as well as a variety of ways of displaying negative numbers.

In commercial programming, a leading minus sign is not used for a negative number; the number may be put into a different output column (credit), be output with a trailing minus sign or a trailing CR (credit), or be enclosed in parentheses. The program below gives the user a choice of methods, as well as the option of a floating dollar sign (a $ placed just to the left of the first valid character). The output field must be wide enough to store the number, the inserted commas, the negative output code, and the floating dollar sign. The program places the output characters into an output array so that the array can include more than one value; the actual output of the array is done in the calling program.

```
         SUBROUTINE  MONEY  (VALUE, OUTSTR, NEND,NCOL, IOP)
C
C      Abstract:  returns an edited money value with commas, optional
C                          floating dollar sign and negative codes.
C                 blank when zero.
C                 overflowed fields filled with asterisks.
C
C      VALUE:    double precision real to be edited
C                          limited to +/- $99,999,999.99
```

```
C      OUTSTR:    character variable in which output is to be placed
C      NEND:      end position in the output string OUTSTR
C      NCOL:      number of columns in output string for edited value
C      IOP:       option:  positive for floating '$'
C                                negative for no '$'
C                          +/-1,  sign suppression
C                          +/-2,  trailing '-'
C                          +/-3,  trailing 'CR'
C                          +/-4,  enclosing parentheses
C
       CHARACTER  MYCHAR, WRKSTR*16, OUTSTR*(*)
       DOUBLE PRECISION    VALUE, X
C
C         MYCHAR:    function to return character code for digit
C         X:         temporary working double precision variable
C         WRKSTR:    temporary working character variable
C
C                    determine first column in output string
       NFIRST = NEND - NCOL + 1
       IF  (NFIRST .LT. 1)  NFIRST = 1
C                    blank out work, output strings
       WRKSTR = ' '
       OUTSTR(NFIRST:NEND) = ' '
C                      if zero, all done  (blank when zero)
       IF  (DABS (VALUE) .LT. 0.005D+00)  RETURN
C                      move rounded value to work variable, save sign
       X  = DABS (VALUE) + 0.005
       IS = DSIGN (1.0D+00, VALUE)
C                      check range of option and value
       JOP = IABS (IOP)
       IF  (JOP .LE. 0  .OR.  JOP .GT. 4  .OR.
      1     X    .GE. 99999999.995D+00)          THEN
           DO 20  I = NFIRST,NEND
   20      OUTSTR(I:I) = '*'
           RETURN
       ENDIF
C                         loop to generate digits, place into work string
       DO 40  I = 1,10
           DIVSOR = DBLE(10) ** (8-I)
           IDIGIT = X / DIVSOR
           X      = X  -  DBLE (IDIGIT) * DIVSOR
   40  WRKSTR(I+6:I+6) = MYCHAR (IDIGIT)
C                         remove leading zeros, except last three positions
       DO 60  NI = 7,13
           IF  (WRKSTR(NI:NI) .NE. '0')  GO TO 80
   60  WRKSTR(NI:NI) = ' '
       NI = 14
C                  determine number of characters, check actual length
   80  NCHAR = 16 - NI + 2
C                        add for negative codes
       IF  (JOP    .EQ.  2)    NCHAR = NCHAR + 1
       IF  (JOP    .GT.  2)    NCHAR = NCHAR + 2
C                        add for floating dollar sign, if desired
       IF  (IOP    .GT.  0)    NCHAR = NCHAR + 1
C                        add for commas
       IF  (NI     .LT. 12)    NCHAR = NCHAR + 1
       IF  (NI     .LT.  9)    NCHAR = NCHAR + 1
       IF  (NCHAR .GT. NCOL)  THEN
           DO 100  I = NFIRST,NEND
  100      OUTSTR(I:I) = '*'
           RETURN
       ENDIF
```

```
C                          reset string, inserting commas
C
C         columns:    1  2  3  4  5  6  7  8  9 10 11 12 13 14 15 16
C         before:    |  |  |  |  |  |  | n| n| m| m| m| n| n| n| m| m|
C         after:     |  |  |  | n| n| ,| m| m| m| ,| n| n| n| .| m| m|
C
      WRKSTR(4:5)   = WRKSTR(7:8)
      IF  (WRKSTR(5:5) .NE. ' ')   WRKSTR(6:6)   = ','
      WRKSTR(7:9)   = WRKSTR(9:11)
      IF  (WRKSTR(9:9) .NE. ' ')   WRKSTR(10:10) = ','
      WRKSTR(11:13) = WRKSTR(12:14)
      WRKSTR(14:14) = '.'
C                          find first used column
      DO 120   NFUSED = 1,12
         IF  (WRKSTR(NFUSED:NFUSED) .NE. ' ')  GO TO 140
  120 CONTINUE
      NFUSED = 13
C                          set in dollar sign, if desired
  140 IF  (IOP .GT. 0)  THEN
         NFUSED = NFUSED - 1
         WRKSTR(NFUSED:NFUSED) = '$'
      ENDIF
C                  shift for negative indicator and set if needed
      IF  (JOP .EQ. 2)  THEN
         NFUSED = NFUSED - 1
         WRKSTR(NFUSED:15) = WRKSTR(NFUSED+1:16)
         IF  (IS .GE. 0)  WRKSTR(16:16) = ' '
         IF  (IS .LT. 0)  WRKSTR(16:16) = '-'
      ENDIF
      IF  (JOP .EQ. 3)  THEN
         NFUSED = NFUSED - 2
         WRKSTR(NFUSED:14) = WRKSTR(NFUSED+2:16)
         IF  (IS .GE. 0)  WRKSTR(15:16) = ' '
         IF  (IS .LT. 0)  WRKSTR(15:16) = 'CR'
      ENDIF
      IF  (JOP .EQ. 4)  THEN
         NFUSED = NFUSED - 2
         WRKSTR(NFUSED+1:15) = WRKSTR(NFUSED+2:16)
         IF  (IS .GE. 0)  WRKSTR(16:16)            = ' '
         IF  (IS .LT. 0)  WRKSTR(16:16)            = ')'
         IF  (IS .LT. 0)  WRKSTR(NFUSED:NFUSED) = '('
      ENDIF
C                  transfer to output string and return
      NEW = NEND - (16 - NFUSED)
      OUTSTR(NEW:NEND) = WRKSTR(NFUSED:16)
      RETURN
      END
```

The code begins by determining the first column in the output string from the ending columns and the number of columns to be used. It then blanks out the work string and the returned string. If the transmitted value is 0 (with a tolerance of $0.005), the blank string is returned. To modify this routine so that it outputs $0.00 instead of blanks when zero appears, it is only necessary to remove one statement:

```
   IF  (DABS (VALUE) .LT. 0.005D+00)    RETURN
```

Note the use of double-precision constants. (They were described in Chapter 4, section 4.4.)

The code continues by placing the rounded absolute value into a working location, X, and saves the sign of the value as either 1 or −1. It then goes on to check the option selected to assure that it is one of the possible four choices. The value is next checked to see if it is within the 10-digit limit. If either of these checks reveals an error, the returned string is filled with asterisks.

The DO 40 loop breaks the value down into individual digits and then into characters using the function MYCHAR (presented in section 12.4). The DO 60 loop removes all leading zeros except the last three (the one preceding the decimal point and the two after it), so that all values less than $1.00 will show a leading zero (such as $0.12). To eliminate the zero before the decimal point, the DO 60 statement should have limits of 7 and 14; thus, 12 cents becomes $.12.

The number of output characters is then calculated, adjusting for the necessary commas, the negative code, and the optional floating dollar sign. If the number of columns allocated is not large enough, the returned string is filled with asterisks to indicate an overflow error.

Next, the work string is modified to include the commas where necessary. Then the dollar sign is placed in the work string, if that option was selected. The string is shifted to make room for any trailing negative code; even positive values are shifted so that they line up with the negative numbers, although the negative code columns are left blank. If the value is negative, the negative code(s) are inserted. The final work string is then transferred into the output string in the columns desired.

As an example of how the routine might be used, assume that we wish to print out totals for two columns of numbers with floating dollar signs and the parentheses option for negative numbers. The annotation *TOTALS* will be in columns 1 through 6, and the output values will be in columns 11 to 24 and 27 to 40 after skipping a line.

```
      CHARACTER  LINOUT*40
      DOUBLE PRECISION  TOTALS(2)
            |                |
            |                |
            |                |
      LINOUT = 'TOTALS'
      CALL MONEY (TOTALS(1), LINOUT, 24,14, 4)
      CALL MONEY (TOTALS(2), LINOUT, 40,14, 4)
      WRITE   (5,2000) LINOUT
 2000 FORMAT  ('0', A40)
```

The output character variable must be cleared before it is used again to wipe out previous values placed into it. Here, the insertion of the short string *TOTALS* at the beginning of the entire string automatically blanks out the rest of the string.

Next we will look at another string-building routine which receives the date as three integer numbers and generates an output string with the date written out.

```
C                      Subroutine Date:  converts from numeric to alpha
C
      SUBROUTINE  DATE  (INDATE, OUTSTR)
C
      CHARACTER  MONTHS(12)*9, OUTSTR*18, MYCHAR
      DIMENSION  INDATE(3)
C
      DATA  MONTHS/'January  ', 'February ', 'March    ',
     1             'April    ', 'May      ', 'June     ',
     2             'July     ', 'August   ', 'September',
     3             'October  ', 'November ', 'December '/
```

```
      C
      C                         place month into string
            LENGTH = LNSTR (MONTHS (INDATE(1)))
            OUTSTR = MONTHS(INDATE(1))(1:LENGTH)
            LENGTH = LENGTH + 2
      C                         place day into string
            IF  (INDATE(2) .GE. 10)  THEN
                OUTSTR(LENGTH:LENGTH) = MYCHAR (INDATE(2) / 10)
                LENGTH = LENGTH + 1
            ENDIF
            OUTSTR(LENGTH:LENGTH) = MYCHAR (MOD (INDATE(2), 10))
      C                      comma and year
            LENGTH = LENGTH + 1
            OUTSTR(LENGTH:LENGTH)     = ','
            OUTSTR(LENGTH+2:LENGTH+3) = '19'
            OUTSTR(LENGTH+4:LENGTH+4) = MYCHAR (INDATE(3) / 10)
            OUTSTR(LENGTH+5:LENGTH+5) = MYCHAR (MOD (INDATE(3), 10))
      C                         return
            RETURN
            END
```

Exercises

12.6a   Modify subroutine DATE to transmit back a character string of length 72. Include an additional argument which selects an option to left-justify, right-justify, or center the date within the string. Also write a driver program to test the routine.

12.6b   Write subroutine MONEY0, a modification of subroutine MONEY, to output monetary values to the nearest dollar. Output a 0 if the value is less than $0.50.

12.6c   Write subroutine MONEYK, a modification of subroutine MONEY, to output monetary values to the nearest $1000. Output a 0 if the value is less than $500.

(See section 12.7 for additional exercises of this type.)

12.7   CHAPTER REVIEW

This chapter has introduced us to a whole new world of programming techniques. The methodology permits the writing of very sophisticated string-handling programs and gives the programmer some powerful tools for developing highly detailed output.

The chapter began with a very brief description of internal codes used on the computer. Although they will be transparent to the novice programmer, the experienced programmer will encounter internal codes not only for the storage of data but also for the control of I/O devices. *Device drivers* are subprograms used to convert desired options to the hardware codes needed by the device; and, to complicate the issue, these hardware codes are not standardized but vary from manufacturer to manufacturer. That is why many I/O devices are not compatible with each other and, if no driver is available on the system or in the software, that device will not work properly. Fortunately, a small number of controls are standardized, such as the audible signal and the form feed for the printer, so these may be included within a FORTRAN program without any problems.

The chapter concentrated on the internal manipulation of strings and substrings, providing the reader with the tools to modify or combine strings. The reader is welcome to use any of the many useful functions included in the chapter, since they are not copyrighted. Every attempt was made to write code that was not dependent on which internal code (ASCII or EBCDIC) the manufacturer chose for the computer. If there is a problem, the reader has been given the tools to look at the codes and make any required adjustment to the program.

Emphasis is placed on editing data and arguments sent to subprograms, because that is where most data errors occur. Going beyond the range of a string (such as assigning a character to position -2) not only can result in a wrong answer, it may bomb out a program and freeze up the operating system so that a reboot is necessary.

The use of internal files saves a significant amount of programmer effort. The chapter mentions the old instructions from FORTRAN 66, DECODE and ENCODE; although they may still be found in old programs, there is no reference to them in FORTRAN 77. They were similar to the access to the external files: DECODE reads a specified number of characters from a character array in A2 format according to an associated FORMAT statement, much like a READ; ENCODE writes a specified number of characters to an array in A2 format according to a FORMAT statement, just like a WRITE statement does. One typical use is to read input into a character array, edit for correct characters, and either display a message indicating the incorrect characters (something the ERR= clause cannot do by itself) or read the internal file into the desired FORMAT. (Exercises 12.4g, 12.4h, and 12.4i relate to this scheme, as do some of the exercises that follow in this section.)

The two application routines in the previous section and the exercises to follow demonstrate the techniques that are used to produce artistic and detailed output with a language as simplistic in its basic I/O as FORTRAN. It is expected that the reader will find the exercises below a bit more challenging than those which are primarily numeric in nature!

The topics covered in this chapter include:

Topics	Section
Alphameric codes	12.1
ASCII	12.1, 12.3
Baudot	12.1
Concatenation	12.2
DECODE/ENCODE	12.5
EBCDIC	12.1, 12.3
Edited output	12.6
Hollerith code	12.1
INDEX	12.3
Internal files	12.5
LEN	12.3
Subprograms	12.4
Substrings	12.2

Exercises

12.7a   Write a program to accept as input seconds since midnight (0 to 86399) and to output the number of hours, minutes, and seconds since midnight. Sample input and output include:

Input	Output
86399	23 hrs 59 min 59 sec
7220	02 hrs 20 min
3603	01 hrs 03 sec
125	02 min 05 sec
120	02 min
5	05 sec
0	[blank line]

12.7b   Write a program that accepts an integer number of units and outputs a breakdown in gross, dozen, and units (1 gross = 12 dozen = 144 units). Sample input and output include:

Input	Output
512	3 gross, 6 dozen, 8 units
120	10 dozen units
118	9 dozen, 10 units
290	2 gross, 2 units
288	2 gross units

12.7c   Write a program to input an integer monetary value from 1 to 99 cents and to output an alpha message of the equivalent change. Note the need for singular and plural strings.

Input	Output
42	1 quarter, 1 dime, 1 nickel, 2 pennies
51	2 quarters, 1 penny
10	1 dime

12.7d   Write a program to input centimeters as a real number. Convert it to feet and inches (using the conversion factor 2.54 centimeters = 1 inch), rounding to the nearest eighth-inch. Sample I/O should include:

Input	Output
100	3 feet, 3-3/8 inches
499	16 feet, 4-1/2 inches
8	3-1/8 inches
61	2 feet
127	4 feet, 2 inches

12.7e   Write a program to input label information consisting of a name and a two-line address, placed on a single input line with two plus signs (+) to separate the three lines. Then reformat to a six-line (1″) label, with line 1 blank, the name on line 2, the address on lines 3 and 4, and lines 5 and 6 blank. The information should be left-justified on the three printed lines and, of course, the plus signs removed.

12.7f   Write a program to accept names in the following format:

Columns	Description
1–10	First name
12	Middle initial
14–29	Last name

The output should have the name "packed"; i.e., only a single blank between the first name and middle initial, a period after the middle initial, and a single blank before the last name.

12.7g   To represent January 20, 1993, date input may be entered in the following forms:

```
02Jan93    2jan93    02JAN93
```

Write a subprogram to accept the 7-character string and to return an array of three integer numbers representing the month, day, and year (the latter without the century).

12.7h   Write a program to read in a text file and determine a frequency distribution of the length of the words in the file; i.e., a count of the number of 1-letter words, 2-letter words, and so forth up to 12 letters, putting all larger words into the 12-letter count. Assume that there are hyphenated words. For simplicity, assume that any nonalphabetic character (except the hyphen) separates words.

12.7i   Write a program which inputs a line of data from the keyboard that is supposed to consist of five pieces of integer data in list-directed form (delimited by commas or spaces). The program must make sure that there are five fields; assume that all fields must be defined numerically and none left blank. Then make sure that all of the characters within the fields are valid for integers (use function INTERR from exercise 12.4g for this). If there are errors, prompt for a reentry of the record. If there are no errors, write the data to a disk file using a format of 5I6.

12.7j   Write a program to read in five fields of formatted integer data (assume 5I6) and check for valid characters. Initially read into an internal file and echo-check that file. Then output a record immediately following the echo check with a pointer (use a caret, ˆ) to any invalid character. If there are no errors, read from the internal file into the desired 5I6 format, add the numbers, and display all six values.

12.7k   Generate a file consisting of two fields:

1. The numbers 0 to 20, 30, 40, 50, 60, 70, 80, 90, 100, and 1000
2. The description of each of these values in words

A partial file would appear as:

```
   0 No
   1 One
   2 Two
   3 Three
   |   |
   |   |
  90 Ninety
 100 Hundred
1000 Thousand
```

Write a program that will read in a real positive value up to 999999.99 and output the amount in words. Use the following as examples of how the final string should appear:

Value	Output
999999.99	Nine Hundred Ninety Nine Thousand Nine Hundred Ninety Nine & 99/100 Dollars
7000.00	Seven Thousand & 00/100 Dollars
17120.10	Seventeen Thousand One Hundred Twenty & 10/100 Dollars
0.54	No & 54/100 Dollars
90002.63	Ninety Thousand Two & 63/100 Dollars

This program might be modularized into the following parts:

1. A routine to input the number/word file and set up the strings for later use, with an array to store the length of each
2. A breakdown routine to change the dollars into the desired denominations
3. A search function to locate the word string wanted
4. A routine to add each string into an output string

13

Additional FORTRAN Instructions

CHAPTER OUTLINE

CHAPTER OBJECTIVES

- To show the methods of accessing different data file structures.

- To demonstrate the use of some advanced formatting specifications.

- To describe some of the obsolete versions of the GO TO statement and how they can be replaced with structured commands.

- To present a complete description of the less-used instructions and capabilities available in FORTRAN for the advanced user.

STATEMENT OF THE PROBLEM

This chapter covers a variety of instructions. Most are useful extensions of previously covered statements. Some are useful only in specialized programming systems and applications. And some are considered obsolete because of their lack of structure and should be avoided; nonetheless, they are presented here for sake of completeness.

The section on disk files (13.1) is critical for a full understanding of the files covered so far and of files to be used in the subsequent chapters. Direct access files are extremely important, since they are the only efficient method for accessing large files and data bases quickly without overflowing memory.

The reader should find section 13.2 quite useful for report writing. Although the additional FORMAT capabilities presented there have limited application, they sometimes easily solve a particular problem the programmer runs into.

Just as the use of the regular GO TO should be avoided, so should the constructs in section 13.3. Although these constructs can be put in structured form, other methods are preferred; they are also described in the section.

The PAUSE instruction has definitive practical application in a number of situations, some of which are described in section 13.4.

COMPLEX variables, presented in section 13.5, are used in scientific calculations where one needs to define values that include the square root of negative numbers. Readers familiar with complex number calculations will find this section extremely useful.

The advanced linkage statements shown in section 13.6 are useful in some programming systems, as they provide greater flexibility and program management.

The structure of this chapter is such that each section is a complete entity within itself; there is not a continuously developing program within. As a result, each section becomes a supplement to an earlier part of the text (a table of the prerequisite chapters is given below). You may find it useful to jump ahead to this chapter, cover the supplement, and then return to the chapter covering the main topic without disturbing the continuity of the text.

Chapter 13 Section	Prerequisite Chapter
13.1: Disk File Access Methods	7
13.2: Additional FORMAT Capabilities	7
13.3: Other Forms of the GO TO	5
13.4: PAUSE	7
13.5: COMPLEX Variables	4
13.6: Advanced Subprogram Linkage	8

13.1   DISK FILE ACCESS METHODS

In the earlier chapters, disk files were treated no differently than input from the keyboard and output to the printer or screen was treated; i.e., sequentially, one record after another. There are ways in which files may be structured for more efficient access. This section will look at files in more detail and develop the necessary techniques.

13.1.1 Sequential Access Files

By now you should be familiar with this kind of file, although each medium stores files slightly differently. These files are often referred to as SAM (sequential access method) files. These files can exist on disk, on cards, as printer or screen output, and as keyboard input. We are primarily concerned with how they appear on disk (as disk files) and how our programs can read from them and write to them.

On disk, although transparent to the programmer, SAM files are stored in as compact a way as possible in order to save disk storage space. And, since these are the files worked on by editing programs, they also save memory space. When we think of a file record stored on a card or printed on a page, we think in terms of a record of either 80 columns or 132 columns, which is the maximum size of those media. But when a line of data or a program statement is entered at the keyboard, one hits the RETURN key as soon as the nonblank input is completed. To save space, each SAM file record is stored only up to the last nonblank column, followed by a character (or characters) representing end-of-line (EOL). On some systems, embedded groups of blanks are replaced with a *blank counter,* a control which indicates a group of blanks and a counter. Thus, all of the blanks which make up the record are not stored and the file is compressed. The computer user is completely unaware of this process, unless the file is "dumped" through a utility program that outputs it just as it is stored. Otherwise, the displaying or outputting of the record shows a complete, properly spaced line for each record.

The Digital Equipment Corporation uses yet another method, in which each record starts with a character counter followed by the characters in the record; there is no EOL indicator. As a result, a magnetic tape produced on one of DEC's computers cannot be read on another manufacturer's computer.

Because of the unevenness of the SAM records, in order for the computer to search out a particular record, it must start at the beginning of the file and read records, counting EOL codes, until it gets to the desired record. (This is almost like trying to find a particular song on a cassette tape; some cassette players will search out the "quiet" spaces between the songs, each one representing an EOL.) SAM files are not designed for random access.

The mechanism used in accessing SAM files is a *record pointer* which contains the location in the file of the beginning of the *next* record to be accessed. When the file is first opened, the record pointer points to the beginning of the first record. Each time a record is input/output, the pointer is modified to point to the beginning of the next record. When an output file is closed, an end-of-file mark is written in the next record being pointed to, placing it after the last data record.

13.1.2 BACKSPACE and REWIND

FORTRAN does, however, provide some facility to skip around within SAM files. There are two instructions—BACKSPACE, which moves the pointer back one record; and REWIND, which moves the pointer back to the beginning of the file (the first record). The syntaxes are:

```
REWIND n   and   BACKSPACE n
```

where *n* is the file number.

Below is a useful program which allows the examination of a SAM file, displaying records in order, moving back a number of records, or returning to the beginning of the file. The program prompts for the file name, allowing it to be used to examine any file. Of course, the program prevents backspacing before the first record or displaying beyond the end of file.

```
      C                       SAM file access
        C
              CHARACTER   LINE*75, NAMEFL*16
        C
        C                       get name of file and open
              WRITE    (*,1000)
         1000 FORMAT   ('0','Enter file name'/' ',16('_'))
              READ     (*,1002, END=900)  NAMEFL
         1002 FORMAT   (A16)
              OPEN     (2, FILE=NAMEFL)
              IREC = 1
        C                       select option
              DO 100  N = 1,20000
                  WRITE    (*,1010)  IREC
         1010      FORMAT   ('0', 'File pointer at record', I5/
              1              ' ', 'Enter +n to output n records'/
              2              ' ', '      -n to backspace n records'/
              3              ' ', '       0 to rewind'/
              4              ' ', '       EOF character to terminate')
                  READ     (*,*, END=900, ERR=80)  IOP
        C                       rewind
              IF  (IOP .EQ. 0)  THEN
                  REWIND  2
                  IREC = 1
              ENDIF
        C                       backspace records
              IF  (IOP .LT. 0)  THEN
                  NB = 1, IOP
                  IF  (NB .GT. ((IREC - 1))  NB = IREC - 1
                  IF  (NB .GT. 0)  THEN
                      DO 20  I = 1,NB
                          BACKSPACE 2
                          IREC = IREC - 1
           20         CONTINUE
                  ENDIF
              ENDIF
        C                       output records
              IF  (IOP .GT. 0)  THEN
                  DO 40  I = 1,IOP
                      READ    (2,1020, END=60)  LINE
         1020          FORMAT  (A75)
                      WRITE   (*,1022)  IREC, LINE
         1022          FORMAT  (I3, 1X, A75)
           40         IREC = IREC + 1
              ENDIF
              GO TO 100
        C                       end-of-file detected, rewind, reread
           60 WRITE    (*,1060)
         1060 FORMAT   ('0','End-of-File')
              REWIND 2
```

```
                          DO 70  I = 1,IREC-1
            70            READ   (2,1020)
                          GO TO 100
      C                                    invalid character
            80            WRITE  (*,1080)
          1080            FORMAT ('0','Invalid character entered')
      C
        100 CONTINUE
      C
      C                                 termination
        900 CLOSE (2)
                          STOP
                          END
```

There is one special construction placed in the program to compensate for a method of implementation used by one of the systems on which this program was tested. After detecting end-of-file, it was not possible to execute a BACKSPACE without getting an error; apparently the system turns the EOF indicator on and tests it before executing any other I/O command using that file. However, the REWIND did work and apparently did turn off the EOF indicator. The solution was, as shown in the program, to REWIND and reread all of the records up to but not including the EOF, leaving the indicator off until another attempt was made to read the EOF.

13.1.3 Direct Access Files

Direct (or random) access files are structured with all records of the same length so that the computer can access any record by moving to a calculated position in the file. For example, for a file of 20 records, each record 80 bytes long, the computer calculates (using a file mapping function) that the second record begins at the 81st byte, the third at the 161st byte, etc. Thus it is easy to jump to any record and I/O it quickly. When accessing a direct access (called a DAM, or direct access method) file, the size of the record must be specified when the file is opened and the record number when the file is accessed. This requires a number of new clauses in the OPEN and I/O commands. First, the OPEN statement must look like this:

```
    OPEN  (UNIT=n, FILE=namefl, ACCESS='DIRECT', RECL=nn)
```

or

```
    OPEN  (n, FILE=namefl, ACCESS='DIRECT', RECL=nn)
```

The RECL= clause is the record-length cause, with *nn* being the number of processor-dependent units. This latter unit is a function of the manufacturer's specification and usually will be in bytes, 16-bit words, or 32-bit words.

When an ACCESS= clause is not present in the OPEN statement, the default is ACCESS=SEQUENTIAL; record length is irrelevant for a sequential file.

Second, the I/O statement should contain a reference to the record number. There are two notations for this; the three more formal ones are:

```
WRITE  (UNIT=n, REC=i)  i/o list
WRITE  (REC=i, UNIT=n)  i/o list
WRITE  (n, REC=i)  i/o list
```

where *n* is the logical unit number (as usual) and *i* is the record number being accessed. When keywords (UNIT=, REC=, etc.) are used, they may be in any order; when not, the logical unit number must be the first value in the parentheses.

If the REC= clause is not specified, the file is accessed as a SAM file. The record pointer works the same way as described above, pointing to the record after the one just input/output (or to the first record when the file is first opened).

Information may be filed in one of two ways, formatted or unformatted. A formatted file is one in which the information is stored by characters and is readable directly. An unformatted file is stored with the information in the internal binary code used by the computer; this is only readable to the computer and to the programmer familiar with the binary storage of data, with the information usually dumped in hexadecimal (or octal) notation. The advantage of storing in pure binary is that the I/O is significantly faster because no translation of the data from one coding system to another is required in either input or output. In addition, there is usually a savings in storage space, since binary data can be stored in fewer bytes. With sequential files, unless specified differently, formatted files are the default. With direct access files just the opposite, unformatted files are assumed. Thus, another clause must be added to the OPEN statement for a formatted direct access file:

```
OPEN  (n, FILE=namefl, ACCESS='DIRECT', RECL=nn, FORM='FORMATTED')
```

Also, the I/O statement must include a reference to that format; the three more formal ones are:

```
WRITE  (UNIT=n, REC=i, FMT=m)  i/o list
WRITE  (UNIT=n, FMT=m, REC=i)  i/o list
WRITE  (n,m, REC=i)  i/o list
```

In FORTRAN 66, an apostrophe was used to indicate the record number and would appear as:

```
WRITE  (n,m'i)  i/o list.
```

When keywords are used, as in the formal definition, the phrases may be placed in any order, but the abbreviated form requires that the first value following the logical unit number be the format reference number (if one is needed). Of course, keyworded and nonkeyworded references may be intermixed as long as the rules about the unkeyworded logical unit and format references are followed. For example, in the more elaborate READ statement, one could find combinations like these:

```
READ  (REC=I, UNIT=9, FMT=1002, ERR=920)  X, Y, Z
READ  (ERR=920, UNIT=9, FMT=1002, REC=I)  X, Y, Z
READ  (9, REC=I, FMT=1002, ERR=920)  X, Y, Z
READ  (9,1002, REC=I, ERR=920)  X, Y, Z
```

With a direct access file, the END= clause is invalid. Thus there is no way to determine the number of records in a DAM file during input, as with a SAM file. The three available alternatives are:

1. Use a fixed number of records. This is not an efficient method for a file that expands and contracts over a large range.
2. Place a dummy EOF record containing a sentinel value after the last valid record. The program must read the entire file and test each record for the EOF; the number of valid records is 1 less than the position of the EOF record.
3. Use an initial record (record 1) to contain a record counter indicating the number of records in the file. The valid records start at record 2. This is generally a preferred method, since it involves much less execution time. However, the data record number must be adjusted by 1 to access the desired physical record.

There is yet one other clause used in the OPEN statement that must be examined: the STATUS= clause.

STATUS='OLD'	The file exists, usually an input file. It could also be an old output file being written over (destroying the old information).
STATUS='NEW'	The file is to be created, usually an output file. If specified as NEW, the file must not exist.
STATUS='SCRATCH'	The file is temporary and can be written to and read from; the file is automatically deleted at the end of program execution.
STATUS='UNKNOWN'	Intended to cover the case of an output file that may or may not exist. If it exists, then the new output is written over it, as if STATUS='OLD'; if it does not exist, it is created as if STATUS='NEW'. However, the implementation of this clause is processor-dependent and may not work according to the intention just stated. This condition is the default.

Thus, the OPEN statement used above for output should read:

```
     OPEN   (UNIT=n, FILE=namefl, ACCESS='DIRECT', RECL=nn,
    1                 FORM='FORMATTED', STATUS='NEW')
```

Direct access files are necessary if those files are very large and it would be necessary, but impractical, to read them into memory in their entirety. By being able to read or write selected records, the program can access the data it needs with a minimum of memory (and also a significant reduction in execution time compared to reading and writing a large SAM file).

**13.1.4
INQUIRE**

On all systems, an attempt to use STATUS='OLD' to open an input file that does not exist can only cause the program to bomb out. Since STATUS='UNKNOWN' is not always implemented as described above, it is often necessary for the programmer to test for the existence of an output file and open it accordingly. The INQUIRE statement gives the programmer the ability to check for the existence of any file. In more complex situations, the INQUIRE statement can also be used to check the conditions under which a file has been previously opened, such as direct or sequential, formatted or unformatted, etc. We will apply the statement only in the simple case to determine if a file exists or not:

```
INQUIRE (FILE='file name', EXIST='status')
```

'*status*' is a logical variable set as either *.TRUE.* if the file exists or *.FALSE.* if it does not. As an example, the program segment below:

1. Checks for the existence of an input file. If the file is not found, the program displays an error message and then terminates execution; if found, it opens the file.
2. Checks for the existence of an output file, opening it as 'OLD' if it does exist and as 'NEW' if it doesn't.

```
      LOGICAL IEX
C                     check existence of input file and open
      INQUIRE (FILE='DATAIN', EXIST=IEX)
      IF (.NOT. IEX) THEN
          WRITE (*,1000)
 1000     FORMAT ('0','File does not exist  -  execution aborted!')
          STOP
      ENDIF
      OPEN (UNIT=3, FILE='DATAIN', STATUS='OLD', FORM='FORMATTED')
C                     check existence of output file and open
      INQUIRE (FILE='DATAOUT', EXIST=IEX)
      IF (IEX) THEN
          OPEN (UNIT=4, FILE='DATAOUT', STATUS='OLD')
        ELSE
          OPEN (UNIT=4, FILE='DATAOUT', STATUS='NEW')
      ENDIF
```

13.1.5 ENDFILE

This statement, accompanied by file unit number, is used to truncate the file. Unfortunately the implementation of this statement in various dialects of FORTRAN 77 is not consistent but is system-dependent; the reader may have to consult the FORTRAN manuals for the system being used for necessary details.

When an existing file is written over and the new file is shorter than the previous version (fewer records being written than had been there before), what happens to the rest of the records? To prevent access to the obsolete records at the end, it is necessary to place an EOF mark after the last of the new records. This prevents reading beyond that point. There is also a need to conserve disk space, so it would be efficient for the unused leftover records to be deleted. That is the purpose of the ENDFILE statement: to write an EOF mark and allow the operating system to cut off (truncate) the file at that point to save storage space.

When closing a SAM file which had been opened for writing, some systems automatically place the EOF mark after the last record written—but some do not. For those that do not (such as Prime and VAX), the ENDFILE is necessary. The user can easily check to see whether such a statement serves any purpose by running exercise 13.1a, given later in this section.

Since the user must implement an end-of-data mechanism in the writing program by one of the three methods to be described in the next section, there is no real need to truncate a DAM file. However, a formatted DAM file can be displayed or printed and then the entire file, even the leftover records beyond the user's end-of-file, will output. For aesthetic purposes, as well as to save disk space, it is wise to use the ENDFILE, *but only after writing the last record.*

(Note: the ENDFILE cannot be used with DAM files on the VAX.)

Some systems may require that a REWIND be issued after the ENDFILE because the latter statement may leave the file pointer behind the end-of-file, causing a file access error when another record access is attempted.

13.1.6 Initializing Direct Access Files

DAM files must be generated by a program. They cannot be set up with an editor because editors generate compressed SAM files and DAM files must have a fixed record length. Furthermore, these files must be initialized by writing data, even worthless data, to the file before it can be read. Some systems require a sequential write of the initial records, while others will allow a random write and will leave space for the undefined records. Some systems allow the user to create the file in the operating system, which then sets aside the required space for the file. Under any circumstances, if information is not written to every record in the file at some time, garbage will exist in those undefined records and can lead to error. Thus all records should be initialized appropriately.

One of the easiest approaches to generating DAM files is to read a SAM file which contains the desired data in the format and order wanted and then write that data to a DAM file. The DAM file can be formatted or unformatted. As an example, the general-purpose program below can be used to initialize one of the DAM files to be used in Application Program 4, Parking Violations. The license plate file is to be a DAM file and, for ease of later searches, is sorted by license plate number. The SAM and DAM file structure is as follows:

Columns	Description
1– 8	License plate number (alphameric)
11–28	Name of car owner (alphameric)
31–48	Address of car owner (alphameric)
51–62	Town (alphameric)
64–65	State code (alphameric)
66–70	Zip code (numeric)

The SAM file can be created in an editor and, since most operating systems provide a file sort routine, the records can be entered in any order and sorted later.

Because this is to be a variable-length DAM file, the first record will contain the number of records. That number is critical, because any attempt to read beyond the end of the file (or before the beginning of it) will cause a bomb-out. Thus any accessing program must know that count.

File PLATE.SAM

```
I WRENCH   Montgomery Scott    418 Argyle Street   Vancouver     WA98661
LOGIC 2    *@#%#@* Spock        314-159 Pi Place    Schenectady   NY12301
MD BONES   Leonard McCoy        77 Bourbon Avenue   Aragon        GA30161
NCC 1701   James T. Kirk        31 Rand Court       Storm Lake    IA51101
```

```fortran
C                        Convert SAM file to DAM file
C                            number of records placed in first record
C
C                        define number of bytes per processor unit
      PARAMETER  (NUMBPR = 1)
C
      CHARACTER   LINE(80), NAMEIN*16, NAMOUT*16
      LOGICAL     EXST
C
C                        get names of input and output files
      WRITE    (*,1000)
 1000 FORMAT  ('0','Enter names of input and output files'/
     1         ' ', 16('_'), 2X, 16('_'))
      READ      (*,1002)  NAMEIN, NAMOUT
 1002 FORMAT          (A16, 2X, A16)
      INQUIRE  (FILE=NAMEIN, EXIST=EXST)
      IF  (.NOT. EXST)  STOP  'file does not exist'
C                        get number of bytes in file
      WRITE    (*,1004)
 1004 FORMAT  ('0','Enter number of bytes in record')
      READ     (*,*)  NUMBYT
C                        adjust to processor units, rounding up
      LENREC = (NUMBYT + (NUMBPR-1)) / NUMBPR
C                        open files
      OPEN  (UNIT=2, FILE=NAMEIN, STATUS='OLD')
      OPEN  (UNIT=3, FILE=NAMOUT, STATUS='UNKNOWN', ACCESS='DIRECT',
     1             RECL=LENREC, FORM ='FORMATTED')
C                        loop through SAM file, writing to DAM file
      DO 20  I = 1,20000
          READ    (2,1010, END=40) (LINE(J), J=1,NUMBYT)
 1010     FORMAT  (80A1)
   20 WRITE   (3,1010, REC=I+1) (LINE(J), J=1,NUMBYT)
      STOP  'more than 20000 records'
C
C                        truncate file after writing last record
   40 ENDFILE  3
C                        write number of records in record 1
      NREC = I - 1
      WRITE    (3,1040, REC=1)  NREC
 1040 FORMAT  (I6)
      WRITE    (*,1042)  NREC
 1042 FORMAT  ('0', I6,' records written to DAM file')
C                        close files and terminate
      CLOSE (2)
      CLOSE (3)
      STOP
      END
```

The resulting DAM file looks identical (except for the record count in the first record) if printed or displayed; but the internal structure is different, allowing a program to access it by record number in any order.

When looking at the DAM file below, the reader should distinguish between data record number and physical record number. Because the first record contains the record counter, data record 1 is in physical record 2, data record 2 is in physical record 3, etc. Unless this is understood, some of the programs to come will be difficult to understand.

File PLATE.DAM

```
      4
I WRENCH   Montgomery Scott   418 Argyle Street   Vancouver    WA98661
LOGIC 2    *@#%#|#@* Spock     314-159 Pi Place    Schenectady  NY12301
MD BONES   Leonard McCoy       77 Bourbon Avenue   Aragon       GA30161
NCC 1701   James T. Kirk       31 Rand Court       Storm Lake   IA51101
```

13.1.7 Accessing Direct Access Files

The program below indicates how the file is accessed. This is a simple program to open the file and read the number of valid records. The user then has the ability to display a record by selecting its number and the ability to modify all of the fields in the record except the key to the record, the sorted license plate number. The record is modified by writing directly to it (using the record number); there is no need to rewrite the whole file just to update particular records. That is one of the major advantages to DAM files, significantly speeding up execution by reducing disk access to a minimum.

```
      C                      Access to DAM file PLATE.DAM
      C
            CHARACTER   LINE*70, NEW*18
      C
      C                      columns and number of columns for fields 2 - 6
            DIMENSION   NCOLS(3,5)
            DATA  NCOLS/ 11,28,18, 31,48,18, 51,62,12, 64,65,2, 66,70,5/
      C
      C                      open file and read number of records
            OPEN   (UNIT=3, FILE='PLATE.DAM', STATUS='OLD',
           1               ACCESS='DIRECT',   RECL=70, FORM='FORMATTED')
            READ   (3,1000, REC=1)  NREC
       1000 FORMAT (I6)
            WRITE  (*,1002)  NREC
       1002 FORMAT ('0',I5,' records in file')
      C                      prompt for record number
            DO 60  NTIMES = 1,20000
               WRITE   (*,1004)
       1004    FORMAT  ('0','Enter record number  (EOD to end)')
               READ    (*,*, END=90)  IREC
      C                      read record (if valid) and echo check
               IF (IREC .GT. 0 .AND.  IREC .LE. NREC)  THEN
                  READ    (3,1006, REC=IREC+1)  LINE
       1006       FORMAT  (A70)
                  DO 20 NCHANG = 1,10
                     WRITE   (*,1010)  LINE(1:28), LINE(31:70)
       1010          FORMAT  (' ',A28/ ' ',10X,A40/
           1                  '0','Enter 0 for next record'/
           2                  ' ','     1 to modify name'/
           3                  ' ','     2 to modify address'/
           4                  ' ','     3 to modify town'/
           5                  ' ','     4 to modify state code'/
```

```
      6                         ' ,'          5 to modify zip code')
                       READ     (*,*, END=60)  NUM
                       IF  (NUM .EQ. 0)  GO TO 60
                       IF  (NUM .LE. 5)  THEN
                          NC1 = NCOLS(1,NUM)
                          NC2 = NCOLS(2,NUM)
                          NC  = NCOLS(3,NUM)
                          WRITE   (*,1012)  ('_', I=1,NC)
   1012                   FORMAT  (' ','Enter new information'/' ',18A1)
                          READ    (*,1014)  NEW
   1014                   FORMAT  (A18)
                          LINE(NC1:NC2) = NEW
                          WRITE   (3,1006, REC=IREC+1)  LINE
                       ENDIF
     20            CONTINUE
                ELSE
                   WRITE  (*,1020)
   1020            FORMAT  (' ','INVALID RECORD NUMBER')
             ENDIF
     60 CONTINUE
   C                         termination
     90 CLOSE   (3)
        STOP
        END
```

The execution of this program is very user-friendly because the user does not have to know the field definitions (columns) and the length of the fields. These are kept in an array NCOLS, which is defined in the DATA statement. The prompt displays only as many underline characters as there are columns in the field, so that the user knows the limit on the input. The information is read into a buffer, NEW, and then be moved into the appropriate columns in the record; a substring cannot be input directly unless the format field is exactly the same size, which would require four separate READs and FORMATs in the above program.

Below is a sample run of the program in which the town and zip code of one of the registrants is modified:

```
        4 records in file

  Enter record number  (EOD to end)
  4
  NCC 1701  James T. Kirk
            31 Rand Court         Dubuque         IA52001


  Enter 0 for next record
        1 to modify name
        2 to modify address
        3 to modify town
        4 to modify state code
        5 to modify zip code
  3
  Enter new information
  _____
  Dubuque
  NCC 1701  James T. Kirk
            31 Rand Court         Dubuque         IA52001
```

```
          Enter 0 for next record
                1 to modify name
                2 to modify address
                3 to modify town
                4 to modify state code
                5 to modify zip code
          5
          Enter new information
          _____
          52001
          NCC 1701   James T. Kirk
                     31 Rand Court        Dubuque        IA52001

          Enter 0 for next record
                1 to modify name
                2 to modify address
                3 to modify town
                4 to modify state code
                5 to modify zip code
          0

          Enter record number   (EOD to end)
          ^Z
          Stop - Program terminated.
```

Additional examples appear in the next chapter with the full solution of Application Program 4, Parking Violations.

Exercises

13.1a Write a program to open and write a SAM file for a variable number of records. Do not use the ENDFILE statement. (Each record could be as simple as 'RECORD nnnn', with *nnnn* being the index of the DO loop.) The program should prompt for the number. On the first run, use about 100 records. Display the file to the screen and also check the directory to see the amount of storage. Then rerun the program with 10 records, *writing over the same file*. Again display the file and check its size. If the file displays more than 10 records or if the size of the stored file has not been reduced, the ENDFILE statement should be added to your program.

13.1b Revise the program in exercise 13.1a to write to a DAM file without the ENDFILE statement and check the file after both runs. Then try it with the ENDFILE on the shorter run and see if it makes a difference. If it does, always use it on your system.

13.1c Revise the sample program which accesses the DAM file PLATE.DAM to provide a delete record option. Then delete the record from the file by moving all the records after it forward one record and adjusting the record counter in the first record. Make sure you test deleting the last record—which, obviously, requires no record movements. The ENDFILE can be used, but only after a read (to make sure that the information is not overwritten) or a write to the last valid record; the record pointer will be pointing to the record after it and the end-of-file will be written in the right location.

13.1d   Revise the program in exercise 13.1c to accept additions to the file. Be sure to place the record in the right place so that the sorted quality is maintained. Move the other records and revise the counter.

13.1e   Revise the program in exercise 13.1d to access the records by license plate number rather than record number. For full sophistication, the search can be binary.

13.1f   Write a program to read through PLATE.DAM and generate a key/record sort array based on the zip code. Sort the array. Then generate a SAM file by passing through the sorted array and accessing the record numbers in the new order from the DAM file and writing them one at a time to the SAM file. The SAM file should have a title and headings.

13.2   ADDITIONAL FORMAT CAPABILITIES

Many aspects of the FORMAT statement have been covered earlier, primarily in Chapter 7 and in discussions of the use of that statement in subsequent chapters. Here a few more capabilities are added that provide the programmer with mechanisms for more flexible I/O.

13.2.1
Integer Edit Descriptor with Digit Control: Iw.m

The simple **Iw** edit descriptor specifies the field width, the number of columns for the value. The programmer also has the ability to specify the minimum number of digits output by modifying the form to **Iw.m**, where w is still the field width and m is the minimum number of digits; blank when zero is specified with $m = 0$. This is best shown by the following examples:

Value	Format	Columns 123456 output	Format	Columns 123456 output
64	I4	64	I4.3	064
0	I4	0	I4.0	[blank]
−1280	I6	−1280	I6.5	−01280

The use of a leading zero is very handy in numeric date output where it is desired that the months and days always have two digits, outputting, for example, 01/01/92 instead of 1/ 1/92. The coding appears as:

```
      DIMENSION  IDATE(3)
                :
                :
      WRITE   (*,1000)  IDATE
 1000 FORMAT  (' ', I2.2,'/',I2.2,'/',I2.2)
```

The last specification for the year provides two-digit output through the first decade of the next century.

This facility has no effect on input.

**13.2.2
Zero/Blank
Option: BN
and BZ**

The normal action when reading numeric data is to assume that all blank columns are ignored, including leading, trailing, and embedded blanks. The only exception is that an all-blank field is interpreted as a zero. However, the programmer has control over this. The insertion of the BZ specification any place in the FORMAT will force the compiler to treat any input blanks as zeros; the effect may be reversed by inserting the specifier BN. Each new FORMAT is treated as a new entity and is not affected by the specifications in a previous FORMAT.

(There is an available clause in the OPEN statement—BLANK = NULL and BLANK = ZERO, corresponding to the **BN** and **BZ** FORMAT specifiers—which specifies the default for any unspecified FORMAT. If the clause does not appear in the OPEN statement, or if there is no OPEN statement, BLANK = NULL is the default.)

As an example, assuming the following code:

```
      READ    (1,1000)  I, J, K, L
 1000 FORMAT  (I6, BZ, 2I6, BN, I6)
```

with the input data:

```
                                    111111111122222
          columns:   12345678901234567890234
                      1 2    1 2    1234   1234
```

will yield:

```
    I = 12,    J = 10200,   K = 12340,   L = 1234
```

**13.2.3
Additional
Positional
Editing: TLc
and TRc**

In addition to the **T** format described in Chapter 7, section 7.4, that tabs to an absolute column location, there are two other versions which tab to a column location relative to the last column input/output. For example, if a programmer wishes to input the values of A, B, and C in columns 11 to 20, columns 31 to 40, and columns 1 to 10, respectively, one of the ways of doing this would be:

```
      READ    (2,1000)  A, B, C
 1000 FORMAT  (T11,F10.2, TR10,F10.2, TL40,F10.2)
```

The pointer which indicates the columns to be input/output is moved to column 11 by the **T11**, where the value of A is read from the next 10 columns (11 to 20). The pointer is now at column 21. The **TR10** moves the pointer right 10 columns, to column 31, where the value of B is read from columns 31 to 40. The pointer is now at column 41. The **TL40** moves it left to column 1, where the value of C is read from the next 10 columns (1 to 10). The only limitation is that a TL cannot move the pointer left of column 1.

This capability is also useful in output formats.

**13.2.4
Sign Edits: S, SP,
and SS**

In most implementations of FORTRAN, a leading plus sign never appears in output before an integer or real number, but it may appear within the exponent in exponential format. However, it is possible to force the leading plus sign by using the specifier **SP** within the FORMAT statement. All positive numbers following that point will show a plus sign wherever such a sign is optional. The **SS** specifier suppresses the sign in all optional positions, and the use of the S specifier returns the compiler to its system-dependent status, usually equivalent to the **SS** condition. For example:

```
      DATA  X/ 12.34/
      WRITE    (*,1000)  X, X, X, X
 1000 FORMAT  (' ',E12.4, SP,E12.4, SS,E12.4, S,E12.4)
      STOP
      END
```

would yield:

```
 .1234E+02  +.1234E+02   .1234E+02    .1234E+02
```

or:

```
 .1234E 02  +.1234E+02   .1234E 02    .1234E 02
```

depending on the implementation.

13.2.5
Scaling: kP

As an aid to the input and output of very large and very small real numbers, FORTRAN provides a scale factor, represented here by k. This k is a positive or negative number that specifies the power of 10 which will be applied to the value—the number of places the decimal point will be moved—during the I/O operation. The scale factor, once specified in a FORMAT statement, applies to all of the following real specifications in that FORMAT statement until a new scale factor is encountered. To return to no scaling, a factor of $0P$ may be entered.

During input, the value read is *divided* by the power of 10, but only if the value is not in exponential format. Where an exponent is explicitly stated, scaling does not apply. The following code:

```
      READ     (*,1000)  A, B, C, D, E
 1000 FORMAT  (F8.2, 2P,2F8.2, -1P,F8.2, 0P,F8.2)
```

with the data:

```
 12.34   12.34 12.34E0   12.34    12.34
```

will store:

```
 12.34,  0.1234, 12.34,  123.4,   12.34
```

for: A   B   C   D   E

During output, the value stored is *multiplied* by the power of 10 if it is output in real (F) format. If output in exponential (E) format, the location of the decimal point is shifted in the output but the value of the exponent is adjusted so that the value is maintained.

```
      X = 12.34
      WRITE    (*,1000)  X, X, X, X, X, X
 1000 FORMAT  (' ',F10.2,E10.2, 2P,F10.2,E10.2, -1P,F10.2,E10.2)
```

will yield:

```
 12.34 0.12E+02  1234.00 12.34E+00     1.23  0.01E+03
```

**13.2.6
Exponent
Control: Ew.dEe**

FORTRAN also provides the facility to control the number of digits in the exponent when outputting in exponential format. The following example indicates the use of the additional **Ee** specification added to the usual **Ew.d** specification.

```
      X = 12.34
      WRITE   (*,1000) X, X, X
 1000 FORMAT  (' ',E12.4, E12.4E1, E12.4E3)
      STOP
      END
```

yields:

```
0.1234E+02  0.1234E+2 0.1234E+002
```

**13.2.7
FORMAT
Specifiers**

The ASSIGN statement (described fully in the next section) assigns a statement number to a variable. It can be used to assign FORMAT statement numbers to a variable included in an I/O command. The following program segment illustrates this use:

```
            :
      IF  (I .LT. J)  ASSIGN 1002 TO IFRMT
      IF  (I .GE. J)  ASSIGN 1004 TO IFRMT
      WRITE   (*,IFRMT) I, J
            :
 1002 FORMAT  ('0','Condition 1', 2I6)
 1004 FORMAT  ('0','Condition 2', I6, I12)
```

**13.2.8
Embedded
FORMATs**

It is possible to embed the FORMAT right into the I/O command. Rather than supplying a FORMAT statement number, the FORMAT itself is placed in its stead, enclosed in apostrophes and parentheses. The following code segment is an alternative to the above code:

```
      IF  (I .LT. J)  WRITE  (*,'(''0'',''Condition 1'', 2I6)')  I, J
      IF  (I .GE. J)  WRITE  (*,'(''0'',''Condition 2'', I6, I12)')  I, J
```

Note the double apostrophes required inside the embedded FORMAT!

**13.2.9
FORMAT
Identifiers**

A FORMAT identifier is a character variable or array containing the characters which make up a valid FORMAT statement. Since it is possible to input data into character variables or to modify them, the programmer has the ability to modify FORMATS during execution. In previous versions of FORTRAN where this was possible, they were called "run-time FORMATS."

In simplest form, a code sequence might look like:

```
CHARACTER*11  FRMT1
        :
DATA  FRMT1/ '(1H0, 2I10)'/
        :
WRITE (1, FRMT1) I, J
```

Additionally, FORTRAN 77 provides the facility to modify the FORMAT within the program:

```
FRMT1(10:10) = '2'
```

and now is specifying 2 fields of 12 columns with (1H0, 2I12).

The ability to input a FORMAT into a character variable allows the program to read in a data file which contains, as its first record, the input FORMAT to be used. Characters in the FORMAT beyond the closing parentheses are ignored, so there is no problem when reading into a long character variable. For example, the program segment:

```
      CHARACTER*66  INFRMT
      INTEGER*2     IDATA(2000)
            :
      READ  (3,1000)  INFRMT
 1000 FORMAT  (A66)
      READ  (3,INFRMT, END = 120)  (IDATA(I), I=1,2000)
      STOP 'excessive data'
  120 NREC = I - 1
            :
```

with the data:

```
                            111111111122222
        columns   12345678901234567890901234
                  (4I6)
                      123       52    1546    8852
                    32767    26852 -19058    -881
                       -1     -850    1175            etc.
```

will read in four fields of six columns per record.

Review Questions

13.2a   The following input data:

```
                            11111111112
      Columns   1234567890123456789.0
      Data         2 4 6      34.8718963
```

is acted upon by

```
      READ    (*,1000)  I, J, K, L,  A, B
 1000 FORMAT  (BZ, I5, I2,  BN, TL6, I5, I2,  T11, -4P, 2F5.1)
```

What values will be stored for each of the variables?

13.2b   Show what output is generated by the following coding:

```
      DATA   I,  J,    X,      Y/
     1          10, 20, 12.34, 123.45/
      WRITE   (*,1002)  I, J, X, Y
 1002 FORMAT  (' ', I4.4, I4, TR12, E10.4E1, SP, -2P, F10.2)
```

13.2c   Show the output generated by the program below:

```
      DATA  J, K, L/ 2, 8, 3/
 1000 FORMAT  (' ', I5, I10)
 1002 FORMAT  (' ', I10, I5)
      IF  (J*L .LT. K)  THEN
              ASSIGN  1000 TO IFRMAT
          ELSE
              ASSIGN  1002 TO IFRMAT
      ENDIF
      WRITE   (*,IFRMAT)  J, K, L
      STOP
      END
```

13.2d Rewrite the statements below with embedded FORMATs:

```
      READ     (2,1000)  X, Y, Z
1000 FORMAT   (F10.2)
      WRITE    (3,1002)  X, Y, Z
1002 FORMAT   (3F10.2)
```

13.2e Determine the values placed in each of the four array locations in the program segment below:

```
      CHARACTER*66  INFRMT
      DIMENSION     DATA(4)
C                   input routine
      READ (3,1000)  INFRMT
1000 FORMAT  (A66)
      READ (3,INFRMT)  DATA
                :
```

with the data:

```
                                1111111111222222222233333333334
columns:  12345678901234567890123456789012345678'90
          (2F10.2)
                 123        52      1546      8852
               32767     26852    -19058      -881
                  -1      -850      1175   5789146
                9763    824763       -18      7132
```

13.3 OTHER FORMS OF THE GO TO

The GO TO statement was defined as an unconditional branch. There are two other forms of that statement that might be defined as "semiconditional" branches; i.e., a limited number of restricted possibilities. These statements implement the CASE construct found in more modern languages but lack the inherent structure. (The CASE statement is included in Fortran 90; see Chapter 6A, section 6A.8.) The use of these statements is not recommended because, if not properly coded, they are capable of destroying a program's structure. As an alternative, more structured code avoiding the use of the GO TO is shown below.

13.3.1 Computed GO TO

The computed GO TO specifies an array of statement numbers to which a branch can be made and a variable index that indicates which branch will be taken. The syntax of the statement is:

```
GO TO  (n1, n2, n3, n4, ..., nm),  index
```

where the n's are the statement numbers and *index* a positive integer variable in the range 1 to m.

The branch taken corresponds to the value of the index in the sense that if the index is 1, the branch is made to the first statement number in the list; if it is 2, the branch is made to the second statement number in the list, and so forth up to the mth statement number. If the value of the index is less than 1 or greater than m, processing continues with the next sequential statement, effectively ignoring the GO TO.

The statement is very useful when branching to a number of different processing sections within the same program. Below is a very simple example illustrating how the statement is used. The user is prompted to enter two real numbers and an integer option from 1 to 5 to instruct the program as to the calculation to be done on these numbers.

```
      C                         Computed GO TO example
      C
            DO 80  NTIMES = 1,2000
                WRITE    (*,1000)
      1000      FORMAT  ('0','Enter two real numbers (EOD to end)')
                READ     (*,*, END=90)  X, Y
                WRITE    (*,1002)
      1002      FORMAT  (' ','Enter 1 to add'/
          1               ' ','      2 to subtract'/
          2               ' ','      3 to multiply'/
          3               ' ','      4 to divide'/
          4               ' ','      5 to exponentiate')
                READ     (*,*, ERR=5, END=90)  IOP
                IF (IOP .EQ. 4  .AND.  Y .EQ. 0.00)  IOP = 0
                GO TO (10, 20, 30, 40, 50), IOP
      C                             error branch
          5     WRITE    (*,1005)
      1005      FORMAT  (' ','INVALID OPTION')
                GO TO 80
      C                             process data
          10    Z = X + Y
                GO TO 60
          20    Z = X - Y
                GO TO 60
          30    Z = X * Y
                GO TO 60
          40    Z = X / Y
                GO TO 60
          50    Z = X ** Y
      C                             output answer
          60    WRITE    (*,1060)  Z
      1060      FORMAT  (' ',F10.4)
          80 CONTINUE
      C
      C                         termination
          90 STOP
             END
```

The menu displays five options. The user enters a number and, if that number is in the range of 1 to 5, the appropriate branch is executed by the computed GO TO. If the entered value is outside the range, the error message is displayed. Attempted division by zero is prevented by resetting the option to an invalid value, forcing a branch to the error message. Likewise the READ statement protects against the entering of a real or nonnumeric entry with the ERR= clause. Hopefully the code is idiot-proof; i.e., any type of entry is under program control, no matter how unsuitable.

**13.3.2
Assigned
GO TO**

The syntax of the assigned GO TO,

```
      GO TO k
```

where k is an integer variable, seems to indicate that we utilize a variable branch; but this is not the case. First of all, that variable is only allowed to contain a statement number that is in the program and that statement number must be assigned to the variable by a special statement, ASSIGN, which can assign only statement numbers to these special variables. In fact, there is a second version of the assigned GO TO which lists the possible statement numbers that can be assigned to the variable; it appears in the form:

```
GO TO k, (n1, n2, n3, n4, ..., nm)
```

The list serves as documentation for the possible branches that may be taken.

We can rewrite the above code using the assigned GO TO rather than the computed GO TO:

```
C                        Assigned GO TO example
C
        DO 80   NTIMES = 1,2000
          WRITE   (*,1000)
1000      FORMAT  ('0','Enter two real numbers  (EOD to end)')
          READ    (*,*, END=90) X, Y
          WRITE   (*,1002)
1002      FORMAT  (' ','Enter 1 to add'/
     1             ' ','      2 to subtract'/
     2             ' ','      3 to multiply'/
     3             ' ','      4 to divide'/
     4             ' ','      5 to exponentiate')
          READ    (*,*, ERR=5, END=90)  IOP
                       ASSIGN  5 TO IBRNCH
          IF  (IOP .EQ. 1)  ASSIGN 10 TO IBRNCH
          IF  (IOP .EQ. 2)  ASSIGN 20 TO IBRNCH
          IF  (IOP .EQ. 3)  ASSIGN 30 TO IBRNCH
          IF  (IOP .EQ. 4   .AND.
     1          Y .NE. 0.0)  ASSIGN 40 TO IBRNCH
          IF  (IOP .EQ. 5)  ASSIGN 50 TO IBRNCH
          GO TO IBRNCH
C                         error branch
5         WRITE   (*,1005)
1005      FORMAT  (' ','INVALID OPTION')
          GO TO 80
C                         process data
10        Z = X + Y
          GO TO 60
20        Z = X - Y
          GO TO 60
30        Z = X * Y
          GO TO 60
40        Z = X / Y
          GO TO 60
50        Z = X ** Y
C                         output answer
60        WRITE   (*,1060)  Z
1060      FORMAT  (' ',F10.4)
80      CONTINUE
C
C                         termination
90      STOP
        END
```

The alternative form of the assigned GO TO is:

```
GO TO IBRNCH (5, 10, 20, 30, 40, 50)
```

The assigned GO TO is preferable to the computed GO TO in only a few limited application situations.

13.3.3
Structured
Replacement

However, other structures provide superior code to either of the GO TO variations above. Thus, the above program could be recoded as:

```
C                           Computed GO TO simulated
C
        DO 20  NTIMES = 1,2000
           WRITE   (*,1000)
1000       FORMAT  ('0','Enter two real numbers  (EOD to end)')
           READ    (*,*, END=90) X, Y
           WRITE   (*,1002)
1002       FORMAT  (' ','Enter 1 to add'/
     1             ' ','      2 to subtract'/
     2             ' ','      3 to multiply'/
     3             ' ','      4 to divide'/
     4             ' ','      5 to exponentiate')
           READ    (*,*, ERR=20, END=90) IOP
           IF  (IOP .EQ. 4  .AND.  Y .EQ. 0.0)  IOP = 0
           IF  (IOP .GE. 1  .AND.  IOP .LE. 5)   THEN
C                          process data
              IF  (IOP .EQ. 1)  Z = X + Y
              IF  (IOP .EQ. 2)  Z = X - Y
              IF  (IOP .EQ. 3)  Z = X * Y
              IF  (IOP .EQ. 4)  Z = X / Y
              IF  (IOP .EQ. 5)  Z = X ** Y
C                          output answer
              WRITE   (*,1004)  Z
1004          FORMAT  (' ',F10.4)
           ELSE
C                          error message
              WRITE   (*,1006)
1006          FORMAT  (' ','INVALID OPTION')
           ENDIF
20      CONTINUE
C
C                          termination
90      STOP
        END
```

Review Questions

13.3a   In the code given below, determine the final value of *N*.

```
        N = 0
        DO 100  I = 1,6
           GO TO (20, 40, 40, 20, 60), I
20         N = N + 1
              GO TO 100
40         N = N + 10
              GO TO 100
60         N = N + 1000
100 CONTINUE
```

13.3b In the code given below, determine the final value of N.

```
DATA X, Y/   -2.00, 8.00/
IF (X .GE. 0.00)  ASSIGN 20 to NST
IF (X .LT. 0.00)  ASSIGN 40 to NST
GO TO NST (20, 40)
20    IF (Y .GE. 0.00)  N = 2
      IF (Y .LT. 0.00)  N = 0
          GO TO 60
40    IF (Y .GE. 0.00)  N = 0
      IF (Y .LT. 0.00)  N = -2
60 PRINT *, N
```

13.4 PAUSE

The PAUSE statement allows the programmer to cause a temporary halt in the operation of a program. The PAUSE may include a number of up to five digits or a character constant to present a display on the screen:

```
PAUSE  8    or    PAUSE  'programmed pause'
```

Execution continues with the entering of a system-dependent command, such as CONTINUE or RESUME.

An alternative method, requiring less input effort to restart, is to request input (which can consist of just a carriage return) in the following manner:

```
     WRITE    (*,1000)
1000 FORMAT   (' ','Press RETURN to continue display')
     READ     (*,1002)  IDUMMY
1002 FORMAT   (A1)
```

This type of coding is useful to stop a screen from scrolling after displaying 20 lines, for example, so that the user has time to read the data and then proceed to the next screen.

The PAUSE is very useful in an operation wherein printer output is sent directly from the computer. Here, temporary halts are used for changing forms and for testing forms lineup:

```
     PAUSE  'Change to check forms'
     DO 20  NTIMES = 1,20
        WRITE   (3,1000)
1000    FORMAT  (////'   ***     *****.**      **/**/**'//////////)
        WRITE   (*, '('0','Approve?  (Y/N)')')
        READ    (*, '(A1)', END=990) IYN
        IF (IYN .EQ. 'Y' .OR. IYN .EQ. 'y') GO TO 40
 20 CONTINUE
        STOP  'checks cannot be lined up properly'
C
 40              print checks

     PAUSE  'Remove check forms'
```

13.5   COMPLEX VARIABLES

The variable type COMPLEX is used to store complex numbers, numbers which consist of two values: one real, the other imaginary. Complex numbers are used in many scientific and engineering applications. FORTRAN contains the necessary commands and techniques to manipulate these specialized arithmetic constructs.

A complex number is one of the form: $a + bi$, where a and b are real variables and i is the square root of -1. The first term, a, is called the real part of the number and, since it is usually accepted that one cannot take the square root of a negative number, the second term, b, is called the imaginary part. Although the notation includes a plus sign, the two terms cannot be added because they are of two completely different types; the geometrical interpretation of the imaginary part places it into a different dimension than the real part.

13.5.1 Assignment

Complex numbers can be manipulated in the following ways:

Added	$(a + bi) + (c + di) = (a + c) + (b + d)i$
Subtracted	$(a + bi) - (c + di) = (a - c) + (b - d)i$
Multiplied	$(a + bi) * (c + di) = (ac - bd) + (ad + bc)i$
Divided	$(a + bi) * (c + di) = \dfrac{(ac + bd)}{c^2 + d^2} + \dfrac{(bc - ad)}{c^2 + d^2}i$

using the standard FORTRAN operators; however, mixed-mode expressions should be avoided, since they tend to lead to errors.

Complex numbers may be multiplied or divided by a real scaler (a noncomplex number) and may be exponentiated to an integer power. For example:

$5(2.42 + 3.25i) = 12.10 + 16.25i$
$(2.42 + 3.25i) ** 3 = (2.42 + 3.25i) * (2.42 + 3.25i) * (2.42 + 3.25i)$

There are intrinsic functions available for computing with complex numbers, such as:

CABS $(a + bi)$ which yields the real scaler $\sqrt{a^2 + b^2}$
CONJG $(a + bi)$ which yields the conjugate complex number $(a - bi)$

as well as CSQRT, CEXP, CLOG, CSIN, and CCOS. All of these functions accept one complex argument and (except for CABS) return a complex value.

FORTRAN stores two real values in each variable defined as COMPLEX. Such definition can be made as with any other type, either implicitly or explicitly; furthermore, these variables may also be arrays. COMPLEX constants are pairs of real numbers enclosed in parentheses:

```
COMPLEX  A, B, C, D
A = (5.62, 8.17E-03)
B = (-2.0, 0.25)
C = A - B
D = CSQRT (A * B)
```

There are three intrinsic functions for mode change from COMPLEX, each of which accepts one complex argument:

INT: conversion, with truncation, of real part to integer value
REAL: conversion of real part to real value
AIMAG: conversion of imaginary part to real value

and one intrinsic function for mode change to COMPLEX:

CMPLX: conversion of integer, real, or double-precision to complex:
      —one argument yields a real part with imaginary part = 0
      —two arguments (must be same type) yield both real and imaginary parts

```
COMPLEX  A, B
A = (2.5, 8.40)
I = INT (A)          yields 2
X = REAL (A)         yields 2.5
Y = AIMAG (A)        yields 8.4
B = CMPLX (Y, X)     yields (8.4, 2.5)
```

13.5.2 I/O and Application

I/O of complex variables requires two real format specifications for each complex variable. For example, to output the above two complex variables A and B:

```
      WRITE   (*,1000)  A, B
1000 FORMAT  ('  ',  4F10.2)
```

places the real and imaginary parts of A in columns 1–10 and 11–20 and of B in columns 21–30 and 31–40.

The classic sample program used to illustrate the usefulness of complex variables is the solution of quadratic equations, wherein the equation to be solved is in the form:

$$y = Ax^2 + Bx + C$$

with A, B, and C called the coefficients of the equation. The formulas used to solve for the two possible values of x (the points where the curve crosses the x-axis; i.e., $y = 0$, are:

$$x1 = \frac{-B + \sqrt{B^2 - 4AC}}{2A}$$

and

$$x2 = \frac{-B - \sqrt{B^2 - 4AC}}{2A}$$

The term $B^2 - 4AC$ is called the discriminant; if it is negative, it means that there are no "real" solutions; i.e., the curve does not cross the x-axis. Furthermore, in FORTRAN the square root of a negative number is a destructive error. However, if the discriminant is converted to a complex number and the CSQRT function is used, the equations will yield a real and an imaginary part corresponding to the correct solutions; if the value is positive or zero, the CSQRT function yields a complex number whose real part is the appropriate scaler square root and whose imaginary part is zero. The complex solution becomes:

$$x1 = \frac{-B}{2A} + \frac{\sqrt{B^2 - 4AC}}{2A} i$$

and

$$x2 = \frac{-B}{2A} - \frac{\sqrt{B^2 - 4AC}}{2A} i$$

In the sample program below, the three coefficients (A, B, and C) are read in as real and converted when necessary to complex using the function CMPLX. The program also protects itself against division by zero by checking the value of A and using alternative logic if A is zero, which reduces the equation to that of a straight line. A sample run is also shown.

```
      C                          Test 13K:   Solution of Quadratic Equation
      C
            COMPLEX   D, X1, X2
      C
      C                   loop through input
         20 WRITE    (*,1020)
       1020 FORMAT  ('0','Solution of Quadratic Equation'/
          1          ' ','Enter coefficient values for A, B and C')
            READ    (*,*, END=90)  A, B, C
            IF  (A .NE. 0.00)  THEN
               D  = CSQRT (CMPLX (B ** 2) - CMPLX (4.0 * A * C))
               X1 = (CMPLX (-B) + D) / CMPLX (2.0 * A)
               X2 = (CMPLX (-B) - D) / CMPLX (2.0 * A)
               WRITE    (*,1022)  A, B, C, X1, X2
       1022    FORMAT  (' ', 9X,'A', 9X,'B', 9X,'C', 8X,'X1', 16X,'X2'/
          1             ' ', 3F10.2,          2(F10.2,',',F6.2,'i'))
            ELSE
               X = -C / B
               WRITE    (*,1024)  A, B, C, X
       1024    FORMAT  (' ', 9X,'A', 9X,'B', 9X,'C', 11X,'X'/
          1             ' ', 3F10.2,          F12.2)
            ENDIF
            GO TO 20
      C
         90 STOP
            END
```

```
Solution of Quadratic Equation
Enter coefficient values for A, B and C
3,4,6
          A           B           C          X1                   X2
        3.00        4.00        6.00       -.67,   1.25i        -.67,  -1.25i

Solution of Quadratic Equation
Enter coefficient values for A, B and C
3,4,-6
          A           B           C          X1                   X2
        3.00        4.00       -6.00        .90,    .00i      -2.23,    .00i

Solution of Quadratic Equation
Enter coefficient values for A, B and C
0,4,6
          A           B           C           X
         .00        4.00        6.00       -1.50

Solution of Quadratic Equation
Enter coefficient values for A, B and C
^Z
Stop - Program terminated.
```

Review Question

13.5a   Show the output resulting from the program below:

```
C                      Complex Numbers
C
        COMPLEX  A(4), B(4)
        REAL     R(4)
C
        A(1) = (6.40, -2.50)
        A(2) = CMPLX (2,5)
        A(3) = CONJG (A(1))
        A(4) = 5.0 * A(1)
C
        B(1) = A(1) + A(2)
        B(2) = A(1) - A(2)
        B(3) = A(1) * A(2)
        B(4) = A(1) / A(2)
C
        R(1) = REAL  (A(4))
        R(2) = AIMAG (A(4))
        R(3) = REAL  (INT (A4)))
        R(4) = CABS  (A(2))
C
        WRITE   (*,1000) (A(I), B(I), R(I), I=1,4)
   1000 FORMAT  (' ', 5F10.3)
C
        STOP
        END
```

13.6   ADVANCED SUBPROGRAM LINKAGE

The commands illustrated here provide the advanced programmer with some of the subprogram features normally available only in assembly language. These features provide more efficient code and better management of the various parts of a programming system.

**13.6.1
ENTRY**

It is possible to place a number of subprograms into one programming unit and access each one independently from the calling program. These subprograms may each be completely independent of one another or may share some of the code. For example, the method used for computing sines can also be used for computing cosines if the angle whose cosine is wanted is complemented [cosine A = sine$(90 - A)$]. Thus it is very efficient to include the coding for both routines within one programming unit.

Suppose we have a system in which three area routines are required: one for right triangles, one for rectangles, and one for circles. The input is in feet and two outputs are returned, square feet and acres. Since the routines are quite small and can share some of the code, it is efficient to combine them, as follows:

```
C                  Subroutine ATRNGL:  area of right triangle
C                  Entry       ARCNGL:  area of rectangle
C                  Entry       ACRCLE:  area of circle
C
      SUBROUTINE  ATRNGL  (SIDE1, SIDE2, SQFT, ACRES)
      SQFT = 0.5 * SIDE1 * SIDE2
          GO TO 100
C
      ENTRY        ARCNGL  (SIDE1, SIDE2, SQRT, ACRES)
      SQFT = SIDE1 * SIDE2
          GO TO 100
C
      ENTRY        ACRCLE  (RADIUS, SQFT, ACRES)
      SQFT = 3.14159 * RADIUS * RADIUS
C
  100 ACRES = SQFT / 43560.0
C
      RETURN
      END
```

The subprograms are accessed with the usual CALL statements:

```
      CALL ACRCLE  (R, FEET, ACRES)

      CALL ATRNGL  (X, Y, FEET, ACRES)

      CALL ARCNGL  (X, Y, FEET, ACRES)
```

ENTRY can be used with external functions as well as subroutines. In fact, functions and subroutines may be grouped within the same program unit. During the linking operation, only the programming unit (file) need be linked in, not each of the subprograms within that unit.

**13.6.2
Alternate
RETURN**

The normal return from a subroutine is to the statement following the accessing statement in the calling program. However, FORTRAN provides for the possibility of a return to another statement in the calling program by including in the argument list (in both calling and called programs) additional terms to provide the necessary linkage to a different statement.

In the calling statement, the additional arguments are the statement numbers for the alternate returns; these statement numbers are preceded by ampersands (&) to indicate that they are statement numbers and not constants. Since the locations of these statements are to be passed to the called program, the argument list therein need only indicate dummy arguments in the form of asterisks (*).

The partial mainline and subroutine below demonstrate how this is done and why it can be a very useful procedure.

```
        CALL COMPUT  (X, Y, Z, &800, &820)
C               computations

        STOP    'End of Run'
C               error stops
    800 STOP    'INVALID INPUT DATA'
    820 STOP    'DIVISION BY ZERO ATTEMPTED'
        END
        SUBROUTINE  COMPUT  (A, B, C, *, *)
C               edit data
        IF  (B .LT. 0.00)  RETURN 1
        IF  (B .EQ. 0.00)  RETURN 2
C               computation

        C = A/B
C               normal RETURN
        RETURN
        END
```

The unannotated RETURN causes a return to the statement in the calling program immediately following the CALL. However, the RETURN 1 causes a return to the first statement number in the list (the fourth argument), statement 800; and the RETURN 2 causes a return to the second statement number in the list (the fifth argument), statement 820.

Alternate returns cannot be used with functions.

13.7 CHAPTER REVIEW

This chapter tends to be a hodgepodge, since it covers a number of unrelated topics. None of them are large enough for their own chapter, but all must be covered for a comprehensive treatment of the FORTRAN language. They were covered, however, in order of importance. The material on files will be used in the next chapter. The material on FORMATs may be of only passing interest at this time, but it will become quite useful if you go on to more advanced or professional work. The additional GO TOs were covered only for background, much as a knowledge of Old English would aid the reader of Chaucer and Shakespeare. The PAUSE is a useful statement when writing in a professional environment; but most programmers already know how to use the keyboard to stop the screen from scrolling when they want to freeze the screen.

The topics covered in this chapter include:

Topic	Section
Alternate RETURN	13.6.2
ASSIGN	13.2.7, 13.3.2
Assigned GO TO	13.3.2
BACKSPACE	13.1.2
COMPLEX	13.5
Computed GO TO	13.3.1
Direct access files	13.1.3, 13.1.6, 13.1.7
Embedded FORMATs	13.2.8
ENTRY	13.6.1
Exponent control	13.2.6
FORMAT identifiers	13.2.9
FORMAT specifiers	13.2.7
Integer edit descriptor	13.2.1
INQUIRE	13.1.4
PAUSE	13.4
Positional editing	13.2.3
RETURN, alternate	13.6.2
REWIND	13.1.2
Scaling	13.2.5
Sequential access files	13.1.1, 13.1.2
Sign editing	13.2.4
Zero/blank edit option	13.2.2

14 Advanced Programming Systems

CHAPTER OBJECTIVES

- To present another method of memory allocation and explain how it is used to transmit information between elements of a programming system.

- To indicate the problems involved when working with large arrays and data structures.

- To show some of the more advanced techniques of using subprograms available to the sophisticated programmer.

- To detail a complete programming system.

STATEMENT OF THE PROBLEM

Since Application Program 4: Parking Violations uses a number of advanced techniques not always covered in an introductory text, it has been saved for this chapter covering the final topics in our presentation of FORTRAN. Also, it is a complete programming system application using a number of new commands and techniques.

The treatment of COMMON and BLOCKDATA was held for this chapter because their application is most effective in programming systems wherein the subprograms are to be used only within that system and not as general subprograms accessible by many calling modules. However, these topics can also be covered as a sequel to the chapters on subprograms and one-dimensional arrays.

The topic of EQUIVALENCE might have been covered very early in the text, inasmuch as it is really an extension of ASSIGNMENT. However, it is better understood once users are familiar with the mapping function. Employed quite often in the early days of computers as a memory-saving device, EQUIVALENCE has now been reduced to a convenience. Again, though, in the right application, that convenience can save a great deal of coding effort.

This chapter also has a very important comment (see section 14.2) about how the computer lays out large arrays of data in excess of 64 kilobytes (65536 bytes). It is one of those warnings a reader sees in language manuals which doesn't seem to mean much, until a program generates garbage data in otherwise correct code. We advise you to carefully read and file that information in the back of your memory as an important debugging consideration.

14.1 ADVANCED SUBPROGRAM COMMANDS

All languages have facilities which seem to be of limited usefulness but do serve specific purposes. This section looks at two of them: (1) INTRINSIC and EXTERNAL and (2) SAVE.

14.1.1 INTRINSIC and EXTERNAL

The INTRINSIC statement allows the programmer to use an intrinsic function as supplied in the system library (with the exception of the type conversion, lexical relationship, and minimum and maximum functions) as arguments to a subprogram. The EXTERNAL statement allows the programmer to indicate that an argument to a subprogram is a user-written subprogram. As examples, the programming system below uses the intrinsic functions SIN and COS and the user-written function PERI to determine the two sides and perimeter of a triangle from the hypotenuse and one angle.

```
C                        Sides and Perimeter of a Triangle
C
        PARAMETER   (D2R = 3.14159 / 180.00)
        EXTERNAL    PERI
        INTRINSIC   SIN, COS
C
        DO 20  NTIMES = 1,2000
            WRITE    (*,1000)
  1000      FORMAT   ('0','Enter hypotenuse, angle (degrees')'
            READ     (*,*, END=90) HYPOT, ANGLE
            ANGLE = D2R * ANGLE
            CALL TRIANG  (HYPOT, ANGLE, SIN,  OPPOS)
            CALL TRIANG  (HYPOT, ANGLE, COS,  ADJCNT)
            CALL TRIANG  (HYPOT, ANGLE, PERI, PERIM)
            WRITE    (*,1002) OPPOS, ADJCNT,      PERIM
  1002      FORMAT   (' ',    'Sides =', 2F8.2,'    Perimeter =', F8.2)
     20 CONTINUE
```

```
C
  90 STOP
     END
                 SUBROUTINE  TRIANG  (H, A, F, S)
C
     S = H * F (A)
     RETURN
     END
                 FUNCTION  PERI (A)
C
     PERI = SIN(A) + COS(A) + 1.00
     RETURN
     END
```

On the first call to TRIANG, the argument SIN is defined as an intrinsic FORTRAN function, not a regular variable. In the subroutine, the third argument is the SIN function and the assignment appears to the computer as:

```
     S = HYPOT * SIN (ANGLE)
```

At the second call, the third argument is the COS function and the assignment is evaluated as:

```
     S = HYPOT * COS (ANGLE)
```

At the third call, the computer first views the assignment as:

```
     S = HYPOT * PERI(ANGLE)
```

Since PERI is also a function, it must be evaluated before TRIANG will work, extending the assignment to:

```
     S = HYPOT * (SIN (ANGLE) + COS (ANGLE) + 1.00)
```

Because FORTRAN has no reserved words, the names of the intrinsic functions may be used as programmer-designed variable names. Only if the name is defined as INTRINSIC or appears in an arithmetic expression looking like a function (with a list of arguments) will the compiler recognize it as such. In fact, the programmer can also define the intrinsic name as EXTERNAL and supply his or her own routine, provided that function name is included when linking.

The INTRINSIC and EXTERNAL statements must appear before any executable statements.

14.1.2
SAVE

Variables which appear in only one module of a programming system are called local variables. Those appearing in COMMON (see next section) or in argument lists are called global variables. (It is the location that is global, not the variable; it is possible to use the same variable name in two routines and, as long as they are not related through either COMMON or the subprogram argument lists, they are local to each routine.) The rules of FORTRAN state that any value in a local variable appearing in a subprogram need not be saved by the system when the RETURN is executed.

Although most systems do save local variables and most programmers do expect that to happen (because of the tradition of many previous versions of the language), it is safer to resort to the proper mechanism: to use a statement called

SAVE any time that a subprogram will be called more than once and a value (or values) in it must not be destroyed. The variables listed after the SAVE statement are preserved after the execution of the routine and its value can be safely reaccessed upon returning to the subprogram. If SAVE appears without a variable list, all local variables in the subprogram are saved.

As an example, a subprogram is presented below which is used to compare a key against the records in a sequential file and return the information in that record. Since the subprogram will be used in many applications, it is efficient to have the subprogram also read in the file, thereby serving a dual purpose. However, it would be wasteful to read in the file each time the subprogram is accessed.

A good solution is to read in the file only the first time the subprogram is accessed and not thereafter. The coding places a logical variable in the routine which is initialized as .FALSE. in a DATA statement. The logical is set to .TRUE. when the file is read. Since a DATA statement is *not* executable, reentering the subprogram will *not* reset the variable to .FALSE. but will leave it as .TRUE. However, a SAVE is needed to ensure that the variable, as well as the data read from the file, is not destroyed between calls to that routine.

In this sample, the subprogram will read in the entire sequential file only on the first entry. This file consists of an account number and the amount in that account. On all accesses, including the first, the subprogram will search the entire file for that account, returning the amount if found and a value of -9999.00 if not found.

In the program it is necessary to save only those variables which are not in the argument list and which will be needed on future calls. However, the instruction SAVE with no variables listed will save all local variables, which in this case would also include the index, I. It is always safer to save all variables, although a selective SAVE is a good form of documentation.

```
      SUBROUTINE  FNDAMT  (KEY, AMT)
C
      LOGICAL     FILEIN, IEX
C
      DIMENSION   IACCNT(10000), BALANC(10000)
C
      SAVE  FILEIN, IACCNT, BALANC, NUMACT
C
      DATA  FILEIN/ .FALSE./
C
C                 on first entrance, check existence of input file,
C                     if there, open and input
      IF  (.NOT. FILEIN)  THEN
          INQUIRE  (FILE='BALANC', EXIST=IEX)
              IF  (.NOT. IEX)  STOP  'BALANC does not exist'
          OPEN (UNIT=11, FILE='BALANC', FORM='FORMATTED',STATUS='OLD')
C
C                     input routine
          READ    (11,1000, END=20) (IACCNT(I), BALANC(I), I=1,10000)
 1000     FORMAT  (I5, F9.2)
              CLOSE  (UNIT=11)
              STOP  'Excessive input  -  execution aborted'
   20     CLOSE   (UNIT=11)
          NUMACT = I - 1
          FILEIN = .TRUE.
      ENDIF
```

```
C
C                              enter here after first time
C                                 search through file
        DO 100  I = 1,NUMACT
            IF  (KEY .EQ. IACNT(I))  THEN
                AMT = BALANC(I)
                RETURN
            ENDIF
    100 CONTINUE
        AMT = -9999.00
C                          termination
        RETURN
        END
```

14.2 COMMON

In the treatment of subprograms in earlier chapters, an argument list was used to transmit information back and forth between calling and called programs. In that mechanism, the address of the variable, the constant, or the temporary location in which an expression is evaluated is transmitted to the called program and the called program utilizes that address in order to access the information.

An alternative method used to transmit information within a programming system utilizes an area in memory common to all modules. In most computers, the memory is laid out for execution of a program by placing the necessary parts of the operating system in low memory and building the executable program above it, usually in the order of mainline, followed by its subprograms, and then the system subprograms. The so-called COMMON area now being referred to usually begins at the top of memory and works down (in decreasing memory addresses).

In modern virtual memory machines and in computers that use memory bank switching, the addressing scheme is not as rigid and may use increasing addressing starting at some system-defined location. To the programmer, the method of storage of COMMON is transparent and the absolute addressing scheme does not matter; but the relative one, the one which associates variables in the multiple COMMON lists, does. Increasing addressing is assumed in this discussion only because it is easier to demonstrate. For example, in this code:

```
DOUBLE PRECISION  X
COMMON  I, J, K(4), X, Y, Z
```

the relative addresses (offset) from the beginning of the section of memory assigned to COMMON will be (in decimal):

Variable	Bytes	Offset
I	4	0
J	4	4
K(1–4)	16	8
X	8	24
Y	4	32
Z	4	36

A subprogram in the same system with the specifications:

```
DOUBLE PRECISION  T
COMMON  L(5), M, T, A(2)
```

would relate to the earlier common in the following way:

Offset	COMMON 1	COMMON 2
0	I	L(1)
4	J	L(2)
8	K(1)	L(3)
12	K(2)	L(4)
16	K(3)	L(5)
20	K(4)	M
24	X	T
32	Y	A(1)
36	Z	A(2)

This can be shown graphically, with each box equal to 4 bytes:

```
  I      J     K(1)   K(2)   K(3)   K(4)    X                 Y      Z
┌──────┬──────┬──────┬──────┬──────┬──────┬──────┬──────┬──────┬──────┬──────┐
│      │      │      │      │      │      │      │      │      │      │      │
└──────┴──────┴──────┴──────┴──────┴──────┴──────┴──────┴──────┴──────┴──────┘
  L(1)   L(2)   L(3)   L(4)   L(5)    M      T                A(1)   A(2)
```

As you may surmise, it is critical that the order of variables in the COMMON list agree in type. Note that the integers, reals, and double-precision reals (as well as any other kind of variable) must correspond, although the variable names need not be the same and arrays and single variables can be mixed.

There is an alternative method of specifying an array in COMMON by using the DIMENSION statement and then listing only the array name:

```
DOUBLE PRECISION   T
DIMENSION  L(5), A(2)
COMMON     L, M, T, A
```

One of the disadvantages of COMMON is that arrays must be specifically defined; variable array sizes are not possible. Thus, subprograms using COMMON lose their generality and cannot be used except with mainlines with arrays of exactly the same size. Considering the emphasis on general-purpose subprograms stressed throughout the text, this seems like a reversal of position. But because there are times when subprograms are specific and COMMON is more convenient (and sometimes necessary), its use must be considered. One of the advantages of using COMMON is that the variables in the COMMON list need not be in the argument list of either the calling or the called module.

Below is a simple programming system which will be converted to COMMON:

```
C                       Triangle Computations
C
      DIMENSION  SIDES(3), ANGLES(3)
C
C                  loop through input
      DO 20  NTIMES = 1,20000
         WRITE  (*,1000)
```

```
1000      FORMAT  ('0','Enter two sides, included angle')
          READ    (*,*, END=90) SIDES(1), SIDES(2), ANGLES(3)
          CALL COMPTR (SIDES, ANGLES, PERIM, AREA)
          WRITE   (*,1002) (SIDES(I), ANGLES(I), I=1,3)
1002      FORMAT  ('0','    Sides    Angles'/ (' ',2F10.2))
          WRITE   (*,1004) PERIM, AREA
1004      FORMAT  (' ','Perimeter =', F9.2/
     1             ' ','Area =',     F14.2)
   20 CONTINUE
C
   90 STOP
      END




      SUBROUTINE  COMPTR  (S, A, P, R)
C
      DIMENSION  S(3), A(3)
C
      PARAMETER  (PI = 3.14159)
      D2R (X) = X / 180.0 * PI
      R2D (X) = X * 180.0 / PI
C
C                 convert known angle to radians
      A(3) = D2R (A(3))
C                 get other side (3) by law of cosines
      S(3) = SQRT (S(1)**2 + S(2)**2
     1                  - 2.0 * S(1) * S(2) * COS (A(3)))
C                 get other angles (1 and 2) by law of sines
      A(1) = ASIN (SIN (A(3)) / S(3) * S(1))
      A(2) = ASIN (SIN (A(3)) / S(3) * S(2))
C                 get perimeter and area
      P = S(1) + S(2) + S(3)
      R = 0.5 * (S(1) * S(2) * SIN (A(3)))
C                 convert angles back to degrees
      DO 20  I = 1,3
   20 A(I) = R2D (A(I))
C                    return
      RETURN
      END
```

When converted to use COMMON, the routines become:

```
C                    Triangle Computations
C
      COMMON  SIDES(3), ANGLES(3), PERIM, AREA
C
C                 loop through input
      DO 20  NTIMES = 1,20000
          WRITE   (*,1000)
1000      FORMAT  ('0','Enter two sides, included angle')
          READ    (*,*, END=90) SIDES(1), SIDES(2), ANGLES(3)
          CALL COMPTR
          WRITE   (*,1002) (SIDES(I), ANGLES(I), I=1,3)
1002      FORMAT  ('0','    Sides    Angles'/ (' ',2F10.2))
          WRITE   (*,1004) PERIM, AREA
1004      FORMAT  (' ','Perimeter =', F9.2/
     1             ' ','Area =',     F14.2)
   20 CONTINUE
```

```
      C
         90 STOP
            END



            SUBROUTINE  COMPTR
      C
            COMMON  S(3), A(3), P, R
      C
            PARAMETER  (PI = 3.14159)
            D2R (X) = X / 180.0 * PI
            R2D (X) = X * 180.0 / PI
      C
      C                   convert known angle to radians
            A(3) = D2R (A(3))
      C                   get other side (3) by law of cosines
            S(3) = SQRT (S(1)**2 + S(2)**2
           1                   - 2.0 * S(1) * S(2) * COS (A(3)))
      C                   get other angles (1 and 2) by law of sines
            A(1) = ASIN (SIN (A(3)) / S(3) * S(1))
            A(2) = ASIN (SIN (A(3)) / S(3) * S(2))
      C                   get perimeter and area
            P = S(1) + S(2) + S(3)
            R = 0.5 * (S(1) * S(2) * SIN (A(3)))
      C                   convert angles back to degrees
            DO 20  I = 1,3
         20 A(I) = R2D (A(I))
      C                   return
            RETURN
            END
```

The COMMON equivalence table is:

Offset	Bytes	Type	Mainline	COMPTR
0	12	Real array	SIDES (1–3)	S (1–3)
12	12	Real array	ANGLES (1–3)	A (1–3)
24	4	Real	PERIM	P
28	4	Real	AREA	R

Note the removal of the argument lists in both the subroutine header and the CALL statement.

The COMMON list in the mainline must be complete, allocating all the space to be used for the COMMON area. The subprograms need only list the variables they need; but since the location in the list is critical, it is often necessary to use "dummy" (unused) locations to preserve the location (offset) in the list. The "safe" way is to duplicate the COMMON list in all modules of the system to avoid the possibility of error.

Furthermore, a combination of COMMON and argument list might be used. For example, in the above system:

```
C                       Triangle Computations
C
        COMMON  SIDES(3), ANGLES(3)
                        |
                        |
            CALL COMPTR (PERIM, AREA)
                        |
        END
        SUBROUTINE  COMPTR (P, R)
C
        COMMON S(3), A(3)
                        |
                        |
        END
```

is one of the valid combinations.

COMMON may also be used with functions to reduce the number of variables in the argument list. A function whose input arguments are completely contained within COMMON may appear with no argument list. The accessing statement retains the parentheses, but the list is empty. The header of the accessed function need not contain the parentheses. For example, assume a function EXMPLE which receives two input arguments, both contained in COMMON. The accessing and accessed partial programs might appear as:

```
C                       Mainline
        COMMON  A, B
                |
                |
        X = EXMPLE()
                |
                |
        END


C                       Function
        FUNCTION  EXMPLE
        COMMON  A, B
C
        EXMPLE = 5.0 * A  -  2.0 * B
C
        RETURN
        END
```

The use of COMMON does have an advantage during execution in that the memory locations are set during compilation and do not have to be transmitted during execution; thus the program will execute faster.

There is one guideline which most professional programmers follow: COMMON is useful when a large number of modules and a large number of variables are to be transmitted; usually the variable names will be the same in all modules, so that the COMMON statement(s) can be duplicated to avoid errors. This also avoids long argument lists.

And now a serious warning! On some systems, large arrays (exceeding 64K = 65536) must be defined in COMMON and not just in the DIMENSION statement. This is due to the method in which the software accesses the memory banks. Since many computers, especially micros and minis, use banks of memories—usually in 64K modules—rather than being able to address the full memory at any time, an array which spills over from one bank to another can lead to an access problem. Furthermore, the programmer should check the FORTRAN manual for his or her machine very carefully, since the compiler may require that programs with large arrays have an additional option included with the compile (and link) command.

Another problem is that an array element cannot cross over from one memory bank to another nor can an I/O command read or write across a memory break. Thus large arrays must be set up so that they can be input/output properly. A character array of:

```
CHARACTER*60  BIGA(1100)
```

will cross over a 64K memory break. An attempt to write or read element BIGA(1093), the element over the break, will lose information, even if in COMMON. Likewise, an integer array:

```
COMMON  IRAY(60,300)
```

using an implied DO loop to write one record:

```
WRITE   (8,1000)  (IRAY(J,I), J=1,60)
```

will not write part of that array correctly when the computer tries to switch 64K memory banks.

The only possible solution is to set up arrays so that the elements and records break at the memory bank border. Whereas $65536/60 = 1092.2666$, we know that $65536/64 = 1024$, which is an integer. Thus:

```
CHARACTER*64  BIGA(1100)
```

will work, as will:

```
COMMON  IRAY(64,300)
```

since 64 four-byte integers total 256, a factor of 65536.

Review Questions and Exercises

14.2a   For the COMMON statements below, set up an equivalency table similar to the ones given in the text above. All relate to the same programming system:

```
CHARACTER*12  CCC
COMMON  A(5), B(2), I(7), CCC
CHARACTER*12  C12
COMMON  T, U, V, W, X, Y, Z, I1, I2, I3, I4, I5, I6, I7, C12
COMMON  R(7), J(2)
CHARACTER*12  ICH
COMMON  DUMMY(6), Q, M, IDUMMY(6), ICH
```

14.2b   Revise exercise 9.8c by placing all the arrays into COMMON; also add to COMMON the number of records and the variable used for the subscript of the arrays. Then revise the modules LOCAPT and INVERSE by removing the argument lists completely, and revise the module EDIT by removing the argument for distance. Adjust the CALL statements accordingly.

14.2c Revise exercise 9.8d by placing all the arrays into COMMON except the totals and use that COMMON in the subprograms. The functions may have as few as zero arguments. Revise so that the argument lists are reduced as much as possible.

14.2d Revise exercise 10.7a by placing all of the input values, the egg and cost arrays, the number of input records, the total cost, and the customer cost in COMMON. Write an input subroutine that opens the file, inputs all the records, and closes the file. Then include a calculational subroutine to compute the customer cost and total cost. Neither of the subroutines should require an argument list. The access to subroutine BRKDWN need not change.

14.2e Revise exercise 10.7c by placing the needed arrays into COMMON. Then place the code for the output generation into a subroutine. No argument list should be needed.

14.2f Revise exercise 10.7e by placing the needed arrays and the record pointer into COMMON, both in the mainline and in subroutines BBCALC and BBSTAT. Remove the argument lists entirely. (An earlier version, exercise 8.8a or 9.8a, may be used as a starting point.)

14.3 NAMED COMMON AND BLOCK DATA

Very large programming systems usually have a very large number of variables listed in COMMON. However, this tends to become unwieldy because there are often subprograms which will be using only a small number of those variables and a long variable list may be confusing to the programmer. One solution is a dummy array:

```
Mainline:      COMMON  I, J, K(5), L(5), X, Y
Subroutine A:  COMMON  M, N, IDUMMY(10), A, B
Subroutine B:  COMMON  I, J, K(5), L(5), DUMMY, B
```

But another method is available that is more sophisticated and elegant.

COMMON can be reduced to separate blocks. Each block is named so that the blocks may be distinguished from one another, and each block is stored in a distinct location in memory. All of the COMMON blocks must appear in the mainline, but only those blocks needed by a particular subprogram need be present in that subprogram.

One of the blocks may be unnamed, equivalent to the COMMON described in the previous section. An alternative notation for blank COMMON includes a pair of slashes with nothing between them:

```
COMMON  // X(20), Y(20), Z(20), NUMPTS, NERR
```

Unnamed (or blank) COMMON may also appear in a subprogram when needed.

Naming a COMMON block means placing that name between two slashes at the beginning of the COMMON list. The name used can be any identifying name which is not the same as any subprogram, either user-written or system; it can be the same as a variable name, even one in the COMMON block. This new approach leads to COMMON statements like these:

```
Mainline:      COMMON   I, J, Y
               COMMON   /INTEGER/   K(5), L(5)
               COMMON   /REAL/      X

Subroutine A:  COMMON   M, N, B
               COMMON   /REAL/ A

Subroutine B:  COMMON   I, J, B
               COMMON   /INTEGER/ K(5), L(5)
```

where there are unnamed or blank COMMONs for the variables present in all three routines and named COMMONs for the variables used in only one subprogram.
Another example is:

```
COMMON   X(20), Y(20), Z(20), NUMPTS, NERR
COMMON /GROUPA/   TEMPRT(20), PRESSR(20), HUMID(20)
COMMON /GROUPB/   MESSGE(10,14), ITIME(3), IDATE(3)
```

where the first line is the unnamed or blank COMMON and there are two blocks of named COMMON: GROUPA and GROUPB. Blank COMMON, if it exists, is usually placed first.
The subprograms in the system might have:

```
SUBROUTINE  A
COMMON   X(20), Y(20), Z(20), NUMPTS, NERR
COMMON /GROUPA/   TEMPRT(20), PRESSR(20), HUMID(20)
        :
        :
```

and

```
SUBROUTINE  B
COMMON   X(20), Y(20), Z(20), NUMPTS
COMMON /GROUPB/   MESSGE(10,14), ITIME(3), IDATE(3)
        :
        :
```

Note that variables unused in the subprograms located at the end of the blank COMMON may be left off. However, named COMMON must be identical in all routines in which it appears.
Generally, the variables used in all routines are placed in blank COMMON and those which appear only in some routines are placed in named COMMON.
In the triangle computation program presented in section 14.1, the COMMON might have been broken down as follows:

```
C                          Triangle Computations
C
      COMMON  /INPUT/   SIDES(3), ANGLES(3)
      COMMON  /OUTPUT/ PERIM,    AREA
                   |
                   |
                   |
      CALL COMPTR
                   |
      END
```

```
         SUBROUTINE  COMPTR
   C
         COMMON  /INPUT/  S(3), A(3)
         COMMON  /OUTPUT/ P,    R
                          |
                          |
                          |
         END
```

One very critical difference between the two types of COMMON is in the treatment of the DATA statement. Blank COMMON cannot predefine data using that statement; named COMMON can, but only by using a special routine called BLOCK DATA. (Because FORTRAN ignores blanks, the statement can also be written BLOCKDATA.) This latter module is like a subprogram in that it is a separate module and is linked into the mainline, but it is not called (i.e., there is no CALL statement). It is used only to initialize variables in named COMMON and can consist only of the following statements:

BLOCK DATA	required header
IMPLICIT	optional
PARAMETER	optional
DIMENSION	required if necessary
COMMON	required
DATA	required
END	required

Below is a simple, but practical, use of BLOCK DATA to place error messages into variables to be used in a programming system. A simple test program is also given. The BLOCK DATA is compiled separately and then linked into the mainline.

```
         BLOCK DATA
   C
         CHARACTER*20  MESSGE(6)
   C
         COMMON  /MSGES/  MESSGE, NUMMSG
   C
         DATA  MESSGE/'File does not exist ', 'Excessive data      ',
        1                'Invalid character   ', 'Data out of range   ',
        2                'Data overflow       ', 'Program error       '/
         DATA  NUMMSG/ 6/
   C
         END


   C                  Test of Block Data
   C
         CHARACTER*20  MESSGE(6)
   C
         COMMON  /MSGES/  MESSGE, NUMMSG
   C
         DO 20  NTIMES = 1,2000
            PRINT *, 'Enter number from 1 to 6'
            READ   (*,*, END=90)  NUM
            IF  (NUM .LT. 1  .OR.  NUM .GT. NUMMSG)  GO TO 90
            PRINT *,  MESSGE(NUM)
      20 CONTINUE
   C
      90 STOP
         END
```

The BLOCK DATA statement may also contain an optional name, but it must not conflict with the name of any subprogram, user-written or system, or any executable program. For example, the above program may have been headed with:

```
BLOCK DATA  INITMS
```

The named COMMON group in BLOCK DATA may also contain variables not defined in the DATA statement. In other words, the above routine would also have been valid with the statement:

```
COMMON  /MSGES/  MESSGE, NUMMSG, OTHERS
```

This allows for the need to keep named COMMON identical in length in all routines.

Exercises

14.3a Write a BLOCK DATA module containing the names of the 12 months. Use an array of 12 nine-character variables called MONTHS, placed into named COMMON, also named MONTHS. Place the months right-justified in the fields, with leading, not trailing, blanks for month names having fewer than nine characters. Write a test program to check out the module which accepts a number from 1 to 12 and displays the month.

14.3b Modify the system written in exercise 14.2d to use named COMMON and blank COMMON. Named COMMON should contain the variable for total cost and the customer cost array; they should be initialized to zero in a BLANK DATA module.

14.4 EQUIVALENCE

This statement, which equates memory locations of variable names, allows the programmer to:

1. Lay out memory in a desired fashion
2. Overlay arrays to save memory
3. Simulate a data structure
4. Have multiple names for the same location

Usually the first property is not of much interest to anyone other than system programmers who might be interfacing with machine or assembly language code; it is also sometimes useful in reducing the code necessary for sophisticated I/O. Applications of that type will not be described, but their use should become obvious from the forthcoming discussion.

The second property is extremely useful in computers with limited memory. In situations where two or more large arrays are not needed simultaneously, they can share the same location. This is no different than two people sharing the same car if they use it at different times. The two (or more) arrays are dimensioned and then equated by "lining up" an element from each, such as:

```
DIMENSION   AR1(50,200),  AR2(16000)
EQUIVALENCE (AR1(1,1),    AR2(1))
```

Thus AR1(1,1) shares a memory location with AR2(1); AR1(2,1) with AR2(2); AR1(3,1) with AR2(3); and so forth up to AR1(50,200) and AR2(10000). The array elements from AR2(10001) to AR2(16000) do not share the memory with any other variables. Because of the way arrays are stored, the same relationship would occur if we used:

```
EQUIVALENCE  (AR1(2,1), AR2(2))
```

or

```
EQUIVALENCE  (AR1(1,2), AR2(51))
```

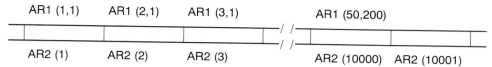

"Sharing a memory location" actually means that the machine is addressing a memory location by more than one variable name. In the above relationship, the code:

```
AR1(2,1) = 12.45
PRINT  *, AR2(2)
```

would yield the output 12.45.

The syntax of the EQUIVALENCE statement is to follow that command with groups of array elements or single variables, separated by commas and enclosed in a set of parentheses. A third array may be set equivalent to two previously "lined up" arrays by either a second EQUIVALENCE or by a single one with the three entered. For example:

```
DIMENSION    I(10), J(8), K(6)
```

with

```
EQUIVALENCE  (I(4), J(1)), (I(1), K(2))
```

is the same as:

```
EQUIVALENCE  (I(4), J(1), K(5))
```

with both leading to this memory layout:

I(1)	I(2)	I(3)	I(4) J(1)	I(5) J(2)	I(6) J(3)	I(7) J(4)	I(8) J(5)	I(9) J(6)	I(10) J(7)	J(8)
K(1)	K(2)	K(3)	K(4) K(5)	K(6)						

Any incorrect equivalences which lead to a "memory warp," such as:

```
EQUIVALENCE  (I(4), J(1)), (I(1), K(2)), (J(2), K(2))
```

will generate an error message during compilation.

Properties 3 and 4 are illustrated by the following example. Assume an input record consisting of five integer values:

Elements 1–3: date (month, day, year)
Element 4: low temperature for the day
Element 5: high temperature for the day

A program using this data structure might look like:

```
      DIMENSION  INREC(5), IDATE(3)
C
      EQUIVALENCE  (INREC(1), IDATE(1)),  (INREC(4), LOW),
     1                               (INREC(5), IHIGH)
C                         input record
      READ    (*,*)  INREC
      MEAN  = (LOW + IHIGH) / 2
      WRITE   (*,1000)  IDATE, MEAN
 1000 FORMAT  (' ', 'Date: ',I2,'/',I2,'/',I2, '    Mean =',I3)
```

Property 4 also allows the equivalence of two or more single variables, such as:

```
      EQUIVALENCE  (IHIGH, IHGH),  (NUMREC, NREC)
```

This is very useful when correcting spelling errors or for improving program documentation.

Review Questions

14.4a   A program consists of the following statements:

```
      DIMENSION  I(10),  J(5)
C
      EQUIVALENCE  (J(1), I(4)), (KK, I(1)), (LL, I(5))
C
      DO 20  N = 1,10
   20 I(N) = N
C
      PRINT *, J, KK, LL
C
      STOP
      END
```

Describe fully the memory layout and the values output.

14.4b   For the following memory layout:

```
      DIMENSION    I(5,30), J(8,4,2), K(100)
      EQUIVALENCE  (I(1,1),  J(1,1,1), K(1))
```

determine the total memory locations (assuming 4-byte storage for each integer variable) required both without and with the EQUIVALENCE and calculate the memory saved therein.

14.5   A PROGRAMMING SYSTEM

Finally, you are ready for the most sophisticated programming system presented in this text, the application program involving billing for unpaid traffic tickets. The system consists of four mainlines, two specific subprograms, and two general-purpose subprograms. The system requires three files:

File 1: VIOLAT.DAT: a SAM file consisting of three fields:

Field Description	Columns
2-character violation code	1– 2
30-character violation description	5–34
2-digit fine	39–40

Sample File

```
OV   Overtime unmetered parking      5
OM   Overtime parking at meter       5
PD   Parked in driveway             25
PF   Parked at fire hydrant         50
PB   Parked in bus stop             25
PX   Parked in crosswalk            20
PR   Parked in restricted area      30
PT   Parked on railroad tracks      40
PH   Parked in handicapped spot     40
P2   Parked across two spots        15
```

File 2: PLATE.DAT: a DAM file with record-count header and detail records consisting of six fields, sorted on the first

Field Description	Columns
8-character license plate number	1– 8
18-character name of car owner	11–28
18-character address	31–48
12-character town	51–62
2-character state code	64–65
5-digit zip code	66–70

Sample File

```
      4
I WRENCH   Montgomery Scott    418 Argyle Street   Vancouver    WA98661
LOGIC 2    *@#%##@* Spock      314-159 Pi Place     Schenectady  NY12301
MD BONES   Leonard McCoy       77 Bourbon Avenue    Aragon       GA30161
NCC 1701   James T. Kirk       31 Rand Court        Storm Lake   IA51101
```

File 3: OUTSTN.DAT: an unsorted DAM file with record-count header and detail records consisting of 5 fields:

Field Description	Columns
8-character license plate number	1– 8
1-character deletion code (nonblank if fine is paid)	10
8-character date	11–18
2-character violation code	19–20
2-digit fine	21–22

Sample File

```
        8
LOGIC 2    02/28/92P215
I WRENCH   02/28/92PT40
NCC 1701   03/01/92PH40
I WRENCH   03/22/92OM 5
I WRENCH   03/23/92OM 5
MD BONES   03/23/92OV 5
MD BONES   03/23/92PH40
NCC 1701   03/23/92PT40
```

In both DAM files, the first record has a count of the number of records following (see section 13.1f), with the detail records starting at record 2; the record count does not include the first record. (We advise that you study the full description of the programming system in Appendix A, especially the file structure, prior to examining the various programming modules below.)

The two general-purpose subprograms are:

1. FUNCTION IASRCH (CHRAY, NREC, KEY): a search routine which receives a character array, the number of records in that array, and a character key of the same number of characters as the array to match against. It returns the record number of the found record or zero if not found. (No solution is provided because of its similarity to exercise 11.4c.)

2. SUBROUTINE ASORT (CHKEY,NREC,NITEM, ICARRY,INDI, RCARRY,INDR): an ascending character sort with the same arguments as the sort algorithm presented in Chapter 11. (No solution is provided because of its similarity to exercise 11.3d.)

The first module, FUNCTION NUMVIO, provides the caller with two features: (1) read violations from disk file into memory and (2) get location (subscript) of particular violation in arrays. It is usual to refer to the collection of the three arrays read in as a table since there is a correspondence between the records of each; i.e., the first record of each of the three correspond, the second record likewise, etc. A multidimensional array could not be used because of the different types of arrays. The use of COMMON in this programming system reduces the argument list in both calling and called programs.

**Parking
Violations**

```
      C                         Function NUMVIO
      C
            FUNCTION  NUMVIO  (VCODE)
      C
      C   Abstract:  on first entry, reads in violation description file into
      C                   COMMON arrays for code, description and fine.   On
      C                   all entries, returns subscript of violation.
      C
      C   Input:      VCODE    Violation code (Character * 2)
      C
      C   Output:     NUMVIO   Subscript of violation in table.  Return 0 if
      C                            violation not in table.  (Integer)
      C
            CHARACTER*2    VCODE, VIOCOD
            CHARACTER*30   VDESCR
            LOGICAL        FILEIN
      C
            COMMON   VIOCOD(20), VDESCR(20), IFINE(20), NVIO
      C
            SAVE     FILEIN
            DATA     FILEIN/ .FALSE./
      C
      C                     if first input, read in violation table
            IF  (.NOT. FILEIN)  THEN
                 FILEIN = .TRUE.
                 OPEN   (4, FILE='VIOLAT.DAT, STATUS='OLD', FORM='FORMATTED')
                 DO 40  I = 1,20
        40       READ   (4,1040, END=60) VIOCOD(I), VDESCR(I), IFINE(I)
      1040       FORMAT               (A2,      2X,   A30, 4X,  I2)
                     STOP  'excessive data in VIOLAT.DAT'
        60       CLOSE  (4)
                 NVIO = I - 1
            ENDIF
      C                     get subscript of entry
            DO 80  NUMVIO = 1,NVIO
                 IF  (VCODE .EQ. VIOCOD(NUMVIO))  RETURN
        80 CONTINUE
      C                     violation not found;  return 0
            NUMVIO = 0
            RETURN
            END
```

Since this is an ongoing application, there is no need to test for the existence of the file VIOLAT.DAT. In most cases, that file would be generated and so protected that it could not be accidentally erased. This is a standard procedure with files that seldom require changes.

The logical FILEIN is used to indicate whether it is the first access of the routine. If it is, the file is opened, read, and closed. The search is sequential because the violation codes may not be alphabetized. The arrays are large enough for future expansion.

The second module reads in part of the license plate file. Since the file may be too large to read into memory entirely, by reading in the field that serves as the key to the file—the unique key that identifies the record—that key serves as an index which can later be searched. Named COMMON was used here just for variety.

When reading the file, the record accessed is one higher than the record number of the data, since the first record in the file contains the count of the number of records following it. Thus data record 1 is at physical (file) record 2, data record 2 at physical record 3, etc. The file was not closed in the routine because it will be accessed later by the calling programs.

```
C                     Subroutine NUMLIC
C
      SUBROUTINE  NUMLIC
C
C     Abstract: opens file PLATE.DAM, returns index, number of records
C
      COMMON  /PLATE/ PLATE(20000), NPLATE
C
      CHARACTER*8  PLATE
C
C                     scan license plate file for agreement
      OPEN    (7, FILE='PLATE.DAT', STATUS='OLD', FORM='FORMATTED',
     1          ACCESS='DIRECT', RECL=70)
      READ    (7,1000, REC=1)  NPLATE
 1000 FORMAT  (I6)
          IF  (NPLATE .GT. 20000)  STOP  'excessive data in PLATE.DAT'
      DO 20  I = 1,NPLATE
   20 READ  (7,1020, REC=I+1)  PLATE(I)
 1020 FORMAT              (A8)
      RETURN
      END
```

The first mainline (Project 4, Module 3) provides the ability to add violations to the file OUTSTN.DAT. The call to NUMLIC reads the plates on PLATE.DAT into the array PLATE. Then the file OUTSTN.DAT is opened and the number therein input. The input to the program is from the keyboard:

```
C           Project 4, Module 3:  Update Outstanding Violation File
C
      CHARACTER*1   DELCOD
      CHARACTER*2   VCODE, VIOCOD
      CHARACTER*8   PLATE, PLATIN, DATE
      CHARACTER*30  VDESCR
C
      LOGICAL  ERROR
C
      COMMON  VIOCOD(20), VDESCR(20), IFINE(20), NVIO
      COMMON /PLATE/ PLATE(20000), NPLATE
C
      DATA    DELCOD/ ' '/
C
C                 open PLATE.DAT and get plates
      CALL NUMLIC
C                 open OUTSTN.DAT
      OPEN    (8, FILE='OUTSTN.DAT', ACCESS='DIRECT', FORM='FORMATTED',
     1          STATUS='OLD',      RECL=22)
      READ    (8,1000), REC=1)  NOUTST
 1000 FORMAT  (I6)
```

```
C
C                              loop through input
          DO 20  NTIMES = 1,20000
                WRITE   (*,1002)  NPLATE, NOUTST
     1002       FORMAT  ('0',I6,' license plates records and',
    1                         I4,' outstanding violations on file'/
    2                    ' ','Enter new license plate  (EOD to terminate)'/
    3                    ' ','_____')
                READ    (*,1004, END=900)  PLATIN
     1004       FORMAT  (A8)
                ERROR = .FALSE.
C                        check against license plate file
                IREC = IASRCH (PLATE, NPLATE, PLATIN)
                IF  (IREC .EQ. 0)  THEN
                    WRITE   (*,1006)
     1006           FORMAT  (' ','LICENSE PLATE INFORMATION NOT ON FILE')
                    ERROR = .TRUE.
                ENDIF
C                        input violation
                IF  (.NOT. ERROR)  THEN
                    WRITE   (*,1008)
     1008           FORMAT  (' ','Enter violation code'/' ','__')
                    READ    (*,1010, END=900)  VCODE
     1010           FORMAT  (A2)
                    NV = NUMVIO (VCODE)
                    IF  (NV .EQ. 0)  THEN
                        WRITE   (*,1012)
     1012               FORMAT  (' ','INVALID VIOLATION CODE')
                        ERROR = .TRUE.
                    ENDIF
                ENDIF
C                        display fine, get date
                IF  (.NOT. ERROR)  THEN
                    WRITE   (*,1014)  IFINE(NV)
     1014           FORMAT  (' ','Fine = $',I2/
    1                         ' ','Enter date'/
    2                         ' ','__/__/__')
                    READ    (*,1004, END=900)  DATE
C                        update file
                    NOUTST = NOUTST + 1
                    WRITE   (8,1016, REC=NOUTST+1)
    1                         PLATIN, DELCOD, DATE, VCODE, IFINE(NV)
     1016           FORMAT  (A8, 1X, A1,     A8,    A2,           I2)
                    WRITE   (8,1000, REC=1)  NOUTST
                ENDIF
       20 CONTINUE
C                        close files and terminate
      900 CLOSE   (7)
          CLOSE   (8)
          STOP
          END
```

After a plate number is entered and the error indicator is turned off, the array PLATE is searched for an entry; if it is found, the record number is in IREC, otherwise the error indicator is turned on. If the plate exists, the violation code is entered and it is checked with function NUMVIO for a match; on the first access to the function, the file VIOLAT.DAT is read in and the number of violations on the file, NVIO, determined. If no match is found, the error indicator is turned on.

If no error has occurred, the value of the fine assigned to that violation is displayed and the user is prompted to enter the date. The file is updated by adding the record to the next available location in the DAM file (following the previous last record), and the new record counter is written to record 1. This last write is not really necessary until the end of the run. It is a safety precaution in case of a bombout or a power outage; at the end of any transaction, the file is up to date. The program continues to accept data until the end-of-data character is entered.

The fourth module of the application is similar to the third in its initial coding. This module accesses the files and displays any records corresponding to the input license plate. In addition, it totals the fines on the outstanding tickets. It also gives the user the ability to indicate whether a fine has been paid.

```
C               Project 4, Module 4:  Displays Outstanding Violation File
C
        CHARACTER*1   DELCOD
        CHARACTER*2   VCODE, VIOCOD
        CHARACTER*4   PAID
        CHARACTER*8   PLATE, PLATIN, PLATFL, DATE
        CHARACTER*30  VDESCR
        CHARACTER*70  NAMADR
C
        LOGICAL   ERROR
C
        COMMON  VIOCOD(20), VDESCR(20), IFINE(20), NVIO
        COMMON /PLATE/ PLATE(20000), NPLATE
C
        DIMENSION  INDEX(100)
C
C                      open PLATE.DAT and get PLATES, NPLATE
        CALL NUMLIC
C                      open OUTSTN.DAT and get number of records
        OPEN  (8, FILE='OUTSTN.DAT', ACCESS='DIRECT', FORM='FORMATTED',
       1          STATUS='OLD',       RECL=22)
        READ    (8,1000, REC=1)  NOUTST
 1000 FORMAT  (I6)
        WRITE   (*,1002)
 1002 FORMAT  ('0','Display of Outstanding Violations')
C                      loop through input
        DO 100 NTIMES = 1,20000
          WRITE   (*,1004)
 1004     FORMAT  ('0','Enter license plate  (EOD to terminate)'/
       1          ' ','_____')
          READ    (*,1006, END=900)  PLATIN
 1006     FORMAT  (A8)
          ERROR = .FALSE.
C                          check against license plate file
          IREC = IASRCH (PLATE, NPLATE, PLATIN)
          IF  (IREC .EQ. 0)  THEN
            WRITE   (*,1008)
 1008       FORMAT  (' ','LICENSE PLATE INFORMATION NOT ON FILE')
            ERROR = .TRUE.
          ENDIF
```

```
C                               display record
            IF  (.NOT. ERROR)  THEN
                READ     (7,1010, REC=IREC+1)  NAMADR
  1010           FORMAT  (A70)
                WRITE    (*,1012)  NAMADR(11:28), NAMADR(31:48),
     1             NAMADR(51:62), NAMADR(64:65), NAMADR(66:70)
  1012           FORMAT  (' ','Name:      ',A18/
     1                    ' ','Address: ',A18/
     2                    ' ', 9X,A12, 2X,A2, 2X,A5/)
C                         scan outstanding violation file
                ITFINE = 0
                NUMOUT = 0
                DO 20  I = 1,NOUTST
                    READ     (8,1014,REC=I+1)
     1                       PLATFL, DELCOD, DATE, VCODE, JFINE
  1014               FORMAT  (A8,1X, A1,     A8,   A2,       I2)
                    IF  (PLATIN .EQ. PLATFL)  THEN
                        NUMOUT = NUMOUT + 1
                        INDEX(NUMOUT) = I + 1
                        IF  (DELCOD .EQ. ' ')  THEN
                            PAID = '     '
                          ELSE
                            PAID = 'Paid'
                        ENDIF
                        ISUB = NUMVIO(VCODE)
                        WRITE    (*,1016)
     1                      NUMOUT,   DATE, VDESCR(ISUB), JFINE, PAID
  1016                   FORMAT  (' ',I3,'. ',A8,  2X,A30,   I5,2X,A4)
                        IF  (DELCOD .EQ. ' ') ITFINE = ITFINE + JFINE
                    ENDIF
  20            CONTINUE
                IF  (ITFINE .EQ. 0)  THEN
                    WRITE    (*,1020)
  1020               FORMAT  (' ','No outstanding tickets on file')
                  ELSE
                    WRITE    (*,1022)  ITFINE
  1022               FORMAT  (' ','Total outstanding fines:', I26//
     1                        ' ','Enter number of violation if paid, '
     2                                         '0 to return')
                    READ   (*,*, END=100)  N
                    IF  (N .GT. 0  .AND.  N .LE. NUMOUT)  THEN
                        READ     (8,1014,REC=INDEX(N))
     1                           PLATFL, DELCOD, DATE, VCODE, JFINE
                        DELCOD = '*'
                        WRITE    (8,1014,REC=INDEX(N))
     1                           PLATFL, DELCOD, DATE, VCODE, JFINE
                    ENDIF
                ENDIF
            ENDIF
  100 CONTINUE
C                       close files and terminate
  900 CLOSE   (7)
      CLOSE   (8)
      STOP
      END
```

Again the user is prompted to enter the license plate, and again the array PLATE is searched for a match. If a match occurs, the program reads the plate file (using REC = IREC + 1 because the first record contains the record counter) and displays the record therein (name and address). It then lists all of the outstanding tickets by scanning file OUTSTN.DAT looking for a match. Whenever it finds a match to the plate which has not been paid (delete code DELCOD blank), it displays the violation with the description and fine (with the subscript obtained from NUMVIO) and a total of the outstanding fines.

The user is then given the option of indicating that the fine has been paid by inputting a nonzero number corresponding to the listed violations. If so indicated, the delete code (DELCOD) is changed to a nonblank character and the record is rewritten to the file. Note the use of the array INDEX which stores the physical (file) data record number so that the file may be updated easily.

Module 5 reads the outstanding violation file first by reading in only the plate number. It then performs a key/record sort on the plate number with the physical record number in the array IREC. The resulting displayed output appears in license plate order, with subtotals for each plate. Again the physical record number is used in the carry-along array for quick access. The look-ahead method is used for level breaks, and grand totals are displayed at the end.

```
C              Project 4, Module 5:  Sort Outstanding Violation File
C
       CHARACTER     DELCOD*1,      VCODE*2
       CHARACTER*8   PLTOUT(10000), DATE
C
       DIMENSION  IREC(10000)
C
       DATA       ISBTOT, IGRTOT/ 2*0/
C
C                   open outstanding file
       OPEN    (8, FILE='OUTSTN.DAT', ACCESS='DIRECT', FORM='FORMATTED',
     1           STATUS='OLD',    RECL=22)
       READ    (8,1000)  NOUTST
  1000 FORMAT  (I6)
C                   read in plates and set record number
       DO 20  I = 1,NOUTST
           READ   (8,1002, REC=I+1)  PLTOUT(I)
  1002     FORMAT  (A8)
    20 IREC(I) = I+1
C              sort  (see exercise 11.3d for alphameric sort)
       CALL ASORT (PLTOUT,NOUTST,1, IREC,1, RCARRY,0)
C              output
       DO 100  I = 1,NOUTST
           READ (8,1020,REC=IREC(I))  DELCOD, DATE, VCODE, JFINE
  1020     FORMAT             (9X, A1,    A8,  A2,      I2)
           IF  (DELCOD .EQ. ' ')  THEN
               WRITE  (*,1022)  PLTOUT(I), DELCOD, DATE, VCODE, JFINE
  1022         FORMAT  (' ',A8, 2X,A1, 2X,A8, 2X,A2, I5)
               ISBTOT = ISBTOT + JFINE
               IF  (I        .EQ. NOUTST      .OR.
     1             PLTOUT(I) .NE. PLTOUT(I+1))  THEN
                   WRITE  (*,1024)  ISBTOT
  1024             FORMAT  (' ','Subtotal:',I21/)
                   IGRTOT = IGRTOT + ISBTOT
                   ISBTOT = 0
               ENDIF
           ENDIF
   100 CONTINUE
       WRITE  (*,1100)  IGRTOT
  1100 FORMAT  (' ','Grand Total:', I18)
```

```
C                            close files and terminate
      CLOSE   (8)
      STOP
      END
```

In this module, a paid fine resulted in an indicator being turned on within the violation record. It would have been possible, but very inefficient, to have packed the file each time a fine was paid. It is much more efficient to pack all of the paid violations at one time. The final module is used to do just that. The methodology used is to write directly over the existing records. Since records are being eliminated, the records being kept are moving to an earlier position in the file; thus when the record is rewritten, the program will not be writing over a record not yet read. This method would *not* work if records were being added to the file; then two files would have to be used if it were not possible to bring the entire file into memory.

Two pointers are used here, one to point to the old record and one to point to the new. Since all records will be read, the old pointer is controlled by the DO loop; the new pointer gets updated only when a fine remains unpaid; i.e., the delete code is blank. (The reader is advised to play computer with this routine, especially when the file is emptied.) For efficiency, a file write takes place only when a record moves.

```
C             Project 4, Module 6:   Pack Outstanding Violation File
C
      CHARACTER*22  OUTSTN
C
      DATA       IPTNEW/ 0/
C
C                    open data file
      OPEN    (8, FILE='OUTSTN.DAT', STATUS='OLD', ACCESS='DIRECT',
     1             FORM='FORMATTED',  RECL=22)
      READ    (8,1000, REC=1)  NOUTST
 1000 FORMAT  (I6)
C                    loop through file
      DO 20  IPTOLD = 1,NOUTST
         READ    (8,1002, REC=IPTOLD+1)  OUTSTN
 1002    FORMAT  (A22)
C                         check delete code
         IF  (OUTSTN(10:10) .EQ. ' ')  THEN
            IPTNEW = IPTNEW + 1
C                            write only if record moving to new location
            IF  (IPTOLD .NE. IPTNEW)
     1            WRITE  (8,1002, REC=IPTNEW+1)  OUTSTN
         ENDIF
   20 CONTINUE
C                      write number of records
      WRITE  (8,1000, REC=1)       IPTNEW
C                      read and write last record, then endfile, close
      READ    (8,1002, REC=IPTNEW+1)  OUTSTN
      WRITE   (8,1002, REC=IPTNEW+1)  OUTSTN
      ENDFILE  8
      CLOSE   (8)
      WRITE   (*,1020)  NOUTST, IPTNEW
 1020 FORMAT  ('0',I5,' records in old file,',
     1              I6,' records in new file')
      STOP
      END
```

In order to make the ENDFILE truncate the file correctly, it is necessary to write the last record on the file. Since the program may not do that (if no records are deleted), the safe way is to read and write the last record under any circumstances and then use the ENDFILE.

14.6   CHAPTER REVIEW

With the completion of this chapter, you have now been exposed to a thorough treatment of the FORTRAN language. There is little more that can be gathered from reading; experience is the best teacher from here on out.

This section does not contain any exercises, since the following chapter is devoted exclusively to that; there the reader will get some real experience!

The topics covered in this chapter include:

Topic	Section
BLOCK DATA	14.3
COMMON	14.2, 14.3
Direct access files	14.5
EQUIVALENCE	14.4
EXPLICIT	14.1
INQUIRE	14.5
INTRINSIC	14.1
Named COMMON	14.3
SAVE	14.1
Sequential access files	14.5

15

Advanced Projects

CHAPTER OBJECTIVES

- To present a series of challenging and useful projects for developing the programming skills of the reader.

- To acquaint the reader with the methodologies used in the professional programming environment.

15.1 INTRODUCTION

There is a significant difference between the environments in which students and professional programmers work. It is often quite a shock when a recent graduate enters the work force and finds that what had been considered difficult programs are insignificant exercises compared with the extensive programming systems encountered in a production environment.

This is not meant to degrade the student's efforts, since the learning process never ends. Even after more than a quarter-century of working with the language, as both a teacher and a professional, the author continues to develop new FORTRAN techniques. In the early days of FORTRAN, the programs written were even simpler than those presented in this text, but as time progressed, written programs expanded. It is fair to say that you have a great deal of catching up to do.

On the other hand, even with the rough tools available in the early days, it was easier for the professional then because there was very little catching up to do. There were very few large programs (remember, computer memories were very limited in size) and, when one was available, it was often distributed with the computer by the manufacturer as a sales enticement. Also, users were supplied with the source code so they could study the techniques other programmers used. There was little concern then about "stolen" code because we all shared our new programs by giving them away or publishing them in technical journals.

Programmers then, as now, learned by studying the code of other programmers and also contributed to the discipline by sharing techniques they had developed. The major difference between then and now is that with so little to learn, it was far easier to become an "expert" then!

Although in this chapter we will not be able to provide the equivalent of 30 years of experience, we can give you a glimpse into the more interesting types of programs that have been or could be written.

15.2   DEVELOPING A SUBPROGRAM LIBRARY

One of the most important tools in the professional programmer's toolbox is a collection of subprograms which have been thoroughly debugged and are available for immediate inclusion into any programming system which can use it. Throughout, this text has presented a number of useful subprograms, both as demonstration programs and as exercises for the reader. In some cases, a program has been assigned a distinct name; in other cases, that assignment was left to the reader.

Below is an alphabetized list of the useful subprograms from the earlier chapters. The asterisk (*) means that the subprogram is unnamed in the text and is now being assigned a name for identification purposes. The three types of subprograms are:

A: Arithmetic statement function
F: Function subprogram
S: Subroutine

The locations are given either as a chapter section (Sec) or as an exercise (Ex).

Name	Type	Description	Location
ANGLES	S	Determine angles from 3 sides	Ex 8.5h
ARCTAN	F	Extended arctangent routine	Ex 8.8c
AREAC (*)	A	Radius to area of circle	Ex 8.3d
AREART (*)	A	Area of right triangle	Ex 8.3i
AREATR (*)	A	Area of any triangle (multiple)	Ex 8.3j
ASORT	S	Ascending 12-character sort (2-D)	Ex 11.3d
AVGINT	F	Real average of integer array	Sec 9.6, 10.5
AVGSTD	S	Returns average, standard deviation	Ex 9.6e
AVINT2	F	Real average integer 1-, 2-D array	Sec 10.5
AZBE	S	Converts azimuth to bearing	Ex 8.8c
BEAZ	F	Convert bearing to azimuth	Ex 8.8c
BIGGER	S	Swap two reals if out of order	Ex 8.5j
BIT32	S	Returns bits from 32-bit integer	Ex 9.6h
BRKDWN	S	Integer breakdown of value	Sec 9.6
COSEC (*)	A	Cosecant	Ex 8.3f
COTAN (*)	A	Cotangent	Ex 8.3f
D2R	A	Degrees to radians	Ex 8.3g
DATE	S	Converts numeric (3) to alphabetic	Sec 12.6

Name	Type	Description	Location
DMS2R (*)	F	Converts deg., min., sec. to radians	Ex 8.4b
EGGBRK	S	Break units to gross, dozen, units	Ex 8.5e
ERRMSG	S	Error message display	Ex 8.5a
EXAMIN	S	Determine same, different sign, parity	Ex 8.5f
EXTDIG	F	Extracts a digit from long integer	Ex 8.8e
FACTL	F	Double-precision factorial	Sec 8.4
GETVAL	F	Returns real number from string	Ex 12.5a, Sec 12.5
GRADE	F	Returns letter grade from integer	Ex 9.6d
HEXCHR	F	Number to hexadecimal character	Ex 12.4f
IAND	F	AND relationship for two integers	Ex 9.6j
IASORT	S	Ascending integer sort	Ex 11.3c
IB2SRC	F	Binary search of 2-D integer array	Ex 11.4b
IBSRCH	F	Binary search of integer array	Ex 11.4a
IDSORT	S	Descending integer sort (2-D)	Sec 11.3
IISIGN (*)	F/A	Compare signs of two integers	Ex 8.4d
IMAX	F	Maximum of integer array	Ex 9.6a
IMIN	F	Minimum of integer array	Ex 9.6a
INITIA	S	Initialize integer array with constant	Ex 9.6f
INT32	F	Generates 32-bit integer from bits	Ex 9.6i
INTAV2	F	Integer average of item in 2-D array	Ex 10.5f
INTRAN	F	Generate random numbers within limits	Ex 8.6a
INVMRX (*)	S	Invert a square matrix	Ex 10.5b
INVRSE	S	Distance, azimuth, between two points	Ex 8.8c
IOMTRX (*)	S	I/O any size matrix	Ex 10.5a
IOR	F	OR relationship for two integers	Ex 9.6j
IPARTY (*)	F	Compare parities of two integers	Ex 8.4e
IRND (*)	A	Rounded integer division	Ex 8.3c
ISORT	S	Ascending integer sort (2-D)	Sec 11.3
ISRITE	F	Determine if a right triangle	Ex 8.4f
L2U (*)	S	Lower to upper case	Ex 12.4a
LMAXR	F	Returns location of maximum in real array	Sec 10.5
LNSTR	F	Determine active string length	Sec 12.4
LOCAPT	S	Point from given point with azimuth and distance	Ex 8.8c
LSRITE	F	Determine if a right triangle	Ex 8.4g
M2HM	S	Converts minutes to hours and minutes	Sec 9.7
MILAGE	S	Computes miles/gallon, cost/mile	Ex 8.5g
MINMID (*)	F	Returns minutes from midnight	Ex 8.4a
MONEY	S	Generates edited money string	Sec 12.6
MONTH	F	Determine number of months since datum	Ex 8.8b
MTRXAD	S	Matrix addition	Ex 10.5c
MTRXAR	S	Matrix arithmetic	Ex 9.6g
MTRXSM	S	Sums of columns and rows of matrix	Ex 10.5e
MYCHAR	F	Returns internal character code	Sec 12.4
NBLANK (*)	F	Returns number of blanks in string	Ex 12.4b
NTIMES	F	Occurrences of character in string	Ex 10.4d
NUMFIB (*)	F	Return nth term of Fibonacci series	Ex 8.4h
R2D	A	Radians to degrees	Ex 8.3g
R2DMS	S	Radians to degrees, minutes, seconds	Ex 8.5b
RANRML	F	Generate normally distributed values	Ex 8.6a
RDSORT	S	Descending real sort (2-D)	Sec 11.3
RMAX	F	Maximum of real array	Ex 9.6a
RMIN	F	Minimum of real array	Ex 9.6a
RND2	F	Round single-precision real number to exactly 2 places	Sec 8.4
ROOT	A	Square root of sum of squares	Sec 8.3
RSORT	S	Ascending real sort (2-D)	Sec 11.3
SALARY	F	Hours, rate to salary with overtime	Ex 8.4c
SECANT (*)	A	Secant	Ex 8.3f

Name	Type	Description	Location
SMALER	S	Swap two reals if out of order	Ex 8.5j
STATS	S	Sum, average, max, min of real array	Ex 9.6b
SUMDIG (*)	A	Sum of digits	Ex 8.3h
SWAP	S	Swap two reals	Ex 8.5k
TAX (*)	F	Calculate graduated tax	Ex 9.6c
TIMBRK	S	Converts real time to hours, minutes	Ex 8.5c
TIMDIF	S	Computes differences in two times	Ex 8.5d
TIMHIT (*)	F	Determine when projectile hits ground	Ex 8.4i
U2L	S	Upper to lower case	Sec 12.4

You should be impressed by this rather long list. You may even be surprised when you see the amount of learning you have accomplished!

In a number of places throughout this chapter, we will refer to the routines listed in the table. Again, as in Chapter 8, we mention the possibility of storing subprograms in what are called *subprogram libraries*, which make the linking process simpler. However, since this is so system-dependent, we cannot discuss this topic at length but can only refer you to the reference material for your own system.

15.3   PARSING

When computers were new, the majority of input, both programs and data, was done using punch cards. The keypunch—the machine that punched the cards—had an indicator to show what column was being accessed. Thus it was not difficult to put information in exact columns.

The early operating systems expected the commands to be entered in specific columns and thus had no difficulty breaking down an instruction into its various parts. Assembly languages then (and some still do) require that the instruction parts be placed in specific columns. It was only when FORTRAN arrived on the scene that the concept of a format-free instruction became necessary. In such an instruction, the location of its parts (except for statement numbers) was not defined; spacing was not critical, and blanks might be used as desired. Variable names could be of any length and did not need to be padded with blanks to maintain an exact location within the instruction line.

The languages BASIC and COBOL also allowed format-free instructions (with some restrictions as to the starting column). RPG, on the other hand, designed for very small computer memories, required fixed-format instructions. However, the use of terminals for system command entry made fixed-field instructions inconvenient. Furthermore, many operating systems started to allow multiple forms of an instruction and the use of abbreviations. For example, entering DIR or DIRECTORY, T or TYPE, R or RUN, Y or YES (or y or yes) would yield the same response.

Parsing is the breaking down of a line of characters into *tokens*. For example, COPY RND2.FOR RND2.OLD is the kind of command used to back up a FORTRAN source file before making a change. This line is parsed into three tokens: the command and the two file names. Since blanks may be inserted at will and the file names may vary from one to multiple characters, the program which reads this line must parse it into three variable-length tokens. Furthermore, if one of the fields is numeric, it might be necessary to convert the value from character to integer or real.

Exercise

15.3a   Write a subroutine to accept an input line in characters and the maximum number of fields (or tokens) to be returned; the subroutine should return each of the tokens as a string, a type code for each token, and a value depending upon the type of information. The subroutine header and glossary are as follows:

```
C                         Subroutine PARSE:  general purpose parsing routine
C
      SUBROUTINE PARSE (LINEIN, MAXTOK, STROUT, TYPOUT, VALOUT, NUMTOK)
C
C                         glossary
C                         ========
C     LINEIN:   input string, length defined in calling program
C     MAXTOK:   maximum number of tokens returnable, defined in
C                  calling program by dimension size
C     STROUT:   array of 16-character tokens, limited by MAXTOK
C     TYPOUT:   array of type codes, one for each token
C                  'C' = character string
C                  'R' = real number
C                  'I' = short integer
C                  'J' = long integer
C                  'O' = numeric overflow (greater than 16 characters)
C     VALOUT:   array of double precision returned values
C                  if 'C', length of string (up to last non-blank)
C                  if 'R', real number, double precision
C                  if 'I' or 'J', integer valued double precision real
C                  if 'O', value returned = 0.00
C     NUMTOK:   number of tokens found in input line
C                  may exceed MAXTOK
C
```

Although LINEIN may be any width, it usually will be 80 columns so it can accept a screen-width input line. The purpose of NUMTOK is to prevent array overflow. STROUT is set at 16 characters as a compromise; it might have been set to any value, but 16 characters will accommodate a significantly long string as well as long integers and double-precision reals. TYPOUT returns an indicator to show the type of information found; this is useful in editing the input to ensure that the proper kind of data has been entered. VALOUT is made double-precision so that it is unlimited in the value which can be returned. NUMTOK returns the actual amount of tokens found; if it exceeds MAXTOK, it indicates that additional unexpected tokens have been found.

To test this routine, one might write a driver such as:

```
C                TPARSE:  mainline driver to test PARSE & PARSED
C                                                  subroutines
      PARAMETER  (MAXTOK = 10)
C
      CHARACTER*80      LINEIN
      CHARACTER*16      STROUT(MAXTOK)
      CHARACTER* 1      TYPOUT(MAXTOK)
C
      DOUBLE PRECISION  VALOUT(MAXTOK)
```

```
C
C                         input data
      DO 40  I = 1,20000
      WRITE   (*,1020)
 1020 FORMAT  ('0','Enter input line')
      READ    (*,1022, END=90)  LINEIN
 1022 FORMAT  (A80)
C                         call parsing routine
      CALL PARSE  (LINEIN, MAXTOK,  STROUT, TYPOUT, VALOUT, NUMTOK)
C                         check number of pieces of data
      IF  (NUMTOK .GT. MAXTOK)     THEN
          PRINT *, NUMTOK-MAXTOK,' excessive data fields'
          NUMTOK = MAXTOK
      ENDIF
C                         output results
      WRITE   (*,1026)   NUMTOK,
     1          (I, STROUT(I),TYPOUT(I),VALOUT(I),VALOUT(I), I=1,NUMTOK)
 1026 FORMAT  (' ',I2,' tokens'/
     1          (' ',I2,': ',A16, 2X,A1, 2X,F16.2, E20.10))
   40 CONTINUE
C
   90 STOP  'end of test'
      END
```

It accepts an 80-character input line and displays the results of the parsing. VALOUT is printed twice: once as decimal for easy reading, then in exponential for extremely large or extremely small real numbers.

There are a few points that need discussion here. First of all, the use of the LNSTR function from our previously written subprograms would be very useful here in determining the length of our input line; there is no need to scan through the trailing blanks once all the entered data has been converted. Then all the return fields (STROUT, TYPOUT, and VALOUT) should be blanked or zeroed out so that no information is left in those fields from previous calls to the routine.

One of the ways of determining if a string can be converted to a number is to attempt to do so using the READ with an internal file (see section 12.5) containing the string. If there are characters in the string that cannot be converted, the ERR= clause is triggered and the program can branch around that code which would treat numeric information. On the other hand, if the READ is successful, the program can now continue to process the data as numeric. There is one caveat, however; the entry of a plus sign, a minus sign, or a decimal point, even with no digits around it, is converted to a zero. Thus some additional logic will be needed so as not to treat one of those symbols, if entered alone (in a string of length one), as a numeric field.

The program must distinguish between real and integer numbers, and also between long and short integers. Long integers must not be outside the range $-2,127,483,648$ and $+2,147,483,647$; short integers must not be outside the range $-32,768$ and $+32,767$. Integer values outside the long integer range are treated as reals. In any case where there are more than 16 characters in the token, this is treated as an overflow and no numeric value is to be generated.

Extensive testing must be done, especially of integer values. The code must be so written (using the appropriate FORTRAN library functions) that extremely small or extremely large reals are not typed as integers. Test also for no input and for excessive input (more than 10 tokens in the above test program).

Sample Test Run

Note: Example done on Microsoft FORTRAN compiler using PC.

```
TPARSE


Enter input line
2147483649 2147483645 32769 32767 2E03 STRING
 6 tokens
 1: 2147483649        R      2147483649.00    .2147483649E+10
 2: 2147483645        J      2147483645.00    .2147483645E+10
 3: 32769             J           32769.00    .3276900000E+05
 4: 32767             I           32767.00    .3276700000E+05
 5: 2E03              I            2000.00    .2000000000E+04
 6: STRING            C               6.00    .6000000000E+01


Enter input line
123456789.123456789
 1 token
 1: 123456789.123456  O              19.00    .1900000000E+02


Enter input line
^Z

end of test
```

15.4 A PARSE EDITOR

One of the advantages of entering data in alphameric format and using the parsing routine is that the program will never bomb out due to an invalid FORMAT or to invalid characters. However, it is still possible to input bad data with insufficient separation of tokens (no blank space between them) or invalid numeric data when such data is expected. The editing process is now in the hands of the programmer. Subroutine PARSE returns enough information that we can determine if the amount of data expected has been input and if the expected type of data in each token is correct. The variables MAXTOK and NUMTOK allow the calling program to check for either insufficient data or excessive data and the array TYPOUT for the type of data.

Since most applications will be expecting data in a prescribed pattern, or maybe a number of patterns (such as two character strings followed by a short integer, then another character string, and finally a real number), a subprogram to check the type of data and return error indications would prove very useful. We would expect that routine to be called immediately after the call to PARSE and to display or print (depending upon the output device) any appropriate error messages, as well as an error counter.

In order to edit the data, the editing routine needs the array of type codes as determined in PARSE, an edit mask (an array of expected type codes), and the number of tokens. In addition, the routine should be supplied with a logical unit number of the output device being used, either the display terminal or the printer output file; a negative value can be used to suppress any output from the routine. The routine should return the number of overflow tokens and the number of erroneous fields.

Exercise

15.4a   Write a subroutine to edit the type codes generated by subroutine PARSE. The subroutine header and glossary are as follows:

```
C                 Subroutine PARSED:   edit parsed tokens
C
        SUBROUTINE  PARSED (TYPOUT,EDITMS,NUMTOK, INDOUT, NUMOVF,NUMERR)
C
C         glossary
C         ========
C     TYPOUT:   array of type codes, one for each token
C                 'C' = character string
C                 'R' = real number
C                 'I' = short integer
C                 'J' = long integer
C                 'O' = numeric overflow, value not returned
C     EDITMS:   array of editing codes (mask) to check against TYPOUT
C                 if blank of 'C', no check done
C                 if 'R', TYPOUT of 'R', 'I' or 'J' acceptable
C                 if 'J', TYPOUT of 'I' or 'J' acceptable
C     NUMTOK:   number of tokens being checked
C     INDOUT:   if positive, write error message to that device
C     NUMOVF:   number of numeric overflow fields
C     NUMERR:   total number of errors, including overflows and types
C
```

Include possible error messages for "Overflow in field *nn*" and "Invalid data in field *nn*," where *nn* is the token number.

A hierarchy of data must be considered. If character data is expected, any kind of data except overflow meets that criterion. If real values are expected, any kind of numeric value, real or integer, likewise meets that criterion. Finally, if long integers are expected, both long and short integers are acceptable. Thus, in order of restriction, from highest to lowest, the hierarchy is:

1. Overflow
2. Short integer
3. Long integer
4. Real
5. Character

An expanded version of TPARSE is needed to test this routine:

```
C       TPARSE:  mainline driver to test PARSE & PARSED subroutines
C
        PARAMETER  (MAXTOK = 10)
C
        CHARACTER*80  LINEIN
        CHARACTER*16  STROUT(MAXTOK)
        CHARACTER* 1  TYPOUT(MAXTOK), EDITMS(MAXTOK)
C
        DOUBLE PRECISION   VALOUT(MAXTOK)
```

```
      C
      C                         input data
            DO 40  I  =  1,20000
            WRITE   (*,1020)
       1020 FORMAT  ('0','Enter input line')
            READ    (*,1022, END=90)      LINEIN
       1022 FORMAT  (A80)
      C                         call parsing routine
            CALL PARSE  (LINEIN, MAXTOK,  STROUT, TYPOUT, VALOUT, NUMTOK)
      C                         check number of pieces of data
            IF  (NUMTOK .GT. MAXTOK)      THEN
               PRINT *, NUMTOK-MAXTOK,' excessive data fields'
               NUMTOK = MAXTOK
            ENDIF
      C                         output results
            WRITE   (*,1026)   NUMTOK,
           1            (I, STROUT(I),TYPOUT(I),VALOUT(I),VALOUT(I), I=1,NUMTOK)
       1026 FORMAT  (' ',I2,' tokens'/
           1          (' ',I2,': ',A16, 2X,A1, 2X,F16.2, E20.10))
      C                         edit input
            WRITE   (*,1028)   ('-', I=1,NUMTOK)
       1028 FORMAT  ('0','Enter edit mask'/ ' ',80A1)
            READ    (*,1030, END=90)      EDITMS
       1030 FORMAT  (80A1)
            CALL PARSED (TYPOUT, EDITMS, NUMTOK, 0, NUMOVF, NUMERR)
            IF  (NUMERR .GT. 0)  THEN
               PRINT *, NUMERR,' error(s) in above data'
               IF (NUMOVF .GT. 0)  WRITE   (*,1034)  NUMOVF
       1034        FORMAT  (' ',20X,'including', I3,' overflow error(s)')
            ENDIF
         40 CONTINUE
      C
         90 STOP   'end of test'
            END
```

Note the new additions in this routine, the array EDITMS and its input. The prompt for the entry of the mask will display the number of dashes corresponding to the number of tokens just above the entry line as a guide to the user.

Again, test this programming system thoroughly with all of the possible combinations imaginable. Shown below is the test run from the previous section with the parse editor inserted.

Sample Test Run

Note: Example done on Microsoft FORTRAN compiler using PC.

```
TPARSE


Enter input line
2147483649 2147483645 32769 32767 2E03 STRING
 6 tokens
 1: 2147483649         R      2147483649.00       .2147483649E+10
 2: 2147483645         J      2147483645.00       .2147483645E+10
 3: 32769              J           32769.00       .3276900000E+05
 4: 32767              I           32767.00       .3276700000E+05
```

```
    5: 2E03                   I            2000.00        .2000000000E+04
    6: STRING                 C               6.00        .6000000000E+01

Enter edit mask
------
IRCJRI
Invalid data in field  1
Invalid data in field  6
        2 error(s) in above data


Enter input line
123456789.123456789
 1 token
    1: 123456789.123456  O                  19.00        .1900000000E+02

Enter edit mask
-
R
Overflow in field  1
        1 error(s) in above data
                 including  1 overflow error(s)


Enter input line
^Z

end of test
```

15.5   A SIMPLE CALCULATOR

Once the parsing routine and editor are tested and debugged, there are many routines in which they can be used. As an example, let us write a number of calculator routines which accept as input alternating tokens of values and operators and performs calculations on them, very much like an electronic calculator. The operators we will use are:

+	addition
−	subtraction
*	multiplication
/	division
^	exponentiation

Although the first four operators are the standard ones used in FORTRAN, the caret (^) has been borrowed from BASIC so that there is a single character operator for exponentiation instead of the double character used in FORTRAN (**).

Sample input might be:

    3.2 ^ 2.4 / 8.35 * -15.24 + 118

and should yield the result:

    94.09686357

There are some problems that must be addressed. The operation codes must be edited to ensure that they are one of the five above, otherwise the calculation cannot be done. Division by zero must be prevented, otherwise the program will bomb out. Likewise, exponentiation of a negative number to nonintegral powers cannot work. Thus, such tests must be included in the program. The program should contain the error messages:

```
ERROR:  invalid characters
ERROR:  division by zero attempted
ERROR:  invalid exponentiation
```

leading to terminating the calculation and returning to the prompt for another input entry.

Exercises

15.5a Write a calculator program to compute in the order of the equation (without regard to priority). Assume each operator must be surrounded by one or more blanks. The header and specification information are:

```
C               Program CALC1:  simple sequential calculator
C
      PARAMETER  (MAXTOK = 39)
C
      CHARACTER*80  LINEIN
      CHARACTER*39  EDITST
      CHARACTER*16  STROUT(MAXTOK)
      CHARACTER* 1  TYPOUT(MAXTOK), EDITMS(MAXTOK), OPRATN(5)
C
      DOUBLE PRECISION   VALOUT(MAXTOK), ANSWER
C
      EQUIVALENCE  (EDITMS(1), EDITST)
C
      DATA  OPRATN/ '+', '-', '*', '/', '^'/
      DATA  EDITST/ 'RCRCRCRCRCRCRCRCRCRCRCRCRCRCRCRCRCRCRCR'/
C
```

Since an 80-character input line could yield 20 single-digit values and 19 operators, the maximum number of tokens was set at 39. Note the use of the EQUIVALENCE statement, which aligns the array of 39 characters needed for the edit mask with a single 39-character string. This simplifies the specification of the string, since it would be necessary to specify each of the 39 characters within its own set of apostrophes if EDITMS were placed in the DATA statement. The use of the array OPRATN simplifies the editing of the operators. Additional variables may be added when so desired.

The displayed output should probably be both in decimal format for easy reading and in exponential format with many decimal places for greater accuracy. For debugging purposes, the program might contain intermediate output to show the value of ANSWER as each calculation is done.

One pitfall to watch out for is that of inputting a combination of characters that is not what the user intended but which yields a valid answer. It might be thought that the entry: "1+2 / 4," which was intended to be "1 + 2 / 4," would yield the result 0.75, but actually it will yield 25 because "1+2" as numeric input will be interpreted by FORTRAN as the equivalent of 1.00E+02. The parse editor will find that "1+2" is a valid numeric token.

Of course, the entries: "1+ 2 / 4" and "1 +2 / 4" should yield errors, since the operator is not a separate token. *(Note: The quotes used in this example are not part of the input but were inserted to show the beginning and end of the input string.)*

Sample Test Run

```
Enter calculation    (ctrl-Z to terminate)
3 + 1 / 5 ^ 2
Answer =               .64       .6400000000E+00

Enter calculation    (ctrl-Z to terminate)
3+1 / 5 ^ 2
Answer =              36.00      .3600000000E+02

Enter calculation    (ctrl-Z to terminate)
3+1/5^2
Invalid data in field 1
ERROR:   invalid characters

Enter calculation    (ctrl-Z to terminate)
3 + 1 / 0 ^ 2
ERROR:   division by zero attempted

Enter calculation    (ctrl-Z to terminate)
3 + 1 / -5 ^ 2.4
ERROR:   invalid exponentiation

Enter calculation    (ctrl-Z to terminate)
^Z

end of program
```

15.5b   Expand the above program to allow for the input of an equation with the option of blanks surrounding the operators. The suggested method is to add a subprogram to expand the input line, so that it has blanks around the operators, and then send it to the same logic used in exercise 15.5a. One difficulty is to allow a minus sign attached to a value not to be separated from it, otherwise the number will be modified.

This new program will be able to handle input of any kind except the implied exponential; i.e., 3+1 will yield 4, not 30.

Sample Test Run

```
Enter calculation    (ctrl-Z to terminate)
3 + 1 / 5 ^ 2
Answer =               .64       .6400000000E+00

Enter calculation    (ctrl-Z to terminate)
3+1 / 5^2
Answer =               .64       .6400000000E+00
```

```
        Enter calculation    (ctrl-Z to terminate)
        3+1/5^2
        Answer =             .64      .6400000000E+00

        Enter calculation    (ctrl-Z to terminate)
        3+1/-5^2
        Answer =             .64      .6400000000E+00

        Enter calculation    (ctrl-Z to terminate)
        ^Z

        end of program
```

15.5c Expand the above program so that it calculates according to the arithmetic priorities: exponentiation first, then multiplication and division, then addition and subtraction. Where priorities are equal, order of calculation is from left to right. For example, $3+1/5^2$ now has the answer 3.04.

15.6 CALENDAR CALCULATIONS

In many areas of data processing, calculations require the number of days between two given dates. Because the number of days in the year is not constant, and the days in the months also vary, the calculation of duration in days is not straightforward. Thus a technique is needed to provide such a calculation.

Many computer systems provide subprograms to return current date and time (based on the clock built into the system). However, they do not provide an elapsed time period in days which might be used to compute the number of days between two dates. Astronomers use a measurement called the *Julian Period,* the number of days since noon, January 1, 4713 B.C. The concept was developed in 1582 by Joseph Scaliger and named after his father, Julius Scaliger (there is no relationship to the Julian calendar, which is named after Julius Caesar). The same kind of period would be useful to programmers. If we can determine the number of days from a given base date for two different dates, the difference between those numbers is the elapsed number of days.

Actually, any date will do, but for our purposes we are better off if we use some base closer to our own time. I suggest Monday, January 1, 1940, inasmuch as it gives us a leap year and a decade-beginning year which begins on the first day of the (work) week, Monday. Even if we restrict ourselves to a short integer with its limit of 32767, it encompasses more than 88 years, until the year 2028.

In the series of exercises below, two subprograms are to be developed to aid our calculations and then three practical programs which utilize them.

Exercises

15.6a Write a function subprogram which returns the number of days since Monday, January 1, 1940. The input consists of three integers: the month, the day, and the last two digits of the year. If the year is a number less than 40, add 100 to extend into the next century. However, the program should be limited to the range 1940 to

2028. The program must adjust for leap years (every fourth year) and for dates after February 28. (This basic algorithm will fail in the year 2100, which is not a leap year!) The function header might be:

```
FUNCTION NUMDAY (IM, ID, IY)
```

Test your function carefully by writing a driver test program. Below is some sample data:

Date	Days	Date	Days	Date	Days
01/01/40	0	03/01/40	60	01/01/41	366
02/28/40	59	12/31/40	365	01/01/90	18,263

15.6b   Write a subroutine DYOFWK which accepts the date as three integers (as in the above exercise) and returns a nine-character string containing the day of the week, right-justified. For example, the date 01/01/90 would return "   Monday". This subroutine calls the above function and, using the MOD function, determines the day of the week. The same testing driver used in the previous exercise can be expanded to test this subprogram also.

15.6c   Write a program to compute the interest and total due on a loan compounded daily. The daily interest rate is the annual interest rate divided by 365.25. The compound interest formula is:

Total = Principal * (1 + rate) ** Number of Days
Interest = Total − Principal

The total and interest should be rounded to the nearest penny. Input can be free format. A sample run is shown below:

```
Enter amount of loan and annual interest rate (%)
12000,10

Enter starting and ending dates of loan
month, day, year,  month, day, year
1,1,90,1,1,91

Interest          = $   1260.96
Total to be repaid = $  13260.96
```

15.6d   Write a program which produces a printed schedule of loan payments. The input is the principal and the annual interest rate, plus the day the loan is made and the desired day of payment. The minimum monthly payment is calculated as $25 per $1000 borrowed, rounded up to the next $1000; for example, a loan of $11,250 would have a minimum payment of $25 times 12 (thousand) = $300. The program should edit to ensure that the user meets or exceeds that minimum.

The program must determine the interest on a daily basis based on the balance left after the last payment. The program must cycle through each month, with the first payment taking place *after* the date of the loan; for example, if the loan is made on the 15th of the month and the desired payment day is the 10th of the month, the first payment must be placed in the next month. Input is from the keyboard and might appear as:

```
Enter amount of loan and annual interest rate (%)
15000,12

Minimum payment is $  375

Enter amount you wish to pay
400

Enter date of loan   (month, day, year)
3,15,90

Enter desired day of payment  (1—28)
10

 48 payments required
```

A sample (partial) output is shown below:

```
                   Loan Payment Schedule

Principle =  15000.00                         Interest = 15.00%
Date of Loan:    3/15/90               Payable on day 10 of month


Payment   Due on:           Days   Interest   Payment   Balance

                                                        15000.00
    1     Tuesday    4/10/90   26    128.66    400.00   14728.66
    2     Thursday   5/10/90   30    145.86    400.00   14474.52
    3     Sunday     6/10/90   31    148.15    400.00   14222.67
    .        .          .       .       .         .         .
    .        .          .       .       .         .         .
   46     Monday     1/10/94   31      8.95    400.00     482.93
   47     Thursday   2/10/94   31      4.94    400.00      87.87
   48     Thursday   3/10/94   28       .81     88.68        .00
```

Note how the final payment must be adjusted so that the balance becomes zero.

15.6e Write a program to accept the year as input and to output a list of the dates of the Fridays in that year. This is very handy when checking out a payroll week ending date, should that week end on Friday.

15.6f Write a program to accept the year as input and to output a printer file with a calendar broken down into weeks, as below:

```
        January 1992                              July 1992

   S   M   T   W   T   F   S                  S   M   T   W   T   F   S
                   1   2   3   4                              1   2   3   4
   5   6   7   8   9  10  11                  5   6   7   8   9  10  11
  12  13  14  15  16  17  18                 12  13  14  15  16  17  18
  19  20  21  22  23  24  25                 19  20  21  22  23  24  25
  26  27  28  29  30  31                     26  27  28  29  30  31


        February 1992                            August 1992

   S   M   T   W   T   F   S                  S   M   T   W   T   F   S
                               1                                          1
   2   3   4   5   6   7   8                  2   3   4   5   6   7   8
                   .                                          .
                   .                                          .
                   .                                          .
```

Test to ensure that the program works for leap years and for years in which some of the months extend over six weeks.

15.6g Set up a file of dates for birthdays, anniversaries, and other events that require an annual greeting card. For birthdays and anniversaries, include the year of occurrence so that the appropriate number can be generated. Events like Valentine's Day, without an age attached, should be entered without a reference beginning year. Write a program to print a "tickler" list of dates not to be forgotten. The input should be the current (or upcoming) year; the output should be a chronological list of all of the events, including the age of the birthday celebrant or the anniversary year.

15.7   CONCLUSION

The projects presented above are only a tiny sample of the kinds of programs that can be written for fun or profit (or both). Although the ones above require no special knowledge, others of interest to the reader may require some technical background. Certainly, the best way to use a computer is to solve problems which come up in other subjects. It is hoped that every college student will be given computer training early enough in his or her college career (if not in high school) so that the skills learned can be used in upper-level courses.

You should look for applications in any course that has a quantitative aspect, such as mathematics, science, economics, statistics, accounting, etc. You might also look at your hobbies and other interests for challenging exercises, such as inventories of household goods, budgeting, depreciation schedules, auto cost analysis, income and tax analysis, name and address lists, and so on.

Furthermore, any computer system with additional peripherals, such as graphic screens or plotters, will usually have a FORTRAN interface (a series of callable subprograms) available which gives the user the pleasure of writing graphics routines. Many personal computers have speakers with the ability to generate some simple forms of music.

In addition, you should be aware that FORTRAN can call assembly language routines on almost all computers, opening up a whole new series of possibilities because such routines allow access directly to the hardware. Some manufacturers provide standardized subprogram calling sequences to other languages available on the system, allowing the FORTRAN programmer to call subprograms in other languages such as C, compiled BASIC, and even COBOL; likewise, those languages can call routines written in FORTRAN.

There is a whole world out there full of problems to be solved—a world full of employment possibilities and fun!

Appendix A
Application Problems

The applications contained in this appendix represent the "end product" of this text in that their solutions will be developed as we go through each of the chapters. Each application has a reference to the chapter (in parentheses) indicating where the solution is complete.

 APPLICATION 1: BOWLING SCORES

This application uses a sequential access file of bowling scores and contains 3200 scores, assuming 40 bowlers and 80 scores per bowler. If you don't know what bowling is, let me just say that it is a very frustrating game in which the scores range from 0 to 300. These scores are to be analyzed and a graph of their distribution produced.

A.1.1
(Chapter 10)

The analysis program reads the entire bowler file into a two-dimensional array of (80,40). It then determines the average for each bowler, and outputs the highest average and the number of the bowler who achieved it. It also outputs the lowest score, with the number of the bowler who scored it and the game number in which it was scored. In addition, it outputs a list of the bowlers who bowled a 300 game.

A.1.2
(Chapter 10)

The above program also does an analysis of the distribution of the games into the following ranges:

0 to 50	171 to 210
51 to 90	211 to 250
91 to 130	251 to 290
131 to 170	291 to 300

Each of the ranges and the number of games scored in each range is output.

APPLICATION 2: COMPUTER TIME ACCOUNTING

The following programming system requires a mainline and two subprograms, which are used to produce a report of computer time used and the charges made. The program uses an input file with the following file structure:

```
Record 1:      Columns   1- 9: month (alphameric)
                  "      11-14: year
Records 2 − n: Columns   1- 2: user number (range 1 to 20)
                  "       4- 5: day of month (range 1 to 28, 30 or 31)
                  "       7-10: log-on time, minutes since midnight
                                (range 0 to 1439)
                  "      12-15: log-off time, minutes since midnight
                                (range, 0 to 1439)
```
If log-off time is less than log-on time, log off is assumed to be on the next day.

A.2.1
(Chapter 9)

```
      SUBROUTINE M2HM (MIN, NEWHRS, NEWMIN)
C
C
C         Abstract:  reduces minutes to hours and minutes
C
C         Input:     MIN        minutes since midnight
C
C         Output:    NEWHRS     hours since midnight
C                    NEWMIN     remainder of minutes
C
C         Example:  if MIN = 535, NEWHRS = 8 and NEWMIN = 55
```

A.2.2
(Chapter 9)

```
      FUNCTION  CMPCST (MIN, RATE)
C
C         Abstract:  computes the cost of computer time from the minutes
C                       used
C
C         Input:     MIN        minutes since midnight
C                    RATE       basic rate per minute
C
C         Output:    CMPCST     based on RATE * MIN for first 120 minutes
C                               and 80% of RATE for balance of minutes
C
C         Example:  if MIN = 90  and RATE = 2.50, CMPCST = 90 * 2.50
C                   if MIN = 150 and Rate = 2.50,
C                      CMPCST = 120 * 2.50  +  0.80 * 30 * 2.50
```

A.2.3
(Chapter 11)

The mainline program reads the file and generates a chronological report. It uses an array MT(9,2000) to input the array and hold the calculated values as follows:

$MT(1,n)$ = user number
$MT(2,n)$ = day of month
$MT(3,n)$ = log-on time, in minutes since midnight
$MT(4,n)$ = log-off time, in minutes since midnight
$MT(5,n)$ = time used in minutes = log-off − log-in. If log-off is less than log-on, add 1 day (1440 minutes) to log-off time.
$MT(6,n)$ = log-on time, in hours and
minutes since midnight
$MT(7,n)$ =
$MT(8,n)$ = time used, in hours and
minutes
$MT(9,n)$ =

An additional array is required to hold the generated costs.
The mainline is written in modular form:

Module 1: Input of up to 2000 records, using the END= clause to terminate the read. If excessive data, terminate with an error message.
Module 2: Calculation of items 5 to 9 in array MT and of the cost. Also, the total time usage and cost will be necessary.
Module 3: Output report in the following format, with times in hours and minutes:

```
COMPUTER TIME USAGE REPORT FOR aaaaaaaaa, 199n


User  Day    Time    Usage      Cost

 nn    n    nn.nn    nn.nn      nn.nn
 nn    n    nn.nn     n.nn       n.nn
  n    n    nn.nn    nn.nn     nnn.nn
 nn   nn    nn.nn     n.nn      nn.nn
  .    .      .        .          .
  .    .      .        .          .
 nn   nn    nn.nn    nn.nn     nnn.nn

Totals             nnnn.nn  nnnnnn.nn
```

A.2.4
(Chapter 11)

The above data is resorted by user, day, and log-on time. An additional report is amended with subtotals by user for time usage and cost and grand total for all records. The subtotal is printed to the right of the cost columns and a line skipped before a new user.

APPLICATION 3: AUTOMATED TELLER MACHINE

Automated teller machines are used by banks to dispense cash in multiples of $10. The user of the machine inputs the account number and the amount desired. The program calculates the number of each denomination of bills needed to meet that amount and keeps a record of the money distributed by account and by denomination. There is also a fee made chargeable against the account, but not deducted from the money given out.

A.3.1
(Chapter 9)

This subprogram will appear in a number of versions, some specific, until this general-purpose routine is developed.

```
        SUBROUTINE  BRKDWN (AMOUNT, NUMDEN, VALDEN, NUMINT)
C
C       Abstract:  reduces a value to denominations
C
        INTEGER  AMOUNT, NUMDEN, VALDEN(6), NUMBIL(6), LEFT
C
C          Glossary: AMOUNT:   amount to be broken down
C                    NUMDEN:   number of denominations, limit 6
C                    VALDEN:   value of those denominations
C                    NUMBIL:   number of units in the denominations
C                    LEFT:     working variable
C
C       Example:  AMOUNT = 180
C                 NUMDEN =   3
C                 VALDEN =  50, 20, 10, 0, 0, 0
C                 NUMBIL =   3,  1,  1, 0, 0, 0
C
```

A.3.2
(Chapter 8)

```
     FUNCTION  CALCFEE  (IAMT)
C
C         Abstract: calculates a fee to be applied to the account
C
C         Input:    IAMT      amount of money dispensed
C
C         Output:   CALCFEE   fee charged according to:
C                               if IAMT <  $100, fee = $2.00
C                               if IAMT >= $100, fee = 2% of IAMT
C
```

A.3.3
(Chapter 10)

The mainline:

1. prompts for a numeric account number and amount. It uses the ERR= clause to ensure that data is numeric and END= clause to terminate input.
2. verifies that the amount is a multiple of 10, displaying an error message and returning for another read if not.
3. accesses subroutine BRKDWN to get breakdown of bills to be dispensed and function CALCFEE to determine fee to be charged. It then displays the results.
4. writes a record to a sequential access file containing the following items:

   account number
   amount
   number of $50 bills dispensed
   number of $20 bills dispensed
   number of $10 bills dispensed
   fee applied

All but the last item is integer.

A.3.4
(Chapter 10)

Another mainline reads the above sequential file and outputs a printed report in the following format:

```
                 Transaction  Register

        Account     Amount  $50  $20  $10      Fee

           nnnnn       nnn    n    n    n      n.nn
           nnnnn        nn    n    n    n      n.nn
             :           :    :    :    :       :
             :           :    :    :    :       :
           nnnnn       nnnn   nn   n    n     nn.nn

        Totals:      nnnnn  nnn  nnn  nnn   nnnn.nn
```

APPLICATION 4: PARKING VIOLATIONS

A parking ticket system consists of two permanent files, one to detail the information necessary for describing and charging for parking violations and the other to keep a record of car registrations in a state. A third temporary file keeps track of all outstanding (unpaid) tickets.

The parking violation description file is a sequential file and is structured as follows:

> Columns 1– 2: violation code (alpha)
> Columns 5–34: violation description (alpha)
> Columns 39–40: amount of fine (integer)

and has the following entries:

OV	Overtime unmetered parking	5
OM	Overtime parking at meter	5
PD	Parked in driveway	25
PF	Parked at fire hydrant	50
PB	Parked in bus stop	25
PX	Parked in crosswalk	20
PR	Parked in restricted area	30
PT	Parked on railroad tracks	40
PH	Parked in handicapped spot	40
P2	Parked in two spots	15

The license plate file is a direct access file and has the following structure:

> Columns 1– 8: License plate number (alpha)
>   "   11–28: Name of car owner (alpha)
>   "   31–48: Address of car owner (alpha)
>   "   51–62: Town
>   "   64–65: State code
>   "   66–70: Zip code

The data is sorted by license plate. The first record in the file contains the record count; the first data record is in physical record 2.

The file for outstanding traffic violations is also a direct access file and has the following structure:

Columns   1– 8: License plate number (alpha)
"   10: Deletion code: nonblank if fine is paid and record is to be deleted
"   11–18: Date (alpha) nn/nn/nn
"   19–20: Violation code
"   21–22: Fine

This file is unsorted. It also contains the record count in the first record.

A.4.1
(Chapter 14)

```
      FUNCTION  NUMVIO (VCODE)
C
C         Abstract: on first entry, reads violation description file
C                   into COMMON arrays for code, description and fine.
C                   On all entries, returns subscript of violation.
C
C         Input:   VCODE    Violation code  (Character*2)
C         Output:  NUMVIO   Subscript of violation in table.  Return
C                           0 if violation not in table.  (Integer)
C
      CHARACTER*2   VCODE, VIOCODE
      CHARACTER*30  VDESCR
C
      COMMON  VIOCOD(20), VDESCR(20), IFINE(20), NVIO
```

A.4.2
(Chapter 14)

```
      SUBROUTINE  NUMLIC
C
C         Abstract: opens PLATE.DAT,
C                   places index, number of records into COMMON
C
      COMMON   /PLATE/ PLATE(20000), NPLATE
```

A.4.3
(Chapter 14)

The mainline program accepts keyboard input and updates the outstanding violation file. The input for each record includes the license plate number, the violation code, and the date; the program leaves the deletion code blank and inserts the appropriate fine into the record.

A.4.4
(Chapter 14)

Another mainline program accepts as input a license plate number from the keyboard and displays all tickets, paid and unpaid, as well as the name and address of the violator. The total outstanding fines are also displayed. The program then gives the user the option of indicating the payment of an outstanding fine; the file is updated for any payment by setting the deletion code to nonblank.

A.4.5
(Chapter 14)

Another mainline program produces a listing of all unpaid violations sorted by license plate, with subtotals by license plate. To save memory, a key/record sort is used in which the license plate is the key and the record number in the file the integer carry-along; after sorting, the order of the record numbers is the order in which the file should be read.

A.4.6
(Chapter 14)

Another mainline program generates an updated outstanding violation file in which the paid violations (the records marked for deletion) are eliminated. This is done with a single file by simply writing over the records to be deleted in a simple packing procedure.

Appendix B
Intrinsic Functions

The Intrinsic Functions are functions provided within the FORTRAN library and are part of the language. They may thus be accessed as a regular function and are brought into the program automatically during the linking operation.

In FORTRAN 66 and the FORTRAN 77 subset, the functions have specific argument types. In the full FORTRAN 77 language, there are generic names which act on all types of arguments, adjusting the returned value to the appropriate type. For example, the generic name ABS will convert to the specific functions IABS, ABS, DABS, or CABS, depending on the mode of the argument (integer, real, double-precision, or complex) and return an answer in the corresponding type. However, in any place in which the mode of the function is not apparent, such as when it is an argument itself, the specific name should be used.

In the table below, the functions are listed in four categories: FORTRAN 66, FORTRAN 77 subset (77s), FORTRAN 77 (77), and FORTRAN 77 generic (77g). The last contains the generic name where it exists; where it does not, the specific name may be used. Some FORTRAN 66 implementations may contain functions now appearing in FORTRAN 77. The type codes used are as follows:

C	Complex
D	Double-precision
A	Character
I	Integer
L	Logical
R	Real

B.1 MODE CONVERSION

Description	66	77s	77	77g	Mode	Arguments	
Conversion to integer truncating if numeric				INT	I	I	1
		INT	INT	INT	I	R	1
	IFIX	IFIX	IFIX	INT	I	R	1
			IDINT	INT	I	D	1
				INT	I	C	1
		ICHAR	ICHAR		I	A	1
Conversion to real	REAL	REAL	REAL	REAL	R	I	1
	FLOAT	FLOAT	FLOAT	REAL	R	I	1
				REAL	R	R	1
			SNGL	REAL	R	D	1
				REAL	R	C	1

447

Description	66	77s	77	77g	Mode	Arguments	
Conversion to double-precision				DBLE	D	I	1
				DBLE	D	R	1
				DBLE	D	D	1
				DBLE	D	C	1
Conversion to complex if two arguments, must be of same type				CMPLX	C	I	1 − 2
				CMPLX	C	R	1 − 2
				CMPLX	C	D	1 − 2
				CMPLX	C	C	1 − 2
Conversion to character				CHAR	A	I	1
Nearest integer, rounding		NINT	NINT	NINT	I	R	1
			IDNINT	NINT	I	D	1
Imaginary part of a complex number			AIMAG		R	C	1
Double-precision product			DPROD		D	R	2

B.2 ARITHMETIC MANIPULATION

Description	66	77s	77	77g	Mode	Arguments	
Truncation	AINT	AINT	AINT	AINT	R	R	1
			DINT	AINT	D	D	1
Nearest whole number		ANINT	ANINT	ANINT	R	R	1
			DNINT	ANINT	D	D	1
Remaindering (modulo function)	MOD	MOD	MOD	MOD	I	I	2
	AMOD	AMOD	AMOD	MOD	R	R	2
			DMOD	MOD	D	D	2
Positive difference a1−a2 if a1>a2 0 if a1<a2	IDIM	IDIM	IDIM	DIM	I	I	2
	DIM	DIM	DIM	DIM	R	R	2
			DDIM	DIM	D	D	2
Absolute value	IABS	IABS	IABS	ABS	I	I	1
	ABS	ABS	ABS	ABS	R	R	1
			DABS	ABS	D	D	1
			CABS	ABS	R	C	1
Square root	SQRT	SQRT	SQRT	SQRT	R	R	1
			DSQRT	SQRT	D	D	1
			CSQRT	SQRT	C	C	1
Conjugate of a complex argument			CONJG		C	C	1
Transfer of sign ABS(a1) if a2 >= 0 −ABS(a1) if a2 < 0	ISIGN	ISIGN	ISIGN	SIGN	I	I	2
	SIGN	SIGN	SIGN	SIGN	R	R	2
			DSIGN	SIGN	D	D	2
Choosing largest value	MAX0	MAX0	MAX0	MAX	I	I	>1
	AMAX1	AMAX1	AMAX1	MAX	R	R	>1
			DMAX1	MAX	D	D	>1
	AMAX0	AMAX0	AMAX0		R	I	>1
	MAX1	MAX1	MAX1		I	R	>1
Choosing smallest value	MIN0	MIN0	MIN0	MIN	I	I	>1
	AMIN1	AMIN1	AMIN1	MIN	R	R	>1
			DMIN1	MIN	D	D	>1
	AMIN0	AMIN0	AMIN0		R	I	>1
	MIN1	MIN1	MIN1		I	R	>1

B.3 MATHEMATICAL FUNCTIONS

Description	66	77s	77	77g	Mode	Arguments	
Exponentiation (e^a)	EXP	EXP	EXP	EXP	R	R	1
			DEXP	EXP	D	D	1
			CEXP	EXP	C	C	1
Natural logarithm (base e)	ALOG	ALOG	ALOG	LOG	R	R	1
			DLOG	LOG	D	D	1
			CLOG	LOG	C	C	1
Common logarithm (base 10)	ALOG10	ALOG10	ALOG10	LOG10	R	R	1
			DLOG10	LOG10	D	D	1
Sine	SIN	SIN	SIN	SIN	R	R	1
			DSIN	SIN	D	D	1
			CSIN	SIN	C	C	1
Cosine	COS	COS	COS	COS	R	R	1
			DCOS	COS	D	D	1
			CCOS	COS	C	C	1
Tangent		TAN	TAN	TAN	R	R	1
			DTAN	TAN	D	D	1
Arcsine		ASIN	ASIN	ASIN	R	R	1
			DASIN	ASIN	D	D	1
Arccosine		ACOS	ACOS	ACOS	R	R	1
			DACOS	ACOS	D	D	1
Arctangent	ATAN	ATAN	ATAN	ATAN	R	R	1
			DATAN	ATAN	D	D	1
		ATAN2	ATAN2	ATAN2	R	R	2
			DATAN2	ATAN2	D	D	2
Hyperbolic sine		SINH	SINH	SINH	R	R	1
			DSINH	SINH	D	D	1
Hyperbolic cosine		COSH	COSH	COSH	R	R	1
			DCOSH	COSH	D	D	1
Hyperbolic tangent	TANH	TANH	TANH	TANH	R	R	1
			DTANH	TANH	D	D	1

B.4 CHARACTER MANIPULATION

Description	66	77s	77	77g	Mode	Arguments	
Length of a character variable			LEN		I	A	1
Index of a substring			INDEX		I	A	2
Lexically greater than or equal		LGE	LGE		L	A	2
Lexically greater than		LGT	LGT		L	A	2
Lexically less than or equal		LLE	LLE		L	A	2
Lexically less than		LLT	LLT		L	A	2

Appendix C
Character Code Tables

As discussed in section 12.1, there are two major coding methods for characters: ASCII (American Standard Code for Information Interchange) and EBCDIC (Extended Binary Coded Decimal Interchange Code). Complete tables for each code follow. The tables include:

Character or abbreviation (mnemonic)
Keyboard entry to enter the character (ASCII only)
Binary code (7-bit for ASCII, 8-bit for EBCDIC)
Octal code (ASCII only)
Decimal code
Hexadecimal code
Definition

ASCII

The user will find ASCII to be the more commonly used code, since its internal structure is more logical; it is found in almost all terminals and printers, even in those systems that use EBCDIC internally in memory. ASCII was defined as a 7-bit code, but with the transition to a byte (8-bit) standard, those systems that have made the conversion to 8-bit ASCII (most of the microcomputers, for example) have an additional 128 codes available; however, these codes are defined individually by the manufacturer and do not fit into any general pattern. The additional codes are used primarily for graphics characters (symbols) or foreign language letters and symbols not used in English.

ASCII Terminal character	key	Equivalent Forms binary	oct	dec	hex	Definition of Use
NUL	CTRL/@	0 000 000	000	0	0	filler; null
SOH	CTRL/A	0 000 001	001	1	1	start of heading; home position
STX	CTRL/B	0 000 010	002	2	2	start of text
ETX	CTRL/C	0 000 011	003	3	3	end of text
EOT	CTRL/D	0 000 100	004	4	4	end of transmission
ENQ	CTRL/E	0 000 101	005	5	5	enquiry
ACK	CTRL/F	0 000 110	006	6	6	acknowledge
BEL	CTRL/G	0 000 111	007	7	7	bell or audible
BS	CTRL/H	0 001 000	010	8	8	backspace; ← arrow
HT	CTRL/I	0 001 001	011	9	9	horizontal tabulation
LF	CTRL/J	0 001 010	012	10	A	line feed; ↓ arrow
VT	CTRL/K	0 001 011	013	11	B	vertical tabulation; ↑ arrow
FF	CTRL/L	0 001 100	014	12	C	form feed; clear screen
CR	CTRL/M	0 001 101	015	13	D	carriage return
SO	CTRL/N	0 001 110	016	14	E	shift out
SI	CTRL/O	0 001 111	017	15	F	shift in
DLE	CTRL/P	0 010 000	020	16	10	data link escape
DC1	CTRL/Q	0 010 001	021	17	11	device control 1
DC2	CTRL/R	0 010 010	022	18	12	device control 2

| ASCII Terminal | | Equivalent Forms | | | | |
character	key	binary	oct	dec	hex	Definition of Use
DC3	CTRL/S	0 010 011	023	19	13	device control 3
DC4	CTRL/T	0 010 100	024	20	14	device control 4
NAK	CTRL/U	0 010 101	025	21	15	negative acknowledge
SYN	CTRL/V	0 010 110	026	22	16	synchronous idle
ETB	CTRL/W	0 010 111	027	23	17	end of transmission block
CAN	CTRL/X	0 011 000	030	24	18	cancel
EM	CTRL/Y	0 011 001	031	25	19	end of medium
SUB	CTRL/Z	0 011 010	032	26	1A	substitute
ESC	CTRL/[	0 011 011	033	27	1B	escape
FS	CTRL/\	0 011 100	034	28	1C	file separator
GS	CTRL/]	0 011 101	035	29	1D	group separator
RS	CTRL/^	0 011 110	036	30	1E	record separator
US	CTRL/__	0 011 111	037	31	1F	unit separator
SP	SPACE	0 100 000	040	32	20	space; blank
!	!	0 100 001	041	33	21	exclamation mark
"	"	0 100 010	042	34	22	double quote
#	#	0 100 011	043	35	23	number symbol
$	$	0 100 100	044	36	24	dollar symbol
%	%	0 100 101	045	37	25	percent symbol
&	&	0 100 110	046	38	26	ampersand
'	'	0 100 111	047	39	27	single quote; apostrophe
(	(	0 101 000	050	40	28	left parenthesis
)	)	0 101 001	051	41	29	right parenthesis
*	*	0 101 010	052	42	2A	asterisk
+	+	0 101 011	053	43	2B	plus symbol
,	,	0 101 100	054	44	2C	comma
-	-	0 101 101	055	45	2D	minus symbol; hyphen
.	.	0 101 110	056	46	2E	period; decimal point
/	/	0 101 111	057	47	2F	divide symbol; slash; virgule
0	0	0 110 000	060	48	30	digit zero
1	1	0 110 001	061	49	31	digit one
2	2	0 110 010	062	50	32	digit two
3	3	0 110 011	063	51	33	digit three
4	4	0 110 100	064	52	34	digit four
5	5	0 110 101	065	53	35	digit five
6	6	0 110 110	066	54	36	digit six
7	7	0 110 111	067	55	37	digit seven
8	8	0 111 000	070	56	38	digit eight
9	9	0 111 001	071	57	39	digit nine
:	:	0 111 010	072	58	3A	colon
;	;	0 111 011	073	59	3B	semicolon
<	<	0 111 100	074	60	3C	less than symbol; left caret
=	=	0 111 101	075	61	3D	equal symbol
>	>	0 111 110	076	62	3E	greater than symbol; right caret
?	?	0 111 111	077	63	3F	question mark
@	@	1 000 000	100	64	40	at sign
A	A	1 000 001	101	65	41	uppercase letter A
B	B	1 000 010	102	66	42	uppercase letter B
C	C	1 000 011	103	67	43	uppercase letter C
D	D	1 000 100	104	68	44	uppercase letter D
E	E	1 000 101	105	69	45	uppercase letter E
F	F	1 000 110	106	70	46	uppercase letter F
G	G	1 000 111	107	71	47	uppercase letter G
H	H	1 001 000	110	72	48	uppercase letter H
I	I	1 001 001	111	73	49	uppercase letter I
J	J	1 001 010	112	74	4A	uppercase letter J
K	K	1 001 011	113	75	4B	uppercase letter K
L	L	1 001 100	114	76	4C	uppercase letter L

| ASCII Terminal | | Equivalent Forms | | | | Definition of Use |
character	key	binary	oct	dec	hex	
M	M	1 001 101	115	77	4D	uppercase letter M
N	N	1 001 110	116	78	4E	uppercase letter N
O	O	1 001 111	117	79	4F	uppercase letter O
P	P	1 010 000	120	80	50	uppercase letter P
Q	Q	1 010 001	121	81	51	uppercase letter Q
R	R	1 010 010	122	82	52	uppercase letter R
S	S	1 010 011	123	83	53	uppercase letter S
T	T	1 010 100	124	84	54	uppercase letter T
U	U	1 010 101	125	85	55	uppercase letter U
V	V	1 010 110	126	86	56	uppercase letter V
W	W	1 010 111	127	87	57	uppercase letter W
X	X	1 011 000	130	88	58	uppercase letter X
Y	Y	1 011 001	131	89	59	uppercase letter Y
Z	Z	1 011 010	132	90	5A	uppercase letter Z
[	[	1 011 011	133	91	5B	left bracket
\	\	1 011 100	134	92	5C	back slash; back slant
]	]	1 011 101	135	93	5D	right bracket
^	^	1 011 110	136	94	5E	circumflex; ↑ up arrow
___	___	1 011 111	137	95	5F	underscore; underline
`	`	1 100 000	140	96	60	back quote; grave accent
a	a	1 100 001	141	97	61	lowercase letter a
b	b	1 100 010	142	98	62	lowercase letter b
c	c	1 100 011	143	99	63	lowercase letter c
d	d	1 100 100	144	100	64	lowercase letter d
e	e	1 100 101	145	101	65	lowercase letter e
f	f	1 100 110	146	102	66	lowercase letter f
g	g	1 100 111	147	103	67	lowercase letter g
h	h	1 101 000	150	104	68	lowercase letter h
i	i	1 101 001	151	105	69	lowercase letter i
j	j	1 101 010	152	106	6A	lowercase letter j
k	k	1 101 011	153	107	6B	lowercase letter k
l	l	1 101 100	154	108	6C	lowercase letter l
m	m	1 101 101	155	109	6D	lowercase letter m
n	n	1 101 110	156	110	6E	lowercase letter n
o	o	1 101 111	157	111	6F	lowercase letter o
p	p	1 110 000	160	112	70	lowercase letter p
q	q	1 110 001	161	113	71	lowercase letter q
r	r	1 110 010	162	114	72	lowercase letter r
s	s	1 110 011	163	115	73	lowercase letter s
t	t	1 110 100	164	116	74	lowercase letter t
u	u	1 110 101	165	117	75	lowercase letter u
v	v	1 110 110	166	118	76	lowercase letter v
w	w	1 110 111	167	119	77	lowercase letter w
x	x	1 111 000	170	120	78	lowercase letter x
y	y	1 111 001	171	121	79	lowercase letter y
z	z	1 111 010	172	122	7A	lowercase letter z
{	{	1 111 011	173	123	7B	left brace
|	|	1 111 100	174	124	7C	vertical bar; logical OR
}	}	1 111 101	175	125	7D	right brace
~	~	1 111 110	176	126	7E	tilde
DEL	DEL	1 111 111	177	127	7F	delete; rub out

EBCDIC   In the EBCDIC table below, only the standardized characters are given; thus not all 256 available codes are present. This code derives partially from the old 6-bit code used in IBM keypunches and thus lacks the more logical arrangement found in ASCII. For example, one finds a difference of one between all letters of the alphabet with the exception of I to J and R to S, where the differences are 8 and 9, respectively. Also, the sorting order based on the numeric values will place lowercase letters before uppercase ones and letters before digits. Furthermore, when stored in byte mode or in any configuration that places the desired character first followed by blanks, the letters and numerals will store as negative numbers (look at the binary or hex representations, which show that the first, or sign, bit is on), sorting the letters and numerals before the special characters, most notably the blank. Special sorts are required when using EBCDIC code directly; however, the lexical functions, which sort in the correct order, provide the programmer with a better option.

EBCDIC char	hex	Equivalent Forms binary	decimal	Definition of Use
NUL	00	0000 0000	0	filler; null
SOH	01	0000 0001	1	start of heading; home position
STX	02	0000 0010	2	start of text
ETX	03	0000 0011	3	end of text
SEL	04	0000 0100	4	select
HT	05	0000 0101	5	horizontal tab
RNL	06	0000 0110	6	required new line
DEL	07	0000 0111	7	delete
GE	08	0000 1000	8	graphic escape
SPS	09	0000 1001	9	superscript
RPT	0A	0000 1010	10	repeat
VT	0B	0000 1011	11	vertical tab; ↑ arrow
FF	0C	0000 1100	12	form feed; clear screen
CR	0D	0000 1101	13	carriage return
SO	0E	0000 1110	14	shift out
SI	0F	0000 1111	15	shift in
DLE	10	0001 0000	16	data link escape
DC1	11	0001 0001	17	device control 1
DC2	12	0001 0010	18	device control 2
DC3	13	0001 0011	19	device control 3
RES/ENP	14	0001 0100	20	restore; enable presentation
NL	15	0001 0101	21	new line acknowledgment
BS	16	0001 0110	22	backspace
POC	17	0001 0111	23	program-operator communication
CAN	18	0001 1000	24	cancel
EM	19	0001 1001	25	end of medium
UBS	1A	0001 1010	26	unit backspace
CU1	1B	0001 1011	27	customer use 1
IFS	1C	0001 1100	28	interchange file separator
IGS	1D	0001 1101	29	interchange group separator
IRS	1E	0001 1110	30	interchange record separator
IUS	1F	0001 1111	31	interchange unit separator
DS	20	0010 0000	32	digit select
SOS	21	0010 0001	33	start of significance
FS	22	0010 0010	34	field separator
WUS	23	0010 0011	35	word underscore
BYP/INP	24	0010 0100	36	bypass; inhibit presentation
LF	25	0010 0101	37	line feed
ETB	26	0010 0110	38	end of transmission block
ESC	27	0010 0111	39	escape
	28	0010 1000	40	reserved
	29	0010 1001	41	reserved
SM/SW	2A	0010 1010	42	set mode, switch
FMT	2B	0010 1011	43	format
	2C	0010 1100	44	reserved
ENQ	2D	0010 1101	45	enquiry

EBCDIC char	hex	Equivalent Forms binary	decimal	Definition of Use
ACK	2E	0010 1110	46	acknowledge
BEL	2F	0010 1111	47	bell
	30	0011 0000	48	reserved
	31	0011 0001	49	reserved
SYN	32	0011 0010	50	synchronous
IR	33	0011 0011	51	index
PP	34	0011 0100	52	presentation position
TRN	35	0011 0101	53	transparent
NBS	36	0011 0110	54	numeric backspace
EOT	37	0011 0111	55	end of transmission
SBS	38	0011 1000	56	subscript
IT	39	0011 1001	57	indent
RFF	3A	0011 1010	58	required
CU3	3B	0011 1011	59	customer use 3
DC4	3C	0011 1100	60	device control 4
NAK	3D	0011 1101	61	negative acknowledge
	3E	0011 1110	62	reserved
SUB	3F	0011 1111	63	substitute
SP	40	0100 0000	64	space; blank
RSP	41	0100 0001	65	required space
¢ or [	4A	0100 1010	74	cents symbol on IBM; left bracket on Burroughs
.	4B	0100 1011	75	period; decimal point
<	4C	0100 1100	76	less than sign; left caret
(	4D	0100 1101	77	left parenthesis
+	4E	0100 1110	78	plus symbol
|	4F	0100 1111	79	logical OR
&	50	0101 0000	80	ampersand
! or]	5A	0101 1010	90	exclamation mark on IBM; right bracket on Burroughs
$	5B	0101 1011	91	currency symbol
*	5C	0101 1100	92	asterisk
)	5D	0101 1101	93	right parenthesis
;	5E	0101 1110	94	semicolon
¬	5F	0101 1111	95	logical NOT symbol
-	60	0110 0000	96	minus sign; hyphen
/	61	0110 0001	97	slash
|	6A	0110 1010	106	vertical line
,	6B	0110 1011	107	comma
%	6C	0110 1100	108	percent symbol
___	6D	0110 1101	109	underscore
>	6E	0110 1110	110	greater than sign; right caret
?	6F	0110 1111	111	question mark
`	79	0111 1001	121	grave accent; back quote
:	7A	0111 1010	122	colon
#	7B	0111 1011	123	number sign
@	7C	0111 1100	124	at sign
'	7D	0111 1101	125	prime; apostrophe
=	7E	0111 1110	126	equal sign
"	7F	0111 1111	127	quotation marks; double quote
a	81	1000 0001	129	lowercase letter a
b	82	1000 0010	130	lowercase letter b
c	83	1000 0011	131	lowercase letter c
d	84	1000 0100	132	lowercase letter d
e	85	1000 0101	133	lowercase letter e
f	86	1000 0110	134	lowercase letter f
g	87	1000 0111	135	lowercase letter g
h	88	1000 1000	136	lowercase letter h
i	89	1000 1001	137	lowercase letter i

EBCDIC char	hex	Equivalent Forms binary	decimal	Definition of Use
j	91	1001 0001	145	lowercase letter j
k	92	1001 0010	146	lowercase letter k
l	93	1001 0011	147	lowercase letter l
m	94	1001 0100	148	lowercase letter m
n	95	1001 0101	149	lowercase letter n
o	96	1001 0110	150	lowercase letter o
p	97	1001 0111	151	lowercase letter p
q	98	1001 1000	152	lowercase letter q
r	99	1001 1001	153	lowercase letter r
~	A1	1010 0001	161	tilde
s	A2	1010 0010	162	lowercase letter s
t	A3	1010 0011	163	lowercase letter t
u	A4	1010 0100	164	lowercase letter u
v	A5	1010 0101	165	lowercase letter v
w	A6	1010 0110	166	lowercase letter w
x	A7	1010 0111	167	lowercase letter x
y	A8	1010 1000	168	lowercase letter y
z	A9	1010 1001	169	lowercase letter z
{	C0	1100 0000	192	opening brace
A	C1	1100 0001	193	uppercase letter A
B	C2	1100 0010	194	uppercase letter B
C	C3	1100 0011	195	uppercase letter C
D	C4	1100 0100	196	uppercase letter D
E	C5	1100 0101	197	uppercase letter E
F	C6	1100 0110	198	uppercase letter F
G	C7	1100 0111	199	uppercase letter G
H	C8	1100 1000	200	uppercase letter H
I	C9	1100 1001	201	uppercase letter I
}	D0	1101 0000	208	closing brace
J	D1	1101 0001	209	uppercase letter J
K	D2	1101 0010	210	uppercase letter K
L	D3	1101 0011	211	uppercase letter L
M	D4	1101 0100	212	uppercase letter M
N	D5	1101 0101	213	uppercase letter N
O	D6	1101 0110	214	uppercase letter O
P	D7	1101 0111	215	uppercase letter P
Q	D8	1101 1000	216	uppercase letter Q
R	D9	1101 1001	217	uppercase letter R
\	E0	1110 0000	224	reverse slash; back slash
S	E2	1110 0010	226	uppercase letter S
T	E3	1110 0011	227	uppercase letter T
U	E4	1110 0100	228	uppercase letter U
V	E5	1110 0101	229	uppercase letter V
W	E6	1110 0110	230	uppercase letter W
X	E7	1110 0111	231	uppercase letter X
Y	E8	1110 1000	232	uppercase letter Y
Z	E9	1110 1001	233	uppercase letter Z
0	F0	1111 0000	240	digit zero
1	F1	1111 0001	241	digit one
2	F2	1111 0010	242	digit two
3	F3	1111 0011	243	digit three
4	F4	1111 0100	244	digit four
5	F5	1111 0101	245	digit five
6	F6	1111 0100	246	digit six
7	F7	1111 0111	247	digit seven
8	F8	1111 1000	248	digit eight
9	F9	1111 1001	249	digit nine

Appendix D

Answers to Selected Review Questions and Exercises

For purposes of compactness, many of the program solutions in this appendix lack the spacing, comments, and other documentation usually shown in the text. In this way, more solutions can be presented within the pages allocated. The reader's indulgence is requested.

Exercise 3.1b

```
      output message
PRINT *, '+-------------------------------------------+'
PRINT *, '|      High Security Programming Area        |'
PRINT *, '|                                            |'
PRINT *, '|             NO BUGS ALLOWED                |'
PRINT *, '+-------------------------------------------+'
STOP  'end-of-run'
END
```

Review Question 3.2a

a. CHRCTR   valid
b. 123ABC   invalid: begins with nonalphabetic
c. REAL   valid
d. LETTER   valid
e. FORTRAN   invalid: more than standard six characters
f. PL/1   invalid: contains invalid character (/)
g. NUMBER   valid
h. C*B*L   invalid: contains invalid character (*)
i. $10   invalid: contains invalid character ($)

Review Question 3.2b

```
CHARACTER  STATE*2, TOWN*18, COMMNT*50          70 bytes
        or
CHARACTER*2   STATE
CHARACTER*18  TOWN
CHARACTER*50  COMMNT
```

Review Question 3.2c: $3 * 5 + 2 * 7 + 12 + 14 = 55$ bytes

Review Question 3.4d: YONEW

Review Question 3.5a

a. D more than six significant digits
b. J greater than 32767
c. E 0.00000517662
d. I
e. X invalid character ($)
f. D more than six significant digits
g. E 720000000000000000.0
h. D *D* exponential notation forces double-precision storage
i. X invalid character (,)
j. X invalid characters (blank and /)
k. E

Review Question 3.5b

a. 45.72
b. 18.75
c. 29.9
d. 240000.0

e. 1.876532
f. 9.95
g. 0.7526
h. 834.57665

Review Question 3.5c

a. 0.12545E+03
b. −0.208E−06
c. 0.10E+00

d. 0.1871098D+05
e. 0.2147483647D+10
f. −0.32768E+05

Review Question 3.6a

a. C
b. I
c. I

d. I
e. I
f. D

g. D
h. D
i. I

j. J
k. R
l. I

Review Question 3.6b

```
IMPLICIT INTEGER          (A-B, E)
IMPLICIT REAL             (C, X-Z)
IMPLICIT DOUBLE PRECISION (M)
IMPLICIT CHARACTER*2      (P, S)
IMPLICIT CHARACTER*16     (F, N)
```

Exercise 3.8c

```
C       computer questionnaire, input from file
        CHARACTER  SERIAL*1, MONTOR*10, PRINTR*12
        INTEGER    MEMORY, HARDSK, DRIVES, AMOUNT
        REAL       SIZEDS
        OPEN  (2, FILE='EX0308C.IN')
        READ  (2,*) MEMORY
        READ  (2,*) HARDSK
        READ  (2,*) DRIVES, SIZEDS
        READ  (2,*) SERIAL
        READ  (2,*) MONTOR
        READ  (2,*) PRINTR
        READ  (2,*) AMOUNT
        CLOSE (2)
```

```
     PRINT *, 'Customer desires:'
     PRINT *, '  Memory',MEMORY,'K  with', HARDSK,'m hard disk'
     PRINT *, '  ', DRIVES, SIZEDS,' diskette drive(s)'
     PRINT *, '  Serial communications adaptor - ', SERIAL
     PRINT *, '  ', MONTOR,' monitor and a ',PRINTR,' printer'
     PRINT *, '  For  $',AMOUNT
     STOP  'end-of-run'
     END
```

Sample Input File   *Sample Output File*

```
2048
110
1,3,50
'Y'
'Color'
'Dot Matrix'
2250
```

```
Customer desires:
  Memory        2048k  with         110m hard disk
               1        3.500000 diskette drive(s)
  Serial communications adaptor - Y
  Color       monitor and a Dot Matrix    printer
  For  $       2250
end-of-run
```

Exercise 3.11d

```
C          display file line with ruler
     CHARACTER*50  LINE
C                  read line from file
     OPEN  (2, FILE='EX0311C.OUT')
     READ  (2, *)  LINE
     CLOSE (2)
C                  display ruler and line
     PRINT *, '          1        12        23        34        45'
     PRINT *, '12345678901234567890123456789012345678901234567890'
     PRINT *, LINE
C                  termination
     STOP  'end-of-run'
     END
```

Review Question 4.1a

a. 54	d. 104,967	g. 6	j. 0.0123457
b. 144	e. 3	h. 0	
c. 1302	f. 0	i. −3	

Review Question 4.1b

a. N * (N − 1) / 2
b. (I + J) / (K + M)
c. I + J / (K + M)
d. J**3 − 4 * M * N
e. I / K**M or I * K**(−M)

Review Question 4.1c

a. $\dfrac{I}{J} - K$ b. $I + J * \dfrac{K}{M} * N$ c. $(I + J) * \dfrac{K}{(M * N)}$ d. $\dfrac{J}{K} + \dfrac{M}{L}$

e. $M * N ** 3 + K ** J$

Review Question 4.2a

I = −86   J = −57   K = 143   L = 170   M = 54   N = 19

Review Question 4.2b

A = 18.7   B = 23.2   N = 7   I = 0   J = 1   K = −18   C = 7   D = 6.0

Exercise 4.2f

```
C       number to various powers
    PRINT *, 'Enter a positive integer number'
    READ  *,  NUMBER
    ISQUAR = NUMBER**2
    ICUBE  = NUMBER**3
    XNUMBR = NUMBER
    SQUART = XNUMBR**0.5
    CUBERT = XNUMBR**(1.0/3.0)
    PRINT *, ISQUAR, ICUBE, SQUART, CUBERT
    STOP  'end-of-run'
    END
```

Review Question 4.3a

	S1	S4	S8
a.	1	1234	1234
b.	F	FORT	FORT
c.		HI	HI

Review Question 4.5a

a. −5.0	g. −3.4	m. 5.0	s. 8
b. 87.0	h. 3	n. −2.50	t. 7.0
c. −6.0	i. 0	o. 23	u. 0.00
d. 88.0	j. 6.20	p. 23.0	v. 1.0
e. 2	k. 5	q. −2	w. 0.0
f. −2	l. 22.7	r. 7	x. 1.0

Exercise 4.5d

```
C       prove trigonometric identity
    PRINT *, 'Enter degrees as integer'
    READ  *,  IDEG
    RADIAN = REAL(IDEG) / 180.0 * 3.14159
    TEST   = SQRT (SIN (RADIAN) ** 2  +  COS (RADIAN) ** 2)
    PRINT *, IDEG, TEST
    STOP  'end-of-run'
    END
```

Exercise 4.5g

```
C       rounded tax
    PRINT *, 'Enter (real) cost'
    READ  *,  COST
    TAX   = 0.08 * COST
    ROUND = ANINT (100.0 * TAX) / 100.0
    PRINT *, TAX, ROUND
    STOP  'end-of-run'
    END
```

Exercise 4.5h

```
C       grade analysis
     PRINT *, 'Enter five (integer) examination grades'
     READ *, IG1, IG2, IG3, IG4, IG5
     MAX = MAXO (IG1, IG2, IG3, IG4, IG5)
     MIN = MINO (IG1, IG2, IG3, IG4, IG5)
     AVG = REAL (IG1 + IG2 + IG3 + IG4 + IG5) / 5.0
     PRINT *, MAX, MIN,AVG
     STOP  'end-of-run'
     END
```

Exercise 4.5n

```
C       number of digits
     PRINT *, 'Enter integer number'
     READ *, NUMBER
     PRINT *, INT (ALOG10 (REAL (IABS (NUMBER))) + 1.0)
     STOP  'end-of-run'
     END
```

Exercise 4.8d

```
C       temperature analysis
     PRINT *, 'Enter high and low temperatures for day (integer)'
     READ *, IHIGH, ILOW
     MEAN = (IHIGH + ILOW) / 2
     IDDAY = IDIM (65 - MEAN, 0)
     PRINT *, MEAN, IDDAY
     STOP  'end-of-run'
     END
```

Exercise 5.3g

1. Input SALARY
2. If SALARY < 100.00
     TAX = 0.02 * SALARY
   Else if SALARY >= 300.00
     TAX = 10.00 + 0.05 * (SALARY-300.00)
   Else
     TAX = 2.00 + 0.04 * (SALARY-100.00)
3. NET = SALARY - TAX
4. Display TAX, NET

Exercise 5.3h

1. Input SALARY, ACCUM
2. If (ACCUM + SALARY) <= 50,000
     TAXABLE = SALARY
3. If (ACCUM + SALARY) > 50,000
     TAXABLE = 50,000 - SALARY'
4. If TAXABLE < 0, TAXABLE = 0
5. TAX = 0.08 * TAXABLE
6. Display TAX

Exercise 5.5c

```
C           test intrinsic function IDIM
     20 PRINT *, 'Enter two integers'
            READ    (*,*, ERR=60, END=90) I, J
            K = IDIM (I, J)
            PRINT *, 'IDIM of (',I,',',J,') =',K
               GO TO 80
C                         error branch
     60     PRINT *, 'Error in input'
C                         return for more data
     80 GO TO 20
C                         termination
     90 STOP  'end-of-run'
        END
```

Exercise 5.6e

```
C          music times
       DATA   ITOTSC/ 0/
C                        input loop
    20 PRINT *, 'Enter time as mm.ss'
          READ  (*,*, ERR=60, END=90)  TIME
          MINUTE = TIME
          ISECND = 100.0 * (TIME - REAL (MINUTE)) + 0.5
          ITOTSC = ITOTSC + ISECND + 60 * MINUTE
       GO TO 80
C                        error processing
    60     PRINT *, 'ERROR IN INPUT  -  re-enter'
C                        return for more data
    80 GO TO 20
C                        final calculation
    90 TIME = REAL (ITOTSC / 60)  +  REAL (MOD (ITOTSC, 60)) / 100.0
       PRINT *, TIME
       STOP  'end-of-run'
       END
```

Exercise 5.7b

```
C          analyze parity
    20 PRINT *, 'Enter two integers:'
          READ  (*,*, ERR=60, END=90) I, J
          K = IABS (I + J)
          IF  (MOD (K,2) .EQ. 0)  PRINT *, 'SAME PARITY'
          IF  (MOD (K,2) .NE. 0)  PRINT *, 'OPPOSITE PARITY'
             GO TO 80
C                        error processing
    60     PRINT *, 'ERROR IN INPUT  -  re-enter'
C                        return for more data
    80 GO TO 20
C                        termination
    90 STOP   'end-of-run'
       END
```

Exercise 5.8c

```
C          tax calculations
       DATA   TOTSAL, TOTTAX/ 2 * 0.00/
    20 PRINT *, 'Enter salary'
          READ  (*,*, ERR=60, END=90)  SALARY
          IF  (SALARY .LT. 100.00)  THEN
             TAX = 0.02 * SALARY
           ELSE IF  (SALARY .LT. 300)  THEN
             TAX = 2.00 + 0.04 * (SALARY - 100.00)
           ELSE
             TAX = 10.00 + 0.05 * (SALARY - 300.00)
          ENDIF
          SALNET = SALARY - TAX
          TOTSAL = TOTSAL + SALARY
          TOTTAX = TOTTAX + TAX
          PRINT *,  SALARY, TAX, SALNET
             GO TO 80
C                        error processing
    60     PRINT *, 'ERROR IN INPUT  -  re-enter'
C                        return for more data
    80 GO TO 20
C                        termination
    90 PRINT *, TOTSAL, TOTTAX
       STOP  'end-of-run'
       END
```

Exercise 5.9b

```
C          salary analysis
       LOGICAL  ST, DT, OT
    20 PRINT *, 'Enter hours worked'
          READ  (*,*, ERR=60, END=90)  HOURS
          ST = HOURS .LE. 40.00
          DT = HOURS .GT. 60.00
          OT = .NOT. (ST .OR. DT)
          IF  (ST)  PRINT *, 'STRAIGHT TIME'
          IF  (DT)  PRINT *, 'DOUBLE TIME'
          IF  (OT)  PRINT *, 'OVERTIME'
             GO TO 80
C                         error processing
    60    PRINT *, 'ERROR IN INPUT  -  re-enter'
C                         return for more data
    80 GO TO 20
C                         termination
    90 STOP  'end-of-run'
       END
```

Exercise 5.10d

```
C          quadratic equation
    PRINT *, 'Enter values for a, b, c'
    READ  *, A, B, C
    IF  (A .EQ. 0.00  .AND.  B .EQ. 0.00)  THEN
        PRINT *, 'Invalid Input'
     ELSE IF  (A .EQ. 0.00)  THEN
        X = -C / B
        PRINT *, 'x =', X
     ELSE
        D = B*B  -  4.0 * A * C
        IF  (D .GE. 0)  THEN
            X1 = (-B + SQRT(D)) / (2.0 * A)
            X2 = (-B - SQRT(D)) / (2.0 * A)
            PRINT *, 'x1 =',X1,'          x2 =',X2
        ELSE
            XR = -B / (2.0 * A)
            XI = SQRT(-D) / (2.0 * A)
            PRINT *, 'x1 =',XR,' +',XI,' i'
            PRINT *, 'x2 =',XR,' -',XI,' i'
        ENDIF
     ENDIF
    ENDIF
    STOP  'end-of-run'
    END
```

Review Question 6.1a

a. 13   b. 0   c. 3   d. 4   e. 10

Review Question 6.1b

a. 720   b. 17   c. 30   d. 5

Exercise 6.1d

```
C          Fibonacci series
       PRINT *, '        Term         Value'
       IPREV = 1
       PRINT *, '           1 ', IPREV
       ILAST = 1
       PRINT *, '           2 ', ILAST
       DO 100  I = 3,20
           IVALUE = IPREV + ILAST
           PRINT *, I, IVALUE
           IPREV = ILAST
   100 ILAST = IVALUE
       STOP  'end-of-run'
       END
```

Exercise 6.2a

```
C          salary calculations with data file
       LOGICAL  INVLHR, INVLRT
C                    initialize error counters
       DATA  NHRERR, NRTERR, NCHERR/ 3 * 0/
C                    open input file
       OPEN  (2, FILE='EX0602A.IN')
C          loop through input
       DO 80  I = 1,2000
           INVLHR = .FALSE.
           INVLRT = .FALSE.
           READ    (2,*, ERR=60, END=90)  IHOURS, RATE
           IF  (IHOURS .LT. 1  .OR.  IHOURS .GT. 80)  THEN
               NHRERR = NHRERR + 1
               INVLHR = .TRUE.
           ENDIF
           IF  (RATE .LT. 3.75  .OR.  RATE .GT. 60.00)  THEN
               NRTERR = NRTERR + 1
               INVLRT = .TRUE.
           ENDIF
           IF  (INVLHR .AND. INVLRT)  THEN
               PRINT *, I, IHOURS, RATE, '  Invalid hours and pay'
            ELSE IF  (INVLHR)  THEN
               PRINT *, I, IHOURS, RATE, '  Invalid hours'
            ELSE IF  (INVLRT)  THEN
               PRINT *, I, IHOURS, RATE, '  Invalid rate of pay'
            ELSE
               PRINT *, I, IHOURS, RATE
           ENDIF
           GO TO 80
C                    invalid character in data
    60     NCHERR = NCHERR + 1
           PRINT *, I, '  Invalid character in input record'
C                    return for more data
    80 CONTINUE
C                    termination
    90 CLOSE (2)
       PRINT *, I-1,' records read with', NHRERR,' hour errors,'
       PRINT *, NRTERR,' rate errors and', NCHERR,' invalid records'
       STOP  'end-of-run'
       END
```

Exercise 6.3a

a. 6 36 216   b. 6 36 216   c. 5 25 125

Exercise 6.4c

```
C       table of factorials
        INTEGER*4  IFACT
        PRINT *, '      Number    Factorial'
        DO 40  I = 1,10
           IFACT = 1
           DO 20  J = 1,I
   20      IFACT = IFACT * J
   40 PRINT *, I, IFACT
        STOP  'end-of-run'
        END
```

Exercise 6.7a

```
C           Newton's method for square roots
C                  loop through input
        DO 80  I = 1,20000
           PRINT *, 'Enter value whose square root is wanted'
           READ    (*,*, ERR=60, END=90)  XN
           IF  (XN .LE. 0.00)  GO TO 60
           APPROX = XN
           DO 20  ITRIAL = 1,50
                ROOT = (APPROX + XN/APPROX) / 2.0
                PREC = ABS (ROOT - APPROX) / ROOT
                PRINT *, ITRIAL, ROOT, PREC
                IF  (PREC .LT. 0.000001)  GO TO 80
                APPROX = ROOT
   20      CONTINUE
           PRINT *, 'Program error!'
               GO TO 80
C                  invalid character or value
   60      PRINT *, 'Invalid characters or value <= 0.00'
C                  return for more data
   80 CONTINUE
C                  termination
   90 STOP  'end-of-run'
        END
```

Review Question 7.4a

Line 1 of new page, columns 21–25: TITLE
Line 3,   columns 14–21: Headings
Line 3,   columns 25–32: Headings
Line 5,   columns 1–14: Identification
Line 5,   columns 31–36: Detail

Exercise 7.4g

```
C          tick-tack-toe
        DO 40  I = 1,3
           DO 20  J = 1,3
   20      WRITE   (5,1020)
 1020      FORMAT  (' ', '      |      |')
   40 IF  (I .LT. 3)  WRITE  (5,1040)
 1040 FORMAT  (' ', '------|------|------')
        STOP  'end-of-run'
        END
```

Exercise 7.5f

```
C          date conversion
           CHARACTER*2, MONTH, DAY, YEAR
           WRITE   (5,1000)
 1000 FORMAT   ('0','Enter:')
           WRITE   (5,1002)
 1002 FORMAT   (' ','Month Day Year')
           WRITE   (5,1004)
 1004 FORMAT   (' ','__    __  ____')
           READ    (5,1006)  MONTH, DAY, YEAR
 1006 FORMAT   (A2, 4X, A2, 4X, A2)
           WRITE   (5,1008)  MONTH, DAY, YEAR
 1008 FORMAT   (' ',A2,'/',A2,'/',A2)
           STOP  'end-of-run'
           END
```

Review Question 7.6a

	I	J	K
a.	1	789	999
b.	0	8765	100
c.	0	0	0
d.	12	4567	123

Review Question 7.6b

	I	J	K
a.	1278	9	9999
b.	987	4321	0
c.	0	0	0
d.	12345	8901	2345

Review Question 7.6c

	I	J	K
a.	127	89	99
b.	98	7654	321
c.	0	0	0
d.	1234	5678	9012

Review Question 7.6d

	I	J	K
a.	127	9	99
b.	98	21	0
c.	0	0	0
d.	1234	1	45

Review Question 7.6e

	I	J	K
a.	1	9	127
b.	0	1	98
c.	0	0	0
d.	12	1	1234

Review Question 7.6g

```
                                     11111111112
                     columns:  12345678901234567890
                               -12    12345    9876
                                -12****9876
                                 -12,12345,9876
                                 9876    -12   12345
                               **123459876
                                  -12  ****   9876
                               GO TO = ******
```

Review Question 7.6h

```
FORMAT  (' ', 3I8)
FORMAT  (' ', I3, I7, I6)
FORMAT  (' ', 3I6)
FORMAT  (' ',I3, T8,I5, T4,I4)
FORMAT  (' ', I4, 2I6)
FORMAT  (' ', I3, ',',I5, ',',I4)
FORMAT  (' ', I3, '-',I5, '-',I4)
FORMAT  (' ','X = ', I2, ' -',I5, 1X,I3)
```

Review Question 7.7a

	X	Y
a.	12.34	0.1234
b.	87.4256	0.00
c.	15200000.0	0.00000325
d.	20.2	8765.4321
e.	1.0	0.01
f.	1.0	1.0

Review Question 7.7b

```
                    111111111122222222223333333
    columns:  123456789012345678901234567890123456
              -12.500   123.450********      0.000
              -12.50    123.45879050.00      0.00
              -0.1E+02   0.1E+03   0.9E+06 -0.3E-03
               0.E+02    0.E+03    0.E+06   0.E-03
                 -13.      123.   879050.       0.
              -12.50123.45******   0.00
```

Review Question 7.9a

Letter	Page	Line
A	1	3
B	1	8
C	2	1
D	2	3
E	2	6
F	2	8
G	3	1

Review Question 7.10b

	R1	R2	R3	R4
a.	27.45	117.42	37.11	105.64
b.	27.45	82.37	117.42	−3.76
c.	27.45	82.37	53.21	117.42
d.	27.45	82.37	53.21	0.00
e.	27.45	82.37	37.11	40.50
f.	117.42	−3.76	105.64	100.00
g.	27.45	82.37	−.12	77.91
h.	27.45	−3.76	37.11	105.64
i.	27.45	−.12	37.11	−9.99

Exercise 8.3b

```
C     arithmetic statement function to convert real to two decimal places
      RND2 (X) = ANINT (100.0 * X) / 100.0
      DO 20  I = 1,20000
         READ    (*,*, END=90)  Y
   20 PRINT *, Y, RND2(Y)
   90 STOP  'end-of-run'
      END
```

Exercise 8.4c

```
C          Function for salary calculations
      FUNCTION  SALARY (HOURS, RATE)
      IF  (HOURS .GE. 0.00  .AND.  RATE .GE. 0.00)  THEN
          IF  (HOURS .LE. 40.0)  THEN
              SALARY = HOURS * RATE
            ELSEIF  (HOURS .LE. 60.00)  THEN
              SALARY = 40.0 * RATE  +  (HOURS - 40.0) * RATE * 1.5
            ELSE
              SALARY = 40.0 * RATE  +  20.0 * RATE * 1.5  +
     1                        (HOURS - 60.0) * RATE * 2.0
          ENDIF
        ELSE
          SALARY = 0.00
      ENDIF
      RETURN
      END
C
C                 DRIVER
      DO 20  I = 1,20000
         PRINT *, 'Enter hours, rate (real)'
         READ    (*,*, END=90)  H, R
   20 PRINT *, SALARY (H,R)
   90 STOP  'end-of-run'
      END
```

Exercise 8.5f

```
C         Subroutine to analyze numbers
          SUBROUTINE  EXAMIN (I, J, SAMSGN, SAMPAR)
          LOGICAL  SAMSGN, SAMPAR
          SAMSGN = ISIGN       (1,I) .EQ. ISIGN       (1,J)
          SAMPAR = IABS (MOD (I,2)) .EQ. IABS (MOD (J,2))
          RETURN
          END
C                      DRIVER
          LOGICAL  SMSGN, SMPAR
          DO 20  I = 1,20000
              PRINT *, 'Enter two numbers'
              READ     (*,*, END=90) M, N
              CALL EXAMIN (M, N, SMSGN, SMPAR)
       20 PRINT *, 'Same sign:', SMSGN,',    parity:', SMPAR
       90 STOP  'end-of-run'
          END
```

Exercise 8.6d

```
C         Generate random data, write to file
          CHARACTER AMPM
C                     seed random number and open output file
          IDUMMY = RND(21717)
          OPEN  (3, FILE='EX0806D.OUT')
          DO 20  I = 1,100
              MONTH  = INTRAN (1,12)
              IDAY   = INTRAN (1,30)
              IYEAR  = INTRAN (1988,1992)
              IHOUR  = INTRAN (1,12)
              MINUTE = INTRAN (0,59)
              IAMPM  = INTRAN (1,2)
                     IF  (IAMPM .EQ. 1)  AMPM = 'A'
                     IF  (IAMPM .EQ. 2)  AMPM = 'P'
              AMOUNT = RND(0) * 1000.00  + 1.0
       20 WRITE     (3,1020) MONTH, IDAY, IYEAR, IHOUR, MINUTE, AMPM, AMOUNT
     1020 FORMAT   (I2, 1X,I2, 1X,I4, I2, 1X,I2, 1X,A1, 3X,F10.2)
          CLOSE  (3)
          STOP  'end-of-run'
          END
```

Exercise 8.8b

```
C         Accounts Receivable
          DATA  TOT30, TOT60, TOT90, TOTGR/ 4 * 0.00/
C                      request date of report
          PRINT *, 'Enter date for report as 4-digit number (moyr)'
          READ *, MDATE
          IDATUM = MONTH (MDATE)
          PRINT *, 'Number of months =', IDATUM
C                       open files and write headings
          OPEN  (2, FILE='EX0808B.IN')
          WRITE  (*,1000) MDATE
     1000 FORMAT ('1','Accounts Receivable for ', I4/
         1        '0','Invoice  Date    Amount  Discount Surcharge',
         2        '     Total Age')
```

```
C                         loop through input
      DO 20  I = 1,20000
            READ    (2,1002, END=90)  INV, IDATE, AMOUNT
 1002       FORMAT  (I4, 2X, I4, F10.2)
            MONTHS = MONAGE (MDATE, IDATE)
            CALL ADDCHG (AMOUNT, MONTHS, DISCNT, SRCHRG)
            FNLAMT = AMOUNT - DISCNT + SRCHRG
            IF (MONTHS .EQ. 0)  THEN
                  TOT30 = TOT30 + FNLAMT
               ELSE IF  (MONTHS .EQ. 1)  THEN
                  TOT60 = TOT60 + FNLAMT
               ELSE IF  (MONTHS .EQ. 2) THEN
                  TOT90 = TOT90 + FNLAMT
               ELSE
                  TOTGR = TOTGR + FNLAMT
            ENDIF
            WRITE    (*,1004)  INV, IDATE, AMOUNT, DISCNT, SRCHRG, FNLAMT,
     1                         MONTHS
 1004       FORMAT  (' ', I7, I6, 4F10.2, I4)
   20 CONTINUE
C
   90 WRITE    (*,1090)  TOT30, TOT60, TOT90, TOTGR
 1090 FORMAT  ('0','Aging:   30 days   60 days   90 days      > 90'/
     1          ' ', 6X,      4F10.2)
      CLOSE (2)
      STOP  'end-of-run'
      END
C
C         Function MONTH:  returns number of months since December 1987
      FUNCTION  MONTH (MOYR)
      MO = MOYR / 100
      IY = MOD (MOYR, 100)
      MONTH = 12 * (IY - 88)  +  MO
      RETURN
      END
C
C         Function MONAGE:  determines number of months between two dates
      FUNCTION  MONAGE (MOYR1, MOYR2)
      MONAGE = MONTH (MOYR1) - MONTH (MOYR2)
      IF (MONAGE .LT. 0)  MONAGE = 0
      IF (MONAGE .GT. 3)  MONAGE = 3
      RETURN
      END
C
C         Subroutine ADDCHG:  returns additional charges
      SUBROUTINE  ADDCHG (AMOUNT, MAGE, DSCNT, SRCHRG)
      RND2 (A) = ANINT (100.0 * A) / 100.0
      DSCNT  = 0.00
      SRCHRG = 0.00
      IF (MAGE .EQ. 0)  DSCNT  = RND2 (0.02 * AMOUNT)
      IF (MAGE .EQ. 2)  SRCHRG = RND2 (0.05 * AMOUNT)
      IF (MAGE .EQ. 3)  SRCHRG = RND2 (100.00 + 0.08 * AMOUNT)
      RETURN
      END
```

Review Question 9.2a

a. 19	c. 90	e. 11	g. 100
b. 19	d. 21	f. 301	h. 201

Review Question 9.3a

a.	1	2	3	4	5
b.	4	3	6	7	8
	9	10			
c.	1	2	3	4	5
	6	7	8	9	10
d.	1	6	2	7	3
	8	4	9	5	10
e.	6	7	8	3	4
	5				
f.	6	1	8	3	10
	5				
g.	1	4	2	5	

Review Question 9.3b

a.	10	1	3
	9		
b.	6	7	8
	9	10	
	1	2	3
	4	5	
c.	6	7	8
	9	10	
	1	2	
	3	4	
	5		

Review Question 9.3c

a. all values of J and K
   J = 1, 2, 3, 6, 7
   K = 8, 11, 12, 13, 16
b. J(1:3) = 1, 3, 7
   K(1:3) = 2, 6, 8
c. J(2) = 6, J(4) = 7
   K(1) = 1, K(3) = 2, K(5) = 3
d. J(2) = 7, J(4) = 6
   K(1) = 3, K(4) = 1
   J(4) = 4, J(2) = 7

Exercise 9.3f

```
C          tax table
      PARAMETER  (RATE = 0.08)
      DIMENSION  AMOUNT(100), TAX(100)
      DO 20  I = 1,100
          AMOUNT(I) = REAL (I) / 100.00
   20 TAX(I) = ANINT (AMOUNT(I) * RATE * 100.00) / 100.00
      WRITE   (*,1020)  (AMOUNT(I), TAX(I), I=1,100)
 1020 FORMAT  ('1',' Amount      Tax'/ (' ', 2F8.2))
      STOP  'end-of-run'
      END
```

Exercise 9.4a

```
C           using DATA statement
        DIMENSION  X(20)
        DATA  X/ 5 * -1.00,  10 * 0.00,  5 * 1.00/
        WRITE   (*,1000)  X
  1000 FORMAT  (' ',10F7.1)
        STOP  'end-of-run'
        END
```

Exercise 9.4e

```
C           social security taxes
        DO 20  I = 1,20000
            PRINT *, 'Enter salary, accumulation'
            READ  (*,*, END=90)  SAL, ACC
    20 PRINT *, 'FICA tax = $', FICATX(SAL,ACC)
    90 STOP  'end-of-run'
        END
C
        FUNCTION FICATX (SALARY, ACCUM)
        DATA  RATE, ACCMAX/ 0.825, 54000.00/
        IF  (ACCUM + SALARY .LE. ACCMAX)  FICATX = RATE * SALARY
        IF  (ACCUM          .LT. ACCMAX    .AND.
     1      ACCUM + SALARY .GT. ACCMAX)
     2                               FICATX = RATE * (ACCMAX - ACCUM)
        IF  (ACCUM          .GE. ACCMAX)  FICATX = 0.00
        RETURN
        END
```

Exercise 9.5d

```
C           tabulating votes
        DIMENSION  IN(12), NTOT(12), PCTOT(12)
        DATA       NTOT/ 12 * 0/
C                      open file,  read number of candidates
        OPEN    (2, FILE='EX0905D.IN')
        READ    (2,*)  NCAN
C                      loop through input
        DO 80  I = 1,20000
            READ    (2,1000, END=90)  IN
  1000      FORMAT  (12I4)
            IF  (NCAN .LT. 12)  THEN
                NN = NCAN + 1
                Do 20  J = NN, 12
                    IF  (IN(J) .NE. 0)  THEN
                        WRITE   (*,1002)  IN(J), I, J
  1002                  FORMAT  ('0',I4,' invalid votes for candidate',
     1                            I3,' in data record',I4)
                        STOP  'Data error'
                    ENDIF
    20          CONTINUE
            ENDIF
            NSUM = 0
            DO 40  J = 1,NCAN
                NTOT(J) = NTOT(J) + IN(J)
    40      NSUM = NSUM + NTOT(J)
            DO 60  J = 1,NCAN
```

```
     60      PCTOT(J) = REAL (NTOT(J)) / REAL (NSUM) * 100.0
             WRITE    (*,1060)  (IN(J), J=1,NCAN)
   1060      FORMAT   ('0','New votes:  ', 12I5)
             WRITE    (*,1062) (NTOT(J), J=1,NCAN)
   1062      FORMAT   (' ','Total votes:', 12I5)
     80 WRITE    (*,1080) (PCTOT(J), J=1,NCAN)
   1080 FORMAT  (' ','Percentages:', 12F5.1)
C
     90 CLOSE (2)
        STOP  'end-of-run'
        END
```

Exercise 9.6c

```
C           function for taxes
C                   loop through input
        DO 80  N = 1,20000
C                   prompt and input
          WRITE   (*,1000)
   1000   FORMAT  (' ', 'Enter income     ctrl-Z to terminate')
          READ    (*,*, END=90)  XINCM
C           access subroutine
          TAX = TAXFNC (XINCM)
C           output
          WRITE   (*,1060)  XINCM, TAX
   1060   FORMAT  (' ', 'For income of', F10.2,', tax = ', F8.2)
     80 CONTINUE
C           termination
     90 STOP
        END
C           Function  TAXFNC: computes graduated income tax
        FUNCTION  TAXFNC (X)
C     Tax program based on the following table:
C     Income                      Tax
C     ------                      ---
C          up  to   $8,000              2% of income
C       $8,000  to  $12,000      $160 +  4% in excess of  $8,000
C      $12,000  to  $20,000      $320 +  5% in excess of $12,000
C      $20,000  to  $40,000      $720 +  8% in excess of $20,000
C      greater than $40,000     $2320 + 10% in excess of $40,000
C
        DIMENSION  RANGE(5),  BASE(5),  RATE(5)
        DATA   RANGE/  0.00, 8000.00, 12000.00, 20000.00, 40000.00/
        DATA   BASE/   0.00,  160.00,   320.00,   720.00,  2320.00/
        DATA   RATE/   0.02,    0.04,     0.05,     0.08,     0.10/
C                   find proper range
        DO 40   I = 1,4
          IF  (X .LE. RANGE(I+1))        GO TO 60
     40 CONTINUE
        I = 5
C                   compute tax
     60 TAXFNC = BASE(I)  +  RATE(I) * (X - RANGE(I))
        RETURN
        END
```

Review Question 10.1a: I = 15, J = 96, K = 270, L = 10

Review Question 10.2a

a. 0	c. 14	e. 55	g. 70
b. 8	d. 18	f. 60	h. 71

Exercise 10.2c

```
C                             storing mapping location in array
C
      DIMENSION  M(5,4,2)
C
      NUMBER = 0
      DO 20  I = 1,2
         DO 20  J = 1,4
            DO 20  K = 1,5
               NUMBER = NUMBER + 1
   20 M(K,J,I) = NUMBER
C
      WRITE   (*,1020)  M
 1020 FORMAT  (' ', 20I3)
C
      STOP  'end-of-run'
      END
```

Review Question 10.3a

a. A(1,1), A(3,1), A(5,1), A(7,1), A(9,1),
A(1,2), A(3,2), A(5,2), A(7,2), A(9,2),
A(1,3), A(3,3), A(5,3), A(7,3), A(9,3)

b. A(1,1), A(1,3), A(5,1), A(5,3), A(9,1), A(9,3)

c. A(1,5), A(2,5), A(3,5), A(1,6), A(2,6), A(3,6),
A(1,7), A(2,7), A(3,7), A(1,8), A(2,8), A(3,8)

d. A(1,1,1), A(2,1,1), A(3,1,1), A(4,1,1),
A(1,3,1), A(2,3,1), A(3,3,1), A(4,3,1),
A(1,1,4), A(2,1,4), A(3,1,4), A(4,1,4),
A(1,3,4), A(2,3,4), A(3,3,4), A(4,3,4)

e. A(1,1,1), A(1,1,4), A(1,3,1), A(1,3,4),
A(2,1,1), A(2,1,4), A(2,3,1), A(2,3,4),
A(3,1,1), A(3,1,4), A(3,3,1), A(3,3,4),
A(4,1,1), A(4,1,4), A(4,3,1), A(4,3,4)

f. A(1,3,1), A(1,3,2), A(1,4,1), A(1,4,2), A(1,5,1), A(1,5,2)

Review Question 10.3b

```
      WRITE   (*,1000)  ((J(K,L), L=1,5), K=1,3)
 1000 FORMAT  (' ', 5I10)
```

Review Question 10.3c

```
      WRITE   (*,1000)  J
 1000 FORMAT  (' ', 3I10)
```

Review Question 10.3d

```
      DO 20  NP = 1,52
   20 WRITE   (*,1020)  ((J(NC,NL,NP), NC = 1,4), NL = 1,7)
 1020 FORMAT  ('1'/(' ', 4I10))
```

Review Question 10.3e

```
      DO 20  NP = 1,4
   20 WRITE   (*,1020)  ((J(NP,NC,NL), NC = 1,7), NL = 1,52)
 1020 FORMAT  ('1'/(' ', 7I10))
```

Review Question 10.3f

```
a.    DO 20  NGROUP = 1,3
             DO 20  NGRADE = 1,8
      20 READ    (*,*)  IGRADE(NGROUP,NGRADE)
b.    DO 20  NGROUP = 1,8
             DO 20  NGRADE = 1,3
      20 READ    (*,*)  IGRADE(NGRADE,NGROUP)
```

Exercise 10.3g

```
C           Tax Table
      DIMENSION  TAXES(2,100)
      PRINT *, 'Enter tax rate in percent'
      READ  *,  RATE
      DO 20  I = 1,100
          TAXES(1,I) = REAL(I) / 100.00
   20 TAXES(2,I) = RATE / 100.00 * TAXES(1,I)
      WRITE   (*,1020)  RATE
 1020 FORMAT  ('0',25X,'TAX TABLE for',F6.2,'%'/
     1          '0', 4('Amount    Tax', 6X)/)
      DO 40  I = 1,25
          WRITE   (*,1022)  ((TAXES(J,K), J=1,2), K=I,100,25)
 1022     FORMAT  (' ',4(2F6.2, 6X))
          IF  (MOD (I,5) .EQ. 0)  PRINT *
   40 CONTINUE
      STOP  'end-of-run'
      END
```

Exercise 10.4b

```
C          grade analysis with subprograms
      DIMENSION  IGRADE(7,101), IAVERG(6)
C                  read in data
      CALL GRADIN  (IGRADE, NREC)
C                  fill in rest of array
      DO 60  I = 1,NREC
          IGRADE(5,I) = (2*(IGRADE(2,I)+IGRADE(3,I)+IGRADE(4,I))+3) / 6
          IGRADE(6,I) =              (IGRADE(3,I)+IGRADE(4,I) +1) / 2
   60 IGRADE(7,I) = MAX0 (IGRADE(4,I), IGRADE(5,I), IGRADE(6,I))
C                  averages
      DO 100  I = 1,6
  100 IAVERG(I) = IAVROW(IGRADE, NREC, I+1)
C                  output report
      CALL GRDOUT  (IGRADE, NREC, IAVERG)
C                  termination
      STOP  'end-of-run'
      END
C                  Subroutine  GRADIN:  inputs data
      SUBROUTINE  GRADIN  (IGRADE, NREC)
      DIMENSION  IGRADE (7,101)
C                  open file, input data
      OPEN    (2, FILE='EX1004B.IN')
      DO 20  I = 1,101
   20 READ    (2,1020, END=40)  (IGRADE(J,I), J=1,4)
 1020 FORMAT  (4I4)
          STOP 'excessive input'
   40 CLOSE   (2)
      NREC = I - 1
      RETURN
      END
```

```
C                       Function IAVROW:  function to get average of matrix row
      FUNCTION  IAVROW (MATRX, NUMREC, NUMITM)
      DIMENSION  MATRX(7,101)
      IAVROW = 0
      DO 20  I = 1,NUMREC
   20 IAVROW = IAVROW + MATRX(NUMITM,I)
      IAVROW = IAVROW / NUMREC
      RETURN
      END
C                       Subroutine  GRDOUT:  displays report
      SUBROUTINE  GRDOUT (IGRADE, NREC, IAVERG)
      DIMENSION  IGRADE(7,101), IAVERG(6)
C                       output report
      WRITE   (*,1100)  ((IGRADE(J,I), J=1,7), I=1,NREC)
 1100 FORMAT  (' ','Number     1     2     3    A13   A23 Final'//
     1          (' ', 7I6))
      WRITE   (*,1102)  IAVERG
 1102 FORMAT  ('0','Averages', I4, 5I6)
      RETURN
      END
```

Exercise 11.2e

```
C             ascending alphameric sort subroutine
      CHARACTER*16  ARRAY(6)
      DATA  ARRAY/'Los Angeles      ','San Francisco    ',
     1            'San Luis Obispo ','San Diego        ',
     2            'Bakersfield     ','Hollywood        '/
      WRITE   (*,1000)  ARRAY
 1000 FORMAT  (' ', 4A16)
      CALL ASORT  (ARRAY, 6)
      WRITE   (*,1000)  ARRAY
      STOP  'end-of-run'
      END
C         Subroutine ASORT:  ascending alpha sort
      SUBROUTINE  ASORT  (AR, NREC)
      CHARACTER*16  AR(*), TEMP
      NMIN1 = NREC - 1
C                       loop through positions to be filled
      DO 40  I = 1,NMIN1
         LMIN = I
C                       compare with following positions
         IPLUS1 = I + 1
         DO 20  J = IPLUS1,NREC
            IF  (LLT (AR(J), AR(LMIN)))  LMIN = J
   20    CONTINUE
C                       interchange, if necessary
         IF  (I .NE. LMIN)  THEN
            TEMP      = AR(I)
            AR(I)     = AR(LMIN)
            AR(LMIN)  = TEMP
         ENDIF
   40 CONTINUE
C                       return
      RETURN
      END
```

Exercise 11.4a

```
C          binary search function
      DIMENSION  IACCNT(101), BALANC(101)
C                    open file, input data
      OPEN    (2, FILE='EX1104A.IN')
      DO 20  I = 1,101
   20 READ     (2,1020, END=40)  IACCNT(I), BALANC(I)
 1020 FORMAT  (I4, F10.2)
      STOP  'excessive input'
   40 NREC = I-1
      PRINT *, NREC
      CLOSE   (2)
C                    loop through input
      DO 80  I = 1,10000
      WRITE   (*,1040)
 1040    FORMAT  ('0','Enter desired account number')
      READ    (*,*, END=90)  JACCNT
      LREC = IBSRCH (IACCNT, NREC, JACCNT)
      IF  (LREC .GT. 0)  THEN
          WRITE   (*,1042)  BALANC(LREC)
 1042       FORMAT  (' ','Balance = $',F10.2)
        ELSE
          PRINT *, 'Account not found'
      ENDIF
   80 CONTINUE
C                    termination
   90 STOP  'end-of-run'
      END
C
C       Function IBSRCH:  binary search of integer array
      FUNCTION IBSRCH  (IA, NR, ISRCH)
      DIMENSION  IA(*)
C
      NPASS = ALOG (REAL (NR)) * 1.4427  +  1.00
      LBOT = 1
      LTOP = NR + 1
C                    loop through search
      DO 20  I = 1,NPASS
      IBSRCH = (LBOT + LTOP) / 2
      IF  (ISRCH .LT. IA(IBSRCH))  THEN
          LTOP = IBSRCH
        ELSE IF  (ISRCH .GT. IA(IBSRCH))  THEN
          LBOT = IBSRCH
        ELSE
          RETURN
      ENDIF
   20 CONTINUE
C                    return 0 if not found
      IBSRCH = 0
      RETURN
      END
```

Review Question 12.2a [Underscore indicates blank space]

a. Status_is_good____

b. Status:_Good__&__B

c. Enter_G,_B_or_I___

d. __Bad_Status_____

e. __Indifferent_Stat

Exercise 12.2d

```
C           convert dates to words
      CHARACTER   MONTHS(12)*9, INSTR*6, OUTSTR*18
      DIMENSION   LENGTH(12)
      DATA  MONTHS/ 'January  ', 'February ', 'March    ',
     1              'April    ', 'May      ', 'June     ',
     2              'July     ', 'August   ', 'September',
     3              'October  ', 'November ', 'December '/
      DATA  LENGTH/  7, 8, 5,  4, 3, 4,  4, 6, 9,  7, 8, 8/
C
      DO 20  I = 1,20000
         WRITE   (*,1000)
 1000    FORMAT  ('0','Enter date:'/ ' ', '__/__/__')
         READ    (*,1002, END=90) MO, INSTR
 1002    FORMAT  (I2, A6)
         IF  (MO .GT. 0 .AND.  MO .LE. 12)  THEN
            L = LENGTH(MO)
            OUTSTR = MONTHS(MO)(1:L) // ' ' // INSTR(2:3) // ', 19'//
     1                                         INSTR(5:6)
            PRINT *, OUTSTR
         ELSE
            PRINT  *, 'Invalid month'
         ENDIF
   20 CONTINUE
C
   90 STOP  'end-of-run'
      END
```

Review Question 12.3a

a. 5   d. 0   g. 0
b. 2   e. 0   h. 10
c. 0   f. 0   i. 5

Exercise 12.4c

```
C           driver for counting specified character
      CHARACTER   LINE*60, SEARCH
      DO 40  I = 1,20000
         WRITE   (*,1020)
 1020    FORMAT  ('0','Enter up to 60 characters:'/ ' ', 60('_'))
         READ    (*,1022, END=90)  LINE
 1022    FORMAT  (A60)
         WRITE   (*,1024)
 1024    FORMAT  ('0','Enter desired character')
         READ    (*,1026)  SEARCH
 1026    FORMAT  (A1)
         N = NAPEAR (LINE, SEARCH)
   40 WRITE   (*,1040)  N, SEARCH
 1040 FORMAT  (' ', I4,1X,A1,'''s in above line')
   90 STOP  'end-of-run'
      END
C
C           Function NAPEAR:  counts specified character in string
      FUNCTION NAPEAR  (STRING, IC)
      CHARACTER  STRING*(*), IC
C                 get size of transmitted character variable
      LENGTH = LEN (STRING)
      NAPEAR = 0
```

```
C                    loop through string
      DO 20   I = 1,LENGTH
           IF   (STRING(I:I) .EQ. IC)   NAPEAR = NAPEAR + 1
   20 CONTINUE
C                    return
      RETURN
      END
```

Exercise 12.4f

```
C            decimal to hexadecimal conversion
      CHARACTER  HEXCHR, OUTSTR*4
      DO 60   NTIMES = 1,20000
          PRINT *, 'Enter integer in the range 0 to 32767'
          READ    (*,*, END=90)  NUMBER
          IF  (NUMBER .GE. 0  .AND.  NUMBER .LE. 32767)  THEN
              OUTSTR = '    '
              N = NUMBER
              DO 40   I = 1,4
                  IDIV = 16 ** (4-I)
                  INUM = N / IDIV
                  OUTSTR(I:I) = HEXCHR (INUM)
   40             N = MOD (N, IDIV)
              WRITE    (*,1040)  OUTSTR
 1040         FORMAT  (' ', A4)
          ENDIF
   60 CONTINUE
   90 STOP   'end-of-run'
      END
C
C                    Function HEXCHR:  returns hexadecimal character
      CHARACTER*1  FUNCTION  HEXCHR (N)
      CHARACTER*16  HEXCOD
      DATA         HEXCOD/ '0123456789ABCDEF'/
      HEXCHR = HEXCOD (N+1:N+1)
      RETURN
      END
```

Exercise 13.1f

```
C          key sort of file from DAM to SAM
      CHARACTER*70 LINE
      DIMENSION    IZIP(400), ICARRY(400)
C                    open file and read in zips
      OPEN    (2, FILE='PLATE.DAM', ACCESS='DIRECT', FORM='FORMATTED',
     1                             STATUS='OLD',    RECL=70)
      READ    (2,1000, REC=1)  NREC
 1000 FORMAT  (I6)
      DO 20   I = 1,NREC
          READ    (2,1002, REC=I+1)  IZIP(I)
 1002     FORMAT  (65X, I5)
   20 ICARRY(I) = I
C                    sort
      CALL ISORT  (IZIP,NREC,1, ICARRY,1, RCARRY,0)
```

```
C                      write new file
      OPEN    (3, FILE='PLATE.ZIP')
      WRITE   (3,1030)
 1030 FORMAT  (10X, 'License Plates sorted by Zip Code'///
     1            'Plate     Name               Address',13X,
     2                'Town          STZip'/)
      DO 40  I = 1,NREC
         IREC = ICARRY(I) + 1
         READ    (2,1040, REC=IREC)  LINE
   40 WRITE   (3,1040)  LINE
 1040 FORMAT  (A70)
      CLOSE   (2)
      CLOSE   (3)
C                      termination
   90 STOP   'end-of-run'
      END
```

Review Question 13.2a

I = 2040, J = 60, K = 246, L = 0, A = 348700.0, B = 18963000.0

Review Question 13.2b

```
                     1111111111222222222233333333334
Columns: 12345678901234567890123456789012345678907890
         0010   20             0.1234E+2      +1.23
```

Review Question 13.2c

```
                       111111
         Columns:   123456789012345
                       2           8
                       3
```

Review Question 13.2d

```
      READ   (*,'(F10.2)')  X, Y, Z
      WRITE  (*,'(''0'', 3F10.2)')  X, Y, Z
```

Review Question 13.2e: 1.23, 0.52, 327.67, 268.52

Review Question 13.5a

```
    6.400     -2.500     8.400     2.500     32.000
    2.000      5.000     4.400    -7.500    -12.500
    6.400      2.500    25.300    27.000     32.000
   32.000    -12.500     0.010    -1.276      5.385
```

Review Question 14.2a

Variable	Type	Offset	Bytes
A(5)	Real array	0	20
B(2)	Real array	20	8
I(7)	Integer array	28	28
CCC	Character	56	12

Variable	Type	Offset	Bytes
T	Real	0	4
U	Real	4	4
V	Real	8	4
W	Real	12	4
X	Real	16	4
Y	Real	20	4
Z	Real	24	4
I1	Integer	28	4
I2	Integer	32	4
I3	Integer	36	4
I4	Integer	40	4
I5	Integer	44	4
I6	Integer	48	4
I7	Integer	52	4
C12	Character	56	12

Variable	Type	Offset	Bytes
R(7)	Real array	0	28
J(2)	Integer array	28	8

Variable	Type	Offset	Bytes
DUMMY(6)	Real array	0	24
Q	Real	24	4
M	Integer	28	4
IDUMMY(6)	Integer array	32	24
ICH	Character	56	12

Index

Note: Boldface numbers identify the pages where the major discussion of the topic is presented.

Summary of FORTRAN Commands (Continued)

ASSIGNMENT

ASSIGNMENT: causes the storage of a value in a memory location

```
TOTAL = COST + TAX
```
Chapter 4

ASSIGN: assigns a statement number to a specialized branching variable

```
ASSIGN 20 TO IBRANCH
```
Chapter 13

CONTROL

CONTINUE: no operation statement used to hold a statement number

```
30 CONTINUE
```
Chapter 6

DO: repetition instruction used to control a loop

```
DO 100  I = 1,10,2
```
Chapter 6

GO TO..:   unconditional branch

```
GO TO 200
```
Chapter 5

IF: conditional branch

```
IF  (I .LT. J)  K = I + J
```
Chapter 5

IF..:   multi-conditional branch structure called the Block IF

THEN   indicates block of instructions where condition is true
ELSE IF   alternate condition
ELSE   indicates block of instructions where conditions are false
ENDIF   end of Block IF

```
IF  (I .LT. K)  THEN
    PRINT *, 'I < K'
  ELSE IF  (I .GT. J)  THEN
    PRINT *, 'I > J'
  ELSE
    PRINT *, 'I = J'
ENDIF
```
Chapter 5

PAUSE: causes a suspension of execution requiring manual intervention to continue

```
PAUSE 'change printer forms'
```
Chapter 13

STOP: returns control of computer to operating system

```
STOP 'end of run'
```
Chapter 2